KU-236-631

OXFORD MONOGRAPHS ON
LABOUR LAW

General Editors: Paul Davies,
Keith Ewing, Mark Freedland

JUST WAGES FOR WOMEN

UNIVERSITY OF WINCHESTER
LIBRARY

Oxford Monographs on Labour Law

General Editors: Paul Davies, Fellow of Balliol College, Oxford and Reader in Law at Oxford University; Keith Ewing, Professor of Public Law at King's College, London; and Mark Freedland, Fellow and Tutor in Law at St John's College, Oxford.

This series is the first new development in the literature dealing with labour law for many years. The series recognizes the arrival not only of a renewed interest in labour law generally, but also the need for a fresh approach to the study of labour law following a decade of momentous change in the UK and Europe. The series is concerned with all aspects of labour law, including traditional subjects of study such as industrial relations law and individual employment law, but it will also include books which examine the law and economics of the labour market and the impact of social security law upon patterns of employment and the employment contract.

Titles already published in this series

The Right to Strike
K. D. EWING

Legislating for Conflict
SIMON AUERBACH

Justice in Dismissal
HUGH COLLINS

Pensions, Employment, and the Law
RICHARD NOBLES

UNIVERSITY RSITY OF
WINC~~EST~~

4. 012153

AUTHOR

| Acc DATE | 13 JAN 1998 |

HOUSE OF COMMONS
LIBRARY

DISPOSED OF
BY AUTHORITY

WITHDRAWN FROM
THE LIBRARY

UNIVERSITY OF
WINCHESTER

KA 0344765 0

HOUSE OF COMMONS LIBRARY

LOCATION

AUTHOR

Acc DATE

Just Wages for Women

UNIVERSITY OF WINCHESTER
LIBRARY

AILEEN McCOLGAN

CLARENDON PRESS · OXFORD
1997

Oxford University Press, Great Clarendon Street, Oxford OX2 6DP

Oxford New York
Athens Auckland Bangkok Bogota Bombay
Buenos Aires Calcutta Cape Town Dar es Salaam
Delhi Florence Hong Kong Istanbul Karachi
Kuala Lumpur Madras Madrid Melbourne
Mexico City Nairobi Paris Singapore
Taipei Tokyo Toronto Warsaw
and associated companies in
Berlin Ibadan

Oxford is a trade mark of Oxford University Press

Published in the United States by
Oxford University Press Inc., New York

© Aileen McColgan 1997

All rights reserved. No part of this publication may be reproduced,
stored in a retrieval system, or transmitted, in any form or by any means,
without the prior permission in writing of Oxford University Press.
Within the UK, exceptions are allowed in respect of any fair dealing for the
purpose of research or private study, or criticism or review, as permitted
under the Copyright, Designs and Patents Act, 1988, or in the case of
reprographic reproduction in accordance with the terms of the licences
issued by the Copyright Licensing Agency. Enquiries concerning
reproduction outside these terms and in other countries should be
sent to the Rights Department, Oxford University Press,
at the address above

British Library Cataloguing in Publication Data
Data available

Library of Congress Cataloging-in-Publication Data
McColgan, Aileen.
Equal pay in labour law / Aileen McColgan.
p. cm. — (Oxford monographs on labour law)
Includes bibliographical references.
1. Equal pay for equal work—Law and legislation—Great Britain.
2. Discrimination in employment—Law and legislation—Great Britain.
3. Women—Employment—Law and legislation—Great Britain.
I. Title. II. Series.
KD3102.M377 1997
344.7301'2153—dc21 97–12929

ISBN 0–19–826588–3

1 3 5 7 9 10 8 6 4 2

Typeset by Graphicraft Ltd., Hong Kong
Printed in Great Britain by
Biddles Ltd. Guildford and King's Lynn

UNIVERSITY OF WINCHESTER

344.01
mCC

03447650

'It is generally allowed, that we do our work much neater, cleaner, and better, than the men; and, I am informed, that, notwithstanding the inferiority of their work, they have extorted from their master a considerable addition to the established prices.'

Letter to *The Times* from a 'taylor's widow', 14 May 1806.

To mum and dad and to little Caoimhe, who took rather less time to produce than this book.

Editors' Preface

This is the fifth title in the series of Oxford Monographs on Labour Law, established to promote the publication of books which will make a distinctive contribution to the study of labour law. For this purpose we have deliberately adopted a wide and open-ended view of the subject, with existing titles exploring the relationship between labour law and labour history, social security law, pensions law, and legal philosophy. It is expected that future titles will continue in this vein, thereby fulfilling our ambition that books in the series will not necessarily adopt a formal or legalistic approach but will draw upon contributions made by other disciplines, whether it be industrial relations, political science, or economics. We continue to expect that books in the series will not concentrate exclusively on legal developments in Britain, conscious as we are of the great importance of European labour law, as well as the growing interest in the labour laws of EU member states, as well as in comparative labour law generally.

Against this background we take great pleasure in the publication of Aileen McColgan's study of equal pay for women: we were extremely pleased that she, as a well known author in the field, agreed to permit her book to be included in the series. The work is an outstanding example of the type of writing which we hoped the series would stimulate and encourage, taking an established problem of British labour law but subjecting it to rigorous scrutiny in a fresh, highly original, and extremely impressive new light. In the course of doing so the author assesses the experience of British and European labour law in the context of developments in Canada and Australia, and draws imaginatively on the research of economists and industrial relations specialists. The breadth and depth of the research, together with penetrating criticisms and balanced judgments convince us that this is by some way one of the most important contributions to the literature about the role of the law in regulating the remuneration of women.

PLD
KDE
MRF

27 May 1997

Acknowledgements

Many, many thanks to Professor Keith Ewing, without whom I would never have written this book; King's College and the Canadian High Commission which funded the necessary research; Professor Hugh Collins and Simon Deakin who supported my grant applications and all those at the Pay Equity Commission, Osgoode Hall Law School, and the University of Toronto who made me so welcome. Thanks especially to Cathy, the librarian at the Pay Equity Commission, and to Judy Fudge at Osgoode Hall.

Table of Contents

List of Tables

IDT	Industrial Disputes Tribunal
ILO	International Labour Organization
IRC	Industrial Relations Commission
IRLR	Industrial Relations Law Reports
IRS	Industrial Relations Services
IT	Industrial Tribunal
KB	Law Reports, King's Bench Division
LFS	Labour Force Survey
LGA	Local Government Act 1988
LSE	London School of Economics and Political Science
NBIR	National Board on Prices and Incomes
NCCL	National Council For Civil Liberties
NES	New Earnings Survey
NHS	National Health Service
NJC	National Joint Council
OECF	Organisation for Economic Cooperation and Development
PEA	Pay Equity Act 1987
PEC	Pay Equity Commission
PEHT	Pay Equity Hearings Tribunal
PER	Pay Equity Reports
PSI	Policy Studies Institute
QB	Law Reports, Queen's Bench Division
RRA	Race Relations Act 1976
SCELI	Social Change And Economic Lifestyle Initiative
SDA	Sex Discrimination Act 1975
SI	Statutory Instrument
TUC	Trades Union Congress
TUPE	Transfer of Undertakings (Protection of Employment) Regulations 1985
UK	United Kingdom
UN	United Nations
WLR	Weekly Law Reports
WIRS	Workplace Industrial Relations Survey

[1]
Introduction

The twenty-ninth of December 1996 marked the twenty-first anniversary of the implementation both of Britain's Equal Pay Act 1970 and of the Sex Discrimination Act 1975. As such, it is an appropriate juncture at which to consider British women's position within the labour market. The focus of this book is on the pay inequality which persists between men and women in Britain. It is not possible to divorce the issues of pay inequality and of wider labour market discrimination, and the history and implementation of the Sex Discrimination and Race Relations Acts, as well as that of the Equal Pay Act, will be considered. But the most significant mark of labour market inequality must lie in the relative thickness of men's and women's pay packets and, in particular, of the wage disadvantage suffered by some groups of women, including those from ethnic minorities and those who work part-time. Access to income dictates not only the standards of living which individuals and families can afford and the extent to which they can be free from dependence upon the state; it also has a very significant impact on the balance of power within the private sphere. Unequal access to income has repercussions throughout women's lives.

Just as many men are more equal than women, so some women are more equal than others. Women whose skins are not white and those with dependent children are particularly disadvantaged in terms of the wages they earn. So, too, are women who are other than middle class. The distinctions between these and other groups of women, and the inter-relationship between race and sex discrimination, will be highlighted in Chapter 2. But just as women differ from each other, so they share a number of common features almost irrespective of their race, class, and family responsibilities. All women's wages are lower than those of equivalently skilled and qualified men; all women are vulnerable to stereotypical assumptions about their aptitudes and their commitment to work, in particular, about the potential impact of their current or future children upon their work; all women are vulnerable to sexual harassment. Despite the factors which distinguish women from each other, it is still possible to discuss the disadvantages that women suffer as a group. Some women have benefited more than others from two decades of equal opportunities legislation. But even those women who have gained most in terms of access to highly paid, sex-integrated, or predominantly male jobs have frequently done so by making private sacrifices which are not required of their male colleagues (in particular, by remaining childless). And those women who have risen to the top in female-dominated professions earn less than do their equivalents in male-dominated jobs.

In the twenty-one years in which equal pay and sex discrimination legislation have been in place in the United Kingdom, women have substantially increased their share of higher paid occupations—namely managerial and administrative jobs and the professions. They have seen their wages rise, relative to those of men, by almost 30 per cent (from 63 per cent of men's average hourly rate in 1970 to almost 80 per cent in 1995) and have, very recently, won the right to maternity leave regardless of length of service. Those women (almost half of all female workers) who work on a part-time basis are now entitled to the same statutory employment protection as full-time workers, and compensation for sex discrimination, introduced in 1975, is no longer (by contrast with unfair dismissal compensation) subject to any upper limit.

All of these changes have taken place within a relatively short space of time. There is no denying that women's employment rights have radically increased in that time. But for all of this, women still earn a great deal less than men (if full-time and part-time women workers are considered together, about 70 per cent of men's hourly wages). Occupational segregation has remained almost constant to date and women are still concentrated, for the most part, at the bottom of the wage hierarchy. A few women have broken through one or more layers of glass ceiling, but the majority remain in jobs which, however demanding and skilled, pay less than those jobs in which men work.

Britain, of course, is not unique in this respect. British women share their disadvantage with women all over the world. In 1986 the International Labour Organization's (ILO's) Committee of Experts reported that, despite widespread ratification of Convention No 100 (the Equal Pay Convention) and at the end of the United Nations' (UN's) Decade for Women, there was a 'continuing and, sometimes, widening gap between men and women workers' in terms of their pay.[1] In 1992 the ILO reported small gains in women's workplace position in a number of countries worldwide, but complained of 'backsliding' elsewhere. Women in Iceland, for example, did better than those anywhere else in the world with 90.6 per cent of men's wages in 1988. But even they had seen this figure decline from 94.1 per cent in 1984. Women in the United States, Canada, Australia, Belgium, the United Kingdom, Czechoslovakia, France, the former West Germany, and New Zealand all saw some improvement in their relative wages during the 1980s. But, according to the ILO's Director-General

---

[1] ILO, *Equal Remuneration* (Geneva: ILO, 1986); ILO 72nd Session Report III (4b); General Survey of the Reports on Convention No. 100, para. 2.

(Michel Hansenne), the movement experienced was much too small to be considered meaningful progress. Further, women in Japan, Denmark, Luxembourg, the Netherlands, and Switzerland all lost ground during these years. It was clear, Hansenne said, that many societies 'have given only lip service to the idea of equal pay for equal work'.[2]

In 1993 the UN Human Development Report found that: '[w]omen, half the world's population, did two thirds of the world's work, earned one tenth of the world's income and owned one hundredth of the world's property'—this despite the commitment to wage equality contained both in the Universal Declaration of Human Rights 1948 and in the International Convention on Economic and Civil Rights 1966.[3] The UN Report went on to record that 'there is still no country that treats its women as well as its men'.[4]

British women may not suffer many of the evils perpetrated upon women elsewhere: here female genital mutilation is an unusual occurrence, sex-selective abortion is far from the norm, and girl children are rarely abandoned to their fates. But for all of the human rights advantages British women enjoy, relative to women elsewhere, they have in common the fact of their financial disadvantage. Just as British women earn around 80 per cent of men's hourly and 70 per cent of men's weekly wage so, in the late 1980s, Japanese, Korean, and Sri Lankan women earned 50 per cent, 53 per cent, and 76 per cent respectively of the daily male wage; Jamaican, Cypriot, and Colombian women 55 per cent, 60 per cent, and 85 per cent respectively of men's weekly wages; and Chilean, Costa Rican, and Kenyan women 47 per cent, 69 per cent, and 80 per cent of men's monthly wages. Women in developed countries did no better, relative to men, than those in the developing world.[5]

This book traces the attempts made by UK governments, frequently under pressure from the EC, to improve women's position at work. Its primary focus is on women's pay but, given that part of women's wage disadvantage stems from their position within the workforce, it also looks at the attempt made by the Sex Discrimination Act to tackle the wider issues of discrimination at work. In addition, because ethnic minority women are particularly disadvantaged at work, it considers the Race Relations Act in terms both of what it actually aimed to do and what it achieved for ethnic minority women in particular. The review of UK discrimination legislation, its aims and impact, is carried out in Chapters 3 to 5 which follow the comprehensive survey of women's current position and pay set out in Chapter 2. Chapter 2 aims to draw attention to the

---

[2] The *Courier-Journal*, 21 Sept. 1992.

[3] Art. 23(2) and Art. 7(a)(i)—the first embraces equal pay for equal work, the second 'fair wages and equal remuneration for work of equal value'.

[4] *US News and World Report*, 28 Mar. 1994.

[5] ILO, *International Labour Review* (Geneva: ILO, 1992), vol. 131, 388–9.

differences between various groups of women (in particular, part-time and full-time women workers, white women and women of various ethnic minority groups) as well as to those issues which unite women in general.

Chapter 6 explores the reasons which underlie the gender–pay gap and questions the extent to which this gap should be seen as evidence of discrimination. It then considers how the gap might most effectively be tackled; i.e. whether by legislation directed specifically at the issue of pay or, instead, at the labour market segregation uncovered in Chapter 2. Chapters 7 to 9 examine three very different mechanisms addressed at tackling the gender–pay gap in particular, or inequality in wages more generally —these consist of specific 'pay equity' legislation as exemplified by the Pay Equity Act 1987 of Ontario, Canada; the collective wage regulation which, until recently, characterized the Australian labour market; and the regulation of minimum wages common to a number of EU Member States and carried out in the UK until recently, albeit in a far from comprehensive form, by means of the Wages Council system and a number of wage-regulation mechanisms including the Fair Wages Resolutions of the House of Commons and the more widely applicable provisions of Schedule 11 to the Employment Protection Act 1975 and its predecessors. Chapter 10 attempts to draw some lessons from the experience here and elsewhere to suggest how the problem of women's lower wages might best be addressed in the UK.

I. CURRENT EQUAL PAY LAW

In order to lay the ground for the critique of UK equal pay law which follows, it is necessary to outline the present state of that law. The first point relates to the complexities involved: in addition to the Equal Pay Act 1970 (as amended by the Equal Pay (Amendment) Regulations 1983), any survey of the law relating to equal pay must also take into account EC provisions—in particular, Article 119 of the Treaty of Rome and Council Directive 75/117 (Equal Pay). To the extent that UK law is compatible with the EC provisions, the former should be relied upon. But in those cases where UK legislation is inadequate (where, for example, the 'pay' whose inequality is challenged takes the form of unfair dismissal compensation which is covered by neither the Equal Pay nor the Sex Discrimination Act), EU law can be relied upon either for the purposes of interpreting the UK legislation consistently with it or, where this is not possible, directly. In this latter case the position regarding pay is unusual in employment law terms: whereas most EU employment provisions take the form of directives which can be relied upon by the individual, if at all, only against the state (whether as employer or otherwise[6]), Article 119 of the Treaty (and, to the extent that it serves only to apply Article 119, the Equal Pay Directive) can be relied upon as against private sector employers too. The role of EU law is further discussed in Chapter 4.

As if all this were not sufficiently complex, some equal pay cases should be taken under the Sex Discrimination Act, rather than the Equal Pay Act. The latter Act regulates only inequality in contractual terms: where the payment whose inequality is challenged is gratuitous (as, in *Garland* v. *British Rail Engineering Ltd.*,[7] in which the disputed 'pay' consisted of gratuitous travel concessions), the Sex Discrimination Act should be relied upon. The latter Act may also be used in respect of contractual benefits of a non-monetary form, so long as no claim is possible under the 1970 Act (i.e. where no comparator is available for the purposes of an Equal Pay Act claim). This matter is further discussed in Chapter 5.

(A) CLAIMING EQUAL PAY

British legislation imposes an individual model of 'equal pay'. The legal challenge to existing pay structures comes only from those employees directly affected by them, and then only if they can tailor their challenge within the narrow legal framework of the equal pay claim. There is no obligation upon employers to review pay structures for evidence of discrimination and, while some trade unions have been in the forefront of the struggle to improve women's pay, no recognized legal role for them.[8]

In order to challenge her rate of pay an individual woman (or man) must select a comparator of the opposite sex who is paid more than she (or he) is but whose work is equivalent in one of three ways: i.e. is either 'like' (broadly similar) work to that done by the claimant, or has been 'rated as equivalent' to hers by a job evaluation scheme carried out (or agreed) by her employer, or is of equal or less value than the work done by her. The final of these three claims has been possible only since the implementation of the 1983 amending regulations (discussed in Chapter 4).

The comparator chosen must be one who is *actually*, rather than merely *apparently* of the opposite sex. This emerged from a recent decision of the Employment Appeal Tribunal (*Collins* v. *Wilkin Chapman Ltd*[9]). Ruling on an appeal brought by an employer, the EAT declared that neither the Equal Pay Act nor Article 119 could be relied upon to claim equal pay with a comparator who appeared to be a man but who was in fact

---

[6] Cases 6, 9/90 *Frankovich & Bonifaci* v. *Italy*, [1991] ECR I–5357.

[7] Case 12/81 [1982] ECR 359.

[8] The EOC's powers to issue non-discrimination notices extend to 'discriminatory practices' (indirectly discriminatory practices even in the absence of a specific victim), but (see Ch. 5) this provision has shown itself to be something of a dead letter.

[9] (1995) 23 *Equal Opportunities Review Discrimination Case Law Digest* (EORDCLD) 12.

a transsexual and biologically, therefore, a woman. Mummery J declared himself content not only that the letter of the law required this decision but that, in addition, the *principle* of equal pay was not violated by such a difference in payment. This reasoning is rather hard to follow, excusing as it would even a deliberate policy, on the part of an employer, of paying an apparently male (but, unbeknown to the employer, biologically female employee) more than comparable women *because* he was (thought to be) a man. Nevertheless, given that such an employer would not be in breach of the Equal Pay Act during a period when, by sheer chance, no men were employed but women's wages were still deliberately held down *because* they were women, such a conclusion is perhaps not surprising. In any case, it is perhaps an issue of more philosophical than practical importance.

The complaint must be made in connection with 'employment' in the wide sense used also in the Sex Discrimination Act and the Race Relations Act—employment 'under a contract of service or of apprenticeship or a contract personally to execute any work or labour'.[10] Statutory office-holders are not entitled to claim under the Equal Pay Act.[11] But all other public employees are so entitled.[12]

Not only is the equal pay claimant obliged to put forward a comparator who fits one of these three sets of criteria but the comparator must, in addition, be employed by the same or an associated employer[13] as the equal pay claimant and at the same establishment in Great Britain or one 'at which common terms and conditions are observed either generally or for employees of the relevant classes'.[14] In *Leverton* v. *Clwyd County Council* the House of Lords interpreted this to permit a claim in respect of a comparator whose contract of employment was governed by the same collective agreement (this situation was, in fact, described by Lord Bridge as the 'paradigm, though not necessarily the only example, of . . . common terms and conditions'[15]). The House of Lords did not indicate in that case that *precisely* the same terms and conditions must be imposed by the collective agreement in respect of each place of work, but the Court of Appeal took a narrow view in *British Coal Corporation* v. *Smith* and refused a claim in respect of comparators who, although governed by the same

---

[10] EqPA, s. 1(6)(a).

[11] Inserted at the report stage, 800 HC Debs. 505–11 (22 Apr. 1970).

[12] See Sched. 2 to the House of Commons Disqualification Act 1975.

[13] The very narrow definition adopted by the EqPA has been held by the EAT, in *Scullard* v. *Knowles & Southern Regional Council for Education and Training* [1996] IRLR 344, to be inconsistent with the broader approach taken by the ECJ in relation to Art. 119's employment 'in the same establishment or service' with the effect that wider claims can be taken under Art. 119 (which does not restrict 'associated employers' to companies as is the case under the 1970 Act).

[14] EqPA, s. 1(6). Northern Ireland is covered by almost identical provisions.

[15] [1989] IRLR 28, 31, the case is further discussed in Ch. 4.

nationally agreed terms and conditions, enjoyed in addition locally negotiated bonuses.[16] This decision was recently reversed by the House of Lords,
which reinstated the broad approach taken in the *Leverton* case.[17]

A woman may choose more than one comparator for an equal pay
claim, and might be well advised to do so in order to multiply her chances
of success.[18] But this tactic is not without its pitfalls: in *Leverton v. Clwyd*
the House of Lords *per* Lord Bridge counselled industrial tribunals to:

be alert to prevent abuse of the equal value claims procedure by applicants who
cast their net too wide over a spread of comparators. To take an extreme case,
an applicant who claimed equality with A who earns £X and also with B who
earns £2X could hardly complain if an Industrial Tribunal concluded that her
claim of equality with A itself demonstrated that there were no reasonable grounds
for her claim of equality with B.[19]

The reluctance of their Lordships to permit multiple-comparator claims
is perhaps understandable, given the delays and expense associated with
the investigation of equal pay claims, in particular where the claim is one
of equal value (which, until recently, required an independent expert's
report if it was to succeed). But there are real difficulties in choosing an
appropriate comparator, particularly in an equal value claim, when information on pay and job requirements is hard to come by outside heavily unionized workplaces. In addition, as is noted in Chapter 7, even independent
experts rarely share similar approaches to the evaluation of jobs.

(B) 'LIKE WORK', 'WORK RATED AS EQUIVALENT', AND 'WORK OF EQUAL VALUE'

The three possible types of claim consist, as was mentioned above, of
'like work', 'work rated as equivalent', and 'work of equal value'. 'Like'
work is defined by section 1(4) of the Equal Pay Act as work which

is of the same or a broadly similar nature . . . the differences (if any) between
[the jobs] . . . not [being] of practical importance in relation to terms and conditions of employment; and accordingly in comparing [the jobs] regard shall be
had to the frequency or otherwise with which any such differences occur in practice as well as to the nature and extent of the differences.

In introducing the Equal Pay Act, Barbara Castle was keen to stress that
'like work' went well beyond the 'same job', a definition which she

---

[16] [1994] IRLR 342.   [17] [1996] IRLR 404.

[18] This is true particularly in equal value cases and where a material factor defence might
cover one, but not another, comparator.

[19] In Dec. 1994 the Green Paper, *Resolving Employment Rights Disputes: Options for Reform*
(London: HMSO, 1994), Cm 2707, suggested that equal value applicants be limited to a
single comparator. The suggestion has not been acted upon, perhaps in part as a result of
EOC opposition.

claimed was 'so restrictive that it would merely impinge on those women, very much in the minority, who work side by side with men on identical work'.[20] Hence, she claimed, differences between jobs had to be 'of practical importance' in order to preclude a 'like work' finding. We shall see in Chapter 3 that the approach of the tribunals has not always been as Mrs Castle envisaged it.

Work will be regarded as having been 'rated as equivalent', according to section 1(5), if the jobs of the applicant and her comparator(s) have been given equal value in a job evaluation scheme which has considered the demands made upon all or any employees in an undertaking or group of undertakings under headings such as skill, effort, and decision-making, and which has been agreed by the parties thereto.[21] 'Equal value' does not mean *exactly* equal value—the Employment Appeal Tribunal accepted in *Springboard Sunderland Trust* v. *Robson* that, if the scheme assigned value within bands (100–120 points, for example, or 410–449, as in *Springboard*), then the placing of two jobs within a single band (in *Springboard*, at 410 and 428) was sufficient to render them 'equivalent' for the purposes of section 1(2)(b).[22] Jobs will also be taken to have been rated as equivalent if they would have been given the same value under the scheme but for the fact that different values were assigned, according to sex, to the same levels of effort, skill, and decision-making, etc. In order for an employee to be entitled to claim under section 1(5), the job evaluation scheme in question must have been *analytical* in form (that is, it must have considered jobs under various sub-headings, such as skill, effort, and decision-making, rather than comparing them in the round[23]). An applicant can only rely on a *discriminatory* job evaluation scheme to claim equal pay if she claims that the scheme directly and obviously discriminated by assigning different values to the same levels of skill, effort, decision-making, etc. according to whether the job-holder was male or female.

In order to succeed in a claim based on a (non-discriminatory and analytical) job evaluation scheme, the scheme must have been accepted by both sides (employer and employees or representative trade union) but need not actually have been applied to the pre-existing pay structures. So, for example, in *O'Brien* v. *Sim-Chem Ltd*, the House of Lords found in favour of the applicant women, whose jobs had been rated as equivalent to those of their male comparators, but whose employers had failed to implement the new structure because of the Government's income policy.[24] Overturning the decision of the Court of Appeal, their Lordships

---

[20] 795 HC Debs. 915 (9 Feb. 1970).

[21] *Arnold* v. *Beecham Group Ltd* [1982] IRLR 307.   [22] [1992] IRLR 261.

[23] *Bromley* v. *H & J Quick Ltd* [1988] IRLR 249.

[24] [1980] IRLR 373. The CA's decision is at [1980] IRLR 151 and it in turn overturned the EAT's decision (at [1978] IRLR 398) allowing the appeal against the decision of the industrial tribunal.

Table 2.4 — proportion of women in full-time jobs, 1995

industrial sector	manual	non-manual
agriculture, hunting, and forestry	10%	34%
mining and quarrying	*	*
manufacturing	21%	29%
electricity, gas, and water supply	*	39%
construction	*	24%
trade, vehicle repair, and goods	15%	43%
hotels and restaurants	43%	50%
transport, storage, and communication	7%	34%
financial intermediation	*	50%
real estate renting and business	15%	44%
public administration, defence, and compulsory social security	17%	47%
education	37%	62%
health and social work	62%	75%
other community, social, and personal service	25%	47%

source: NES, 1995, tables 54–57[29]
* Not recorded by the NES

Table 2.5 — distribution of full-time employees by occupation, 1995

occupation	men	women
managerial and administration	18.4%	12.0%
professional	10.5%	11.3%
associate professional and technical	8.5%	11.1%
clerical and secretarial	9.5%	36.2%
craft and related	17.5%	3.3%
personal and protective services	6.1%	9.2%
selling	4.5%	6.2%
plant and machine operatives	17.1%	7.0%
others	7.9%	3.6%

source: NES, 1995, tables 86 & 87

for much of the difference in the occupational distribution of men and women. It appears that, while (very broadly) similar proportions of men and full-time women work in areas such as selling, the professions, and personal and protective services, the 'middle' portion of men and women

[29] The LFS does not give the breakdown of full-time and part-time, manual and non-manual men and women by sector. For this reason, NES figures are used. However, these underestimate the proportion of women, in particular, of manual women workers.

is absorbed by skilled and semi-skilled manual and by junior to inter-mediate non-manual work respectively.

But table 2.5 gives only a partial idea of the extent to which jobs are segregated by sex. Even within broad categories such as 'managerial and administration', 'professional', and 'selling', men and women do very different jobs. In 1989, for example (according to Department of Employment figures), women graduates'

first job was most likely to be in personnel, health, or social work. More than 20 per cent of new graduates chose these fields. Finance and legal work were also popular while marketing, administration, and science and engineering each attracted 10 per cent of the new graduate women. Men's first choice, made by more than 30 per cent, was scientific or engineering work.[30]

In 1995, two-thirds of women professionals, but only 28.2 per cent of professional men, were teachers, and over 50 per cent of women associate professionals, but only 7.9 per cent of men, worked in health care.[31]

Although women managers increased their share of all management jobs from between 12 and 14 per cent in 1980 to 21–24 per cent in 1990, they occupy a narrow range of these jobs. Men are spread throughout the ten managerial categories from personnel (where they occupied 76.3 per cent of jobs in 1990) to property (with 98.7 per cent). By contrast, women are concentrated within four categories in which, in 1990, they accounted for between 23.7 per cent (personnel) and 9.3 per cent (financial and legal) of managers.[32] And just as women managers are concentrated in a narrow range of occupational specialisms, so too they are unevenly distributed across the industrial sectors. In 1993, for example, while 34 per cent of all managers were women, three of the ten LFS sectors contained too few women managers to be counted, and the proportion of women managers in the other seven sectors varied from 13 per cent in construction and 17 per cent in metal goods to 34 per cent in distribution, hotels, and catering and 53 per cent in 'other services'.[33]

Within the sales and 'personal and protective services', too, men and women perform very different functions. In 1995, over 80 per cent of

[30] V. Hammond and V. Holton, 'The Scenario for Women Managers in Britain in the 1990s: Competitive Frontiers: Women Managers in the Triad' (1993) 23 *International Studies of Management & Organization*, citing Department of Education and Science Statistical Bulletin, *First Destination of Graduates* (HMSO, London, 1991).

[31] For teachers the figures were 66.2% for full-time women professionals and 67.7% for all women professionals—NES 1995, tables 86 & 178, the figures for men are from table 87. 52% of full-time women associate professionals and 58.4% of all worked in health.

[32] P. Gregg and S. Machin, *Is the Glass Ceiling Cracking? Gender Compensation Differentials and Access to Promotion Among UK Executives* (National Institute of Economic and Social Research, 1993), Discussion Paper No 50, 13.

[33] *Employment Gazette*, Sept. 1994, LFS 4. The 10 sectors consisted of agriculture, farming, etc.; energy and water supply; other mineral and ore extraction; metal, engineering, vehicles, etc.; other manufacturing; construction; distribution, hotels, etc.; communication & transport; banking, insurance, finance, etc.; other services.

women who worked in sales did so as sales assistants or check-out operators (67.1 per cent of full-time women sales workers) while only 7.5 per cent (17.9 per cent of full-time women) were sales representatives. Over half the men who work in sales, on the other hand, were sales representatives and fewer than a third were sales assistants and check-out operators.[34] The same pattern is evident in 'personal and protective services': in 1995, over 50 per cent of the men in this broad occupational group worked in security and protective services in comparison with 7.5 per cent of full-time women and under 4 per cent of all women (the figures for part-time women in this narrower sector were too low to be included in the New Earnings Survey). By contrast, 45 per cent of full-time women but only 9 per cent of men worked in health and related jobs and 20.1 per cent of women but an insignificant number of men worked in childcare.[35]

Just as men and women are segregated within broad occupational groups, so too occupational sex segregation is prevalent within industrial sectors. We saw above (table 2.4) that men dominate manual jobs in all but one of the industrial sectors. And even when non-manual work within sectors is considered in isolation, men and women do different jobs. A recent survey by BECTU found, for example, that, while its male members worked as producers, directors, sound and lighting engineers, and camera operators, women were concentrated in departments such as wardrobe, makeup, hair, costume, production support, and research/writing.[36] And women in banking, insurance, etc. are almost exclusively to be found at the bottom of the occupational hierarchy—in 1985, women accounted for 56 per cent of Midland Bank staff, 60 per cent of the clerical grades, 16 per cent of appointed staff, and a mere 1.8 per cent of group managers.[37] In the insurance business, too, women are generally employed as secretaries and clerical staff, while men work as supervisors and managers.[38]

(B) PART TIME WOMEN WORKERS

Introduction

Part-time workers account for an increasing proportion of the workforce and are an overwhelmingly female group. The number of part-time jobs has more than doubled, for both men and women, since 1971, and now accounts for almost 30 per cent of the total number of jobs, almost half (46.4 per cent) of the jobs held by women.[39] Almost 25 per cent of all

---

[34] NES 1995, tables 86, 87 & 173.   [35] *Ibid.*

[36] Survey by M. Woolf and S. Holly, 'Employment Patterns and Training Needs' 56 *Equal Opportunities Review* 8.

[37] IDS, *Maternity and Paternity Leave* (IDS Study 351, 1985), cited by D. Collinson, D. Knights, and M. Collinson, *Managing to Discriminate* (London: Routledge, 1990), 19.

[38] Collinson, Knights, and Collinson, n. 37 above.

[39] *Employment Gazette*, 'Part-time Working in Great Britain—an Historical Analysis', Dec. 1994, 473.

employees work part-time (the increasing proportion of those with second jobs accounts for the disparity between jobs and workers) and in
1994 women accounted for 86 per cent of part-time workers and held
81 per cent of part-time jobs.[40] Forty-four per cent of all women workers
work part-time. When the mothers of dependent children are considered
in isolation, this proportion rises to 65 per cent.

The age profile of part-time women differs substantially from that of
part-time men. In 1992, for example, 39.2 per cent of the 11 per cent
of men who worked part-time were aged between 16 and 24 (many of
them were students). For women, the proportion was a mere 11.5 per
cent. By contrast, 21.9 per cent and 40.7 per cent of part-time women
workers were aged 25–34 and 35–49 respectively: this compared with
8.9 per cent and 9.1 per cent of men. Forty-seven per cent of part-time
women workers were the mothers of children aged 15 and below.[41]

Industrial Segregation

Table 2.6 shows the distribution, according to the LFS, of male full-time
and female full-time and part-time employees across industrial sectors.

Table 2.6 — distribution of employees by industrial sector, 1996

industrial sector	as % of full-time male and female and part-time female employees		
	full-time women	full-time men	part-time women
agriculture, hunting, and forestry	0.7%	1.9%	0.6%
fishing	0.03%	0.04%	0.01%
mining and quarrying	0.1%	0.6%	0.03%
manufacturing	15.9%	27.8%	4.6%
electricity, gas, and water supply	0.5%	1.2%	0.1%
construction	1.5%	6.9%	1.1%
trade, vehicle repair, and goods	13.2%	15.2%	21.8%
hotels and restaurants	4.1%	2.8%	10.4%
transport, storage, and communication	4.5%	8.8%	1.8%
financial intermediation	7.0%	4.2%	2.4%
real estate renting and business	13.1%	12.8%	11.1%
public admin., defence, and compulsory social security	8.3%	6.5%	3.7%
education	10.3%	4.2%	14.6%
health and social work	16.6%	3.5%	21.8%
other community, social, and personal service	4.1%	3.4%	5.8%

source: LFS, 1996, table 1.4

[40] LFS, Spring 1994.
[41] *Employment Gazette*, 'Part-time Employment and Attitudes to Part-time Work', May
1993, 213.

Part-time women's pattern of industrial distribution is quite distinct from that of full-timers. Part-time workers are particularly concentrated in trade, vehicle repair, and goods; in education; health, and social work, and in hotels and restaurants. In virtually all sectors (the only exception is financial intermediation), full-time women's distribution is closer to that of men than is the pattern for part-timers.

Table 2.7 shows the composition of the workforce (in terms of men, full-time and part-time women) by industrial sector.

Table 2.7 — workforce composition by industrial sector, 1996

industrial sector	men	full-time women	part-time women
agriculture, hunting, and forestry	75.7%	14.6%	9.8%
fishing	69.9%	23.3%	8.2%
mining and quarrying	88.4%	9.5%	2.2%
manufacturing	70.8%	23.3%	5.9%
electricity, gas, and water supply	77.4%	18.7%	4.0%
construction	83.2%	10.5%	6.3%
trade, vehicle repair, and goods	48.9%	20.9%	30.2%
hotels and restaurants	38.0%	19.1%	43.0%
transport, storage, and communication	72.4%	20.3%	7.3%
financial intermediation	44.7%	42.1%	13.0%
real estate, renting, and business	52.2%	27.2%	20.3%
public admin., defence, and compulsory social security	50.6%	35.6%	13.8%
education	28.4%	31.8%	39.7%
health and social work	18.0%	38.0%	44.0%
other community, social, and personal service	46.1%	23.4%	30.0%

source: LFS, 1996, table 1.4

Part-time women comprise 21.2 per cent of workers overall according to the LFS. Table 2.7 shows that part-timers account for a representative proportion of the employees in only one sector (real estate, etc.[42]) and are over-concentrated (relative to their position in the workforce as a whole) in five of the fifteen sectors—in these sectors they account for an average 37.3 per cent of the workforce (176 per cent of their expected strength), while in all other sectors they account for only 7.8 per cent of the workforce (around a third of their expected strength).

---

[42] Accounting for between 80 and 120% of their expected proportion (16.9–25.3%).

Occupational Segregation

Tables 2.8 and 2.9 show, respectively, the proportion of part-time women in the manual and non-manual workforces in the various industrial sectors (with the equivalent figures for full-time women for the purposes of comparison), and the proportion of part-time women in each occupational group (with those of full-time women and of men for comparison). The figures for tables 2.8–2.10 are taken from the NES which, as was mentioned above, under-estimates the number of part-time women by about one fifth, and, in particular, under-counts those in low-paid manual work. The LFS does not, however, disaggregate the occupational figures for full-time and part-time women, so the NES statistics have to be used here.

Table 2.8 — women as % of workers by industrial sector, 1995

industrial sector	full-time women		part-time women	
	manual	non-manual	manual	non-manual
agriculture, hunting, and forestry	10%	34%	*	*
fishing	*	*	*	*
mining and quarrying	*	*	*	*
manufacturing	19%	28%	6%	6%
electricity, gas, and water supply	*	39%	*	*
construction	*	22%	*	10%
trade, vehicle repair, and goods	13%	30%	16%	32%
hotels and restaurants	25%	39%	49%	22%
transport, storage, and communication	7%	31%	4%	9%
financial intermediation	*	44%	*	12%
real estate, renting, and business	11%	38%	25%	14%
public admin., defence, and compulsory social security	10%	40%	36%	14%
education	13%	41%	64%	34%
health and social work	29%	47%	54%	38%
other community, social, and personal service	18%	35%	28%	25%

source: NES, 1995, tables 54–57
* not recorded by the NES

Whereas full-time women workers account for a greater proportion of non-manual workers than of manual workers in every industrial sector, the pattern for part-timers is very different. Leaving aside the four sectors in which the numbers of part-time women (or, at any rate, of those earning at least £68 per week) are too insignificant to be recorded, and despite the under-counting of part-time manual workers, part-time women are more concentrated in manual than in non-manual jobs in six of the remaining ten sectors. Together, these sectors employ over 65 per cent of those part-time women workers whose existence is recorded by the NES.

It is already clear that part-time women work in different jobs from those of full-time women workers. This is further confirmed by table 2.9 which shows the distribution of full-time and part-time women across the different occupational categories and table 2.10 which shows the composition, in terms of full-time men and women and part-time women, of each occupational group.

Table 2.9 — distribution of male and female employees by occupation, 1995

occupation	men	full-time women	part-time women
managerial and administration	18.4%	12.0%	2.7%
professional	10.5%	11.3%	6.7%
associate professional and technical	8.5%	11.1%	9.1%
clerical and secretarial	9.5%	36.2%	23.4%
craft and related	17.5%	3.3%	1.4%
personal and protective services	6.1%	9.2%	20.2%
selling	4.5%	6.2%	15.2%
plant and machine operatives	17.1%	7.0%	3.0%
others	7.9%	3.6%	18.4%

source: NES, 1995, tables 86, 87 & 183

Table 2.10 — men and women as % of occupation

occupation	full-time men	full-time women	part-time women
managerial and administration	69.4%	26.5%	4.2%
professional	52.7%	33.2%	14.1%
associate professional and technical	45.2%	34.6%	20.2%
clerical and secretarial	23.6%	52.4%	24.1%
craft and related	87.5%	9.6%	2.8%
personal and protective services	30.9%	27.0%	42.1%
selling	27.6%	21.9%	38.2%
plant and machine operatives	76.3%	18.2%	5.5%
others	44.8%	12.0%	43.2%

source: NES, 1995, tables 86, 87 & 183

Save in clerical and secretarial work, part-time women's occupational distribution (table 2.9) is less similar to that of men than is the case for full-time women workers. The NES, upon which tables 2.9 and 2.10 are based, put part-time women's share of the total employed workforce at 19.8 per cent in 1995 (this compared with 21.1 per cent according to the LFS[43]). On this measure, part-time women were proportionately represented in only one occupational group (associate professional and technical), are under-represented in four (where they accounted in 1995 for one third of their expected strength), and were over-represented in the other four (where they accounted for almost twice their expected strength).

And just as the broad occupational groups do not fully capture the different occupational distributions of full-time men and women workers, so the same is true of part-time and full-time women. Whereas, in 1995, health associate professionals accounted for just over half of full-time women associate professional and technical workers, the figure for part-time women associate professional and technical workers was closer to three-quarters (nurses alone accounted for 41 per cent and 80 per cent respectively of full-time and part-time women within this broad occupational group). Two-thirds of full-time women in sales, but 93 per cent of part-time women, worked as check-out operators and sales assistants.

In order to estimate the extent to which the NES is inaccurate as regards part-time women (not least as regards pay, considered below), it would be useful to compare it to the LFS. But the LFS does not disaggregate part-time and full-time women by occupation, and, although it does supply statistics by occupation for part-timers and full-timers separately, it does not distinguish in these between full-time and part-time men (the latter being a group ignored by the NES).

(C) ETHNIC MINORITY WOMEN

Introduction

Just over 6 per cent of women aged between 16 and 59 in Great Britain are from one or other of the ethnic minority groups ('ethnic minority' being defined as other than white). The term 'ethnic minority' is used here because the statistics upon which this section is based disaggregate this group into 'black', 'Indian', 'Pakistani and Bangladeshi', etc. Whereas the term 'black' is commonly used to include people of Asian, African, and Carribean extraction, 'ethnic minority' is used here in order to distinguish the total group of those not wholly of Caucasian extraction from those who are of African and/or Carribean extraction.[44]

---

[43] Further, given that the NES statistics ignore its own estimates (in 1995) of 4.2% part-time men in the workforce, this works out at $19.8 \times 95.8/100 = 19\%$.

[44] See R. Bhavnani, *Black Women in the Labour Market: A Research Review* (Manchester: EOC, 1994), for discussion of the terminology.

the only women to work in any substantial numbers in manufacturing are white and Indian; that a disproportionately high proportion of black and mixed/ other women work in the service industries; that black women are under-represented and Indian women over-represented in distribution, hotels, and catering; and that very high and low proportions of black and Indian women respectively work in 'other services' (mainly administration, education, health, and welfare).

Occupational Segregation

Similar proportions of white and ethnic minority women work in non-manual jobs, although the position differs substantially between the different ethnic minority groups. In 1993, for example, non-manual women accounted for 70 per cent of white and 67 per cent of ethnic women workers, but between 62 per cent (Indian) and 73 per cent (Pakistani/ Bangladeshi and mixed/other) of particular ethnic minority groups had non-manual jobs.[66] The most recent available break-down of women by ethnic group and occupation is shown in table 2.17.

Table 2.17 — women by occupational and ethnic group, 1993

	white	ethnic minority	black	Indian	Pakistani/ Bangladeshi	mixed/ other
professional	2%	5%	3%	5%	3%	6%
intermediate	30%	31%	33%	26%	36%	35%
skilled non-manual	37%	33%	33%	34%	25%	38%
skilled manual	8%	7%	6%	7%	8%	8%
part skilled	17%	19%	14%	24%	26%	9%
unskilled	6%	5%	11%	4%	2%	3%

source: LFS, 1993[67]

Table 2.17 does not distinguish between full-time and part-time workers. But Irene Bruegel, who examined the LFS statistics for 1987–9, found that, if the greater tendency of ethnic minority women to work full-time is taken into account, the disparities between white and ethnic minority women are starker than they otherwise appear. Again, the occupational groupings are different from those employed by the other tables in this chapter but it is possible to discern the difference in occupational status between black and white women workers. Breugel's findings are displayed in table 2.18.

---

[66] Ethnic Groups and the Labour Market (1994), n. 50 above, 66% of black women had non-manual jobs.
[67] *Ibid*. 153 fig. 3. These include employees and self-employed and are estimates only.

Table 2.18 — occupational status of black and white full-time women workers

	black	white
professional, employers, and managers	5%	24%
intermediate non-manual	28%	29%
junior non-manual	25%	33%
skilled manual	8%	4%
personal service	13%	5%
semi-skilled manual	15%	4%
unskilled	2%	0%
white collar	58%	86%
manual	30%	9%

source: Breugel[68]

Despite having a higher level of qualifications than white women, black women are much more likely to work in manual jobs (in particular, in semi-skilled work) than are equivalent white women (that is, white full-time women workers). They are also much less likely to be employed in the upper strata of professional and managerial jobs and themselves to be employers.

(D) WOMEN AND WORKPLACE SEGREGATION

The foregoing section has concentrated on segregation at the level of industrial sector and occupation. Little research has been conducted on sex segregation at the level of the actual *workplace*, but that which is available from the Workplace Industrial Relations Survey (WIRS) indicates that workplaces are generally sex-segregated.[69]

Millward and Woodland extracted information on sex segregation at the level of the workplace from the 1990 WIRS which covered over 2,000 establishments in Britain. Although it excluded establishments employing fewer than twenty-five employees, it included material about all other sizes of establishment. Millward and Woodland found that employment was highly sex-segregated for all occupational groups (skilled, semi-skilled, and unskilled manual workers; clerical, administrative, and secretarial workers; supervisors and foremen; junior technical and professional

---

[68] Breugel, n. 15 above, 54, table 4.
[69] More is available from the US. See, e.g. F. Blau, *Equal Pay in the Office*; W. Bielby and J. Baron, 'A Woman's Place Is with Other Women: Sex Segregation Within Organizations' in B. Reskin (ed.), *Sex Segregation in the Workplace: Trends, Explanations, Remedies* (Washington, DC: National Academy Press, 1984). See also Hakim (1996), n. 2 above, 151–2.

employees; senior technical and professional employees; and middle and senior management).[70]

Women also tend to be employed in different *types* of workplaces from those in which men work. According to Millward, predominantly female workplaces tend to be small—typically they had between twenty-five and forty-nine employees (smaller workplaces being excluded from WIRS data)—they have labour costs which accounted for more than 50 per cent of total costs; they tend to provide local rather than national service; and their managers report very good relations with the workforce and high productivity in comparison with competitors. Men's workplaces, by contrast, tend to be either small (employing fewer than 100 workers) and in the private sector, or very large (having at least 100,000 employees), and often state-owned; and to serve monopolistic product markets.[71]

WIRS data showing that women are more likely to be found in small workplaces are supported, in relation to very small workplaces, by LFS results. In 1994, for example, 22 per cent of all women workers in Great Britain but only 16 per cent of men were found in workplaces with fewer than eleven employees.[72]

If workplaces are considered in terms of the occupational groups therein, the pattern of sex segregation becomes even more apparent. In 78 per cent of all workplaces, skilled manual workers were at least 95 per cent single sex (in 65 per cent of workplaces they were exclusively male, in 9 per cent exclusively female, and in 4 per cent, 95–9 per cent male). In 67 per cent and 62 per cent of workplaces semi-skilled manual workers and middle and senior managers respectively were at least 95 per cent single-sex, and only two of the eight categories (unskilled manual and junior professional/ technical/sales) were less than 95 per cent single-sex in 50 per cent of workplaces.[73]

---

[70] N. Millward and S. Woodland, *Gender Segregation and Male/Female Wage Differences* (London, LSE Centre for Economic Performance, 1995), Discussion Paper No 220, 12. In the NHS, too, IHSM Consultants, *Creative Career Paths in the NHS: Report No. 1: Top Managers* (report for the NHS Women's Unit) reported that women managers were over-represented in provider units, men in purchaser units. Even where men were found in provider units they were underrepresented in the less prestigious community, elderly, and learning disability services.

[71] N. Millward, *Targeting Potential Discrimination* (Manchester: EOC, 1995), 6–7. See also M. Curran, *Stereotypes and Selection: Gender and Family in the Recrutment Process* (London: HMSO, 1985) EOC. Report.

[72] *Employment Gazette*, Dec. 1994, LFS 1.

[73] Millward, n. 71 above, 8, table 2.1. Semi-skilled manual workers were exclusively male and female in 52% and 11% of workplaces respectively, and were almost exclusively male and female in a further 3% and 1%. For managers the figures were 53%, 8%, and 95–99% male in 1%. Note that in some of the smaller workplaces there may be very small numbers of employees in one or more of the occupational groups. WIRS classifies occupations into unskilled, semi-skilled and skilled manual; clerical administrative and secretarial; supervisors; junior professional/technical/sales; senior professional/technical/sales and middle and senior managers.

What is true in respect of women workers generally is even more so as regards part-time workers. Part-timers, who are overwhelmingly female, tend to be concentrated together, and research has shown 'evidence of a strong association between "part-time using" and "female using" industries'.[74] Part-time workers are also, like women generally, clustered in small workplaces: 'the higher the proportion of part time employment; the smaller' the workplace.[75] As far as gender segregation *within* workplaces is concerned, too, Millward reports that: '[w]orkplaces with over 40 per cent of their employees working part-time had much more segregation among the manual workforce than other workplaces'.[76]

Ethnic minority workers are also, according to the WIRS, segregated by workplace. The survey does not distinguish between male and female ethnic minority workers, or between people of different ethnic minority groups. Nevertheless Millward reports, on the basis of the 1990 results, that fully 61 per cent of workplaces surveyed had no ethnic minority workers, and in only 15 per cent of workplaces did ethnic minority workers account for at least 5 per cent of the workforce.[77] Ethnic minority workers were more likely to be found in larger workplaces; in recently established and non-union workplaces; in nationalized industries and textiles, clothing, medical, and catering services; in workplaces in which managers rated both productivity and employee relations as relatively poor. There was no apparent relationship between the proportion of women and the proportion of ethnic minority workers in establishments.

III. WOMEN AND PAY

(A) INTRODUCTION

We have considered where women and men are found within the labour force (in terms both of industry and occupation) and, to the extent that differences exist, have considered the relative positions of full-time and part-time women workers, white and ethnic minority women. The purpose of this section is to introduce the issue of the gender–pay gap, to consider it as it affects full-time and part-time women workers, white and black women workers, and to begin to explore where and why the gap arises. Just as in the previous section, full-time and part-time workers, white and ethnic minority women, will be considered separately.

[74] D. Blanchflower and B. Corry, *Part-time Employment in G.B.: An Analysis Using Establishment Data* (London: HMSO, 1987), Department of Employment Research Paper No. 57, 56.
[75] *Ibid.* 13.   [76] Millward, n. 71 above, 13.   [77] *Ibid.* 17.

Full-time women workers earn, on the latest figures, 79.9 per cent of full-time men's hourly and 72.3 per cent of their weekly pay.

Industrial Segregation and Pay

We saw, above, that full-time women are distributed differently across the various industrial sectors from men. The ranking of industrial sectors in terms of overall average wages (i.e. taking into account the wages of men and women, full-time and part-time) is shown in table 2.19.[78]

Table 2.19 — industrial sectors by salary, 1995

industrial sectors
financial intermediation
mining and quarrying
electricity, gas, and water supply
education
real estate, renting, and business
public administration, defence, and compulsory social security
manufacturing
construction
transport, storage, and communication
health and social work
other community, social, and personal service
trade, vehicle repair, and goods
agriculture, hunting, and forestry
hotels and restaurants

source: NES, 1995, tables 54–57, 172 & 177
fishing is not recorded as a category by the NES

At first sight women's position looks satisfactory. If table 2.19 is compared with table 2.2 we can see that fully 39.3 per cent of full-time women workers, as against 29.5 per cent of men, work in the six top-paying industrial sectors and that fractionally fewer women than men (22.1 per cent: 23.3 per cent) work in the four lowest-paying sectors. Yet women earn considerably less than men. The explanation lies in the relative wages of men and women *within* the various sectors, displayed in table 2.20.

Table 2.2 showed that full-time women are most concentrated in health and social work, followed by manufacturing, then by trade, vehicle repair, and goods, real estate, education, and public administration. Together

[78] No statistics are available for part-time men.

Table 2.20 — full-time women's hourly pay by sector, 1995

industrial sectors	as % of men's wages in sector	as % of all men's wages
financial intermediation	54.3%	92.1%
mining and quarrying	*	*
electricity, gas, and water supply	77.9%	92.1%
education	87%	117%
real estate, renting, and business	71.7%	84.4%
public administration, defence, and compulsory social security	75%	82.8%
manufacturing	70.7%	66%
construction	94.2%	71.8%
transport, storage, and communication	88.8%	77.2%
health and social work	76.8%	79.7%
other community, social, and personal service	85.1%	77.3%
trade, vehicle repair, and goods	87%	62.7%
agriculture, hunting, and forestry	97.8%	57.9%
hotels and restaurants	82.3%	51.9%

source: NES, 1995, tables 54–57
* not recorded. Fishing is not recorded as a category by the NES

these sectors employ almost 80 per cent of all full-time women workers. Four of them pay relatively well. But in four of these sectors, full-time women workers earn less than 80 per cent of the hourly rate enjoyed by their male colleagues. And only in education do women earn more than the (overall) average male hourly wage.

Manual workers generally earn lower wages than non-manual workers. It is useful, therefore, to consider whether women's wages are held down, within industrial sectors, by their concentration into low-paid manual jobs. Table 2.21 shows full-time male and female manual workers, as a proportion of full-time male and female workers respectively, in the various industrial sectors in 1995.

Men comprise the bulk of manual workers in almost all fourteen industrial sectors, and in no sector do a larger proportion of full-time women than of full-time men work in manual jobs.[79] Whatever the reason for women's lower average pay within the various industrial sectors, it is not the result of their concentration into manual jobs. The pay of full-time manual and non-manual women workers, relative to that of comparable men in the same sectors, is shown by table 2.22.

[79] Men account for between 100% (financial intermediation; mining and quarrying; electricity, gas, and water supply; construction) and 19% (health and social work) of manual workers by sector. On average (in 1995), they comprised 71% of manual workers in each industrial sector, 92% of full-time manual workers (NES, 1995, tables 54–57 & 172).

Table 2.21 — proportion of workers in manual jobs by sex and industrial sector, 1995

industrial sector	women	men
financial intermediation	*	4%
mining and quarrying	*	55%
electricity, gas, and water supply	*	53%
education	5%	14%
real estate, renting, and business	9%	30%
public admin., defence, and compulsory social security	4%	16%
manufacturing	53%	64%
construction	*	65%
transport, storage, and communication	23%	66%
health and social work	19%	30%
other community, social, and personal service	23%	45%
trade, vehicle repair, and goods	13%	38%
agriculture, hunting, and forestry	46%	80%
hotels and restaurants	59%	65%

source: NES, 1995, tables 54–57
* not recorded. Fishing is not recorded as a category by the NES

Table 2.22 — manual/non-manual women's pay by sector, 1995

industrial sector	same sector		all	
	manual	non-manual	manual	non-manual
agriculture, hunting, and forestry	88.6%	78.4%	45.8%	69.6%
mining and quarrying	*	*	*	*
manufacturing	70.3%	64%	52.8%	80.6%
electricity, gas, and water supply	*	63%	*	92.1%
construction	*	61.1%	*	71.8%
trade, vehicle repair, and goods	76.9%	64.2%	48.3%	64.8%
hotels and restaurants	81.5%	77.8%	41.7%	66.6%
transport, storage, and communication	95.9%	67%	67%	80.3%
financial intermediation	*	53.3%	*	92.1%
real estate, renting, and business	80.6%	61.7%	49.9%	87.6%
public admin., defence, and compulsory social security	82.7%	70.9%	57.4%	83.9%
education	79.5%	82.3%	47.9%	120.6%
health and social work	80%	71.5%	48.5%	87.2%
other community, social, and personal service	70.5%	76.5%	44.7%	86.4%

source: NES, 1995, tables 54–57
* not recorded. Fishing is not recorded as a category by the NES

Women's lower earnings are explicable more by reference to their pay, relative to those of men, *within* the various industrial sectors (and, in turn, within manual and non-manual hierarchies therein) than by their distribution *between* those sectors or between manual and non-manual jobs. Full-time manual women workers earned, in 1995, between 70.3 per cent and 95.9 per cent of the hourly wages of manual men in the same sectors—the latter figure is high but represents one of only two sectors in which such women earned 85 per cent or more of their male colleagues' wages. Together these sectors employ a mere 6 per cent of full-time women manual workers. In 1995 the manufacturing industry employed 44.6 per cent of all full-time manual women workers, health and social work a further 17.4 per cent and trade, vehicle repairs, etc. and hotels and restaurants 8.4 per cent each. Within these sectors manual women earned between 70.3 per cent (manufacturing) and 81.5 per cent (trade, etc.) of their male colleagues' wages. Non-manual women were concentrated in health and social work, trade, vehicle repairs, etc., education, and real estate where they earned between 61.7 per cent (real estate) and 82.3 per cent (education) of non-manual male hourly rates.[80] The only category of female workers who earned more than the average male hourly rate was full-time non-manual women workers in education. But even these women earned considerably less than full-time non-manual male workers in the same sector.

It could be argued, of course, that women (whether manual or non-manual) may perform very different work from that done by their male colleagues. This is, no doubt, true to a significant extent, although table 2.23 shows that women are paid considerably less than men within the same occupational groups.

Table 2.23 — full-time women's hourly pay by occupation, 1996

occupation*	women's wages
managerial and administration	70.9%
professional	90.6%
associate professional and technical	79.0%
clerical and secretarial	94.1%
craft and related	67.9%
personal and protective services	70.6%
selling	67.8%
plant and machine operatives	76.9%
others	78.2%

source: NES, 1996, tables 8 & 9
* ranked in order of overall average wages

[80] With 17.3%, 14.1%, 12.7%, and 12.3% respectively, between them these sectors employ 56.4% of non-manual women full-time workers. A further 12%, 10.2%, and 9.7% respectively are found in public administration, financial intermediation, and manufacturing. Figures taken from the NES 1995, tables 56 and 57.

And even when occupations are considered at a greater degree of dis-aggregation, women continue to be paid considerably less than men. Within the broad category of 'managers and administrators', for example, there are six sub-categories of management for which both male and female earnings are listed.[81] Within these subcategories, women earn between 58.5 per cent (general managers and administrators in national and local gov-ernment, large companies, and organizations) and 89.2 per cent (man-agers in transport and storage) of men's hourly rate. The hourly earnings of women, relative to men, averaged over the seven categories is 72.9 per cent, only slightly better than the average figure for women managers and administrators generally. And if the level of disaggregation is taken still further and earnings examined on the basis of the twelve sub-sub-categories for which statistics are available on both men's and women's earnings, the relative hourly rate for women varies between 63.7 per cent (Bank, Building Society, and Post Office Managers) and 95.4 per cent (Civil Service Executive Officers), the average being 76.0 per cent. Again, this marks an improvement over the figure (70.9 per cent) for women managers generally, but is a very long way from being equal.

What is true in respect of management is also true when the other large occupational groups are disaggregated. In no case do the disaggregated figures remove the gender–pay gap within the occupations (i.e. in no case do they show that the gender–pay gap at the broad occupational level results from men's and women's different specializations within the occu-pation). In most cases (associate professional and technical, personal and protective services, sales, craft and related, and other) the lower-level ana-lysis serves to locate part of the gap in the different sub-occupational dis-tributions (this does not, of course, explain *why* some of those specialisms pay more than others), but in other cases this level of analysis either leaves the gap unaltered (plant and machine operatives) or serves only to increase it (professional, clerical and secretarial).[82]

Occupational Segregation and Pay

Women and men do not, typically, get paid the same, even when they are engaged in the same (broad categories of) jobs. But men and women

---

[81] This goes some way to refuting Hakim's suggestion, n. 2 above (1996), 178, that gender–wage gaps in broad occupational classifications are due in large part to the differ-ent types of job occupied by men and women within those broader classifications.

[82] The figures for sub-occupational and sub sub-occupational level are, respectively, pro-fessional: 72.9–97.3% and 77.7–97.8%, with averages of 84.6% and 85.1%; associate pro-fessional and technical: 64–94.2% and 59.1–97.3% with averages of 84.4% and 85.2%; clerical and secretarial: 75.8–92.9% and 75.7–97.7% with averages of 84.5% and 86.7%; per-sonal and protective: 80.7–103% and 80.8–126.4% with averages of 88.7% and 94.4%; sales: 80.2–89.3% and 77.6–100% with averages of 83.8% and 88.6%; plant and machine operat-ives: 70–83.8% and 61.3–85.9% with averages of 76.2 and 76.5%; craft and related: 72.4–85.4% and 68.7–92.7% with averages of 84.5% and 86.7%; other: 79.8–95% and 81.7–100% with averages of 88.1% and 92.8%

do not, for the most part, do the same jobs. We saw from table 2.5 above that women in general, and full-time women in particular, are concentrated in occupational and clerical work, an occupational group which employs few men. Table 2.24 shows the ranking of the nine occupational groups in terms of pay, and the wages of full-time women within them.

Table 2.24 — full-time women's hourly pay by sector, 1995

occupation*	women's wage
managerial and administration	109.5%
professional	135.5%
associate professional and technical	99.1%
craft and related	52.7%
plant and machine operatives	52.8%
selling	57.7%
personal and protective services	55.6%
others	45.9%
clerical and secretarial	67.4%

source: NES, 1995, tables 8 & 9
* ranked in order of overall average wages[83]

Tables 2.5 and 2.24 show that women are concentrated in the lowest paid occupations (pay being measured in terms of the average wages of all workers, rather than of women workers alone). Clerical and secretarial work, which absorbs the highest proportion of full-time women workers, is the lowest-paid of all occupations.[84] And while the second largest group of full-time women workers is found in the highest paid occupation (managerial and administrative), in 1995 fractionally under 50 per cent of all full-time women were concentrated in the three lowest-paid occupations (clerical, personal and protective services, and other), as against less than a quarter of men, and 37.8 per cent of full-time women (but 55.3 per cent of men) were found in the top four occupations.

The issue of different specialisms within broad occupational groups was discussed above. This, in turn, has an impact upon women's relative pay within the various groups. The concentration of women managers into

---

[83] The figures for professional, plant and machine operatives, personal and protective services, other, and clerical and secretarial fell from 1995 to 1996.

[84] It is clear from the relatively high wages of women within that occupation that the wages for the occupation as a whole were depressed by the absence of highly paid men. Indeed there is evidence from Australia that, by working in predominantly female occupations, women actually maximize their wages (i.e. that while overall levels of pay are lower in predominantly female occupations, the wages earned by women are actually higher)— see F. Vella, 'Gender Roles, Occupational Choice and Gender Wage Differentials' (1993) 69 *Economic Record* 382. This is further discussed in Ch. 6.

four of the ten categories of manager was a major factor, according to research carried out by Gregg and Machin, behind the pay gap between male and female managers.[85] The NES, too, shows that the occupational sub-categories into which women are concentrated are often (but not invariably) less well-paid than those in which men are found. Within management, for example, women are half again as likely as men (23 per cent: 15 per cent) to be found in the service industries which paid only two-thirds of the average managerial and administrative wage in 1995; within the personal and protective category 52 per cent of men work in the protective services (which paid 119 per cent of the average wage in 1995), while 45 per cent of women work in health and related services (which paid 86 per cent); within the craft and related category 44 per cent of men work in relatively highly paid metal and electrical occupations while 65 per cent of women work in the poorly paid textiles category; and within selling occupations, nearly 60 per cent of men work as relatively well paid brokers and sales representatives while two-thirds of women work as sales assistants.[86] But this pattern is not uniform: women in the clerical and secretarial category are concentrated in the relatively well-paid secretarial/personal assistants/typists/word processor-operator sub-category, while men tend to be found in the poorest paying category (store and despatch clerks and storekeepers); professional women are overwhelmingly concentrated in teaching which paid (men) 110 per cent of the average professional salary, while many men work as engineers which paid only 89 per cent of the average in 1995.[87] And in the categories both of plant and machine operatives and associate professional and technical staff, the disparity in wages would appear to arise more as a result of differential payment of men and women in the same sub-categories than of women's concentration in lower paying subcategories.[88]

[85] Gregg and Machin, n. 32 above, 13.

[86] Wages are calculated on the basis of men only in order to counteract, as much as possible, the downward impact of women's wages in predominantly female jobs—tables 86 and 87. Within craft and related, men are concentrated in metal machining, fitting, and instrument making, with 25% of men and 110% of average pay, electric/electronic trades with a further 19% and wages of 113%, while women are concentrated in textiles which pays 83% of the average male wage in craft and related—women earn only 75% of that. Brokers and sales representatives account for 7% and 51% of men in sales and pay 132% and 123% of the average male wage in the broad occupational group—in sales assistant jobs men earn 63% of average male salary for the broad occupation.

[87] While there is no figure for male wages in the secretarial, etc. category, women working in it earn 111% of the average female hourly rate in the clerical and secretarial category. 35% of clerical/secretarial men are store and dispatch clerks/store-keepers, where they earn 86% of the average male wage for the category. Finally, 66% of women teach, 3% are engineers—men are more evenly spread between the two (28% and 35% respectively).

[88] Among plant and machine operatives there is a reasonably small salary range with men relatively evenly spread, save for their concentration (29%) as road transport operatives who earn only 86% of the average male hourly rate for the broad occupational category—women are concentrated predominantly in sub-occupations paying slightly more than the male average in the category but in which they earn only about three-quarters of the male rate; in

The issue of why women's jobs pay less than men's, and of why women who do the same (even narrowly defined) jobs as men still earn lower wages, is addressed below. First, however, we will consider the issue of part-time women and pay.

(c) PART-TIME WOMEN WORKERS

It was pointed out, above, that New Earnings Survey statistics for part-time women workers should be treated with particular caution. The one-in-five of all part-time women who, according to NES estimates, are excluded from the NES statistics are those women who are particularly badly paid: those part-time women workers included in the NES might be regarded as the relatively advantaged four-fifths.[89] Despite this, the NES statistics show that part-time women fare considerably worse both than men and than women who work full-time.

Industrial Segregation and Pay

The distribution of part-time women workers between the various industrial sectors is shown in table 2.6 above. When the overall ranking of the sectors in terms of pay is considered, part-time women's position is less advantageous than that of full-time women. Only 31.9 per cent of part-time women fall within the top six earning industrial sectors and considerably more (38.6 per cent) are within the bottom four sectors in terms of pay (the figures for full-time women were 39.3 per cent and 22.1 per cent, and for men were 29.5 per cent and 22.7 per cent respectively). And, just as full-time women earned less than men within the various sectors, so this was the case (and considerably more so) for part-time women. The figures for 1995 are at table 2.25.

If table 2.25 is compared with the equivalent results for full-time women (at table 2.20 above) it can be seen that part-time women are disadvantaged in terms of pay by comparison with full-timers. Full-time women workers earn between 54.3 per cent and 92.4 per cent of the hourly rates of men in the same sectors (and, in ten of the thirteen sectors for which figures are available, earn at least 75 per cent of men's rates) and between 51.9 per cent and 117 per cent of all men's average hourly rates (in nine of the thirteen, over 70 per cent). Part-time women, by contrast, earn a low of 43.4 per cent and a high of only 73.3 per cent of the hourly rates earned by men in the same sectors (in only two of the eleven sectors for

associate professional and technical, while women are overwhelmingly more concentrated in the relatively low paying (86%) health associate jobs (52%, 8% of men), there is not a great deal of difference in the spread between high and low paid areas save that more men work in the business and financial area (17%: 7%), where they earn a staggering 154% of the average and in which women earn only 63% of the male rate).

[89] See text to n. 16 above—the NES estimates for the numbers of those excluded are probably significantly too low.

Table 2.25 — part-time women's hourly pay by sector, 1995

industrial sectors*	as % of men in sector	as % of all men
financial intermediation	43.4%	73.6%
mining and quarrying	*	*
electricity, gas, and water supply	*	*
education	55.3%	74.3%
real estate, renting, and business	50%	58.9%
public administration, defence, and compulsory social security	60.3%	66.6%
manufacturing	58.1%	54.2%
construction	73.3%	63.8%
transport, storage, and communication	68.2%	59.2%
health and social work	63.4%	65.8%
other community, social, and personal service	56.3%	51%
trade, vehicle repair, and goods	64.3%	46.3%
agriculture, hunting, and forestry	*	*
hotels and restaurants	63.2%	39.9%

source: NES, 1995, tables 54–57, 172 & 177
* not recorded. Fishing is not recorded as a category by the NES

which statistics are available earning more than 65 per cent) and between 39.9 per cent and 74.3 per cent of all men's average hourly rates (in only two sectors, over 70 per cent, and over 60 per cent in a total of five).

In order to consider why part-time women do so badly, it is useful to compare the proportion of part-time and full-time women engaged in (relatively poorly paid) manual jobs within each sector.

Part-time women are much more likely to be engaged in manual work than are full-time women—the only exception is in trade, vehicle repair, etc., where the difference is marginal. This may have some effect in holding down part-time women's wages, relative both to those of full-time women and of men. But the pattern is not clear: part-time women are anywhere between seven and a half times as likely (public administration) and fractionally more likely (trade) to be engaged in manual work than are their part-time colleagues. And full-time women earn between 121 per cent (health and social work) and 151 per cent (other community, social, and personal service) of part-time women's hourly rates. There is no apparent relationship between the relative proportions of full-time and part-time women engaged in manual work within each industrial sector, and the relative advantage of full-time women workers, in terms of pay, in the sectors. It seems rather that, just as full-time women earn consistently less than men, whether they are engaged in manual or in non-manual work, so the same is true as between part-time and full-time women workers. This can be seen in table 2.27.

Table 2.26 — proportion of women in manual jobs by sector, 1995

industrial sector	full-time women	part-time women
financial intermediation	*	*
mining and quarrying	*	*
electricity, gas, and water supply	*	*
education	5%	26%
real estate, renting, and business	9%	36%
public admin., defence, and compulsory social security	4%	30%
manufacturing	53%	60%
construction	*	*
transport, storage, and communication	23%	37%
health and social work	19%	36%
other community, social, and personal service	23%	40%
trade, vehicle repair, and goods	13%	14%
agriculture, hunting, and forestry	46%	*
hotels and restaurants	59%	87%

source: NES, 1995, tables 54–57 & 183
* not recorded. Fishing is not recorded as a category by the NES

Table 2.27 — part-time women's pay by sector

industrial sector	manual	non-manual
financial intermediation	*	*
mining and quarrying	*	*
electricity, gas, and water supply	*	*
education	88.8%	71.8%
real estate, renting, and business	80.1%	79.3%
public admin., defence, and compulsory social security	82.1%	89.3%
manufacturing	91.7%	76.3%
construction	*	88.9%
transport, storage, and communication	88.1%	73.9%
health and social work	100%	87.0%
other community, social, and personal service	91.5%	67.2%
trade, vehicle repair, and goods	91.3%	72.1%
agriculture, hunting, and forestry	*	*
hotels and restaurants	92.8%	71.9%

source: NES, 1995, tables 54–57 & 177
* not recorded. Fishing is not recorded as a category by the NES

Even when manual and non-manual women are considered separately, part-time manual workers' wages vary between fractionally over 80 per cent (real estate, etc.) and 100 per cent (health and social work), and non-manual workers' between 67.2 per cent (other community, social, and personal services) and 89.3 per cent (public administration, etc.) of full-time manual and non-manual workers' respective hourly rates. Just as was the case with full-time male and female workers (see Table 2.2 above), the differences between the wages of part- and full-time women workers (and, thence, between the hourly rates of part-time women and full-time men) are at least in part the result of differential payment of workers doing the same broad types of work (manual or non-manual) in the same industrial sectors, as well as of any differences in occupational and/or manual/non-manual distribution. This point is underlined when the relative hourly rates of men and part-time women in the same occupations are considered.

Within most of the occupational sub-categories part-time women earn in the region of 90 per cent of full-time women's hourly rate (in eighteen of the twenty-seven shared occupational sub-categories, between 85 per cent and 94 per cent; in a further five, between 95 and 99 per cent; in two each, under 84 per cent and over 100 per cent). And if the statistics are disaggregated to the sub-sub-category level, fourteen of the thirty-eight categories of part-time women earn between 85 and 94 per cent of full-time women's wages, a further 12 per cent, between 95 per cent and 99 per cent, nine over 100 per cent and three under 84 per cent. Occupational distribution does not differ markedly, as between part-time and full-time women workers, at the sub-occupational level (i.e. when differences at the broad occupational level are ignored and full-time and part-time women considered only within those broad categories). Part-time professional women benefit from their greater degree of concentration

Table 2.28 — part-time women's hourly pay by occupation, 1995

occupation	relative to men	relative to women
managerial and administration	58.4%	82.4%
professional	92.3%	101.4%
associate professional and technical	71.3%	90.6%
clerical and secretarial	81.3%	88.0%
craft and related	63%	92.9%
personal and protective services	64.8%	88.8%
selling	51.7%	77.6%
plant and machine operatives	71.4%	92.4%
others	73.5%	92.9%

source: NES, 1995, tables 86 & 178

within teaching, coupled with the relatively high pay in that area (full-time women earning 106 per cent of the normal 'professional' hourly rate and part-time women earning 102 per cent of the hourly rate of full-timers); part-time women in sales suffer from their greater concentration (94 per cent) into the relatively (and absolutely) poorly paid sales assistants/check-out sub-category and their absence from the relatively well paid area of sales representation (in which full-time women, 18 per cent of whom work in this category, earn 142 per cent of the average female hourly rate in sales).

Occupational Segregation and Pay

Just as full-time women workers are concentrated in lower-paying occupations than are men, so the same is true (and to a significantly greater extent) of part-time women workers. Part-time women are found mainly in occupations such as clerical and secretarial work, personal and protective services, 'other occupations', and selling: these occupations occupy the lowest four places in the occupational pay hierarchy shown in table 2.22 and between them employ at least 77.2 per cent of part-time women workers (the true figure is considerably higher than this, since the most underpaid women are least likely to be included in the NES statistics), as against only 55.2 per cent of female full-time workers.

The picture looks even more grim when the hourly wages of part-time women workers within the various occupational categories are considered at table 2.29. When considered together with table 2.9 above, it shows that more than half of all part-time women workers who appear in the NES earn less than half the average hourly male wage.

Table 2.29 — part-time women's hourly pay by occupation, 1995

occupation	relative to all men
managerial and administration	88.7%
professional	139.5%
associate professional and technical	89.7%
craft and related	48.8%
plant and machine operatives	49.2%
selling	44.7%
personal and protective services	49.5%
others	43.8%
clerical and secretarial	60%

source: NES, 1995, tables 86, 87 & 178

(D) ETHNIC MINORITY WOMEN

Introduction

At first glance, ethnic minority women do not appear to be disadvantaged, in comparison to white women, when it comes to pay.

Table 2.30 — hourly pay of women by ethnic group, 1994

	white	ethnic minority	black	Indian	Pakistani/ Bangladeshi	mixed/ other
£ per hour	£6.40	£6.31	£6.77	£5.77	£5.15	£6.17
as % of white		98.6%	105.8%	90.2%	80.5%	96.4%

source: LFS, 1994[90]

But Irene Breugel pointed out, in relation to 1987–9 statistics, that the hourly pay of ethnic minority women is inflated, in comparison to white women, both by their greater tendency to work full-time, and by their relative over-concentration in the higher-paying metropolitan areas of the UK.[91]

Applying Breugel's approach to more recent statistics the following results emerge. All part-time women earn an average 74.9p per hour for every pound earned by full-time women. Table 2.14 shows that 54 per cent, of white women but 67 per cent, 66 per cent, 62 per cent, 73 per cent, and 73 per cent of ethnic minority, black, Indian, Pakistani/Bangladeshi, and mixed/other women respectively work full-time. If each group is given the same full-time/part-time distribution as white women and their hourly rates adjusted accordingly, the hourly wages of women look like this.

Table 2.31 — hourly pay by ethnic group adjusted for part-time/full-time distribution, 1994

	white	ethnic minority	black	Indian	Pakistani/ Bangladeshi	mixed/ other
£ per hour	£6.40	£6.09	£6.55	£5.64	£4.89	£5.85
as % of white		95.2%	102.3%	88.1%	76.4%	91.4%

source: LFS, 1994[92]

Only black women are paid more than white women when the greater propensity of white women to work part-time is taken into account. And if the figures are adjusted again to take into account the geographical distribution of the various ethnic groups of workers the picture changes once

---

[90] Ethnic Groups and the Labour Market (1995), n. 49 above, 257, fig. 5.
[91] N. 15 above.
[92] Ethnic Groups and the Labour Market (1995), n. 49 above, 257, fig. 5.

more. The geographical distribution of workers by ethnic group, together with the average hourly wages for full-time women workers in each region (expressed as a percentage of the average throughout Great Britain) is shown in table 2.32.

Table 2.32 — ethnic minority workers as % of economically active population, 1994–5

Region	ethnic minority workers	female wage as % of average female wage
Great Britain	4.8%	100%
North	1.3%	89.5%
Yorkshire and Humberside	3.1%	89.5%
East Midlands	3.6%	88.8%
East Anglia	1.7%	90.9%
South East	9.0%	115.1%
Greater London	18.8%	130.4%[93]
South West	1.2%	93.6%
West Midlands	7.0%	91.3%
North West	3.2%	94.1%
Wales	1.0%	92.2%
Scotland	0.9%	95.0%

source: LFS, Spring 1994 & NES, 1995[94]

The economically active from ethnic minority groups generally are concentrated most of all in Greater London and, to a lesser extent, in the South East generally and in the West Midlands. In Greater London, where ethnic minority workers are most concentrated, wages are almost a third as high again as the national average.

Table 2.32 does not disaggregate the various ethnic minority groups but table 2.33 shows that each of the ethnic minority groups is more concentrated in the South East than are white workers, the concentration being particularly marked for black workers. Table 2.34 goes on to display in detail the distribution of black and white workers across the country.

Assuming that economically active men and women within different ethnic groups are similarly distributed around the country (i.e. that if 55 per cent of Indian workers are found in the South East, then 55 per cent both of economically active Indian men and of economically active Indian women are found in the South East, and that, if 10.8 per cent of the economically active black population is in the West Midlands, that this

---

[93] In the rest of the South East women earn 101.1% of the average female wage.
[94] Ethnic Groups and the Labour Market (1995), n. 49 above, 259, fig. 6.

Table 2.33 — % of economically active population in South East by ethnic group, 1994

	All	white	ethnic minority	black	Indian	Pakistani/ Bangladeshi	mixed/ other
South East	32%	31%	61%	73%	55%	43%	66%

source: LFS, Spring 1994[95]

Table 2.34 — % of black and white economically active population by region, 1994

Region	white	ethnic minority	black	Indian	Pakistani/ Bangladeshi	mixed/ other
North	5.4%	1.4%	*	*	*	*
Yorkshire and Humberside	8.9%	5.6%	3.3%	7.5%	12.0%	4.9%
East Midlands	7.5%	5.5%	4.4%	9.8%	*	*
East Anglia	4.1%	1.4%	*	*	*	*
South East	30.9%	60.7%	72.6%	54.5%	43.5%	66.0%
Greater London	10.4%	47.6%	63.3%	40.7%	32.9%	47.0%
Rest of S.E.	20.5%	13.0%	9.2%	13.8%	10.2%	19.3%
South West	8.9%	2.1%	*	*	*	*
West Midlands	9.2%	13.7%	10.8%	20.1%	17.6%	5.6%
of which metropolitan	4.1%	11.8%	9.2%	17.6%	16.2%	3.5%
elsewhere	5.1%	1.9%	*	2.5%	*	*
North West	11.0%	7.2%	4.6%	5.8%	5.8%	6.0%
Greater Manchester/ Merseyside	6.7%	5.5%	4.1%	4.3%	11.1%	4.9%
Rest of North-West	4.4%	1.7%	*	*	5.1%	*
England	85.8%	97.7%	99.2%	98.7%	95.8%	94.4%
Wales	4.9%	0.9%	*	*	*	*
Scotland	9.4%	1.6%	*	*	*	3.5%

source: LFS, 1994[96]
* not recorded

applies equally to economically active black men and women), it is possible to calculate what the average hourly rates of ethnic minority women would be if they shared the same pattern of geographical distribution as white women.

Taking first table 2.33, which shows the proportion of economically active people in the various ethnic groups who are located in the South East, and table 2.32, which shows the rates of pay in the various regions, the average hourly rate of women in the South East is 115.1 per cent of

[95] *Ibid.* figs. 6 & 6a.   [96] *Ibid.* table 9.

the overall average and of women elsewhere is 92.7 per cent.[97] If the proportions of ethnic minority women working in the South East are redistributed to match the pattern for white women, the average hourly rates of ethnic minority women drop to the levels shown in table 2.35.

Table 2.35 — hourly pay by ethnic group adjusted for part-time/full-time work and geographical distribution, 1994

	white	ethnic minority	black	Indian	Pakistani/ Bangladeshi	mixed/ other
£ per hour	£6.40	£5.71	£5.98	£5.35	£4.76	£5.42
as % of white		89.1%	93.5%	83.6%	74.4%	84.7%

source: LFS, 1994[98]

It is possible to consider the geographical issue in much more detail using table 2.34. Again, assuming that the overall geographical concentration of economic activity is accurate for women, as well as for workers generally, distributing black women in the same geographical pattern as white women would have a profound impact on their hourly wage rates. Whereas at present, and holding constant for full-time/part-time work, black women earn 102.3 per cent of white women's wages, the geographically adjusted rate is a mere 94.4 per cent.[99] The adjusted rates for ethnic minority, Indian, Pakistani and Bangladeshi, and mixed/ other women are 83.8 per cent, 81.1 per cent, 79.0 per cent and 90.2 per cent: the higher value of the adjusted than the unadjusted rate for Pakistani and Bangladeshi women might well be due to the large gaps in the available data.

[97] In Great Britain generally the average female hourly wage is £7.14 and the female workforce is 94.9% white and 5.1% ethnic minority (see Ethnic Groups and the Labour Market (1995), n. 49 above—this takes into account relative proportions of ethnic minority and white women aged 16–59 and of different economic activity rates between them) of which respectively 31% and 61% work in the South East. This means that, overall, 32.53% work in the South East with average wages of £8.22 which means that average wages elsewhere are £6.62.

[98] *Ibid.* 257, fig. 5.

[99] This figure is reached by determining the figure reached by adding (individually for ethnic minority/black/Indian/Pakistani and Bangladeshi/mixed and other, and white women) the sums of the relative hourly rate in various geographical areas (where 100% is the GB average hourly rate for women) and the proportion of the economically active ethnic group which is found in that area. The 'constant' figure for black women's wages, for example, is then determined by using the equation X[(proportion of black women in region A) (wages in region A) + [(proportion of black women in region B)(wages in region B) + [(proportion of black women in region C)(wages in region C), etc] = 102.3[(proportion of white women in region A) (wages in region A) + [(proportion of white women in region B) (wages in region B) + [(proportion of white women in region C) (wages in region C), etc]. The value of X (96.31) is then applied to the distribution of white women to find the wage which black women would earn if distributed likewise.

Finally, Irene Breugel argues that ethnic minority women are younger than white women, with the effect that they have higher average education levels which, in turn, yield an upward impact on pay.[100] Even without considering this issue in the kind of detail used in relation to full-time/part-time work and geographical location, it is clear from the foregoing discussions that the superficially high earnings of black and other ethnic minority women do not withstand scrutiny, and that the headline statistics, suggesting as they do that there is little cause for concern about the relative pay of black and other ethnic minority women, serve to mask a significant pay gap when like is compared with like.

Industrial Segregation and Pay

The foregoing section merely established the levels of pay which women from the various ethnic groups earn in the labour market. In this section and the next the relationship between those rates of pay and women's industrial and occupational distribution by ethnic group is explored. Given the relatively small numbers involved (particularly, by virtue of their very low rates of recorded economic activity, in the case of Pakistani and Bangladeshi women), the statistics are far from comprehensive and only a few general points can be made.

Table 2.16, above, showed the industrial distribution of women by ethnic group, and table 2.36 shows the average hourly rates earned by full-time women in each of those sectors in 1995.

Taking first the manufacturing/services division, white and ethnic minority women generally have quite similar distributions between these major categories (13 per cent: 83 per cent and 13 per cent: 85 per cent respectively), but when the ethnic minority groups are disaggregated the picture

Table 2.36 — average hourly female pay by industrial sector, 1995

industrial sector	wage
manufacturing	£6.94
metal goods, engineering, vehicles	£6.72
other manufacturing	£7.00
construction	£6.05
services	£7.51
distribution, hotels, catering	£5.48
transport and communication	£7.20
banking, insurance, and finance	£7.73
other services	£8.13

source: NES, 1995, tables 54–57

[100] Breugel, n. 15 above, 55.

changes quite considerably with only Indian women being represented other than negligibly in the manufacturing category. Given the disparity between the average hourly rates of (full-time) women in manufacturing and in services (according to the 1994 LFS, £6.94 and £7.51 respectively), white women's and, to a greater extent, Indian women's pay should be held down relative to that of other women.[101] If the position within manufacturing is considered, ethnic minority women generally and Indian women in particular are considerably more concentrated in the higher-paid 'other manufacturing' sub-category than are white women: this, too, should exert a downward influence upon white women's relative wages.

Turning towards the distribution of those working in services, rather more ethnic minority women than white women (30.6 per cent and 27.7 per cent respectively of those in the service industries) work in the lowest paid category, and rather fewer (50.6 per cent and 53 per cent respectively) in the highest paid. This might be expected to hold wages down for ethnic minority women generally. But when ethnic minority women are looked at in more detail, a different pattern emerges. Black women are considerably less likely than white women to work in the lowest paid category and considerably more likely to work in the highest paid (17.6 per cent and 63.7 per cent respectively of those in the service industries) while, for Indian women, the position is reversed (with 42.9 per cent in the lowest paid category and only 37.7 per cent in the highest). The figures for Pakistani and Bangladeshi women are too low to allow any conclusions to be drawn and the mixed/other category of women shares a similar distribution with that of white women.

From this, one would expect ethnic minority women generally and mixed/other women to have roughly comparable wages with those of white women, black women to have a slight edge on white women when it comes to pay, and Indian women to be somewhat disadvantaged, all else (i.e. full-time/part-time ratios; geographical distribution, etc.) being equal. We saw in the text after table 2.35 above that, when other factors are held constant, ethnic minority women generally and mixed/other women earn about 90 per cent and 85 per cent respectively of white women's wages and black women's wages lag behind those of white women by more than 5 per cent, Indian women's by over 15 per cent.

Occupational Segregation and Pay

It may be the case, of course, that the different occupational distributions of white and ethnic minority women contribute to the pay gap between them. Our task is not helped at this point by the fact that those occupational

---

[101] The relatively small numbers of Pakistani and Bangladeshi women in this formal labour market make it difficult to reach conclusions about this group.

categories by which the breakdown of workers by ethnic group are avail-able are not the same as those by which pay statistics are produced. Nevertheless, between them the professional and intermediate categories in table 2.17 (which shows occupational distribution by ethnic group) roughly correspond with those of 'professional', 'manager', and 'associate professional and technical' in the New Earnings Survey.[102] It is possible to say, as a result, that women working in the professional and inter-mediate categories are likely to be relatively well paid in comparison with other women (see tables 2.24 and 2.29). Table 2.17 informs us that 32 per cent of white women and 36 per cent of ethnic minority women are to be found within these relatively well paying professions and that, with-in the ethnic minority group, as many as 41 per cent of 'mixed/other' women and 39 per cent of Pakistani and Bangladeshi women, together with 36 per cent of black women but only 31 per cent of Indian women are found within these categories.

The skilled non-manual category broadly corresponds to the clerical and secretarial group which, although the worst paid of all occupations for men and women together, nevertheless is placed just below profes-sional, managerial, and associate professional and technical in the hier-archy of female wages. Here white women have an edge over every group except for that of mixed/other, while Pakistani and Bangladeshi women lag well behind. At the bottom of the pay hierarchy come partly skilled and unskilled work which account for similar proportions (23 per cent, 24 per cent and 25 per cent respectively) of white, ethnic minority, and black women workers (although the proportion of unskilled black women workers well outstrips that in other groups); for a slightly greater propor-tion (28 per cent) of Indian and Pakistani and Bangladeshi women workers (though here the partly skilled very substantially outweigh the unskilled) and for very few (12 per cent) of mixed/other workers.

The occupational distribution of women suggests that mixed/other women should enjoy a considerable advantage over all the other groups of women workers, and that black women should have some advantage over white women. Indian women, given their slight disadvantage at both the top and the bottom of the occupational hierarchy, might be expected to do a little less well than white women, and the position of Pakistani/Bangladeshi women is more difficult to predict—it would depend upon the relative importance of their advantage at the top of the hierarchy and their disadvantage in skilled manual at the bottom of the hierarchy. But again, these predictions bear little relation to reality. It would appear, then, that the relative pay of ethnic minority women, both generally and within different ethnic groups) is affected by factors other than those relating to their occupational and industrial distribution.

[102] Ethnic Groups and the Labour Market (1994), n. 50 above, technical note at 159.

IV. WOMEN AND WORK—SPECIAL FACTORS AFFECTING WOMEN

(A) INTRODUCTION

We have considered men's and women's occupational and industrial distribution and seen that, at least on the face of it, the pay gap between them cannot fully be explained in terms of differences at these levels of distribution. Possible reasons behind the pay gap between men and women (more precisely, behind the pay *gaps* between full-time men and women workers, part-time women and full-time workers, women from the various ethnic minority groups and white men and women) will be discussed later. But first it is useful to consider the particular factors that affect women as workers and which render them quite distinct from men in the labour market.

This approach can be criticized on the basis that distinguishing 'women' and 'men', for the purpose of exploring possible links between their different labour market behaviours and their different rates of pay, serves to perpetuate the conceptualization of women as always 'other', the notion that women are best understood by comparison with the male standard. In this particular context, however, the male standard includes the happy factor of enhanced pay to which women, as a group, do not have access. That this state of affairs requires explanation and, at least on the face of it, redress, could be regarded as the primary premise of this book.

This is not to claim that the male pattern of work or pay should be regarded as the ungendered 'norm'. If men are indeed paid more than women for reasons which relate to the difference of sex, this may be as much the result of a male pay 'bonus' as it is the result of a female pay 'discount'. In addition, the extent, if any, to which particular groups of men benefit from the bonus, together with the effect, if any, of the discount on particular groups of women, may depend not only upon the degree to which these groups share the attributes of 'male' and 'female', but also upon other factors such as ethnicity, age, and social class. But to the extent that explanation and potential redress of the male–female pay gap(s) requires comparisons to be drawn between the working lives of women and those of men, it is suggested that such comparisons serve to expose a problem which already exists (i.e. that women earn less because, by virtue of their being women, they neither behave like nor are treated like men) rather than perpetuating the ideology that women *should* behave like men or be treated like men, or that the different ways in which men and women behave should be seen properly to give rise to different treatment and/or different outcomes resulting from similar treatment. My purpose is to explore the ways in which women are disadvantaged, particularly in relation to pay, in terms both of their labour market treatment and of the outcomes of that treatment. In order to do this, it is necessary to compare women with men, as well as with each other.

In the foregoing sections I stressed the differences between particular groups of women workers. But, in the same way as ethnic minority women share similarities in terms of higher unemployment levels and lower rates of part-time work than white women, even at the same time as they differ hugely between themselves when it comes to qualification levels, relative rates of pay, and industrial distribution; so women workers generally share some characteristics which distinguish them from male workers, while at the same time varying greatly between themselves. The purpose of this section is to set out some of the features which are, to a greater or lesser extent, generally shared by women workers.

The first, and most obvious, of these features is that women earn less than men. With the exception only of manual workers under the age of 18 and women working full-time in the 'security guards and related occupations' category (who, in 1995, earned a staggering 129 per cent of the hourly rate earned by men in the same occupational sub-category[103]), every group of women workers, whether they are defined on the basis of age, occupation, industrial distribution, formal qualifications, or any other factor, earn less than equivalent men. Women also work shorter hours than men (both in terms of basic and overtime work), a factor which might be expected to explain their lower pay, save for the fact that the pay gap exists at the level of hourly, as well as weekly, pay and that it persists where overtime payments are excluded from consideration. When all women workers are taken into account, women worked only 70.3 per cent of men's weekly hours in 1995. And even when full-time workers alone are considered, women worked only 90.2 per cent of men's weekly hours in 1996. The extent of part-time working by women in the UK is such that, overall, they have the lowest ratio of weekly hours to those worked by men anywhere in the EU except for the Netherlands, where an even greater proportion of women work part-time. And if the hours worked by full-time men and women are considered in isolation, women in the UK have the shortest weekly hours, relative to those of men, anywhere in the EU. Such are the hours demanded of full-time workers in the UK, however, that full-time British women workers combine having the shortest working weeks *relative* to those of men with having the longest working weeks, in *absolute* terms, of any women in the EU. This latter honour they share with British men who outwork their nearest competitors, the Portuguese, by almost three hours a week (45.4: 42.7) and the EU male average (41.1) by over four hours.[104]

---

[103] This in turn had the effect of bringing up women's hourly rate in the security and protective services sub-category to 106%—also in 1995, for the first time, women in the professional occupations n.e.c. sub-category earned more than their male colleagues—101%.

[104] Central Statistical Office, *Social Trends 1994* (London: HMSO, 1995), 71, table 4.15.

Women in Britain are overwhelmingly more likely than men to work part-time. They are also more likely, whether they work full-time or part-time, to engage in all of the various types of 'flexible' working except self-employment than are men. In 1994, for example, 15.4 per cent and 9.7 per cent full-time female and male workers worked 'flexi-time' (9.1 per cent and 7.3 per cent respectively of part-timers) and 4.7 per cent and 1.1 per cent of female and male full-timers were engaged in 'term-time' working (10.3 per cent and 4.9 per cent of part-timers).[105]

Much of the difference in working time between men and women workers relates to family responsibility. Women's working lives, for the majority who have children, are typically the scene of extraordinary disruption with movements between full-time and part-time work and one or more periods of economic inactivity.[106] Men, by contrast, unless they are afflicted by involuntary unemployment, usually remain in full-time work from the beginning of their working lives until they retire. The impact of motherhood on women's working lives will now be considered.

(B)   WOMEN, WORK, AND FAMILY RESPONSIBILITIES

Introduction

One of the most striking contrasts between men's and women's paid employment is in their patterns of economic activity by age. Whereas the proportion of men who are working or formally seeking work rises steadily with age until 45, thereafter declining slowly to 54 before dropping swiftly (see figure 2.1), the participation rates for women are depressed between the ages of 20 and 34. Women, like men, reach peak participation rates at 35 to 44 and decline slowly, then dramatically, in the following decades. But the years between 20 and 34 vary enormously according to sex, as do the overall participation rates of men and women. Figures 2.1 and 2.2 display the 1993 economic activity rates according to age and sex. The rates for all men and women over the age of 16 were, respectively, 71.9 per cent and 52.6 per cent in that year—in 1971 these figures had stood at 80.5 per cent and 43.9 per cent.[107]

The difference in the pattern of economic activity between men and women, as well as in the overall levels of activity (note the different ranges on the graphs' vertical axes), is associated with child-bearing and rearing: whereas this process has little impact on the working lives of men (save that it tends to be associated with increased working hours), for women the story is very different. Many women take time out of the labour market

---

[105] *Social Trends 1995*, Spring 1994 LFS, table 4.16.

[106] For discussion of the Women and Employment Survey see J. Martin and C. Roberts, *Women and Employment: A Lifetime Perspective* (London: HMSO, 1984); S. Dex, *Women's Occupational Mobility: A Lifetime Perspective* (London: Macmillan, 1987).

[107] In 1994, according to *Social Trends 1996*, table 4.4, 72.6% and 53% respectively.

Figure 2.1 — 1993 economic activity rate by age for men aged 16 and over

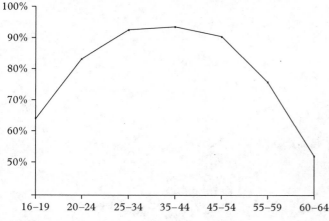

source: LFS, 1993, table 4.4

Figure 2.2 — 1993 economic activity rate by age for women aged 16 and over

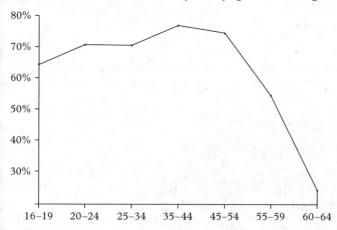

source: LFS, 1993, table 4.4

in order to have children, and most of those who return do so, at least in the short term, on a part-time basis. The pattern of full-time and part-time working is not evident from figure 2.2 above but can be seen in figures 2.3 and 2.5 which, respectively, illustrate women's full-time and part-time work by their age and the age of their youngest dependent children. Figure 2.4 illustrates men's part-time and full-time work by age.

When the full-time/part-time division is taken into account the difference between male and female patterns of work is even greater. Whereas only a relatively small proportion (11 per cent) of men work part-time

Figure 2.3 — women's pattern of part-time and full-time work by age, 1993–5

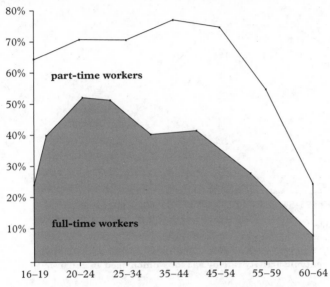

source: LFS 1993, table 4.4 & NES, 1995, tables 184 & 130[108]

Figure 2.4 — men's pattern of full-time and part-time work by age, 1993–4

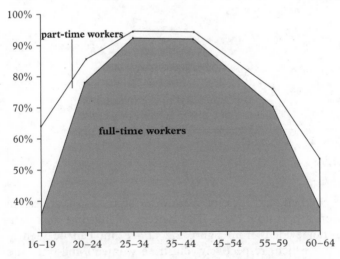

source: LFS, 1993 & 1994

---

[108] Part-time workers are underestimated due to the use of NES figures, but full-time workers' numbers are also underestimated because these figures, but not those for part-timers, exclude those without earnings in the pay period (about 7.5%).

and, of them, 40 per cent are under 25 and students, part-time work remains common throughout women's lives. Full-time working peaks (both
as a proportion of women working and as a proportion of all women) in
the early twenties (and even here it accounts for only about half of all
women), and declines rapidly between the mid-to-late twenties and the mid-
thirties. Meanwhile, from about thirty, the number of women working part-
time (again, both as a proportion of women working and as a proportion
of all women) increases rapidly until they reach the age of about forty,
after which time matters remain relatively stable for a further decade. Full-
time working never really recovers after women's child-bearing years—at
no stage after about 29 do as many as 50 per cent of women work full-
time, and after about 45 not even 40 per cent do. Men, by contrast, almost
exclusively work full-time between the ages of 25 and 60.

It should be noted at this point that figures 2.1 to 2.5 indicate what
men and women of each age were actually doing in any particular year,
rather than what women currently in their twenties, thirties, or sixties
either did in the past or may be expected to do in the future. Cohort
studies of economic activity by age are not carried out in the LFS but
Peter Elias used evidence from the 1980 Women and Employment Survey

Figure 2.5 — women's pattern of work according to age of youngest child, 1987–9

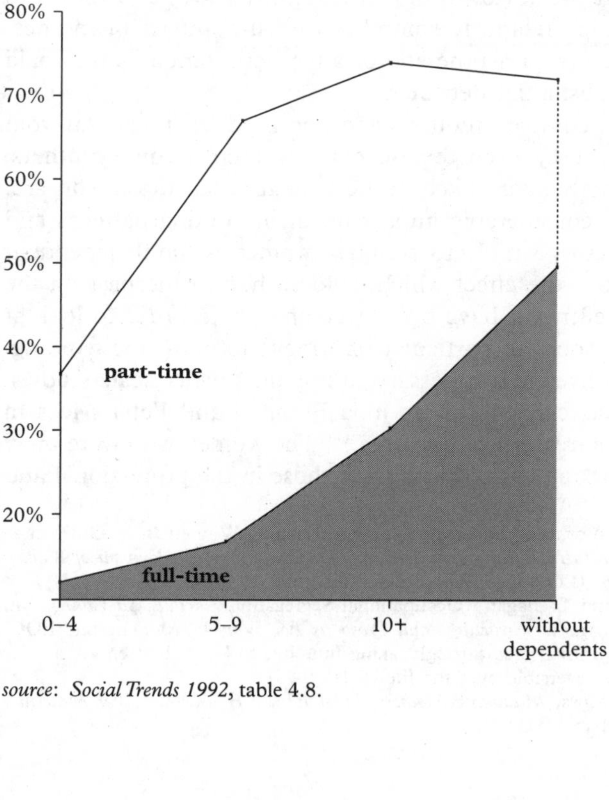

source: *Social Trends 1992*, table 4.8.

to trace the occupational histories of three groups of women who were aged, respectively, 35–9, 40–9, and 55–9 in 1980. Elias found:

a tendency nowadays for young women to enter better jobs than was the case in the 1960s. . . . [e]verything goes fine for the first five to ten years or so, with an increasing proportion of the age group [35–39 in 1980] entering better paid jobs. Then suddenly, between the ages of 23 and 30 years, the proportion of the age group working in well paid jobs drops dramatically. The counterpart of this decline is [in] . . . the proportion of [the] age group who are working part-time in below average earnings occupations. Remarkably, there is an equal proportion of women moving into part-time employment in below average paid jobs at the age of 30 in 1981 as was the case in 1951.[109]

The 1980 Women and Employment Survey suggests that the pattern of women's working lives was similar for those born just after the First and subsequent to the Second World Wars: while the latter group were more likely to begin their working lives in well-paid jobs, they were just as likely to experience a significant backward move as a result of motherhood.

The Impact of Part-Time Working

The impact of the child-bearing break in women's working lives and, to an even more significant extent, of any move towards part-time work thereafter are profound. Whereas the career paths of high-status women who take only a short break (for example, maternity leave) and return to full-time work can cope relatively smoothly with the impact of mother-hood, women who return part-time and/or after a substantial gap in paid employment suffer substantial detriment.

It is not possible to compare mothers and non-mothers in general from the LFS material because, given that so many women become mothers, those who are not mothers are likely to be younger than those who are: this itself will have a considerable impact on their working patterns and pay. Nor is it satisfactory simply to compare women without dependent children to those with—the effect which children had in the past on the former group may well never have been overcome.[110] In order to look at the impact of motherhood, in particular of a move to part-time working, on women's working lives it is necessary to rely on smaller scale studies.

One such study was carried out by Julia Brannen and Peter Moss in the mid-1980s in the Greater London area.[111] The women who were most likely to return to work after childbirth were those in the professional and

[109] P. Elias, 'Part-time Work and Part-time Workers: Keeping Women In or Out?' in S. McRae (ed.), *Keeping Women In: Strategies to Facilitate the Continuing Employment of Women in Higher Level Occupations* (London: Policy Studies Institute, 1990).

[110] See e.g. J. Rubery and C. Fagan, 'Occupational Segregation . . . *Plus Ça Change?*' in R. Lindley (ed.), *Labour Market Structures and Prospects For Women* (Manchester: EOC, 1994), 40 'disadvantages women face through taking time out to have children . . . appear to be cumulative and non-reversible over the life cycle'.

[111] J. Brannen and P. Moss, *Managing Mothers: Dual Earner Households After Maternity Leave* (London: Unwin Hyman, 1991).

managerial occupations. In all, 77 per cent of women returned to work after maternity leave but 34 per cent of these resigned shortly thereafter (31 per cent of these did not find another job within three years of the birth) and only 54 per cent of the 77 per cent (42 per cent of the total sample) continued to be employed in their old jobs in a full-time capacity after maternity leave. A further 11 per cent of the returners (9 per cent of the total sample) returned to their old jobs on a part-time basis directly after maternity leave.

Of all the women who were employed at some time in the three years after the birth of their child, 24 per cent had experienced downward occupational mobility (two-thirds of this was due to mobility *between*, as distinct from *within*, occupations) while only 17 per cent had moved upwards (78 per cent within and 22 per cent between occupations). By contrast, 29 per cent of the men in the study (which considered only those mothers who had been in a dual-earning partnership at the time of the birth) had moved upwards occupationally and only 5 per cent had moved down.[112] The danger of downward mobility was not shared equally between women: whereas only 7 per cent of the women who returned to the same employer immediately after maternity leave (whether full-time or part-time) experienced downward mobility, and 20 per cent actually saw their position improve in the three years following childbirth; the figures were 45 per cent and 23 per cent for women who resigned after maternity leave and thereafter found new jobs, and 60 per cent and 0 per cent for women who resigned at childbirth and subsequently found new work. Those women who were likely, on this account, to suffer most severely as a result of motherhood (those who took prolonged breaks from paid employment after childbirth) were excluded from the sample which considered only those women who had returned within three years.[113]

Downward mobility typically occurred between occupations when professional or managerial women (particularly the latter) moved into clerical, manual, or sales jobs, frequently in order to work part-time.[114] When downward movement took place within occupations, too, it was frequently the result of a request for part-time hours. The impact of downward mobility was considerable: 'nearly two thirds of the [affected workers] worked on a temporary, casual or self-employed basis and three-quarters were part-time . . . many did not qualify for any maternity leave, maternity pay, paid holidays, or sick pay'.[115] Upward mobility between occupations generally resulted from a beneficial change of employer after an initial return after maternity leave, while upward movement within occupations was associated with continuous employment with the pre-childbirth employer.

The impact on earnings of childbirth and its associated labour market interruptions has been estimated by Joshi and Davies as being as high as

---

[112] *Ibid.* 150. See also Martin and Roberts, and Dex, both n. 106 above.
[113] Brannen, n. 111 above, 57, table 5.1.
[114] Brannen, n. 111 above, 58.   [115] *Ibid.* 65.

57.4 per cent of women's lifetime earnings after the age of 25.[116] Jane
Waldfogel, too, found that, whereas single childless women earned 95 per
cent of single childless men's wages in the UK in the period 1985 to
1988, the ratio for married mothers to fathers was a mere 60 per cent.[117]
Waldfogel followed a cohort of women who were 17 years old in 1975
until 1991, when they were 33. She found that, while those who remained
childless increased their earnings (relative to those of men) from 78 per cent
in 1978 to 90 per cent in 1988, all the women taken together saw their
wages fall from 76 per cent to 73 per cent over that period and women who
were mothers earned 71 per cent of men's wages in 1978 and a mere 65
per cent in 1988.[118] Women earned 82 per cent of male earnings at 23 but
only 71 per cent at 33: the latter figure was held down mainly by mothers
whose earnings fell from 70 per cent of 23-year-old men's in 1981 to 64
per cent in 1991, as against non-mothers' 84 per cent in both years.

Motherhood and Class

The behaviour of women after the birth of children differs according to
their occupational status. Women in the professional/employer/manager
category are much more likely to return to work quickly after the birth
and are much more likely to return to full-time work than are other
mothers. Women's labour market behaviour by occupational status is
displayed at figures 2.6 to 2.10 according to the age of their youngest
dependent child.

In 1987–9, women in the professional/manager/employer category were
between 1.9 and thirty times as likely as women in the other occupational categories to have returned to work full-time within four years of
their most recent birth, and only between 67 per cent and 81 per cent as
likely to remain economically inactive for that period. The greatest differences at this stage were those between women in the highest occupational
strata and manual workers, whether semi- or unskilled, at the bottom. This
remained true for the mothers of children aged as young as 5 to 9 as regards
their respective likelihood of working full-time and part-time, although
unskilled manual workers were actually closer than any other group to
professional/managerial/employer women in having a very low likelihood
(around one in five) of being economically inactive. By the time children
reached 10 the greatest contrast was, once again, between women at the top
and the bottom of the occupational hierarchy: the former were much more

[116] H. Joshi and H. Davies, *Childcare and Mothers' Lifetime Earnings: Some European
Contrasts* (London: Centre for Economic Policy Research, 1992) Discussion Paper No. 600,
table 4. The estimate is based on a typical woman having two children and compares with
earnings losses of only 1% in France.
[117] J. Waldfogel, *Women Working For Less: A Longitudinal Analysis of the Family Gap*
(London: LSE, 1993), LSE, Suntory and Toyota International Centre for Economics and
Related Disciplines, Discussion Paper WSP 93, 3.
[118] *Ibid.* 11.

Figure 2.6 — pattern of work of women professionals/employers/managers according to age of youngest child, 1987–9

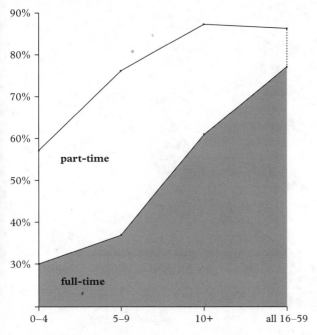

source: *Social Trends 1992*, table 4.8.

likely to work full-time, much less likely to work part-time and to be economically inactive than the latter, and the contrasts between unskilled manual workers and professional/managerial/employers were particularly acute.

Lone Mothers

When women with dependent children are considered separately according to whether they are 'lone' parents or not ('lone' being defined to exclude those who are cohabiting), the impact of motherhood on women's patterns of work is seen to be particularly acute for those without partners. In 1990, for example, while lone mothers constituted 15 per cent of all mothers they accounted for only 12 per cent of economically active mothers and 11 per cent of those in employment (they did, however, account for 14 per cent of mothers who worked full-time as against 9 per cent of those working part-time). Part of the disparity in economic activity rates results from the different composition of the 'lone' and 'not lone' groups of mothers: the former are younger (accounting for one-third of mothers aged between 25 and 34 in 1990, under 10 per cent of those aged 35 to 44 and 14 per cent of those between 45 and 59) and less well qualified (accounting for 15 per cent of all mothers but only

Figure 2.7 — pattern of work of women intermediate and junior non-manual workers according to age of youngest child, 1987–9

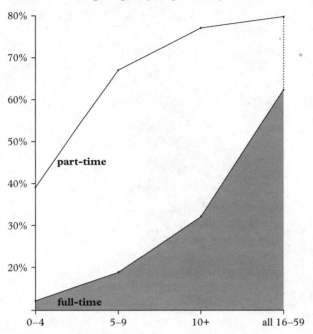

source: *Social Trends 1992*, table 4.8.

10 per cent of those whose highest qualification was post 'A' level, 14 per cent of those whose highest qualification was 'A' level, 13 per cent of 'O' level, 17 per cent below 'O' level, and 20 per cent of those with no qualifications). But even when age is held constant, lone mothers' economic activity rates remain well behind those of other mothers.[119] And when highly qualified mothers are considered in isolation, those with partners are more likely to be economically active than those without.

In stark contrast to the picture for married and co-habiting mothers, lone mothers' employment and economic activity rates have actually fallen over the two decades to 1990. Whereas in 1971, 52 per cent of lone and 39 per cent of other mothers were in paid employment, by 1984 these figures stood at 39 per cent and 48 per cent and, in 1990, at 39 per cent and 61 per cent.[120] The rates of economic activity (including unemployment) for lone and other mothers stood at 50 per cent and 56

[119] All statistics taken from *Employment Gazette*, 'Lone Parents and the Labour Market: Evidence from the Labour Force Survey', Nov. 1992, 559. See 562 table 2 for comparisons of 15% with A levels, etc.

[120] J. Brown, *Why Don't They Go to Work? Mothers on Benefit* (London: HMSO, 1989), Social Security Advisory Committee Research Paper 2, table 2.1—includes only those women with dependent children (under 16).

Figure 2.8 — pattern of work of women skilled non-manual workers according to age of youngest child, 1987–9

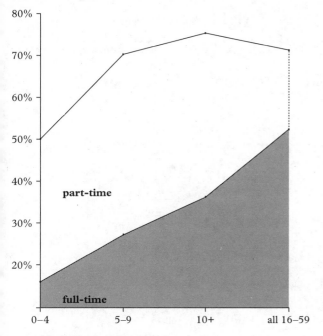

source: *Social Trends 1992*, table 4.8.

per cent in 1984, and at 49 per cent and 66 per cent in 1990.[121] The fall in economic activity and employment rates is partly the result of changes in the composition of the 'lone mother' category (in particular, of a substantial increase in the proportion of lone mothers aged between 25 and 34 and those having children under 5[122]) but also in part related to falls in economic activity within the various age categories of lone mothers relative to other mothers. So, for example, while the employment rates of other mothers of children under 5 increased by 96 per cent between 1981 and 1990 (their full-time employment rates by 180 per cent to 14 per cent and their part-time rates by 94 per cent to 31 per cent); the employment rates of lone mothers of very young children actually fell by 19 per cent (to 22 per cent, their full-time rates were down by half to 8 per cent and their part-time rates up 30 per cent to 13 per cent).[123] And even highly qualified lone mothers, the group of lone mothers most likely to be economically active and employed, reduced their level of economic

---

[121] 1984 and 1990 figures taken from 'Lone Parents and the Labour Market', n. 119 above, table 6.
[122] One-third in 1981 to a half in 1990. See generally 'Lone Parents and the Labour Market', n. 119 above.
[123] *Ibid.* table 6.

Figure 2.9 — pattern of work of women semi-skilled manual workers according to age of youngest child, 1987–9

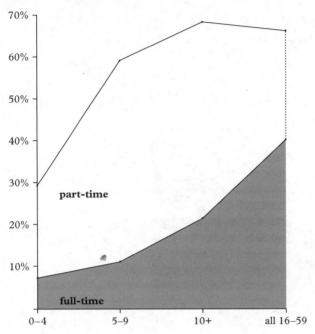

source: *Social Trends 1992*, table 4.8.

activity by ten percentage points between 1984 and 1990 (from 82 per cent to 72 per cent) at a time when other mothers increased their rates of economic activity by nine points (from 66 per cent to 75 per cent).

(c) WOMEN AND TRADE UNIONS

Women are less likely to be members of trade unions than are men. In 1994, for example (according to the Labour Force Survey), 36 per cent of male employees but only 30 per cent of women employees were members of trade unions. The disparity in membership seems to be associated predominantly with women's part-time working (38 per cent of all full-time employees, but only 21 per cent of part-time employees were trade union members)—when this is taken into account it seems that women who work full-time are as likely to belong to trade unions as their full-time male colleagues.[124]

The gap between male and female levels of union membership is much less pronounced today than it was even six years ago. In 1989, for example,

---

[124] *Employment Gazette*, 'Trade Union Membership and Recognition: Data from the 1994 LFS', May 1995, 191.

Figure 2.10 — pattern of work of women unskilled manual workers according to age of youngest child, 1987–9

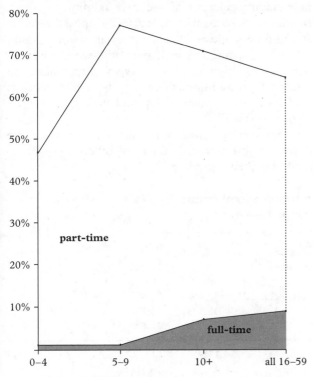

source: *Social Trends 1992*, table 4.8.

44 per cent of male and 33 per cent of female employees were trade union members. Since then, the gap has been reduced predominantly by the faster decline in the level of male than of female trade union membership.[125]

Despite the decline in the male–female gap, union membership is less common in most of the occupational groups in which women are concentrated than those which men dominate. With the exception of professional and associate professional and technical occupations which boast, respectively, 52 per cent and 48 per cent union membership and relatively high female concentrations, and managerial and administrative work, which combines a high degree of 'maleness' with a low level of union membership (24 per cent), 'female' jobs tend to be associated with lower levels of unionization than male jobs. So, for example, 40 per cent of craft and related workers but only 28 per cent of clerical and secretarial workers, 45 per cent of plant and machine operatives but a mere 11 per cent of sales workers, were members of trade unions.[126]

[125] 'Trade Union Membership and Recognition', n. 124 above, table 1.
[126] *Ibid.* table 2.

The disaggregation of union membership by occupational group does not, of course, explain why women (more particularly, part-time workers) are less likely to be trade union members than are men (full-time workers). It may be that women who work part-time are less well-disposed towards trade unions than are full-time workers. But lower levels of trade union membership might equally be connected with part-time workers' occupational and/or industrial distribution or with the types of workplaces in which they are concentrated. In addition, there may be a link between women's lower levels of trade union membership and their shorter average periods of continuous service.[127]

Some speculation is, however, possible, not least as a result of the statistics in table 2.37 which illustrates trade union membership by occupational group separately for men and women.

Table 2.37 — trade union membership by sex and ocupational group, 1994

trade union membership	men	women
managerial and administration	19.5%	19.4%
professional	38.4%	56.4%
associate professional and technical	33.6%	52.9%
clerical and secretarial	35.9%	24.7%
craft and related	28.7%	27.8%
personal and protective services	39.6%	22.2%
selling	11.9%	11.2%
plant and machine operatives	42.5%	33.1%
others	32.4%	24.2%

source: LFS, 1994[128]

By contrast with the general relationship between the percentage of women by occupation and the proportion of trade union members within the occupation, table 2.37 shows that women in some of the broad occupational groups are as likely, and sometimes considerably more likely, to be trade union members than are men. This is particularly the case in the professional and associate professional occupations while in managerial, craft, and selling jobs the proportion of male and female trade union members is similar, and only in clerical and secretarial, personal and protective services, plant and machinery, and other service jobs are men considerably more likely than women to belong to trade unions.

Table 2.37 suggests that levels of trade union membership may be as much related to the jobs that people do as to any gender-related (or even

---

[127] Trade union membership increases with length of service—11% at 0–6 months' service in 1994, steadily increasing through 17% at 1–2 years and 38% at 5–10 years to 60% at 20 years or more).

[128] *Social Trends 1995* (London: HMSO, 1995), table 4.22.

part-time/full-time related) attitude towards trade unions, a suggestion supported by the widely disparate levels of trade union membership in the public and private sectors (62 per cent and 23 per cent respectively) and in large and small workplaces (17 per cent and 42 per cent in workplaces having less than and at least twenty-five employees respectively).[129] The greater levels of unionization in the public sector operate so as to increase the proportion of women union members (women being more concentrated in the public sector than men) while the lower levels of unionization in small workplaces serve to reduce it (the same being true in respect of women and small workplaces).

Many of the benefits of union membership, of course, depend upon whether or not the union is recognized by the member's employer, in which case some of those benefits may accrue also to those employees who are not themselves union members. The distribution of men and women, and even of full-time and part-time employees, between workplaces at which unions are and are not recognized is much more balanced than are men's and women's, full-timers' and part-timers' levels of union membership. In 1994, for example, 49 per cent of male and 47 per cent of female employees, 51 per cent of full-time and 40 per cent of part-time employees, worked in workplaces in which one or more unions was recognized for collective bargaining purposes. Looking at the private sector alone, however, 39 per cent of men and 27 per cent of women, 38 per cent of full-time and 21 per cent of part-time employees, worked in union-recognizing workplaces.

It is clear that women and, in particular, part-time workers in the private sector are considerably less likely to have access to the benefits of collective bargaining than are (full-time) men. But if the public and private sectors are considered together, the statistics might be taken to suggest that, as far as union recognition is concerned, men and women are in broadly similar positions regardless of the issue of union membership. Such a view would be mistaken. The statistics concerning recognition do not show which employees are affected by collective bargaining—it is perfectly possible, as a result, that in a workplace in which 98 per cent of machine operatives are male and 100 per cent of clerical staff female, collective bargaining takes place for plant but not for clerical staff (according to Rubery and Fagan the engineering agreement, the largest national private sector agreement, covered only manual workers, thereby excluding predominantly female clerical etc. workers[130]). In such a case, the fact that clerical staff are in a workplace with union recognition (even the fact that clerical staff are in a union) is likely to have little impact on their terms and conditions of employment.

[129] 'Trade Union Membership and Recognition', n. 124 above, does not disaggregate membership by sex within the public and private sectors.
[130] J. Rubery and C. Fagan, 'Equal Pay Policy and Wage Regulation Systems in Europe' (1994) 25(4) *Industrial Relations Journal* 281, 292, n. 37.

The LFS shows that, in 1994, 25 per cent of union non-members (together with 91 per cent of union members) worked in workplaces in which a union was recognized. It is possible that the 25 per cent of union non-members should be seen as 'free-riders' who gain the advantage of collective bargaining without the costs of union membership. It is equally possible that part of this 25 per cent is not in a position to undertake the costs or reap the benefits of collective bargaining. In order to capture this factor the LFS included a question in 1993 on whether the worker was able to join a recognized union at his or her workplace. The responses suggested that 61 per cent of employees were, and that only 3 per cent of employees worked in a workplace in which a trade union was recognized, but were not themselves covered by any collective agreement. The LFS urged great caution in respect of these results, pointing out that the 61 per cent figure would, 'somewhat implausibly, suggest that there had been an increase in [collective bargaining] coverage between 1990 and 1993' (WIRS results for the former year were available for comparison). The WIRS results for 1993 suggested that only 54 per cent of employees in workplaces having at least twenty-five workers (which are more likely than smaller workplaces to recognize trade unions) were in a position to join recognized trade unions, and 13 per cent of employees worked in workplaces with recognition without being covered by any collective agreement. This latter figure is more likely to be correct than the LFS's 3 per cent.[131]

Table 2.38 suggests that workers in predominantly female occupational groups are less likely to belong to unions in workplaces in which unions are recognized for the purpose of collective bargaining than those

Table 2.38 — degree of union membership and workplace recognition by occupational group

	union members	workplace recognition
managerial and administrative	24%	41%
professional	52%	69%
associate professional and technical	48%	61%
clerical and secretarial	28%	49%
craft and related	40%	46%
personal and protective	30%	43%
sales	11%	26%
plant and machine operatives	45%	53%
others	29%	44%

source: Employment Department[132]

[131] *Employment Gazette*, 'Trade Union Recognition: Data From the 1993 LFS', 450–1, Dec. 1994, 441.
[132] *Ibid.* table 6 and 'Trade Union Membership and Recognition' (1995), n. 124 above.

in predominantly male groups (in sales, for example, more than twice as many work in workplaces with recognition than actually belong to a union, in clerical and secretarial work almost twice as many, but in plant and machinery and in craft and related work, only 20 per cent more.[133] This might, as was pointed out above, suggest that workers in predominantly female occupational groups are more likely to 'free-ride'. It might equally suggest that they are less able to benefit from membership of a recognized trade union.

(D) THE IMPACT OF EMPLOYMENT POLICIES ON WOMEN

Women are more likely to be found in the public sector than are men, a factor which operates so as to increase their levels of trade union membership and the extent to which they work in workplaces where trade unions are recognized. Concentration in the public sector has these and other advantages—rates of pay for manual workers are, for example, relatively high in comparison with those in the private sector and the gender–pay gap is lower in the public than in the private sector.[134]

But there is one very significant disadvantage associated with public sector employment. As a result of compulsory competitive tendering initiatives, many of those who work within it are subject to, at best competition from, and at worst the threat of absorption into, the private sector. Some indication of the effect that this has had on low-paid workers, in particular upon women, can be seen in the facts of the *Ratcliffe* v. *North Yorkshire County Council* case decided in 1995 by the House of Lords.[135] While the decision can be seen as a blow for the principle of equal pay, the facts which gave rise to it cannot.

The *Ratcliffe* case arose from the compulsory competitive tendering (CCT) imposed on local authorities by the Local Government Act 1988. In order to continue to provide particular services including school catering local authorities are required, *inter alia*, to do so via a 'direct service organization' (DSO) which bids for the work in competition with such other operators as may come forward. The local authority is forbidden, in determining which organization shall be awarded the tender, to 'act in a manner having the effect or intended or likely to have the effect of restricting, distorting or preventing competition'. In particular, the Local Government Act 1988 forbids local authorities to consider workers' terms and conditions in allocating contracts.[136] The DSO must keep its finances separate from those of the authority generally (although it remains in law part of the authority) and, if it is successful in the bid, must 'debit and

---

[133] For managerial staff, 1.7 times as many but the categories are hardly comparable given the differences in individuals' bargaining strength.
[134] See NES 1995, table 1.   [135] [1995] IRLR 439.
[136] Local Government Act 1988 (LGA), s. 17(5)(a).

credit items' to the rest of the authority 'assuming it were an independent contractor'. The local authority is forbidden to 'top up' the finances of the DSO which must, further, provide the return on capital (currently 5 per cent) specified by the Secretary of State.

Prior to August 1991, 'dinner ladies' had their terms and conditions of employment regulated in accordance with the National Joint Council (NJC) for Local Authorities Services (Manual Workers). The job evaluation scheme on which these terms and conditions were based had rated the job done by the applicants as being of equivalent value to those of their various comparators.

In 1990, North Yorkshire County Council put its school meals service out to tender. The DSO bid for the first of the six geographical areas was successful, but the second was not, the tender having been undercut by an outside contractor. The DSO became concerned that failure to secure the remaining areas would increase its administrative costs proportionately. Its major cost was kitchen labour (51 per cent of the total) and its manager decided that, in order to ensure success in the remaining four areas, these labour costs would have to be reduced by 25 per cent. This entailed not only a reduction in kitchen workers' hourly rate, but the abolition of their retainer payments and a reduction in their hours, holiday, and sickness pay. The DSO won the remaining tenders, sacked the kitchen staff, and offered to re-employ them on these impoverished terms. Their equal pay comparators, by contrast, were either in jobs which had not been put out to tender or which had been retained by the council without any substantial reduction in terms and conditions.

The decision in *Ratcliffe* turned upon whether 'market forces', which had impelled the employers to slash the pay of the (almost exclusively female) 'dinner ladies' but not of their predominantly male jobs held by their comparators, could function as a defence to the equal pay claim. The House of Lords ruled that the defence could only succeed to the extent that the market forces were sex-neutral—i.e. either impacted equally as between men and women or, if they impacted unequally, to the extent that reliance upon them for the purpose of wage-setting was nevertheless 'justifiable' (this issue is discussed in Chapter 1). Given that the uneven pressure upon the council in terms of predominantly male and predominantly female jobs arose from the ability of private sector tenderers to undercut wages in the latter but not the former jobs because of 'the general perception in the UK, and certainly in North Yorkshire, that a woman should stay at home to look after her children and if she wants to work it must fit in with that domestic duty', the defence had to fail.

From a lawyer's point of view the decision in *Ratcliffe* can be seen as a victory. But, although the Transfer of Undertakings (Protection of Employment) Regulations (TUPE) require, where they apply, that the incoming tenderer take on the workers formerly employed by the council, and

do so on the same terms and conditions (save as far as pensions are concerned) as those provided by the council, it would appear from *Ratcliffe*
that this is not in practice what occurs. There are a number of flaws in
the protection afforded by TUPE.

- TUPE has only recently been accepted as being relevant to the
  contracting-out provisions so many former public sector employees
  have already lost their jobs or been forced to accept lower rates in
  the private (or, in a *Ratcliffe*-type scenario, the public) sector;
- the exclusion of pensions from TUPE arms incoming employers
  with bargaining power to undercut other terms and conditions;[137]
- TUPE does not prevent incoming tenderers from undercutting
  public-sector wages in the long term by freezing terms and conditions
  of existing staff and by taking new staff on at lower rates—TUPE
  protects only transferred employees and only does so in terms of their
  contracts at the time of transfer;
- incoming employers do not have to employ all the public sector staff
  affected by the transfer—they can rationalize and reduce the total
  number of incoming and existing staff;[138]
- not all workers are protected from dismissal/enforced change to their
  terms and conditions by the incoming employer. The decision of the
  EAT in *Milligan and Another* v. *Securicor Cleaning Co. Ltd* (that the
  qualifying periods do not apply to dismissals connected with transfers
  of undertakings) cannot be relied on given the subsequent decision
  by the Court of Appeal in *MRS Environmental Services Ltd* v. *Marsh*,
  in which the qualifying periods were upheld in this context;[139]
- there is no way of telling how long the protection afforded by TUPE
  lasts—incoming employers could perhaps exert pressure on transferred employees some time after the transfer in order to rationalize
  their terms with other staff. Once the protection of TUPE has expired
  any unfair dismissal claims arising as a result of such pressure could
  be met with a claim, by the employers, of the need to reorganize as
  'some other substantial reason' within section 57 of the Employment
  Protection (Consolidation) Act 1978. In such cases, the requirements
  imposed by tribunals upon employers in respect of the dismissals
  appear to be low indeed.[140]

[137] See *Adams and Ors.* v. *Lancashire County Council and BET Catering Services Ltd.* [1996]
IRLR 154 for discussion of the exclusion, but see also *Wilson* v. *St Helens Borough Council*
[1996] IRLR 320 for restrictions on the extent to which employees can bargain away the
protection afforded by the transfers regulations.
[138] Given the existence of the ETO defence.
[139] [1995] IRLR 288. The decision in *MRS* v. *Marsh* is reported at *The Times*, 22 July
1996.
[140] See, e.g. the discussion in S. Deakin and G. Morris, *Labour Law* (London: Butterworths, 1995), 458–61.

Perhaps more significant than any of these factors is the apparent trend of the ECJ against applying Council Directive 77/187 (Acquired Rights), which TUPE is intended to implement in the UK, in the contracting-out context. Whereas, in the early 1990's, the message from decisions such as *Dr Sophie Redmond Stichting* v. *Bartol*[141] was that the Acquired Rights Directive applied to almost any conceiveable change in the control of work, such as that which occurs when work is contracted-out, the trend more recently appears to have been towards restricting the protection afforded by the Directive. This trend began with the decision in *Rygaard Ledernes Hovedorganisation* v. *Dansk Arbejdsgiverforening* (1995),[142] in which the ECJ ruled for the first time that a transfer fell outside the protection of the Directive, and has continued subsequently with the decisions in *Henke* v. *Gemeinde Schierke & Verwaltungsgemeinschaft 'Brocken'* and *Süzen* v. *Zehnacker Gebäudereingung GmbH Krankenhausservice*.[143] In view of the fact that TUPE was amended in 1993 precisely so as to reflect what was understood to be the (wide) approach of the Acquired Rights Directive, it is unlikely in the long term that TUPE would continue to afford a higher degree of protection than the Directive. If the decisions in *Rygaard*, *Henke* and *Suzen* do indicate a reversal by the ECJ, it is likely that TUPE will also cease to apply in many contracting-out situations.

The facts which gave rise to *Ratcliffe* cannot, of course, be taken without more to be indicative of any general problem. But research recently conducted on behalf of the EOC suggests that compulsory competitive tendering has had a significant negative impact upon women. The study, which looked at the effects of CCT in local government (in particular, in the areas of building cleaning, refuse collection, education catering, and sports and leisure management) compared pre- and post-CCT employment levels and gender–pay gaps.[144] The bulk of the contracts (76 per cent) were retained by the local authorities, 15 per cent had gone to DSOs and 10 per cent to private contractors. The study found that overall employment levels fell by 21 per cent between pre-contract and post-contract measurements. But the impact of CCT was not uniform: employment in building cleaning, refuse collection, and education catering fell by 29 per cent, 23 per cent, and 10 per cent respectively, whereas levels in sports and leisure management rose by 5 per cent.

Women, because they formed the large bulk (93 per cent) of workers affected by CCT, suffered more job losses than men. But the impact of CCT was not even as between men and women employed: women suffered 96 per cent of job losses and female employment declined by 22 per cent by contrast with the male decline of 12 per cent. In building cleaning

---

[141] Case 29/91, [1992] IRLR 366.

[142] Case 84/94 [1996] IRLR 51.

[143] Case 298/94, [1996] IRLR 701 and case 13/95 [1997] IRLR 255.

[144] *Equal Opportunities Review* 'The Gender Impact of Compulsory Competitive Tendering', 61, 19. Community care was examined also but contracting out began later and gender specific figures were not available and so the sector is excluded here.

and education catering, male employment actually increased (by 40 per cent and 41 per cent respectively) while female employment fell (by 31 per cent and 11 per cent).

Part-time employment, too, declined by 22 per cent whereas full-time employment declined by only 12 per cent and part-time workers who retained their jobs suffered average cuts in their weekly hours of 25 per cent and 16 per cent in the predominantly (99 per cent) female areas of building cleaning and education catering but retained pre-CCT hours in the predominantly (98 per cent) male area of refuse collection.[145]

Just as the squeeze on part-time hours varied between sectors, so too did the effects of CCT on pay. Whereas wage levels in (male) refuse collection increased after 1988–9, with 90 per cent of local authorities retaining NJC rates (where the contracts were won by DSOs) and half the DSOs improving bonus schemes, wage levels failed to improve, and in some cases actually declined, in (female) catering and cleaning. The impact by gender also varied between the local authority, DSO, and private contractors—whereas the former tended to retain NJC rates for workers subject to CCT the DSOs generally introduced a lower rate for female-dominated areas and private contractors all paid lower rates. 'In the privatised contracts, bonuses, overtime payments and unsocial hours payments for evening and weekend work were rarely paid to manual women workers'.[146]

The outlook for women employed in the public sector can only be described as bleak. The National Health Service and Community Care Act 1990 extended CCT to community care and the Local Government Act 1988 to white collar work. It appears, from the study outlined here, that the 'market forces' unleashed by CCT operate to reduce the terms and conditions enjoyed by workers in predominantly female jobs, both directly when contracts are awarded to the private sector and, even when jobs are retained in the public sector, as a result of the threat of under-cutting. And what is true for women in the public sector is true more generally in the increasing drive towards 'flexibility'. In particular, research recently published by the TUC suggests a decline in the real earnings of the lowest-paid part-time workers over the last few years.[147]

V. CONCLUSION

This chapter has considered where women are situated within the labour market today and the levels at which the gender–pay gap is felt—i.e. not simply as an average figure for all men and all women, or all male and

---

[145] In each of the predominantly female areas women accounted for 99% of the workers pre-contracting out, 98% and 99% respectively after CCT; in the male areas women accounted for 2% of employees pre-contracting, 1% after.

[146] The Gender Impact of Compulsory Competitive Tendering, n. 141 above, 20.

[147] TUC, n. 16 above.

female full-time and/or part-time workers respectively, and explained by men's and women's concentration in different jobs, different industries—but between men and women doing the same jobs, working in the same industries, working even for the same employers.

It has also explored a number of factors, among them public-sector employment and part-time working, which particularly affect women as workers, and has attempted to distinguish between groups of women on the basis of their varying experiences in the labour market. We have seen that women in general, and ethnic minority women in particular, can be characterized as disadvantaged, at least in terms of pay. Women are also segregated into predominantly female jobs and industries, and ethnic minority women are further segregated by occupation and industry. While many differences are apparent between full-time and part-time women workers, white and ethnic minority women workers, professional and manual women workers, women are linked to some extent by their under-payment, relative to men.

The following three chapters turn to consider the existing legislation directed at sex and (to a lesser extent) race discrimination and, in particular, at pay inequality. Although the provisions of the Race Relations Act are considered, the main focus is on the Equal Pay Act 1970 and the Sex Discrimination Act 1975: these pieces of legislation, in contrast to the Race Relations Act 1976, were specifically directed at women in the labour market, and this, in turn, is the focus of this book. In order to judge the success of these pieces of legislation their aims, together with the history of their implementation, will be discussed—success has to be measured on the legislation's own terms as well as more broadly in terms of its effect on the labour market in order that the potential impact upon the labour market of legislation generally, as well as of these pieces of legislation in particular, can be assessed.

[3]

The Equal Pay Act 1970

I. A HISTORY

(A) INTRODUCTION

The Equal Pay Act 1970 came into force on 29 December 1975. The Act was given Royal Assent some five-and-a-half years before, but its implementation was delayed in order to give employers the opportunity to prepare for the extra costs (estimated to be as much as 18 per cent of the then annual wage bill in the clothing sector, and up to 32 per cent in individual firms[1]), and men a chance to get used to the idea.

The Equal Pay Act was not the first piece of legislation to deal with discrimination against women. In 1918, the Representation of the People Act first gave women the vote, but applied only to those over 30 who were university graduates, householders, or the wives of householders. Dissatisfaction with the scope of women's enfranchisement led to the passage, in 1919, of the Sex Disqualification (Removal) Act, which declared:

Section 1
  A person shall not be disqualified by sex or marriage from the exercise of any public function, or from being appointed to or holding any civil or judicial office or post, or from entering or assuming or carrying on any civil profession or vocation.

The Sex Disqualification (Removal) Act might have been used to open women's path into employment and to challenge the common operation of marriage bars (the practice of sacking women when they got married). But as Breen Creighton pointed out in 1979, it had no impact in the employment field and was considered only twice by courts in cases when employment discrimination was at issue.[2] In the first of these, *Price* v. *Rhondda Urban District Council* (1923), a woman dismissed in pursuance of the marriage bar applied to teachers argued, *inter alia*, that her employers had breached the 1919 Act. Eve J ruled against her, stating baldly that 'I cannot accept that view' and demanding that the court '[c]onsider the absurdity to which such a conclusion might lead'.[3] The Act did

---

[1] Barbara Castle, 795 HC Debs. (9 Feb. 1970), col. 924.
[2] W. Creighton, *Working Women and the Law* (London: Mansell, 1979), 66 ff.
[3] [1923] 2 Ch 372, 391.

UNIVERSITY OF WINCHESTER
LIBRARY

not again fall to be considered in relation to employment discrimination until the decision of the Court of Appeal in *Nagle* v. *Fielden* (1966).[4] In that case, Salmon LJ declared that the plaintiff's claim, that the Jockey Club's refusal to license women trainers breached the 1919 Act, 'is certainly arguable', although he found it unnecessary to decide the case on that ground. The window of opportunity opened by Salmon LJ was not thereafter used.

Such employment legislation as dealt with women prior to 1970 required *special*, rather than non-discriminatory, treatment for them. In 1842, for example, women and girls were prohibited from working underground. And two years later the regulation of women's (but not men's) working hours began in earnest. While such legislation was perhaps driven in part by genuine concern for women's welfare (and, so far as the restriction of working hours was concerned, also by the desire to reduce the hours worked by all), many commentators took the more cynical view that its major impetus lay in the desire to protect men from undercutting and to restrict women's freedom of movement (and thus the opportunities for sin available to the lower classes).[5]

The Equal Pay Act was also partly the result of concerns that women's lower wages presented a threat to men's job security. But this Act, by contrast with earlier employment legislation, required that women be treated the *same* as men. Not in all things—while the Act extended beyond pay itself to all contractual terms, it did not address discrimination in areas such as recruitment, training, promotion, or dismissal (save to the extent that these were governed by contractual terms); nor, as originally drafted, did it preclude discrimination in contractual terms on the grounds of marriage (it would not, for example, have prevented the operation of a contractual term requiring women employees to resign on getting married). But the Equal Pay Act 1970 was the first piece of legislation clearly to outlaw discrimination against women in the employment sphere.

'Equal pay' was not a new issue in 1970. In the 1850s the more radical sections of the press had carried articles condemning women's underpayment, and the matter of equal pay had been discussed by the TUC as early as 1875.[6] It was also the subject of a unanimous resolution in 1888: 'in the opinion of this Congress it is desirable, in the interests of both men and women, that in trades where women do the same work as men, they should receive the same payment'.[7] It may have been entirely

---

[4] [1966] 2 QB 633.

[5] See, e.g. Creighton, n. 2 above, 19 ff.; A. Morris and S. Nott, *Working Women and the Law: Equality and Discrimination in Theory and Practice* (London: Routledge, 1991), 33.

[6] See generally A. Russo and C. Kramarae, *The Radical Women's Press of the 1850s* (New York: Routledge, 1991), Ch. 4; I. Ford, 'Women's Wages' in M. Roberts and T. Mizuta, (eds.), *The Exploited: Women and Work* (London: Routledge/Thoemmes Press, 1993).

[7] Creighton, n. 2 above, 90. See generally P. Paterson and M. Armstrong, *An Employers' Guide to Equal Pay* (London: Kogan Page, 1972), esp. Ch. 2.

by chance that the resolution listed men's interests before those of women. But the order is consistent with the tone of most early debates about equal pay. Women's underpayment was seen, primarily, as men's problem—while women were available at rates of pay lower than those which a man would receive, men were always vulnerable to displacement. It was this fear which made the Association of Engineering Workers insist upon equal pay as early as 1894–5 and which motivated some of the early proponents of equal pay in the Civil Service. In 1921, for example, the mover and seconder of a motion calling for equality of pay in the Civil Service (Major Hills MP and Lieutenant-Colonel Sir S. Hoare MP) spoke respectively of the 'dangers of undercutting . . . women degrading men's wages, and, above all . . . a most bitter and uncomfortable sex war'; and of the possibility that, without such equality, the Civil Service would follow the trend in teaching (where unequal wages were paid) and become a female profession.[8] And in the United States, Henry Ford's male workers downed tools during the Second World War on discovering that women were being paid 50 cents to their 85 cents per hour: 'Ford eventually conceded the equal pay principle, but did not hire another woman until the 1970s.'[9]

The TUC passed over forty resolutions in the seventy-five years after 1888, but did not begin to favour legislative intervention on unequal pay until the 1960s. Meanwhile, the matter had been debated with almost monotonous regularity in the House of Commons. Members would pass resolutions supporting the principle of pay in the public service (the first of these was in May 1920, while private sector intervention was not considered until the 1940s, and then the idea was rejected by the Asquith Committee); the government of the day would either dismiss the claim on economic grounds or appoint a Committee or Royal Commission to consider it before declaring its support for the principle but regretting that economics forbade its implementation, and would generally promise a review in a matter of years. This would happen, again the application of the principle would be rejected on economic grounds, and, eventually, MPs would make another stand.[10] Twice (in 1936 and 1944) MPs actually

[8] 145 HC Debs. (5 Aug. 1921), cols. 1894 & 1902. See also 302 HC Debs. (7 June 1935), col. 2211—Sir Clifton Brown, introducing the Salaries and Wages (Sex Equality) Bill stated that: 'men have been increasingly nervous of what they believe to be the unfair competition of women' and, cols. 2240–2, Eleanor Rathbone MP stated that: 'it has been one of the satisfactory features of the debate that this claim has been put forward quite as much in the interests of men as of women'.

[9] P. Nash and L. Gottheil, 'Employment Equity: a Union Perspective', 2 *Canadian Labor Law Journal* 49, 50.

[10] In 1921, e.g. a motion was dropped on the promise of review within three years (145 HC Debs. (5 Aug. 1921), col. 1947; in 1924 (176 HC Debs. (24 July 1924), col. 1491) Philip Snowden, Chancellor of the Exchequer, stated that the position had been reviewed (without a committee having been established) and equal pay rejected on the grounds of cost; in 1929 Fredrick Pethwick-Lawrence, Financial Secretary to the Treasury, announced a Royal Commission (229 HC Debs., 9 July 1929, col. 672); six years later Mr Duff-Cooper, Financial Secretary to the Treasury, dismissed the Salaries and Wages (Sex Equality)

voted in favour of equal pay in the Civil Service. Twice the then Prime Ministers (Baldwin and Churchill) promptly made their resistance to equal pay an issue of confidence, and secured votes in their favour.[11]

In 1944 the Equal Pay Campaign Committee was set up. It co-ordinated over forty national groups which were agitating for equal pay. According to one report, many of the committee's 'activities and techniques later became a model for inter-group co-operative efforts towards equal pay in other countries'.[12] The committee, which brought together trade unions, professional organizations, party and non party-political and women's and feminist organizations, continued until a Conservative administration adopted a rolling programme of equal pay in the Civil Service in 1955. Between that year and 1961, 'equal pay' (i.e. the same rate for men and women doing the *same job*) was awarded to teachers, non-industrial Civil Servants, and non-manual local government employees (professionals such as doctors had been in receipt of it as early as 1936, in line with the government's policy of echoing outside rates which were, for doctors, the same regardless of sex[13]). This left unaffected the relative salaries of women manual employees in the public sector, and of many in the private sector. But in 1964 a Labour Government was elected on the promise of equal pay for all, in 1968 the Ford machinists struck for equal pay, and by 1970 the Equal Pay Act was in place, if not in force.[14]

The arguments employed in favour of the Equal Pay (No 2) Bill (the Equal Pay Bill had been introduced in July 1968 and again in December 1969 by Christopher Norwood MP, but never made it to a second reading[15]) related more to justice for women than to protection for men, although Lena Jeger, Labour MP for Holborn and St Pancras South, also stressed that it was 'a step towards eliminating the dangers of undercutting'.[16] But the Bill, according to Jeger, was

about poor women. It is about the more than 50 per cent of working women who earn less than 5 shillings an hour. There has been equal pay for some time for clever, articulate, professional women. Today we are talking about poor women . . . the women who do the lowest paid, most drudging jobs in society.[17]

Bill, primarily on economic grounds (302 HC Debs., 7 June 1935, col. 2245); one month later a committee was set up to consider the issue of wage inequality (304 HC Debs., 25 July 1935, cols. 1996–7) and 9 months thereafter a Resolution to put the 1920 Resolution into action moved (310 HC Debs., 1 Apr. 1936, col. 2017). In 1944 Prime Minister Churchill announced a Royal Commission (399 HC Debs. (9 May 1944) col. 1710); in 1946 the government pronounced equal pay right in principle but too expensive (423 HC Debs. (1 June 1946)), a position reiterated in 1952 (500 HC Debs., 16 May 1952, col. 1791).

[11] 310 HC Debs. (6 Apr. 1936), col. 2444.
[12] *Equal Pay for Equal Work* (New York: UN, 1960).
[13] 318 HC Debs. (7 Dec. 1936), cols. 1650–1.
[14] Paterson and Armstrong, n. 7 above, 23–4.
[15] 769 HC Debs. (23 July 1968), col. 286 and 792 HC Debs. (2 Dec. 1969), col. 1309.
[16] 795 HC Debs. (9 Feb. 1970), col. 970.   [17] *Ibid.*, col. 971.

And Barbara Castle (then Secretary of State for Employment and Productivity), declared the implementation of equal pay 'a basic act of justice . . . another historical advance in our struggle against discrimination'.[18] 'We intend', she said, 'to make equal pay for equal work a reality; and, in doing so, to take women workers progressively out of the sweated labour class'.[19] A noble sentiment indeed. But what was meant by 'equal pay'? The early campaigns, and those supporters primarily concerned with men's employment security, demanded simply that women be paid equally when engaged in the *same jobs* as men. The CBI followed this tradition in pressing for the equal pay obligation to apply only when men and women were doing the same work. The TUC, on the other hand, argued that women should be paid the same for work of equal *value*. Mrs Castle declared the former approach (which she took to be that embodied in Article 119 of the Treaty of Rome) too narrow, the latter (that proposed by the ILO) 'far from satisfactory', 'too abstract a concept to embody in legislation'.[20] Her aim was to 'eradicate discrimination in pay in specific identifiable situations by prescribing equally specific remedies'. This, she said, would do 'all that can be done in legislation, and goes far beyond anything in the law of other major countries'.[21] It was aimed at producing the same *result* as that mandated by International Labour Organization (ILO) Convention No 100: 'remuneration established without discrimination based on sex' and would, as a result, allow the United Kingdom to ratify that convention (some twenty years after its adoption by the ILO).[22]

(B) THE EQUAL PAY (NO 2) BILL OF 1970

According to Barbara Castle, who introduced the legislation, the Equal Pay Act would entitle women to equal pay (and other contractual terms) with those men 'in the same employment' who were engaged on 'like' work—that is, work which was broadly similar to theirs, or on work which had been rated as of equivalent value by a job evaluation scheme.[23] The scheme could have been carried out unilaterally by the employer or in co-operation with one or more trade unions, but employers were under no obligation to conduct or co-operate in any job evaluation.

[18] *Ibid.*, col. 914.   [19] *Ibid.*   [20] *Ibid.*, cols. 915–16.
[21] *Ibid.*, col. 917.
[22] *Ibid.*, cols. 915–16. The UK was the 72nd state to ratify (in 1971, with Chile and the Netherlands)—by 1986, according to the report of the General Survey by the Committee of Experts on the Application of Conventions and Recommendations, *Equal Remuneration* (Geneva: ILO, 1986), 4, the Convention was 'among the most widely ratified by countries from all regions of the world' (107 countries having ratified by that date).
[23] The Act applied, and still applies, to men as well as to women, but it was clear from its introduction in the House that it was directed primarily at the underpayment of women. It will be referred to in this manner.

In order to succeed in an 'equal pay' claim, a woman would have to point to a man (or men, or if a man claimed, a woman or women) who enjoyed more favourable pay or other contractual term(s) and who was employed on like work/work rated as equivalent. Claims could be made only as against comparators 'in the same employment'—that is, who were employed (i) by the same or an associated employer *and* (ii) at the same establishment or at different establishments 'at which common terms and conditions [were] observed either generally or for employees of the relevant classes'.[24]

If a claimant satisfied the tribunal that her chosen comparator was so employed and if the employer did not successfully defend the claim (of which more between notes 67 and 90 below), the tribunal would then declare that an 'equality clause' had been implied into her contract entitling her to the more favourable pay or other contractual term enjoyed by her comparator. This approach made it necessary that the woman could point to an *actual* man, with whose contract hers could be assimilated, rather than claiming merely that she *would have been* granted more favourable contractual terms had she been a (hypothetical) man instead of a woman.

In addition to these individual claims, the Equal Pay (No 2) Bill also provided that women were entitled not to suffer discrimination on the basis of sex 'where their terms and conditions of employment are laid down in collective agreements, statutory wages orders or employers' wage structures'. In other words, the common practice by which employers maintained overtly discriminatory 'male rates' and 'women's rates' had to cease. But the provision would apply only to *overtly* discriminatory rates and would not prevent employers from renaming grades which remained in substance 'male' and 'female'. Nor would it require that employers integrate groups of workers previously excluded from the collective bargaining structure into it, although it would require that an overtly declared 'female rate' for jobs outside a collective agreement was raised to that of the lowest 'male rate' either within or outside the agreement. This aspect of the Act was to be enforced by the Industrial Court (by the time the Act came into force, the Central Arbitration Committee) to which collective agreements could be referred by one of the parties thereto or by the Secretary of State, pay structures by the employer or the Secretary of State.

The Bill did not propose to create an absolute entitlement to equal pay where like work or work rated as equivalent was established. According to the Secretary of State, there was no intention to 'prohibit differences in pay between a woman and comparable male workers which arise because of genuine differences other than sex between her case and theirs'.[25] The

[24] EqPA, s. 1(6).   [25] 795 HC Debs. (9 Feb. 1970), col. 920.

Bill, therefore, allowed an employer to defend a claim (once the woman had satisfied the burden of proving like work/work rated as equivalent) on the basis that the difference in pay/other contractual terms was 'genuinely due to a material difference (other than the difference of sex) between her case and his'.[26] This would be for the employer to prove and, according to Mrs Castle, would allow employers to pay according to:

length of service, merit, output and so on . . . provided that the payments are available to any person who qualifies regardless of sex . . . such payments must be related to actual differences in performance of service. . . . It will not be permissible for an employer to discriminate between men as a class and women as a class, because he believes that in some way women generally are of less value to him as workers than men.[27]

Mrs Castle was upbeat about the likely impact of the legislation. There were, she said, about 8.5 million women employees, of whom one million already received equal pay. Three million more, she estimated, were engaged on broadly similar ('like') work to men, and 2.5 million of the 3.8 million workers covered by Wages Councils were women. Of the remaining two million women employees, some would be covered by job evaluation schemes (she estimated that such schemes covered about 30 per cent of all employees[28]), and still others would benefit from the 'halo' effect created by the rising wages of women engaged in mixed-sex jobs. '[P]ockets of discrimination' would remain where employers succeeded in evading the legislation. But it was for women to 'organise to put a stop' to such practices. It was 'no part of [the Secretary of State's] job to make it unnecessary for women to join a trade union'.[29] And this, together with the new Act, would (it seemed from the tone of Mrs Castle's speech) be sufficient to tackle the problem of women's underpayment.

Not only was the Secretary of State for Employment and Production happy with the coverage afforded by the Equal Pay (No 2) Bill, she was also apparently content with the enforcement mechanisms provided. Industrial tribunals, she declared, would afford a 'speedy, informal and accessible' means of redress.[30] One MP was even more convinced of the ease with which the legislation could be applied. Albert Booth questioned whether it was necessary to involve the industrial tribunals at all, suggesting that, in equal pay cases, 'there will not be quite the same necessity for someone to have a grasp of the law as there is in industrial tribunal cases'.[31]

The Equal Pay (No 2) Bill underwent some amendments in committee and in debate in the House of Commons. But its progress was a remarkably happy one, both sides of the House largely united in the view that

---

[26] EqPA, s. 1(3).   [27] 795 HC Debs. (9 Feb. 1970), col. 920.   [28] *Ibid.*, col. 919.
[29] *Ibid.*, cols. 928–9.   [30] *Ibid.*, col. 918.
[31] 800 HC Debs. (22 Apr. 1970), cols. 572–3.

legislation was long overdue. Some sniping went on about which party had been to the fore in supporting equal pay for women, and uncertainties were expressed both that the Bill went too far, and that it did not do enough. Tory MP Robert Carr, while welcoming legislative intervention on the issue, at once complained of 'fussy interventionism' and claimed that equal opportunities legislation was required to block employers' likely attempts to replace newly-expensive women with male workers; Liberal Dr Winstanley MP warned that the battle for equality had far to go, and that many women operated in a separate labour market which would go largely untouched by the 'equal pay for like work' model; and Labour Member Frederick Lee mentioned 'the situation of women who carry out jobs that are not usually regarded as carrying men's rates'.[32] But, with one exception (Ronald Bell MP, who claimed that 'the market mirrors the truth', and that women's lower wages were the result of their poorer work[33]), the House seemed unanimous in its support for legislation. Even Margaret Thatcher, doyenne of the free market, congratulated Barbara Castle on introducing the Bill, argued that market forces were not sufficient to ensure equitable pay for women, and concluded for the opposition by declaring:

So many people have supported the idea of equal pay for so long that one wonders at the continuing inequality of payment between men and women. I believe that the Bill will lead to better pay for many jobs, and I support it as another step in the equal pay process.[34]

(c) INITIAL IMPACT OF THE EQUAL PAY ACT

So matters progressed smoothly, the Equal Pay (No 2) Bill became the Equal Pay Act with barely a whisper of opposition and, within a year, the United Kingdom finally ratified ILO Convention No 100 of 1951. At the end of 1975 the Equal Pay Act became binding on employers, trade unions, and wage-fixing bodies. Agricultural Wages Boards, which had for decades laid down 'male' and 'female' rates (women's hourly rates were typically 75 per cent of men's until 1971, when they began to be set at 80 per cent[35]); made the pay scales for some grades of agricultural workers 'unisex' from 1974 (outside these grades, women continued to

[32] 795 HC Debs. (9 Feb. 1970), cols. 933, 939, 990, and 952 respectively.
[33] *Ibid.*, cols. 956 ff.   [34] *Ibid.*, cols. 1019, 1923, and 1027.
[35] In 1946, e.g. the Agricultural Wages Regulations laid down male rates of 80 shillings for a 48-hour week, 107/6 for 60 hours. The female rate was 55 shillings for a 44-hour week, 60 shillings where the more usual 48-hour week was worked. By 1968, the Agricultural Wages Board laid down minima of between 231 and 254 shillings per week for men, between 173/6 and 191 shillings for women, and by 1971 rates of £14.80 to £16.28 applied to men, £11.84 to £13.02 to women. Statistics published by the Ministry of Labour and National Service Statistics Department.

receive 80 per cent of male rates); and, at the end of 1975, imposed a single minimum for all workers. Wages Councils, likewise, replaced sex-specific minimum rates of pay with a single scale applicable to all. Women's pay shot up: those working in both manual and non-manual jobs in industry experienced a 10 per cent rise (relative to men) between 1970 and 1976.[36] By far the greater part of that increase took place towards the end of this period. This can be seen from table 3.1 below, which shows the proportionate rises in male and female wages (both on a weekly and hourly basis) between October 1969 (before the Act was passed) and October 1976 (by which time it had been in place for just under a year). In total, women's wages rose, between 1969 and 1976, by 335 per cent (342 per cent on an hourly basis) as against men's rise of 270 per cent (285 per cent hourly). Women's wage increases therefore outstripped men's by a factor of 5:4 (weekly, 6:5 hourly).

Table 3.1 — relative increases in full-time men's and women's pay 1969–1976

	average weekly		average hourly		female/male		hours/week	
	male	female	male	female	weekly	hourly	male	female
1969–70	13%	16%	15%	16%	123	107	45.7	37.9
1970–1	10%	13%	13%	14%	130	108	44.7	37.7
1971–2	16%	16%	15%	15%	100	100	45.0	37.9
1972–3	14%	16%	13%	16%	114	123	45.6	37.7
1973–4	19%	28%	20%	29%	147	145	45.1	37.4
1974–5	23%	27%	27%	28%	117	104	43.6	37.0
1975–6	12%	19%	11%	17%	158	154	41.0	37.4

source: Department of Employment *Gazette*, 1977.[37]

The 5:4, 6:5 figures are rather less impressive when one takes into account the fact that women were starting from a lower base (about 50 per cent of men's weekly and 55 per cent of men's hourly average in 1970[38]) and that, therefore, their wages had to increase more as a percentage of themselves than men's simply in order not to fall further behind men's wages. But the Government appeared content with the progress of the Act. In July 1976, at which point the Act had been in force for a mere seven months, a Department of Employment Minister stated that, while:

[36] ILO *Women at Work* (Geneva: ILO, 1979), 9–10.

[37] The 5th and 6th cols. indicate the rate at which the increase in female wages surpassed that in male wages where 100 indicates equal rates of improvement between men and women from previous year); average hours worked are in 1970, 1971, 1972, 1973, 1974, 1975, and 1976; the statistics upon which the table is based are taken from the Department of Employment *Gazette*, Mar. 1977, 241.

[38] NES 1970, tables 1, 3, 4, & 5.

In the last round [of pay talks] a significant sum had to be allowed for the implementation of equal pay because it was known that large numbers of women were not getting equal pay. Although there are still some women who are not getting what they are entitled to under the Act, the overall sum required to meet their needs is much smaller than last year.[39]

The effect of the faster rate of increase in men's than in women's pay (outlined at table 3.1) is illustrated in table 3.2 which shows women's wages, relative to those of men, between 1970 (when the Equal Pay Act was passed) and 1984 (when it was amended, an issue discussed in Chapter 4).

Table 3.2 — full-time women's pay as a percentage of comparable men's, 1970–84[40]

	average hourly rates			average weekly rates		
	all	manual	non-manual	all	manual	non-manual
1970	63%	61%	52%	56%	50%	50%
1975	71%	68%	61%	62%	58%	58%
1976	73%	71%	63%	64%	61%	60%
1977	74%	72%	63%	65%	61%	61%
1978	72%	72%	61%	63%	61%	59%
1979	71%	70%	61%	62%	69%	58%
1980	72%	71%	61%	63%	61%	59%
1981	73%	70%	62%	65%	61%	59%
1982	72%	69%	61%	64%	60%	59%
1983	72%	70%	61%	65%	61%	59%
1984	73%	70%	62%	66%	61%	59%

source: NES 1970–84, tables 86 & 87

It is clear from this table that women's pay did improve, relative to that of men, in the period 1970–6. It improved significantly—more significantly, in fact, than it had done at any other time before; and more significantly than it has done since. Such an increase in women's earnings is not to be sneezed at and was described by economists Zabalza and Tzannatos as 'remarkable'. The 'improvement cannot be attributed to shifts in female employment from low to high paying sectors of the economy . . . . By far the major factor . . . is an increase in relative pay within industries and within occupations, and this is the case for both contracting and expanding sectors.'[41]

[39] J. Coussins, *The Equality Report* (London: NCCL Rights for Women Unit, 1976), 8.
[40] Hourly rates are without overtime, weekly with.
[41] A. Zabalza and Z. Tzannatos, *Women and Equal Pay: The Effects of Legislation on Female Employment and Wages* (Cambridge: Cambridge University Press, 1985), 9 and 1–7.

But for all of this improvement, in 1976 women earned an average of only 73 pence (again, taking full-time workers' hourly rates) for every pound earned by men. And if manual and non-manual women workers are considered separately, the picture was still worse. Women manual workers earned only 71 pence for every pound earned by their male colleagues (again, taking only the hourly rate for full-time employees), and non-manual women workers a mere 63 pence. (The higher rate of pay earned by non-manual workers and the over-concentration of women, relative to men, in non-manual jobs, explains why *all* women's pay, relative to that of *all* men, was, and remains, higher than that of either manual or non-manual women workers relative to their male counterparts.)

Not only did a substantial gender–pay gap survive the Equal Pay Act, but table 3.2 shows that the gap actually *increased* after 1976. Between 1976 and 1979 women's relative hourly earnings in all categories decreased, as did the relative weekly figure for women taken as a whole. Zabalza and Tzannatos put this decline down to the removal of incomes policies (see Chapter 9) which had increased women's wages slightly in 1976 and 1977 and to the increased supply of female labour which had resulted from the improvement in women's wages.[42] The Equal Opportunities Commission's (EOC's) *Annual Reports* for 1978 and 1979 expressed alarm over the fall (in hourly earnings, from a high of 75.5 per cent in 1977 to 73.9 per cent in 1978 and 73 per cent in 1979). And the EOC was not isolated in its concern—in 1979, Incomes Data Services claimed that 'women's first response [to the Equal Pay Act and the Sex Discrimination Act] has modulated over four years from hope to something near disenchantment'; and reported disillusionment with and within the EOC: the 'EOC, true to their structure, to the careful balance of interests they represent—indeed to their own express policy—were bent on persuading not militant campaigning. . . . Yet this slow, careful start has made a painful impression on working women, some of them in the Commission itself.'[43]

In 1980 the EOC's *Annual Report* noted a rise in women's relative hourly rate to 73.5 per cent, but went on: 'the reality is that women's relative earnings have now stabilised at around 73 per cent and that they are unlikely to show any further substantial improvement'.[44] This view was reiterated in 1981 and 1982, in which years women's earnings had again risen to 74.8 per cent only to fall again to 73.9 per cent. In 1982 the EOC claimed that 'the marked progress towards equal pay between 1970 and 1977 had been effectively halted in the last five years . . . the Commission does not attach any great significance to small yearly fluctuations'.[45] And in the same year, the ILO publication *Women at Work* claimed that

---

[42] *Ibid.* 68–9.

[43] Incomes Data Services, *Equal Pay, Sex Discrimination, Maternity Rights* (London: IDS, 1979), 1 & 2.

[44] EOC, *Annual Report 1980*, 1.   [45] EOC, *Annual Report 1982*, 1.

women in the United Kingdom were 'gradually losing their fight for equal pay'.[46]

The ILO cited evidence not only of a relative decline in general terms but also of a fall, in many important female occupations, to pre-1975 relative wage levels from a peak in 1977. In only five of the seventeen predominantly female occupations identified by the ILO had wages improved, relative to the average male wage, between 1975 and 1981. While women in these jobs (shop assistants, typists, secretaries/short hand typists, primary school teachers, and managers) had gained between 1.7 per cent and 6.4 per cent in the six years after the implementation of the Equal Pay Act; eight female occupational groups had actually lost ground in that time[47] (these included professional women supporting management; nurses; telephonists; caterers, cleaners, and hairdressers; and home and domestic helpers).

Manual women workers did particularly badly in this continuing backlash. Not only did their hourly rates fall from 72 per cent to 69 per cent of manual men's between 1978 and 1982, but women in some parts of the country did extremely poorly. In East Anglia and North West England, women manual workers fell behind by only 2 per cent, and in the South East, East, and West Midlands by 4 per cent. But manual women in Scotland saw their hourly rates fall from 72 per cent of men's to 67 per cent in four years, while the rate for manual women in the South West declined by a massive 11 per cent, from 73 per cent to only 62 per cent of that for men.

Nor were British women doing well by international standards. Figures published by the ILO showed that, while they fared better (relative to their men) than women in the Republic of Korea, Ireland, Luxembourg, and Switzerland (and, in 1981, than women in Greece or Kenya), they did less well, in both years, than women in Belgium, Finland, France, West Germany, the Netherlands, New Zealand (all of whom earned between 70 and 80 per cent of men's hourly rates in 1981), and substantially worse (relative to men) than women in Australia, Denmark, Norway, Burma, Sri Lanka, El Salvador, and Sweden (80 to 90 per cent in 1981).[48]

It should be noted that changes in the gathering of statistics in 1983 had the effect of increasing women's relative earnings: prior to this year the rates had been calculated for women over 18, and for men of 21 and above; from 1983 the rates referred to all employees on *adult rates*. In 1983, in which year both sets of statistics were collected, the new approach

[46] N. 36 above, 6. The ILO based its claim on the NES 1981, *Labour Research*, Jan. 1982, and the *Employment Gazette*, May 1982.

[47] The major source of the wage gap was, according to the ILO, the concentration of women in the lowest paid jobs (3 of the 17 predominantly female occupations paid less than half the average male wage).

[48] N. 36 above, 6. Statistics taken from the ILO (1982) *Yearbook of Labour Statistics*, table 17A.

gave women a 1.5 per cent advantage (on weekly rates) over the old: thus 1.5 per cent of any gain made by women in the period since 1982 is due to the statistics themselves, rather than to any real change in their relative position.[49]

The EOC continued to press for changes to the Act—in 1978 the Commission complained of the 'rigidity' of the requirement for a male comparator, and of the failure of the Act to deal with indirectly discriminatory pay practices and to allow for 'equal value' comparisons—these complaints were reiterated in one form or another until 1983 when the appointment of a new 'chairman' appeared, on the evidence of the annual reports at any rate, to be accompanied by a change to a more 'softly softly' approach. In any event, that year saw the introduction of the Equal Pay (Amendment) Regulations which, as we shall see in Chapter 4, became law in January 1984.

II. SHORTCOMINGS OF THE EQUAL PAY ACT 1970

Why did the Equal Pay Act have such a limited effect? It might be argued that the gap which remained between men's and women's wages was not the result of discrimination, and so could not be addressed by legislation aimed at eliminating discrimination. This particular explanation is much favoured by free-marketeers who reason that discrimination is inefficient and will, therefore, be eliminated if free reign is given to the market. These arguments are considered in more detail in Chapter 6. Suffice it to say at this point that more plausible explanations relate to the inadequacy of the legislation itself and, to a lesser extent, to the manner of its application by the courts.

The Equal Pay Act aimed only at the crudest forms of pay discrimination against women. In practical terms it required only that women be paid the same as men when they did effectively the *same work* in the *same organization*. It did not set out, save in two very limited respects, to address the low payment of women in *female* jobs (whether those jobs were in mixed-sex or in segregated workplaces). Unless a job done by a woman or women within an organization could be regarded as 'like work' with one done by a man or men, no claim was possible except where the jobs had been rated as equivalent under an existing job evaluation scheme, or where the collective jurisdiction of the CAC could be called into play (this is discussed in the text following note 90 below). It is clear from Chapters 2 and 6 that women are, and in the 1970s were, largely segregated into different jobs from those which are typically done by men. Job

---

[49] The weekly statistics improved by 1.5% for all women (increasing from (65–66.5%), by 1% for manual women (61.2–62.2%) and by 1.4% for non-manual women (59.1–60.5%).

evalution schemes were rare and, given the very crude understanding of indirect discrimination prevalent until at least the mid-1980s (see further Chapter 3), unlikely to have been gender-neutral. The result was that equal pay claims were, for the most part, permitted only to those women who did the same jobs as men. And in any cases where substantial numbers of women were engaged in the same work as men, it is likely that male wages were themselves held down by the availability of cheap female labour. There was no sense, then, in which the Equal Pay Act could be regarded as entitling women to discrimination-free wages, much less as securing such wages for them.

Perhaps even more serious than the limitations of the Equal Pay Act as regards occupational sex segregation was its non-application, save in very limited circumstances, to pay differences which arose between workplaces. Again, this limitation could be circumvented under the collective provisions but, as we shall see in the text following note 89 below, these provisions had a very limited impact and would benefit, in this context, only those women covered by a multi-employer agreement. Such women, typically, would not have been among the most disadvantaged.

We saw, above, that the Act permitted (and to this day permits) comparisons to be made, broadly, between men and women employed in the same workplace by the same employer.[50] We also saw, in Chapter 2, that, for the most part, men and women work in different industries, different workplaces. This was as true in the 1970s as it is today (see Chapter 5). The fact that the Equal Pay Act addressed itself only to those pay disparities which arose between workplaces meant, again, that it was of very limited value to the many women who worked, and work, in predominantly female workplaces. Even where such women could find a comparator (and again, the likelihood of this was much reduced by the narrow scope for comparison under the Equal Pay Act as originally implemented) the men with whom they could compare themselves were likely to be relatively poorly paid by virtue of their position in predominantly female, and therefore low paying, workplaces.[51]

The other glaring defect of the Equal Pay Act was its application solely to pay differentials associated with sex. We saw in Chapter 2 that Indian, black, Pakistani and Bangladeshi women, women of mixed race and of other ethnic origins are all at a significant disadvantage, in comparison with white women, when it comes to pay. The same is true for ethnic minority men. Yet the Equal Pay Act made no attempt to address the

[50] Strictly, 'the same establishment' is somewhat broader than the same workplace—see EPA, s. 1(6) and the discussion of *Leverton* v. *Clwyd County Council* [1989] IRLR 28 and *BCC* v. *Smith* [1996] IRLR 404 in Ch. 1. Claims can also be made against comparators employed by associated employers—see also Ch. 1.

[51] See N. Millward and S. Woodland, *Gender Segregation and Male/Female Wage Differences* (London: LSE, 1995), Centre for Economic Performance Discussion Paper No 220, discussed in Ch. 6.

race–pay gap and the Race Relations Act 1976, while applicable to pay, was not specifically directed at it. The 1976 Act is discussed in Chapter 5. Here we turn to consider the other shortcomings of the 1970 Act in rather more detail.

(A) INDIVIDUAL MECHANISMS

Establishing Equivalence

The Equal Pay Act allowed comparisons between the wages of women and those of men, working in the same employment, whose jobs had been rated as equivalent by a job evaluation scheme. But such schemes were designed primarily to justify existing wage hierarchies and so were unlikely to assign equal value to male and female jobs. Even if a scheme had done so prior to 1970, the advance notice given to employers of the Equal Pay Act's implementation would have given them ample opportunity to replace the scheme or alter the parameters of the equally-rated male and female jobs to render them 'unequal'.

An Employers' Guide to Equal Pay, a book published in 1972, contains a section entitled 'avoidance' in its chapter 'Implementing the Act—Strategies for Management'.[52] The section, which draws a distinction between 'avoidance' (which is 'not illegal') and 'evasion' (which is), states that 'any book dealing with equal pay is bound somewhere to put on record some of the ways in which management is likely to arrange its affairs if it believes that the impact of the [Equal Pay] Act will harm its business'.[53] It goes on to list these 'more negative responses to equal pay that could be made under the legislation as it is framed at present'. The list (which predated the Sex Discrimination Act 1975) includes 're-grading jobs on the basis of the degree to which the work is light or heavy, which would automatically discriminate against women . . . eliminating, or at least reducing, jobs performed by both men and women so as to avoid direct comparisons', maintaining different terms and conditions at different plants 'to discourage comparison between establishments', and refusing to engage women 'on the grounds, justified or unjustified, that increased absenteeism and higher rates of turnover would make them a less economic proposition than men paid at the same rates'.[54]

Research conducted by Snell and others in the late 1970s/early 1980s suggested that many employers adopted a number of these 'minimization' techniques. Among the organizations whose responses to the Equal Pay Act were studied, eleven out of a total of twenty-seven (separating manual and non-manual workers) either failed to comply with the legislation or reduced the benefit to women by adopting minimization techniques. Such techniques included the replacement of male and female wage-scales in the same grade with a variety of 'unisex' grades, women being placed in

[52] Paterson and Armstrong, n. 7 above, 53.   [53] *Ibid.*   [54] *Ibid.* 54.

the lower grades and men in the higher ones; the reduction of women's piece-work rates to compensate for the 'equal pay' increase in their basic rates; the replacement of 'male' and 'female' piece-work schemes with 'heavy' and 'light', all men being classified as 'heavy' and all women as 'light'; the increase of female rates to a notional 'male rate' which, by the completion of implementation, had had its rate depressed and had no men remaining in it; and the increase of the 'female rate' to the lowest 'male rate' which was depressed during the implementation period relative to other male rates but whose male incumbents had their rates redcircled. The researchers concluded that:

Despite greater systematization of pay, there were still *de facto* male and female grades and/or rates within many unisex pay structures. The lower grades in clerical structures were almost always all women and the manual structures of 15 [of 19] organizations contained rates on which it would have been rare to find a man. These reflected the continuing segregation of jobs and, in some cases, employers' minimizing strategies.[55]

An Employers' Guide to Equal Pay also suggested that employers could refuse to introduce job evaluation 'because it could encourage equal pay claims' although, given the ease with which job evaluation can be manipulated to serve chosen ends (an issue discussed in depth in Chapter 7), employers who instituted job evaluation schemes with knowledge of the Equal Pay Act could take steps to ensure that unwanted equivalences were not found between male and female job classes. The Act did allow some room for challenge to discriminatory job evaluation schemes, section 1(5) providing that:

A woman is to be regarded as employed on work rated as equivalent with that of any men if . . . her job and their job . . . would have been given an equal value but for the evaluation being made on a system setting different values for men and women on the same demand under any heading.

But this covered only the most blatantly discriminatory evaluation systems and provided no scope for challenge to a system which undervalued (or failed entirely to take account of) the types of skill primarily associated with female jobs (of which more in Chapter 7 below). The extent to which this influenced what Snell reported as 'the greater use of job evaluation' in the years following the implementation of the Equal Pay Act is a matter for speculation.[56]

As far as the 'like work' provisions of the Act were concerned, Barbara Castle had claimed that 'like work' was much less restrictive than 'the

---

[55] M. Snell, P. Glucklich and M. Povall, *Equal Pay and Opportunities: A Study of the Implementation and Effects of the Equal Pay and Sex Discrimination Act in 26 Organisations* (London: Department of Employment, 1981), Research Paper No 2, 51–5 and 56.

[56] *Ibid.* 56.

same work', and stressed that differences between jobs must be 'of practical importance' in order to preclude a 'like work' finding.[57] But Jean Coussin's *Equality Report*, published in 1976, declared that 'the high failure rate [72 per cent] of claims in 1976 was largely due to tribunals interpreting the words ["broadly similar"] in an unnecessarily narrow way'.[58] The report instanced cases such as *Amey* v. *Tidmars & Sons*, in which a tribunal refused to accept that the jobs of a curtain cutter and a blind cutter were 'broadly similar'. Curtain cutting involved the marking and cutting of fabric with scissors or shears, whereas blind-cutting, which involved the use of a knife, was considered 'a heavier and generally bigger operation'.[59] In another case, a woman warehouse assistant's claim was rejected on the ground that her comparator sometimes stood in for driving duties when the van driver was absent, and had on occasion undertaken 'personal errands' for the management.[60]

To these examples might be added the decisions in *Brodie & Anor.* v. *Startrite Engineering Co. Ltd* and in *Eaton Ltd* v. *Nuttall*.[61] In the first of these cases the tribunal rejected a 'like work' claim by female drill operators using as their comparator a male drill operator. The male drill operator selected as well as fitted a particular machine part, and could do minor repairs on his own machine. He earned 1.42 times the hourly rate earned by the women. History does not record why the man was, and the women were not, deemed capable of performing these additional functions.[62] And in *Eaton Ltd* v. *Nuttall*, the difference in the value of items looked after by a male and a female production scheduler led the EAT to allow an employer's appeal despite the fact that the only other female production scheduler in employment, who was paid the same rate as the applicant, had replaced a man who had been paid on the same (higher) rate as that paid to the one male production scheduler whose rate of pay was known. It is perhaps unfortunate that this was not seen by the EAT as sufficient to undermine the employer's attempts to prove that the difference in value relied upon was 'of practical importance'.

The decision of the Employment Appeal Tribunal, in *Capper Pass* v. *Lawton* (October 1976), was welcomed by Coussins for its adoption of a 'wide liberal approach' to the question whether jobs were 'broadly similar' (the EAT declared that no account should be taken, in determining

---

[57] 795 HC Debs. (9 Feb 1970), col. 918.

[58] Coussins, n. 39 above, 22. The 72% failure rate refers to the 261 cases heard until 17 Nov. 1976.

[59] *Ibid.* 28.

[60] *Hutchinson* v. *UU Textiles Ltd*, reported in Coussins, n. 39 above, 28.

[61] [1976] IRLR 101 and [1977] IRLR 71.

[62] The employers may have shared the view, expressed by one of the respondents to a Department of Employment Study undertaken in the late 1970s/early 1980s (Snell *et al.*, n. 55 above, 58, that: '[w]omen are not machine sophisticated . . . it would not be worth training them' (the woman, unlike men operating the same machine, was not trained to change tools).

the question of 'like work', of 'trivial differences or differences not likely in the real world to be reflected in the terms and conditions of employment'[63]), but the *Equality Report* pointed out that the EAT's detailed guidance in that case 'is no certain guarantee that some industrial tribunals will make no mistakes in the future'.[64]

This fear proved well-founded. Despite similar decisions by the EAT in *Electrolux Ltd* v. *Hutchinson & Ors* and the Court of Appeal's approval of *Capper Pass* in *Shields* v. *Coomes (Holdings) Ltd* in 1977, the attrition rate for equal pay cases remained at extremely high levels—in 1977, 64 per cent of cases heard by tribunals were dismissed; in 1978, 78 per cent; in 1979, 83 per cent; in 1980, 85 per cent; in 1981, 78 per cent and in 1982, 85 per cent.[65] Many cases failed because the applicants failed to satisfy the tribunal on the issue of 'like work'—the proportion ran at 72 per cent of dismissals in 1978 and 48 per cent in 1979. And while this proportion declined in 1980 and thereafter, Alice Leonard's survey of industrial tribunal decisions in 1980–2 revealed that some tribunals were still approaching the 'like work' issue in an extremely narrow way. In *Judging Inequality*, Leonard cites one case in which the jobs performed by a male and a female rates rebate officer were found not to be 'like' because only the woman deputized for her superior during his absence, and only the man completed an annual statistical return to the Department of the Environment.[66] In another case, a tribunal ruled that a woman bingo caller was not entitled to equal pay with that of a male bingo caller—the two called different types of bingo games for part of each day and briefly performed different tasks to 'complete the day's activities'.[67] Neither of these decisions appears on its face to be consistent with Barbara Castle's view that 'like work' was a great deal wider than 'the same work'.

The Employers' Defence—Disguised and Indirect Discrimination

It is clear from the foregoing that, at least as far as individual women were concerned, the likelihood of establishing equivalence (the *sine qua non* of the equal pay claim) was slim. And even in those cases in which 'like work' or 'work rated as equivalent' was made out, the 'material difference' defence presented problems from the earliest days. In *Hobson* v. *Rowntree Mackintosh Ltd*, for example, a tribunal denied that a woman who operated a machine which put cellophane wrappings on boxes of Black Magic was entitled to equal pay with men who operated machines wrapping

[63] *Capper Pass Ltd* v. *Lawton* [1976] IRLR 366, 367–8.

[64] Coussins, n. 39 above, 27.

[65] Statistics taken from the EOC *Annual Reports* for the relevant years. *Electrolux Ltd* v. *Hutchinson & Ors* is at [1976] IRLR 410 and *Shields* v. *Coomes* at [1978] IRLR 263.

[66] *Coley* v. *Hinkley and Bosworth Borough Council*, cited by A. Leonard, *Judging Inequality: The Effectiveness of the Tribunal System in Sex Discrimination and Equal Pay Cases* (London: Cobden Trust, 1987), 57.

[67] *Goy* v. *Clifton Bingo Club*, cited by Leonard, n. 66 above.

Kit Kat bars. Because the men were handling unwrapped chocolate, their 'responsibility to their employers' was 'of a different nature' from that of the woman. The *Equality Report* points out that Rowntree had altered its pay structure to 'comply' with the Equal Pay Act by replacing 'male piece-work' and 'female piece-work' grades with 'general piece-work' grades, and placing all the men in 'general piece-work' grade A which served to maintain their pre-Equal Pay Act advantage. The decision of the tribunal did nothing to challenge this.

Perhaps of more general interest were the 'red circle' cases. Many employers, it seems, responded to the impending implementation of the Equal Pay Act by revising sex-specific pay structures into unified structures, but also by protecting the wages of men whose jobs were accorded reduced pay as a result of the revised structure ('red-circling' them). Whereas the approach adopted by Rowntree would perpetuate discriminatory wages for new employees (assuming that new male employees would be placed within 'grade A', and that women employees would not be so placed), 'red-circling' is usually specific to the incumbent of the job, rather than to the job itself. 'Red circles' may last as long as the red-circled person remains at work (i.e.(s)he may continue to receive pay rises in line with other employees), or they may be phased out by the practice of freezing the pay of the red-circled employee until the rate appropriate to the job has caught up with the rate paid to that particular incumbent of it.

'Red-circles' are usually triggered by the demotion of an employee, or the down-grading of his or her job, in circumstances where industrial goodwill or some other factor makes it in the employer's interests to preserve that employee's former rate of pay. Where this happens (where, for example, a skilled factory worker is injured at work, with the effect that he cannot perform his former job and is transferred to less skilled work generally carrying a lower wage rate), the retention of the employee at the former wage rate will not generally give rise to any discrimination issue. Where, on the other hand, the downgrading of the work done by the employee is the result of an 'equal pay' policy (where, for example, the employer equalizes formerly 'male' and 'female' 'factory hand' scales at the lower, female rate and then 'red-circles' all the male factory hands' wages at the level of the former male scale), the existence of a 'red circle' cannot logically be viewed as being a difference 'not the difference of sex' as required by the Equal Pay Act. The widespread use of such tactics would, indeed, delay the achievement of equal pay even between men and women doing the same work for years or even decades, until such time as all the protected men had died, retired, or otherwise ceased to be employed in those jobs.

Logic did not, however, prevent tribunals in the early days of the Act from accepting 'red circle' defences along these lines. In *Bedwell & Ors.* v. *Hellerman Deutsch Ltd* (the first 'red-circle' case heard by an industrial

tribunal), the woman applicant claimed equal pay with a man who performed similar work. Prior to the implementation date of the Act the
women had all been paid on an hourly (women's) rate, while men enjoyed
superior 'staff' status. After a job evaluation exercise, all those doing the
job were placed on (sex unspecific) hourly rates, but the men who had
previously enjoyed staff status were retained on a higher hourly rate to
reflect their previous position. An industrial tribunal rejected the woman's claim, the chairman opining that: 's.1(3) of the Act is included *for
this very purpose*, i.e. to enable employers to overcome immediate practical difficulties in complying with the Act' (my emphasis).[68] This might
have come as come surprise to the framers of the Act: Barbara Castle
had declared that section 1(3) was intended to permit differentials based
on 'length of service, merit, output and so on . . . *provided* that the payments are available to any person who qualifies *regardless of sex*' (my emphasis).[69] The very issue in *Bedwell* was that *only* men could qualify for
the additional payments, as only they had been eligible for staff status.

In *Snoxell and Davies* v. *Vauxhall Motors Ltd* the Employment Appeal
Tribunal expressed doubt about the decision in *Bedwell*, Phillips J stating that:

it cannot be right to justify the variation in pay by another variation between the
man's and the woman's contract [the fact that the man used to have staff status]
which itself requires to be justified as being genuinely due to a material difference
(other than the difference of sex).[70]

In *Snoxell*, the EAT ruled that 'an employer can never establish . . . a
material difference (other than the difference of sex) . . . when it can be
seen that past discrimination has contributed to the variation' in pay
between the woman and her comparator. The employer's defence, that
the difference in pay between female machine parts inspectors and male
inspectors who had been red-circled after an exclusively male grade had
been assimilated into a new unisex pay structure, failed because the difference between the women's case and the men's was itself tainted by
sex—women had not been eligible for the grade in respect of which the
men's wages were red-circled.

The decision in *Snoxell* required a rigorous approach to the question
whether any 'material difference' relied upon by an employer was 'not
the difference of sex' within section 1(3) of the Equal Pay Act, just as
that in *Capper Pass* had required a broad approach to the issue of equivalence. But problems remained, and even after *Snoxell* the courts (up to
and including the Court of Appeal in *Farthing* v. *Ministry of Defence*[71])

---

[68] [1976] IRLR 98, 99.   [69] See Ch. 1.   [70] [1977] IRLR 123, 128.
[71] [1980] IRLR 402. In this case the CA accepted as a material factor 'not the difference of sex' but the fact that the employers had, in the process of eliminating directly discriminatory pay scales, first moved the women from grade 4 to grade 6 of the women's

persisted in a very narrow approach to the issue of discrimination within section 1(3) which, on occasion (as in *Farthing*), led them to accept, as 'material differences', factors which were directly based on sex. But the major difficulty, highlighted by the EOC in its annual reports as early as 1978, was the failure of the Equal Pay Act explicitly to address the issue of *indirect* discrimination. The EAT's exhibition of concern in 1976 (in *Snoxell*) over *disguised* discrimination did not signal a willingness on the part of that court to come to grips with the problem of disparately *impacting* pay practices.

In *Meeks* v. *NUAAW* (1976) an industrial tribunal had been prepared to accept the possibility of an *indirect* discrimination claim under the Equal Pay Act.[72] The case involved a secretary working part-time who claimed that she was entitled to the same rate of pay as that which full-time secretaries enjoyed. The claim failed because there was no male secretary against whom the applicant could compare herself, but the tribunal chair (Bob Hepple) identified the gap in the coverage of the Equal Pay Act as concerning the requirement for a male comparator, rather than the need for *direct* discrimination. The tribunal was satisfied that married women such as the applicant generally had to work part-time, that the applicant herself had to do so, and (on the basis of the NES statistics) that a considerably smaller proportion of women than of men (68 per cent as against 97 per cent) worked full-time. But claims concerning contractual payments had to be made under the Equal Pay Act which required a comparable man from whose contract the equality clause could be drawn.

Bob Hepple may have been prepared to regard the Equal Pay Act as extending to indirect discrimination, but the Employment Appeal Tribunal was not. In *Handley* v. *Mono Ltd*, for example, the Appeal Tribunal (under Slynn J, as he then was) not only ruled that the difference between the hourly rate paid to a part-time woman machinist and that paid to a full-time male machinist was justified by the part-timer's lower contribution to the overall productivity of the company, but also declared: '[t]hat the variation in pay between a [full-time] worker and a [part-time] worker is a material difference which does not depend on the difference in sex is *established* by the fact that [full-time] women . . . were also treated differently from [the applicant]' (my emphasis).[73] Small wonder, then, that many defeats in equal pay cases were due to employers' successful use of the

pay scale (which entitled them to roughly equal pay with men on grade 4 of the male pay scale) then, in response to the women's complaints at being moved down to the unisex grade 4 (where they continued to receive the same wages as they had on grade 6 of the women's pay scale), transferred them up to grade 6 on the unisex scale 'on a personal basis'. The men employed on grade 4 made an equal pay claim but Lord Denning, in the CA, ruled that both the tribunal and the EAT had erred in finding that the variation was due to sex: it came about, rather: 'because of the system which had been adopted to eliminate the difference in pay between men and women'. Waller and Dunn LJJ agreed.

[72] [1976] IRLR 198.   [73] [1978] IRLR 543, 547.

'material difference' defence (39 per cent of cases dismissed in 1977, 19 per cent in 1978, 11 per cent in 1979, 41 per cent in 1980, 29 per cent in 1981, and 18 per cent in 1982[74]).

Slynn J again rejected an indirect discrimination claim in *Durrant* v. *North Yorkshire Area Health Authority and Secretary of State for Social Services* (1978), another case involving a part-time worker.[75] There the EAT ruled that the prohibition of disparately impacting treatment by the Sex Discrimination Act could not be 'transposed' into the Equal Pay Act—this despite the statements of the EAT in *Macarthys Ltd* v. *Smith* and the Court of Appeal in *Shields* v. *Coomes* that the Equal Pay Act should be treated as part of a 'code' of anti-discrimination legislation.[76] The difference between part-time and full-time workers could, according to the EAT, have amounted to the difference of sex only if 'part-time work in the health service was limited *exclusively* to women'. And, given the EAT's refusal in that case to look behind the alleged 'material difference', there was no guarantee that even an exclusively female part-time workforce would have generated a finding of discrimination.

The reluctance of the EAT to countenance equal pay claims where issues of indirect discrimination were involved not only excluded part-time women from the protection of the Equal Pay Act, but also led to the almost automatic acceptance of 'material difference' defences based on the employer's own grading or pay structure. The Court of Appeal required, in *National Vulcan Engineering Insurance Group Ltd* v. *Wade*, that grading structures must, in order to justify a difference in pay between men and women engaged in equivalent jobs, be 'based upon ability, skill, and experience and [be] fairly applied irrespective of sex'.[77] But placement within the grading system under question in the case consisted simply of personal assessment by a manager—according to the EAT the scheme could 'be shown in action to be obscure in certain respects'.[78] Nevertheless the Court of Appeal overturned the EAT's decision, Lord Denning stating that it must have rested on a 'misconception as to the burden of proof'.[79]

The reluctance to look beyond explanations based on grading structures can also be seen in the decision in *Lewis* v. *S.G.S. Inspection Services Ltd* in which an industrial tribunal failed adequately to consider the actual operation of grading structures and their impact on women employees. In the face of evidence of immense differences between the nature of appraisals of the applicant and her male comparator, and of its own finding that the appraisal scheme was erratic in the extreme in its operation, the tribunal recorded merely that '[i]f a man and a woman on the same grade

---

[74] Statistics taken from the EOC annual reports for the relevant years.
[75] [1979] IRLR 401.
[76] The EAT's decision in *Macarthys* v. *Smith* is at [1978] IRLR 10.
[77] [1978] IRLR 225.   [78] Para 18E, cited by the CA, *ibid.* 226.
[79] *National Vulcan* v. *Wade*, [1978] IRLR 225, 227.

get the same number of points in an appraisal they would get the same salary'.[80] The problem was, however, that women were *not* getting the same points as men, and that they were failing to do so in circumstances which ought to have given rise to the suspicion of discrimination.

There were some exceptions in which tribunals rejected grading schemes which very obviously bore the marks of discrimination. One such case was *Graviner Ltd* v. *Hughes* in which the EAT rejected the employer's argument that the different positions of the women 'viewers' and their male comparators within the grading structure was a 'material difference other than the difference of sex'.[81] The grading structure, which had been drawn up to replace a previous discriminatory structure, placed *all* men within the inspector's grade, whether they were inspectors or merely viewers, while placing *all* women viewers within the (lower) 'viewer's' grade.

Notwithstanding the occasional exception such as *Graviner*, in 1980 the EOC reported that the 'trend appears to be for industrial tribunals to take the view that where a *bona fide* grading scheme exists, this constitutes a material difference' and in 1987 Alice Leonard, discussing the results of tribunal research conducted between 1980 and 1982, declared that the area of grading structures was one 'in which the tribunals appear particularly reluctant to find that sex discrimination has occurred'.[82] The same levels of complacency continued to be displayed towards pay differences based on (separate) collective agreements until the Court of Appeal (and subsequently the ECJ) ruled on the *Enderby* case in 1991 and 1993 respectively (see further Chapter 4).

The Employment Appeal Tribunal accepted, in *Jenkins* v. *Kingsgate (Clothing Productions) Ltd* (1981) that indirect discrimination was prohibited by the Equal Pay Act. But this decision came more than five years after the initial implementation of the Act, and it seemed by this stage that much of the momentum had been lost. Even after this, the prohibition of indirect discrimination at the level of theory took a very long time to feed into the actual application of the Act. This is further discussed in the following chapter.

Not only did indirectly discriminatory 'material differences' continue to be accepted by the courts long after *Handley* v. *Mono*, but even those differences which had their roots in historic direct discrimination continued to pass as 'material differences' despite the decision in *Snoxell*. One such case, in which both the EAT and the Court of Appeal found in favour of the employer, was *Methven and Musiolik* v. *Cow Industrial*

---

[80] Leonard, n. 66 above, 59.

[81] (1978) EAT 46/78, cited by IDS, n. 43 above, 41. See also, more recently, the decision in *Latham* v. *Eastern Counties Newspapers Ltd*, 20 Equal Opportunities Review Discimination Case Law Digest (EORDCLD) 11, in which a tribunal rejected the employer's defence that pay differences were due to the application of a performance related pay scheme—the scheme was applied without guidance for the assessors.

[82] *Annual Report*, 9 and Leonard, n. 66 above, 84.

Polymers Ltd.[83] The applicants, who were employed as clerks, claimed equal pay with a male clerk who was the latest incumbent of a job *de facto* reserved for men forced by age or illness to transfer from shop-floor work in the employer's factory, and who retained their higher shop floor wages together with the additional benefits of (white-collar) 'staff' status. This particular job-incumbent had initially taken a slight pay-cut on transfer, being paid the same rate as the job's previous incumbent (a rate which was still higher than that paid to the applicants). He had later received an increase, as a result of a revision of the pay structure, which meant that he was on a higher salary than he would have been had he remained in his previous position.

The tribunal was, in the EAT's view, entitled to decide that he received more than the applicants, not because he was a man but 'because of his age and his illness'.[84] The argument put forward by the applicants, that the comparator's initial receipt of the previous incumbent's wage showed that the rate for the *job* (rather than the comparator's own wage) was red-circled, was not accepted. And although the EAT declared that the tribunal in such cases would have to be satisfied that the job generally filled by red-circled employees was not 'reserved exclusively as a special job for men' if the employer's defence was to succeed, that court did not see fit to state why the fact that this job had always been filled by *men* transferred from the factory did not give rise to at least the suspicion that it was precisely so reserved.[85] Nevertheless, the Court of Appeal upheld the EAT's decision, and did so in a decision which seemed at times cavalier with respect to the issue of discrimination. Dunn LJ was complacent in the face of the employer's evidence that 'I decided that [the comparator's] salary should be the same as [that of the previous incumbent of the job].[86] He was paid that rate because that was the rate paid to the previous man'; and saw no reason to disagree with the tribunal's view that 'the company's appointment of infirm and slightly ageing men to this particular position' amounted to a 'material difference' within section 1(3) of the Act.[87] While both the EAT and the Court of Appeal drew support from the fact that 'women in the company had been offered . . . protection of a similar nature', not one of the judgments delivered by the courts addressed the discrimination inherent in the apparent reservation of this otherwise female (and lower paid) position (of clerk) for *men* (albeit those previously employed elsewhere within the company), paid at a higher rate *because* it was occupied by (these) men and because, presumably, the wages of women clerks were considered to be too low for male employees.

The fact that the male comparator had originally been paid at the rate of the previous incumbent of the post, rather than the slightly higher wages

---

[83] [1979] IRLR 276 (EAT).   [84] *Ibid.* 279.   [85] *Ibid.* 278.
[86] [1980] IRLR 289.   [87] *Ibid.* 292, cited by Dunn LJ.

he had enjoyed in his former job, coupled with the employer's admission that this was regarded as the 'rate for the job', was expressly disregarded by the EAT (on the basis that it would be absurd if a red circle could apply only at the actual rate of pay previously enjoyed, rather than at a slightly lower rate) and, it seems, ignored by the Court of Appeal. But this, together with the fact that his salary was subsequently raised *above* the rate he would have received had he stayed in his previous job, should surely have given rise to a suspicion that the 'male clerk's' position was remunerated *as* a 'man's job', albeit one that was reserved for the old and infirm. The employer's burden in relation to the material factor defence had, it is true, been fixed by the Court of Appeal in *National Vulcan Engineering Ltd* v. *Wade* at the level merely of the balance of probabilities. But it is difficult to see how the employer here satisfied even this, given its apparent failure to point to anything which could counter the suspicion that the comparator's rate here was fixed directly by reference to his sex.

The only example the writer has found of a case in which a woman's wage was fixed by reference to her 'age and infirmity' was *Goldbourne* v. *Prince Regent Laundry Ltd*, in which a tribunal accepted that factors justified her lower, rather than higher, payment.[88]

It was pointed out, above, that the structural limitations of the Equal Pay Act were such that only a relatively small number of women were in a position to benefit from it, at least in so far as its individual provisions were concerned. These provisions did very little to address the wide pay disparities associated with women's occupational and workplace segregation, permitting comparisons to be drawn only, for the most part, between persons engaged in 'like work'. To the structural limitations imposed by the Act itself can be added the difficulties thrown up by judicial interpretation of the legislation: even those women who were potentially in a position to benefit from the 'like work', 'same employment' approach were likely to be frustrated by the very narrow approach taken by the courts to 'like work', together with the generous application of the employer's defence. It should come as no surprise, then, that the number of equal pay applications plummeted from 1742 in 1976 (with 709 tribunal decisions), through 263 in 1979 (seventy-eight decisions) to only thirty-nine in 1982 (with thirteen tribunal decisions).[89] The EOC attributed this decline, not to the elimination of pay discrimination during those years, but to widespread disillusionment with the shortcomings of the Act. In 1981 the EOC's *Annual Report* declared that, because of the 'steady attrition of equal pay cases taken to industrial tribunals over the last six years

---

[88] COIT 456/156 (1976) cited by IDS, n. 43 above, 43.
[89] EOC annual reports for the relevant years. In 1977 there were 942 applications and 492 tribunal decisions; in 1978, 454 applications and 187 decisions; in 1980, 91 applications and 26 decisions and in 1981, 54 applications and 27 decisions.

... the extent to which individual women and men see the Equal Pay Act as providing a remedy worth seeking has reached an·all-time low'.[90]

(B) THE COLLECTIVE MECHANISM

The shortcomings of the Act's individual provisions, coupled with their interpretation by the courts, were such that they provided little incentive for employers to eliminate sex discrimination from their pay structures. In addition, the failure of these provisions to address inter-establishment pay differentials has been discussed. But these difficulties would have been less significant had the collective provisions of the Equal Pay Act proven more effective. These provisions required that 'male' and 'female' rates within collective agreements and workplace pay structures be eliminated and that 'female rates' outside collective agreements be raised to the level of the lowest 'male rate' within the workplace. In addition, Wages Council orders ceased to distinguish between male and female workers.

The potential of these provisions was significant. In particular, where multi-employer collective agreements were in existence, women employed by any of the employers concerned could benefit from the upgrading of 'female rates' within the agreement as a whole. It would thus be possible even for women in exclusively female workplaces to benefit from the Equal Pay Act, as they would also where they were covered by Wages Council orders.[91] Women whose rates of pay were determined by collective agreement could also benefit from the equalization of 'male' and 'female' rates within their workplaces regardless of whether they were employed on 'like work' or 'work rated as equivalent' to that done by men.[92] And even where women were not covered by collective agreement, 'female rates' within workplaces had to be raised to the level of the lowest 'male rate' regardless, again, of the content of the jobs performed by the men and women respectively.

A number of commentators have attributed the greater part of the reduction in the gender–pay gap which took place in the early to mid-1970s to the collective aspects of the Act. Zabalza and Tzannatos, for example, who studied the impact of the (unamended) Equal Pay Act on the employment and wages of women, found:

evidence that collective agreements started to move towards equalisation quite early in the decade, that these increases in relative rates resulted in corresponding and contemporaneous increases in relative earnings, and that the effect on

---

[90] At 1.   [91] *Ibid.* 171, citing Award No 3313.

[92] This was settled, after some confusion, by the CAC in Award No 29 (1976). For a detailed discussion of the collective provisions see P. Davies, 'The Central Arbitration Committee and Equal Pay' [1980] *Current Legal Problems* 170.

average earnings was not confined to the covered sector but also spilled over to non-covered employees.[93]

And one Australian study attributed the success of the UK legislation, relative to that in the United States, precisely to this factor: 'in terms of institutional mechanisms a comparatively centralised wage-fixing system is a more efficient vehicle for implementing equal pay initiatives . . . across the board . . . initiatives such as those seen in Great Britain . . . are the most effective in reducing sex-based differentials'.[94]

Where unions were inclined to press for improvements in women's wages, the Equal Pay Act appears to have given them the wherewithal so to do. But the loopholes in the Act's collective provisions were considerable, and where unions and/or employers were not minded to eliminate discrimination from collective agreements, the enforcement mechanism laid down by the Equal Pay Act left much to be desired. The Central Arbitration Committee (CAC) was given the power to amend discriminatory provisions of collective agreements and pay structures, but the relevant provision of the Act defined that power narrowly. Section 3 provided that: '(1) Where a collective agreement . . . contains any provision applying specifically to men only or to women only, the agreement may be referred . . . to the Central Arbitration Committee . . . to declare what amendments need to be made to the agreement . . . so as to remove that discrimination between men and women.'

References could be made under section 3 by one of the parties or the Secretary of State for Employment in the case of a disputed term of a collective agreement, by the employer or the Secretary of State if the dispute concerned a pay structure. In the early years of the Equal Pay Act, section 3 appeared to hold out real possibilities for radical change. The CAC took a very optimistic approach to the question of its jurisdiction, declaring in its 1977 *Annual Report* that its concern was 'with eliminating discrimination found in collective agreements and pay structures'.[95] This statement of intent was, as Paul Davies pointed out:

broader than the opening words of section 3 might suggest because, whereas collective agreements containing provisions applying specifically to men only or to women only may well be discriminatory as between men and women, collective

---

[93] Zabalza and Tzannatos, n. 41 above, 9. See also Z. Tzannatos and A. Zabalza, 'The Anatomy of the Rise of British Female Relative Wages in the 1970's: Evidence from the New Earnings Survey' (1984) 22(2) *British Journal of Industrial Relations* 177—between 1970 and 1976 the ratio of minimum wages specified in collective agreements for male and female jobs rose from around 0.8 (at which level it had remained stable since 1950) to 1. See also J. Rubery, 'Structured Labour Markets, Worker Organisation and Low Pay' in A. Amsden (ed.), *The Economics of Women and Work* (Harmondsworth: Penguin, 1980), 120.

[94] K. MacDermott, *Pay Equity: A Survey of 7 OECD Countries* (Canberra: Australian Government Publishing Service, 1987), Women's Bureau, Information Paper No 5, 77.

[95] (London; CAC, 1977), cited by Davies, n. 92 above, 172.

agreements which contain no such provisions (and are thus neutral on their face) may also be discriminatory.[96]

It also went far beyond the role envisaged by the Government in 1970: introducing the Act to the House of Commons, Barbara Castle had declared that the powers of the Industrial Court (later the CAC) would be 'confined to removing discrimination which appears on the face' of the agreement.[97] Indeed, the Committee went beyond merely seeking out cynical manipulations such as those in which, for example, 'Grade 1 and Grade 2 replace[d] the previous male clerks and female clerks with no other change' and also amended structures in which, in the CAC's view, insufficient steps had been taken fully to eradicate the effects of past discrimination.[98]

In *Prestcold & APECCS* (1978), for example, the Committee ruled that the extent of pay differentials between apparently gender-neutral grades was tainted by discrimination—historically there had been a large differential between high-paid (male) jobs and low-paid (female) jobs.[99] The CAC ordered that the differentials be reduced. And in *Hy-Mac Ltd & APECCS* (1979) the Committee expressed itself dissatisfied that a reordering of the pay structure designed to eliminate 'male' and 'female' rates had been sufficient to eliminate the historical concept of a woman's rate of pay. But it was this ruling which was condemned by the Divisional Court in *R. v. CAC ex p. Hy-Mac Ltd*, a decision which, in the words of the EOC, put an end to 'the important work which the CAC was doing in the correction of possibly discriminatory collective agreements'.[100]

In *ex p. Hy-Mac*, the Divisional Court ruled that the CAC had exceeded its jurisdiction both by intervening in a collective agreement which did not contain overtly discriminatory 'male' and 'female' payscales, and by playing fast and loose with the Equal Pay Act's (very narrow) restrictions on the nature of amendments it could order to an agreement. Widgery LCJ declared that section 3 required a provision applying specifically to men only or women only in order to found the CAC's jurisdiction. And while Browne LJ stated that the CAC should be allowed to intervene in respect of 'sham' provisions—those applying 'specifically only to men or women, although on [their] face [they do] not'—Davies interpreted this as applying only to the most blatant attempts to avoid the provisions of the Equal Pay Act.

Whatever the finer legal implications of the decision, its apparent effects were profound. The Committee retained its jurisdiction over equal pay

---

[96] McDermott, n. 94 above, 172.   [97] 795 HC Debs. (9 Feb. 1970), col. 920.

[98] *Annual Report 1977* (London: CAC, 1977), cited by Davies, n. 92 above, 173.

[99] CAC Award No 78/830, reported in EOC *Annual Report 1978*, 50.

[100] *Annual Report 1981*, 5. The decision is at [1979] IRLR 461.

until February 1987, when the provisions of the Sex Discrimination Act 1986 stripped it of its powers in this respect. But, just as Davies had predicted in 1980, the decision in *Hy-Mac* did 'render section 3 obsolete'.[101] Between 1976 and 1979 the CAC had ruled on about fifty equal pay cases in all (although these were for the most part towards the beginning of that period). In 1980 the EOC declared that 'the scope and effect of the Equal Pay Act have been reduced as a result of the' *Hy-Mac* decision which had left it 'beyond the powers of the Central Arbitration Committee' to scrutinize collective bargains and pay structures for evidence of indirect discrimination.[102] Between 1981 and 1986 not one case was decided.

In 1987, the final year in which the CAC was able to receive complaints, one decision was reached (*Norwich Union & ASTMS*). In what looked like a final, two-fingered salute to those who had stripped it of its equal pay jurisdiction, the CAC ordered the amendment of a pay structure which, in its view, indirectly discriminated against women as part-timers. In its 1988 *Annual Report* the CAC explained its view that, while section 3 provided no jurisdiction in respect of indirect discrimination, Article 119 of the Treaty of Rome did. The report continued: 'the decision in . . . *Hy-Mac* . . . was taken to close the door, more or less completely, on claims under the Equal Pay Act. . . . It seemed to the majority of the CAC in the Norwich Union case that a fresh look should be taken at this assumption.'

The majority of the CAC, alas, turned out to be mistaken. Its final equal pay decision was, like the decision in *Hy-Mac*, overturned by the Divisional Court on the ground that the Committee had exceeded its jurisdiction.[103] Almost simultaneously, the Sex Discrimination Act 1986 abolished the CAC's jurisdiction and (section 77 of the Sex Discrimination Act 1975) stated that directly *and* indirectly discriminatory terms in collective agreements and in employers' pay structures were void. There were two glaring faults with this provision: (a) women workers generally wish to have their positions *improved* to match those of men, whereas section 77 would simply abolish any additional benefit enjoyed by the men; (b) section 77 lacked any enforcement mechanism and so was a dead letter from the start. In 1993 individuals were given a right of complaint to the industrial tribunal in respect of discriminatory terms of collective agreements.[104] Again while this might assist a woman who wishes to challenge a term which provides that part-timers are to be made redundant

[101] N. 92 above, 177.   [102] At 5.

[103] *Norwich Union & ASTMS*, reported at CAC, *Annual Report 1987*, 13–14. The CAC had applied Art. 119 and considered the question of *indirect* discrimination. The DC ruled that it had the power to consider only direct discrimination.

[104] The relevant provisions are now to be found in s. 77 of the Sex Discrimination Act 1975 and s. 6 of the Sex Discrimination Act 1986 (dealing, respectively, with contracts and collective agreements), as amended by the Trade Union Reform and Employment Rights Act 1993.

first (or, as in *Meade-Hill* v. *British Council*, imposes a very wide mobility clause with which women employees are less likely than men to be able to comply[105]), it does not, in contrast with section 3, allow for the *extension* of benefits to those to whom they are at present (discriminatorily) denied. It is arguable that, in this respect, British law falls short of the requirements of Article 119—in *Kowalska* v. *Freie und Hansestadt Hamburg* (1990), the European Court of Justice ruled that, in the absence of any national legislation providing for the equalization of collectively agreed terms as between men and women, the disadvantaged sex would be entitled to be granted the benefits enjoyed by the advantaged sex.[106] Unless the Sex Discrimination Act, as amended in 1993, is sufficient to implement EU law (which, in general, requires that equalization be upward rather than down[107]), *Kowalska* would continue to apply and a woman who wished to share the advantages granted to men under a collective agreement (rather than to avoid any disadvantage) could, so long as the benefit qualified as 'pay', claim under Article 119 of the Treaty of Rome.[108]

It is rather tempting to romanticize the role of the CAC prior to its abolition, not least because of its final insouciant cheerfulness in the face of its exclusion from the field of equal pay. But even at the height of its interventionist approach, the Committee never considered more than a tiny minority of collective agreements and pay structures. This was partly due to the relative paucity of referrals to the Committee. In 1978 the EOC declared it 'regrettable that there have been instances of trade unions not being prepared to refer agreements which, in the Commission's view, were discriminatory'.[109] And the position with respect to employers' (unilaterally imposed) pay structures was a matter of even greater concern— only the employer and the Secretary of State for Employment had the power of referral in such cases and, while one commentator pointed out that 'there's nothing to stop an employer or union nudging the Secretary of State into action', the EOC reported a marked reluctance on the part of the Secretary of State to make such referrals.[110] In particular, the Department of Employment would consider for referral only pay structures containing *overt* 'male' and 'female' rates, a policy which was at that time 'much more restricted than that adopted by the Central Arbitration Committee'.[111]

---

[105] [1995] IRLR 478.   [106] Case 33/89 [1990] ECR I-2591.

[107] See however the decisions *Coloroll Pensions Trustees Ltd* v. *Russell*, Case 200/91 [1994] ECR I-4389 and *Smith* v. *Avdel Systems Ltd*, case 408/92 [1994] ECR 4435, in which the ECJ ruled that, in respect of pension entitlement, Member States and pension schemes were permitted, respectively, to legislate and amend their rules so as to reduce the benefits enjoyed by men, rather than to increase those available to women.

[108] Widely defined as it is under Art. 119—see *Barber* v. *Guardian Royal Exchange Assurance Group*, case 262/88 [1990] ECR I-1899, *Rinner-Kühn* v. *FWW Spezial-Gebäudereingung GmbH & Co KG* [1989] ECR 2743, *R.* v. *Secretary of State for Employment, ex p. EOC* [1994] IRLR 176.

[109] *Annual Report*, (Manchester: EOC, 1978), 16.   [110] IDS, n. 43 above, 53.

[111] *Annual Report 1978*, 16.

The most radical potential of the collective provisions was in relation to multi-employer collective agreements, where they could tackle discrimination even in predominantly female workplaces. But, even if the spirit as well as the letter of the 1970 Act was respected in the revision of such agreements, many of the lowest-paid women were concentrated in workplaces without collective agreements and so gained nothing from these provisions of the Act.[112] A number of such women would have benefited from the equalization of Wages Council rates. But not all of the lowest paid enjoyed the coverage of Wages Council rates and, even after equalization, women were much more likely to be paid at or near the minimum rates than were men.[113]

Where women were not covered by collective agreements the potential for avoidance of the Equal Pay Act was enormous. Paterson and Armstrong's helpful *Employers' Guide to Equal Pay* had suggested, as early as 1972, that employers who wished to avoid the provisions of the Act could do so by 're-classifying jobs at present carried out only by women at women's rates' so as to open them, theoretically, to men 'although in practice the job descriptions would not correspond with any work at present carried out by men'. This would, the authors explained, allow the minimum rate for these jobs to be lower than the male minimum.[114] We saw, above, that this practice was adopted by a number of employers studied by Snell *et al.* In addition, those researchers found that many women who were entitled under the Act to have their rates equalized with those of men under the 'work rated as equivalent' provisions of the Equal Pay Act, instead received only a smaller increase under section 3 by having their (undifferentiated) 'female' rate equalized only with that of the lowest-paid men.[115]

Even had references been markedly more common than was in fact the case, the structural limitations of the CAC would have rendered it impossible for the Committee to scrutinize *every* collective agreement, *every* pay structure across the nation. The collective provisions of the Act did have a significant impact on the gender–pay gap.[116] But they were never more than a blunt mechanism and their shortcomings, together with those of the Act's individual provisions, meant that there was little incentive for employers (or, where unions were ready to collude, employers and unions) to make more than minor and cosmetic changes to the pay structures and/or collective agreements.

Some employers, certainly, did little more than to translate (for example) the previously typical 'male skilled, male semi-skilled, male unskilled; female' wage categories into 'Grade IV; Grade III, Grade II, Grade I'.

---

[112] See CIR, *Report No 89: Retail Distribution* (London: HMSO, 1974) and discussion at Ch. 6.
[113] See Ch. 9.   [114] Paterson and Armstrong, n. 7 above, 53–4.
[115] Snell *et al.*, n. 55 above, Ch. 3 *passim*.   [116] See text to nn. 93 and 94.

It seems that this was precisely what occurred in Rowntree Mackintosh when the Equal Pay Act came into force—the sex-specific grades were made facially neutral but men were placed on a higher rung than women previously at the same grade (though, given 'male' and 'female' rates, not the same level of pay). The same approach on the part of the employer was apparent in *Graviner Ltd* v. *Hughes* (text to note 81 above). And it would appear from the facts in *Electrolux* v. *Hutchinson* that a similar thing happened within that company—although the grades were on their face sex-neutral, 599 of 600 hourly-paid women were on grade 01 and *not one* of the 1,300 hourly-paid men was on, *or had ever been recruited to* grade 01. According to evidence given to the EAT by the women in that case, men were invariably recruited directly onto grade 10.[117] Whether or not grades 01 and 10 had ever been explicitly labelled 'female' and 'male', it is clear, in effect, that this is what they amounted to. (That Electrolux did little to alter its practices in the wake of this case is suggested by the EOC's issue of a non-discrimination notice to the company in 1979, three years after the tribunal's finding of discrimination.[118])

It should be noted at this point that the EOC's powers of formal investigation (see Chapter 5) could be regarded as an additional collective mechanism for the enforcement of the Equal Pay Act. In particular, the Commission was empowered to issue non-discrimination notices in respect of 'discriminatory practices', i.e. 'the application of a requirement or condition which results in' discrimination unlawful under the 1970 or 1975 Act, 'or which would be likely to result in such an act of discrimination' if those to whom it applied were not all of one sex.[119] This power could have amounted to a significant additional enforcement mechanism but, as we shall see in Chapter 5, went almost unused by the EOC.

The result of the legislation's various shortcomings was, according to the EOC in 1980, that 'only certain forms of direct discrimination in relation to pay are capable of elimination under the Equal Pay Act'.[120] While women were able to challenge *implicitly* (as distinct from *overtly*) discriminatory pay structures in those cases where they could point to a man doing 'like work', and launch an individual claim (as in *Graviner*— though the discrimination would have to be fairly obvious for the grading structure to fail as a 'material difference'), no such claims were possible where men and women were employed on different work, unless a job evaluation scheme was in existence. If such a scheme had rated the woman's work as equivalent, a claim was possible under section 1(2)(b), as it was also where the scheme had failed to do so for reasons which were *on their face* discriminatory. But, as was pointed out above, such cases were rare indeed, and the only course of action open in practice (certainly after

---

[117] [1976] IRLR 410, 412.   [118] EOC, *Annual Report 1981*, 6.
[119] SDA, s. 37(1).   [120] *Annual Report*, 5.

Hy-Mac) would be where *overt* discrimination was apparent in the pay structure or collective agreement. It is far from clear, even in circumstances such as those which became apparent in the *Electrolux, Rowntree*, and *Graviner* cases, whether the requirement for overt discrim-ination would have been satisfied and jurisdiction founded for a CAC ruling on the issue.

The problems associated with the Act were so severe that even the most obvious cases of female under-payment were as likely to be outside as they were to be within its scope. Quite apart from all the women excluded from protection by virtue of their employment in predominantly or wholly female workplaces, many of those in mixed workplaces were outside the scope of the legislation. In 1970 Lena Jeger MP had complained that women's wages in the pottery industry varied between 2 shillings, 1½ pence per hour, and 2 shillings, 3¾ pence per hour:

These highest paid women in the pottery industry include women gilders and decorators who are doing very highly skilled work . . . I cannot find an equivalent for a man doing gilding and patterned work which is so skilled. But the man who packs up the china and carts it to the warehouse has a minimum of 3 shillings, 1½ pence.[121]

Ms Jeger seemed confident that the plight of women such as these would be addressed by the new Act. That her optimism was unfounded is illustrated by *Hopkinson* v. *EP Publishing Ltd*, an early industrial tribunal decision concerning a 'like work' claim. The applicant was paid £23 per week for 'selecting films to fulfill orders, putting the films into cans and splicing them together where necessary . . . [and doing] a certain amount of stock accounting and stock taking'.[122] She selected as her comparator a man who worked in the same packing department and whose job involved [solely] packing books into cartons, for which he was paid £29 per week. The tribunal rejected her claim:

we have a feeling that if there was a job evaluation in this establishment there might be some drastic alteration in the various salaries paid to different employees . . . [the comparator] has his own particular small skills in performing the work of packing . . . the applicant, when she was originally engaged, was doing the work of packing films and did this for the first six years . . . when her job changed about two years ago it was a promotion and involved an increase in pay. . . . In the end, the question for our decision is whether her work and [the comparator's] . . . are the same or of a broadly similar nature . . . we are clearly of the opinion, whatever other merits Mrs Hopkinson may have had as regards her claim to an increase in her rate of pay, that she is not employed on like work with [her comparator].[123]

It seems clear in this case that the tribunal could have reached no other decision. Even with the broadest-brush approach conceivable, the work of

---

[121] 795 HC Debs. (9 Feb. 1970), col. 968.   [122] [1976] IRLR 99, 99.
[123] *Ibid*. 100–1.

UNIVERSITY OF WINCHESTER
LIBRARY

the applicant and her comparator could not sensibly have been regarded as 'similar'. He was engaged in the most unskilled work, little different from that of Ms Jeger's warehousemen. She, on the other hand, performed a variety of functions, some of them skilled and semi-skilled, and even had to handle greater weights (22 lbs as opposed to 11 lbs) than those handled by her comparator. In addition, it was the tribunal's view that in the six years before her promotion 'she had been learning her present job'.[124]

[124] [1976] IRLR 99, 100–1.

[4]
Equal Pay—The European Dimension

I. INTRODUCTION

It should be clear from Chapter 3 that the Equal Pay Act 1970 could not, by the end of the 1970s, be regarded as having been an unqualified success. Progress had ground to a halt, and in some cases had begun to reverse itself, and there were many problems both with the legislation itself and its application in the courts. It appeared that women, as a group, had gained just about all they were going to from the Equal Pay Act. Individual women did make some gains in the industrial tribunals but progress was fairly slow, success on the collective front was limited, and, between 1976 and 1982, full-time women workers' average hourly rate improved by only 2 per cent relative to men's.[1]

There things might have remained but, in 1973, the United Kingdom had joined the European Economic Community. In doing so, the UK accorded Community law supremacy within the national legal system, a fact which has impacted profoundly on the matter of equal pay (at least at the level of theory) as it has on many others.

At the point at which the UK (with the Republic of Ireland) joined the European Community, only one piece of Community legislation governed equal pay. Article 119 of the Treaty of Rome, which came into force in the then Member States in 1957, provided that:

Each Member State shall . . . ensure and subsequently maintain the application of the principle that men and women should receive equal pay for equal work.

For the purpose of this Article, 'pay' means the ordinary basic or minimum wage or salary and any other consideration, whether in cash or in kind, which the worker receives, directly or indirectly, in respect of his employment from his employer.

Equal pay without discrimination based on sex means:

(a) that pay for the same work at piece rates shall be calculated on the basis of the same unit of measurement;

(b) that pay for work at time rates shall be the same for the same job.

---

[1] *Social Trends 1984*, 74.

Barbara Castle had been complacent about the potential impact of Article 119 when she introduced the Equal Pay (No 2) Bill to the House of Commons. Given her view that Article 119 demanded only equal pay for the *same* work and that 'pay' was to be understood in its normal sense, she claimed that the Bill went well beyond its requirements. To the extent that the Bill did not confine itself to a narrow definition of 'pay', but instead covered all contractual terms, she was right (although even this was insufficient in its failure to extend to non-contractual payments and perks, an issue discussed below). Her complacency was to prove most misguided not on the definition of pay itself, but rather on the question of who was entitled to receive it in equal amounts.

Article 119, as has already been stated, referred not to 'work of equal value', as did the International Labour Organization's (ILO's) Convention No 100, but rather to the apparently narrower 'equal work' and, more conservatively still, to 'the same work', 'the same job'. The 1956 *travaux préparatoires* of the Treaty of Rome refer to 'equal pay for equal work or for work of equal value' but the commitment to equal value was controversial and was omitted from the final version of Article 119.[2]

Despite this, as early as 1961 the Member States, recognizing that nothing had been done to achieve equal pay (however so defined) and agreeing to do better began, according to Creighton, to look at Article 119's 'equal pay' 'increasingly . . . in terms of "equal value"'. Although their agreement of December 1961 to achieve pay equality by the end of 1965 ended in failure, the 'equal value' approach was, according to Creighton, 'taken to its logical conclusion by Council Directive 75/117'. In a foretaste of what was to become a familiar approach, the Member State whose resistance to the inclusion of 'equal pay for work of equal value' into the Equal Pay Directive was foremost and most prolonged was the United Kingdom.[3]

Article 1 of Council Directive 75/117 (the Equal Pay Directive) provides that:

the principle of equal pay for men and women outlined in Article 119 . . . means, for the same work or for work *to which equal value is attributed*, the elimination of all discrimination on grounds of sex with regard to all aspects and conditions of remuneration [my emphasis].

Article 2 of the Directive states that:

Member States shall introduce into their national legal systems such measures as are necessary to enable all employees who consider themselves wronged by failure to apply the principle of equal pay to pursue their claims by judicial process after possible recourse to other competent authorities.

---

[2] See C. Hoskyns, *Integrating Gender: Women, Law and Politics in the European Union* (London: Verso, 1996), 56–7.

[3] See also *ibid.*, 88. UK compliance was bought with the words 'to which equal value is attributed' on the understanding that this would be satisfied by the Equal Pay Act.

Neither Article 119 nor the Equal Pay Directive, nor for that matter any other EC Directive either then or now in existence, prohibited race discrimination in pay.

II. IMPACT OF EC LAW

(A) DIRECT IMPACT

The demands of Article 119 and the Equal Pay Directive were eventually to lead to the amendment of the Equal Pay Act in 1983. But even before this time, British women had begun to benefit directly under European Community law. While the European Court of Justice (ECJ) had, in the earliest litigation concerning Article 119, adopted a restrictive approach to the equal pay issue, the picture began to change from the early 1980s. In *Defrenne* v. *Sabena (No 2)* (1976), the Court accepted that Article 119 had both vertical and horizontal direct effect—that it gave rise to individual rights which were enforceable in the courts of the Member States—against both private individuals and the Member States themselves.[4] This was itself significant (sufficiently so that the Court agreed to limit retroactive effect of the decision in much the same way as it did, fifteen years later, in *Barber* v. *Guardian Royal Exchange Assurance Group*[5]), but the application of the principle was limited by the Court's decision that Article 119 could only be relied upon against '*direct and overt discrimination* which may be identified solely with the aid of the criteria based on equal work and equal pay' (my emphasis).[6] By 1981 the ECJ changed its tune and, in *Worringham and Humphries* v. *Lloyds Bank*, accepted that Article 119 could be relied upon to challenge *indirect* as well as *direct* discrimination in pay.[7] This was possible, however, only to the extent that the discrimination could 'be identified solely with the aid of the criteria of equal work and equal pay' set out in Article 119. In the same year the decision in *Jenkins* v. *Kingsgate (Clothing Productions) Ltd* appeared to suggest that indirect discrimination could be challenged under Article 119 only when it was the employer's *intention* to discriminate.[8] But if this was in fact what the Court intended (and it is far from clear that it was[9]), any such

---

[4] Case 43/75 [1976] ECR 455.   [5] Case 262/88 [1990] ECR I–1889.
[6] *Defrenne* v. *Sabena (No 2)*, n. 4 above, para 18.   [7] Case 69/80 [1981] ECR 767.
[8] Case 96/80 [1981] ECR 911 [1981] IRLR 228. The EAT seemed to understand it in this light but ruled that 'it would not contravene s.2 of the European Communities Act if the United Kingdom statutes conferred on employees greater rights than they enjoy under Art. 119' ([1981] IRLR 388, 394) and the IRLR commentary suggested that 'contrary to . . . what at first sight might be thought from reading the decision, analysis of the judgment indicates that the European Court rejects the argument that Article 119 is violated where the effect of the employer's pay policy is to discriminate against women' ([1981] IRLR 235).
[9] The ECJ did not expressly require that indirect discrimination be intentional but stated, para 15, that the lower payment of part-timers would not 'amount to discrimination . . . unless it is in reality merely an indirect way of reducing the pay of part-time workers on the ground that that group of workers is composed exclusively or predominantly of women'.

requirement has long since been abandoned. In *Bilka-Kaufhaus GmbH* v. *Weber von Hartz* the ECJ declared that:

if . . . a much lower proportion of women than of men work part-time, the exclusion of part-time workers from [an] occupational pensions scheme would be contrary to Article 119 . . . where, taking into account the difficulties encountered by women workers in working full-time, that measure could not be explained by factors which exclude any discrimination on grounds of sex . . . if the undertaking is able to show that its pay practice may be explained by objectively justified factors unrelated to any discrimination on grounds of sex there is no breach of Article 119.[10]

While the language used by the ECJ in *Bilka* is permissive (i.e. it appears to grant employers permission to do what they could not otherwise do[11]), its *effect*, and its subsequent expression in cases such as *Rinner-Kühn* v. *FWW Spezial-Gebäudereinigung GmbH*, *Handels-og Kontorfunktionærernes Forbund i Danmark* v. *Dansk Arbejdsgiverförening (acting for Danfoss)*, and *Nimz* v. *Freie und Hansestadt Hamburg*, was restrictive: employers were instructed that they could not adopt disparately impacting pay practices unless they could justify them in line with increasingly rigorous tests.[12] This test was set out in *Bilka-Kaufhaus* as follows: the determination of whether disparately impacting pay practices were objectively justified within Article 119 was a matter for the national courts which should decide in favour of employers where the practices 'correspond to a real need on the part of the undertaking, are appropriate with a view to achieving the objectives pursued and are necessary to that end'.[13]

In *Rinner-Kühn* the ECJ ruled that the non-availability of state rebates by reason of part-timers' perceived lower degree of integration into the workforce was not even *potentially* capable of amounting to objective justification of the decision to deny them access to sick pay.[14] In *Danfoss* the same court demanded that payment on the basis of training and flexibility must be justified, where it impacted disparately according to sex, in terms of the worker's ability to do his or her particular job, and the court's willingness in that case to accept that payment on the basis of seniority would always be objectively justifiable was jettisoned shortly afterwards in the *Nimz* case.[15] All of these decisions, relating as they did to the application of Article 119 of the Treaty of Rome, could be relied upon directly by individuals in the various Member States as a result of early decisions such as *Defrenne* and *Worringham*. In the UK context, this influenced the interpretation of the genuine material factor defence established by section

---

[10] Case 170/84 *Bilka-Kaufhaus GmbH* v. *Weber von Hartz* [1986] ECR 1607, 125–6.

[11] This is how *Bilka* was interpreted by the CA in *BCC* v. *Smith and Ors*; *North Yorkshire County Council* v. *Ratcliffe and Ors* [1994] IRLR 342.

[12] Respectively Case 71/88 [1989] ECR 2743; Case 109/88 [1989] ECR 3199; and Case 184/89 [1991] ECR I–297. See also case 33/89 *Kowalska* v. *Freie und Hansestadt Hamburg* [1990] IRLR 447.

[13] *Bilka-Kaufhaus*, n. 10 above, 126.   [14] N. 12 above.   [15] N. 12 above.

1(3) of the Equal Pay Act: where the factor relied upon by the employer
was one which impacted disparately upon men and women, it would not
be a factor 'not the difference of sex' unless reliance upon it was objectively justified in line with the test adopted by the ECJ in *Bilka-Kaufhaus*
and the subsequent cases. This was accepted by the House of Lords in
Rainey v. *Greater Glasgow Health Board*, discussed in the text following note
33 below.

Despite the decisions in *Defrenne* and *Worringham*, difficulties remained
about how wide the scope of Article 119 actually was. On the one hand
the ECJ's declaration, in *Jenkins*, that the Equal Pay Directive's application of the principle of equal pay to 'the same work or . . . work *to which
equal value is attributed*' existed simply to 'facilitate the practical application of the principle' and 'in no way alters the scope of the content of
that principle', suggests that Article 119 mandates equal pay for work of
equal value.[16] On the other hand, that declaration was made in the context of a ruling that, if a claim under Article 119 failed, there was no
separate ground under Article 1 of the Equal Pay Directive. In addition,
the court stressed in that case, as it had in *Macarthys Ltd* v. *Smith* and in
Worringham, that Article 119 was directly applicable where discrimination
'may be identified *solely* with the aid of criteria of equal work and equal
pay referred to by . . . [Article 119], without national or Community measures being required to define them with greater precision in order to permit of their application' (my emphasis)—a requirement which appeared
to preclude the possibility of equal *value* claims under Article 119.[17]

Having said this, this statement, taken from the *Worringham* decision,
was followed almost immediately by the declaration that 'the inequality
between the gross salaries of men and women [in the instant case] is . . .
a source of discrimination contrary to Article 119 of the Treaty since
because of that inequality men receive benefits from which women
engaged in the same work *or in work of equal value* are excluded' (my
emphasis).[18] And in *Macarthys Ltd* v. *Smith*, the comments of the ECJ
were directed towards the suggestion that a woman might claim as against
a hypothetical man in circumstances in which 'comparative studies of entire
branches of industry' would be required in order to establish discrimination.[19] In that case the ECJ confined comparisons made under Article
119 to cases where 'parallels . . . may be drawn on the basis of concrete
appraisals of the work actually performed by employees of different sex

---

[16] N. 8 above, para 22. This conclusion may have surprised the legislators—R. Nielsen
and E. Szyszczak point out (*The Social Dimension of the European Community*, (Denmark:
Handeldhøjkolens Forlag, 1993), 114): 'Art. 1 [of the Equal Pay Directive] intended to
widen the operation of Art. 119 . . . since both the European Parliament and the Economic
and Social Committee urged the EC Commission to widen the original proposals.'

[17] In *Macarthys Ltd* v. *Smith*, case 129/79 [1980] ECR 1275, the ECJ used the first part
of the quotation: 215. The full quotation is taken from *Worringham* n. 7 above.

[18] *Jenkins*, n. 8 above.   [19] *Macarthys*, n. 17 above, 216.

within the same establishment or service'.[20] In *Macarthys*, as in *Worringham*, the court declared not that the direct effectiveness of Article 119 was *limited* to those cases in which 'men and women receive unequal pay for equal work carried out in the same establishment or service' but that such cases were (my emphasis) '*[a]mong* the forms of discrimination which may be . . . judicially identified and, as a result, challenged under Article 119'.[21] These statements appear more to support than to deny the possibility of an equal value claim being launched under Article 119.

In *Pickstone* v. *Freemans plc* the Court of Appeal allowed an equal value claim to be brought under Article 119 but, on appeal to the House of Lords, the case was decided under the Equal Pay Act and Lord Oliver expressed doubts whether an equal value claim would have been possible under Article 119.[22] More recently, the ECJ appear to have abandoned any limitation in the application of Article 119 to equal value claims. The decisions in *Bilka-Kaufhaus*, *Rinner-Kühn*, *Kowalska* v. *Freie und Hansestadt Hamburg* (1990), and *Nimz* were concerned with (indirectly) discriminatory awards of pay (whether sick pay, pensions, or seniority increments) to male and female workers within particular pay structures, in circumstances where no real issue arose whether jobs were 'the same', 'equal', or, indeed, 'of equal value'—all job categories were entitled to X or Y: the only question was whether part-time workers could properly be excluded.[23] But the *Danfoss* case concerned *differential* payments made to men and women engaged in different jobs which were in the same pay grades but whose relative value *could not* have been determined on the basis of Article 119/the Equal Pay Directive alone.[24] The questions put to the ECJ in that case related to the application of European law (in that case, the Equal Pay Directive) to challenge differential payments made 'assuming . . . male and female workers . . . carry out . . . work of *equal value*'. The court raised no objections to direct reliance upon Article 119 in cases concerning work of equal value, and determined most of the issues in favour of the applicants. And more recently still the ECJ ruled, in *Enderby* v. *Frenchay Health Authority and Secretary of State for Health*, that a *prima facie* case was established under Article 119 where jobs of equal value were paid differently according to sex. While no finding concerning value could be made save under the mechanisms laid down by the Equal Pay Act, it seems that Article 119 can give rise to directly enforceable rights once the issue of value has been so determined.[25]

Even before these developments in the area of equal value, the influence of Europe on the equal pay issue had come to be felt. The courts of the

---

[20] *Macarthys*, n. 17 above.   [21] *Ibid.* 215.
[22] [1987] IRLR 218 and [1988] IRLR 357 respectively.   [23] Nn. 10 and 12 above.
[24] *Handels- og Kontorfunktionærernes Forbund i Danmark* v. *Dansk Arbejdsgiverförening (acting for Danfoss)*, n. 12 above.
[25] Case 127/92 [1993] IRLR 591.

Member States are under a general obligation to interpret national legislation, in so far as it is possible, so as to comply with any equivalent European provisions. The extent of the interpretive duty is as yet unclear; early restrictions of it to national legislation passed with the express aim of implementing Community provisions having given way to a more general obligation.[26] What is clear, however, is that where 'pay' is concerned (by contrast with other employment 'treatment' regulated by Council Directive 75/117, the Equal Treatment Directive) the discriminated-against employee can rely *directly* on Article 119/the Equal Pay Directive (subject to the reservations expressed about equal value claims) and can do so regardless of whether she is employed by the state or by a private employer. Article 119 and the Equal Pay Directive (in so far as the latter serves simply to explicate the former) are *horizontally*, as well as *vertically*, enforceable.

How have the Community provisions affected UK equal pay law? The impact of EC law was pointed out in Chapter 1, in which the current legal position was outlined. But it is useful here to provide some overview of the effect of the EC provisions. As early as 1980 the ECJ ruled, in *Macarthys Ltd* v. *Smith,* that a woman was entitled to claim equal pay with her *predecessor* in employment under Article 119.[27] The Court of Appeal, which had referred the issue after deciding that the Equal Pay Act allowed no such claim and that no amount of creative interpretation could change this, accepted that 'the provisions of Article 119 of the Treaty of Rome take priority over anything in our English statute on equal pay which is inconsistent with Article 119'.[28] Macarthys 'had no right to look to our English statute alone' and Mrs Smith was entitled to equal pay with her predecessor, despite the fact that she had brought her claim solely under that statute.

The claim in *Worringham and Humphries* concerned Lloyds Bank's practice of paying young male employees a higher gross salary than that paid to women of equivalent age, in order to remove the effect on their net pay of an obligatory contribution to the bank's pension scheme. The Court of Appeal referred the case to the ECJ on appeal from the EAT's decision that the claim must fail as a result of the exclusion from the ambit of the Equal Pay Act of 'terms related to death or retirement, or any provision made in relation to death or retirement'.[29] The ECJ found that the differential gross salaries breached Article 119 and that the individual

---

[26] *Marleasing SA* v. *La Comercial Internacional de Alimentacion SA*, case 106/89 [1990] ECR I–4135. See G. de Burca, 'Giving Effect to European Community Directives' (1992) 55 *Modern Law Review* 219.

[27] N. 17 above.

[28] [1979] IRLR 316 and [1980] IRLR 209, 210. More recently, a claim has also been permitted with a woman's *successor* as a comparator—*Tyldesley* v. *TML Plastics Ltd* [1996] IRLR 395 (EAT).

[29] EqPA, s. 6(1A)(b). The EAT's decision is at [1979] IRLR 26.

employees could rely directly upon it in these circumstances, a decision replicated in *Garland* v. *British Rail Engineering Ltd* (with regard to gratuitous post-retirement travel concessions falling outside the scope of the Equal Pay Act but interpreted by the House of Lords, subsequent to the decision of the ECJ, to come within the Sex Discrimination Act 1975[30]) and *Barber* v. *Guardian Royal Exchange Assurance Group* (with regard to occupational pensions excluded by the Equal Pay Act).[31] More recently still, the House of Lords has interpreted 'pay' in Article 119 as applying to entitlement to statutory redundancy pay (and, in so doing, rendered unworkable the differential qualifying periods for many statutory protections previously applied to full- and part-time workers). Even before the legislation was amended in the wake of this decision, an individual denied such a redundancy payment for a reason connected with sex (where, for example, she failed to satisfy the longer 'qualifying periods' required of (mainly female) part-time workers), could bypass the Equal Pay Act and claim directly under Article 119.[32]

(B)   THE EQUAL PAY (AMENDMENT) REGULATIONS 1983—
'WORK OF EQUAL VALUE'

For all of the direct input of European law prior to 1984, British women were denied the benefit of Article 119's entitlement to equal pay for work of equal value because, save in cases where their employers had voluntarily carried out job evaluation which showed their jobs to be paid less than those of equal value done by men, no mechanism existed to determine the issue of value.

The UK Government had made no attempt to amend the Equal Pay Act in the wake of the apparent extension to the scope of its obligations regarding equal pay. (This omission was, perhaps, understandable as the final acceptance by the United Kingdom of the 1975 Directive had been, according to one commentator, 'in the belief or hope that' the amended text—which replaced 'work of equal value' with 'work to which equal value is attributed'—'would mean that the British Equal Pay Act would not require modification'.[33]) In 1981 the European Commission brought proceedings against the United Kingdom under Article 169 of the Treaty

[30] [1982] IRLR 111.
[31] N. 5 above.
[32] [1994] IRLR 504. The HL left open the question whether compensation for unfair dismissal fell within the scope of Art. 119; the EAT shortly thereafter ruled, in *Mediguard Services Ltd* v. *Thame* [1994] IRLR 504, that it clearly did, but the CA disagreed in *R.* v. *Secretary of State for Employment, ex. p. Seymour-Smith* [1995] IRLR 464, as did the HL which referred the question to the ECJ, *The Times*, 14 March 1997. The Employment Protection (Part-time Employees) Regs. 1995 (SI 1995 No 31)—equalized the qualifying periods for full-time and part-time workers, see (1996) 25 *Industrial Law Journal* 43 for an explanatory note.
[33] Hoskyns, n. 2 above, 88.

of Rome for failure to implement the Directive and the UK Government's argument that the existence of an equal value claim (albeit one dependent on a job evaluation scheme which no employer could be required to undertake) was sufficient to satisfy the Directive's obligation failed to persuade the ECJ.[34] The ECJ ruled that the words 'work to which equal value is attributed' meant 'work of equal value' and that the United Kingdom, in making such claims contingent on the employer's having voluntarily undertaken a job evaluation scheme, was in breach of its obligations under the Directive. Equal value must be assessed 'notwithstanding the employer's wishes, if necessary in the context of adversary proceedings' and the Directive required Member States to invest an authority with jurisdiction to determine the equal value issue.[35] The United Kingdom was obliged to amend the Equal Pay Act accordingly.

The amendments were made by the Equal Pay (Amendment) Regulations 1983, which came into force on 1 January 1984.[36] The Regulations paved the way for women to take equal value claims, but did so with rather poor grace. The requirement for legislative amendment afforded an opportunity for more wide-scale revision of the equal pay legislation—in particular, the Government could have responded to the concerns expressed by the Equal Opportunities Commission (EOC) and others about the need for a male comparator, the uncertainty which still prevailed about indirectly discriminatory 'material differences', and the effective death of the collective 'equal pay' mechanism. But the Government addressed none of these problems (nor did it tackle the issue of inter-establishment pay comparisons), introduced an 'equal value' procedure widely condemned at the time for its complexity, and sought to *widen* the employer's defence (at least in the context of the equal value claim) to a finding of equality between a woman and her comparator.

A woman could claim equal pay with a man or men 'in the same employment' (see Chapters 1 and 3 above) who was or were engaged in work which was of equal value to hers. But while a finding of equal value could not be made by a tribunal until it had received the report of an independent expert appointed by it to consider the relative worth of the jobs done by the woman and her comparator(s), the tribunal could *dismiss* an equal value claim without reference to such an expert.[37] It *must* do so if the woman's job had already been rated as being of different value from that done by her comparator by a job evaluation scheme so long as there were 'no reasonable grounds for determining that the evaluation . . . was . . . made on a system which discriminates on grounds of sex'.[38] Not only this, but the tribunal should dismiss without further ado

---

[34] *EEC Commission* v. *United Kingdom*, case 61/81 [1982] ECR 2601.
[35] *Ibid.* 339–40 and 340.   [36] SI 1983/1794.
[37] EqPA, s. 2A(1)(b). Experts are appointed from a panel selected by ACAS.
[38] EqPA, s. 2A(1) & (3).

any claim in respect of which 'it is satisfied that there are no reasonable grounds for determining that the work is of equal value'.[39]

The Regulations did not only allow the dismissal of equal value claims as 'hopeless' at the preliminary hearing stage; they also allowed employers to make use of the 'material factor' defence at this stage. An employer could, at the preliminary hearing, deny that the woman's work was of equal value but claim that, even if it was, the pay differential was justified on the grounds of X or Y. And if the tribunal declined to accept the defence at this stage, the employer could use it (or another 'material factor' defence), if the jobs done by the woman and her comparator(s) were eventually determined to be of equal value. This did not merely give employers 'two bites at the cherry' (an issue since resolved, see Chapter 1)—there are real difficulties with determining the question of the material factor defence in the absence of a finding on the issue of value. While an employer might allege that a particular characteristic of a woman's chosen comparator justified his higher pay, without the evidence of an independent expert it is hard to tell whether such a characteristic is actually important, and whether it outweighs, for example, the significantly higher value which may be assigned to the woman's job.[40]

Finally, the Regulations provided a wider defence for equal *value* claims than existed at the time in respect of like work/work rated as equivalent claims. The Equal Pay Act, before amendment, allowed an employer to defend an equal pay claim by showing that the difference between the applicant's wages and those of her comparator was 'genuinely due to a material factor which is not the difference of sex [and which is] . . . a material difference between the woman's case and the man's'.[41] The requirement that the material factor be 'a material difference between the woman's case and the man's' had been taken, by the Court of Appeal in *Clay Cross Ltd* v. *Fletcher*, to preclude reliance upon 'market forces' to justify pay differences between men's and women's work.[42] According to Lord Denning MR, the 'material difference' upon which an employer sought to rely had to relate 'to the personal equation of the woman as compared to that of the man . . . irrespective of any extrinsic forces which led to the variation in pay'.[43] This being the case, genuine material differences could include a:

much longer length of service . . . superior skill or qualifications . . . bigger output or productivity . . . or [placement] . . . owing to downgrading, in a protected pay category . . . [but a]n employer cannot avoid his obligations under the Act by saying: 'I paid him more because he asked for more', or 'I paid her less because she was willing to come for less'. If any such excuse was permitted, the Act would be a dead letter.[44]

---

[39] EqPA, s. 2A(1)(a)—subsequent amendments are discussed in Ch. 1.
[40] The first, but not the second, point has been addressed by subsequent amendments discussed in Ch. 1.
[41] EqPA, s. 1(3)   [42] [1979] ICR 1.   [43] *Ibid*. 5.   [44] *Ibid*.

Nor, according to Lord Denning, could employers be permitted to claim that they had to match a male employee's previous salary, even if he were the only applicant for the job: '[t]hose are reasons personal to the employer. If any such reasons were permitted as an excuse, the door would be wide open. Every employer who wished to avoid the statute would walk straight through it.'[45]

The government was determined, in extending the Equal Pay Act to permit equal value claims, that employers should be able to defend such claims by reference to market forces.[46] Alan Clark MP, in a marked departure from the Thatcher line of some thirteen years earlier, declared 'I feel that it is safe to rely on the market'.[47] Section 1(3) was amended to require only that the pay difference was due 'to a material factor which is not the difference of sex'; and that the factor '*must* be a material difference between the woman's case and the man's' where like work/work rated as equivalent had been established; but only '*may* be such a material difference' where work of equal value was concerned. The distinction became something of a dead letter when the House of Lords decided, in *Rainey* v. *Greater Glasgow Health Board* (1986) (a claim involving like work), that the Court of Appeal in *Clay Cross* had been 'unduly restrictive of the proper interpretation of s. 1(3)'; that 'material' meant 'significant and relevant'; that the differences between 'her case and his' under section 1(3) 'may well go beyond what is not very happily described as "the personal equation"'; and may, 'where there is no question of intentional sex discrimination', extend to 'economic factors affecting the efficient carrying on of the employer's business or other activity'.[48]

Returning to the Regulations themselves, they were widely criticized at the time of their passage. Barry Jones MP (the Opposition spokesman) characterized them as 'legal gobbledegook . . . algebraic mystery—a small print bonanza for specialists . . . a daunting, obtuse maze of a measure and truly a stumbling block to a female complainant and her advisers'.[49]

The House of Lords went so far as to pass an amendment to the Regulations which declared that they were not in conformity with European Community law. The amendment, proposed by Lord McCarthy, was prompted primarily by concerns relating to the 'no reasonable grounds' provision and the widening of the 'material difference' defence.[50] But the Government was unmoved by their Lordships' pleas. Its device of introducing the amendments to the Equal Pay Act by means of a statutory instrument under the European Communities Act 1972 had the effect that no substantive amendments could be tabled to them, and only ninety minutes were allowed for debate in each of the Houses of Parliament. There was

---

[45] *Ibid.*   [46] Alan Clark MP, 46 HC Debs. (20 July 1983), col. 484.
[47] *Ibid.*, col. 486.   [48] [1987] IRLR 26, *per* Lord Keith, 29.
[49] 46 HC Debs. (20 July 1983), col. 488.
[50] 445 HL Debs. (5 Dec. 1983), cols. 882–90 and 894–930.

some suggestion at the time that Alan Clark, then Under-Secretary of State for Employment, was less than sober when he introduced the regulations to the House of Commons on the evening of 20 July 1983. Clare Short, from whom the suggestion came, was obliged to withdraw it. She did so on the basis that 'the House understands that I meant what I said'.[51]

Whatever the truth about Mr Clark's precise state of sobriety (and he admits in his diaries to having attended a wine tasting which he left, at 9.40 pm, with a 'muzzy' head and with only twenty minutes in which to come to grips with the 'virtually unmarked and unexcised' text of the Regulations which he was to introduce to the House[52]), there was little doubt about his attitude towards equal pay. Despite his assertion that the government was 'committed to the full implementation of the [equal pay] directive', his tone gave rise to opposition claims that he was less than enthusiastic.[53] His response was to admit that 'a certain separation between express and implied beliefs is endemic among those who hold office'.[54] No such shackles bound Tony Marlow MP, who protested that the Equal Pay Act, as amended, stood as 'an open invitation to any feminist, and harridan or any rattle-headed female with a chip on her bra strap to take action against her employer. . . . This is a charter for petticoat lawyers.'[55]

The 1983 Regulations were introduced with a certain lack of grace. But, for all of the criticism aimed at them by the opposition and the government's own backbenchers, the Equal Pay Act, as amended, at least allowed women to claim equal pay in respect of work which was of equal value to that performed by their male colleagues. The change was significant. Despite the hope expressed by Lena Jeger MP that the Act would help 'the women who do the lowest paid, most drudging jobs in society', in practice the Act's main beneficiaries were women who worked in mixed-sex occupations and who, on the whole, were not as poorly paid as those in predominantly female jobs. While some of those in 'women's jobs' would have benefited from the equalization upwards of statutory minimum wage rates and from the Act's requirement that sex-specific rates of pay be eliminated from collective agreements and pay structures, many more did not.

The major problems consisted of the Act's application, in general, only to women who did the *same* work as men and who, further, did it in the same workplace for the same employer. As was pointed out in Chapter 3, many women were engaged in very predominantly female organizations in which no male comparators were available. These women were in a position to benefit from the 1970 Act only where they were covered by a multi-employer collective agreement whose 'male' and 'female' rates had to

---

[51] 46 HC Debs. (20 July 1983), col. 483.
[52] A. Clark, *Diaries* (London: Weidenfeld & Nicholson, 1993), 30 ff.
[53] 46 HC Debs. (20 July 1983), cols. 479–80.   [54] *Ibid.*, col. 481.
[55] *Ibid.*, col. 491.

be equalized. Many other women, although employed in the same work-place as men, had different jobs. These women could benefit directly under the Act only if their employer had voluntarily chosen to conduct a job evaluation scheme (this was perhaps least likely to have happened in the poorest-paying workplaces); or if the 'female rate' in the collective agreement or pay structure was brought up to the level of the lowest 'male rate', whether by agreement or as a result of Central Arbitration Committee (CAC) intervention. But section 3, which provided the CAC with jurisdiction, was hobbled by its application only to pay structures which discriminated *on their face*, and the CAC's attempts to widen its application were thwarted by the Divisional Court in *R.* v. *Central Arbitration Committee, ex p. Hy-Mac* (discussed in Chapter 3).[56] And while the minimum rates of pay laid down by Wages Councils and the Agri-cultural and Scottish Agricultural Wages Boards benefited some of those at the bottom of the wage pile, they did not apply to all low-paid workers and were, in any case, frequently flouted by employers. (See Chapter 9 for discussion of this.)

Prior to 1984, those women who suffered the lowest rates of pay—those segregated into female jobs—received less benefit from the Act than did their relatively better-off sisters who worked in mixed-sex occupations and workplaces. While the implementation of 'equal pay for work of equal value' did little to avail those women who were segregated into predom-inantly female workplaces, it did hold out the possibility of improvement to women who worked in mixed-sex workplaces but who had previously been denied equal pay adjustments by the lack of men doing like work or work rated as equivalent by the employer.[57]

The UK legislation was seen as 'state of the art' by many comment-ators. While US legislation mandated equal pay for *like* work it did not refer to the concept of 'equal value' and the Supreme Court's decision in *County of Washington* v. *Gunther*, although it allowed pay discrimination claims under Title VII of the Civil Rights Act 1964 (which, being wider than the Equal Pay Act 1982, was not restricted to comparisons between men and women doing the *same* job[58]), was concerned with *deliberate* dis-crimination by the employer.[59] Even this was later put in doubt by the Supreme Court's restrictive decision in *Wards Cove Packing Co.* v. *Antonio*.[60]

One commentator went so far as to complain that the provision which blocked equal value claims where a job evaluation system had rated the jobs of the woman and her comparator as unequal threatened to be unduly

---

[56] [1979] IRLR 461.
[57] Although the requirement that women and their comparators were 'in the same employ-ment' was to deny many women claims. This is discussed in the text following n. 84 below.
[58] See generally D. Fields and K. Morrison, 'Comparable Worth: The Next Step to Pay Equity Under Title VII' (1985) 62 *Denver University Law Review* 417.
[59] 452 US 161 (1981).   [60] (1989) 109 S Ct. 2115.

disruptive of existing pay structures.[61] Such an approach was perhaps unduly optimistic. But for all of the criticisms deservedly levelled at the Equal Pay Act, the introduction of the equal value claim was a significant event in women's struggle for equal pay. Such a claim could cut across pay disparities between 'male' and 'female' jobs and could at last require that the worth of *women's* work be recognized. Women could claim equal pay with men whose jobs were different from theirs, with men whose jobs had never been accepted by the employer as being of the same value. The Act, as amended, did not require that pay structures or collective agreements were overtly discriminatory before women could seek redress. Women could compare themselves with any man in their workplace, could compare themselves even with men who worked at another workplace but for the same or an associated employer.

III. THE IMPACT OF THE EQUAL VALUE CLAIM

If women were truly underpaid by virtue of their sex, then it might be supposed that the implementation of equal value legislation, coupled as it was with a broad approach both to 'pay' and to the issue of discrimination (direct and indirect) should have improved their position very significantly. Any disparities resulting from the underpayment of women by comparison with men working for the same employers should have been eliminated, and only those stemming from workplace segregation and any non-discriminatory factors should remain. But if anyone held her breath in the expectation of dramatic change, she must long since have expired. In 1984, women's hourly rates improved by 1 per cent to 73 per cent (the Regulations had come into force on 1 January of that year), and they improved again by 1 per cent in 1985. Thereafter, they remained at 74 per cent in 1986 and dropped to 73 per cent in 1987. This was hardly evidence of re-ordered pay structures across the United Kingdom.

In the years since 1987 the position has improved—in each of the years to 1996, women's relative hourly earnings have increased. But the rate of increase has slowed—in the four years to 1991 women's relative hourly earnings increased by 4.4 per cent: between 1991 and 1996 the increase was only 2.1 per cent. If the pace of change continues as it has since 1987, women will have reached parity (in terms of hourly rates) by 2024. If progress continues at the average rate we have seen over the past twenty years, the relevant date would be 2050.[62]

   [61] M. Rubenstein, 'Discriminatory Job Evaluation and the Law' (1985–6) 7 *Comparative Labour Law* 172, 178.
   [62] Reuters' *World Service*, 27 June 1995, quoting *The Times* on a Labour Research Department report.

Again, however, the picture is rather less rosy (if, indeed, 'rosy' is an apt word to describe the prospect of waiting around for between twenty-seven and fifty-three years[63]) when it is examined closely. First of all, the statistics cited refer to *all* full-time women workers. As we saw earlier, women are disproportionately concentrated in the relatively higher paying non-manual sector, a factor which makes their relative earnings as a group higher than the earnings of both manual and non-manual women workers relative to manual and non-manual men respectively. The improvements in the hourly and weekly earnings of manual women considered separately (relative to men in the same category) have been much less dramatic. This is illustrated by Table 4.1.

Table 4.1 — full-time women's pay as a percentage of comparable men's, 1987–96[64]

	average hourly rates			average weekly rates		
	all	manual	non-manual	all	manual	non-manual
1987	73.4%	71.1%	61.2%	66.1%	62.2%	59.1%
1988	74.9%	70.8%	62.2%	66.8%	61.6%	59.7%
1989	76.0%	71.5%	63.1%	67.6%	61.9%	60.3%
1990	76.6%	72.0%	63.5%	68.2%	62.4%	60.7%
1991	77.8%	71.3%	66.5%	69.7%	62.9%	63.0%
1992	78.8%	71.5%	67.3%	70.9%	63.4%	64.1%
1993	78.9%	71.9%	67.4%	71.5%	64.6%	64.3%
1994	79.5%	72.5%	67.9%	72.2%	64.8%	65.0%
1995	79.6%	72.8%	68.2%	72.0%	64.6%	65.0%
1996	79.9%	72.5%	68.6%	72.3%	64.8%	65.1%

source: NES 1987–95, table 1

While both 'all women' and non-manual women experienced roughly a 7 per cent relative rise in hourly and a 6 per cent relative rise in weekly earnings in the nine years to 1996, manual women workers saw their hourly and weekly rates increase by just over 1 per cent and just under 3 per cent respectively. The steady increase in the disparity between manual and non-manual wages (in 1984, manual workers earned 72 per cent of non-manual workers' hourly and 83 per cent of their weekly rates, by 1996 this had declined to 61 per cent and 72 per cent respectively[65]),

[63] 'Rosy' is, though, appropriate in comparison with the position regarding representation of women in Parliament. According to the Reuters' *World Service* (*ibid*), at the current rate of progress equal representation will take a further 200 years.
[64] Hourly rates exclude overtime payments; weekly rates include them.
[65] Figures taken from NES 1984 & 1996, table 1. The 1984 figures themselves represented a decline from 1979 at which time manual workers earned 86% of non-manual workers' hourly rate (manual women 79% of non-manual women's and manual men 70% of non-manual men's) and 99% of their weekly rate (manual women and men 83%). In 1984

and women's greater relative concentration in non-manual jobs (in 1984, 75 per cent of full-time women workers, but only 43 per cent of full-time men, had non-manual jobs—in 1995 these figures stood at 80 per cent and 53 per cent respectively[66]) explains the relative increase in women's wages to a significant extent.[67]

Just as some predominantly female occupational groups had seen their wages fall between 1975 and 1981, so the decline continued until 1994. Women nurses did very well, their hourly rates increasing from 75 per cent of the average male wage in 1981 to 96 per cent in 1994, and the weekly rates for women primary school teachers increased marginally, from 103 per cent of the average male weekly wage in 1981 to 106 per cent in 1991.[68] But wages for full-time receptionists, telephonists, shop assistants, and secretaries either remained stable or declined slightly in the thirteen years from 1981; those for home and domestic helpers plummeted from 57 per cent to 46 per cent and of sewing machinists from 52 per cent to 46 per cent of the average male hourly rate. And women who worked in catering, cleaning, and hairdressing saw their wages drop until 1990 when they ceased to be included as a distinct group in the New Earnings Survey. Overall, of the eighteen occupational groups included in the NES until 1990, women's wages in two of the four predominantly female categories declined, relative to the average male weekly wage, between 1977 and 1990 as they did also in three of the five groups in which women accounted for between 25 per cent and 49 per cent of the workforce.[69]

manual women earned 71% of non-manual women's hourly and 75% of their weekly rate, while manual men earned 63% of non-manual men's hourly and 73% of their weekly rate. The 1996 figures represented a decline of around 2% since 1995.

[66] NES 1984, table 87—51% of part-time women and 68% of all women worked in non-manual jobs (tables 87 and 173). The figures for men are from NES 1995, table 87—66% of part-time women and 75% of all women workers—(tables 86 and 173, the figures for men are from table 86).

[67] The trend towards women in non-manual jobs is recognized by J. Waldfogel, *Women Working For Less: A Longitudinal Analysis of the Family Gap* (London: LSE, 1993) LSE Suntory and Toyota International Centre for Economics and Related Disciplines, Discussion Paper W.S.P./93, 2. Waldfogel cites the EOC's *Women and Men in Britain* (London: HMSO, 1991) and L. Katz, G. Loveman, and D. Blanchflower, *A Comparison of Changes in the Structure of Wages in 4 OECD Countries* (paper presented at the National Bureau of Economic Research Comparative Labour Markets Conference, Cambridge 1992—now NBER Working Paper No 4297, Cambridge, Mass. NBER, 1993). The other factor Waldfogel mentions (citing J. Schmitt, 'The Changing Structure of Male Earnings in Britain, 1974–1988' in R. Freeman and L. Katz (eds.), *Changes and Differences in Wage Structures* (Chicago, Ill.: University of Chicago Press)), is the slower wage growth experienced by less educated men. Both of these factors echo current developments in the US according to Katz *et al.*, above.

[68] Figures taken from the NES tables.

[69] Decline in professionals allied to education, welfare, and health (89% to 88% weekly) and catering, cleaning, and hairdressing (53% to 47%), improvement in clerical and related (61% to 62%) and selling (47% to 52%). Painting, assembling, etc.—down from 58% to 52%, materials processing (excluding electricity) 55 to 51% and making and repairing (54 to 49%)—in professions allied to management and administration up from 96% to 113% and in management excluding general management, 67% to 81%.

Jill Rubery suggests that much of the improvement in women's relative wages has resulted 'from [the] changing occupational composition of women workers and not through an enhancement of the value attached to female jobs'.[70] This is supported by the statistical evidence from recent years. Not only do women account for a much greater proportion of managers (27.6 per cent as against 14.3 per cent[71]) and a somewhat greater proportion of professionals now than they did in 1984, but women have also moved into the higher paying jobs within these broad occupational categories.[72] This trend would appear to have played a considerable part in the increase in women's relative pay.

In 1991, for example, full-time women managers earned 65.6 per cent of male managers' weekly wages: in 1995 this had improved to 68.5 per cent.[73] On the one hand this might suggest that the position of women managers generally has improved in that time. But closer examination of the statistics suggests that this is not the case. In 1991, women comprised a higher proportion of managers in four areas than they did in management as a whole and five of a total of twenty-six management occupations accounted for 59.4 per cent of all women managers.[74] Women in the former category earned 83.1 per cent of the weekly wages earned by men in the same occupations while women in the later category earned 72.2 per cent.[75] In 1995, those women in the same occupations earned 81.7

---

[70] J. Rubery, *Wage Determination and Sex Segregation in Employment: Report for the UK* (1993) Report for the Network of Experts on the Situation of Women in the Labour Market, cited in J. Rubery and C. Fagan, 'Equal Pay Policy and Wage Regulation Systems in Europe' (1994) 25(4) *Industrial Relations Journal* 281, 281. See also J. Rubery and C. Fagan, 'Occupational Segregation . . . *Plus Ça Change?*' in R. Lindley (ed.), *Labour Market Structures and Prospects For Women* (Manchester: EOC, 1994). For an analysis of changes in the US, see E. Sorensen, *Exploring the Reasons Behind the Narrowing Gender Pay Gap in Earnings* (Washington, Urban Institute Press, 1991). Sorensen posits that a great deal is down to occupational movement and highly paid women, though some also due to decline in discrimination.

[71] The figures are taken from tables 86 and 87 for the relevant years—the classifications have changed—'management' excluding general management up to 1990 and including it thereafter and the categorization of a number of jobs changing between 1990 and 1991. But the figures for women in management in 1990 were 21.1% and in 1991 23.8% so the effect of the changes in classification have been much less important than changes in the sex composition of management.

[72] The gains for women as professionals look much less impressive (38.7% in 1995 as against 35.1% in 1984) but, prior to changes in classification in 1991 the 'professional' grouping included job categories now included in the 'associate professional and technical' category. The change in classification between 1990 and 1991 had the effect of reducing the number of women 'professionals' from 11,643 to 4,980, their proportion from 37.1% to 36.1%—this change in classification partly masks the upward trend which occurred both between 1984 and 1990, and between 1991 and 1995.

[73] NES 1991 & 1995, tables 86 & 87.

[74] Local Government officers, advertising and public relations managers, personnel, training, and industrial relations managers and Civil Service executive officers—all statistics come from 1991 and NES 1995, tables 86 & 87.

[75] Save that one occupation was not listed for the men—this accounted for 13.4% of all women in the four categories. Again, one group had no male comparator—this accounted for 26.9% women concerned.

per cent and 74.7 per cent respectively of their male colleagues' salaries.[76] However, the ten highest-paid managerial occupations accounted for 46.4 per cent of all women managers in 1991 (52.3 per cent of men)—a figure which had increased to 52.8 per cent of women (54.3 per cent of men) in 1995.

These statistics suggest that the increase in women managers' average salary has as much to do with the movement of women into the higher paying areas of management as with any increase in the wages in those management jobs typically performed by women. This observation is borne out for professional women too—whereas women professionals earned 81.6 per cent of their male colleagues' weekly wages in 1995 in comparison with 78.6 per cent in 1991, 13 per cent of women professionals were employed in the top ten salaried professions in 1995—up from a mere 2.9 per cent in 1991 (for men the figures were 32 per cent and 31.2 per cent respectively).[77]

To the extent that these figures indicate that some women have broken through the 'glass ceiling', this is of course to be welcomed. On the other hand, it holds little comfort for the majority of women workers who are not to be found clinging to the upper reaches of the job ladder. Those women who have reached the top are often single and most usually child-less. In 1995, for example, over 50 per cent of women television producers over the age of 40 were childless as were 50 per cent of women in top management positions in the NHS, but only 7 per cent of men. Twenty-three per cent of these top women managers but only 2 per cent of men were single.[78] 'Success', if it is on such terms, will be unpalatable to many.

The other very significant omission from the 80 per cent hourly and 72 per cent weekly figures is that of *part-time* women workers. We saw in Chapter 2 that part-timers earn very inferior rates and, accounting as they do for almost 50 per cent of women workers, can hardly be dis-missed as an insignificant minority.[79] In 1972, part-time women workers earned only 52 per cent of the male full-time worker's hourly wage. By 1976 this had improved to only 59 per cent, and by 1982 the hourly rate

[76] By this time women accounted for a greater than representative proportion of four fur-ther occupations—the latter category now accounted for 56.5% of all female managers while 22.4% were left out of the calculation.

[77] Women's salaries in the 5 occupations in which they were over-represented relative to the professions as a whole rose from 86.5% of men's weekly rates in 1991 to 88.3% in 1995—librarians are omitted because of their lack of a male comparator but comprised only 2.1% of the whole—those 3 occupations which accounted for 64.6% of all women profes-sionals in 1991 (62.4% in 1995) (secondary and primary school teachers and social workers/ probation officers) paid women 86.4% of men's weekly rates in 1991, 88.2% in 1995. Prior to 1991, there were too few categories containing women to work on.

[78] The *Scotsman*, 29 Aug. 1995; IHSM Consultants, *Creative Career Paths in the NHS: Report No 1: Top Managers* (report for the NHS Women's Unit).

[79] See also 'The Flexible Workforce and Patterns of Working Time in the UK', *Employ-ment Gazette*, July 1994, 239.

had slipped to 57 per cent. The movements in wage rates after 1982 are detailed in table 4.2.

Table 4.2 — women's hourly pay as a percentage of full-time men's, 1982–96

	part-time			full-time
	all	manual	non-manual	all
1982	57.0%	61.9%	50.2%	71.9%
1983	57.2%	62.4%	50.6%	72.2%
1984	57.7%	62.5%	51.0%	73.4%
1985	57.8%	62.6%	51.0%	73.9%
1986	56.9%	62.8%	49.6%	74.1%
1987	56.3%	63.1%	48.6%	73.4%
1988	56.2%	63.1%	48.3%	74.9%
1989	57.1%	63.1%	49.5%	76.0%
1990	57.3%	63.2%	49.5%	76.6%
1991	58.2%	63.4%	51.5%	77.8%
1992	58.5%	63.8%	51.8%	78.8%
1993	58.5%	64.5%	51.7%	78.8%
1994	58.7%	65.0%	52.0%	79.5%
1995	59.6%	64.8%	52.7%	79.6%
1996	58.2%	64.1%	51.1%	79.9%

source: NES 1982–96, tables 86, 87 & 178

Again, there is a stark contrast both between the relative hourly rates of full-time and part-time women workers in 1996 (around 80 per cent and 60 per cent respectively), and between the rates of improvement of the two groups since 1987 (6.5 per cent and 2 per cent respectively). Non-manual women workers do particularly badly as part-timers, earning only 51 per cent of the hourly (full-time) male rate (again, an improvement of only 2.5 per cent from 1987), and part-time manual women workers, while they do significantly better (relatively) than both non-manual women and 'all women' part-timers, still earn only 1 per cent more of the full-time manual male rate than they did in 1987 and 16 per cent less (relative to manual men) than all full-time women workers do (relative to all men).

It is also important to note that the figures cited in tables 4.1 and 4.2 are taken from the New Earnings Surveys for the relevant years. This is significant because the statistics used in that survey actually omit the lowest paid workers who, according to TUC research, have experienced a decline in their real wages in recent years.[80] This issue was discussed in detail in Chapter 2.

[80] TUC, *The New Divide: Part Time Workers' Pay in the 90s* (London: TUC, 1995).

Just as in 1976 and 1981, British women continue to do less well than many of their sisters elsewhere. In particular, the European Commission's *Memorandum on Equal Pay for Work of Equal Value*, published in 1994, reveals that non-manual women workers in Britain earn only 54.2 per cent of men's monthly rate, a figure which contrasts with the 84.5 per cent earned by women in Denmark.[81] The only women who fare (marginally) worse are manual workers in Ireland and Luxembourg, while Danish non-manual women workers earn 85 per cent and French manual women workers over 80 per cent of their male colleagues' monthly and hourly rates. The document further points out that, in some Member States, the pay gap was widening as a result of economic difficulties. In the United Kingdom, the decline in the relative earnings of many manual women (see Chapter 3) continued in the ten years to 1988 and, although they have generally kept pace with those of male manual workers since 1988, this has been against a backdrop of steep decline relative to the wages of non-manual workers.[82]

IV. DEFICIENCIES IN THE EXISTING LEGISLATION

The reasons behind British women's particular disadvantage in the labour market will be discussed in Chapter 6. But here it is useful to consider why the Equal Pay Act, as amended, has had so small an impact on women's relative pay. Again, before turning to the arguments frequently heard that the gender-gap has its roots in factors other than discrimination, it is useful to consider the law itself. In the period between July 1984 and December 1994, almost 8,000 equal value claims involving 565 employers were lodged.[83] Of the 119 cases involving just under 1,000 applicants which resulted in the appointment of an independent expert, twenty-one cases involving a total of 399 applicants awaited the expert's report at the end of 1994. A further sixty-seven cases involving 371 applicants were withdrawn or settled, either with or without the report of an independent expert.[84] Only twenty-one cases resulted in success for some or all of the applicants at the tribunal—together these cases involved around 150 applicants.

---

[81] (1994), EC Comm. Denmark's consistently high female wages are coupled with the highest female participation rate in the EC (in 1991 this stood at 61%, the UK was second with 52% while the average EC participation rate was 42%).

[82] *Ibid.* In England and in Scotland manual women's hourly rate fell from 72.5% of the hourly male rate to 71% and 70% respectively. NES 1988 & 1995, tables, 1, 108, & 110: manual women workers' hourly rates fell from 58.1% to 54.7% of all workers' hourly wages; 49% to 46.8% of all non-manual workers' hourly, and 65.7% to 58.7% of non-manual women's hourly.

[83] *Equal Opportunities Review* 58, 11, 'Equal Value Update'.

[84] Of these, 53 cases involving over 260 applicants were settled.

The provisions of the Act, together with the relevant European legislation and case law, are discussed elsewhere, and the briefest summary will suffice to point to the inadequacies of the existing law as an instrument with which to tackle women's underpayment (assuming for the moment that women's *lower* levels of payment do actually constitute *underpayment* related to sex). In examining the existing law it is useful first to consider the problems associated with the legislation *itself*, and then to consider the difficulties which have arisen in the application of that legislation by the courts. Again, we consider the legislation here on its own terms, i.e. applying as it does only to sex discrimination and not to race discrimination in pay.

(A) THE LEGISLATION

Workplace Focus

Some of the most fundamental inadequacies of the Equal Pay Act become apparent when the law outlined in Chapter 1 is considered together with the pattern of women's labour market participation (discussed in Chapter 2). In the first place, it should be apparent from Chapter 2 that women are found in different industries and workplaces, as well as in different occupations, from those which men occupy. The last of these is within the remit of the Equal Pay Act, providing that a male comparator whose job is of *equal* value to that done by the applicant can be found. But no claim is possible under the Act, save where the woman and her comparator work in the 'same employment'—a definition even narrower, for all practical purposes, than one which demands only that they be employed by the same employer. Certainly, except in the case of associated employers, no claim is possible in relation to a comparator employed by a different person or organization, whether that comparator works at the applicant's workplace or elsewhere.[85] The significance of this has been mentioned several times throughout this chapter and Chapter 3.

Comparator-Based Approach

The second major problem associated with the Act lies in the narrowness of its approach. By the time the equal pay amendments were introduced the CAC's power to adjudicate *collective* equal pay disputes was, although not yet abolished, effectively a dead letter (see Chapter 3 above). The only legal recourse in respect of pay discrimination lay in an individual complaint to an industrial tribunal, whether that complaint was based on a claim of 'like work', 'work rated as equivalent', or the new 'work of equal value'. The new claim depended, as did the old, upon the woman

---

[85] See *Scullard* v. *Knowles & Southern Region Council for Education and Training* [1996] IRLR 344 for a decision that the Equal Pay Act's narrow definition of 'associated employers' is out of line with the requirements of Art. 119.

establishing a disparity between her wage and that of an *equal* (in one of the three senses) man or men. No complaint was available regarding *generalized* underpayment of women within a firm or industry: jurisdiction was available to the tribunal only in respect of *individual* comparators.

Women's difficulties in selecting an appropriate comparator are exacerbated in the context of equal value claims. The equal value claimant has to assert that her job is as valuable as that done by a particular man; yet the determination of value is an *ex post facto* question for the tribunal to decide, generally on the basis of an independent expert's report.[86] The applicant cannot know what view such an expert may take—nor can she even know upon what system (s)he may base that view (see Chapter 7 for further discussion of this point).[87] 'Like work' and 'work rated as equivalent' claimants have to gamble on the fact that an employer may be able to put forward a 'material difference', and 'like work' claimants on whether particular differences between their jobs and those of their comparators may be sufficient to render the jobs not 'broadly similar'. But 'equal value' claimants are in a much more difficult position—they have no certain grounds upon which to select an appropriate comparator.

The difficulty in choosing a comparator stems, in essence, from the failure of the Act to allow for proportionate value claims—the first step for the equal value claimant is to establish *equality* and, without this, the claim must fail. While a woman may claim equal (but not greater) pay than that received by a man doing *less valuable* work (and even this took a decision of the ECJ to determine[88]), there is no provision for the applicant whose job is paid 50 per cent of the salary, and rated as 90 per cent as valuable, as that of her male comparator. A tribunal may (but does not have to) accept 'equal value' where an independent expert has rated jobs at 100 per cent and 98 per cent, or at 400 and 420 points on a scale of 200 to 600, but it is unlikely that a 10 per cent differential in the assigned values could found a determination of equal value. So, even in the face of the strongest evidence that differentials between jobs were maintained at high levels because of arguments about men needing a 'family wage', women working for 'pin money'; the claimant who fails to establish *equality* of value between her job and that of a man has no legal means of challenging the employer's discriminatory practices. Nor is even the amended Act of any assistance to women working in very predominantly female workplaces. These women, who are among the lowest paid of *all* women (see Chapter 2), have almost no chance of finding an appropriate comparator.

---

[86] Until 1996, such a report was a prerequisite to a finding of equal value—see further Ch. 1.

[87] A. Plumer, *Equal Value Judgments: Objective Assessment or Lottery* (Coventry: University of Warwick, School of Business Studies Industrial Research Unit, 1992), Warwick Papers in Industrial Relations No 40. Reported at 45 *Equal Opportunities Review* 4–5.

[88] *Murphy* v. *Bord Telecom Eireann*, case 157/86 [1988] ECR 673.

The Equal Pay Act's individuality of approach is evident in this demand for a direct comparison between an individual woman and a man. More than one similarly situated woman may, of course, bring a claim; and the woman or women may name more than one comparator (see Chapter 1 for the problems associated with this). This has been a characteristic of much trade union activity in the area of equal pay—trade unions have initially attempted to 'bargain equality' and, in the face of employer intransigence, have effectively brought mass claims on behalf of the women (this, at least, is the practice—in theory the women bring their own claims). But these claims are not 'mass actions' properly so-called—they may end up being heard by a host of different industrial tribunals which reach contradictory conclusions on the facts.[89] And while representative cases can be heard and the decisions in them applied across all the applicants, this course of action requires the agreement of the parties to each case. In 1989 the EOC reported that such agreement was 'often' lacking.[90] Where cases are heard individually, or where only some of the women underpaid by virtue of a particular pay practice, or in comparison with a particular man, file cases, there is no provision for a successful claim to apply to anyone other than the applicant herself.

The Cost of 'Equal Pay'

Not only does the requirement for individual claimants give rise to difficulties in determining appropriate comparators, it also acts as a disincentive to complaints. The direct financial costs of equal value claims are high (particularly now that both employer and employee generally commission their own experts to balance the views of the independent expert[91]), and the fear of victimization prevents many potential claimants from pursuing their cases. The EOC's *Annual Reports* have often attributed drops in the numbers of cases brought to tribunals to down-swings in the economy and the resulting increased fear of unemployment. Such fear would appear well founded: studies of those who have brought sex discrimination and/or equal pay cases have shown that applicants suffer heavy penalties in the form of job losses and deterioration in their working conditions:[92] of the seventy successful equal pay and sex discrimination claimants in Alice Leonard's 1980–4 study, only seventeen remained in employment

---

[89] EOC, *Equal Pay . . . Making it Work* (Manchester: EOC, 1989), 9 cites *Whitmore and Alcock* v. *Frayling Furniture Ltd* (Birmingham IT 1985), *Holden & Ors.* v. *Buoyant Upholsterers Ltd* (Manchester IT, 1985) and *White & Ors.* v. *Alstons (Colchester) Ltd* (London North IT, 1985).

[90] See *Equal Pay . . . Making it Work*, n. 89 above, 10.

[91] *Ibid.*, 11. The cost of equal value claims rivals that of 'complex high court litigation'.

[92] See further A. Leonard, *Pyrrhic Victories: Winning Sex Discrimination and Equal Pay Cases in the Industrial Tribunals, 1980–1984* (London: HMSO, 1987). See also J. Gregory, *Trial by Ordeal: A Study of People who Lost Equal Pay and Sex Discrimination Cases in the Industrial Tribunals During 1985 & 1986* (London: HMSO, 1989).

at the time of her survey. And even if a woman is willing to bring her claim, legal aid is unavailable (and will, even if this changes, remain unavailable to the vast majority of industrial tribunal applicants in view of the extremely low income limits), and the resources of the EOC and trade unions are limited. Particularly in view of the fact that employers do not have to extend the pay increase resulting from a successful claim to other, similarly situated, women, the financing of equal pay claims may be a questionable use of resources by both the EOC and trade unions.

Individualistic Approach

But the absurdity of the individual approach is perhaps most apparent in the manner of the legislation's approach to *systemic* pay discrimination. It is almost certainly the case (this is discussed further in Chapter 6) that women's underpayment stems, not only from deliberate discrimination against individuals, but from structural assumptions about the value of women's work and their position in the workforce, and from traditional notions of the 'family wage' (available, of course, exclusively to men). Pre-1975 pay structures operated to the disadvantage of women, relating men's wages to family needs, but women's, at best, to the requirements of an individual. Trade unions embraced the notion of the 'family wage' at the same time as they pressed for men to be rewarded on the basis of effort.[93] And even those economists who embraced the 'marginal productivity' theory of wage setting, claiming that wages were dependent on the worker's utility to the employer, abandoned this theory when it came to explaining women's lower wages. To the extent that they were unable to explain women's lower wages in terms of their lower productivity (the result of their lack of employment opportunity and training), they justified them in terms of subsistence theory.[94] Whatever the ideology surrounding men's wages, women's salaries were depressed by virtue of the assumption that they were not responsible for others; that, indeed, they were subsidized by male family members and so did not have to receive even subsistence wages.

The Equal Pay Act did little to challenge the shape of the pay structures resulting from these assumptions. The Act does not prohibit the discriminatory under-payment of women *because* they are women in the

[93] The TUC retained the policy of bargaining in respect of a 'family wage' until 1960 and, even more recently, the 'family wage' argument has resurfaced in the Government's purported justifications for the abolition of the minimum wage, See, e.g., 213 HC Deb. (3 Dec. 1992), col. 139, Mr Michael Forsythe MP: '80 per cent of wages councils workers are in households with two or more wage earners. The biggest source of poverty is not low pay.' For a critique of this approach see R. Dickens *et al.*, 'Wages Councils: Was There a Case for Abolition?' (1993) 31 *British Journal of Industrial Relations* 515.

[94] F. Edgeworth, 'Equal Pay to Men and Women for Equal Work' (1922) 32 *Economic Journal* 431; 'Women's Wages in Relation to Economic Welfare' (1923) 33 *Economic Journal* 487.

absence of a suitable male comparator. Even the 'equal value' claim depends upon the *initial* determination that a woman's job is in fact of equal value to that of her male comparator, and the question whether the employer's overall pay practices are such as to disadvantage women (and, in particular, the incumbents of female-dominated jobs) arises only if the employer puts forward that pay structure as a material factor defence. If this does happen, the tribunal is dependent on the evidence of the employer and employee/trade union in order to determine whether the 'pay structure' factor is a factor which is 'not the difference of sex'. Although the burden of proof is on the employer to establish that the difference between the man's pay and the woman's pay is due to a factor not being the difference of sex, the burden is not a heavy one and arguments about the preponderance of women in low-paid grades or the impact of market forces on the pay in particular (male-dominated) grades appear often to be beyond the grasp of tribunals and, in particular, the EAT.

Among the cases in which this lack of grasp became apparent were *Reed Packaging Ltd* v. *Boozer*, and *Enderby* v. *Frenchay* (discussed in the text accompanying notes 106–10 and 121–4 below). In both of these cases, the Employment Appeal Tribunal was confronted with employers' claims that pay disparities resulted from the determination of pay in accordance with separate structures regulating the jobs of the applicants and those of their comparators. On both occasions the EAT accepted this as sufficient to amount to a material factor defence without considering whether the determination of this pay disadvantaged women as a group; *why* this was the case; and whether the employers were justified in determining pay in this fashion. It was clear, in both cases, that men did better out of the bargaining structures than did women, but the potential significance of this appeared entirely to escape the notice of EAT.

The Equal Pay Act appears to start from the presumption that discrimination in pay is *not* widespread: hence the individual, complaints-based mechanism. The apparent presumption against discrimination is evident in the individual complaint mechanism adopted. It is also clear in the legislation's strong favouring of the *status quo* even where equal value has been established, or before the applicant has had a chance to make out her claim on this point: not only did the amendments widen the 'material difference' to a 'material factor' defence where equal value claims are concerned (see Chapter 2), but they allowed the defence to be pleaded before the determination of value, and they allowed claims to be thrown out at the preliminary hearing, either because of the successful use of this defence or because there were 'no reasonable grounds' upon which to determine that the jobs were of equal value. This, in turn, could be established either by virtue of the fact that a job evaluation scheme had rated the jobs as unequal or because, in the eyes of the tribunal, the claim was 'hopeless'.

Overview

The result of these shortcomings is that:

(a) no challenge is possible in respect of pay differentials which arise between male- and female-dominated workplaces. It can be seen from Chapter 6 that such disparities in payment are common—in 1980 '[t]he higher was the female proportion of the manual workforce the lower was the level of pay for semi-skilled and skilled workers';[95] in 1995 '[w]here the establishment's workforce is 60 per cent or more female, semi-skilled workers' pay is approximately 30 per cent lower than in an establishment with at least 80 per cent males'.[96] These disparities remain unchallengeable under the Equal Pay Act;

(b) an employer may (subject to the future interpretation of the House of Lords' decision in *Ratcliffe* v. *North Yorkshire County Council* (see Chapters 1 and 6) defend an equal pay claim on the ground that he had to pay the male comparator more than the woman in order to persuade him to accept or remain in the job (this, effectively, was the scenario which Lord Denning found unthinkable in *Clay Cross*);

(c) the employer may run this argument even before a tribunal has determined the relative value of the jobs (thus not being given the chance to find out that the woman's job is one-and-a-half times more valuable (in terms of the demands made upon her) than that performed by the man—such a finding may raise doubt whether his 20 per cent pay advantage could genuinely be said to result from the 'genuine material factor' relied upon);

(d) the woman's claim may be thrown out at the preliminary hearing because the employer's job evaluation scheme rated it as less valuable than that done by her comparator. The scheme may have failed to rate it as equal on grounds that were themselves discriminatory, but this will not assist the woman unless the manner of the discrimination consisted in 'setting different values for men and women on the same demand under any heading' (section 1(5)) or in setting different or coincidental values 'on different demands under the same or different headings . . . [the difference or coincidence not being] justifiable irrespective of the sex of the person on whom those demands are made' (section 2A(3)). This particular provision is hardly a model of clarity, but does suggest that the failure of a job evaluation scheme to take into account factors that are particularly characteristic of female jobs (while giving weight to the

---

[95] W. Daniel and N. Millward, *Workplace Industrial Relations in Britain: The ED/PSI/ ERSC Survey* (London: Heinemann Educational, 1983).

[96] N. Millward and S. Woodland, *Gender Segregation and Male/Female Wage Differences* (London: LSE Centre for Economic Performance, 1995), Discussion Paper No 220, 16.

characteristics associated with male jobs) would be outside the scope of the Act. In such circumstances, an equal value claim could be blocked by a discriminatory job evaluation system (see *Neil and Ors.* v. *Ford Motor Co.*, discussed in Chapter 1. And in *Miller* v. *J. H. Fenner* a tribunal required the applicant to establish that the scheme discriminated on the grounds of sex in order that her claim could proceed—this approach was not adopted by the later Court of Appeal decision in *Bromley* v. *H. and J. Quick Ltd*, discussed in the next section below);[97]

(e) tribunals may dismiss claims on the residual 'no reasonable grounds' basis for reasons which are themselves rooted in discriminatory assumptions about the value of women's work. Baroness Seear, debating the amending Regulations in the House of Lords, pointed out that the equal value claim

> will be an affront to common sense because they will be quite contrary to what in the past has been normal practice. . . . The *whole point* is that it will reverse the pecking order at any rate in certain cases, and will not at first sight seem reasonable to many people (my emphasis).[98]

It is unfortunate, then, that the Regulations left tribunals with the power to dismiss 'unreasonable' claims, particularly in view of the fact that the industrial tribunal is composed, in the majority, of the very people (employer and trade union nominees) most likely to have a robust, 'common-sensical' approach to the question of equal pay.

These issues are addressed further in the next section below, when we come to consider the application of the amended Act in the courts. The last matter which will be mentioned here is the appalling complexity of the law relating to equal pay. Not only is the legislation tortuously drafted, but UK law does not stand alone—requiring to be interpreted in accordance with and applied together with EC provisions. Even assuming that such an individualistic, establishment-centred, and equal (rather than proportionate) value-dependent scheme could impact on women's relative underpayment (again, assuming for the moment that women *are* under-paid in any meaningful sense); the complexities involved in making a claim are such that the potential effect of equal pay law is radically undermined.

The same can be said, unfortunately, in respect of the judicial approach. The application of the equal pay legislation by the domestic courts (and, in particular, by the EAT) has appeared at times driven by a determination to frustrate even the most conservative interpretation of the principle of equal pay.

[97] Glasgow IT 1985, discussed in EOC, *Equal Pay*, n. 89 above. *Bromley* v. *Quick* is at [1988] IRLR 249.
[98] 445 HL. Debs. (5 Dec. 1983) cols. 901–2.

(B) JUDICIAL APPLICATION

Delays

Equal value claimants face ridiculous delays. The latest available figures show average delays of over two-and-a-half years in equal value cases—even this pales into insignificance in comparison with *Pickstone* v. *Freemans plc* (in which over seven years elapsed between the first industrial tribunal hearing and the determination of the equal value issue), and *Enderby* v. *Frenchay*, which was first heard by an industrial tribunal in November 1986 and finally referred to an independent expert in December 1995 (by which stage the government had expended £400,000 of taxpayers' money resisting the claim). The Government finally conceded that the applicant's work was of equal value to that of her comparators in April 1997, although it declared its intention to fight other, related, claims.[99] The 1,286 applicants in *British Coal Corporation* v. *Smith* waited four years before their case reached a tribunal at which the chair pointed out that, given their average age, many of them would have died before the independent expert reported. The employer appealed, and there was a further two-and-a-half year delay by which stage only 17 per cent of the women were still employed by British Coal.[100]

While the EAT has been ready to condemn the delays associated with equal value claims, Wood J describing them as 'scandalous', and the procedures giving rise to them as 'fouling the proper administration of the law', that tribunal's major response has been to encourage the dismissal of claims at the preliminary hearing (before the assessment of value) and to do so, on occasion, even where this is inconsistent with the wording of the Act.

One example of this is provided by the EAT's decision in *Bromley* v. *Quick*.[101] Section 2A of the amended Act requires tribunals to reject equal value claims where the woman's job has been rated as unequal in value to that of her comparator under a job evaluation scheme which complies with section 1(5) of the Act. Section 1(5) also regulates the type of job evaluation scheme upon which a woman can *found* an equal pay claim (where the scheme has rated her job as equivalent to that of her comparator). In *Eaton Ltd* v. *Nuttall* (a 'work rated as equivalent' case), the EAT decided that section 1(5) required that the scheme be one which was 'thorough in analysis and capable of impartial application'.[102] A study which 'requires the management to make a subjective argument concerning the nature of the work before the employee can be fitted into the appropriate place in the appropriate salary grade, would seem to us not to be a valid study for the purpose of subsection (5)'.[103]

[99] Equal Value Update, n. 83 above. The cost of the *Enderby* case is reported at 66 *Equal Opportunities Review* 3.
[100] The HL referred the matter back to the tribunal for the determination of the equal value issue in May 1996 [1996] IRLR 404, over *10 years* after the first claims were lodged.
[101] [1987] IRLR 456.   [102] [1977] IRLR 71.   [103] *Ibid.* 74, *per* Phillips J.

In *Bromley* v. *Quick* however, the EAT ruled that equal value claims could be blocked by reference to a *non-analytical* job evaluation scheme, carried out by the employers, which had assigned a lower value to their jobs than to those of their comparators. The scheme in question had relied upon benchmark jobs and, ultimately, the creation of a 'felt fair' hierarchy ('an order in accordance with the general level of expectation as to the value of jobs') which had been used to slot into the hierarchy those jobs which had not been chosen as benchmarks.[104] A number of these jobs, including most of those done by the appellants and all of those done by their comparators, had been evaluated on a 'whole job' rather than a factor basis, and had been evaluated without benefit of job descriptions. Further, a number of female jobs which had initially been rated as higher than male jobs had had their positions within the hierarchy lowered, in the final result, in line with the 'felt fair' test. Still, the EAT took the view that the woman's claims were blocked by section 2A.

The EAT's decision on this issue was overruled by the Court of Appeal.[105] So, too, was its interpretation of section 2A(2)(b) which provides that the job evaluation relied upon by the employer must be one which 'there are no reasonable grounds for determining . . . was . . . made on a system which discriminates on grounds of sex'. The EAT decided, contrary to the apparently clear meaning of this section, that the tribunal could dismiss an equal value claim even where there *were* 'reasonable grounds' for determining that the job evaluation system had discriminated on the basis of sex, so long as the tribunal itself decided that no such discrimination had occurred. Such was the concern of the EAT with unfounded, time-wasting, and expensive 'equal value' claims, it seems, that it was more than happy to dismiss arguable cases at drop of a hat.

The same approach was taken by the EAT in *Reed Packaging Ltd* v. *Boozer* and in *Davies* v. *McCartneys*.[106] In the first of these cases, the EAT overruled as perverse the decision of a tribunal to appoint an independent expert to assess the relative value of the clerical jobs performed by the (staff) applicants and the (hourly paid) comparators. The employer had sought to rely upon the existence of separate, negotiated, pay structures governing the jobs to justify the difference in pay, a defence rejected by the tribunal on the ground that:

the principles of equal pay do not take kindly to the somewhat artificial differences between staff and hourly-paid workers which are the product of historical development . . . there is no internal machinery to allow a staff employee to compare herself with an hourly-paid worker. . . . If a tribunal were to allow this defence at this stage, it would mean that these particular women would not be able to break through the artificial machinery which, so far as the internal machinery

---

[104] N. 101 above *per* Sir Ralph Kilner Brown, 459.   [105] N. 97 above.
[106] [1988] IRLR 833 and [1989] IRLR 439.

is concerned, denies them the opportunity of pursuing claims to equal pay with a selected male employee. If there was a single structure they would, of course, be able to do so.[107]

The EAT was so concerned with the costs associated with equal value cases that it overruled the tribunal's decision and dismissed the women's case (the case is further discussed in the next paragraph below). In doing so, the court gave *carte blanche* to employers to continue operating the same old systems which, as a matter of fact, resulted in women's lower payment and erected additional barriers to women seeking to cut across those systems and have their work paid on the basis of its value. The preoccupation with costs and delays is in one sense admirable—there is every reason for the equal value procedure to be simplified and stream-lined and unnecessary costs eliminated. But to seek the reduction of costs and delays by throwing out cases before they have been properly evaluated is as sensible a way of going about this as attempting to save legal aid costs by abolishing criminal trials and imprisoning suspects on the word of a complainant or a police officer. The interests of justice, not to say the application of the principle of equal pay, would have been better served had the EAT made more of an effort to facilitate applicants' already tortuous passage through the procedures laid down by the Equal Pay Act, rather than concentrating on throwing out potentially valid claims at first base.

In *Davies* v. *McCartneys*, too, the EAT upheld a tribunal's decision to dismiss a claim at the preliminary hearing, and did so partly because the applicant was 'just a secretary'.[108] The tribunal had reached its decision partly on the basis of the employer's material factor defence (which, in turn, put forward issues related to the value of the jobs themselves and therefore, according to one reading of the House of Lords in *Leverton* v. *Clwyd County Council*, inappropriate for consideration under the material factor defence).[109] The EAT insisted that all and any factors were suit-able for assessment under the material factor defence. Not only this, but the EAT found that the tribunal had 'in effect' decided that there were no grounds for a determination that the jobs of Ms Davies and her com-parator were of equal value. The man performed a 'much more demand-ing and responsible role' (being a 'market clerk') than the applicant, whose duties, the tribunal had found, were 'not exceptional for a secretary' and whose knowledge of the field in which she worked did not 'extend beyond that which most secretaries would pick up in such an environment'.[110] In view of the fact that the concept of equal value was thought likely

---

[107] Cited by Wood J in the EAT [1988] IRLR 833 at 836.   [108] [1989] IRLR 439.
[109] [1989] IRLR 28, *per* Lord Bridge, 32. Lord Bridge placed some emphasis on the fact that the hours worked would *not* be a matter for the independent expert whose examina-tion, he suggested, was concerned with *qualitative* rather than *quantitative* matters and that, therefore, this issue was appropriate to be considered under s. 1(3).
[110] Para. 24, cited by the EAT, n. 108 above, 441.

radically to disrupt existing pay structures, this approach to its application seems rather less than impressive.

Indirect Discrimination

The application of the law in this area has been poor in the extreme. We saw in Chapter 3 the initial refusal by the UK courts to accept that the 1970 Act prohibited indirect discrimination in pay. This reluctance, which persisted well after the EAT's decision in *Jenkins* v. *Kingsgate*, manifested itself most recently in the demands made by the EAT in *Enderby* v. *Frenchay* and in *BCC* v. *Smith* that, in order to found a successful claim under the Equal Pay Act, discrimination be evidenced by reference to sex-based *causes*, rather than *effects*. In the first of these cases the applicant's claim was dismissed because the cause of the disparity was that her comparators were engaged in different jobs—women could be pharmacists and psychologists, too, so no discrimination had occurred. And in *British Coal Corporation* v. *Smith*, the EAT ruled that the pay difference resulted from the separation of pay structures 'for which there was no sexually discriminatory reason . . . there is no discriminatory factor, no tainting of sex in the negotiating machinery relevant to the [women] . . . which requires any explanation or justification'.[111]

The problem with the EAT's approach in these cases was that it was accepting as a material factor defence a mere *explanation* of why a difference arose. Yes, the disparity between male and female wages arose because they did different jobs which were governed by different pay structures. But the very fact that this arrangement resulted in lower wages for women itself raised an inference of (at least) indirect discrimination, one that the employer could avoid only by showing that reliance upon these disparately impacting pay structures was justified within the test developed by the European Court of Justice in *Bilka-Kaufhaus*, *Rinner-Kühn*, *Danfoss*, and *Nimz* (see further Chapter 1 and the text accompanying notes 4–32 above). To accept the fact of men's and women's different jobs and/or pay structures (assuming equality of value) as excusing differences in pay completely confounds the purpose of 'equal value' legislation. It is to be hoped that the decision of the House of Lords in *Ratcliffe* v. *North Yorkshire* (see Chapter 1) will alter the approach to the section 1(3) issue. Whether this happens in practice, however, remains to be seen.[112]

Respect for Existing Pay Structures

The concern of the lower courts not to disrupt existing pay structures was made evident by the EAT's decision in *Hayward* v. *Cammell Laird*

---

[111] [1993] IRLR 308, 316.   [112] [1995] IRLR 439.

Shipbuilders Ltd, in which Popplewell J refused to permit a claim which, on appeal, the House of Lords was content came within the 'natural and ordinary' meaning of the legislation. The case, which turned on the question whether pay should be 'equal' in *overall* terms (taking into account benefits such as free meals, etc.) or at the level of *each element* of the 'pay package', was decided by the EAT on the basis that the latter approach 'would necessarily involve leap-frogging, [and] would in the view of the industrial members of this court result in widespread chaos in industry and inflict grave damage on commerce'.[113] The House of Lords, permitting Ms Hayward's appeal, preferred the 'natural and ordinary' meaning of the legislation and embraced the approach which the lower courts had said would lead to 'absurd and unreal consequences'.[114]

We have already come across Baroness Seear's argument, in the House of Lords, that 'the *whole point* of equal pay for work of equal value . . . is that in some cases it will be an affront to common sense. . . . The *whole point* is that it will reverse the pecking order' (my emphasis).[115] Obviously, if equal value legislation was rendered necessary by the tendency of existing pay structures to discriminate against women, then the elimination of discrimination in pay will lead to a reordering of pay structures.

The significance of this legislation, however, appears at times to have been lost on those whose task it is to apply the law, and there have been marked indications of reluctance to upset the apple-cart even at the expense of statutory interpretations which render the Equal Pay Act a nonsense. In *Leverton* v. *Clwyd*, for example, the applicant (a nursery nurse) sought parity with men employed by the defendant council in other establishments. Section 1(6) of the Act permits cross-establishment comparisons where (and only where) the man and woman are employed by the same or associated employer 'at establishments in Great Britain . . . at which common terms and conditions of employment are observed either generally or for employees of the relevant classes'.

The drafting of section 1(6) is, perhaps, less than clear. But whatever else it could be taken to mean, logic dictates that the one interpretation which *must* be incorrect is that the woman and the man with whom she seeks to compare herself are employed on the same or similar terms. If this was indeed the case, the woman would have nothing about which to complain under that Act, as the wrong at which the Act is addressed is the application of *different* contractual conditions to comparable male and female employees.

Staggeringly, however, this apparently impossible interpretation was precisely that which the EAT embraced in *Leverton* v. *Clwyd*.[116] When the decision reached the House of Lords, Lord Bridge characterized section

---

[113] [1986] IRLR 287, 291.   [114] [1988] IRLR 257, 261–2.
[115] 445 HL Debs. (5 Dec. 1983), col. 896.
[116] Unreported. The decision of the HL is at n. 109, above.

1(6) as 'clear and unambiguous' and declared that to require 'a "broad similarity" between the woman's terms and conditions of employment and those of her claimed comparators . . . frustrates rather than serves the manifest purpose of the legislation'.[117]

But such frustrations of purpose remained the EAT's *forte* long after Lord Bridge's chastisements. In *Benveniste* v. *University of Southampton*, a 'like work' case decided in 1988, the EAT upheld the decision of a tribunal that the point of a payscale on which a lecturer had been placed by her employers was not a contractual term (but a matter at the discretion of the employer), and that a complaint relating to her pay was, therefore, outside the scope of the Act's provisions.[118] In the view of the tribunal, no term of Dr Benveniste's contract was less favourable than those enjoyed by her comparators. This decision was one of the most bizarre ever reached under the Equal Pay Act—if it was to be widely applied, pay would almost never be a contractual matter and would (quite apart from being legally vulnerable to reduction at the whim of the employer[119]) invariably be incapable of challenge under the Act. Absurd as the decision was, the EAT upheld it, and it took a further appeal before the applicant's claim that she was employed under a less favourable contractual term than those of her male colleagues was recognized.[120]

Nor did the EAT's preoccupation with keeping apple-carts upright end here. The extent to which pay structures and collective agreements have typically been regarded as sufficient, almost without more, to found 'material factor' defences has already been remarked. In *Reed Packaging* v. *Boozer*, discussed in the section above, the EAT accepted as a 'material factor defence' the existence of separate pay structures governing the claimant and her comparator.[121] But by putting forward this defence the employers had done no more than to state that the women were paid less than their comparators because the pay structure adopted by the employer said so. The tribunal had found that there was no discrimination *within* the individual pay structures. But there were wide differences *between* the structures, and the employer had not justified these.

The proper approach would have required the EAT to determine whether reliance on these separate pay structures *in fact* disadvantaged women and, if so, whether the employer was justified (within *Bilka-Kaufhaus*) in relying on this system of pay determination nevertheless. Instead, the EAT

---

[117] *Ibid.*, 31 *per* Lord Bridge. The HL subsequently had to rule again on a similiar issue in *BCC* v. *Smith* [1996] IRLR 404, 408–9, in which the CA demanded that *precisely* similar terms apply as between establishments before s. 1(6) be satisfied: the HL ruled that this approach undermined the purpose of the legislation.

[118] Case EAT/400/86 (Transcript) 28 July 1987, *Lexis*. The decision of the CA is reported at [1989] IRLR 123.

[119] That it is clearly not is evident from a succession of cases, not least of them the decision of the HL in *Rigby* v. *Ferodo Ltd* [1987] IRLR 516.

[120] N. 118 above, 126.   [121] [1988] IRLR 833.

failed to consider the impact of the collective bargaining structures on male and female staff respectively and relied on the decision of the Court of Appeal in *National Vulcan Engineering Insurance Group* v. *Wade* to declare that a single grading scheme was capable of constituting a material factor defence.[122] The EAT, further, declared itself 'reinforced' in its view by the decision of the House of Lords in *Rainey* v. *Greater Glasgow Health Board*: the present case 'shows an objectively justified administrative reason and therefore a material factor which was genuine or sound'.[123] But this finding of objective justification was made without reference to the very factor (disparate impact on male and female staff) which, if it was found, should have required justification by the employer.[124]

The EAT held, in essence, that the fact that a pay structure paid a woman less than a man (the very issue forming the subject matter of the woman's complaint) could be justified on the basis that she was paid less than the man in accordance with the pay structure. Such an approach undermines the very purpose of the equal value legislation, but was reiterated by the EAT in *Enderby* v. *Frenchay*, even where it was clear that relationship between the structures was such that women were disadvantaged as a matter of practice.[125] In that case Wood J declared that the Equal Pay Act was not 'intended to disrupt the well-tried and established negotiating machinery which is totally untainted by gender'.[126] Certainly the Act was not intended to interfere with gender-neutral pay disparities. To assume without more, however, that the vast pay disparities between (overwhelmingly female) senior speech therapists and (predominantly male) senior clinical psychologists and hospital pharmacists came about 'by chance not by gender' was disingenuous in the extreme.[127]

The *Enderby* decision, with many of the EAT's other decisions, has been put right on appeal, Dr Enderby finally winning her claim in April 1997. But the impact of the many adverse decisions upon the effectiveness of the Equal Pay Act should not be underestimated. To the extent that such decisions regarded existing pay structures, particularly those resulting from

---

[122] [1978] IRLR 225.   [123] [1988] IRLR 833, 838.

[124] Such an approach was apparently anticipated by R. Townshend-Smith. In 'Equal Pay and the Material Factor/ Difference Defence' (1987) 16 *Industrial Law Journal* 114, 116, he states that the recognition by the HL of the concept of indirect discrimination in the context of the s. 1(3) defence 'should mark the beginning of a new era of judicial sympathy to the aims and methods of anti-discrimination legislation; this writer, for one, will believe it when he sees it.'

[125] [1990] IRLR 44. See also the decision of the EAT in *Lloyds Bank Plc* v. *Fox* (EAT/556/89 (Transcript) 30 July 1992, *Lexis*). V. Gay remarks, in 'Collective Bargaining as a Material Factor Defence in Equal Value Cases' (1989) 18 *Industrial Law Journal* 63, 63, that collective bargaining was, at the time of the decision in *Reed* v. *Boozer*, a 'current vogue' for employers to argue as a genuine material factor defence.

[126] [1990] IRLR 44, 61.

[127] *Ibid.* 59. 'Equal Value Update,' n. 83 above, 9 reports that, in the NHS in 1988, staff nurses were paid less than electricians, and senior enrolled nurses paid considerably less than technical officers in the architecture department.

the different collective bargaining patterns of male- and female-dominated job categories, as sufficient to justify payment differentials between men and women (as in *Reed* v. *Boozer* and, prior to its appeal from the EAT, *Enderby* v. *Frenchay*), the right to equal pay was rendered largely meaningless. Much of the pay inequality between men and women stems precisely from the fact that men's and women's wages have, over the years, been established separately from each other, whether directly by the imposition of overtly 'male' and 'female' rates or, more commonly, by the differential wage-setting processes employed in respect of predominantly male and female jobs. While the approach adopted by the EAT in *Reed* and in *Enderby* would not necessarily prevent challenge to the former, it did block any effort to eradicate the impact of the latter. In addition, the approach taken by the EAT in *Davies* v. *McCartneys* sends the message that women should not attempt to overturn established and commonplace pay differentials, regardless of the reasons for which such differentials developed over time: where a pay differential is regarded as normal, the message is, no challenge to it will succeed.

The combined effect of these approaches is to restrict the Equal Pay Act, in practice, to tinkering with the occasional pay anomaly or blatant piece of discrimination. Given the huge delays associated with equal value claims, the staggering costs involved, and the levels of commitment required from prospective applicants, it is somewhat surprising that the Equal Pay Act has given rise even to as many claims as it has. Certainly there was, at least until decisions such as that of the ECJ in *Enderby* and the House of Lords in *Ratcliffe* and in *Smith*, little incentive for the applicant, particularly one unsupported by a trade union, to challenge entrenched inequalities in pay. Even today the applicant, whether supported or not, faces an uphill struggle. Even where, as in *Enderby*, she finally succeeds, her victory is an individual one, and has no direct application to the many other women who may share her position.

V. CONCLUSION

In the face of all of these factors, together with others such as the failure of the Act to allow cross-employer comparisons or comparisons based on proportional value and the unavailability at present of any collective mechanism for the elimination of pay discrimination, it is inappropriate to claim that the remaining gender–pay gap is free from the effects of sex discrimination. We saw in Chapter 2 that women work in different occupations, industries, and workplaces from those in which men are found. The Equal Pay Act addresses only those differences which arise at the level of the workplace, and then does so only imperfectly. In particular, for the first eighteen years of the Act's operation, pay differences which arose from differential collective bargaining strength or historically as a result of different pay structures governing typically 'male' and 'female' jobs, were outside the scope of challenge.[128] The shortcomings of this approach have been recognized in recent years, but huge difficulties remain as a result of the complexities of the Equal Pay Act itself and of the relationship between it and European law; the problems of establishing comparability, particularly where the 'equal value' claim is relied upon (the removal of the requirement for an independent expert in this regard may, in fact, make the situation worse—see Chapter 1); and the non-application of the Act to pay differences which arise between men and women employed in different workplaces (save where they are nevertheless regarded as being 'in the same employment'—see Chapter 1).

How the remaining gender–pay gap might be explained and how, if at all, it might be addressed by law is a topic to which we shall turn in Chapter 6. But first it is necessary to consider the Sex Discrimination Act. The issue of equal pay (or the problem of unequal pay) does not exist in a vacuum. Just as the Equal Pay Act is sister to the Sex Discrimination Act 1975, so the issue of discrimination other than in contractual terms is sister to that discrimination which is covered by the terms of the 1970 Act. We saw, in Chapter 2, the extent to which the workforce is segregated along the lines of sex (and race). We also saw the relationship between this and pay. Changes in sex segregation could impact on women's relative levels of pay, and sex segregation may itself be the result of discrimination. In order to assess whether, and to what extent, discrimination is a factor in sex segregation, and to consider the possible role of legislation aimed at reducing sex segregation in tackling the gender–pay gap, we will consider the content and impact of the Sex Discrimination Act 1975. In discussing this Act, some reference will also be made to the Race Relations Act 1976 where relevant to the issue of black women's pay.

---

[128] *Reed* v. *Boozer*, *Enderby* v. *Frenchay*, discussed in the text to nn. 121–7, above. This approach was not laid to rest until the decision of the ECJ in *Enderby*, n. 125 above. Even after this, some traces of the old approach could be seen in the decision of the EAT in *BCC* v. *Smith*, n. 110 above, overruled by the HL on appeal, n. 100 above.

[5]

The Sex Discrimination Act 1975 and Race Relations Act 1976

I. INTRODUCTION

The Equal Pay Act, as originally implemented, required that men and women were paid equally when they were employed by the same employer and engaged in the same work or work which the employer had accepted as being of equal value. But it did nothing to prevent employers from circumventing the equal pay obligation by refusing to employ women (or indeed men), or from employing them only in exclusively male or female jobs to which no job evaluation scheme had been applied.[1] Nor, as we saw in Chapter 3, did the Equal Pay Act contain any prohibition on race discrimination.

It was partly in recognition of the 1970 Act's shortcomings that the Sex Discrimination Act, which became law on 29 December 1975 (the same day on which the Equal Pay Act 1970 was implemented), was passed. The Race Relations Act (which received the Royal Assent on 22 November 1976) was not primarily concerned with the issue of pay, the White Paper on which it was based barely referring to this matter at all but focusing, in the employment field, primarily upon discrimination in recruitment and promotion and, in general terms, upon the inadequacies of the preceding race discrimination legislation (the Race Relations Acts 1965 and 1968).[2] Nevertheless, the Act's provisions did extend to cover discrimination in pay.

According to *Equality for Women* (the White Paper which preceded the Sex Discrimination Act), the 1975 Act was intended 'to eliminate anti-social practices; to provide a remedy for the victim of unfair discrimination and indirectly to change the prejudicial attitudes expressed by discrimination'.[3] That such change was long overdue was evident from the tone

---

[1] Nor, even after its amendment to mandate equal pay for work of equal value, did it prevent employers from ensuring that 'male' and 'female' jobs remained separate and unequal.
[2] Department of Employment, *Race Discrimination* (London: HMSO, 1975), Cmnd. 6234.
[3] Department of Employment, *Equality for Women* (London: HMSO, 1974) Cmnd. 5724, 5.

adopted by some of its opponents. Ivor Stanbrook MP, who made the penultimate speech during the Bill's passage through the Commons, summarized his main objections to the legislation thus:

it leaves out of account those considerations of human nature which apply to relations between the sexes. . . . The Bill takes no account of the fact that most women are mothers, naturally endowed as the best home makers, and better endowed than men to look after children. In the world of their homes and their families women can find satisfying lives fulfilling, influential and complete in a world in which the fact that there are few women serving in public positions is of no significance to them.[4]

The Sex Discrimination Act did not only prohibit discrimination in employment, with which we are here concerned, but also extended to cover education, housing, and the provision of goods, facilities, and services (including financial facilities such as mortgages). The Race Relations Act, too, covered these areas and included the criminal offence of incitement to racial hatred.[5] Both Acts went much further than the Equal Pay Act whose concern, as is evident from the title, lay exclusively in the area of employment.

Both the 1975 and the 1976 Acts were the product of decades of agitation. The Sex Disqualification (Removal) Act 1919 had removed formal legal barriers to women's employment and holding of public office, and the Race Relations Acts of 1965 and 1968 had prohibited discrimination, the first primarily in places of public resort and the second more generally. But the provisions of these Acts were limited indeed: the 1919 Act did not even prohibit the operation of the marriage bar (see Chapter 3), much less discrimination in employment more generally. And the earlier Race Relations Acts were rendered largely ineffective by the severe limitations placed upon individual enforcement and the highly circuitous mechanism for administrative enforcement, as well as by the limited scope of their prohibitions on discrimination.[6]

The marriage bar was finally removed on the recommendation of a subcommittee of the National Whitley Council in 1946, but this did nothing to affect its (less common) operation in the private sector or the reservation of some jobs for men alone. Numerous attempts were made (notably by Baronness Seear) to introduce legislation regulating sex discrimination in the twenty-five years from 1946, but it was not until the early 1970s that a Conservative administration published a Green Paper on the subject. Before the government could act on the relatively limited proposals

[4] 893 HC Debs. (18 June 1975), col. 1611.
[5] Previously contained in the 1965 Act but extended here by the removal of the requirement for intention to stir up racial hatred and implemented as an amendment (s. 5A) to the Public Order Act 1936.
[6] See generally I. MacDonald, *Race Relations: The New Law* (London, Butterworths, 1977).

set out in the paper, a Labour government was elected. It published its own White Paper and, six months later, introduced the Sex Discrimination Bill to the House of Commons. The new legislation was wider than that proposed by the previous government.

Given the chronology involved, it is clear that the passage of the Sex Discrimination Act was not motivated by any proof of failure of the Equal Pay Act. Nevertheless, some indication of the narrowness with which the latter addressed the issue of discrimination is evident from the discussion in Chapter 2. In particular, the 1970 Act did not make it unlawful for employers to avoid the equal pay obligation by segregating men and women into sex-specific jobs—while the provision of explicitly sex-based pay structures could be challenged under section 3 of the Act, there was nothing (save, for a while, the extra-jurisdictional supervision of the Central Arbitration Committee (CAC)—see Chapter 3) to prevent an employer from maintaining de facto separate pay scales for male and female workers by deliniating jobs along the lines of sex and paying them accordingly. National Council for Civil Liberties (NCCL) publications claimed that employers were getting around the provisions of the Equal Pay Act by tinkering with pay scales and reducing the overlap between male and female jobs (in relation to the latter, in line with advice given by employers' organizations such as the Engineering Employers' Federation) and that 'over the past five years whilst the principle of equal pay has supposed to have been put into effect there has been an increasing tendency for work to become separated [by sex], especially in manual jobs'.[7] The Department of Employment itself produced evidence of women workers' substitution by men in manufacturing between 1967 and 1975.[8]

The Race Relations Act of 1976 was the result both of the recognized shortcomings of the 1968 Act and of the desire to harmonize the legislative approaches to race and sex discrimination.[9] The race discrimination White Paper suggested fear of disorder if the disadvantages suffered by ethnic minority Britons were not addressed and the link between the control of immigration and the integration of existing immigrants was explicit in the Parliamentary progress of the Bill.[10] Much of the opposition to the Race Relations Bill was concerned with its focus upon discrimination against ethnic minorities already in Great Britain rather than, as many on the Conservative side would have preferred, concentrating on stemming the flow of further immigration.[11]

[7] P. Hewitt, *Rights for Women* (London: NCCL, 1975), 37–40; NCCL, *The Sex Discrimination Act* (London: NCCL, 1975), 7.

[8] Z. Hornstein, *Trends in Female Employment 1967–75* (London: Department of Employment, 1977).

[9] MacDonald, n. 6 above.

[10] See further ibid, 4–7. Roy Jenkins, introducing the Bill, dwelt on the link—see 906 HC Debs. (4 Mar. 1976), cols. 1547 ff.

[11] See, e.g. William Whitelaw MP, 906 HC Debs. (4 Mar. 1976), cols. 1568–74.

II. PROVISIONS OF THE 1975 AND 1976 ACTS

(A) THE SCOPE OF 'DISCRIMINATION'

Section 1 of both the Sex Discrimination and the Race Relations Acts defined discrimination to include not only the *direct* but also what came to be known as the *indirect* form. Direct discrimination was defined as less favourable treatment 'on the ground of' sex or on 'racial grounds', the latter being defined by the Race Relations Act as grounds of 'colour, race, nationality or ethnic or national origins'.[12] Indirect discrimination occurred when a requirement or condition was applied to the applicant, as to others, where the application of this requirement or condition was to the applicant's detriment because he or she could not comply with it; where a considerably smaller proportion of that applicant's sex or racial group than of others could comply with the requirement or condition; and where the requirement or condition was not justifiable irrespective of the sex, colour, race, nationality, or ethnic or national origins of the person to whom it is applied.[13]

The inclusion of indirect discrimination had not been envisaged by the government at the time of its publication of the sex discrimination White Paper which preferred the view that only intentional discrimination should be prohibited: 'to understand the meaning of unlawful discrimination, it is essential not to confuse motive with effect'.[14] But within the six-month period during which the legislation was drafted Roy Jenkins, then Secretary of State for the Home Department, had visited the United States and been familiarized with the decision of the Supreme Court in *Griggs* v. *Duke Power Company*, in which Title VII of the Civil Rights Act 1964 was interpreted to prohibit 'not only overt discrimination, but also practices that are fair in form but discriminatory in operation'.[15] On his return Mr Jenkins declared that 'the Bill would be too narrow if it were confined to direct and intentional discrimination'.[16] The race discrimination White Paper subsequently instanced the failure of previous legislation to include this concept as one of the reasons for its limited success.[17]

The Race Relations Act (but not the Sex Discrimination Act) specifically defined deliberate segregation as direct discrimination and, for the purposes of employment-related matters only, the Sex Discrimination Act prohibited discrimination on the ground of a person's married (but not marital) status as well as on the ground of sex.[18] In addition to the

---

[12] SDA & RRA, ss. 1(1)(a), RRA, s. 3(1).   [13] SDA & RRA, ss. 1(1)(b).

[14] *White Paper*, n. 3 above, para. 33.

[15] 401 US 424 (1971), 43—the provision prohibited discrimination in employment on the grounds, *inter alia*, of sex and race.

[16] 889 HC Debs. (26 Mar. 1975), col. 513.   [17] N. 2 above, para 35.

[18] SDA, s. 1(2). For criticism of the Government's refusal to extend protection to single persons see, e.g. Jo Richardson MP, 889 HC Debs. (26 Mar. 1975), cols. 553–4 and Lynda Chalker MP, 889 HC Debs. (26 Mar. 1975), col. 570.

prohibition of direct and indirect discrimination, both Acts included within their definition of discrimination 'victimization':[19] that is, less favourable treatment accorded on the ground that someone had taken action under that Act (or, for the purposes of the Sex Discrimination Act, under the Equal Pay Act.)

Discriminatory Advertisements and Practices, Instructions, Inducement, and Assistance

In addition to prohibiting (in the circumstances specified below) direct and indirect discrimination on the grounds of sex, race, or being married, and victimization; the 1975 and 1976 Acts also prohibited discriminatory advertisements; the issue of instructions to discriminate; the application of pressure to discriminate; the provision of assistance to discriminate; and 'discriminatory practices', which were defined to consist of 'the application of a requirement or condition which results in [unlawful indirect sex or race discrimination] *or which would be likely to result in such an act of discrimination*' if those to whom it applied were not all of one sex or if they included people of any particular racial group (my emphasis).[20] This last provision, which the Sex Discrimination Act applied only to sex (i.e. not to marital) discrimination and which allowed the Equal Opportunities Commission (EOC) or the Commission for Racial Equality (CRE) alone to take action (and only after a formal investigation and by means of a non-discrimination notice—see the section after note 177 below), proved controversial in the passage of the 1975 Act. According to John Fraser, Under-Secretary of State for Employment, it was aimed at 'unintended discrimination [which is] . . . so deeply entrenched or so overwhelmingly effective that it is practically invisible and, therefore, may not give rise to any single individual complaint'.[21]

Employers' Vicarious Liability

The Sex Discrimination Act (echoed by the Race Relations Act) established a scheme of vicarious liability, sections 41 and 32 respectively providing that '[a]nything done by a person in the course of his employment shall be treated for the purposes of this Act as done by his employer as well as by him, whether or not it was done with the employer's knowledge or approval' (the Race Relations Act did not extend this to criminal offences created by the Act). Liability was in each case subject to a defence if the employer proved 'that he took such steps as were reasonably practicable to prevent the employee from doing that act, or from doing in the course of his employment acts of that description'.[22]

---

[19] Types of protected action are found in the SDA, s. 4, RRA, s. 2.
[20] SDA, ss. 38, 39, 40, 42, & 37(1) and RRA, ss. 29, 30, 31, 33, & 28 respectively.
[21] 906 HC Debs. (4 Mar. 1976), col. 1430. See cols. 1431–3 and 1434–5 for opposition.
[22] SDA, ss. 41(1) & (3). S. 41(2) applied vicarious liability to agents. See also RRA, s. 32(1), (3) & (2).

(B) PROHIBITED DISCRIMINATION

Discrimination by Employers

Discrimination in employment was prohibited by sections 6 and 4 respectively of the 1975 and 1976 Acts which made it unlawful for a person 'in relation to employment by him at an establishment in Great Britain' to discriminate on the grounds of sex or on racial grounds[23] at the point of hire (or failure to hire), during employment in the context of training, promotion, or access to benefits, facilities, or services and the subjection of employees to any other detriment, and in dismissal. The Race Relations Act, but not the Sex Discrimination Act, also prohibited discrimination in the terms of employment (this being covered by the Equal Pay Act 1970).

Sections 6 and 4 were reasonably comprehensive, the 1975 Act extending its prohibition of discrimination to all aspects of employment with the exception of pensions, other retirement-related matters, and contractual terms concerning remuneration, and the 1976 Act covering even these. The definition of employee adopted by the Acts was also wider than in other legislation, 'employment' being defined as 'employment under a contract of service or of apprenticeship or a contract personally to execute any work or labour'.[24] In addition, both Acts prohibited discrimination against partners, prospective partners, and contract workers in terms similar to those applied to employees;[25] and extended their provisions to cover discrimination by 'qualifying bodies' and in vocational training and trade union membership,[26] as well as education, housing, and the provision of goods, facilities, and services. The provisions regulating vocational training permitted some positive action where men, women, or persons of a particular racial group were under-represented or where people were perceived to be in special need of training 'by reason of the period for which they have been discharging domestic or family responsibilities to the exclusion of regular full-time employment'.[27] Trade unions, too, while generally bound not to discriminate on grounds of race or sex, could target membership drives and training for trade union positions by sex or race in circumstances of under-representation. The Sex Discrimination Act, further, permitted discrimination in order to secure representation by sex on elected bodies.[28]

(C) DISCRIMINATION NOT PROHIBITED BY THE ACTS

For all the scope of the Sex Discrimination and Race Relations Acts, neither set out to prohibit every manifestation of discrimination. The 1975

---

[23] Or, see above, on the ground that someone was married or had previously taken any protected action under the relevant Act.

[24] SDA, s. 82(1); RRA, s. 78.   [25] SDA, ss. 11, 9, & 5, RRA, ss. 10, 7, & 4.

[26] SDA, ss. 12, 13, & 14 and RRA, ss. 11, 12, & 13.   [27] SDA, s. 47.

[28] SDA, s. 49.

Act did not apply to social security or to tax[29] (these areas were not the scene of officially sanctioned race discrimination) and contained numerous exceptions to the principle of non-discrimination (in addition to those already mentioned, these included 'protective' legislation and acts done 'for the purpose of safeguarding national security'). Crucially, also, the Act did nothing to address the practical hurdles, such as lack of access to affordable and reliable childcare, which prevented women from competing in the labour market on an even playing field with men.[30]

The failure of the Act to address the wider factors associated with women's disadvantage in the workplace as well as, more generally, in terms of access to capital and income, was the subject of criticism from MPs and the NCCL. Most women were not, the NCCL argued, in a position to benefit from the provisions of the Act: in order to be able to compete with men on men's terms (this, according to the NCCL, being the approach taken by the Act), women had to have access to adequate maternity leave and allowances (at the time, entitlement to maternity pay was affected by marital status), to suitable childcare, and to equal social security provision.[31] Further:

any Sex Discrimination Act which was seriously intended to end [women's oppression] would have to ensure the stopping up of loopholes in the Equal Pay Act by guaranteeing equal pay to those who have not already got it . . . would have provided for restructuring areas of employment so that women were not ghettoised in some sectors and denied admittance to others . . . would have to ensure that women were able to take advantage of the improved mortgage and loan facilities by guaranteeing a minimum wage tied to increases in the rate of inflation.[32]

Roy Jenkins, introducing the Bill, accepted that the legislation was 'a necessary pre-condition for an effective equal opportunity policy, but . . . not a sufficient condition'.[33] But he took the view that the wider measures required were not the responsibility of government alone and was prepared merely to call for 'a profound shift in the attitudes and actions of all of us'.[34] Three months later Barbara Castle, then Secretary of State for Social Services, blocked attempts to include social security provisions in Council Directive 76/207 (the Equal Treatment Directive).[35]

[29] For criticism of this see 889 HC Debs. (26 Mar. 1975), cols. 549, 582, 560, and 585. See also col. 516 for the government's response.

[30] SDA, ss. 43, 44, 7, & 51, and 45, 46, & 52 respectively. Ss. 7 & 51 were narrowed by the SDA 1986 and the Employment Act 1989.

[31] NCCL, n. 7 above, 2. See also 889 HC Debs. (26 Mar. 1975), cols. 538 & 567. That none of these matters were addressed enabled the government of the day to present the Act as a 'no cost' piece of legislation (*ibid.*, col. 516).

[32] N. 7 above, 1.

[33] 889 HC Debs. (26 Mar. 1975), cols. 524–5. See also Dame Shirley Summerskill at 889 HC Debs. (26 Mar. 1975), cols. 615–16.

[34] Roy Jenkins, *ibid.*

[35] C. Hoskyns, *Integrating Gender: Women, Law and Politics in the European Union* (London: Verso, 1996) 105. Hoskyns notes that the Secretary of State was the only woman at the relevant meeting and alone stood out against the inclusion of social security provisions.

Even in those areas which were covered by the Sex Discrimination Act, some discrimination remained lawful. The most significant exclusion from the prohibition on discrimination was that of provisions relating to death or retirement.[36] In addition section 7 set out a variety of cases in which sex would be regarded as a 'genuine occupational qualification' and sections 17 to 21 permitted discrimination (to varying extents) in the cases of police and prison officers, ministers of religion, midwives, and mineworkers.

The provisions concerning mineworkers and midwives have since been repealed, but the exemptions provided in the cases of police and prison officers and ministers of religion remain, as do all but one of the 'genuine occupational qualifications' (GOQs) laid out by section 7. The GOQs, broadly, covered selection for dramatic performance; 'decency or privacy' in jobs where physical contact was required or men [or women] would be exposed to a job holder while undressed or using sanitary facilities; 'live in' jobs where the employer had reasonably failed to provide separate sleeping or sanitation quarters for women [men]; jobs in single sex, caring, or detention institutions in relation to which sex discrimination was reasonable; 'personal services' jobs which could most effectively be provided by a man [woman]; jobs in which there were legal restrictions upon women's employment (this provision was repealed in 1989); jobs likely to involve duties to be performed outside the United Kingdom 'in a country whose laws or customs are such that the duties could not, or could not effectively, be performed by a woman'; and jobs which were 'one of two to be held by a married couple'. The Sex Discrimination Act also excluded from its scope employment in private households and by employers employing no more than five persons.[37]

Although the genuine occupational qualifications applied 'where some of the duties of the job . . . as well as where all of them' fell within the categories listed above, the 1975 Act provided that they did not apply where an employer had sufficient male [female] staff to fulfil those duties without 'undue inconvenience'.[38] Nor, once a woman had been accepted for a job in respect of which a genuine occupational qualification could otherwise have applied, could that GOQ be relied upon by an employer save, if relevant, in relation to promotion, training, or transfer.

The exceptions permitted by the Race Relations Act were considerably narrower than those allowed under the Sex Discrimination Act (in

Her objections 'made no reference to advantages or disadvantages for women, but were based on a purely governmental view of the likely costs and disruption', citing B. Castle, *The Castle Diaries 1974–76* (London: Weidenfeld, 1980), 418–20.

[36] SDA, ss. 6(4), 11(4), & 12(4). These provisions were amended and the original exemption from the provisions of the Act of employers and partnerships of fewer than six persons abolished by SDA 1986, s. 1, in the wake of ECJ rulings against the UK.

[37] SDA, s. 6. The former was narrowed and the latter repealed by the SDA 1986.

[38] SDA, s. 7(3). This did not apply to the last of these categories and (SDA, s. 7(4)), did not apply in either the private household or married couple exceptions.

particular, not extending to retirement ages, pensions, insurance, small employers, or private clubs having at least twenty-five members). In addition to the exclusion from the prohibition of discrimination of acts done under statutory authority[39] and some exceptions covering charities, sports, and national security,[40] GOQs were permitted to cover authenticity in dramatic performance or other entertainment, modelling, restaurant or bar work, and 'personal services', the latter on similar lines to the 1975 Act. The Act did not apply in Northern Ireland[41] nor did it apply (save as regards victimization) to employment in private households—this exclusion, unlike that in the Sex Discrimination Act, remains.[42] The Race Relations Act applied *ab initio* to small employers (with five or fewer employees) but allowed certain public bodies to restrict employment to persons of particular birthplace, nationality, descent, or residence.[43]

(D) RELATIONSHIP WITH THE EQUAL PAY ACT

The Sex Discrimination Act

The new legislation did not, as the NCCL pointed out, substantially improve the existing position in respect of entitlement to equal pay. It did not extend the circumstances in which equal pay could be claimed (in particular, did not entitle women to equal pay for work of equal value), nor did it permit claims in cases where the lack of a comparable man rendered a money-based claim under the Equal Pay Act impossible. Section 6(6) provided that the Sex Discrimination Act's prohibition on discrimination 'does not apply to benefits consisting of the payment of money when the provision of those benefits is regulated by the woman's contract of employment'; and sections 6(5) and 8(3), (4), and (5) provided that the Act did not apply in relation to the terms (whether relating to money or not) upon which jobs were offered or to the (non-monetary) terms of employment if the employer would have been able to establish under the Equal Pay Act that a genuine material factor defence operated.

To the extent that a woman's complaint was concerned with a contractual term relating to money, then, the Sex Discrimination Act did not avail her. But where the contractual term was not one relating to money, or where the money claimed was not connected with a contractual term, a claim could be launched under the Sex Discrimination Act if no comparator was available for an Equal Pay Act claim: the Sex Discrimination

---

[39] RRA, s. 41. This prevented the Act from applying in the immigration field.

[40] RRA, ss. 9, 34, 39, & s. 42. See also RRA, ss. 36 & 6.

[41] On 19 March 1997, Privy Council Assent was granted to the Race Relations (Northern Ireland) Order, which extends the provisions of the 1976 Act to N. Ireland.

[42] RRA, s. 4(3).

[43] See the Race Relations (Prescribed Public Bodies) Reg. 1984, SI 1984/218.

Act, unlike its earlier sister legislation, allowed claims based on the treatment of a hypothetical man.

The Race Relations Act

The Race Relations Act 1976, by contrast, contained no provisions regulating areas of overlap with the Equal Pay Act. The latter Act's failure to address underpayment associated with race had the effect that black and other ethnic minority women could launch race—(as distinct from sex—) based pay claims only under the Race Relations Act. To this end, section 4(2) of the 1976 Act prohibited discrimination 'in the terms of employment' afforded to employees as well as in the terms on which employment was offered. But, judging from the Parliamentary debates surrounding the passage of the Race Relations Bill, little thought was given to the process by which pay discrimination might be addressed. Indeed, leaving aside a brief mention of the problem of unequal pay in the race discrimination White Paper, the issue of pay inequality was not addressed at all in the discussions preceding the 1976 Act. The extent to which the Race Relations Act has, despite this, been used to challenge pay discrimination is addressed below.

(E) ENFORCEMENT AND REMEDIES

The Sex Discrimination and Race Relations Acts provided for enforcement both by the individual alleging discrimination and, in particular circumstances, by the EOC and the CRE, created by the 1975 and 1976 Acts respectively. The remedies open to individuals in respect of employment discrimination were to be awarded, for the most part, by industrial tribunals, and included declarations, compensation orders, and recommendations 'that the respondent take within a specified period action appearing to the tribunal to be practicable for the purpose of obviating or reducing the adverse effect on the complainant of any act of discrimination to which the complaint relates'.[44]

If a complainant succeeded at industrial tribunal the Acts did not provide for the remedies of reinstatement or re-engagement (theoretically the primary remedies in unfair dismissal cases) although they did (until 1993 and 1994 respectively[45]) apply the maximum compensation limit in unfair dismissal cases to compensation for unlawful sex and race discrimination. No award was to be made in those cases where the discrimination established took the indirect form 'if the respondent proves that the requirement or condition in question was not applied with the intention of treating the claimant unfavourably on the ground of his sex or marital status'. But

---

[44] SDA, s. 65; RRA, s. 56.
[45] Sex Discrimination and Equal Pay (Remedies) Regs. 1993 SI 1993/2798; Race Relations (Remedies) Act 1994.

what precisely was meant by 'intention' in this context was not clear. If it required that the treatment be motivated by the sex or marital status of the complainant, it is arguable that the discrimination would better be regarded as direct, albeit covert, discrimination. But if this was the case, no case of indirect discrimination would give rise to compensation.

The matter was not satisfactorily resolved until the decision in 1995 of the Employment Appeal Tribunal in *London Underground* v. *Edwards*, in which that court ruled (in a claim under the Sex Discrimination Act) that an intention to apply the disputed requirement or condition to the complainant, coupled with knowledge of its effect on her as a member of the group upon which the requirement or condition impacted disadvantageously, was sufficient evidence from which an intention to discriminate against her could be inferred.[46] The Sex Discrimination Act was amended within a year to permit compensation for unintentional indirect discrimination[47] but, although the *Edwards* approach has been applied to the Race Relations Act by the EAT in *J. H. Walker* v. *Hussain & Ors.*, no legislative amendment of that Act has taken place and the requirement for intention remains.[48]

The 1975 and 1976 Acts also contained provisions permitting the county (or sheriff) court to revise unlawful discriminatory terms of a contract.[49] Section 6 of the Sex Discrimination Act 1986 provided, further, that any unlawfully discriminatory term of a collective agreement or 'rule made by an employer for application to all or any of the persons who are employed by him or who apply to be, or are, considered by him for employment' would be void.[50] The shortcomings of this provision have been discussed in Chapter 3, together with its amendment by the Trade Union Reform and Employment Rights Act 1993.

(F) THE EOC AND CRE

The individual's legal means of redress, in respect of discrimination in the employment field, lay through the industrial tribunal system (after the normal attempts by the Advisory Conciliation and Arbitration Service (ACAS) to conciliate). But the Sex Discrimination and Race Relations Acts also established, respectively, the EOC and the CRE. These bodies had the power to assist individuals as well as to carry out investigations and to initiate legal action on their own behalf. Such action could include applying for injunctions against 'persistent discrimination' as well as suing

---

[46] [1995] IRLR 355.

[47] The Sex Discrimination and Equal Pay (Miscellaneous Amendments) Regs. 1996, SI 1996 No 438, which came into effect on 26 Mar. of that year.

[48] [1996] IRLR 11.   [49] SDA, s. 77; RRA, s. 72.

[50] SDA 1986, s. 6(1)(b). Deakin and Morris (S. Deakin and G. Morris, *Labour Law* (London: Butterworths, 1995), 576–7) question the compatability of Art. 4(b) of the Equal Treatment Dir. with the abolition of the CAC jurisdiction.

in respect of discriminatory advertisements and instructions and pressure to discriminate.[51]

III. IMPACT OF THE ACTS

(A) INTRODUCTION

The focus of this book is predominantly on the issue of pay, and it is with those matters most closely related to pay that this chapter is concerned in evaluating the Sex Discrimination and Race Relations Acts. In some cases the relationship between the Acts and pay differences will be obvious—if, for example, all women or women from a particular racial group are excluded from all jobs paying more than £X,000 per year, then their overall wage levels will be held down relative to those of men and women of other racial groups respectively. But the relationship is much wider than this: if women's access (or some women's) access, to jobs in some areas is impeded by discrimination, their supply to those jobs which do not discriminate in terms of access will be greater and, as a result, their wages will be depressed.

We saw in Chapter 2 that women (and, in particular, part-time workers) are segregated into a narrower and different range of jobs and industries from those in which men predominate, and that those jobs and industries in which women work tend to pay less than those in which men are found. Deliberate discrimination by employers is not the only form of discrimination which will restrict women's employment (or the employment of women from particular racial groups): sexual and racial harassment are useful mechanisms by which men (white people) can preserve male (white) enclaves; clothing and appearance rules can impact on the perceived status of male and female employees and, as a result, on their relative chances of advancement (or, in the case of women from particular ethnic groups, can preclude their employment); and, perhaps most important of all, the structuring of many jobs as full-time and inflexible (save at the initiative of the employer) excludes most of those women with family responsibilities from access to them.

The position of women in the workplace was the subject of much comment during the passage of the Sex Discrimination Act 1975. Roy Jenkins complained that:

five times as many boys as girls take up apprenticeships. . . . Fewer girls than boys go on to higher education. . . . Less than one seventh of our medical profession are women. Women are a majority in the teaching profession, but, nonetheless, only two fifths of our primary school head teachers are women.[52]

---

[51] SDA, s. 71; RRA, s. 62. SDA, s. 73; RRA, s. 64. SDA, s. 72; RRA, s. 63.
[52] 889 HC Debs. (26 Mar. 1975), col. 512.

Renée Short MP pointed out that there were only

three women on the boards of the main retailing companies in Britain . . . only two women on the boards of the leading 1,000 companies in industry . . . not one woman director or managing director among the top firms . . . less than two per cent of the membership of the Institute of Directors are women . . . women are conspicuous by their absence in the top echelons of industry.[53]

And Roderick McFarquhar remarked that 'only 7.5 per cent of the non-clerical jobs in Whitehall are done by women' and that Britain was '22nd on the international civil service equality table, just below Guatemala and a fraction above Syria'.[54]

It was envisaged in the mid-1970s that the Sex Discrimination Act would reduce sex-segregation. But Renée Short claimed that, without 'a considerable shift in opinion and positive discrimination', 'men were likely to take the majority of top jobs for the next twenty years'.[55] Over twenty years have passed since the implementation of the Sex Discrimination Act, and in that time Short's words have been proven correct. More women have scaled the upper reaches of the employment ladder than was the case during the 1970s. But nothing even remotely resembling equality has yet been achieved.

By 1992, female membership of the Institute of Directors had increased only to 6.5 per cent. In 1971–2 female membership of the Institute of Banking stood at 1.2 per cent, the Law Society at 3.2 per cent, of the Institute of Chartered Accountants of England and Wales at 1.6 per cent, and of the Chartered Institute of Building at 0 per cent. By 1992, female membership had reached 2.5 per cent, 24.5 per cent, 12 per cent, and 1.6 per cent respectively.[56] In 1975 there were only two women on the boards of Britain's leading 1,000 companies and no female directors or managing directors among the top firms. In 1989, only twenty-one of the largest 200 industrial companies in the United Kingdom had women members on their company boards (twenty-four women in all, of which eighteen appointments were as either part-time or non-executive directors[57]). And two years later, Britain's top 100 companies still did not employ a single woman chief executive between them. Women remain conspicuous by their absence from the top.

Nor is it only the very top from which women remain excluded. In 1993–4, women still accounted for only one-fifth of apprentices.[58] Women

---

[53] Ibid., col. 574.   [54] Ibid., col. 566.   [55] Ibid., col. 575.

[56] Of those members of the Law Society with a practising certificate, 33.3% of all members.

[57] V. Hammond and V. Holton, 'The Scenario for Women Managers in Britain in the 1990s' (1993) 23 International Studies of Management & Organization 71.

[58] 'Women and Training: Data from the Labour Force Survey', Employment Gazette, Nov. 1994, 391. The same point is made by D. Meulders, R. Plasman, and V. Vander Stricht, Position of Women on the Labour Market of the EC (Aldershot: Dartmouth, 1993), 116 on Irish youth wages.

have closed the gap with men in terms of education and now account for 40 per cent of doctors (almost three times their proportion in 1975), but they still account for a mere 17 per cent of NHS hospital consultants (as few as 4 per cent of surgeons), just over half of primary school and only 30 per cent of secondary school headteachers[59] (but 81 per cent and 49 per cent of primary and secondary school *teachers* respectively). Although far more women are now employed in the Civil Service than were in 1975, in 1987 women accounted for 75 per cent of clerical assistants (the lowest-paid grade in the Civil Service), 37 per cent of executive officers (the lowest level of management), and a mere fifty (5 per cent) of the 1,000 posts in the top four management grades.[60]

Some women have made significant gains in the years since the implementation of the Sex Discrimination Act. It may be that their progress was due in part to the existence of anti-discrimination legislation. But in general only a very particular type of woman scales the higher reaches of the job ladder—we saw in Chapter 2 that success is frequently limited to childless women who have been able, like many men, to pursue their careers unimpeded by the demands of motherhood. The wider picture which emerges when the position of women in the workforce is considered is, again as we saw in Chapter 2, one of segregation both in terms of occupation and also in terms of industrial sector. When part-time women workers are considered separately from full-time women a yet more segregated pattern emerges. And even when relatively mixed industrial sectors or occupational groups are considered, segregation at the workplace and job levels is extremely pronounced.[61]

What of ethnic minority women? Neither the debates concerning the Sex Discrimination Act nor those which preceeded the passage of the Race Relations Act contained reference specifically to the labour market position of black and other ethnic minority women. The White Paper on race discrimination did recognize that 'coloured' women, while less likely than white women to be employed, were proportionately more concentrated in full-time employment, that they were 'more heavily concentrated in the lower socio-economic groups, more likely to combine full-time work with having dependent children, and that they worked longer hours than white women'. But with this exception the White Paper did not specifically address the problems faced by ethnic minority women. And the only discussion of ethnic minority women in the Parliamentary debates consisted of Enoch Powell's warnings about their tendency to produce more children than white women; Iain Dudley-Smith's concerns about West Indian

---

[59] 58 *Equal Opportunities Review* 6–7, 54% of paediatric consultants.

[60] Hammond and Holton, n. 57 above.

[61] See N. Millward and S. Woodland, *Gender Segregation and Male/Female Wage Differences* (London, LSE Centre for Economic Performance, 1995), Discussion Paper No 220; J. Martin and C. Roberts, *Women and Employment: A Lifetime Perspective* (London: HMSO, 1984). Occupational segregation at the workplace level is far more pronounced: 63% of women and 80% of men worked in jobs done only by their own sex.

women's production of illegitimate children and their subsequent immigration claims; and Michael Alison's complaint that many 'West Indian mothers go out to work not just part-time but whole-time, leaving many West Indian children alone for long periods'.[62] The employment prospects, much less the relative pay, of ethnic minority women were evidently not at the forefront of legislators' minds.

(B) CHANGES IN OCCUPATIONAL AND INDUSTRIAL SEGREGATION

Women have increased their representation throughout the workforce as a whole quite considerably (from about eight million to just over ten and a half) since the implementation of the 1975 Act. All else being equal, it might be expected that this increase would have taken place across the board, both in terms of industries and occupations. Tables 5.1 and

Table 5.1 — changes in the proportion of women by occupation 1971–2000

	1971	1981	1991	2000*
corporate managers and administrators	17.2%	20.3%	30.5%	39.6%
managers/ employers in agriculture and services	25.0%	27.7%	33.0%	34.2%
science and engineering professionals	2.5%	6.1%	9.8%	13.4%
health professionals	23.3%	25.2%	35.0%	39.3%
teaching professionals	54.3%	58.0%	61.1%	63.1%
other professional occupations	17.7%	21.7%	32.3%	34.2%
science and engineering associate professionals	10.8%	15.2%	22.5%	29.9%
health associate professionals	86.4%	87.9%	88.4%	88.3%
other associate professional occupations	23.7%	28.5%	38.9%	44.0%
clerical occupations	56.5%	63.5%	68.5%	72.3%
secretarial occupations	96.2%	95.9%	96.6%	95.7%
skilled construction trades	0.5%	1.0%	1.3%	1.4%
skilled engineering trades	2.1%	1.7%	2.0%	2.3%
other skilled trades	21.6%	18.3%	17.3%	12.0%
protective service occupations	7.3%	12.4%	15.6%	14.6%
personal services occupations	72.7%	75.6%	78.2%	78.9%
buyers, brokers, and sales representatives	10.1%	14.4%	24.0%	28.7%
other sales occupations	72.3%	77.5%	79.3%	79.8%
industrial plant and machine operatives, etc.	34.9%	32.2%	29.3%	22.3%
drivers and mobile machine operatives	4.2%	3.7%	5.1%	4.9%
other occupations in agriculture, etc.	22.8%	21.8%	22.9%	21.3%
other elementary occupations	41.9%	52.1%	56.3%	54.8%

source: Lindley and Wilson[63]
* projected

---

[62] At 906 HC Debs. (4 Mar. 1976), cols. 1582 ff and. 1582–94 and 914 HC Debs. (8 July 1976), col. 1661 respectively. See also Alison at 906 HC Debs. (4 Mar. 1976), cols. 1650 ff.
[63] R. Lindley and R. Wilson (eds.), *Review of the Economy and Employment 1992/3: Occupational Assessment* (Coventry: Institute for Employment Research, University of Warwick,

Table 5.2 — changes in the proportion of women by industrial sector 1971–2000

	1971	1981	1991	1995*	2000*
agriculture	14.8%	14.4%	14.8%	14.5%	14.5%
mining etc.	4.3%	5.7%	8.9%	10.0%	10.1%
utilities	15.9%	20.0%	23.5%	22.7%	22.6%
metals, minerals, etc.	15.5%	16.2%	16.6%	16.8%	16.7%
chemicals	26.9%	27.4%	30.4%	31.0%	31.0%
engineering	22.0%	20.6%	20.5%	20.2%	20.1%
food, drink, and tobacco	39.4%	39.9%	40.4%	39.9%	40.0%
textiles and clothing	60.0%	60.3%	57.8%	58.7%	58.9%
other manufacturing	29.5%	29.0%	29.2%	28.3%	28.1%
construction	5.0%	7.5%	8.6%	8.3%	8.3%
distribution etc.	43.6%	46.4%	46.9%	46.3%	46.4%
transport and communication	15.7%	18.2%	20.6%	20.9%	21.1%
banking, insurance, etc.	41.4%	43.4%	44.1%	43.6%	43.5%
miscellaneous services	48.7%	54.5%	53.1%	53.5%	53.5%
health and education	70.3%	72.4%	74.3%	75.0%	74.7%
public administration	33.0%	38.0%	41.1%	42.0%	43.0%
manufacturing	29.4%	28.2%	28.4%	28.2%	28.0%
whole economy	34.4%	38.4%	41.5%	42.2%	43.1%

source: Lindley and Wilson[64]
* projected

5.2 indicate the changes which have occurred in the sex composition of occupations and industries since 1975. The categories used are slightly different from those employed in Chapter 2 and the overall proportion of women in the economy is considerably lower on these figures than that reported in that chapter. Nevertheless, the important issue here is the comparison of the data over time rather than any comparison between these figures and those in Chapter 2.

Occupational Segregation

Changes in occupational segregation have occurred in the wake of the Sex Discrimination Act. Of the twenty-two occupational groups featured, women accounted for a larger proportion of nineteen groups in 1991 than they did in 1971 and will account for a larger proportion of eighteen in 2000, according to projections, than in 1971. In only three and four groups respectively do (or will) women account for a lower proportion

1993) reproduced in R. Wilson, 'Sectoral and Occupational Change: Prospects for Women's Employment' in R. Lindley (ed.) *Labour Market Structures and Prospects for Women* (Manchester: EOC, 1994), 25.

[64] *Ibid.*

of employees in 1991 and in 2000 than in 1971, prior to the passage of the Act.

In 1971, women accounted for a disproportionately high number of those in seven of the occupational groups (a proportionate number only of those in one group—industrial plant and machine operatives—and a disproportionately low number of those in the remaining fourteen). Between 1971 and 1991 women's dominance of these seven occupations increased substantially, their average representation rising from 68.6 per cent to 75.5 per cent. The projected figures for 2000 suggest that that trend will continue.[65]

Women have also increased their level of representation in male-dominated occupational groups. In 1971, the average representation of women among the fourteen male-dominated occupations listed in table 5.1 was a mere 13.5 per cent. By 1991 that proportion had increased to 20.7 per cent and by 2000 it is expected to have reached 22.8 per cent. This is an improvement upon the position in 1971 but, particularly given the significant increase in women in the economy as a whole (from 34.4 per cent in 1971 to a projected 43.1 per cent in 2000), is hardly spectacular. And, despite improvements in occupational categories such as management, health, and 'other' professionals and 'other' associate professionals, women remain very under-represented (achieving less than two-thirds of their expected proportion) in many jobs, notable among them professional and associate professional jobs in science and engineering, all the skilled trades and protective service occupations. While the position in the former two categories has improved somewhat since 1971 (and is expected to continue so to do), women account for a lower proportion of those working in the skilled trades now than they did then, and their representation in the protective service occupations, though up from 1971, is expected to decline.

Even in those cases where women make advances into previously male-dominated occupations, the resulting reduction in sex segregation may occur only at the broad occupational level. It was pointed out in Chapter 2 that the real pattern of segregation is considerably more pronounced than is apparent at the level of these broad occupational and industrial groupings. Categories such as 'management', 'professional occupations', 'sales', and 'personal services' hide a variety of sex-segregated sub-categories. This point is addressed to some extent by table 5.1 which distinguishes a number of sub-categories. But neither it nor table 5.2 illustrates the extent to which women managers are clustered in poorly paying sectors such as management and proprietorship in service industries (in which women managers earned only 73 per cent of the average male hourly wage, 85 per cent of the average hourly rate for non-manual women workers,

---

[65] 76.1% in 2000.

in 1995[66]), or the extent to which women in banking are to be found predominantly at the bottom of the job hierarchies.

Across the board, women are typically to be found in positions subordinate to those which men occupy. In 1994, for example, women accounted for 44 per cent of personnel managers but only 9.5 per cent of personnel directors.[67] This pattern is true of women managers generally. Whereas, in 1993, women accounted for 13 per cent of senior staff in the National Management Survey (this being the lowest level of management), their representation declined with seniority and they comprised just under 13 per cent of section leaders, less than 9 per cent of section and department managers and 7 per cent of function heads respectively, fewer than 5 per cent of senior function heads and 3 per cent of directors, under 2 per cent of Deputy Chief Executives, and less than 1 per cent of Chief Executives. These figures did constitute an improvement since 1973, when less than 1 per cent of directors or function heads, less than 2 per cent of department heads, and under 3 per cent of function heads were women.[68] But the rate of progress could hardly be described as breath-taking.

We saw, above, that the situation is particularly poor at the very top of the ladder. The chief executives and company boards of Britain's top companies are almost exclusively male. In the NHS in 1993, women comprised 69 per cent of 'first-line' managers in the NHS, 55 per cent of middle managers, and 47 per cent of senior managers, and the same picture prevails in the Civil Service.[69] What is true of management is true also in the professions and elsewhere. The situation which prevails among school teachers and doctors has already been described. In 1990, women held 25 per cent of university lecturerships but a mere 5 per cent of chairs.[70] And in 1992, 60 per cent of men solicitors but less than 30 per cent of women were partners, less than 25 per cent of men but 60 per cent of women were assistant solicitors.[71]

The movement of women into corporate management and administration, into professional and associate professional jobs in science and engineering, into jobs as buyers, brokers, and sales representatives, may well be a movement into jobs in which women remain subordinate to men or, at any rate, in which they are denied the bureaucratic status and power exercised by men. In his study of women in banking Michael Savage found that, whereas male managers tended directly to exercise control and/or authority over others, women managers were characterized

[66] NES, tables 74, 75, 86, & 87. This sector accounts for 23% of all full-time women managers, according to NES 1995, table 87, but only 15% of men (table 86).

[67] Survey of 407 companies carried out by Sedgwick Noble Lowndes, reported in 57 *Equal Opportunities Review*, 4.

[68] 1993 National Management Survey reported in EOC, *Women and Men in Britain 1993*, 25.

[69] *Ibid.*   [70] EOC, n. 68 above, 29.   [71] *Ibid.*, 27.

(in common with professionals generally[72]) by the possession of expertise rather than organizational power: 'the increasing numbers of *expert* women in the labour market should not be seen as evidence that women are moving into positions of organizational authority and control, but rather that, as organisations restructure, there is increased room for women to be employed in special niches'.[73]

That this is true more generally is suggested by 1992 statistics on women in management and the professions. Whereas, in that year, women accounted for 32 per cent of all managers, their representation varied from less than 2 per cent of general managers and administrators to around 30 per cent of specialist managers.[74] Commentators including Rubery and Fagan have argued that women's entry into a number of previously high status occupations has been accompanied by a decline in the status and wages associated with those occupations. Rubery and Fagan conducted case studies in relation to teachers, computer professionals, bank clerical workers, civil service administrative and clerical staff, catering workers, and drivers. They reported that:

[s]everal of the case studies yielded examples where women had increased their share of high level jobs precisely at a time of relative downgrading of the pay and status of the occupation. . . . Evidence of changes in the occupational sex mix does not necessarily imply a move towards integration but may herald the development of new occupational subdivisions or indeed a long-term, trend towards feminisation.[75]

In the United States, too, 'the growing number of women who have the title of manager are concentrated lower in chains of command than men are and tend not to supervise men' and, according to one study among a cross-section of workers:

women managers participated in decision making by gathering information and making recommendations but . . . men usually made the final decision . . . men more often had the authority to make decisions about bread-and-butter issues like hiring, firing, promoting and giving raises and were more likely to have had a say in decisions that affected other units. The large number of relatively powerless female managers has led some researchers to question whether women's increasing representation in managerial occupations represents genuine progress, or is what Jerry Jacobs termed the 'glorified secretary' phenomenon, in which employers

[72] See R. Crompton, 'Occupational Trends and Women's Employment Patterns' in R. Lindley n. 63 above, 43.
[73] M. Savage, 'Women's Expertise, Men's Authority: Gendered Organisation and the Contemporary Middle Classes' in M. Savage and A. Witz (eds.), *Gender and Bureaucracy* (Oxford: Blackwell, 1992). Cited by Crompton, n. 63 above, 49.
[74] EOC, n. 62 above, 25.
[75] J. Rubery and C. Fagan, 'Occupational Segregation: *Plus Ça Change . . . ?*' in Lindley, n. 63 above, 36–40.

bestow managerial titles on women but not the responsibilities and authority that usually accompany the titles.[76]

Increases in Female Occupations

Rubery and Fagan also point out that, while '[w]omen have been increasing their share of higher level occupations . . . at the same time female labour has been piling up in more traditional feminised areas'.[77] Much of the growth in female employment can be attributed to expansion of characteristically female occupations. Whereas, between 1971 and 1991, the number of workers employed in craft and related jobs and as plant and machine operatives plummeted by well over a million in each case, the total number of managers and administrators, professionals, and those with associate professional and technical jobs increased in the order of a million, a million, and three quarters of a million respectively. In addition, there were more moderate increases in the numbers of clerical and secretarial workers, those in personal and protective services, and in sales (around 100,000, 500,000, and 300,000 respectively). While increases in the first three categories of workers were shared between men and women, those in the latter tended to be largely the result of expanded female employment. Again, if we consider the proportion of women in each of these occupational groups (taking into account table 2.10) we can see that, with the exception of managerial and administrative jobs, all those occupations which experienced growth between 1971 and 1991 were predominantly female, while the two main losers were very strongly male. Only 'other occupations' bucked this trend with a significant decline (over 500,000 jobs between 1971 and 1991) and a predominantly female workforce.

Changes in Industrial Segregation

Turning now to the question of industrial segregation, we can see from table 5.2 that women were disproportionately represented (relative to their role in the workforce as a whole) in only six sectors of a total sixteen in 1971. Five of these six sectors remained female-dominated in 1995, the average proportion of women in the female-dominated sectors increasing from 50.6 per cent to 52.8 per cent. Matters are expected to remain fairly static until 2000 (public administration becoming slightly female dominated but things otherwise remaining stable).

Not a great deal has changed, in terms of female-dominated industries, since 1971. As far as male-dominated industries are concerned, women

---

[76] B. Reskin and I. Padavik, *Women and Men at Work* (Thousand Oaks: Pine Forge Press, 1994), 94–5 citing B. Reskin, and C. Ross 'Jobs, Authority, and Earnings Among Managers: The Continuing Significance of Sex' (1992) 19 *Work and Occupations* 342 and J. Jacobs, 'Long-Term Trends in Occupational Segregation By Sex' (1992) 95 *American Journal of Sociology* 160.

[77] N. 75 above.

increased their representation in the eight male-dominated industries from 15 per cent to 18 per cent between 1971 and 1991, and the number of industries in which men accounted for at least 80 per cent of workers declined from six to four. Some changes have occurred. But, just as was the case in relation to occupations, much of the growth in female employment can be explained in terms of the expansion of predominantly female industrial sectors rather than in any mass movement of women into previously male-dominated industries. The growth that there has been in female employment can be seen from table 5.2 to have been concentrated primarily in the services sector, while in the manufacturing sector as a whole, and in four of the six sub-sectors therein, the proportion of women in the workforce actually declined between 1971 and 1993 with further declines projected to 1995 and 2000.

Increases in Female Industries

Between 1971 and 1991 the distribution etc., business services, miscellaneous services, and health and education sectors experienced considerable growth (over one and a half million workers in the case of business services, at least a million workers in the others) while all other sectors either remained constant (construction) or reduced either very greatly (engineering, which lost in the region of a million and a half workers) or less dramatically. Not only do women account for a substantial proportion of the workers in sectors such as distribution etc., business and miscellaneous services, and health and education (46.9 per cent, 44.1 per cent, 53.1 per cent, and 74.3 per cent in 1991) but these sectors are also large and account for a huge proportion (as many as 75 per cent[78]) of women. By contrast, the sectors which have experienced decline since 1971 have largely been those dominated by male workers (79.5 per cent of the engineering sector in 1991, 83.4 per cent of those in metals, minerals etc., 85.2 per cent of those in agriculture, and 91.1 per cent of those in mining, etc.) over 55 per cent of whom were, even in 1995, employed in these declining sectors.

Tables 5.3 and 5.4 show the changes in the number of those employed in the various industrial sectors between 1975 and 1995.

Once again, the categories utilized here differ from those in Chapter 2, but the changes over time are evident.

It is clear that women have been the beneficiaries, in terms of employment opportunities, of the changes which have taken place since 1975. The increase in the workforce which has taken place in that time has been entirely due to increased female employment. Not only have female full-time jobs increased by half-a-million, but fully one-and-a-half million full-time (male) workers have been replaced with part-time (female) employees.

[78] In 1995—see table 2.6, but only around 47% of men.

Table 5.3 — distribution of employees across industrial sectors, 1995

industrial sector	all (000s)	men	full-time women	part-time women
agriculture, hunting, and forestry	230	180	30	20
electricity and water supply	280	220	50	10
other mineral and ore extraction	560	420	120	20
metal and engineering	1,860	1,470	320	70
other manufacturing	1,840	1,100	570	170
construction	840	710	80	60
distribution, hotels, catering, etc.	4,560	2,090	910	1,560
transport and communication	1,180	890	210	80
banking, finance, and insurance	2,750	1,370	1,020	380
other	6,950	2,210	2,230	2,510
public administration and defence	1,280	670	410	190
education	1,860	530	600	730
health	1,570	290	600	690
total	21,050	10,650	5,520	4,880

source: LFS 1995, table 1.4[79]

Table 5.4 — changes by industrial sector, 1975–1995

industrial sector	all (000s)	men	full-time women	part-time women
agriculture, hunting, and forestry	−160	−110	−30	−20
gas, electricity, and water supply	−60	−60	n/c	n/c
other mineral and ore extraction etc.	−760	−700	−40	−20
metal and engineering	−1,470	−1,110	−270	−100
other manufacturing	−1,200	−700	−350	−150
construction	−430	−460	+20	+30
distribution etc.	+1,840	+890	+160	+800
transport and communication (not storage)	−310	−320	n/c	−20
banking, finance, and insurance	+1,660	+840	+620	+220
other	+1,330	+160	+440	+730
public administration and defence	−330	−320	−30	+20
education	+80	+110	+50	+70
health	+350	n/c	+50	+300
total	+460	−1,580	+520	+1,510

source: British Labour Statistics 1975, table 56 and LFS 1995, table 1.4[80]

[79] Figs. are rounded up.
[80] Department of Employment. The figures are rounded up and some categories have changed during the period—maximum consistency has been retained but gas was included

But these replacements have not been direct substitutions of male by female employees as discrimination against women has declined: rather, these jobs were created in areas which were already predominantly female. This 'replacement' had in fact begun well in advance of the implementation of anti-discrimination legislation, a 1977 Department of Employment study noting that, between 1967 and 1975, the female workforce had increased by almost 900,000 (this being composed entirely of part-time workers in the service sector[81]). Since 1975, too, with a few very minor exceptions, men and women within any particular sector have experienced similar rates of growth or reduction. But the sectors which have experienced the greatest decline (electricity and water supply, other mineral and ore extraction, and metal and engineering) have been strongly male-dominated in employee terms, while those which have increased (distribution, hotels and catering; banking, insurance, and finance; and 'other') have (with the exception of banking etc. which is mixed) been predominantly female.

(C) IMPACT OF OCCUPATIONAL AND INDUSTRIAL CHANGE

There has been some improvement in the position of women in the labour market over the past two decades. A number of women have moved into relatively highly-paid jobs and, as we saw in Chapter 4, have contributed thereby to the reduction in the gender–pay gap. But for very many other women the picture is considerably bleaker. While the expansion of female-dominated occupations and sectors is good for women's overall employment levels, the quality of the jobs provided by them needs to be addressed. We have already seen that the increase in the numbers of women in management occupations has been associated with declining pay and status levels in those occupations. A similar pattern emerges in the expanding industrial sectors: the largest areas of expansion for female employment since 1975 (banking, finance etc.; distribution, hotels, catering, etc.; education and health) rank second, eleventh and thirteenth, first and sixth respectively in the hierarchy of female wages (see table 2.20).[82] The bulk of the increase for full-time women workers has taken place in banking, finance etc., in which they earn about 90 per cent of the average wage earned by all men.[83] This factor may well explain part of the increase

with electricity and water in 1975, transport and communication did not include storage then but did thereafter, distribution did not then include hotels and restaurants (which were in 'other') but did thereafter.

[81] There was a decline of over 300,000 women in manufacturing and an increase of 1.2 million in services. No substitution of men by women took place—the reverse in fact occurred in manufacturing—see Hornstein, n. 8 above.

[82] 'Eleventh and thirteenth' refer to the separate categories of distribution and hotels and catering.

[83] In education the figure is about 120%, in health, 80%, and in distribution etc. a much poorer 50–60% (trade, vehicles repair, and hotels and restaurants respectively)—the average for all women is about 80%.

in women's average pay, relative to that of men, which has taken place since 1975. But the picture for part-time women workers is much bleaker —the increase in their numbers has taken place largely in distribution, etc., in which they earn only between 40 and 50 per cent of all men's average hourly wage.[84] The movement of women part-time workers into these badly paid sectors may help to explain why their wages have so little improved in the twenty years since the implementation of the Equal Pay Act.

(D) ETHNIC MINORITY WOMEN

Prior to the passage of the Race Relations Act, ethnic minority women were segregated into a narrow range of those occupational and industrial positions in which women more generally were found.[85] This, as we saw in Chapter 2, remains the case. Statistics did not exist, and still do not exist, relating to the number of ethnic minority women members of the Institute of Directors, the Institute of Banking, or the Law Society, or to the numbers of ethnic minority women on the boards of Britain's leading companies. But the number of ethnic minority women who occupy leading public positions is so small that the majority of these women can be individually named with relative ease.

Changes which have occurred since the implementation of the Race Relations Act are, given the relatively small numbers of employees frequently involved and the paucity of material on race in much of the statistical information available, difficult to trace. Reena Bhavnani recently reported that 'there has been little change in the position of black men and women regarding their segregation into lower status, lower paid jobs'.[86] There has been an increase in the number of ethnic minority women employed in the professional/manager/employer class (although ethnic minority women are still under-represented in this class in comparison to white women).[87] But, in common with the picture for women more generally, ethnic minority women tend to be concentrated on the lower rungs, and there is evidence that their movement into these positions (and into sectors such as finance, computing, and banking) has coincided with a down-grading and resegregation process:[88]

---

[84] Table 2.6.

[85] See C. Brown, *Black and White in Britain* (London: Policy Studies Institute, 1984).

[86] R. Bhavnani, *Black Women in the Labour Market: A Research Review* (Manchester: EOC, 1994), 73 citing C. Hakim, *Occupational Segregation: A Comparative Study* (London: Department of Employment, 1979), Research Paper No 9 and Brown, n. 85 above.

[87] Bhavnani, n. 86 above, citing I. Breugel, 'Sex and Race in the Labour Market' (1983) 32 *Feminist Review* 49, 74. See also I. Breugel, 'Labour Market Prospects For Women from Ethnic Minorities' in Lindley, n. 63 above, 61—Breugel claims that ethnic minority women are more likely to be in manual work and less likely to be in professional jobs in the late 1980s than they were a decade before.

[88] Bhavnani, n. 86 above, 76 citing studies for the CRE on teaching, by the King's Fund on doctors and local government evidence.

[d]isadvantaged groups largely increased their access to the professions through the creation of a large number of jobs in professions that were deteriorating in power, prestige, income and authority. . . . The increasing mobility of the black middle class has been explained by the fact that it now serviced the poor and minority populations that had previously been underserved or unserved by white professionals. . . . Many of these areas are highly vulnerable to government funding cuts.[89]

Just as the concentration of ethnic minority (in particular, black) women within the public sector has rendered them especially vulnerable to the impact of government policies such as contracting-out (and, in general, to the employment effects of public expenditure constraints[90]); so, too, the concentration of Asian women in the manufacturing sector (in particular, in textiles, clothing, and footwear) has rendered them especially vulnerable to the job losses and reduced wages which have resulted from the decline of manufacturing over recent decades.[91] Irene Breugel reported, in 1994, that 'ethnic minority women are found to a disproportionate extent in occupations that are in decline and are underrepresented in growth areas' and forecast that, while white women would experience a 9 per cent employment growth to 2000, ethnic minority women could expect their employment prospects to remain static in numerical terms.[92] As Breugel pointed out, the decline in those sectors traditionally responsible for employing large numbers of ethnic minority women might not itself result in an overall drop in the number of ethnic minority women in employment, but might, instead, prompt their movement into those jobs (particularly in the contracted-out parts of the public sector) whose terms and conditions have been reduced by the impact of structural changes in the labour market.

IV. 'CHOICE' OR DISCRIMINATION?

It is one thing, of course, to assert that women's position in the workplace has remained relatively unaltered over the last twenty years and that such changes that have taken place have not been entirely positive. It is another matter to claim that this apparent stasis is the result of discrimination (whether on grounds of race or sex).

[89] *Ibid.*, citing US evidence from N. Sokoloff, *Black Women and White Women in the Professions* (London, New York: Routledge, 1992).
[90] See Ch. 2 for the discussion of the effect of CCT. Breugel, n. 87 above, 67 cites evidence that this has impacted in particular on ethnic minority women: 'the cost of labour market policies may not always show up in increased unemployment for ethnic minority groups; it can take the form of a shift towards ethnic minorities in the profile of poor quality women's employment'.
[91] Between 1970 and 1983, over 320,000 women's jobs (out of a total 620,000) were lost in these sectors alone—Bhavnani, n. 86 above, 72.
[92] N. 87 above, 65–6.

If the differences which persist are the result of discrimination, one might justifiably query whether the employment provisions of the Sex Discrimination and Race Relations Acts can be regarded as having been successful. If, on the other hand, they are the result of different inclinations on the part of men and women, or of women of different racial groups, the only criticism which could be aimed at the Acts, if any criticism were due, would concern the education provisions which might be accused of failing adequately to combat the social stereotyping of male and female, black and white, roles. Even such criticism might be undeserved, in the context of the 1975 Act, if women were, as Ivor Stanbrook suggested, merely complying with 'human nature'.[93]

But it cannot be assumed that the job segregation which remains is the product of women's choices. There is abundant evidence that employers discriminate in hiring workers, both in deciding to take them on at all and in allocating them to particular jobs. Whether the discrimination is motivated by 'taste' (views about whether women, or particular women, should work, and, if so, what jobs they are suited to); statistics (where lack of information about individuals' propensities to quit, slack, etc. causes employers to reach decisions on the basis of the real or perceived propensities of the 'group' to which the individual belongs[94]); or concern over the prejudices of clients or fellow employees; not all employers wish to recruit women, or to recruit them for particular types of job.

One study carried out in 1973, prior to the implementation of the Sex Discrimination Act, found that 89 per cent of the establishments surveyed (which together employed over 100,000 staff) never used women for transport jobs, 63 per cent never used them for skilled manual work, and 47 per cent never employed women as managers. Sixty-two per cent of those who were to be responsible for the formulation of equal opportunities policies thought there were 'jobs in the establishment which *no* woman could do, compared with 14.4 per cent who think there are jobs which

---

[93] 893 HC Debs. (18 June 1975), col. 1611.

[94] See F. Blau, 'Occupational Segregation and Labour Market Discrimination' in B. Reskin (ed.), *Sex Segregation in the Workplace: Trends, Explanations, Remedies* (Washington, DC: National Academy Press, 1984), 122; C. Goldin, *Understanding the Gender Gap* (New York: Oxford University Press, 1991); L. Larwood, E. Szwajkowski, and S. Rose, 'When Discrimination Makes Sense: The Rational Bias Theory' in B. Gutek, A. Stromberg, and L. Larwood (eds.), *Women and Work: An Annual Review* (Newbury Park, Cal.: Sage Publications, 1988) iii; B. Chiplin and P. Sloane, *Tackling Discrimination in the Workplace* (Cambridge: Cambridge University Press, 1982). Larwood *et al.* found strong evidence of statistical discrimination from a number of US studies. Chiplin and Sloane provided evidence that this type of discrimination was practised very overtly prior to the 1975 Sex Discrimination Act—employers frequently used sex, in their dealings with job centres, to 'screen' employees. Men are commonly seen as more 'reliable', at least in terms of staying power, than are women, though no such generalizations are supported by the evidence. Chiplin and Sloane report that, after the implementation of the Sex Discrimination Act 1975, factors such as pay rates and overtime demands were used as 'covert' and increasingly common signals as to the sex of particular jobs.

no man could do. The range of jobs named was very much wider for women than for men'.[95]

This survey predated the 1975 Act. But relatively little has changed in the intervening years. Numerous studies have demonstrated determined and persistent discrimination on the part of employers. Among these studies was one carried out in 1983–5 by David Collinson for the EOC. Concerned specifically with self-proclaimed 'equal opportunities employers' in a variety of sectors, the study uncovered high levels of discrimination in recruitment and promotion. Collinson found that sex discrimination in selection decisions was masked by reference to the issues of *stability*, *flexibility*, and *compatibility*, these factors being applied to favour male or female candidates in line with the sex stereotyping of the job:

the apparently gender-neutral selection criteria . . . are in fact so subjective, impressionistic and vague that they can be used to justify a specific preference for either men or women. Whether women were excluded or preferred, selectors usually explained their choices by either *blaming* women, employees or customers, or by emphasising how women were the *beneficiaries* of gender preferences . . . job sex-typing and candidate stereotyping were often found to be self-fulfilling and self-confirming in their effects on the selection process.[96]

Collinson found that predetermined gender preferences:

were . . . retained regardless of candidates' interview performance . . . highly qualified interviewees who performed well were rejected in favour of candidates with lower qualifications who were less impressive at interview. . . . Even where unsuccessful candidates articulated appropriate answers, for example when women expressed career aspirations, these were treated with scepticism or dismissed in favour of the stereotypes which selectors believed to be more reliable.[97]

Collinson highlighted the consistent emphasis placed on men as breadwinners and women as secondary earners and the frequent denial of jobs to women on the basis of their perceived unreliability.[98] The refusal to employ women persisted even where, as in sales, employers were faced with serious shortages of candidates for 'male' posts, and the insistence on women's unreliability remained in the face of evidence to the contrary.[99] Employers in banking frequently viewed women as 'girls' who were looking for 'jobs' rather than 'careers'.[100] And in the insurance field, 'while men are often channelled into relatively autonomous fields . . . women in insurance tend to be recruited for, and restricted to, the office equivalent of domestic work'.[101] Collinson concluded that:

[95] A. Hunt, *Management Attitudes and Practices Towards Women at Work* (London: HMSO, 1975), Office of Population Censuses and Surveys, 22.
[96] D. Collinson, *Barriers to Fair Selection: A Multi-Sector Study of Recruitment Practices* (London: HMSO, 1988), EOC Research Series, 33.
[97] *Ibid.*, 69.   [98] *Ibid.*   [99] *Ibid.*, 150 & 170.   [100] *Ibid.*, 126.
[101] *Ibid.*, 188–9.

UNIVERSITY OF WINCHESTER LIBRARY

despite anti-discrimination legislation . . . a substantial number of employers, many of whom publicly subscribe to equal opportunities, are still 'managing to discriminate' on the grounds of sex through a variety of recruitment practices . . . job segregation is a central, if often taken-for-granted, aspect of management's control of the labour process.[102]

Margaret Curren also carried out research for the EOC in 1984.[103] She focused on recruitment to clerical and retail occupations which were not strongly sex-typed and which were, as a result, expected to attract both male and female applicants. Curran found, despite employers' awareness of her EOC links and the lack of any prompting on her part on the issue of sex, that the sex and family circumstances of potential recruits featured highly among the list of attributes sought. In all, two-thirds of recruiters for retail jobs and a third of those for clerical jobs expressed a clear preference for applicants of a particular sex. Sex was the fifth most important attribute (of eighteen) in retailing and the tenth in clerical appointments, while family and domestic commitments assumed first and third place respectively. And even where employers were not concerned about the sex of the applicants for the particular job in respect of which the research was carried out, 'most . . . gave indications that they would not regard such preferences as illegitimate'.[104]

Curran found that the initial sex-typing of jobs was related to their wage level and promotion prospects and to whether they afforded access to a pension: ' "[f]emale" jobs were twice as likely as "male" vacancies to be "dead end jobs" . . . "female" jobs were generally found to offer lower rates of pay, inferior pension provisions and lesser prospects of promotion than "male" jobs, and in clerical work they were concentrated in smaller establishments'.[105]

The initial sex-typing of jobs was carried through the advertising, short-listing, and interview stages and 'only a minority of recruitment decisions ultimately resulted in the change of a vacant post from a man's job to a woman's job or vice versa'.[106] Taken together (and even in the absence of an articulated employer sex preference), the promotion prospects, pay, gender of supervisor (where the supervisor was a woman) and of colleagues (where those colleagues were male and of the same grade) composed a 'reasonably reliable indicator (77 per cent accurate) basis for predicting whether the outcome of the recruitment process would be the appointment of a woman or a man'.[107]

[102] Collinson, n. 96 above, 192.

[103] M. Curran, *Stereotypes and Selection: Gender and Family in the Recruitment Process* (London: HMSO, 1985), EOC Report.

[104] *Ibid.*, 22.

[105] *Ibid.*, 24–5. Pension provision was 79%:59% male: female; promotion prospects as expected job characteristic 36%:18%.

[106] *Ibid.*, 47.   [107] *Ibid.*, 49.

Curran's and Collinson's studies are supported by findings made by Alice Scott in retailing and by Crompton and Sanderson in the finance sector.[108] Millward and Woodland reported in 1994 that the levels of sex segregation evident from the Workplace Industrial Relations Survey (WIRS) (50 per cent of workplaces employed only male semi-skilled workers, and two-thirds only male skilled workers[109]) were such that 'we cannot say that employers' hiring practices approximate a random process with respect to gender'.[110] And studies recently conducted in the fields of medicine, law, NHS administration and science, academia, and printing all point to the continuing practice of discrimination in recruitment.[111] Spender and Podmore found that women lawyers were excluded from both formal and informal activities and marginalized by way of a 'more or less conscious and explicit set of assumptions' (in particular, relating to the impact of childbearing on women's continued employment) held by male lawyers. Women's jobs were generally 'lower status, less financially rewarding, less demanding and less "visible"' than those of their male colleagues.[112]

Hilary Homans found that women scientists in the NHS did not have the same job opportunities as were open to men, even when they worked in the same jobs. In common with lawyers, women scientists were disadvantaged by the assumption that they would leave permanently on childbirth. And the view was also often held that male and female scientists had different 'skills' (given that the upper hierarchy consisted largely of men, 'different' obviously equated to 'unequal'): 'it was generally regarded as unproblematic that men should be dominant in men's jobs and women should predominate in the more menial jobs. This was seen to reflect the 'natural' order of things, since women would 'naturally' get pregnant and

---

[108] A. Scott, 'Gender Segregation in the Retail Industry', R. Crompton and K. Sanderson, 'The Gendered Restructuring of Employment in the Finance Sector' both in A. Scott, (ed.), *Gender Segregation and Social Change: Men and Women in Changing Labour Markets* (Oxford: OUP, 1994).

[109] N. Millward, *Targeting Potential Discrimination* (Manchester: EOC, 1995), Research Discussion Series No 11.

[110] N. 61 above, 12.

[111] See generally, A. Spender and D. Podmore, *In a Man's World: Essays on Women in Male-Dominated Professions* (London: Tavistock Publications Ltd, 1987) and D. Collinson, D. Knights, and M. Collinson, *Managing to Discriminate* (London: Routledge, 1990). For discussion of discrimination against women in printing see C. Cockburn, *Brothers* (London: Pluto Press, 1983); for medicine, law, and NHS administration see B. Lawrence, 'The 5th Dimension: Gender and General Practice', A. Spender and D. Podmore, 'Women Lawyers —Marginal Members of a Male-Dominated Profession', J. McAuley, 'Women Academics: A Case Study in Inequality'; and P. Newton, 'Who Becomes an Engineer'? Social and Psychological Antecedents of a Non-Traditional Career Choice' all in Spender and Podmore, n. 111 above. See also J. Lovering, 'Restructuring and the Sex-Typing of Jobs', in Scott, n. 108 above, on a wide variety of establishments and the rigid and inflexible sex-stereotyping of jobs therein by a variety of mechanisms.

[112] Spender and Podmore, n. 111 above, 127.

leave'.[113] Pregnancy, in fact, accounted for the third highest reason for wastage after promotions or sideways moves and total changes of career.

The picture concerning race discrimination is similar. Jenkins' research in the West Midlands found the widespread use of the inherently subjective 'acceptability' criteria in employment decision-making, coupled with endemic racism and the (increasing) use of informal selection methods: '[i]nstead of being formally specified [many criteria of acceptability] are frequently implicit and largely taken for granted . . . racist prejudice is allowed a safe passage into decision making . . . [and] many of these criteria of acceptability may, in their application . . . unobtrusively discriminate'.[114]

Jenkins concluded from his interviews with the managers in the organizations studies that 'many of them will simply regard black people as an unacceptable presence' and found that 'racism and discrimination, although endemic or even routine, are not often highly visible or apparent'.[115] His results were borne out by those of Jewson and others, four years later, who found employment decisions heavily dependent upon notions of acceptability and a 'prevalence of negative stereotypes of ethnic minorities' on the part of employers'.[116] Irene Breugel, too, reports the results of a 1986 Greater London Council (GLC) survey: '[a]s many as one in five of black men and women with qualifications beyond A level . . . are working in jobs which in the main do not demand such qualifications, compared to less than 1 per cent of white men and 10 per cent of white women (including part-time workers)'.[117] This finding is strongly suggestive of discrimination in recruitment.

(A) INDIRECT DISCRIMINATION

Discrimination such as that outlined above should be regarded as direct. But discrimination is even more pervasive in its indirect form. Even among those employers who are equally prepared to employ men or women, 'all things being equal', requirements such as being within particular age limits, being able to work full-time, having particular types or length of experience, all impact adversely upon women employees.

We saw in Chapter 2 that the move to part-time employment which is so commonly associated with motherhood in the United Kingdom exerts a powerful downward force upon women's occupational status

---

[113] H. Homans, 'Man-made Myths: The Reality of Being a Women Scientist in the NHS' in Spender and Podmore, n. 111 above, 91. See also the HL Select Committee on Science and Technology 1995, *Report on Research Careers for Graduate Scientists* (London: HMSO, 1995), which points out 'outdated male attitudes' to the employment of women in that area.

[114] R. Jenkins, *Racism and Recruitment* (Cambridge: CUP, 1986), 236.

[115] *Ibid.* 236–8.

[116] N. Jewson, D. Mason, S. Waters, and J. Harvey, *Ethnic Minorities and Employment Practice* (London: Department of Employment, 1990).

[117] Breugel n. 87 above (1983) 59–60 commenting upon the results of the GLC's London Living Standards Survey 1986.

and their earnings. The general inflexibility of full-time work and the inadequate provision of child-care in the United Kingdom forces many women into part-time work which, in turn, is for the most part restricted to poorly paid and low status jobs.[118]

Discrimination persists against women employees in general. But the situation concerning part-time workers is a great deal worse. Part-time women workers are more segregated, both by occupation and industrial sector, than full-time women workers. Part-time women are frequently over-qualified for the work they do, a factor explained by the common equation, on the part of employers, of part-time jobs with those which are perceived (whether accurately or not) as relatively unskilled, and are paid accordingly.[119] Part-time working is, as can be seen from table 5.3 above, confined for the most part to the service sector. But even within this sector, Rubery et al. found that '[p]art-time jobs are often distinct from full-time jobs in the sense of involving different tasks and responsibilities . . . [and] constitute a distinct and very specific segment of the labour market'.[120] The explanation behind this does not lie in any difference in quality between part-time and full-time workers. Rather, the researchers found, part-time women workers' characteristics 'are more related to stages in the life cycle than to specific labour qualities or credentials'.[121]

We saw in Chapter 2 that women's movement into part-time work after child-bearing is often associated with downward occupational mobility. According to Rubery et al., almost three times as many female part-time as female full-time jobs (and almost twice the proportion of male full-time jobs) were categorized as partly skilled or unskilled.[122] Shirley

[118] Cf. France, e.g., where high quality child-care is abundant and mothers are far more likely to work full-time—see, e.g., A. Dale and J. Glover, An Analysis of Women's Employment Patterns in the U.K., France and the U.S.A. (London: Department of Employment, 1990), Research Paper No 75; M. David and C. Starzec, 'Women and Part-time Work: France and G.B. Compared' in N. Folbre, B. Bergmann, B. Agarwal, and M. Floro (eds.), Issues in Contemporary Economics: Volume 4, Women's Work in the World Economy (New York: New York University Press, 1992). In 1985, women's total labour force participation rates were similar (at 55% and 60% respectively) in France and the UK. In France, however, only 22% of working women worked part-time, in contrast with the 45% figure for the UK.

[119] See B. Burchell and J. Rubery, 'Divided Women: Labour Market Segmentation and Gender Segregation' in Scott, n. 108 above. See also S. Horrell and J. Rubery, Employer's Working Time Policies and Women's Employment (London: HMSO, 1991) EOC 'Research Series and 'Gender and Working Time: An Analysis of Employers' Working Time Policies' (1991) 15(4) Cambridge Journal of Economics 373. Horrell and Rubery argue that the gender of jobs tends to dictate how working hours are organized (and, presumably therefore, how accessible it is to women subsequently) rather than working hours requirements determining the pattern of occupational segregation.

[120] J. Rubery, S. Horrell, and B. Burchell, 'Part-time Work and Gender Inequality' in Scott, n. 108 above, 206.

[121] Ibid.

[122] Ibid. 209–10. The 'skilled' and 'unskilled' categories were taken form the Registar-General's Social Class categories of: (I & II) professional, managerial, and intermediate; (III) skilled manual and non-manual; (IV & V) partly and unskilled manual. On SCELI's own rating: 69%, 42%, and 26% respectively of female part-time, female and male full-time

Dex, too, found that 'the bulk of part-time jobs are at the lower level occupations. Women are often faced with the choice, therefore, of working full-time in order to keep their occupational status, or accepting a loss of occupational status in order to get a part-time job'.[123] Again, women's concentration in these jobs had more to do with their need to work part-time than with any lack of human capital factors on their part. Part-time jobs are not, in general, made available in the more desirable, lucrative, and prestigious occupational and industrial sectors.

Just as women in general experience indirect as well as direct discrimination in the labour market, ethnic minority women experience particular additional forms of indirect discrimination. While ethnic minority women (particularly Pakistani and Bangladeshi women, and those of Chinese or mixed origin) are much less likely to work part-time than are white women, all women with children are subject to the conflicting demands of work and children. In addition, Jenkins found that '[m]any criteria of acceptability are ... profoundly ethnocentric ... [that] the applicant's appearance, "manner and attitude" or (for men) age and marital status ... [impacted upon employment-related decisions]'.[124]

(B) DISCRIMINATION AND EXPECTATIONS

Not only are women subject to direct and indirect discrimination on the part of employer, but the *expectation* of discrimination can result in women's concentration within female dominated jobs and/or workplaces. Women will be less inclined to invest the effort in applying for jobs which they hold little hope of securing than for jobs which are generally filled by women—their 'job search' costs are higher in male-dominated than in female-dominated jobs because a greater proportion of employers in the former category is likely to reject them on the basis of their sex.[125] And even in those cases in which employers might be ready to recruit women, men who work in very predominantly male workplaces and/or jobs are frequently not averse to using sexual harassment to maintain the *status quo*. Women who fight their way into apprenticeships in very male areas such as mechanics, or who enter the macho world of the police constable, risk being harassed by men who insist on labelling them 'slags'—

jobs fell into the lowest of three skill-bands measured but the authors warned that women were more likely than men to underestimate the skill factors associated with their work.

[123] S. Dex, *Women's Occupational Mobility: A Lifetime Perspective* (Basingstoke: MacMillan, 1987), 86.

[124] Jenkins, n. 114 above, 236.

[125] See, e.g., D. Black, 'Discrimination in an Equilibrium Search Model' (1995) 13(2) *Journal of Labor Economics* 309. See also E. Phelps, 'The Statistical Theory of Racism and Sexism' (1972) 62(4) *American Economic Review* 659; M. Spence, *Market Signalling: Information Transfer in Hiring and Related Screening Processes* (Cambridge, Mass.: Harvard University Press, 1974); and K. Arrow, 'The Theory of Discrimination' in O. Ashenfelter and A. Rees (eds.), *Discrimination in Labour Markets* (Princeton, NJ: Princeton University Press, 1973).

neither firefighters nor policemen, construction workers nor barristers have shown unqualified support for the integration of women into their strongly male occupations.[126]

Just as the expectation of discrimination can encourage women to seek work in predominantly female jobs and occupations, so the same is true in respect of women of particular racial groups. Brah found evidence, in relation to South Asian women, that the expectation of racism in the labour market discouraged many from seeking paid work outside the home.[127] And many of those Asian women who were interviewed for Hoel's research on 'sweatshops' in the West Midlands found their employment options constrained by the expectation of discrimination.[128]

The other issue which should not be overlooked is that a woman who decides to work in a field such as, for example, engineering makes a qualitatively different choice from that made by a man deciding to work in the same area (the same is true of men entering very predominantly female jobs and of people entering jobs in which they will form a small minority defined by colour or racial group). The woman (or man) is deciding to work as a very visible minority in an overwhelmingly male (female/white) preserve and, by doing so, to behave in an unfeminine (unmasculine, etc.) manner—the man chooses to work as a man among men and, in so doing, to conform to a very stereotypical version of masculinity. It is simply not realistic, bearing this in mind, to expect women and men to enter occupations in comparable numbers and to ascribe any failure on their part so to do to freely made 'choices'. The same is true in respect of 'choices' made by persons of particular racial groups.

V. SHORTCOMINGS OF THE ACTS

It seems that, at least as far as occupational and industrial segregation is concerned, the Sex Discrimination and Race Relations Acts have had a

[126] See, e.g., 'Nearly half Manchester's police sexually harassed', *Guardian*, 19 Apr. 1995; 'Fireman makes his stand . . .', *Guardian*, 9 June 1994; 'Sex harassment suit tells horror tale' (sexual harassment in the construction industry), *Houston Chronicle*, 23 July 1995. For accounts of organized resistance by men to women's entry into printing, in particular, and 'men's' blue collar jobs more generally, see Cockburn, n. 111 above; J. Rubery, 'Structured Labour Markets, Worker Organisation and Low Pay' in A. Amsden (ed.), *The Economics of Women and Work* (Harmondsworth: Penguin, 1980); S. Walby, *Patriarchy at Work* (Cambridge: Polity Press, 1986); and the *Guardian*, 9 May 1995, on the results of a major study on sexual harassment at the British bar.

[127] A. Brah, ' "Race" and "Culture" in the Gendering of Labour Markets: South Asian Young Muslim Women and the Labour Market' (1993) 19(3) *New Community* 38. See also A. Brah and S. Shaw, *Working Choices: South Asian Women and the Labour Market* (London: Department of Employment, 1992), Research Paper No 91.

[128] B. Hoel, 'Contemporary Clothing "Sweatshops", Asian Female Labour and Collective Organisation' in J. West (ed.), *Work, Women and the Labour Market* (London: Routledge & Kegan Paul, 1982).

limited impact on discrimination in the labour market and such evidence as is available suggests that the latter Act has had little effect on the pay of ethnic minority women.[129] In order to assess why this might be the case it is useful to consider the shortcomings of the Acts, both as they were drafted and as they have been applied by the courts. Here I will focus exclusively upon those provisions concerned with discrimination in employment.

The most obvious candidates for criticism might appear to be the numerous exceptions made by both Acts to the principle of non-discrimination and perhaps, in particular, the numerous GOQs permitted, especially by the Sex Discrimination Act. But the former were not, on the whole, directly related to pay or even to the issue of segregation by race or sex. And, while GOQs could obviously have an impact on segregation, in practice their scope is relatively narrow. The only GOQ of potentially wide effect is that relating to personal services promoting welfare (or, in the context of the 1975 Act, 'welfare or education, or other similar personal services'), at any rate since the removal of the GOQ relating to 'protective' legislation. But this exception operates more to benefit than to disadvantage women and ethnic minority workers (some ethnic minority groups, in particular, sometimes being better served by those of the same racial or ethnic group), and the difficulties experienced with it have owed more to the narrow approach taken to it by the Court of Appeal in *London Borough of Lambeth* v. *CRE* in which that court ruled that the provision would generally apply only to those jobs where there was direct contact between the holder and the recipients of his or her personal services, than to any apparent use of the provision to exclude women or ethnic minority workers.[130] The real problems encountered in the application of the 1975 and 1976 Acts are considered below.

(A) INDIVIDUAL ENFORCEMENT

Victimization

Both the Sex Discrimination and the Race Relations Acts, like the earlier equal pay and race discrimination legislation, adopted a primarily individualistic approach to the problem of discrimination. Just as an individual worker had to pluck up the courage to make a complaint under the Equal Pay Act, so too the individual denied employment or promotion, dismissed, or otherwise subjected to any detriment had to put herself forward in order to take advantage of the Sex Discrimination or Race Relations Act. The difficulties experienced by applicants under the Equal Pay and Sex Discrimination Acts, and the failure of discrimination claims

---

[129] See Breugel, n. 87 above (1983), p. 62 and Bhavnani, n. 86 above, Ch. 7.
[130] [1990] IRLR 231.

to improve the work situation of those who bring them, was mentioned in Chapter 4. There is little reason to suppose that race complainants fare very differently—indeed, it was the recognition of the problems caused by reliance upon the individual enforcement mechanism in previous race relations legislation that underlay the emphasis placed by the 1975 race discrimination White Paper upon the collective enforcement powers of the proposed CRE. And while a woman who suspected that she has been refused employment or dismissed for a discriminatory reason would not stand to lose anything *vis-à-vis* the particular respondent by bringing a claim under either Act, such action might well (particularly if taken in connection with a dismissal) jeopardize her future chances of employment: Alice Leonard's 1980–4 study of successful equal pay and sex discrimination applicants found that about one-third had experienced difficulty in finding subsequent employment, and that all had attributed this difficulty, in part at least, to their claims.[131] In any event, any advantage gained by not being employed by the respondent to a sex discrimination action was at least balanced by the particular difficulties of proof associated with establishing such a discrimination claim.

While the legislature might be praised for having made an attempt to deal with the issue of victimization, the protection actually provided by section 4 of the Sex Discrimination Act (section 2 of the Race Relations Act) seems to have been minimal indeed. Part of the problem rests with the judicial interpretation of the sections: initially the courts required, in order to establish unlawful victimization, that the complainant had been less favourably treated than a person who had not done the act[132] by reason of which the victimization was alleged to have occurred.[133] This approach stripped complainants of any meaningful protection and, in *Aziz* v. *Trinity Street Taxis*, the Court of Appeal ruled that it was incorrect. But their Lordships insisted, nevertheless, that the victimizer's action had been taken '*by reason that* the person victimised' (my emphasis) had done (or intended to, or was suspected of having done or intended to do) one or more of the acts protected by the Race Relations and Sex Discrimination Acts.[134] Where, as in *Aziz*, the court is satisfied that the alleged victimizer would have acted similarly if the act on which less favourable treatment is alleged to have been based had not been related to the Race Relations or Sex Discrimination Act, victimization is not established. The overall effect of this decision is indistinguishable from that achieved by

---

[131] A. Leonard, *Pyrrhic Victories: Winning Sex Discrimination and Equal Pay Cases in the Industrial Tribunals, 1980–1984* (London: HMSO, 1987), 50.
[132] RRA, s. 2(1); SDA, s. 4(1): 'brought proceedings . . . given evidence or information in connection with proceedings . . . otherwise done anything under or by reference to' the relevant Act or 'alleged that the discriminator or any other person has committed an act which . . . would amount to a contravention of' the relevant Act.
[133] *Kirby* v. *Manpower Services Commission* [1980] IRLR 229.
[134] [1988] IRLR 204.

the earlier approach, despite the Court of Appeal's characterization of the latter as 'absurd'.[135]

Proving Discrimination

Particularly in cases where direct discrimination is alleged, direct evidence that the applicant's less favourable treatment was based on his or her sex, rather than on any other factor, is rare: few employers admit such discriminatory conduct in writing or before witnesses. Recognition of this has caused the higher courts to encourage the inference of discrimination from primary facts where less favourable treatment is established 'in circumstances which are consistent with that treatment being based on [sexual] grounds'.[136] The question when such inferences can or should be drawn, and the relationship between such inferences and the burden of proof in discrimination cases, is less clear: decisions such as that in *Chattopadhyay* v. *Headmaster of Holloway School* suggest that the inference *should* be drawn where less favourable treatment is established 'unless the respondent can *satisfy* the industrial tribunal that there is an innocent explanation' (my emphasis). But the Court of Appeal in *North West Regional Health Authority* v. *Noone* took the view that an inference of discrimination was only '*usually* the legitimate inference' from a finding of less favourable treatment, a difference in race and an inadequate or unsatisfactory explanation by the employer' (my emphasis).[137] And the suggestion by the Court of Appeal in *Baker* v. *Cornwall County Council* that differential treatment and a difference in race or sex served to shift the burden of proof to the employer to disprove discrimination[138] was contradicted by the same court in *King* v. *Great Britain China Centre*.[139]

The discrimination complainant must establish that she was treated less favourably (that she failed to be shortlisted, for example, or was dismissed) than a man in the same relevant circumstances.[140] She will generally also have to point to some further factor in order to counter the employer's likely claim that the difference was grounded on 'merit', 'attitude', 'presentation', or some other, frequently untestable, factor (in *Quereshi* v. *London Borough of Newham*, for example, failure to comply with the employer's own equal opportunities policy was insufficient evidence from which to infer discrimination[141]). Section 74 of the SDA (section 65 of the RRA) established a procedure allowing applicants to send the alleged

---

[135] See also *Cornelius* v. *University of Swansea* [1987] IRLR 147, *In Re York Truck Equipment Ltd* EAT/109/88 (Transcript), 20 Oct. 1989, *Lexis*. The decision of the EAT in *Waters* v. *Commissioner of Police of the Metropolis* [1995] IRLR 531 has reduced the protection afforded to complainants still further—see the comments of Richard Townshend-Smith at (1996) 2 *International Journal of Discrimination and the Law*, 137.

[136] *Chattopadhyay* v. *Headmaster of Holloway School* [1981] IRLR 487, 490.

[137] [1988] ICR 813, 822.   [138] [1990] IRLR 194.   [139] [1991] IRLR 513.

[140] Some of the difficulties associated with the demand for the 'same relevant circumstances' are touched upon below.

[141] [1991] IRLR 264.

discriminator a questionnaire asking for an explanation for the less favourable treatment complained of. This was intended to go some way towards easing the burden of proving a discrimination claim,[142] not least in the light of the Government's refusal to place any burden of proof on the employer. But despite the protests of some Conservative politicians that the provision was 'objectionable on the grounds of compulsion to self-incrimination', and that it 'smack[ed] of the Star Chamber',[143] its impact appears to have been relatively slight. Employers can refuse to answer questions on the ground of irrelevance, or because to do so would impose an onerous and undue burden, and an explanation by the employer of any refusal to answer will prevent any adverse inferences being drawn by a tribunal.[144]

The discovery procedure can ease the burden on the discrimination complainant as on other industrial tribunal applicants. The tribunal's power to order the disclosure of documents where this is necessary in order to dispose fairly of the case can be of particular assistance to the employee who wishes to make a discrimination claim: frequently a refusal to recruit or to promote a woman might look innocent in the abstract but will take on a different hue when assessed against a background of similar refusals.[145]

Statistical evidence can be among the strongest weapons available to the discrimination complainant. But employers are not legally obliged to retain or to compile information relating to the sexual or racial composition of their workforces or characteristics of job applicants. Codes of Practice issued by both the EOC and the CRE recommend that employers monitor the sex and race of job applicants; recruits; applicants, and employees selected for promotion, training etc.; and of employees by job, section, and department.[146] If an employer has complied with these guidelines the statistical information collected may be made available to

[142] The procedure can also be used after the tribunal application is made.

[143] Leon Brittan MP, 893 HC Debs. (18 June 1975) col. 1602. See also Ian Percival MP at col. 1598.

[144] Permitted questions are set out in SI 1975/2048 and SI 1977/842—see M. Malone, *Discrimination Law: A Practical Guide for Management* (London: Kogan Page, 1993), 197–8. The tribunal may only draw such inferences as it considers just and equitable where the employer 'deliberately, and *without reasonable excuse*, omit[s] . . . to reply within a reasonable period or [where] . . . his reply is evasive or equivocal' (my emphasis). Where the demands made upon the employer would be oppressive the tribunal will not make a discovery order in respect of it—this being the case, it would certainly be perverse to draw any adverse inference from a refusal to answer—see *West Midlands Passenger Transport Executive* v. *Singh* [1988] ICR 614. See also the EAT's alternative ground for rejecting the appeal in *Carrington* v. *Helix Lighting Ltd* [1990] IRLR 6. On an (unsuccessful) appeal on perversity from a questionnaire inference see *Brighton Borough Council & Anor* v. *Richards*, EAT/431/92, (Transcript), 14 July 1993, *Lexis*.

[145] See the decision of the HL in *Science Research Council* v. *Nasse* [1979] ICR 921.

[146] The Code of Practice for the Elimination of Discrimination on the Grounds of Sex and Marriage and for the Promotion of Equality in Employment, 1985, paras. 37–40 and the Code of Practice for the Elimination of Discrimination on the Grounds of Race and for the Promotion of Equality in Employment 1983, paras. 133–43 respectively.

the complainant and an inference of direct discrimination may be based upon it.[147] But if an employer has failed to collect statistical information (and, as we saw above, most employers do), he or she cannot be required to do so for the purposes of a discrimination complaint.[148]

Just as discovery orders will not be granted so as to require employers to produce statistics that are not already collected, so too such orders will be refused if the tribunal takes the view that the applicant is engaged on a 'fishing expedition' (evidence gathering) or that for any other reason the order is not necessary (as opposed to merely useful) for the fair disposal of the case.[149]

EOC/CRE Assistance

The EOC and CRE were empowered to assist the individual, whether with legal advice, representation, or any other matter. Such assistance could relieve the applicant of such practical concerns as the procedural requirements involved in a discrimination claim and the expense of legal assistance. Not all discrimination complaints apply for assistance. Between 1977 and 1984, for example, there were anywhere between one sixth (1977 and 1978) and almost 100 per cent (1983 and 1984) as many applications for EOC assistance in employment cases as there were applications to the industrial tribunals made and completed within the year.[150] And the Policy Studies Institute's (PSI's) late 1980s research on race discrimination cases suggested that 67 per cent of applicants applied to the CRE for assistance.[151]

Some of those complainants who did not seek the assistance of the relevant Commission may have made an informed choice on the basis of trade union or other support.[152] But many more may not have been aware of the available assistance: although all complainants would come into

[147] *West Midlands Passenger Transport Executive* v. *Singh*, n. 144 above.

[148] *Carrington* v. *Helix*, n. 144 above. According to the EAT, 'failure to comply with the provisions and spirit of the Code[s] of Practice [which recommend monitoring] can be taken into account by a tribunal and when it considers the whole of the case an adverse inference may be drawn'. But tribunals are under no obligation to draw such inferences and the author can find no appellate decision concerning the drawing of inferences from failure to monitor alone.

[149] See, e.g., *British Aerospace plc* v. *Green & Ors.* [1995] IRLR 433 (CA). This is a matter for discretion of the tribunal appealable only on perversity or mistake of law—see *Medallion Holidays Ltd* v. *Birch* [1985] IRLR 406; *Byrne* v. *The Financial Times Ltd* [1991] IRLR 417; *McAndrew* v. *Chemical Bank & Anor.*, EAT/299/94, EAT/574/94, (Transcript) 6 July 1994, *Lexis*.

[150] EOC, *Annual Reports* (Manchester: EOC, relevant years).

[151] C. McCrudden D. Smith, and C. Brown, *Racial Justice at Work* (London: Policy Studies Institute, 1991), 205.

[152] C. Graham and N. Lewis, *The Role of ACAS Conciliators in Equal Pay and Sex Discrimination Cases* (Manchester: EOC, 1985), found that 40% of applicants had applied, half successfully, whereas 28% had trade union support, 16% lawyers, and 17% others including CABs and friends.

contact with ACAS, officers were not under any instructions to inform applicants of the possibility of EOC support until the mid-1980s, and one study carried out in 1981–2 found that such information had been given to less than half of potential beneficiaries (the PSI research found that ACAS did refer unrepresented applicants in race discrimination cases to the CRE).[153]

Even when women did apply for EOC or CRE assistance, help was not always forthcoming. The number of cases in which legal assistance was granted by the EOC (again, these included cases brought under the Equal Pay as well as the Sex Discrimination Act) varied between sixty-eight in 1980 and 417 in 1986. In the former year these accounted for 47 per cent and in the latter 50 per cent of all applications for assistance. Between forty-seven (1979) and 425 (1988) applications for assistance were rejected outright (30 per cent and 57 per cent respectively of total applications). The CRE, by contrast, provided assistance and advice of some sort in 73 per cent of cases in 1990, rising to 83 per cent in 1994 and offered no advice or assistance in only 17 per cent of cases in 1990, declining to 6 per cent in 1994. In the years 1990–4 inclusive, advice and assistance was granted in between 792 (1990) and 1,394 (1994) cases, *in addition to* representation by the CRE which was provided in between 188 (1990) and 388 (1991) cases.[154]

Not only did the EOC reject many applications for assistance but it did so, on occasion, in terms which caused applicants to withdraw their cases.[155] Also indicted by one early commentator were ACAS officers who, according to Jeanne Gregory in 1981, 'unduly pressurized' women to drop discrimination cases.[156] In one study of race discrimination applicants, too, ACAS officers were rated as helpful by only 35 per cent.[157]

(B) DIFFICULTIES IN INTERPRETATION

The problems associated with the 1975 and 1976 Acts did not relate simply to practical issues such as difficulties of proof, fear of victimization, etc. While these were the major hurdles to be overcome in a straight-forward case such as a claim that an employer did not employ women (or black women) for particular posts, or applied different promotion or dismissal criteria to women and men (persons of different racial groups), many

---

[153] Graham and Lewis, n. 151 above, 42; McCrudden *et al.*, n. 152 above, 192.
[154] *Annual Report 1994* (London: CRE, 1994).
[155] *Ibid*: 64.
[156] J. Gregory, 'The Great Conciliation Fraud,' *New Statesman* 3 July 1981 cited by Graham and Lewis, n. 152 above, 65. Cf. L. Dickens, M. Jones, B. Weekes, and M. Hart, *Dismissed: A Study of Unfair Dismissal and the Industrial Tribunal System* (Oxford; Blackwell, 1985) on the point that ACAS officers, being under a statutory duty to promote conciliation, would not regard withdrawal or settlement in negative terms.
[157] V. Kumar, *Industrial Tribunal Applicants Under the Race Relations Act 1976* (London: CRE, 1986).

other aspects of discrimination proved even more difficult to challenge. This additional difficulty stemmed from the definition of discrimination itself. Some indications of the difficulties faced by potential claimants have already been given in relation to the judicial interpretation of the victimization provisions. In the case of direct and indirect discrimination, and even that of marital discrimination, comparable problems arose.[158] And ethnic minority women faced even greater hurdles than white women or ethnic minority men: those discriminated against specifically as black, Asian, or other ethnic minority *women* could not complain of their treatment specifically as ethnic minority women, but would have to bring their claims either as ethnic minority persons, under the Race Relations Act, or as women under the Sex Discrimination Act.[159]

For the purposes of deciding whether a woman (person of any particular racial group) has received *less favourable* treatment, as is required for a finding of direct discrimination under section 1(1)(a) (sex or race discrimination) or 3(1)(a) (discrimination against married persons), the tribunal is instructed to compare the case of the woman (person of the applicant's racial group or married person) with that of a man (person of another racial group or unmarried person—in each case whether real or hypothetical) 'the relevant circumstances in the one case [being] . . . the same, or not materially different, in the other [*sic*]'.[160] The problem of proof has already been considered. But in addition to the practical problems of establishing a direct discrimination claim, the question of what these 'relevant circumstances' are has given rise to enormous confusion, not least in the case of discrimination on the grounds of pregnancy. We saw in Chapter 2 that women's and men's labour market experiences differ most markedly in the aftermath of childbearing. Pregnancy and childbirth (and the potential for them) are the characteristics which, perhaps more than any other, are responsible for women's disadvantaged position in the labour market. Women lose out because they take time out of the paid labour force to bear and look after children, they are discriminated against because employers think they are likely to behave in this way and because women's mothering role results in their perception as secondary, 'pin money' earners. Ethnic minority women suffer from these disadvant-

---

[158] In *R. C. Bick* v. *Royal West of England Residential School for the Blind* [1976] IRLR 326, an industrial tribunal ruled that the provision did not apply in a case in which a woman was dismissed because she was to be married. In addition, no protection is afforded to co-habitees.

[159] This issue formed the basis of a paper by D. Ashiagbor ('The Intersection Between Gender, "Race" and Class in the Labour Market') to the Transformative Labour and Employment Law: Democratic Perspectives in a Changing World Conference at Rutherford College, University of Kent, 6–8 July 1996. Ashiagbor cites C. Crenshaw, 'Demarginalizing the Intersection of Race and Sex: A Black Feminist Critique of Antidiscrimination Doctrine, Feminist Theory and Antiracist Politics' in K. Bartlett and R. Kennedy (eds.), *Feminist Legal Theory* (Boulder, Colo., Westview Press, 1991).

[160] SDA, s. 5(3); RRA, s. 3(4).

ages and, in addition, frequently find themselves the recipients of racial stereotyping (concerning, for example, irresponsible single black mothers, passive downtrodden Asian women) which impedes their prospects in the labour market. We shall consider the problems of interpretation which have arisen in the context of direct discrimination, then in indirect discrimination, and in each case will discuss those issues common to both Acts before mentioning those specific to the sex and race legislation.

Direct Discrimination

(i) Sexual/Racial Harassment

Sexual and racial harassment, whatever the direct motivation of harassers, function as mechanisms by which particular groups of employees (men, for example, or white people) preserve the homogenous nature of their group. We saw, in the text after note 92 above, that the existing sex composition of jobs is frequently used by employers to justify discrimination in recruitment in terms of the compatability (or otherwise) of the prospective candidate. Employers' abdication of responsibility in this provides no defence to a sex discrimination claim (though proof, of course, is another matter). But where sexual harassment by employees is concerned, the position is much less clear. Whereas the fact of sexual or racial harassment will generally be regarded as 'detriment' within section 6(2) (4(2)) of the Act, the question whether it will amount to 'less favourable treatment' is not always so easily answered.[161]

The Court of Sessions ruled, in *Porcelli* v. *Strathclyde Regional Council* that this requirement would be satisfied even if the harassers would have treated a person of the opposite sex to the complainant equally badly, so long as the treatment meted out to her 'was a particular kind of weapon, based upon the sex of the victim'.[162] This went a long way towards defining sexual (and, by analogy, racial) harassment as prohibited discrimination, although it is clear from the decision in *Stewart* v. *Cleveland Guest (Engineering) Ltd* that the battle has not entirely been won.[163] But employers are given considerable scope to abdicate responsibility for harassment by denying that the act complained of was done 'in the course of [the harasser's] employment' so as to found vicarious liability under the Race Relations or Sex Discrimination Act.[164] And employers are afforded a special defence, even where vicarious liability is founded, that they 'took such steps as were reasonably practicable'[165] to prevent the harassment. This defence has been rather generously applied in the past (see, for example,

---

[161] But not invariably—see the decision of the CA in *De Souza* v. *AA* [1986] IRLR 103.
[162] [1986] IRLR 134, 137.
[163] [1994] IRLR 440. See the author's comment on this case at (1995) 24 *Industrial Law Journal* 181.
[164] Ss. 32 & 41 respectively.   [165] S. 32(3) RRA, 41(3) SDA.

the facts in *Balogoblin* v. *London Borough of Tower Hamlets*, but the tribunals appear recently to be taking a more rigorous approach.[166]

(ii) Clothing and Appearance Rules

The need for a comparator, albeit a hypothetical one, in allegations of direct discrimination also caused difficulties in the context of clothing and appearance rules. This issue is, as was mentioned above, far from trivial, because the manner in which an employee is required to present him- or herself can give signals about his or her status which in turn can influence assessments of his or her value as an employee and potential for advancement.[167] It can also deny women (and indeed men) of particular racial groups access to employment where clothing and appearance rules conflict with religious or cultural obligations.

The approach of the courts to this issue has been far from satisfactory. In *Schmidt* v. *Austicks Bookshops Ltd*, the EAT took the view that, so long as *some* clothing or appearance rule was imposed upon both male and female employees, the application of the specifically female (or male) rule to employees of that sex was not to be regarded as discriminatory[168]—the fact that the employer prohibited male employees from wearing tee-shirts was accepted as balancing the requirement not only that women employees wear skirts, but also that they don a smock while in contact with customers. Yet this is precisely the type of clothing difference which will result in the smock-wearer being considered as being of lower status than the un-uniformed employee.

A more appropriate approach to clothing and appearance rules would be based simply on the 'but for' test of direct discrimination adopted by the House of Lords in *James* v. *Eastleigh Borough Council*:[169] where a woman is disciplined or otherwise disadvantaged by reason of her failure to comply with a sex-specific rule, one should ask whether she would have been so treated 'but for' the fact of her sex. The answer is surely no: even if a man would have been similarly disadvantaged for his failure to comply with a sex-specific rule, the content of the rule applicable to him, being sex-specific, should not form part of the 'relevant circumstances' to be considered under section 1(1)(a) of the Sex Discrimination Act. If the legislature had intended to preserve the power of employers to issue sex-specific dress codes, as they intended to preserve the power to restrict certain jobs to persons of one or other sex, then they could have done

---

[166] [1987] IRLR 401. See also *A* v. *Civil Aviation Authority*, 28 EORDCLD 9, *Earlam* v. *MB Ltd & Andrews*, 25 EORDCLD 8–9, and *Dias* v. *Avon County Council*, 25 EORDCLD 8–9.

[167] This argument has been recognized in some US cases e.g., *Carroll* v. *Talman Federal Savings and Loan Association of Chicago*, 604 F. 2d 1028 (1979)—see I. Hare, 'Gender Discrimination and Grooming Codes in the Labour (Super)market (1995) 1 *International Journal of Discrimination and the Law* 179.

[168] [1978] ICR 85. See also *Murphy and Davidson* v. *Stakis Leisure Ltd* (a decision of a Scottish industrial tribunal), S/0534/89 and S/0590/89.

[169] [1990] IRLR 288.

so (perhaps in narrow terms allowing employers to require female, but not male, lifeguards to wear clothing on their upper chests, male but not female employees to wear trousers). This approach has not, however, been accepted by the courts: most recently the Court of Appeal, in *Smith* v. *Safeways plc*, embraced the *Schmidt* v. *Austicks* decision and ruled that 'less favourable' treatment was not established where an employer applied a conventional dress code to male and female employees, regardless of the fact that different rules applied according to the employees' sex.[170]

The major legal problem which has arisen in the application of the Race Relations Act to clothing and appearance rules concerns the lack of fit between the Race Relations Act's definition of 'racial group' and the origin of a number of culture-specific clothing regulations with which women cannot comply consistent with clothing rules imposed by an employer (where, for example, a Muslim woman's compliance with religious clothing restrictions is inconsistent with an employer's dress code). The particular difficulty lies in the 1976 Act's failure to prohibit religious discrimination. 'Racial grounds' is defined to refer to grounds of, and 'racial group' to a group defined by, 'colour, race, nationality or ethnic or national origins'.[171] Whereas discrimination on the ground that someone is black, or Asian, on the ground that she was born in Africa or of Turkish nationality, all come within the Act's prohibition, discrimination against Muslims and other religious groups may not. The House of Lords accepted, in *Mandla* v. *Dowell Lee*, that Sikhs' long, shared history, their cultural tradition, common origin, language and region, common and unique literature, and minority status qualified them as a group defined by ethnic origin. But the question whether any particular group will qualify as one protected by the Race Relations Act may be haphazardly answered.[172] In *Dawkins* v. *Department of the Environment*, for example, the requirement for a *long* shared history was taken by the Court of Appeal to exclude Rastafarians from the definition of 'ethnic group'. And the question whether clothing requirements which preclude Muslim women from complying with their religious obligations will breach the Race Relations Act turns on whether Islam is the dominant faith of the complainant's 'ethnic group'[173] ('ethnic group' being defined other than by reference to faith— see 'Race and Religion' below).

---

[170] [1996] IRLR 456. See also the decision of the CA in *Burrett* v. *West Birmingham Health Authority*, (Transcript) 3 March 1994, *Lexis*.

[171] RRA, s. 3(1) This was wider than the 1968 Act which did not apply to nationality as a result of the decision of the HL in *Ealing LBC* v. *Race Relations Board* [1972] AC 342. But see *Tejani* v. *The Superintendent Registrar for the District of Peterborough* [1986] IRLR 502.

[172] [1983] ICR 385—only the former two were absolute requirements for an ethnic group.

[173] See UK Action Committee on Islamic Affairs, *Muslims and the Law in Multi-Faith Britain: Need for Reform* (London: UK Action Committee on Islamic Affairs, 1993). *Dawkins* is at [1993] IRLR 284. See also *Ahmad* v. *ILEA* [1977] ICR 490 and *Nyazi* v. *Rymans Ltd*, EAT 6/88 (Transcript) 10 May 1988, *Lexis* in which the refusal to allow a Muslim woman time off for religious reasons failed on the ground that Muslims did not qualify as an ethnic group.

Sex Discrimination Act

(i) Pregnancy/Maternity

If women did not give birth to children it is quite possible that they would be in as strong a labour market position as men. It is deeply ironic, then, that it has taken twenty years and several changes of tack by the British courts (the most recent the result of the ECJ ruling in *Webb* v. *EMO Air Cargo (UK) Ltd*) to establish that a woman's pregnant condition (and her need for time off work to give birth) does not constitute 'relevant circumstances' for the purposes of comparing her treatment with that of a man.[174] The legislation originally proposed by the Conservatives expressly excluded such discrimination from the scope of protection but the 1975 Act went so far as to include a provision to the effect that, in determining whether a man had been subject to unlawful sex discrimination, 'no account shall be taken of special treatment afforded to women in connection with pregnancy or childbirth'.[175]

If discrimination based on pregnancy or child-bearing was *not* to be regarded as discrimination based on sex, there would have been no need for such a provision—the employer accused of discriminating against men by providing women with maternity leave or time off for ante-natal care could have defended him- or herself simply by claiming that the failure similarly to advantage men was based on the fact that they were not subject to pregnancy or childbirth.[176] Nor is there any reason why pregnancy or childbirth, or the need for time off in connection with them, should be considered part of the 'relevant circumstances' for the purposes of a direct discrimination claim, these experiences being unique to one sex. But this did not prevent the courts up to and including the Court of Appeal from declaring themselves unable to read any prohibition on pregnancy discrimination into section 1(1)(a) of the Sex Discrimination Act. In *Webb* v. *EMO*, Glidewell, Balcombe, and Bedlam LJJ all agreed with the argument put forward by David Pannick QC (as *amicus curiae* in the EAT) that to do so 'would necessarily distort the meaning of British statute'; would amount to a 'distortion of the meaning of the Sex Discrimination Act'; 'could not be given . . . without distorting the natural meaning of the [Act's] language'.[177] Lord Keith, in the House of Lords, agreed that

---

[174] Case 32/93 [1994] ECR I-3567. See also *Webb* v. *EMO (No 2)* [1995] IRLR 645 (HL). Prior to this see *Turley* v. *Allders Department Stores Ltd* [1980] ICR 66; *Hayes* v. *Malleable Working Men's Club and Institute* [1985] ICR 703; *Webb* v. *EMO* [1990] IRLR 124 (EAT), [1992] IRLR 116 (CA) and [1993] IRLR 27 (HL).

[175] SDA, s. 2(2).

[176] This argument was recognized but not accepted by the EAT in *Webb* v. *EMO*, n. 174 above. Lord Keith addressed the issue in the HL (No 1, n. 174 above.), 30, but did not accept that it supported the argument that pregnancy discrimination in itself amounted to sex discrimination.

[177] N. 174 above, 123, 124, and 126 This being the case, the decision of the HL in *Duke* v. *Reliance Systems Ltd* [1988] IRLR 118 precluded them from finding in the applicant's favour.

the comparison required by section 5(3) of the Act was 'expected unavailability at the relevant time'. The House of Lords amended this view in the wake of the ECJ ruling in this case.

(ii) Part-Time Work

Perhaps the most significant failing of the Sex Discrimination Act, in terms of its approach to direct discrimination, lay in its failure to extend the prohibition upon less favourable treatment beyond women (men) and married people to those who worked part-time. An absolute prohibition against the differential treatment of full-time and part-time workers cannot be read into the law as it stands—for discrimination against part-time workers to be regarded as direct discrimination it would have to be proven that it was motivated by the (female) sex of the workers. In the absence of this, the complainant must rely on the (weaker) indirect discrimination provisions (see 'Indirect Discrimination' below). Yet the single most significant distinction between men and women in the labour market lies in the tendency of the latter, but not of the former, to work part-time. Equally, even those women who do work full-time tend to require a much greater degree of flexibility from their jobs.

One might argue, of course, that absolute protection should not be given to women in these circumstances because there is always some element of choice involved in the assumption of those family responsibilities which impair women's freedom of movement in the labour market (whereas the bare fact of being male or female is a biological given). But no such objections prevented the protection of married persons by the 1975 Act. Nor would the direct protection of part-time workers, or those who needed to work flexibly, necessarily have operated so as to shore up the traditional division of labour between the sexes: men who required, by reason of family responsibilities, to work part-time or flexibly could have been given like protection with that given to part-time or flexible women workers. This would have gone much further to challenge traditional labour divisions than the existing position where the need to rely on the indirect discrimination provisions of the Sex Discrimination Act protects only those who act in conformity with their stereotypical sexual role. The problems with the indirect discrimination provisions of the legislation are considered below.

(iii) Race and Religion

Ethnic minority women are somewhat less likely than white women to work part-time (though—see Chapter 2—this varies between particular ethnic groups). But the Act's failure specifically to prohibit discrimination on the basis of religion, taken together with the relatively narrow approach to 'ethnic origins' (see after note 166 above) means that direct discrimination against women on the grounds that they were Rastafarians or, in some cases, Muslims, would not amount to a breach of the Act. Just as discrimination against part-time workers has to be addressed from the rather circuitous 'indirect discrimination' angle so, too, this approach has to be adopted in relation to race-connected religious discrimination. As we shall see below, even this does not necessarily bring religious discrimination within the ambit of the 1976 Act.

(iv) Race Discrimination in Pay

Although pay-related race discrimination claims could in theory be brought under section 4(2)(a) of the 1976 Act (which forbids discrimination 'in the terms of employment' offered by employers), virtually no pay-related race claims have ever been brought. There has been one case (*Barclays Bank plc* v. *Kapur & Ors.*[178]) in which the Race Relations Act was relied upon to challenge pension arrangements and, no doubt, other cases have been determined at tribunal level. But the appellate records appear bare of any claims on this point.

The reason for this lack of race–pay claims is not difficult to guess at. Unlike the Equal Pay Act, the 1976 Act contains no mechanism for making an equal pay claim. While it might be relatively easy to challenge a pay differential which arose as between two individuals of different race performing exactly the same job or whose jobs had been rated as having the same value by a job evaluation scheme (JES) (although the employer would still, of course, be entitled to rebut any inference of discrimination which arose by pointing to an alternative reason for the disparity), no equivalent exists under the Race Relations Act for the 1970 Act's equal value claim. Nor, by contrast with the position under the 1970 Act, would the fact that the individuals concerned were engaged in comparable work (whether the same or accepted by the employer as equally valuable) itself give rise to a *prima facie* entitlement to equal pay: whereas the 1970 Act mandates equal pay in these circumstances save where the employer can prove reliance upon a *non-discriminatory*, material, pay-related factor, the Race Relations Act would permit differential pay save where the aggrieved employee proves that that pay difference results from race discrimination. Given the horrors associated with attempting to claim equal pay even where this *prima facie* entitlement and a dedicated mechanism exist, it is hardly surprising that few have attempted equal pay claims under the 1970 Act which provides neither. In addition, as noted above, a woman whose pay was held down by the fact that she was a black woman, or a Pakistani woman, or a woman of any other racial group, would be able only to proceed under the Equal Pay Act *or* the Race Relations Act, neither of which would comprehend the specific nature of the discrimination alleged by her.

---

[178] Most recently *(Barclays Bank plc* v. *Kapur & Ors (No 2))* [1995] IRLR 87. The case originally concerned time limits.

Indirect Discrimination

If the definition of direct discrimination caused problems in the application of the Sex Discrimination and Race Relations Acts, the position regarding indirect discrimination was considerably worse. The 1975 and 1976 Acts left a number of matters undefined, among them the question of what was meant by a 'requirement or condition', what constituted a 'considerably smaller proportion' and how rigorous an approach should be taken to the issue of justification. All of these issues have given rise to considerable difficulty in the application of the Acts.

The largest category of cases concerned with indirect discrimination involves women workers disadvantaged (whether by denial of access to particular jobs, unfavourable treatment within their jobs, or discriminatory removal from jobs) by reason of their actual or requested part-time working. But indirect sex discrimination can also arise when employers impose age restrictions on particular jobs, demand particular levels of experience, or apply any other factor which in practice can be shown to disadvantage women workers. And claims of indirect race discrimination can result from the application of clothing and appearance rules or from refusal to permit employees time off for religious reasons.

(i) 'Requirement or Condition'

The 'requirement or condition' problem first became apparent in *Perera* v. *Civil Service Commission (No 2)*, in which the Court of Appeal held that the words applied only to an absolute requirement or 'must' and not to criteria which were merely favoured or preferred.[179] This approach has been applied as recently as 1992 in the EAT's decision in *Brook* v. *London Borough of Haringey*. Dismissing a claim by a number of women who had been selected for redundancy on the basis, *inter alia*, of attendance and seniority factors which were alleged to disadvantage women, Wood J declared that the claimants' failure to score sufficiently highly (on an amalgam of these and other factors) to avoid redundancy was not the result of any 'requirement or condition' which had been applied to them. They had, rather, simply failed to defeat the competition.[180]

Such an interpretation of indirect discrimination is clearly unsupportable as a matter of principle. If an employer prefers (for example) that applicants for a job are prepared to work full-time, any applicant who wishes only to work part-time will have to be better in other respects in order to compete with those who are prepared to work full-time: a part-time woman worker will have to be a better candidate, all else being equal,

---

[179] [1983] IRLR 166, affirmed by the CA in *Meer* v. *London Borough of Tower Hamlets* [1988] IRLR 399, having been doubted meanwhile in *Home Office* v. *Holmes* [1984] IRLR 299.
[180] [1992] IRLR 478.

than a full-time man. Equally, in the *Brooks* case, the claimants would have had to score better than their comparators on the non-discriminatory factors in order to overcome the disadvantage they suffered as a result of the allegedly discriminatory factors. This, surely, should be regarded as satisfying the test laid down by section 1(1)(b).

A further problem with the 'requirement or condition' provision became apparent in *Clymo* v. *Wandsworth Borough Council* in which the EAT ruled that the (absolute) requirement imposed upon a senior librarian that she work full-time could not be considered as a 'requirement or condition' under section 1(1)(b):

in many working structures . . . there will be a grade or position where the job or appointment by its very nature requires full time attendance. At one end of the scale if a cleaner was required to work full time it would clearly be a requirement or condition. Whereas in the case of a managing director it would be part of the nature of the appointment . . . it will be for the employer, acting reasonably, to decide—a management decision—what is required for the purposes of running his business or establishment.[181]

This decision was disapproved of by the Northern Ireland Court of Appeal in *Briggs* v. *North Eastern Education and Library Board* and the EAT, too, appears to have revised its approach more recently. In *Bhudi & Ors.* v. *IMI Refiners* the EAT ruled that a practice of selecting for redundancy those employees who did not work 'normal office hours' amounted to a requirement or condition under section 1(1)(b): i.e. a requirement that, in order to avoid redundancy, employees work 'normal working hours'.[182] This approach does away with much of the difficulty associated with the provision.

(ii) Detrimental Impact

Turning next to the requirement that, in order to establish an indirect discrimination claim, the applicant must show that a 'considerably smaller proportion' of women (or persons of her ethnic group) than of men 'can comply with' the requirement or condition applied: the major difficulty here has been with the appropriate 'pool for comparison'—the selection criteria for the groups of men and women (persons) whose relative abilities to comply with the requirement or condition are to be compared. The interpretation of 'can comply' and 'considerably smaller' have proved less (although not entirely un-) problematic. The former has been interpreted by the House of Lords and more generally to mean 'can in practice comply', 'can comply at the time when the requirement is imposed', 'can

---

[181] [1989] IRLR 241, 247. See also *Francis* v. *BAEO* [1982] IRLR 10 and the decision of the EAT in *Enderby* v. *Frenchay Health Authority & Secretary of State for Health* [1991] IRLR 44.

[182] [1994] IRLR 204. The decision in *Briggs* is at [1990] IRLR 181.

consistently with the customs and cultural conditions of the . . . group'
comply while dispute about the meaning of 'considerably smaller' has
arisen in only a handful of cases.[183]

The failure of the Acts to specify which men and women (persons)
should be compared (e.g. in a recruitment case, whether all men and
women (persons), or all men and women (persons) in the locality, or all
qualified men and women (persons)—either generally or in the locality—
or all qualified men and women (persons) currently seeking work) has
led to contradictory decisions and unnecessary complications for women claiming indirect discrimination. The test should be straightforward
enough—the pool should include all (and only) those men and women
(persons) 'in the same relevant circumstances'. But here, as elsewhere, the
practical application of this test has proven more difficult. Sometimes the
issue barely raises a question and the disparate impact is all but assumed
(this is particularly the case in respect of women and a requirement to
work full-time). But on other occasions tribunals, supported by the higher
courts, have gone so far as to read into the pools chosen for comparison
the very discrimination of which the applicant complains. This is particularly well illustrated by *Clymo* v. *Wandsworth* in which, in the context
of a claim by a senior librarian that her employer's requirement that she
work full-time indirectly discriminated against her as a woman, the EAT
approved the tribunal's choice, as a pool, of senior librarians. This pool
would not, of course, include all those women whose inability to work
full-time excluded them from employment as senior librarians.[184]

The choice of pool adopted will be interfered with by the higher courts
only if it is so wrong as to be perverse[185] and tribunals and the higher
courts have veered between drawing pools for comparison in very narrow
and in very wide terms and between relying upon general knowledge to
decide whether a considerably smaller proportion of women could comply

---

[183] *Mandla* v. *Lee* n. 172 above. The latter is a race case but equally applicable to sex.
See also the decision of the CA in *Commission for Racial Equality* v. *Dutton* [1989] IRLR
8 and of the EAT in *Price* v. *Civil Service Commission* [1978] ICR 27 and in *Clarke* v. *Eley
(IMI) Kynoch Ltd* [1983] ICR 165. Cf. the approach of the EAT in *Clymo*, n. 181 above,
in which Wood J distinguished 'can comply' from 'wishes to comply': and *Turner* v. *Labour
Party* [1987] IRLR 101. On the question of 'considerably smaller' see *Staffordshire County
Council* v. *Black* [1995] IRLR 234 and *R.* v. *Secretary of State for Employment, ex p Seymour-
Smith* [1995] IRLR 464 (CA), currently on appeal to the ECJ from the HL.

[184] Further, Wood J expressed agreement with the tribunal's view that compliance with
the full-time requirement was a matter of choice for the women concerned: 'in every employment ladder from the lowliest to the highest there will come a stage at which a woman who
has family responsibilities must make a choice', n. 181 above, 248. On choice of pools see
also *Fulton* v. *Strathclyde Regional Council*, EAT 949/83 discussed in IDS, op. cit., 27 and
the tribunal's decision in *Edwards* v. *London Underground* at [1995] IRLR 355.

[185] See *Kidd* v. *DRG (UK) Ltd* [1985] IRLR 190, *Greater Manchester Police Authority* v.
Lea [1990] IRLR 372 in which the EAT refused to interfere with an 'imperfect' choice of
pool. For the difficulties relating to the appropriate choice of pool in race cases see *Orphanos*
v. *Queen Mary College* [1985] IRLR 349 (HL).

with a requirement or condition and requiring detailed statistics.[186] Some assistance was provided by the decision of the Court of Appeal in *Jones* v. *University of Manchester* in which Gibson LJ ruled that the pool should include all those people with the qualifications required for the job (this being an appointment case) not including the requirement in dispute.[187] But there will inevitably be cases in which the very expression of the other requirements will itself be problematic and the matter remains one for the discretion of the industrial tribunal.[188]

Particular problems arise in the context of race discrimination claims where the factor behind differential ability to comply with a requirement relates to religion: in such cases it may be very difficult to pinpoint the *racial* (as distinct from religious) group the applicant's membership of which precludes her compliance with the requirement or condition.

An example of this was provided by the facts in *Dawkins* v. *Department of the Environment*, in which Rastafarians were held by the Court of Appeal not to comprise a distinct 'racial group' under the 1976 Act.[189] The claim for direct race discrimination failed on this basis, but even had the applicant attempted a claim of *indirect* discrimination, its success would have turned on whether he could have established that black, or perhaps Jamaican or African-Caribbean persons in Britain would be substantially less likely to be able to comply with a 'no dreadlocks' rule than would others. It is by no means certain that this requirement could have been satisfied. This problem has also been mentioned in the context of clothing and appearance rules, after note 166 above.

(iii) Justification

The final problematic factor in the definition of indirect discrimination is that of justifiability. Early approaches favoured a balance between the detrimental impact of a requirement or condition upon employees affected by it and its benefit to the employer, but differed on whether, in addition, the employer had to show that reliance upon the disparately impacting factor was necessary (*Steel* v. *Union of Post Office Workers and the General Post Office*[190]) or not (*Singh* v. *Rowntree Mackintosh Ltd*[191]). The Court of Appeal's decision in *Ojutiku* v. *Manpower Services Commission* was widely taken to lay down an even less rigorous test, equating justification

---

[186] Examples of the former approach include *Home Office* v. *Holmes* n. 179 above; *Clarke* v. *Eley (IMI) Kynoch Ltd* n. 183 above; *Perera* v. *Civil Service Commission* [1982] IRLR 147; and *Briggs* v. *North Eastern Education and Library Board* n. 182 above. See also *Orphanos* v. *Queen Mary College*, n. 185 above. The latter approach is exemplified by the decision in *Kidd* v. *DRG*, n. 185 above; *Price* v. *CSC*, n. 183 above.

[187] [1993] IRLR 218. See also *Pearse* v. *City of Bradford Metropolitan Council* [1988] IRLR 379.

[188] See, e.g., the facts in *R.* v. *Secretary of State for Education, ex p. Schaffter* [1987] IRLR 53.

[189] N. 173 above.

[190] [1977] IRLR 288.   [191] [1979] IRLR 199.

with the production of 'reasons for doing something which would be acceptable to right thinking people as sound and tolerable reasons for so doing' (*per* Eveleigh LJ); and declaring that that 'justifiable' 'clearly applies a lower standard than the word "necessary"' (*per* Kerr LJ), although Stephenson LJ approved of the approach in *Singh* which he interpreted as requiring a balance between reasonable necessity and disadvantageous impact.[192] Confusion followed as a result of the House of Lord's acceptance of the rather more rigorous *Bilka-Kaufhaus GmbH* v. *Weber von Hartz* test in *Rainey* v. *Greater Glasgow Health Board*, in the context of the Equal Pay Act (their Lordships expressed the view that this would apply also to the 1975 Act but considered neither *Ojutiku* nor the Race Relations Act). On the face of it the 'sound and tolerable . . . to right-thinking people' test which was generally drawn from *Ojutiku* appeared inconsistent with *Bilka-Kaufhaus*. But in *Hampson* v. *Department of Education and Science* the Court of Appeal adopted the approach of Stephenson LJ in *Ojutiku*[193] (and declared that the same test should apply in the Race Relations as in the Sex Discrimination and Equal Pay Acts). Subsequently, the House of Lords in *Webb* agreed,[194] although it remains strongly arguable that this test is considerably less rigorous than that laid down by the ECJ in *Bilka-Kaufhaus* and successive cases[195] (see Chapters 1 and 3 for discussion).

Time Limits and Remedies

The issues considered above are not the only shortcomings which have impaired the effectiveness of the 1975 and 1976 Acts' individual provisions. To them could be added procedural problems such as the very tight time limits which apply to all industrial tribunal applicants and which, despite legislative confidence to the contrary and an express statutory provision allowing extension in cases where it is 'just and equitable', are almost invariably adhered to. This may give rise to particular difficulties for women subject to sexual or racial harassment, many of whom find it extraordinarily difficult to discuss the matter with anyone.

Finally, the remedies available in sex and race discrimination cases have proven less than adequate. Much has been said recently about the very high awards (as much as £299,851 in one case before the loss of pension rights was considered[196]) made to a number of servicewomen sacked on becoming pregnant, not least in view of the contrast between these sums

---

[192] [1982] IRLR 418, 421.

[193] Case 170/84 *Bilka-Kaufhaus* [1986] ECR 1607, *Rainey* [1987] IRLR 26 and *Hampson* [1989] IRLR 69.

[194] [1993] IRLR 27, 30, *per* Lord Keith (with whom the rest concurred).

[195] N. 193 above, and Case 171/88 *Rinner-Kühn* v. *FWW Spezial-Gebäudereinigung GmbH* [1989] ECR 2743; Case 109/88 *Handels- og Kontorfunktionærernes Forbund i Danmark* v. *Dansk Arbejdsgiverforening (acting for Danfoss)* [1989] ECR 3199; and Case 184/89 *Nimz* v. *Freie und Hansestadt Hamburg* [1991] ECR I–297.

[196] *Homerwood* v. *MOD*, 20 EORDCLD 20.

and those available to the war wounded. But these awards serve merely to illustrate the huge losses that discrimination can inflict upon its victims, and these and other recent compensation awards (£30,000 to an Irish lecturer subjected to racial abuse and victimization, £29,000 to a black prison officer who suffered two years of 'appalling' treatment, £35,000 to a woman refused permission to job-share[197]) contrast very clearly with the more usual level of pay-out (the median awards in 1992–3 were £1,416 and £3,333 for sex and race discrimination respectively; in 1991–2 £1,725 and £1,374; and in 1990–1: £1,142 and £1,749). While there has been some indication of substantial increases in awards since the removal of the upper limit on compensation (£11,000 for sex discrimination cases in 1993), the median award in 1993 (excluding Ministry of Defence cases) increased only slightly to £1,748.[198] In 1994 the median and average awards in race discrimination cases rose from £1,500 and £2,824 to £2,500 and £4,596 respectively after the abolition of the upper limit.[199] And although the awards made in race cases tend to be higher than those in sex discrimination cases (this is particularly true in respect of injury to feelings awards, which were 60 per cent higher in race cases in 1995[200]), the success rate is considerably lower. In 1992–3, for example, only 20 per cent of race discrimination applicants succeeded at tribunal (up from 15 per cent in 1991–2 and 1990–1—the average success rate at tribunal between 1977 and 1988 was 18 per cent[201]). The figures in respect of sex discrimination were 34 per cent (up from 26 per cent in 1991–2 and 1990–1).

The existence, until 1993 and 1994, of discrimination compensation caps had an effect on the level of awards beyond acting simply as a cut-off at the upper end. This was particularly evident in the case of awards for injury to feelings: in *North West Thames Regional Health Authority* v. *Noone* the Court of Appeal took the view that £3,000 should be regarded as the upper limit for awards under this heading, bearing in mind the overall statutory maximum of £7,500.[202] Since the removal of the cap, awards for injury to feelings have run as high as £21,000.[203] But the median sex

---

[197] *Equal Opportunities Review* 67, 'The Rising Cost of Discrimination'; *Given* v. *Scottish Power* 22 EORDCLD 1. See also 7, £50,000 settlement to nurse for CRE-backed race claim against Bethlem & Maudsley NHS Trust (no admission of liability from the hospital)—one of the highest settlements yet. See also *Bishop* v. *The Cooper Group plc.* 21 EORDCLD 9— £24,000 for a dismissed apprentice.

[198] *Equal Opportunities Review* 57, 'Taking the Cap off Discrimination Awards', 11, 18. Including MOD cases the median was £1,805. Even in the MOD cases the average award was only £11,000. By early 1996 £55 million had been paid out by the three services, around 120 cases involving awards in excess of £50,000 and 31 awards in excess of £100,000 *Equal Opportunities Review* 66, 2.

[199] 'The Rising Cost of Discrimination', n. 197 above.

[200] *Ibid.* 13—£3,129 as against £1,924 in sex discrimination cases.

[201] McCrudden *et al.*, n. 151 above, 158.

[202] N. 137 above.

[203] See 67 *Equal Opportunities Review*, n. 197 above. See also *A & B* v. *R1 & R2* 21 EORDCLD 9 and *McClenaghan and Rice* v. *British Shoe Corporation Ltd*, 23 EORDCLD 11.

discrimination award made in this category actually fell from £1,750 in 1992 to £1,000 in 1993, although in race cases it rose after abolition of the cap in 1994 from £1,200 to £1,500.

Aggravated damages may be awarded in race discrimination cases as an additional element in the injury to feelings award where the employer has acted in a 'high-handed, malicious, insulting or oppressive' manner[204] and where (Ministry of Defence v. Meredith) there is a link between the employer's exceptional or continuous conduct or motive in committing the wrong and the employee's intangible loss.[205] These damages are awarded in about 3 per cent of successful sex and race discrimination claims— where, for example, an employer waited until after a sexual harassment complainant had been put through the ordeal of cross-examination before admitting the wrong, or answered the section 74 questionnaire in a 'misleading, inconsistent and untruthful' manner.[206] The average aggravated award in discrimination claims in 1995 was £1,857.[207]

Aggravated damages go some way towards penalizing the wrongdoer (as distinct from compensating the victim of the wrong). But their award is very unusual and exemplary damages, which are intended to serve this purpose, are not available in cases brought under the Sex Discrimination or Race Relations Act and the level of compensation awarded to successful complainants cannot act as much of a disincentive to potential discriminators.[208] Research carried out by Gerry Chambers and Christine Horton found that even those employers who were the subject of successful sex discrimination or equal pay claims (and who might, as a result, be expected to be most affected by the law) effected little change in their workplaces as a result.[209] Of the forty employers surveyed, seven became more progressive as a result of the tribunal decision, five became more hostile towards equal opportunities and the remaining employers remained gloriously unaffected by the experience.[210] Only 30 per cent of the employers surveyed, but six of the seven improvers, were in the public sector. The other was a voluntary-sector organization. Chambers and Horton concluded that: 'an adverse tribunal decision is rarely a sufficient incentive on its own to become an equal opportunity employer but . . . it can play

---

[204] Alexander v. Home Office [1988] IRLR 190.

[205] Ministry of Defence v. Meredith [1995] IRLR 539.

[206] Knox v. Lurgan Community Workshop & McConville, 19 EORDCLD 10—£1,500 awarded; Webster v. MOD, 17 EORDCLD 6–7—£1,000 awarded.

[207] 'The Rising Cost of Discrimination', n. 197 above.

[208] City of Bradford Metropolitan Council v. Arora [1991] IRLR 165 (CA) accepted exemplary damages but the CA in Gibbons v. South West Water Services [1993] 2 WLR 507 and the EAT in Deane v. London Borough of Ealing [1993] IRLR 209 refused to award exemplary damages in discrimination cases.

[209] G. Chambers and C. Horton, Promoting Sex Equality: The Role of Industrial Tribunals (London: Policy Studies Institute, 1990).

[210] 40 of 108 cases were successful between 1984 and 1986 in Great Britain—the sample was balanced for public/private and type of claim and number of applicants.

a part among other influences in moving employers in that direction'.[211] Where employers already had equal opportunities policies the researchers found 'little evidence that industrial tribunal decisions led to review' of them.[212]

The apparent lack of impact on employers was attributed in part to the EOC's failure to follow up cases in which employers had been found in breach of the Sex Discrimination Act. In addition, in only six of the thirty cases in which a breach of the 1975 Act was found did tribunals issue recommendations as they were empowered to do so under the Act (major PSI research on race discrimination cases decided between 1986 and 1988 found that recommendations were issued in only 2 per cent of successful cases, and a declaration of rights in a further 1.1 per cent[213]). The low number of recommendations, and the relative ineffectiveness of those issued, was attributed in part to tribunals' lack of expertise on the discrimination issue: it was, Chambers and Horton pointed out, a

practical precondition for making effective recommendations that panels appreciate and understand the origins of discriminatory actions and before making a recommendation have fully analysed the likely effects on the organisation. Many panels are not capable of issuing recommendations because they have a poor grasp of the issues and do not have this appreciation and understanding.[214]

Whether or not recommendations were issued, only seventeen of the forty employers (a mere nine of the twenty-eight private sector employers) took any specific measures to deal with the issues raised by the tribunal, and in six of these cases the measures taken were 'cosmetic or of limited impact only'.[215] The attitude of employers was affected by the size of the award made against them: 'employers who have been required to pay only very small amounts of compensation not only fail to engage in follow-up action, but also regard the tribunal process with disrespect, if not outright disdain'.[216]

In 1995, 5 per cent and 12 per cent of race and sex discrimination awards respectively were for under £400, only 20 per cent and 10 per cent respectively in excess of £5,000.[217] Small wonder, when the practical and legal difficulties facing prospective applicants and the low success rate enjoyed by those who do get as far as a tribunal (see after note 195 above) are taken into account, that the individual enforcement provisions of the 1975 and 1976 Acts have not proved an overwhelming success.

As far as the Race Relations Act is concerned, the available evidence suggests that the legislation has had relatively little impact upon employers save in those cases where they have found themselves under the spotlight

---

[211] Chambers and Horton, n. 209 above, 166.   [212] Ibid. 167.
[213] McCrudden et al., n. 151 above, 153.
[214] Chambers and Horton, n. 209 above, 169.   [215] Ibid. 170.   [216] Ibid. 177.
[217] 'The Rising Cost of Discrimination', n. 197 above.

as far as their compliance is concerned. Any substantial effort at compliance with the 1976 Act would require that the CRE's Code of Practice be consulted: CRE research published in 1989 suggested that fewer than 17 per cent of employers had ever even glanced at the Code of Practice and that, of that 17 per cent, only 40 per cent had analysed the race and ethnic origins of their workforce as the code suggested.[218] But when it comes to the impact of enforcement action, the picture regarding race discrimination appears somewhat brighter than is the case in relation to sex discrimination. Research carried out for the PSI and published in 1991 suggests that race discrimination enforcement measures (whether in the form of an industrial tribunal hearing or a formal investigation) do have a considerable impact upon employers. Apparently in contrast to the position with sex discrimination, 'tribunal cases seemed to be eye-openers for employers, whatever the result of the application, and irrespective of their denial of discrimination'.[219] Employers were deeply concerned, not so much with the remedies available to aggrieved employees, as with the fact of being found to have discriminated on racial grounds: 'this anxiety can be a galvanising influence, leading them to look at their employment policies and practices for the first time with a view to eliminating discrimination'.[220]

The experience of tribunal cases was perceived in very negative terms (although there were no claims that tribunals were biased against employers) and changes were made by respondent organizations in order to avert future claims. The PSI concluded that the findings 'generally suggest more grounds for optimism than the studies of religious and sex discrimination' (although it should be noted that only ten employers were questioned, of whom only five had been respondents in industrial tribunal cases). But the lack of guidance afforded to employers on how to alter employment practices limited the effectiveness of the desire to change.

(C) COLLECTIVE REMEDIES

The problems associated with the individual provisions of the Sex Discrimination and Race Relations Acts might have been less significant if adequate action had taken place on the collective front. The EOC and

---

[218] CRE, *The Race Relations Code of Practice in Employment: Are Employers Complying?* (London: CRE, 1989)—the sample probably over-estimated compliance as it was biased towards large employers.

[219] McCrudden *et al.*, n. 151 above, 262.

[220] *Ibid.* 268. The perception of a case of race discrimination as considerably more serious than one of sex discrimination is not confined to employers—during Parliamentary debates on the Race Relations Bill Jonathan Aitken MP was extremely concerned about the formal investigation powers of the CRE but seemed unconcerned about their replication in the hands of the EOC; quoting Norman Tebbit he declared that 'the Sex Discrimination Act is one of the great laughing stocks of our national life' (914 HC Debs. (8 July 1976), col. 1707).

CRE, as we saw above, were empowered to bring actions on their own behalf in respect of persistent discrimination, etc., and to conduct formal investigations into individuals and organizations. The potentially radical prohibition of discriminatory practices by both Acts, in addition, was enforceable only through the formal investigation procedure.

The solution of contract compliance had been supported by a number of MPs but rejected by the government in favour of an assurance regarding administrative action.[221] Certainly, there was nothing in the 1975 Act to prevent government or other contractors from making it a requirement of any contract that the provisions of that or any other Act were observed by the other contracting party. And section 71 of the Race Relations Act expressly required local authorities 'to make appropriate arrangements with a view to securing that their various functions are carried out with due regard to the need . . . to eliminate unlawful racial discrimination; and to promote equality of opportunity and good relations, between persons of different racial groups'.

Contract compliance policies were widespread amongst local authorities during the 1980s. But central government was hostile to such practices by this stage and section 17 of the Local Government Act 1988 expressly prohibited these and other bodies from taking into account 'non-commercial matters' in making arrangements to contract in respect of public supply and works contracts. Among the matters listed as 'non-commercial' are '(5)(a) the terms and conditions of employment by contractors of their workers or the composition of, the arrangements for the promotion, transfer or training of or the other opportunities afforded to, their workforces'. Section 18 provides a very limited exception relating to the Race Relations Act. But local authorities are not permitted to terminate contracts for failure to comply with the provisions of the Race Relations Act, and not even these limited powers apply in relation to the 1975 Act. Far from being required to ensure compliance with employment legislation, including the Sex Discrimination Act, by those spending or being paid with public funds, many government authorities are prohibited from exercising such a supervisory function.[222]

Positive Action

Just as the government rejected the call for contract compliance in 1975, so, too, it refused to allow positive action except in very narrow circumstances.[223] Some allowance was made for the provision of discriminatory access to training by employers and other bodies and for 'encouraging

---

[221] See 889 HC Debs. (26 Mar. 1975), col. 538 and 893 HC Debs. (18 June 1975), col. 1481 for Jo Richardson's attempted amendment; 893 HC Debs. (18 June 1975), col. 1482 for the response.

[222] See, e.g., *R.* v. *London Borough of Islington, ex. p. Building Employers' Federation* [1989] IRLR 382.

[223] The 1976 Act abolished the former provision permitting employers to discriminate in order to retain a racial balance—see MacDonald, n. 6 above, 46.

women only, or men only [persons of a particular racial group], to take advantage of opportunities' where the training or the opportunities related to work which had exclusively or predominantly been performed by members of the opposite sex (had not been performed by persons of this group) during the previous twelve months. But these provisions could at best be described as minimal, did not in any event allow discrimination in terms of access to jobs (as distinct from encouragement to apply for them), and were rarely taken advantage of by employers or others. In 1987 the EOC criticized the Training Opportunities Scheme for having made no use of its power to direct training towards women, and a study published in the same year found that only seven of the 441 employers surveyed had made any use of section 48.[224] The EOC claimed that the need for positive discrimination was 'overwhelming' to combat the very high degree of segregation in industry which was ascribed to 'shop floor and local trade union resistance to change . . . the absence of women in management and union negotiators . . . [and] women's apathy to career furtherance'.[225] Such action was not forthcoming, and there is little evidence to suggest that the 'take-up' of positive action possibilities has increased in recent years.

The positive action provisions of the Race Relations Act would appear, according to research carried out by Welsh and others in the early 1990s, to have been used rather more than those of the 1975 Act. The research, carried out mainly in the public sector, found that 82 per cent of employers had used advertisements to encourage applications from ethnic minority workers and that 33 per cent had provided targeted training for ethnic minority workers. But the 'targeted' advertisements were generally of the 'all welcome', 'welcome regardless of race' variety, and the study concluded that the use of the provisions was generally 'patchy' and their 'overall impact . . . probably limited'.[226]

EOC/CRE Action

The focus has, to this point, been on those forms of collective action which were not required (indeed, not permitted) by the Sex Discrimination and Race Relations Acts. But the EOC and CRE did have the power to conduct formal investigations and to bring actions in respect of persistent discrimination, discriminatory advertisements, etc. The approaches taken by the EOC and the CRE in this area differ substantially and require separate consideration.

---

[224] EOC, *Review of the Training Opportunities Scheme* (Manchester: EOC, 1978); EOC, *Equality Between the Sexes in Industry: How Far Have We Come?* (Manchester: EOC, 1978).
[225] *Ibid.* 88–9.
[226] C. Welsh, J. Knox, and M. Brett, *Acting Positively: Positive Action Under the Race Relations Act 1976* (Sheffield: Employment Department, 1994), Research Series No 36, 37. The research found that 61% of employers were influenced in their decision to take some form of positive action by the CRE.

Taking the EOC first, its collective powers appear to have made little impact and the Commission has been been subject to much criticism, in particular for its apparent reluctance to carry out formal investigations.[227] By 1979, only one formal investigation had been launched and Incomes Data Services pointed out the contrast between this and the CRE's running total, over a shorter lifespan, of seventeen.[228] Jeanne Gregory records that the EOC's insistence on the 'softly softly' approach had, even by 1977, resulted in dissent among the ranks, threated resignations, and, in 1978, a turnover rate at the Commission which was three times the national average.[229] In 1979 the EOC launched four formal investigations and these were, in turn, followed by a further nine over the subsequent twelve years (only eight of the thirteen concerned employment). Even if these investigations (in only four of which formal non-discrimination notices were issued) had repercussions beyond the immediate employer, it would be stretching a point to claim that they could be regarded as a broad-based attack on discriminatory employment practices.[230]

The EOC should not be held solely responsible for the apparent under-utilization of its powers. According to Honeyball, the procedures which had to be adopted for formal investigations were 'extremely cumbersome and complicated' as a result of 'parliamentary draughtsmanship which is not of the highest order'.[231] In addition, the judiciary made the task of the Commission more onerous than it might otherwise have been by restricting the power of investigation in *London Borough of Hillingdon* v. *CRE*.[232]

Most judicial intervention took place in relation to CRE investigations.[233] But the EOC was badly shaken by proceedings taken by the Provincial Building Society, in connection with a formal investigation, in which pre-

---

[227] See, e.g., J. Coussins, *The Equality Report* (London: NCCL Rights for Women Unit, 1976), 112; S. Honeyball, *Sex, Employment and the Law* (Oxford: Blackwell, 1991).

[228] N. 184 above, 106.

[229] J. Gregory, *Discrimination, Employment and the Law* (LSE: PhD thesis, 1985), 348–54, and see generally Ch. 9.

[230] CRE investigations tended to relate to broader areas than those conducted by the EOC—typical of the former were investigations into Cardiff employers, the hotel industry, and chartered accountancy training: investigations into Dan Air's failure to recruit male cabin staff and into allegations of discrimination in promotion at a number of individual schools were more typical of those carried out by the EOC. See McCrudden *et al.*, n. 229 above, Ch. 3 for details of the CRE's record.

[231] N. 227 above, 13.

[232] [1982] IRLR 424. See also *CRE* v. *Prestige Group plc* [1984] IRLR 166. Some indication of the hostility with which certain of the judiciary viewed the EOC and CRE is evident from Lord Denning's claim, in *Science Research Council* v. *Nasse*, that the CRE's investigative powers enabled it to 'interrogate employers . . . up to the hilt and compel disclosure of documents on a massive scale. . . . You might think that we were back in the days of the inquisition.' Lord Denning's remarks are at [1979] QB 144 (CA). The HL was less belligerent towards the Commission—[1979] ICR 921.

[233] Judicial hostility was apparent from the outset: Lord Halisham likened the CRE's powers to those of the Star Chamber in the HL debate on the Bill (373 HL Debs. (20 July 1976), col. 745).

judice on the part of the Commission was alleged.[234] Finally, the EOC is dependent upon the Government for its funding. Having said this, the CRE is subject to similar constraints, but has displayed a markedly different attitude towards undertaking formal investigations. Indeed, the criticism aimed at the CRE in this regard has been of its over-enthusiastic approach in early years (forty-six investigations launched between 1977 and 1982, of which twenty-four related to employment[235]). The CRE appears to have been considerably more adventurous in its attitude towards formal investigations. And although significant delays were experienced with such investigations, the EOC's investigations were also interminably slow on occasion despite their far smaller number. Nevertheless, part of the CRE's scope for manœuvre in this area was curtailed by judicial decisions,[236] and formal investigations have proved a less than adequate mechanism for the collective challenge of discrimination. This is unfortunate in view of the intention, expressed in the race discrimination White Paper, that the CRE's investigative powers would account for much of the legislative enforcement of the new Race Relations Act.

The EOC and CRE were not limited to conducting formal investigations but were empowered, in addition, to take action against discriminatory advertisements and persistent discrimination, etc. If the EOC's utilization of its formal investigation powers was disappointing, the position with regard to its other powers (action against persistent discrimination, etc.), was even less impressive. In the period 1977–92 the *Annual Reports* record two cases relating to persistent discrimination by employers, two each against employers who persistently instructed job centres to discriminate and who placed discriminatory advertisements, and a handful of cases in which employers capitulated to EOC demands in the face of threatened formal investigations or action relating to instructions to discriminate.[237] More recently, a smattering of cases relating to discriminatory advertisements and inducement and/or pressure to discriminate have passed through the tribunals. But the extreme rarity of actions against persistent discrimination is hard to defend in view of evidence (see text after note 195 above) of employers' common inaction in the aftermath of successful discrimination claims.[238] Employers might well adopt a different attitude if successful discrimination claims were followed up by

[234] See Gregory, n. 229 above, 368–9.
[235] In all, of the 24 investigations started between 1977 and 1982, 8 resulted in nondiscrimination notices; in each of these cases there was an appeal and, of these, four notices quashed (one being substituted by a more limited notice), the other 4 withdrawn on the CRE's agreement to vary—see McCrudden *et al.*, n. 229 above, 76–7.
[236] *Hillingdon* and *Prestige*, n. 232 above.
[237] *Annual Report 1988, 1986,* and *1988* respectively. In 1985, action relating to instructions to discriminate was taken against Barclays, in 1988 against Clarks, and in 1986 a further three were threatened and agreement reached.
[238] Criticized by Chambers and Horton, n. 209 above, 179.

EOC investigation. Again, as with formal investigations, the CRE appears to have been rather more active in these areas: the *Annual Reports* 1990–4, for example, each refer to a number of proceedings started, as well as to agreements reached, in respect of discriminatory advertisements and instructions/pressure to discriminate. Again, however, the power to take action against persistent discrimination appears to have amounted to little more than an empty promise.

VI. CONCLUSION

It is evident from the above that neither the Sex Discrimination nor the Race Relations Acts have been an unmitigated success. In particular, the Sex Discrimination Act has failed to make any substantial impact on the most significant causes of women's inequality in the labour market: namely, their horizontal and vertical segregation within narrow parts of the occupational and industrial spectrum and, most especially, the crippling effects of their movement into part-time work. The evidence relating to employer recruitment practices, in terms of their impact both on women in general and on part-time women workers in particular; the everyday nature of sexual harassment; the persistence of the commonplace distinction between 'real' jobs and those which can be done part-time (for evidence of this one need look no further than the judgment in *Clymo* v. *Wandsworth*), all point to a failure on the part of the 1975 Act to 'create a climate of opinion which will create a momentum in the right direction' to eliminate discrimination[239] (*per* Roy Jenkins MP, Secretary of State for the Home Department, introducing the Sex Discrimination Bill.).

The Race Relations Act, too, has failed to address the very real problems faced by ethnic minority women: in particular, their segregation into a narrow range of low-status jobs in declining industries and occupations, and the impact of these and other factors on their relative levels of pay. With the exception of some movement into professional jobs largely serving ethnic minority client bases, ethnic minority women have experienced relatively little improvement, in terms both of occupational status and relative pay, since the mid-1970s.

That these failures have occurred is not surprising in view of the various shortcomings of the Acts which have been outlined above, most notably: the reliance of both Acts on individual complainants in the absence of legislative support mechanisms; the difficulties of proving discrimination; the non-recognition, for many years, of some of the most commonplace discrimination suffered by women (pregnancy, maternity) *as* sex discrimination coupled with the difficulties associated with the characterization of much other commonplace discrimination (notably, that against part-timers) as indirect; the paucity of the compensation typically awarded.

[239] N. 16 above, col. 516.

The result of these inadequacies, together with the problems relating to EOC and CRE enforcement, is that relatively little has changed over the twenty years in which anti-discrimination legislation has been in force. Segregation persists in terms of both sex and race, and it is clear from the preceding chapters that substantial wage gaps exist both between men and women in general and between women of different ethnic groups. To the extent that the gender–pay (and the race–pay) gap is the result of factors such as women's (and, in particular, part-time women workers' and ethnic minority women workers') lack of access to the variety of jobs that men do, that gap can be seen as testament to the failure of the Sex Discrimination and Race Relations Acts. How this gap may best be addressed is the subject matter of Chapters 7 to 10. Prior to this investigation, Chapter 6 will consider the extent to which the gender–pay gap ought properly to be regarded as the result of 'discrimination' at all.

[6]

Discrimination and Pay

I. INTRODUCTION

The preceding chapters have charted the position of women in the labour market, the history of UK equality legislation, and the impact of this legislation over the past two decades. It would appear that, although the Equal Pay and Sex Discrimination Acts have not *entirely* failed *all* women, neither can they be regarded as resounding successes. Not only are women segregated into different and lower-paid jobs than men (both in terms of occupation and workplace); not only are part-time workers trapped, in large part, in poorly rewarded jobs for which they are over-qualified; but overt sex-typing of jobs according to factors such as pay and promotion prospects remains common. In addition, ethnic minority women remain particularly disadvantaged in the labour market and the Race Relations Act 1976 appears to have had little impact either on the high levels of racial segregation under which many ethnic minority women work or upon their relative levels of pay. Despite over twenty years of legislation aimed at eliminating discrimination in employment, the central planks of women's disadvantage (that is, their segregation into poorly-paying workplaces and their concentration in jobs which pay less than those done by men) remain largely unchanged.

The focus of this book is on pay inequality between women and men, both generally and, in particular, as it impacts upon full-time and part-time women workers, upon white and ethnic minority women workers. But the manner in which equality may best be achieved depends upon the source of the gender–pay gap (and of the particular gaps which comprise it). If the gap results mainly from men and women doing unequal work, it may best be tackled by mechanisms designed to place women workers in more demanding jobs. If, on the other hand, it is attributable more to factors such as the underpayment, relative to job quality, of women's work, a different approach may be required. Once the sources of the gap have been identified, consideration must be given to the extent to which existing legislation has been capable of dealing with that part of it which is attributable to discrimination, and then to the shape which any new approach might adopt.

II. LOCATING WOMEN'S UNDERPAYMENT

(A) SAME WORK, DIFFERENT WAGES

It is clear from Chapter 2 that the gender–pay gap is all-pervasive, that it exists whether women and men are compared within or across industries, within or across occupations. If we consider men and women within the same occupations (tables 2.23 and 2.28, together with accompanying text), we see that full-time women earn between 68 per cent and 94 per cent of the hourly rates earned by men in the same broad occupational categories, part-time women workers between 52 per cent and 92 per cent in 1995. Even when men and women are compared at the lower levels of disaggregation the differences, though reduced, remain. In general, the gender–wage gap is greatest towards the top of the earnings distribution.

Women are paid less than men, and part-time workers less (on an hourly basis) than those who work full-time, even when they are engaged in the same work. But this disparity may arise in one (or both) of two ways: in the first place, women may be differently paid for performing the *same* job in the *same* workplace. If this were the case then the provisions of the Equal Pay Act might be of some assistance, although women's lower rates of payment might be explained by reference to factors such as age/work experience/seniority within the workplace or concentration in lower grades which might (but might not) be discrimination-free. Alternatively, women might be doing the same *jobs* as men, but doing them in female *workplaces*, with the effect that no comparison would be possible under the Equal Pay Act (save if they were employed by the same or an associated employer 'in the same employment', for which see Chapter 1).

Seniority

There is some evidence that men and women are paid differently for performing the *same* work in the *same* workplaces. Where this happens, however, it appears to result from women's lower position within the hierarchy and from the differently impacting nature of 'reward' systems, rather than from straightforward discrimination in basic hourly rates. We saw in Chapter 5, for example, that women managers, teachers, doctors, civil servants, and solicitors are concentrated at lower levels of their respective job hierarchies than are men and women accountants are still only half as likely to become company directors or partners in large firms as are men. Women's hierarchical position results in their pay being held down relative to that of men within those occupations. But this itself should perhaps be regarded as evidence of discrimination. It is clear from the ECJ decisions in *Handels- og Kontorfunktionærnes Forbund i Danmark* v. *Dansk Arbejdsgiverforening (acting for Danfoss)* and in *Nimz* v. *Freie und Hansestadt Hamburg* (see Chapter 1) that experience, seniority, etc. should be rewarded only to the extent that they are actually important to the performance of the particular job where their reward serves to disadvantage women. Similarly, to the extent that promotion depends on such disparately impacting factors as seniority and experience, it is acceptable only if objectively justified within *Danfoss* and *Nimz*. The application of these cases may well raise some questions about, for example, the fact that one in five women accountants who take career breaks for child-bearing reasons are downgraded on return, and that promotion from part-time accountancy work is still unusual, even in the public sector.

Hours

More generally, any link between pay and long service or pay and 'flexibility' results, almost invariably, in lower earnings for women (see table 2.1).[1] Not only are women likely to have been with their current employers for a shorter period than have men, but they are considerably more likely than men to experience labour market interruptions associated with child-bearing and -rearing, and are less likely to be able, as mothers, to change working patterns on demand. Women generally also work less paid overtime, with the result that, where weekly earnings are substantially affected by the amount of overtime undertaken, women's wages suffer. In 1996, for example, 8.4 per cent of men's and 3.4 per cent of women's weekly wages consisted of payments for overtime and shift work.[2] For manual men and women the proportions were 17.6 per cent and 9.1 per cent respectively.[3]

While the practice of paying employees more for working more hours can hardly be disputed, any significant weighting of payment towards hours worked overtime (i.e. by paying substantially enhanced wages for overtime work) will exert a downward force on women's relative pay.[4] Women are not only less likely to be able to take on overtime work (typically being responsible for getting children up in the morning, collecting them from school or childcare, preparing their meals) but, at least where sex segregation is a factor, they are also less likely to be offered it (this is discussed in the text to note 121 below). And if full-time women workers are disproportionately excluded from overtime payments, *part-time* women workers are even more disadvantaged. Hunter and McInnes' study, *Employers' Labour Use Strategies*, found that such workers usually:

---

[1] A. Zabalza and Z. Tzannatos, *Women and Equal Pay: The Effects of Legislation on Female Employment and Wages in Britain* (Cambridge, Cambridge University Press, 1985), 90–2 attribute most of the gender–wage gap to differences in labour market experience and the effects of labour market interruptions on women's wages.

[2] NES 1996, table 1.   [3] *Ibid.*

[4] Industrial Relations Services, *Pay and Gender in Britain: A Report for the EOC (2)* (London: IRS, 1992), found that premia were often restricted in practice to male-dominated jobs.

qualified for overtime payments only after they had exceeded the normal work-ing hours for *full-time* employees . . . the normal working hours which they had to exceed in order to qualify for a premium rate to compensate for disruption to their normal working and leisure pattern was defined in terms not of their own normal experience but that of full-time employees. Given the gender distribution of part-time workers, and the significance . . . attributed to domestic commitments in determining the labour supply position of part-timers, this meant that women who might face considerable inconvenience in working extra unsocial hours, nevertheless received no premium for them unless they were so considerable as to take them beyond the full-time normal hours.[5]

The authors of *Pay and Gender in Britain (2)* reported that part-timers who worked on the (typically exclusively female) 'twilight shifts' were not usually integrated into normal payment structures and that, while part-timers more generally 'are in most cases theoretically eligible for exactly the same terms and conditions as their full-time counterparts on a pro-rata basis, restrictions on certain payments and the working patterns of part-timers mean that they are unlikely to receive payments in the same way as full-timers'.[6]

Discretionary Pay Systems

Paid overtime work and additional payments for shift work account for a larger proportion of manual workers' than of non-manual workers' weekly wages (16.5 per cent: 3.2 per cent in 1996[7]). But the benefit which non-manual women gain from the relative insignificance of these elements of pay is balanced by the impact on their wages of 'performance-related' or 'merit' pay. These forms of payment go unrecorded by the NES.[8] One survey, conducted in Leicester and Reading in 1990, found that four-fifths of organizations related the basic pay of at least some employees to managerial assessment of performance: in 57 per cent of these cases assessment was made on an individual, rather than collective, basis. The use of performance-related pay was twice as common for non-manual as for manual employees (two-thirds of organizations used performance-related pay to determine the wages of non-manual workers, one-third to determine the wages of manual workers), and most common for man-agerial and professional staff (three-quarters of organizations used it for this purpose).[9] And performance-related pay has remained popular: in 1994 the Industrial Society reported that 61 per cent of pay rises made in the finance sector were linked with the assessment of individuals' per-formance. In the public sector the proportion was considerably smaller, at

[5] L. Hunter and J. McInnes, *Employers' Labour Use Strategies—Case Studies* (London: HMSO, 1991), Department of Employment Research Paper No 87, 37.

[6] IRS, n. 4 above, 26–7 and 38.   [7] 1996 NES, table 1.

[8] Save for mainly manual payment by results.

[9] B. Casey, J. Lakey, and M. White, *Payment Systems: A Look at Current Practice* (Sheffield: Department of Employment, 1992), Research Paper No 5.

23 per cent; the average was 43 per cent. Nor does performance-related pay invariably constitute only one of several elements of pay increases: one-fifth of companies (one-third in the finance sector) relied exclusively upon individual assessment to determine pay increases.[10]

Performance-related pay impacts unfavourably upon women's wages. Not only are they less likely to be eligible for such pay, but the calculation of individual wages tends to be done so as to disadvantage women.[11] Case studies undertaken by the Institute of Manpower Studies revealed that managers responsible for determining merit pay valued different attributes in male and female workers, and disproportionately favoured stereotypically male traits in making pay awards. Managers in the finance company surveyed, for example, cited intelligence, dynamism, energy, assertiveness, creativity, powers of persuasion, and ambitiousness as important amongst male staff; thoroughness, organization, dependability, honesty, tactfulness, professionalism, competence, and commitment as valuable in female staff. The factors cited as important in male and female staff are stereotypical attributes of their respective sexes, and the impact of these stereotypical views became apparent when the average wage rises in male- and female-dominated jobs were studied. The incumbents of female-dominated jobs received an average of between 3 and 4 per cent in performance-related pay: for male dominated jobs this figure was between 9 and 10 per cent.[12]

The Equal Opportunities Commission's (EOC's) *Pay and Gender in Britain (2)* also reports that '[t]he most "objective" and formal methods of merit pay and appraisal are likely to be more readily applied to jobs performed by men than to those carried out by women'.[13] In general, little attention was paid by employers to the equality implications of their pay structures: '[m]any of the personnel specialists interviewed told us that pay equality was "not a live issue in our organisation", sometimes in spite

---

[10] Industrial Society, *Managing Best Practice*, reported in the *Employment Gazette*, July 1994, 232.

[11] In common with women lower down the hierarchy who are often excluded, in practice, from bonus payments as well as overtime premia. Women are also less likely to receive incentive pay than are men. Casey *et al.*, n. 9 above, 25 report that 31% of manual women and 40% of manual men received such payments, 17% and 13% of non-manual men and women respectively in 1989. While the use of such payments had increased among non-manual workers and decreased among manual workers since 1983 (using NES statistics), women were consistently less likely to receive them than men.

[12] S. Bevan and M. Thompson, *Merit Pay Performance Appraisal and Attitudes to Women's Work* (Brighton: University of Sussex, 1992), Institute of Manpower Studies Report No 234. Male managers also viewed employees' thoroughness, motivation, dedication, dependability, dynamism, assertiveness, maturity, aggression, and ambition as important in promotion decisions. Three of these factors are among those rated most important in men; two in women. Further, aggression is a stereotypically male trait and men are frequently seen as more mature than women. It is unsurprising, then, that male employees of the finance company were more likely than women with the same appraisal scores to have been offered training and promotion opportunities.

[13] N. 4 above, 2.

of factual evidence that their pay systems might not pass muster if challenged on the equal pay principle . . . many union officials seem to share this view'.[14] Small wonder, then, that according to the recent Social Change and Economic Life Initiative (SCELI) survey women were less likely to receive merit pay and those who did had their pay raised by only 6 per cent in comparison with men's 16 per cent.[15]

Not only does performance-related pay impact negatively on women's relative wages, but the payment of market-related supplements has a similar effect. *Pay and Gender in Britain (2)* reported that:

[p]erformance assessments of women's occupations often focus on the volume/ quantity of work, attitudinal and/or behavioural characteristics and casual judgements by line managers. . . . National level pay data are more likely to be used for 'male' occupations; and local pay data . . . for 'female' occupations. . . . Market supplements, or special salary scales in response to perceived market pressures, are more likely to be paid to occupations in which men predominate. There is also evidence that employers are more likely to consider ending these supplements for women than for men when the labour market eases. A lower ceiling may also be applied when payments are made to women.[16]

Sex Segregation

However great the impact of these factors on the gender–wage gap within sex-*integrated* workplaces, far more important, in explaining the wage difference between men and women doing the same types of job, is the effect of sex segregation *between* workplaces. We saw in Chapters 2 and 5 that women and men are concentrated within different industrial sectors, different workplaces. We also saw (tables 2.22 and 2.26) that women's lower average pay could not (particularly in the case of full-time workers) be explained by virtue of their (broad) industrial distribution, but that, instead, they were consistently paid less (both as manual and non-manual workers) than men working within the same industrial sectors. It could be argued, of course, that women (whether manual or non-manual) may perform very different work from that done by their male colleagues. This is, no doubt, true to a significant extent, although women are paid considerably less than men within the *same* occupational groups.

[14] *Ibid.* 40.
[15] See P. Sloane, 'The Gender Wage Differential' in A. Scott (ed.), *Gender Segregation and Social Change: Men and Women in Changing Labour Markets* (Oxford: Oxford University Press, 1994). The Social Change and Economic Life Initiative was a major study funded by the ERSC and carried out by 35 academics in the early 1990s. Its results are discussed in Scott and in M. Anderson, F. Bechhofer, and J. Gershuny (eds.), *The Social and Political Economy of the Household*; D. Gallie, C. Marsh, and C. Vogler (eds.), *Social Change and the Experience of Unemployment*; J. Rubery and F. Wilkinson (eds.), *Employer Strategy and the Labour Market*; and R. Penn, M. Rose, and J. Rubery (eds.), *Skill and Occupational Change*, all (Oxford: Oxford University Press, 1994).
[16] N. 4 above, 2.

And even when men and women are engaged in different jobs, the question remains whether the existence and extent of the pay gaps between women and men, manual and non-manual workers, are justifiable (whether, to use the terminology of the Equal Pay Act itself, women nevertheless perform work of equal value to that done by men).

The question of 'value' is one to which we shall return. But first, the issue of *workplace* segregation should be addressed. We saw in Chapter 2 that (the broader issue of industrial segregation aside) women and men, full-time and part-time workers, black and white, are found in different workplaces. Millward and Woodland, whose research is discussed there, found that the sex composition both of workplaces and of particular occupational groups within them had a major impact on the level of pay. The pay differences associated with sex were, in fact, 'substantially greater than the premium associated with working in an establishment with recognised trade unions'.[17]

In 1983, Millward and Daniels had reported, on the evidence of the 1980 Workplace Industrial Relations Survey (WIRS), that:

[t]he higher was the female proportion of the manual workforce the lower was the level of pay for semi-skilled and skilled workers. The trend was marked and consistent. *In cases where all manual workers were women, pay levels were only just over half of those in cases where hardly any or no manual workers were women* [my emphasis].[18]

In 1995, Millward and Woodland examined the effect of sex segregation on the wages of unskilled and semi-skilled manual workers, supervisors, and clerical workers. They found that, while the wage levels of female unskilled manual and clerical workers did not appear to decline with an increasingly female establishment, the wage levels of supervisors and semi-skilled workers did: '[w]here the establishment's workforce is 60 per cent or more female, semi-skilled workers' pay is approximately 30 per cent lower than in an establishment with at least 80 per cent males'.[19] Semi-skilled female manual workers also suffered with the increasing concentration of women within their occupational group.

The findings concerning female workers were mixed—it appeared, for example, that unskilled manual and clerical women workers' wages were unaffected by sex segregation. But the results for male workers showed a clearer relationship with sex segregation: '[a]s establishment-level female concentration increases, male earnings fall progressively. The pattern is clear for all occupational groups.'[20] The authors estimated that, for men,

---

[17] N. 4 above, 10.

[18] W. Daniel and N. Millward, *Workplace Industrial Relations in Britain: The ED/PSI/ERSC Survey* (London: Heinemann Educational, 1983).

[19] N. Millward and S. Woodland, *Gender Segregation and Male/Female Wage Differences* (London: LSE, 1995), Centre for Economic Performance Discussion Paper No 220, 16.

[20] *Ibid.*

the wage premiums assiociated with 'working in an establishment where the majority sex of the occupational group is male' were: for unskilled manuals, 29 per cent; semi-skilled manuals, 22 per cent; clericals, 12 per cent; and supervisors, 12 per cent.[21] And Millward's 1995 report for the EOC claimed that, where workplaces were at least 70 per cent female, they were almost three times as likely to employ low-paid workers as where they were predominantly male.[22]

Millward and Woodland's conclusions are supported by a number of other studies which have focused, in particular, on the wages of part-time women workers. We have already seen that women who work part-time are particularly poorly paid. It seems, from WIRS evidence, that much of this gap results from sex segregation. While part-time women workers earn substantially less than both full-time women and men, they are generally paid the same rates *pro rata* as full-time employees doing the same job in the same workplace (in terms of basic wage, though access to benefits such as pensions is more variable[23]). But part-time workers are concentrated in workplaces where poor pay is standard. One study found that work (particularly work seen as women's work) was offered as part-time by employers who could not attract full-timers at the rates they were prepared to pay.[24] Another study found that there was 'evidence of a strong association between "part-time using" and "female using" industries'; and that 'the higher the proportion of part time employment; the smaller [and, hence, more predominantly female] was the establishment'.[25]

(B) DIFFERENT WORK, DIFFERENT WAGES

It is fairly clear that women and men receive different payments in respect of the same kinds of work. The extent to which this can be attributed to 'discrimination' is addressed in the next section below. But for the most part, men and women do not perform the same work, either for the same or for different employers. Not only are women more likely than men to be engaged in non-manual work but, as we saw in Chapter 2, women occupy a different (and much narrower) range of occupations from those in which men work.

The issue of why women's occupations pay less than men's, in particular the question whether women's jobs are less 'demanding' than men's,

---

[21] Cf. Sloane, n. 15 above, 160—'while women earn most in jobs held mainly by men, men earn most in jobs held mainly by women, though the practice is more confused when the sample is split into manual and non-manual categories'.

[22] N. Millward, *Targetting Potential Discrimination* (Manchester: EOC, 1995), Research Series No 11. See also Sloane, n. 15 above.

[23] Hunter and McInnes, n. 5 above.   [24] *Ibid.* 37.

[25] D. Blanchflower and B. Corry, *Part-time Employment in GB: An Analysis Using Establishment Data* (London: Department of Employment, 1987), Research Paper No 57, 56 and 13.

is addressed at the text beginning at notes 50 and 96 below. It should, however, be noted here that such differential payment persists even in cases where employers accept that men's and women's jobs are equally valuable. One particularly notorious example of this arose in the aftermath of the equal value-inspired overhaul of the local authority manual workers' pay structure which took place in the mid-1980s. The overhaul resulted in the upgrading of most of the predominantly female groups with the effect that, according to one commentator: '[i]n terms of basic pay, it can reasonably be argued that . . . female local-authority manual workers have equal pay for work of equal value with their male counterparts'.[26] In terms of take-home pay, however, the story was very different:

bonus payments skew total earnings to such an effect that gender rather than grade is the better indicator of earnings . . . more men have access to bonus schemes and even where there are bonus schemes for both male and female groups the payments to women are usually lower than the payments to men . . . nearly all the high-earning bonus schemes, which could add up to 100% on top of basic pay, were for 'male' jobs.[27]

The gender impact of bonus schemes and other forms of 'add-on' payment is not confined to local authority workers. The EOC's 1991 study, *Pay and Gender in Britain*, reported that bonuses and premium payments were in practice often restricted to those in male-dominated jobs (labourers earning £2,000 less basic wage than word processor operators in one organization took home £1,200 more as a result of overtime payments). Even those organizations which used job evaluation techniques paid little attention to the equal value implications of their pay structures: while most organizations surveyed had reviewed their use of job evaluation schemes in the five years preceding the survey, few did so with equal value considerations in mind.[28]

III. EXPLAINING THE GENDER–PAY GAP

We have seen that the gender–pay gap exists both within and between occupations, within and between industries and workplaces. The next issue which should be addressed relates to *why* this gap exists between men's and women's wages. Is it the case, for example, that men are more skilled, that they have higher levels of education, commitment, and labour market experience than women do? Are men's jobs more demanding, men's

---

[26] S. Hastings, 'Equal Value in the Local Authorities Sector in Great Britain' in P. Kahn and E. Meehan, *Equal Value/Comparable Worth in the U.K. and the U.S.A.* (Basingstoke: Macmillan, 1992), 219.

[27] *Ibid.* Hastings draws her conclusions from the London Equal Value Steering Group's *A Question of Earnings, a Study of the Earnings of Blue Collar Employees in London Local Authorities*, Sept. 1987. The local authority pay structure was overhauled again in early 1997.

[28] IRS, n. 4 above. IRS surveyed 150 organizations in the private and public sectors.

workplaces more productive, than those in which women predominate? Or does the gap persist where skill, education, commitment, etc. are held constant? Is the gap explicable, in other words, in terms of the human capital of men and women workers? Or are men and women workers treated differently when it comes to pay? In subsequent sections we address whether the sources of the pay disparity should be regarded as tainted by discrimination, and the disparities to which they give rise therefore as unlawful; and question how effective the current legislation is at targeting any unlawful discrimination uncovered.

The first question (why does the gap exist?) is usefully addressed in terms of each of issues outlined above. I stated that the wage differences between men and women engaged in the *same* work were explicable in terms of:

- their different levels within occupational hierarchies—women tend to be clustered at the bottom; and
- the fact that men and women are found in different workplaces and that those in which women predominate pay lower wages.

In addition, whether men and women do the same or different work, pay practices may disadvantage women. Such pay practices include:

- heavy reliance of earnings on overtime payments;
- performance-related pay—women are less likely to work in the jobs to which it applies and, even where they do, they are generally awarded lower payments;
- the payment of bonuses, etc., only in those jobs in which men predominate and the disadvantaging of part-time workers.

Finally, women are concentrated in different occupations from men, and these occupations, typically, are lower paid than those in which men predominate.

But why are women clustered at the bottom of the occupations in which they work? Why do the workplaces in which they predominate and the occupations in which they are concentrated pay less than do those in which men are to be found?

Orthodox economists often argue that women are paid less than men for reasons which are related more to women's freely exercised 'choices' than to 'discrimination'. Two of the variations on this theme are (a) human capital theory and (b) compensating differentials theory. These approaches seek to explain why women are segregated into female occupations and female workplaces, and why women are clustered at the bottom of occupational as well as workplace hierarchies. Both attribute the gender–wage gap, in the main, to differences in the *supply* side rather than in the *demand* side of the labour market, i.e. to the actions of *workers* rather than those of *employers*.

UNIVERSITY OF WINCHESTER
LIBRARY

(A) SUPPLY-SIDE EXPLANATIONS

Human Capital Theory

The human capital approach was developed throughout the 1960s by economists such as Gary Becker and Jacob Mincer. Becker, in common with many other proponents of supply-side approaches, takes as a starting point the notion that workers are rational actors who make choices so as to maximize the income earned over an entire lifetime. Since investment in human capital (whether by way of formal education or specialist job-training) is regarded as a cost borne by the worker, the decision whether to acquire any particular set of skills involves a balancing of the future rewards of those skills with the immediate costs. In the early 1960s Becker argued that 'women spend less time in the labour force than men, and therefore have less incentive to invest in market skills'.[29] Further, the types of skills which women 'chose' to acquire would be less labour-market related than those acquired by men: '[a] woman wants her investment to be useful both as a housewife and as a participant in the labour force'.[30]

Solomon Polachek, too, argued that the differences between men's and women's earnings were attributable in the main to the different choices made by them. Not only did women invest less in training, he claimed, but their expectations relating to child-care affected the types of fields they would enter. In particular, he argued, women would avoid the technologically advanced areas of work in which skills would atrophy rapidly during career breaks and would choose those jobs in which discontinuity of employment was least penalized.[31] Women were paid less than men because they had less work experience (itself a form of human capital); because they invested less even when they were at work (knowing that their working lives would be shorter than those of men); and because what skills they did had atrophied during the career breaks associated with childbirth.[32]

Time moves on, and it became apparent, as the decades passed, that the rapid increase in women's employment, together with their gradual

---

[29] G. Becker, 'Investment in Human Capital: A Theoretical Analysis' (1962) 70(5) (II) *Journal of Political Economy* 9, 38.

[30] *Ibid.* 39. See also C. Hakim, *Key Issues in Women's Work: Female Heterogeneity and the Polarisation of Women's Employment* (Athlone, NJ: London Atlantic Highlands, 1996). At 133 Hakim suggests that concentration of women in liberal arts at third level education is motivated by their suitability for homemaking. Hakim also claims, 170, that female occupations are low-skill occupations.

[31] S. Polachek, 'Sex Differences in College Majors' (1978) 31 *Industrial Labor Relations Review* 498; 'Occupational Self-selection: A Human Capital Approach to Sex Differences in Occupational Structure' (1981) 63 *Review of Economic Statistics* 60. See also H. Zellner, 'The Determinants of Occupational Segregation' in C. Lloyd (ed.), *Sex Discrimination and the Division of Labour* (New York: Columbia University Press, 1975), 125.

[32] J. Mincer and S. Polachek, 'Women's Earnings Re-examined' (1978) 13 *Journal of Human Resources* 118; 'Family Investments in Human Capital: Earnings of Women' (1974) 82(2) *Journal of Political Economy* S. 80, 80–1.

penetration into many formerly male occupations, had failed to be accompanied with any dramatic increase in their relative wages. Further than this and despite the fact that women's increased participation in the labour market was accompanied by their falling turnover rates and the closure of the educational gap between men and women, women's wages actually fell in the United States, relative to those of men, between the mid-1950s and the early 1980s and did not exceed their 1955 level until 1986.[33] The lack of improvement in women's wages might, as Becker suggested, have been attributable in part to the increased supply of women to the labour market: not only would this have the effect of increasing competition for women's jobs, thereby driving down wages; it would also reduce women's average work experience, as many of the women entering the labour market would be returning after long periods of absence. But Becker's analysis is contested. In the first place, if all else were equal the increased flow of women to jobs would depress men's as well as women's wages—there would be a general increase in the number of workers available to employers, with the result that wages would be lower. And Francine Blau argues that women's increased participation in the labour market has resulted from their decreased tendency to exit, as well as from their increased tendency to enter, with the effect that the increased proportion of women is not necessarily indicative of a decrease in the average level of experience.[34] Becker himself accepted in the mid-1980s that:

[t]he modest increase in the hourly earnings of women relative to men during the last 30 years . . . has been an embarrassment to the human capital interpretation of sexual earnings differentials . . . the evidence still suggests . . . that the earnings of women and men would not be equal even if their participation were equal.[35]

[33] F. Blau, 'Occupational Segregation and Labour Market Discrimination' in B. Reskin (ed.), *Sex Segregation in the Workplace: Trends, Explanations, Remedies* (Washington, DC: National Academy Press, 1984), 117–18. B. Reskin and I. Padavic, *Women and Men at Work* (Newbury Park, Cal.: Sage Publications/Pine Forge Press, 1994), 103. Not until 1986 did women's median yearly earnings surpass the level (63.9%) they had reached in 1955. Between 1955 and 1986 they fluctuated between 55% and just under 64% of men's. See also F. Blau and A. Beller, 'Trends in Earnings Differentials' (1988) 41(4) *Industrial and Labor Relations Review* S. 13.

[34] F. Blau, n. 33 above, 125–6. Blau relies, *inter alia*, upon J. Mincer, 'Wage Differentials: Comment' in C. Lloyd, E. Andrews, and C. Gilroy (eds.), *Women in the Labor Market* (New York: Colombia University Press, 1979); and C. Lloyd and B. Niemi, *The Economics of Sex Differentials* (New York: Colombia University Press, 1979). See also J. Brannen, G. Mészáros, P. Moss, and G. Poland, *Employment and Family Life: A Review of Research (1980–1994)* (London: Department of Employment, 1994), 4—the proportion of mothers returning to work within 9 months of having their babies increased from one quarter to one half between the late 1970s and the late 1980s—a further sixth of new mothers were economically active within that time.

[35] G. Becker, 'Human Capital, Effort, and the Sexual Division of Labour' (1985) 3(I) (2) *Journal of Labour Economics* S33, S35. See also J. O'Neill, 'Role Differentiation and the Gender Gap in Wage Rates' in L. Larwood, A. Stromberg, and B. Gutek (eds.), *Women and Work: An Annual Review I* (Newbury Park, Cal.: Sage Publications, 1985).

How could this be explained? Becker attributed the remaining gap in part to a difference in *effort*:

[m]arried women with primary responsibility for childcare or other housework allocate less energy to each hour of work than married men who spend equal time in the labor force. . . . Since married women earn less per hour than married men when they spend less energy on each hour of work, the household responsibilities of married women reduce their hourly earnings . . . even when both participate the same number of hours and have the same market capital . . . household responsibilities also induce occupational segregation because married women seek occupations and jobs that are less effort intensive.[36]

Compensating Differentials

The bottom line, for the proponents of human capital approaches, is that women earn less because they are worth less to their employers. The 'compensating differentials' approach, on the other hand, claims that women only *appear* to earn less than men; that different advantages are associated with men's and women's work; and that, when all of these are considered, women have nothing to complain about. Stephen Rhodes, for example, recently claimed that:

[p]art of the wage differential between men and women may be explained by the former's relatively greater interest in obtaining high pay or in taking a leadership role, which generally commands a higher salary . . . men put more emphasis on wages and leadership opportunities . . . women . . . are more apt to stress non-monetary benefits, such as good physical conditions, convenient hours, or rewarding interpersonal aspects of the job—relations with co-workers and supervisors, the opportunity to help others, and the like.[37]

And other commentators have suggested that, 'whereas women may feel underpaid, they may not feel under-compensated', their take-home wages (remunerative compensation) being supplemented by the 'intrinsic compensation' of 'job security and safety issues. . . . The pleasant, sanitised working conditions in many office settings . . . friendships and sociability . . . jobs that allow for social interaction . . . scheduling flexibility . . . job status . . . "cause" or "calling" '.[38]

This approach found favour, too, with Judge Richard Posner in *American Nurses Association* v. *State of Illinois*. 'There are', he claimed:

---

[36] N. 35 above, S52. For a very recent articulation of this approach see Hakim, n. 30 above, 69.

[37] S. Rhodes, *Incomparable Worth: Pay Equity Meets the Market* (New York: Cambridge University Press, 1993), 14. See also M. Killingsworth, 'The Economics of Comparable Worth: Analytical, Empirical, and Policy Questions' in H. Hartmann (ed.), *Comparable Worth: New Directions for Research* (Washington, DC: Academy Press, 1985).

[38] N. Mathys and L. Pincus, 'Is Pay Equity Equitable? A Perspective That Looks Beyond Pay' (1993) 44 *Labor Law Journal* 351, 352–3.

inherent differences in the compensation schemes of traditionally female positions which make those positions more attractive to women. . . . Nurses may have
flexible hours; nursing is a professional occupation which generally provides for
additional benefits through hospital programmes for children and spouses; and
women are more likely than men to appreciate and seek the nurturing aspects of
the position.[39]

I shall merely note Rhodes' apparent assumption that women *choose*
not to be managing directors of oil companies/senior partners of law firms/
presidents of multi-national corporations or the United States, and that
they could reach these positions as easily as men if they wished (cf. Chapter 5). But where is the evidence that women have more attractive/con-
venient/rewarding jobs? How does Rhodes' assertion that women pick more
attractive jobs square with the great variety of female-dominated jobs
across the globe (in Uganda, for example, women dominate charcoal selling; in Nepal, road building; and in Hungary, electronics assembling[40])?
And how are we to be sure that the rewarding aspects of nursing are not
themselves balanced by the joys (hearty exercise, fresh air, limited supervision, etc.) associated with typically male jobs?

(B) ECONOMISTS' APPROACH TO 'DISCRIMINATION'

The extent to which either the 'human capital' or the 'compensating differentials' theories can be considered persuasive is a matter to which we
shall return. The reason traditional economists tend to favour the 'free
choice' approach to the gender–wage gap lies in their advocacy of the free
market. As one non-traditional economist put it: '[a]n economist is, almost
by definition, a person elaborately trained to demonstrate and to preach
that prices and wages are best determined in a free, competitive market
by supply and demand'.[41]

The free market is supposed to be rational—employers will act so as
to maximize profit, and those which fail to do so will not flourish.[42] Gary
Becker, for example, accepts that discrimination occurs, and that discriminating employers enjoy a 'taste' benefit in (for example) employing
only men which, when added to their pecuniary profits, increases their
overall profits.[43] Discriminating employers will, therefore, hire female labour

---

[39] 783 F 2d 716, cited by Mathys and Pincus, n. 38 above, 356. See also Hakim, n. 30
above, 66–71 on part-time working.
[40] Reskin and Padavic, n. 33 above, 56, citing UN statistics.
[41] B. Bergmann, 'The Economic Case for Comparable Worth' in Hartmann, n. 37 above,
71.
[42] For a different approach see Z. Tzannatos, *A General Equilibrium Model of Discrimination
and its Effects on Incomes* (London: LSE, 1986), Centre for Labour Economics, Discussion
Paper 1986.
[43] G. Becker, *The Economics of Discrimination* (Chicago, Ill.: University of Chicago Press,
1957).

only at a discount sufficient to offset the non-pecuniary 'taste' cost or may, alternatively, maximize total 'profits' even by hiring more expensive male labour. But for Becker, and for neo-classical economists generally, discrimination in the hiring practices of employers cannot drive down women's wages in the longer term.[44] While discriminating employers may manage initially to set a market rate for women's wages which is lower than that for men: 'if men and women are equally productive . . . but nevertheless receive different wages in the same job, then an employer who is interested only in pecuniary profits [a non-discriminating employer[45]] will want his . . . workforce to consist entirely of women: otherwise, costs will be higher than the minimum possible'.[46]

Non-discriminating employers who hire female labour at the lower rate will make higher financial profits as a result and will, therefore, eventually drive discriminating employers out of business.[47] And even if discriminating employers make sufficient profit to remain viable, competition among non-discriminating employers for (initially underpaid) women's labour will drive the price of that labour up to the level which reflects women's productivity: 'wages are determined by the market, not by any ex ante determination of relative merit. If women act rationally as a group, they would be able to create a supply and demand ratio that would force the wages for women up to meet that lack of supply'.[48]

That this has failed to happen is evidence that the gender–wage gap is not the product of discrimination by employers (although it may, of course, result from societal expectations relating to women and domestic responsibilities).[49]

(C) TESTING THE ARGUMENTS—HUMAN CAPITAL THEORY

Answering orthodox economists on their own terms and leaving aside, for a moment, issues of discrimination in terms of access to jobs, training, promotion, etc.; can the gender–pay gap be attributed to women's skill, education, and effort levels, or to their preference for jobs which compensate them in terms other than the purely financial? Taking first the human capital arguments, the impact of bonus payments and heavily weighted overtime premia on women's relative rates of pay has already been mentioned: to the extent that they are unequally available to equally

---

[44] The same is true for those who favour the 'statistical discrimination' to the 'taste' approach.

[45] 'Non-discriminating' in terms of employers' personal taste.

[46] Killingsworth, n. 37 above, 91.

[47] See Blau, n. 33 above. For an example of this approach see V. Fuchs, 'Women's Quest for Economic Equality' (1989) 3(1) *Journal of Economic Perspectives* 25, 28 ff. and, more generally, his book of the same name (Cambridge, Mass.: Harvard University Press, 1988).

[48] Mathys and Pincus, n. 38 above, 159.   [49] Killingsworth, n. 37 above.

rated male and female employees, the wage gap between those employees cannot be attributed to women's lower human capital values.

Skill

Research carried out by Jill Rubery and others in Northamptonshire, too, calls into question the idea that pay differences can be attributed, for the most part, to differences in the levels of skill possessed. The study concluded that women workers were paid less not *because* they were concentrated in jobs requiring less skill, but *despite* their working in jobs very similar to those performed by men in different organizations.[50] A redistribution of the skill content of men's and women's full-time jobs would, the study found, reduce the gender–pay gap by only 26 per cent, whereas paying the same for jobs of similar content would slash the gap by 71 per cent.[51]

Rubery *et al.* found evidence that different factors account for at least some part of the pay gap between part- and full-time workers from that between men and women full-time workers. Fully 39 per cent of part-time women workers (in comparison with 19 per cent and 13 per cent respectively of full-time men and women) came within the partly or un-skilled category.[52] Even this should, however, be treated with caution—'the evidence suggests that women, and especially those in part-time jobs, are more likely to underrate the skill and content of their jobs' than are men.[53] And even if skill was assessed in line with the perceptions of jobs' incumbents, paying part-time women the same as men having the same skill would have reduced the hourly pay gap between them by 67 per cent, redistributing the skill content of their jobs only by 24 per cent.[54]

Some explanation of the gender–pay gap is provided by a study conducted in 1990 in the Northern Irish clothing industry.[55] The study found that women were very segregated in terms of occupation: nineteen of every twenty employees worked in occupations which were at least two-thirds same-sex; seventeen in twenty worked in occupations which were at least 90 per cent same-sex. What is perhaps most interesting about this study is its findings on *perceptions* of the skills associated with women's work. Whereas male jobs were viewed as skilled and organized so as to reward the increase of skills with experience, women's jobs were not regarded as skilled: no account was taken of the skills which women brought into the job with them, and women's pay structures were flat. Women were

---

[50] S. Horrell, J. Ruberry, and B. Burchell, 'Unequal Jobs or Unequal Pay?' (1990) 20 *Industrial Relations Journal* 176. Job skills were compared using index allocating points for responsibility, degree of supervision, autonomy, training, & education.
[51] J. Rubery and B. Burchell, 'Part-time Work and Gender Inequality' in Scott, n. 15 above, 216.
[52] *Ibid.* 209.   [53] *Ibid.* 218.   [54] *Ibid.* 216.
[55] E. McLaughlin and K. Ingram, *All Stitched Up: Sex Segregation in the Northern Ireland Clothing Industry* (Belfast: Northern Ireland EOC, 1990).

concentrated in the lowest graded and lowest paid occupations, and were, the study concluded, paid a 'female rate' regardless of actual work.[56]

In 1982 Craig *et al.* reported the findings of a series of case studies in industries from which Wages Councils had been withdrawn. They found that:

[i]n many of the survey firms, in all [but one of the five] . . . industries . . . , there was still no grading for women's jobs even after equal pay. These . . . firms would often recognise differences in skill between the women workers . . . but nevertheless pay all of them at the same rate, justifying the practice on the basis that any differentiation would cause resentment amongst the other women workers. The fact of women's pay being less than men's cannot therefore simply be explained on the grounds that women's work is less skilled, for even within women's work there is little or no differentiation of reward by skill . . . the *predominant influence* on the shape and structure of the pay and employment system was the *sex of the workers* [my emphasis].[57]

And Frank Wilkinson points out, more generally, that:

low pay is generally found in jobs which are socially downgraded and/or those which are performed by classes of workers with low labour market status. Generally skills associated with domestic work or the 'servant classes'—caring, serving, cleaning, cooking, household and office management—and usually performed by women—are afforded low status. Certain manufacturing operations—sewing machine operations, fine assembly work, or work requiring feminine traits (nimbleness of fingers, the capacity to absorb boredom, and so on) which are assessed as having little value.[58]

Training

What about the idea that women invest less in job-related training than do men? The theory here assumes that people choose between relatively 'dead-end' jobs that pay higher rates in the short term but involve little or no training; and jobs whose initial starting salaries are low but whose training and advancement prospects are good (apprenticeships would be a paradigm of the latter). Women, it is argued, choose the former because

[56] See also Parliament of the Commonwealth of Australia, the House of Representatives Select Committee on Legislative and Constitutional Affairs, *Half Way to Equal* (Canberra: Australian Government Publications, 1993), para. 4.6.24: 'One of the major factors underlying pay inequality is the lack of recognition for the skills generally ascribed to women'.

[57] C. Craig, J. Rubery, R. Tarling, and F. Wilkinson, *Labour Market Structure, Industrial Organisation and Low Pay* (Cambridge: Cambridge University Press, 1982), 84.

[58] F. Wilkinson, *Why Britain Needs a Minimum Wage* (London: Institute for Public Policy Research, 1992), 8–9. See also P. Armstrong, 'If Its Only Women's Work It Doesn't Matter So Much' and A. Coyle, 'Sex and Deskilling in the Organisation of the Clothing Industry', both in J. West (ed.), *Work, Women and the Labour Market* (London: Routledge & Kegan Paul, 1982); C. Craig, E. Gansey, and J. Rubery, *Payment Structures in Small Firms: Women's Employment in Segmented Labour Markets* (London: Department of Employment, 1985), Research Paper No 48; R. Crompton and G. Jones, *Deskilling and Gender in Clerical Work* (London: Macmillan, 1984).

they expect to spend less time in the labour market, and so will benefit relatively more from immediate rather than deferred wages, while men choose the latter because they will spend more time working and thereby recouping their initial investments.

As one US critic of the supply-side approaches to the gender–pay gap points out, the proof of such a theory would be that 'female' jobs had higher starting salaries than 'male' jobs, and slower rates of wage growth thereafter.[59] Equally, Polachek's argument that women choose jobs whose skills depreciate less during labour market interruptions would be supported by evidence that women's wages depreciate at a lower rate during interruptions in predominantly female occupations. But Paula England has demonstrated that, in the United States, women's wages appreciate and depreciate at about the same levels whether they are working in predominantly female or other jobs.[60] And predominantly female occupations do not, either in the United States or the United Kingdom, offer higher starting salaries than those which are predominantly male. In fact, the only category of women who are paid more than men is the group of female manual workers aged under 18, who earned 111.5 per cent of comparable male salaries in 1995 (see table 6.1).

Table 6.1 — full-time women's weekly pay relative to those of same-aged men, 1995

women workers	under 18	18–20	21–24	25–29	30–39	40–49	50–59	60–64
manual	111.5%	83.7%	71.7%	72.8%	65.9%	61.0%	62.3%	65.3%
non-manual	*	91.9%	79.6%	79.9%	71.6%	60.4%	57.9%	68.0%
all	103%	87.2%	81.9%	84.8%	78.7%	66.5%	65.9%	74.8%

source: NES 1995, table 130
* not available

The explanation for the relatively high earnings of very young women may well lie in the fact that boys are more likely to be engaged in

[59] See P. England, 'Wage Appreciation and Depreciation: A Test of Neoclassical Economic Explanations of Occupational Sex Segregation' (1984) 62(3) *Social Forces* 72. Zellner, n. 31 above, emphasized that women's jobs would have high starting salaries. For criticism of the human capital approach in this context see also M. Marini, 'Sex Differences in Earnings in the US' (1989) 15 *Annual Review of Sociology* 343 and, on Polachek's theory of depreciation, M. Corcoran, G. Duncan, and M. Ponza, 'Work Experience, Job Segregation and Wages' in Reskin, n. 33 above. On depreciation, see M. Corcoran, 'Work Experience, Labour Force Withdrawls and Women's Wages: Empirical Results Using the 1976 Panel of Income Dynamics' in Lloyd, Andrews, and Gilroy, n. 34 above.

[60] *Ibid.* See also P. England, 'The Failure of Human Capital Theory to Explain Occupational Sex Segregation' (1982) 17(3) *Journal of Human Resources* 358. More recently, P. England, G. Farcas, R. Kilbourne, and T. Dou, 'Explaining Occupational Sex Segregation and Wages: Findings From a Fixed Effects Model' (1988) 53(4) *American Sociological Review* 544 suggests that female-dominated fields pay less initially and subsequently.

(low-paying) apprenticeships (women accounted for only one-fifth of 230,000 apprentices in 1993–4[61]). But the group of women who start work in manual jobs before the age of 18 is relatively very small (76 per cent and 62 per cent respectively of 16- and 17-year-old girls were still in full time education in 1993–4 and, in 1992, less than 10 per cent of 16–17-year-old girls were in full-time work—in 1995, girls under the age of 18 accounted for only 0.22 per cent of all women in full-time employment[62]) and the bulk of women start work in jobs which pay less than those done by men.

In addition, recent surveys of UK employees point to negligible differences in the levels of on-the-job training undertaken by male and female employees. In spring 1995, for example, the Labour Force Survey showed that the women surveyed were more likely than the men to have received job-related training within the past four weeks and that the training which they received was comparable (in terms of length) with that received by their male colleagues.[63] It should be noted, however, that women who work part-time receive less job-related training than both male and full-time female workers, and that women are more likely to pay for their own training than are men.[64] Since access to training is largely controlled by employers, differential levels of training may themselves be regarded as evidence of sex discrimination.

Education

Leaving job-specific skills aside, could it be that women are less educated than men? Zabalza and Tzannatos, dealing with 1975 statistics for the United Kingdom, reported that a combination of time spent in education

---

[61] 'Women and Training: Data from the Labour Force Survey', *Employment Gazette*, Nov. 1994, 391. The same point is made by D. Meulders, R. Plasman, and V. Vander Stricht, *Position of Women on the Labour Market of the E.C.* (Aldershot: Dartmouth, 1993), 116 on Irish youth wages, citing U. Barry, *La Position des Femmes sur le Marché du Travail en Irelande, Evolution entre 1983 et 1989* (1991), Report for the Equal Opportunities Unit of the European Communities, Brussels.

[62] 'Women and Training', n. 61 above, 397–401. 70% and 54% of 16 and 17-year-old boys were in full-time education in 1993–4 and, in 1992, just under 20% of 16–17-year-old boys were in full-time work, 1995 NES, table 130.

[63] *Employment Gazette*, Oct. 1995, LFS 53. 13.7% of men and 15.1% of women had received some training. This has been consistently the case between 1988 and 1995—although in 6 of the 9 broad occupational groups (excepting professional, managerial, and administrative and associate professional and technical) women did marginally (or, in some cases substantially) worse than men. This position would appear to have changed considerably since 1984—see F. Green, 'Sex Discrimination in Job-Related Training' (1991) 29(2) *British Journal of Industrial Relations* 295. On 1984 statistics, Green estimated that women had one third less chance of training, half as great a chance of job specific training. Cf. also *Social Trends* 1995, table 4.32—14.9% of men aged 16–64 and 16.2% of women aged 16–59 were receiving training.

[64] N. 63 above. Failure to train part-timers may itself be regarded as discriminatory—whether it is best tackled by pay regulation, however, is another issue. P. Sloane, n. 63 above, 161 found from the SCELI survey that '[w]omen had slightly less on-the-job training in their current job than men and the return to this was lower than men's'.

Table 6.2 — proportion of employees receiving training within previous four weeks, 1995*

	ongoing	3 years +	6 mths– 3 yrs	2 wks– 6 mths	4 days– 2 wks	2–3 days	1 day
men	17%	11%	19%	9%	8%	15%	21%
women	15%	9%	24%	11%	4%	13%	24%

source: 1995 LFS[65]
* where 100% represents all employees who received some training

and *potential* labour market experience (i.e. time elapsed since leaving school) could account for only 2.7 per cent of the wage gap between men and women.[66] Since women in the workforce were marginally younger than men, having only 23.2 years' potential experience as against men's 24.5, the difference attributable to years of education was less than 2.7 per cent. And given that women's *actual* labour market experience is generally a much smaller proportion of their *potential* labour market experience than is the case for men, the extent to which educational differences accounted for the gender–pay gap would appear to have been very small indeed.[67] Moreover, if education played a small part in 1975, it should play a smaller part today. In that year, 31 per cent of men and 22 per cent of women were qualified to GCE (now GCSE) ('O') level or above.[68] In 1995 the figures were 55 per cent of men and 49 per cent of women respectively. And, whereas women accounted for only 34 per cent of all undergraduates and 42 per cent of full-time undergraduates in 1970–1, by 1995 these proportions had reached 48 and 49 per cent respectively[69]). Men do still have marginally higher qualifications, but the differences are small, and working mothers (who account for 38 per cent of all working women) consist disproportionately of more, rather than less, qualified women.[70] In 1994, 82 per cent of women who had qualifications above 'A' level were economically active. This compared with 48 per cent of mothers who had no qualifications. The greater tendency of less-qualified

---

[65] N. 63 above.

[66] A. Zabalza and Z. Tzannatos, *Women and Equal Pay: The Effects of Legislation on Female Employment and Wages* (Cambridge: Cambridge University Press, 1985), 90—if differences in occupational and industrial position were taken into account, this figure increased to 28.1%—91.

[67] Women have more time out of the labour market than do men. Sloane, e.g. (n. 15 above, 161), reports that married women had around 7 years' less total labour market experience than married men. For single men and women the difference was around one year.

[68] *Social Trends* 1995, 52. See also G. Court, *Women in the Labour Market* (Brighton: Institute of Employment Studies, 1995), Report No 294 for evidence on the closure of the education gap.

[69] *Ibid.* 54.

[70] *Employment Gazette*, 'Mothers in the Labour Market', Nov. 1994, 403. Working mothers include only those women with children under 16.

women to quit the labour market on becoming mothers should go at least some way towards balancing men's marginally higher level of qualifications.

Women are paid less even when they are equally or more highly qualified than men in the sample. In the Northamptonshire study, for example, 26 per cent of the women but only 24 per cent of the men had higher education qualifications. It might, of course, be suggested that women were over-qualified for the jobs that they held—if they were not using their skills they could not expect to be rewarded for them. This was true in the case of part-timers—40 per cent of them had qualifications above the level required for entrance into their current job. But this was not the case for full-time women workers—only 28 per cent of them (compared with 27 per cent of men) were over-qualified in this sense.[71] And research conducted for the NHS Women's Unit showed that (in 1994) senior women NHS managers were better qualified than their male colleagues but were under-represented in senior management and paid less than men in almost every sector.[72] More generally, a large study of university and (then) polytechnic graduates carried out in 1990 (ten years after the subjects graduated) found that salary differences between men and women persisted when degree grades (and experience) were held constant.[73] In Canada, too, 'women in the labour force have more education than men in the labour force, even though women are paid much less. If women were paid for their education as much as men are paid for theirs, women would be much better off'.[74]

Productivity

Any assertion that women's lower pay is the result of a relative lack of qualifications on their part is, it would appear, at least open to question. But perhaps women are, however skilled and educated, less productive than men? This was suggested by Tory MP Ronald Bell, one of the few MPs overtly to oppose the Equal Pay Act 1970.[75] Could Gary Becker be right in asserting that married women (together, presumably, with cohabitees and mothers) put in less effort than men? If women's lowered wages were associated with the demands of hearth and home, one would expect

[71] N. 70 above (1994), 225.

[72] Creative Career Paths in the NHS Report No 1: Top Managers (IHSM Consultants report for NHS Women's Unit, 1994) reported in 56 Equal Opportunities Review 5.

[73] P. Dolton, G. Makepeace, and G. Inchley, The Early Careers of 1980 Graduates (London: Department of Employment, 1990), Research Paper No 78 (a study of over 6,000 graduates). Female university and polytechnic graduates with 3–4 years' experience earned 89% and 82% respectively of equivalent men's wages, those with at least 6 years' experience 84% and 77% respectively. The same pattern can be seen when graduates' grades were held constant: women university graduates earned between 79% (lower seconds and thirds) and 91% (firsts) of equivalent men's wages while women polytechnic graduates earned between 70% ('others') and 87% (undifferentiated seconds) of equivalent men's wages.

[74] J. Gaskell, 'What Counts as Skill?', in J. Fudge and P. McDermott (eds.), Just Wages (Toronto: University of Toronto Press, 1991). Cf. Sloane, n. 15 above, 161.

[75] 795 HC Debs. 966 (9 Feb. 1970).

that younger women would not suffer pay disadvantage. The gender–pay gap certainly increases with age (see table 6.1) to peak at age 50–59 (all women and non-manual women workers, 40–49 for manual women). But Becker's 'flagging housewife' theory would be hard-pressed to account at all for the gap which is evident at 18–20 years. And in the United States:

attempts to measure sex differences in labor-force attachment (including absenteeism and self-imposed restrictions on job choice) and their effect on sex differences in earnings have found these measures to be either unrelated or weakly related to earnings . . . sex differences in self-reports of work effort indicate that women actually allocate more effort per hour to market work than do men . . . social psychological research on internal standards of personal entitlement suggests that, with all else equal, women are likely to allocate more effort to work activities than men do.[76]

Closer to home, Millward and Woodland considered the possibility of differences in productivity in seeking to explain their finding (see Chapter 2) that women who performed the same jobs as men (albeit in different workplaces) do so at lower rates of pay. They found, contrary to the 'human capital' arguments, that predominantly female workplaces were no less productive than those in which men worked: 'establishment performance is not significantly affected by the level of female concentration. We therefore find no support for the hypothesis that higher female concentration is an indicator of lower human capital'.[77]

Experience

The final frequently cited component of 'human capital' is labour market experience. To what extent is the difference between men's and women's wages due to disparities between the length of time they spend in the workforce and/or to the periods of time they spend out of it? It is certainly the case that the gender–wage gap increases with age. Table 6.1, above, shows that in the United Kingdom, as in the United States, women's

---

[76] Marini, n. 51 above, 351. See also M. Hill, 'The Wage Effects of Marital Status and Children' (1979) 14(4) *Journal of Human Resources* 579.

[77] Millward and Woodland, n. 19 above, 21. As interesting as their findings on the human capital issue were Millward and Woodland's comments on their fellow economists. Noting that analysts of the Workplace Industrial Relations Survey (WIRS) data tended not to remark on the wage premium associated with working in predominantly male workplaces, 'save to case female concentration in the role of a proxy measure of low labour quality', they declared the contrast between this assumption and the recognition that the negative wage impact of concentrations of ethnic minority workers could be attributed to discrimination 'difficult to understand' (8–9). Certainly, the economists who attributed lower female wages to lower human capital accumulation appeared to do so simply on the basis that 'one would expect that a higher quality workforce would result in a higher gross weekly pay of the "typical" employee', and that women's wages were lower (8, citing D. Blanchflower, 'Union Relative Wage Effects: a Cross-section Analysis using Establishment Data' (1984) 22(3) *British Journal of Industrial Relations* 311).

wages fall progressively, relative to those of men of the same age, over their lifetimes.[78] In 1995, British manual women workers started off (at under 18) earning more than men of the same age, by 18–20 they earned 83.7 per cent, and by 40–9 only 61 per cent. Women's relative proportion of male manual earnings increased thereafter (62.3 per cent at 50–9 and 65.3 per cent at 60–4), but only because the increase with age in manual men's earnings reversed after 50. Non-manual women workers saw their earnings fall, relative to those of their male contemporaries, from 91.9 per cent at 18–20 through 71.6 per cent at 30–9, to 57.9 per cent at 50–9. Only after women's state pensionable age did they begin to narrow the gap (earning 68 per cent of men's wages at 60–64[79]).

This pattern—in particular, the high level of young women's wages (relative to those of men) is sometimes taken as evidence that the gender–pay gap is not due to any discrimination on the part of employers but, rather, to the decline in women's labour market experience, relative to that of their male contemporaries, which often occurs as a result of childbearing. But even if the increasing gap was due to the effects of labour market experience it would not necessarily be non-discriminatory (men and women might receive different returns on experience, or the extent to which experience is rewarded might be out of proportion, given its disadvantageous impact on women, to its effect on productivity).[80]

We saw in Chapter 5 that, under Article 119, experience may be rewarded only to the extent that it has a demonstrable impact on the ability of the worker to do the job in question. But even if the reward of experience were always regarded as justifiable, Zabalza and Tzannatos estimated (in relation to 1975 statistics) that only about 7 per cent of the gender–wage gap could be attributed to differences in actual labour market experience, although a further 50 per cent was the result of women's labour market interruptions[81] (wages dropped by around 3 per cent for each year

[78] US statistics can be seen in Reskin and Padavic, n. 33 above, 107. In 1991 16–24-year-old women earned more than 90% of their male contemporaries' wages, 25–34-year-olds 80%, 35–44-year-olds 68%, and those over 44, 61%.

[79] This pattern is consistent within broad occupational groups—see NES 1995, tables 128 and 129—the largest weekly gap for full-time women managers and administrators is 40.2% at 50–59 (up from 12.1% at 25–29); for professionals is 20.4% at 40–49 (from 7.4% at 21–24); for associate professionals and technicals is 28.4% at 40–49 (from 18.9% at 21–24); for clerical and secretarial occupations is 22.9% at 40–49 (from 7.1% at 18–20); for craft and related occupations is 44.2% at 50–59 (from 15.4% at 18–20); for personal and protective services, 41% at 50–59 (from 13.7% at 18–20); for sales occupations 47.2% at 40–49 (from 2.5% at 18–20); and, for plant and machine operatives, 34.6% at 50–59 (from 10.2% at 18–20).

[80] Sloane, n. 15 above, 161–2 found that married women had lower returns to experience than married men, although single women had slightly higher returns than single men.

[81] N. 1 above. 7% is reached by subtracting 2.7% (attributable to educational years and potential labour market years differences) from 11.1% (actual labour market experience and educational years). See also P. Miller, 'The Wage Effect of Occupational Segregation of Women in Britain' (1987) 97 Economic Journal 885—Miller's estimate is comparable for

spent out of the workforce, and women averaged seven such years). They left open the question whether this factor should be considered as 'discriminatory' or not, pointing out that in some jobs productivity would decrease substantially with absence (they gave as an example of this computer programming where three years' absence might result in a woman finding 'herself both a bit rusty as far as her programming skills are concerned, and quite at a loss among the new technology developed during her absence'[82]) whereas 'there may be other situations in which technological advances are less dramatic, and (or) in which the skill content of jobs is much lower, where absence from the labour force may have a very insignificant detrimental effect on productive capacity'.[83]

More recently, Jane Waldfogel studied the relationship between married mothers' wages and those of men. The 'mother' category is particularly important—we saw in Chapter 2 that women in this category are most likely to experience labour market interruptions. Waldfogel found that, whereas single childless women earned 95 per cent of single childless men's wages in the United Kingdom in the period 1985 to 1988, the ratio for married mothers to fathers was a mere 60 per cent.[84] She followed a cohort of women who were 17 years old in 1975 until 1991, when they were 33. She found that, while those who remained childless increased their earnings (relative to those of men) from 78 per cent in 1978 to 90 per cent in 1988, all the women taken together saw their wages fall from 76 per cent to 73 per cent over that period, and women who were mothers earned 71 per cent of men's wages in 1978 and a mere 65 per cent in 1988.[85] Women earned 82 per cent of male earnings at 23 but only 71 per cent at 33: the latter figure was held down mainly by the proportion of mothers whose earnings fell from 70 per cent of 23-year-old men's in 1981 to 64 per cent in 1991, as against non-mothers' 84 per cent in both years.

In contrast to the earlier researchers, Waldfogel emphasized her conclusion that human capital differences (in the form of labour market interruptions) explained only part of the wage gap:

only a small proportion of the gender gap . . . is due to differences in characteristics between young men and women . . . if women had the same characteristics

1985. The justifiability of relating wages to experience was assumed by the ECJ in *Handels-og Kontorfunktionærernes Forbund i Danmark* v. *Dansk Arbejdsgiverforening (acting for Danfoss)* [1989] IRLR 532, an assumption revised by that court in *Nimz* v. *Freie und Hansestadt Hamburg* [1991] IRLR 222.

[82] N. 1 above, 14.

[83] *Ibid.* For a critique of the 'rusty skills' explanation see P. Gwartney-Gibbs, 'The "Rusty Skills" Hypothesis', in B. Gutek, A. Stromberg, and L. Larwood (eds.), *Women and Work: An Annual Review III* (Newbury Park, Cal.: Sage Publications, 1988).

[84] J. Waldfogel, *Women Working For Less: A Longitudinal Analysis of the Family Gap* (London: LSE, 1993), LSE Suntory and Toyota International Centre for Economics and Related Disciplines, Discussion Paper WSP/93, 3.

[85] *Ibid.* 11.

they do now but received the same returns as men in the labour market, the gender gap at age 23 would fall 84% (from 19% to 3%) and at age 33 would fall 70% (from 30% to 7%). This means that the much greater part (84% at age 23 and 70% at age 33) of the gender gap is due to differential *treatment* [my emphasis].[86]

Differences in labour market experience, she found, did explain part of the gap (though men also received higher returns for experience than did women[87]). But by the age of 33 '*by far the most important factor* [my emphasis; 53 per cent of the gap] was family status: men received a premium for being married; women suffered for being mothers'.[88]

Conclusions

Much of human capital theory simply does not withstand scrutiny.[89] The gender–pay gap cannot, it seems, be explained by reference to women's lack of education, skills, or commitment to the world of paid employment. In the first place, the theorized relationships appear to depend more on assumptions about women's work than on hard evidence. Secondly, human capital theories fail to explain the abundant evidence that, skills, education, training, labour market experience, etc. held constant, men *still* earn more than women.[90] Paul Gregg and Steve Machin, for example, found that, while women managers were generally younger and had less tenure within their employing organizations than men, the significant gap between male and female managers' earnings did not simply reflect women's relatively junior status.[91] On the contrary 'the gap between their

---

[86] Waldfogel, n. 84 above, 47. Sloane, n. 15 above, 191 found that discrimination accounted for approximately one third of the wage gap between single men and women, one quarter of that between married men and women. It should be noted, however, that Sloane included as factors distinct other than 'sex' (the latter being the measure of discrimination) some, such as marriage and experience, which might themselves be considered discriminatory.

[87] Waldfogel, n. 84 above, 47.

[88] *Ibid.* 48. Sloane, n. 15 above, 169 also found that marriage raised men's but lowered women's earnings.

[89] See also B. Martin, 'Understanding Class Segmentation in the Labour Market: An Empirical Study of Earnings Determination in Australia' (1994) 8(3) *Work, Employment and Society* 357 for a critique of human capital theory in the Australian context.

[90] See, e.g. Dolton *et al.*, n. 73 above. Women were likely to have had more jobs than men since graduation (and, as a result, shorter periods of experience with their current employers) and to have worked for fewer years since graduation. But, whereas men gained with each additional job held (labour market experience held constant), this factor had no impact on women's wages. Salary differentials persisted when men and women's experience levels were held constant (female university and polytechnic graduates with 3–4 years' experience earned 89% and 82% respectively of equivalent men's wages, those with at least 6 years' experience 84% and 77% respectively).

[91] Remuneration Economics, *1990 Salary Survey* (Corby: British Institute of Management, 1991), cited in V. Hammond and V. Holton, 'The Scenario for Women Managers in Britain in the 1990s: Competitive Frontiers: Women Managers in the Triad' (1993) 23 *International Studies of Management and Organization* 71, found that women managers are an average 7 years younger than men managers and have 7 years less service with their current company.

earnings widens as one moves up the corporate ladder'.[92] Even Polachek
and Mincer, among the most convinced of the human capital theorists,
ascribed less than half of the gender–pay gap to differences in male and
female workers' attributes.[93]

Waldfogel's research has already been mentioned. Other recent estimates of the relationship between 'human capital' and the gender–wage gap
in Britain suggest that '[t]he primary reason for women's lower pay is
smaller remuneration for human capital attributes in their jobs: if women's human capital was remunerated at the same rate as men's, their
hourly pay would be substantially—of the order of one fifth—higher'.[94]

If full-time women's hourly remuneration was one fifth higher than at
present (80 per cent), the gender–pay gap would virtually disappear. In
the United States, too, there is evidence that:

white women of childbearing age invest in human capital at a far greater rate
than do their white male contemporaries; black women in the same age group
invest in human capital at about the same rate as their male counterparts. These
statements still hold true if . . . job tenure is treated as a measure of rates of investment in job-specific skills and . . . market experience is treated as a measure
of investment in general labor market skills. If . . . education . . . is also treated as
a measure of human capital investment, the gap in investment rates between men
and women grows wider, since both black women and white women have coeffi-
cients of schooling about twice as large as those of their male counterparts.[95]

[92] P. Gregg and S. Machin, *Is the Glass Ceiling Cracking? Gender Compensation Differentials
and Access to Promotion Among U.K. Executives* (National Institute of Economic and Social
Research, 1993), Discussion Paper No 50, 13. The same finding was made by the Jonathan
Wren Executive (*Women's Pay in the City* (London: Jonathan Wren Executive, 1990), cited
in Hammond and Holton, n. 91 above)—at manager level in the City of London women
earned 3% less than men; at director level the gap was 33%.

[93] J. Mincer and S. Polachek, 'Family Investments in Human Capital: Earnings of
Women' (1974) 82(2) *Journal of Political Economy* 576—even this estimate was based on a
group of 30–44-year-old women whose characteristics are more different to those of men
than are women's on average (see Blau, n. 33 above, 129–30). For empirical critiques of
the human capital approach see, e.g. M. Corcoran, 'The Structure of Female Wages' (1978)
68(2) *American Economic Review* 165—human capital factors explained only 36% of the
gender–wage gap between white men and women, 27% of that between white men and
black women. See also S. Sandell and D. Shapiro, 'An Exchange: The Theory of Human
Capital and the Earnings of Women' (1978) 31(1) *Journal of Human Resources* 103; F. Blau
and M. Ferber, *The Economics of Women, Men and Work* (Eaglewood Cliffs, NJ: Prentice
Hall, 1986); C. Goldin, *Understanding the Gender Gap* (New York: Oxford University Press,
1991); R. Wood, M. Corcoran, and P. Courant, 'Pay Differences among the Highly Paid:
The Male and Female Earnings Gap in Lawyers' Salaries' (1993) 11(3) *Journal of Labor
Economics* 417. The Canadian position is much the same—see T. Wannell, 'Male-female
Earnings Gap among Recent University Graduates', Statistics Canada (1990) *Perspectives* 19.

[94] J. Ermisch and R. Wright, 'Differential Returns to Human Capital in Full-time and
Part-time Employment' in N. Folbre, B. Bergmann, B. Agarwal, and M. Floro (eds.), *Issues
in Contemporary Economics: Volume 4, Women's Work in the World Economy* (New York: New
York University Press, 1992), 208.

[95] D. Boothby, *The Determinants of Earnings and Occupation for Young Women* (New York:
Garland Publishing Inc., 1984), 115. See also the testimony of H. Hartmann and S.
Aaronson of the Institute for Women's Policy Research, before the US House of Repres-
entatives Subcommittee on Select Education and Civil Rights regarding the Fair Pay Act
(Federal Document Clearing House Congressional Testimony, 21 July 1994).

The final point which should be made here relates to ethnic minority women who, as we saw in Chapter 2, are considerably less likely than white women to work part-time and who, in this regard, bear substantially more resemblance to white men than do white women. In addition, some groups of ethnic minority women combine this tendency to work full-time with higher educational achievements than white women or men. Despite all of this, they lag considerably behind white men in terms of wages.

(D) EVALUATING THE 'COMPENSATING DIFFERENTIALS' APPROACH

If human capital theories fail to explain the gender–pay gap, what can be said of the compensating differentials approach? Women are concentrated in the lowest-paid jobs. In 1990 the lowest-paid workers (men as well as women) included nursing auxiliaries and assistants, shop assistants, security guards and patrolmen, bar staff, hospital ward orderlies, road sweepers, sewing machinists, footwear workers, and repetitive assemblers.[96] The highest-paid workers, by contrast, include doctors, lawyers, and bankers. While these jobs are generally recognized as entailing high levels of stress, recent research shows that those at the bottom, rather than the top, of the incomes hierarchy suffer the most stress-related ill health, and the earliest deaths.

Not only do those at the bottom of the wage hierarchy die younger than those at the top, but they are also engaged in dirty and unpleasant work which generally carries more risk of injury than work which is better paid.[97] Bar staff, to take one example, earn the poorest rates of all, yet they are constantly vulnerable to attack from drunken and aggressive customers. They are also liable to criminal prosecution if they serve underage drinkers, and at the same time are under pressure not to alienate potential customers, not to mention trying to avoid being attacked. Security staff are under constant threat of violence; nursing auxiliaries, assistants, and orderlies spend a fair proportion of their time cleaning up excrement; and sewing machinists perform repetitive work of a sort which, although not generally recognized as physically arduous (because it does not often involve lifting heavy weights), is extremely demanding in that it requires workers to adopt uncomfortable positions hunched over their machines, often in cramped and unhealthy conditions. Doctors and lawyers, by contrast, while they may work long hours and shoulder a great deal of responsibility, generally perform their tasks in comfortable surroundings with a network of support and a considerable amount of autonomy and, therefore, control.

[96] Wilkinson, n. 58 above, table 1. Figures taken from the NES.
[97] See, e.g. the *Guardian*, 1 Nov. 1995.

Rhodes claims that predominantly female jobs are associated with 'better supervisors and better relations with co-workers . . . fewer illnesses . . . shorter commutes, easier time off for personal reasons'.[98] His arguments are echoed by the other supporter of the 'compensating differentials' approach cited above. But some of these factors may result simply from the proportion of women in the jobs—women are generally viewed as being more co-operative, less combative than men. The 'fewer illnesses' Rhodes attributes to 'lower risks'. But it is equally possible that any differences in sickness absence levels (if, indeed, women do take less time off—the more common assumption is that they have higher sickness absence records[99]) are associated with women's lower average alcohol intake or, given their lower levels of security in employment (see table 2.1), their increased fear of job-loss.

Rhodes claims that women have 'easier time off for personal reasons', but research carried out among women employed part-time in the United Kingdom suggests that this is not always the case. While part-time workers will have more 'home time' simply by virtue of being part-time, Collinson et al. found evidence that, even when recruitment was taking place to an entirely female (twilight) shift and 'from a tightly controlled labour market predominantly of married women with dependents . . . management was unprepared to make any concessions to their specific needs'.[100] This remark was made, it is true, in relation to one specific firm recruiting for one specific shift, but these conclusions are born out more generally by the findings made by Horrell and Rubery and discussed in Chapter 2—women are not only less likely than men to have access to 'cash' benefits such as pensions, sick-pay, a company car, transport subsidies, discounted goods, finance and/or loans, life assurance, private health care, and recreation facilities, but they are also less likely to benefit from paid time off for domestic reasons.[101] The only time off from which full-time women were as likely as men to benefit, and part-time women workers more likely, was of the unpaid variety.

Rhodes claims that one compensating factor for women's lower payment is that they enjoy 'shorter commutes'. But to accept this as a factor

---

[98] Rhodes, n. 37 above, 14.

[99] R. v. London Borough of Hammersmith and Fulham, ex p. Nalgo & Ors. [1991] IRLR 249.

[100] Collinson, Barriers to Fair Selection: A Multi-Sector Study of Recruitment Practices (London: HMSO, 1988), Equal Opportunities Commission Research Series, 117.

[101] Pensions were available in 73% of male full-time and 68% of female full-time jobs; sick-pay in 66% and 58% respectively; a company car in 30% and 10%; transport subsidies in 31% and 24%; discounted goods in 47% and 40%; finance/loans in 21% and 20%; life assurance in 39% and 19%; private health care in 31% and 22%; recreation facilities in 40% and 36% and paid time off for domestic reasons in 64% and 48% respectively— J. Rubery, S. Horrell, and B. Burchell, 'Part-time Work and Gender Inequality in the Labour Market' in A. Scott (ed.), Gender Segregation and Social Change: Men and Women in Changing Labour Markets (Oxford: Oxford Univeristy Press, 1994), table 6.7.

capable of justifying their lower payment is to beg the question. If women have to live closer to work because their earning potential is lower than that of their partners (as a result of which their work is seen as secondary) and someone has to collect the children from school, the fact that they have shorter commutes cannot be seen as negativing discrimination as a factor in their lower pay. On the contrary, women's greater responsibility for childcare may allow employers to hold women's wages down simply because women will not have the same choice of job opportunities as men. This is discussed further after note 112 below.

Part of what lies behind the 'compensating differentials' approach would appear to be the 'greener grass' attitude. Those who make claims about women's jobs are frequently those who have had little experience of them and who simply make assumptions, based on stereotypical notions, about them. Attitudes towards the worth of women's work are so deeply ingrained that, whereas Stephen Rhodes treats a 'leadership role' as a job factor which requires compensation, in the *American Nurses* case, mentioned above under 'Compensating Differentials', the court seemed to treat nurses' caring role, not as a compensable factor required *by* the job, but as part of the compensation *for* it. Even if we are to work on the (highly questionable) assumption that men are naturally inclined towards leadership and women towards caring, there is no excuse for treating the former as worthy of monetary reward and the latter as a substitute for it.

(E)   ALTERNATIVE APPROACHES TO THE GENDER–WAGE GAP

Why are women paid less than men? To the extent that the gender–pay gap results from women's occupation of lower positions than men in occupational hierarchies, human capital factors may well play a part. Women's concentration in the lower hierarchies of management, medicine, etc., may well be attributable in part to the fact that women working in these jobs are younger, or have less work experience, than their male colleagues. But we saw in Chapter 5 that, twenty years after the implementation of the Sex Discrimination Act, discrimination remains rife in recruitment and promotion decisions. Even in those cases where employers do not consciously discriminate against women, stereotypical assumptions about women's attitudes and commitment are common and reliance upon factors such as labour market experience, continuity of employment, etc., disadvantages women workers.

These issues are discussed in Chapter 5. But whether 'human capital' factors, rather than deliberate discrimination, explain the gender–pay differential which results from vertical segregation within occupations (and whether or not reliance upon these factors should itself be considered 'discriminatory'), they account for a comparatively small part of the gender–wage gap. They do not explain why men's and women's wages differ when skill, education, labour market experience, etc. are held constant. Nor do they explain the existence of payment structures which, by rewarding overtime disproportionately in relation to normal time working, by refusing part-time workers access to fringe benefits, or by restricting 'bonus' schemes or performance-related pay to male-dominated jobs, pay less in respect of 'female' jobs even where they are acknowledged to be equally as valuable as those done by men.

To the extent that the gender–pay gap is not the result of differences in experience, skill, education, working conditions, etc., how can it be explained? We saw in Chapter 2 that women generally do different types of jobs from those done by men and that, whether they work in different or the same occupations as men, they work in different places. The occupations in which women are concentrated pay less than those in which men predominate. Equally, and regardless of any similarity in job content between men and women in different workplaces, the workplaces in which women are employed pay lower rates than those in which men work.

Sex Segregation

More than one piece of research has attributed much of the gender–wage gap to occupational sex segregation. A study carried out by David Blanchflower and Peter Elias in the late 1980s on the employment histories of a cohort of 23-year-old men and women, for example, concluded that the very considerable disparity which existed between men's and women's wages could be explained neither by 'differences in their educational abilities or work histories' nor, in the main, by the childbearing histories of the men and women concerned. The authors found, instead, that it 'reflected the concentration of women's jobs in a narrower range of occupations then men's, with much lower occupational earnings over all age groups for those in full time employment'.[102]

Orthodox economists claim that factors other than level of qualification and years of experience should be taken into account in determining the worth of workers. So, for example, the fact that men work in engineering, technology, science, industry, and commerce while women work in education, health, and welfare, should also be taken account of before any allegations of 'discrimination' are made.[103] Robert Rector, for example, protests that any measurement of human capital made simply by reference to years of schooling or the like:

[102] D. Blanchflower and P. Elias, *The Occupations, Earnings and Work Histories of Young Adults—Who Gets the Good Jobs?* (London: Department of Employment, 1989), Research Paper No 68, 55–7.

[103] This, presumably, is why the authors of the study themselves took the view that only 7% could be attributed to 'residual discrimination': *ibid.* 2.

UNIVERSITY OF WINCHESTER
LIBRARY

leads to absurd conclusions. Example: A male worker, Bill, has 4 years of college and a BS in electrical engineering; a female worker, Anne, has 4 years of college and a BA in English. Both have been employed for 4 years; B works as an engineer and A works as a secretary. Since both workers have 4 years of education and work, wage gap models would expect them to be paid equally.[104]

But Rector's assumption, that any claim for equality between the A and B in his example is so patently absurd as not to require explanation, is questionable. It may well be the case, upon examination, that B's engineering job is more skilled, arduous, and/or responsible than A's secretarial job. It may equally be the case that A is 'composing letters and running the office, but, because she is 'only' a secretary [it is assumed that] the skills involved cannot be too complex'.[105] The British courts do not themselves, on occasion, appear averse to engaging in precisely this kind of reasoning.[106] But regardless of decisions reached in any particular cases, it is clear from the Equal Pay Act that jobs should be assessed, for relative value, in terms *inter alia* of the skill, effort, and decision-making that they entail, rather than by any unreflective assumption concerning appropriate job hierarchies. In asserting the absurdity of any claim to equality of pay, Rector is doing precisely what the advocates of 'equal pay' ('comparable worth' in the United States) are attempting to combat—he is reaching decisions on the relative worth of (stereotypically male and female) jobs on the basis of their titles alone, without attempting to examine those jobs to determine what skills they require, responsibilities and working conditions they impose, demands they make of their occupants.[107]

The question of comparative job 'worth' and how it might be evaluated is addressed in Chapter 7. But Rector is not alone in leaping to assumptions on this issue. Stephen Rhodes cites with approval a paper which claims that men's greater mathematical ability 'successfully accounts for the observed male–female differences in earnings'.[108] What remained unexplained by the authors of the paper was *why* mathematical ability (generally associated with men) should be important in determining earnings

---

[104] Rhodes, n. 37 above, 14 citing R. Rector, 'The Pseudo-Science of Comparable Worth' (1988) 635 *Heritage Foundation Backgrounder* 4.

[105] Gaskell, n. 74 above, 147.

[106] See, e.g. the decision of the EAT in *Davies* v. *McCartneys* [1989] IRLR 439 in which the appellant's claim was dismissed on the ground that her duties were 'not exceptional for a secretary'.

[107] Given the nature of much 'women's work' (nursing, operating a check-out, or otherwise serving in a shop, machining), there is little reason (other than the 'greener grass' theory mentioned in the text to nn. 96–101 above) to suppose that their working lives are more congenial than men's. Rhodes and others may assume that women work in cleaner or more comfortable environments. But this is often the result of failure to see the dirt associated with nursing, the physical discomfort inherent in shop work, the stressful nature of secretarial jobs.

[108] M. Paglin and A. Rufolo, 'Heterogenous Human Capital, Occupational Choice and Male Female Earnings Differences' (1990) 8(1) *Journal of Labor Economics* 123 cited in Rhodes, n. 37 above, note 35 to p. 14.

whereas verbal ability (more commonly seen as a female skill) 'is relatively unimportant in explaining incomes'.

Occupational segregation and its connection with the gender–pay gap are returned to immediately below. But first the question of *workplace* segregation should be considered. Millward and Woodland's research (discussed in Chapter 2 and at 'Sex Segregation' above) shows that women are concentrated in predominantly female workplaces, men in predominantly male ones, and that female workplaces pay less. An orthodox economist would claim that, if the workplaces in which women are to be found pay less than those in which men work, women workers must be less productive, in general, than are men. But Millward and Woodland found that pay differences between male and female workplaces could not be explained in terms of productivity: that those establishments employing women were no different in this respect than were those in which men worked.

If the links between workplace and occupational segregation and the gender–pay gap do not result from differences in human capital between men and women, how can they be explained? Stephen Rhodes would suggest that the poor pay in female-dominated workplaces is balanced by factors such as better physical conditions, more convenient hours and rewarding 'interpersonal aspects of the job'.[109] But the evidence that exists tends to suggest otherwise. Blanchflower and Corry's study, for example, found that part-time workers were concentrated in the same workplaces as were women generally and that those workplaces, in addition to having lower unionization rates than male workplaces, were almost twice as unlikely to have 'formal procedures for dealing with pay and conditions, dismissals or individual grievances'.[110]

Workplaces lacking disciplinary, grievance, and other procedures are not the most secure or congenial environments in which to work and, while women workers and their bosses report more harmonious relations than generally exist in male-dominated workplaces, this may well be because employees who work in small, close-knit, unorganized workplaces cannot afford to be as combative as can men who work in large, impersonal, unionized plants.

Homeworkers, too, perform arduous and frequently skilled work in the most unsatisfactory conditions and often at incredibly low rates of pay.[111] On the one hand it can be argued that they *choose* to accept such conditions in return for the advantages associated with working at home (lack of supervision, ability to combine work with childcare, a degree of flexibility —though the extent to which this latter is a factor of homework varies

---

[109] N. 37 above.   [110] Blanchflower and Corry, n. 25 above, 58–9.
[111] U. Huws, *Home Truths: Key Results from a National Survey of Homeworkers* (Leeds: National Group on Homeworking, 1994), Report No 2.

considerably[112]). But the question remains whether those whose access to the labour market is so restricted by the competing demands under which they operate should not be protected from the exploitation to which they are rendered vulnerable.

If we are to reject the argument that the gender–pay gap is explained, entirely or for the main part, by the differences between men's and women's attributes as workers; and also to reject the claim that women's jobs and/or workplaces offer them the same levels of reward as do men's, when all things are taken into account, how can we explain the persistence of the gender–wage gap? Why do men's jobs pay more than women's? Why, if women are being underpaid in the jobs in which they work, do they not move into the better-paid jobs which are more usually done by men? Why, if women are as 'valuable' workers as are men, does competition for their services not drive their wages up to the male level? The same questions could, of course, be posed in relation to the race–wage gap.

(F) LABOUR FORCE SEGREGATION/WAGE DISCRIMINATION

We saw in Chapter 5 that employer and worker discrimination, the greater cost for women of job search in non-'female' occupations (and for ethnic minority workers in 'white' jobs), and structural constraints on women's employment all continue to contribute to sex (and race) segregation in employment. But it is one thing to attribute segregation in employment to discrimination, and quite another to explain the link between women's segregation and their poor pay, relative to men and, in the case of ethnic minority women, to white women. An orthodox economist might still insist that, whatever the link between discrimination and segregation, the normal forces of supply and demand will eliminate wage-based discrimination— if equally 'valuable' women are paid less than equivalent men, for example, the competition for cheap female labour will be such as to drive women's wages up to the level of their marginal productivity which, assuming women are equally as valuable as men, will be the same level as the male wage. Those employers who do not wish to recruit women will be driven out of business by their reliance on more expensive male labour and will not, in any event, affect the wages of women employed by non-discriminating firms which will compete between themselves for women's labour.[113] It follows, as a result of this, that, if the occupations and workplaces in which women are concentrated are low-paying, these jobs must be less 'valuable' (whether or not this 'value' is capable of measurement),

---

[112] See A. Phizacklea and C. Wolkowitz, *Homeworking Women: Gender, Racism and Class at Work* (London: Sage Publications, 1995).

[113] For a (critical) summary of these arguments see B. Bergmann, 'Does the Market for Women's Labour Need Fixing?' (1989) 3(1) *Journal of Economic Perspectives* 43.

these workplaces less productive, than those in which men are concentrated. The same reasoning could be applied to ethnic minority women and men.

The flaws in this type of argument are not difficult to spot. In the first place, workers are not usually able to switch occupations at the drop of a hat—by the time a speech therapist (for example) becomes aware that she is paid much less at a senior level than are (predominantly male) hospital pharmacists and clinical psychologists it would be quite absurd (contrary to Wood J's advice to Dr Enderby[114]) to demand that she retrain in one of these areas.

Secondly, even if consideration is restricted to less skilled work, or to the same jobs which are performed by lower paid women in one workplace and higher paid men in another, or to currently 'male' and 'female' jobs whose skills are very similar, the notion that women could simply transfer from their jobs to those currently done by men requires (i) that the women *know* about the pay differential; (ii) that openings exist in the men's jobs/workplaces; (iii) that these openings would actually be made available to women who applied. It is submitted that, in practice, all three of these conditions will rarely be fulfilled.

The simple fact is that employers pay women less because they *can*.[115] Women do not have the same freedom of choice or, at a later stage, of movement within the labour market as men do. It is true that men are discriminated against in terms of recruitment (and much has been made of this recently in the wake of the EOC's publication of figures showing that, in 1995, more men than women complained to it of sex discrimination in recruitment). But this discrimination tends to take the form of refusal to employ them in low paid, dead-end jobs which are more usually reserved for women.[116] Women, on the other hand, are excluded from 'men's' jobs because they are unreliable or undeserving (men need 'good' wages more, since they are responsible for families); because they are less able than are men to comply with requirements such as being willing to work 'flexibly', or to work full-time, or to take on overtime work; because they fear discrimination by employers or sexual harrassment by predominantly male co-workers; because only the most determined and single-minded women can survive in 'male' jobs. Ethnic minority women are even more constrained within the labour market by the effects of race discrimination additional to the sex discrimination they experience as women.

Economists are fond of claiming that women *choose* the employment paths which render them less attractive to employers[117] (that is, they *choose* to work part-time, they *choose* to take time out for childbearing and rearing

---

[114] *Enderby* v. *Frenchay Heath Authority* [1991] IRLR 44, 60.
[115] See F. Blau, *Equal Pay in the Office* (Lexington, Mass.: D.C. Health, 1977).
[116] See generally Scott (ed.), n. 101 above.
[117] See also Hakin, n. 30 above, Ch. 5.

purposes, they *choose* to devote more time to their domestic responsibilities than do men). It is true that the bulk (80 per cent[118]) of women who work part-time are not seeking full-time work. Further than this, they generally define themselves as 'wanting' to work part-time. But women do not 'choose' part-time work from a position in which childcare is high-quality and affordable; they do not 'choose' it over full-time work which is flexible to their needs (rather than to the needs of their employers[119]); or from a starting position of equal access with their male partners (if any) to comparably paid work; they do not 'choose' part-time work over other arrangements which would enable one or other parent to take children to and collect them from school, and to take time off work to tend to them when they are sick; or over state-mandated, paid parental leave distributed between parents; they do not 'choose' part-time work in situations where this choice is equally open to the fathers of their children. Many women do not, in other words, 'choose' part-time work freely, from a position which allows them to demand the same benefits and status in part-time jobs as they previously commanded as full-time workers. The 'choice' to work part-time is, for many women, the only practical solution to the problem of combining parenthood with paid employment.[120]

The widespread need, on the part of women, to work part-time (or to preserve some degree of the flexibility required by children's primary carers) constrains their choice of jobs and, at an earlier stage, of occupations. Opportunities for part-time work tend to be very much more common in predominantly female occupations and appear also to be more common in predominantly female workplaces. This could be seen as a case of chicken and egg—if an occupation is largely the preserve of women, employers may be forced to accept part-time working: equally, if an employer accepts (or requires) part-time working, women are more likely to come forward than are men. But Hunter and McInnes' 1991 study, *Employers' Labour Use Strategies*, suggested that:

feminisation leads to peripheralisation . . . occupations, because they are dominated by women are seen to be suitable for temporary or part-time work . . . many of the skills traditionally associated with women's work are seen as readily transferable, capable of application in different workplaces with relatively short learning

---

[118] *Employment Gazette*, Oct. 1994, LFS 3. This compared with 36% of those men working part-time.

[119] The much-vaunted 'term time' working, for example, is open to almost no employees except those who work in the education sector where the schools are only open during term-time anyway. See *Employment Gazette*, 'The Flexible Workforce and Patterns of Working Time in the U.K.' July 1994, 239. In Spring 1993, all but 0.27 million of the 1.1 million employees who work term-times were teachers.

[120] S. Dex, *Women's Attitudes Towards Work* (Basingstoke: Macmillan, 1988) found that the presence of children, lack of childcare, and inequalities in the division of domestic labour had a greater effect on the decision to work part-time than did women's normative attitudes about work.

curves. . . . It is an open question whether these skills *really are* more transferable, or whether this is a question of employers' *perceptions* of them.[121]

Whatever the reasons, the fact is that all but the most highly paid women may be obliged, because of the paucity of high-quality and reasonably-priced childcare coupled with the unequal burden of child-care placed upon them (whether directly or by virtue of their socialized 'choices'), to work part-time in order to cope with children's needs. This has the effect that occupational (and workplace) sex segregation is perpetuated—women are propelled into 'female' jobs partly because those are the jobs which will allow them to perform paid work as well as school-runs, food preparation, and general child-rearing.

Sex-Segregated Labour Markets

Not only are women driven into 'female' jobs (ethnic minority women into 'ethnic minority' jobs) by these direct and indirect forms of discrimination, but their wages are held down, in these jobs, by virtue of their being female. I discussed the issue of part-time work above. Almost half of the women who work in the United Kingdom do so on a part-time basis. Many of these women are extremely disadvantaged when it comes to bargaining power—often their need to restrict their hours of work takes precedence over the rates of pay available. In addition, part-time workers (and women workers more generally) tend to be less able than typically full-time male workers to move homes in order to accommodate the demands of a new or existing job or to commute significant distances. This in turn allows employers to exert monopsonistic power over local labour markets for part-time staff, thus driving wages down. Frequently, prospective part-time women workers have to accept jobs at poor wage levels, if they are to work at all.

The Industrial Relations Services' 1992 report to the EOC *Pay and Gender in Britain (2)*, reported that: '[m]ost of the personnel staff interviewed believed that they did not need to make special recruitment or retention payments or benefits available to part-time workers, as it was assumed that part-time working was, of itself, sufficient inducement and benefit to such employees'.[122]

These relatively disadvantaged, often part-time, women workers create a labour force which, by virtue of its constituents' lack of bargaining power,

---

[121] N. 5 above, 46. See also S. Horrell and J. Rubery, *Employers' Working Time Policies and Women's Employment* (London: HMSO, 1991), EOC Research Series; S. Horrell and J. Rubery, 'Gender and Working Time: An Analysis of Employers' Working Time Policies' (1991) 15(4) *Cambridge Journal of Economics* 373. The authors argue that the gender of jobs tends to dictate how working hours are organized (and, presumably therefore, how accessible they are to women subsequently) rather than working hours requirements determining the pattern of occupational segregation.

[122] N. 4 above, 19.

exerts downward pressure on women's wages. Although it has become clear, in recent years, that high levels of unemployment do not serve to reduce the wage demands of (predominantly white male) 'core' workers (who enjoy relatively high levels of unionization, wages, fringe benefits, and security of employment), the unemployed not in practice being substitutable for this relatively privileged group, there is evidence that the reserve army of part-time and potential part-time women workers impacts on the wages available in predominantly female jobs. Research based on the 1984 WIRS found evidence of employers substituting:

women part-time for full-time workers because they had found recruitment of full-time workers difficult or impossible at the rates of pay the establishment was prepared to offer . . . where occupations were dominated by men, particularly men with skills, either of a manual or non-manual nature, part-time working . . . was not usually considered as a possible option, because of the nature of the male labour supply. These views of the male labour supply position could also be seen in public sector employers' reactions to competitive tendering. While they shifted some women's work from full-time to part-time contracts or reduced the length of the part-time contracts already used, it seems extremely doubtful that they could have responded to pressures on the reorganisation of male manual work . . . in the same way. Usually bonus schemes aimed at increasing labour productivity and reducing the overall number of full-time employees was tried.[123]

The existence of a large reserve of part-time women workers, skilled and unskilled, allows employers to keep the wages in predominantly female occupations low—should full-time women workers cease to be attracted by the rates of pay on offer, their places can be taken by part-time employees. This seems to be the case whether the women concerned are unskilled or semi-skilled manufacturing workers or, as became apparent in *Enderby* v. *Frenchay Health Authority and Secretary of State for Health*, professionally qualified workers. One of the defences put forward by the employers in *Enderby* (and accepted by the EAT) related to 'market forces'.[124] The hospital authority argued, *inter alia*, that the salaries paid to hospital pharmacists were better than those paid to speech therapists because demand for hospital pharmacists outstripped supply. By contrast speech therapy, being almost exclusively female, was opened to part-time workers, with the effect that any shortage of therapists was solved and the NHS did not have to increase their wages.

Women's wages are not only held down by the presence of part-time workers. We saw, above, that women work in different establishments from those in which men work. Above and beyond this, however, women work in different *types* of workplace than do men. Neil Millward reports that predominantly female workplaces were likely not only to have relatively high labour productivity in comparison with their competitors (according

[123] Hunter and MacInnes, n. 5 above, 36 and 46.   [124] N. 114 above.

to managers' reports), but that they also tended to share, *inter alia*, the following characteristics: they were small—typically they had between twenty-five and forty-nine employees (smaller workplaces being excluded from WIRS data); they had labour costs which accounted for more than 50 per cent of total costs; and their managers reported very good relations with the workforce generally. (Part-time, as well as full-time, women workers tend to be concentrated in 'female' workplaces.) Men's workplaces, by contrast, tended to be either small (employing fewer than 100 workers) and in the private sector, or very large (having at least 100,000 employees), and often state-owned; and to serve monopolistic product markets.[125]

It is obvious that workplaces in which labour costs account for the greater part of the total costs are more likely to exercise firm control on wages than are workplaces where other costs are more significant. It is also obvious that workplaces which have to compete in order to sell their products or services are likely to be more concerned about production costs (including the cost of labour) than are workplaces having a monopoly on the production of the goods and/or services they supply.[126]

Wages in women's workplaces are not only held down by virtue of their proportionately high labour costs and exposure to competition. As early as 1974, the Commission on Industrial Relations remarked that industrial organization was most problematic in establishments with, *inter alia*, the following features: small establishments operating in highly competitive markets; establishments having a high proportion of part-time workers; establishments having a high proportion of female workers.[127]

Small establishments, the Commission reported, were more likely to encourage close relationships between employer and employee (hence, perhaps, the managers' perception of harmony in female workplaces) which, in turn, inhibited the development of union organization: 'both [employers and employees] may be less likely to see the need for an outside body to represent employees' separate interests'.[128] The expectation of co-operation, rather than confrontation, is not conducive to a bargaining (as opposed to managerial dictate) mode of running a workplace, determining pay, etc.[129] It is well established that union membership (in particular, its association with collective bargaining) has a significant upward impact on workers'

[125] Millward, n. 22 above.
[126] Ethnic minority workers, too, tend to be found in workplaces with low-paying characteristics: according to Millward, they are concentrated in large, recently-established and non-union workplaces with relatively low productivity and poor employee–manager relations.
[127] CIR, *Report No 89: Retail Distribution* (London: HMSO, 1974).
[128] *Ibid.* para. 80. See Low Pay Unit, *Minimum Wages for Women: An Examination of Women's Earnings in Industries Covered by Wages Councils* (Manchester: EOC, 1980) for discussion.
[129] See also, in the US, L. Schur and D. Kruse, 'Gender Differentials in Attitudes Towards Unions' (1992) 46(1) *Industrial and Labor Relations Review* 89—their study found that structural barriers, rather than any lack of interest or, indeed, family barriers, explained women's lower levels of unionization.

wages.[130] Small wonder, then, that women are less likely to be union members and, particularly within the private sector, to work in establishments in which unions are recognized. (According to the 1994 Labour Force Survey (LFS), 36 per cent of men and 30 per cent of women employees belong to trade unions; 39 per cent of men in the private sector but only 28 per cent of women work in establishments in which trade unions are recognized.[131]) Bearing all this in mind, it should not be too difficult to understand why predominantly female workplaces pay less than those in which men comprise a majority.[132]

Little general evidence is available on race segregation as it occurs at the level of the workplace, but, as was pointed out in Chapter 2, Neil Millward's research for the EOC found that ethnic minority workers tended to be concentrated, not only in larger workplaces and in nationalized industries (the former factor, at least, should have an upward impact on wages) but also in workplaces which were relatively recently established and whose financial performance was poor.[133] The last of these is certain to exert a downward influence on wages, and it is possible that employment in relatively new workplaces might be regarded, depending on the sector, as insecure and likely to be poorly paid. Ethnic minority workers are disproportionately concentrated in textiles, clothing, and catering, rather than in high-technology industries: it may be that in these former sectors new businesses are more likely to operate on particularly narrow margins.

Millward's sparse, but general, WIRS evidence is supplemented by more narrowly focused research such as that carried out by Hoel into 'sweatshops' in the West Midlands which employed very high proportions of Asian women: Hoel found that wages were extremely poor—in many cases below Wages Council minima—and that in many cases the women were tied into this poorly-paid employment not only by loyalty to close-knit communities of which their employers were a part, but also by the expectation of discrimination in the wider labour market.[134]

Finally, women in 'female' occupations and 'female' workplaces are also disadvantaged because the majority of them (and of potential replacement

---

[130] Sloane, n. 15 above, estimates that unionization increases women's wages by 25%.

[131] *Employment Gazette*, 'Trade Union Membership and Recognition: Data from the 1994 LFS', May 1995, 191, table 6.

[132] The relationship between female and non-unionized workplaces is also noted by Casey *et al.*, n. 9 above. Also, even within workplaces, male-dominated groups such as craftworkers and machine operatives were more likely to have wages determined by collective bargaining than were female groups such as clerical staff (19). The link between union density and the extent of the gender–pay gap has been noted by, *inter alia*, J. Fletcher and S. Gill, 'Union Density and Women's Relative Wage Gains' in N. Folbre *et al.* (eds.), n. 94 above.

[133] Millward, n. 22 above, 17.

[134] B. Hoel, 'Contemporary Clothing "Sweatshops", Asian Female Labour and Collective Organisation' in J. West (ed.), *Work, Women and the Labour Market* (London: Routledge & Kegan Paul, 1982).

employees) do not have access to the same levels of social security as do men. Women who are married or co-habiting are not entitled to benefits in their own right so, for many, any wages are better than none at all. This serves to explain, presumably, why the homeworkers who responded to the 1991 survey conducted by the National Group on Homeworking (see Chapter 2) were prepared to work for an average £1.28 per hour, the lowest-paid for as little as 20p per hour. Three-quarters of the women interviewed had dependent children and 16 per cent cared for dependent relatives. Seventy-eight per cent worked at home for reasons associated with care of children or others, a further 7 per cent because of family disapproval of outside work. Only 15 per cent said that they would not experience financial hardship without the income, however meagre, which their work provided.

Some form of minimum is set, for some women, by the cost of child-care, but the costs of formal childcare are so great that women who work in lower-paid jobs are more likely to be dependent (as far as pre-school children are concerned) on informal care arrangements or (in the case of older children) to be working during the hours their children are at school. *Social Trends* 1995 reports that only 15 per cent of pre-school children went to nursery school, 21 per cent to a playgroup, and 8 per cent to a day nursery: by contrast, 21 per cent were looked after by their fathers, 23 per cent by a grandparent, and 21 per cent attended a parent-and-toddler group.

Chapter 5 stressed the importance of recognizing that women in the labour market cannot be perceived as an undifferentiated lump of inter-changeable labourers. Some women (predominantly those without small children) cannot properly be viewed as 'disadvantaged'—they are located in the 'core' group of workers who enjoy relative stability and reasonable prospects.[135] Some have jobs which pay sufficiently well to fund reliable and flexible childcare, and some women are primary household earners and have partners who take prime responsibility for childcare. Other women are economically disadvantaged but, because they are categorized by marriage or co-habitation as economically dependent upon an unemployed male partner, suffer a marginal tax rate of 100 per cent and, as a result, cannot afford to accept work unless it pays more than the state benefits otherwise available. Small wonder, then, that, while women's earnings generally exercise an *equalizing* effect on family incomes (reducing the results of increasingly unequal male earnings[136]), this effect is absent in respect of women whose partners are unemployed.

[135] See generally B. Burchell and J. Rubery, 'Divided Women: Labour Market Segment-ation and Gender Segregation' in Scott (ed.), n. 101 above, 80.
[136] See S. Machin and J. Waldfogel, *The Decline of the Male Breadwinner: Changing Shares of Husbands' and Wives' Earnings in Family Income* (London: LSE, 1994), Discussion Paper WSP 103 and S. Harkness, S. Machin and J. Waldfogel, *Evaluating the Pin Money Hypothesis* (London: LSE, 1995), Suntory-Toyota International Centre for Economics and Related Disciplines WSP 108.

But whatever the differences between women workers, most suffer relative economic loss as a result of bearing children. Many, who need to work part-time in order to juggle the demands imposed by their domestic commitments, can find only work for which they are over-qualified, more desirable jobs requiring full-time work.[137] And even the most privileged women workers may still face discrimination in recruitment, promotion, and pay. Even they may still find themselves judged on the basis of their sex as well as that of their ability, and even they may still work in 'female' jobs, if not in 'female' workplaces, in which their wages are depressed by virtue of their sex.

IV. WHERE DO WE GO FROM HERE?

It is clear from the foregoing that women's wages are held down by a variety of factors which include (i) their lower positions within occupational hierarchies; (ii) the existence of pay structures which disadvantageously impact on women as a result of their greater burden of childcare and domestic responsibilities; (iii) women's segregation into workplaces which, even in respect of jobs done by men elsewhere, pay women lower wages; (iv) their segregation into relatively low-paying, predominantly 'female' occupations. Wages in both women's workplaces and occupations are held down by employers' access to cheap part-time female labour and by the relative lack of bargaining power which results from many women's restricted travel-to-work capacity and inability to conform to the traditional arrangement of working time. In addition, women's workplaces are less likely to be organized and operate under relatively greater competitive pressure than those in which men work—factors which tend to drive down wages.

The next questions to consider are (i) whether the gender–pay gap, to the extent that it results from the relationship between pay and one or all of these factors, should be considered 'discriminatory', and (ii) whether, and if so to what extent and how, it should be addressed by legislation. In answering this latter question we will have to consider the extent to which existing legislation is apt to address the problem.

(A) DISCRIMINATION AND THE GENDER–PAY GAP

To a large extent the answer to this question depends upon the definition of 'discrimination' which is adopted. Economists, for example, argue about whether or not 'statistical' discrimination on the part of employers is

---

[137] Rubery et al., n. 101 above. See also Brannen et al., n. 34 above, 21. 37% of women moved down in occupational level after childbirth (14% up)—downward movement was most common with part-time returners.

properly viewed as 'discrimination'. *Statistical discrimination* takes place when employers judge individuals on the basis of the employment characteristics (real or imagined) of the 'group' to which they belong: sex, race, or any other characteristic is used as a 'screen' to eliminate from consideration potential employees who are perceived to be poor risks. Such screening occurs because employers do not have perfect information about individuals, while it is in employers' interests to select employees who will display particular characteristics (whether commitment, loyalty, staying power, ambition, or anything else). Such discrimination may be based on accurate information about the quitting or other characteristics of groups or may be based on myths. But if 'discrimination' is understood to consist only of the exercise of prejudicial 'tastes' by employers on their own behalf or on the behalf of their customers or other employers, confusion arises whether extrapolation from the (real or mythical) general to the particular can properly be viewed as discriminatory.

Economists are not alone in taking a very narrow view of 'discrimination'. In the United States, too, sex-based pay discrimination can be challenged, in those cases where men and women perform different jobs, only under Title VII of the Civil Rights Act 1964—the Equal Pay Act applies only to men and women who are engaged in the same work.[138] Title VII forbids discrimination on the basis of sex, race, religion, colour, or national origin.[139] In *Griggs* v. *Duke Power Co.* the Supreme Court ruled that the intention to discriminate was not required in order to prove discrimination under Title VII—disparate impact (indirect discrimination) could be made out in the absence of a discriminatory motive. But the Ninth Circuit Court of Appeals ruled, in *AFSCME* v. *Washington*, that an employer's refusal to pay female jobs in line with its own job evaluation scheme (the rates suggested by the scheme were above the 'market' rates for the jobs) was not itself discriminatory: 'reliance on a free market system in which employees in male dominated jobs are compensated at a higher rate than employees in dissimiliar female-dominated jobs is not in and of itself a violation of Title VII, notwithstanding that the . . . study deemed the positions of comparable worth'.[140]

In *American Nurses' Association* v. *Illinois*, too, Judge Richard Posner (himself an economist), declared in the Illinois Court of Appeals that 'to demonstrate such a [discriminatory] purpose (even if the employer failed to pay female dominated jobs in line with a job evaluation scheme) the

---

[138] As amended in 1972.

[139] S. 703(a) applies to employers. The decision in *International Union of Electrical Radio and Machine Workers* v. *Westinghouse Electrical Corp.*, 631 F 2d 1094 (3rd Cir., 1980) allowed Title VII to be applied to cases where like work was not established and the Supreme Court in *County of Washington* v. *Gunther*, 425 US 161 (1981) also applied Title VII where intentional discrimination was found in respect of jobs which were not the same.

[140] 770 F 2d 1401 (9th Cir., 1985), 1408.

failure to act would have to be motivated in part by a desire to benefit men at the expense of women'.[141] The employer's knowledge of, and decision to benefit by, the systemic underpayment of women within an organization would not, of itself, amount to such a motive.[142]

Neither of these approaches to discrimination is satisfactory. Neither is wide enough to comply with the approach to discrimination adopted by European Community law and, in particular, with the approach to pay discrimination required by Article 119 of the Treaty of Rome which, as interpreted by the European Court of Justice (ECJ), prohibits indirect as well as direct discrimination in pay. In keeping with the approach set out by Article 119, I will categorize pay differentials as discriminatory if:

(a) they are attributable *directly* to the difference in sex—if, for example, men are paid more because employers regard them (as a group) as better workers, or as bearing more financial burdens, and set wages which distinguish between all women and all men (or between women and unmarried men, on the one hand, and married men on the other) on that basis. Also regarded as *directly* discriminatory will be pay differentials which exist because women are deliberately denied access to jobs which carry higher wages—where, for example, an employer restricts women to jobs in job category A, employs men in job category B, and pays job category B at a higher rate.

(b) they arise because wages are set on the basis of factors which, although not themselves sex-specific, *in fact* result in different wages being paid to men and women. Examples of this include a practice of paying full-time employees at a higher rate than (predominantly female) part-timers, or of linking hourly wages to factors such as willingness to work flexible (i.e. overtime) hours, or to seniority.[143] But reliance upon any factor which penalizes women in practice will not be regarded as *discriminatory* if it is objectively justifiable in the sense laid down by the ECJ in *Bilka-Kaufhaus GmbH* v. *Weber von Hartz*, i.e. if linking pay to the disputed factor 'correspond[s] to a real need on the part of the undertaking, [is] appropriate with a view to achieving the objectives pursued and [is] necessary to that end'.[144]

---

[141] 783 F 2d 716 (17th Cir., 1986), 722. See also *Wards Cove Packing Co.* v. *Antonio*, 109 S Ct 2115 (1989), in which the Sup. Ct. drastically narrowed its approach to indirect or 'disparate impact' discrimination. The case was widely seen as the final death knell for 'comparable worth' by judicial action in the US.

[142] Cf. interpretation of intention in *London Underground* v. *Edwards* [1995] IRLR 355.

[143] See *Jenkins* v. *Kingsgate* [1981] IRLR 388; *Bilka-Kaufhaus GmbH* v. *Weber von Hartz* case 170/84 [1986] ECR 1607; *Handels- og Kontorfunktionærernes Forbund i Danmark* v. *Dansk Arbejdsgiverforening (acting for Danfoss)* case 109/88 [1989] ECR 3199; *Nimz* v. *Freie und Hansestadt Hamburg* case 184/89 [1991] ECR I-297.

[144] N. 143 above, 125–6.

The second of these definitions of discrimination is particularly important—we saw that economists are frequently inclined to assume, without
more, that pay differences which result from differences in seniority, tenure, etc., should be regarded as 'non-discriminatory'. It should be clear
from Chapters 3 to 5, however, that this is not correct from a UK lawyer's
point of view.

Taking in turn each of the factors which contributes to the gender–pay
gap, should the gender–pay gap, to the extent that it results from each
factor, be considered 'discriminatory'?

Vertical Segregation

It is clear that, to the extent that pay depends upon the occupational
level reached by an individual, discrimination suffered by women in terms
of promotion within the various occupations will impact on the overall
relationship between men's and women's pay. To take an example, the
fact that women accountants are only half as likely to become company
directors or partners in large firms as are their male colleagues was mentioned in Chapter 3. Women's lower status as accountants will not only
impact upon the pay of women accountants relative to that of their male
colleagues, but will also drive down the pay of all women relative to that
of all men (though, obviously, only to a small extent).

It may be the case that women's failure to progress as accountants is
the result of direct discrimination—their employers may regard women
as more suited to occupying subordinate roles, they may be concerned
that clients would not wish to deal with women directors or partners, or
they may regard women as less reliable employees, prone to getting pregnant or taking days off to care for sick children. It may, on the other
hand, be that women accountants who take time out to have children, or
who wish to work part-time for a while, are treated as having disqualified
themselves from promotion with the effect that only a fraction of women
accountants are competing with men on a level playing field. These
women who work continuously and full-time may have as good a chance
of making it to the top as do male accountants.

Economists claim that the reason those women who take time out fail
thereafter to progress at the same rate as men is attributable to their relatively lower levels of human capital—a women who has worked part-
time for a while, or who has taken time out, will have less labour market
experience than a man of the same age and will, therefore, be a less valuable employee. But, to the extent that employers base promotion opportunities, wages, etc. upon such 'human capital' factors, those employers
may be guilty of indirectly discriminating against women—since women
are overwhelmingly less likely to be able (in practical terms) to work
continuously and full-time throughout childbearing and rearing than are
men, penalizing women who fail to work continuously and full-time will

amount to discrimination unless it is 'justifiable'—unless the seniority or continuity of employment which is being rewarded is actually necessary to the job which is being allocated or rewarded (this is further discussed immediately below in relation to pay structures).[145]

To the extent that women's vertical segregation is the result of direct and indirect discrimination, the elimination of discrimination in pay will require the elimination of discrimination, both direct and indirect, in recruitment and promotion. The question of how such discrimination might best be addressed and, in particular, of whether *pay* regulation is the best way to tackle that part of the gender–pay gap which results from vertical segregation (even assuming that segregation is the result of discrimination) will be addressed below.

Pay Structures

The next factor which was identified as contributing to the gender–pay gap was the existence of pay structures which reward employees on the basis of factors such as performance, seniority, 'flexibility', or overtime work or which restrict entitlement to bonus payments, etc., to employees in predominantly male jobs. Should this part of the gap be considered the result of discrimination?

Again, if discrimination is understood to encompass differentially *impacting* (but equal) treatment of men and women employees, as well as different treatment, then pay structures which in practice disadvantage women employees can be seen as discriminatory, at least to the extent that reliance upon them is not justified in line with the tests laid down by the ECJ in *Bilka-Kaufhaus*, *Rinner-Kühn v. FWW Spezial-Gebäudereinigung GmbH*, *Handels- og Kontorfunktionærernes Forbund i Danmark v. Dansk Arbejdsgiverforening (acting for Danfoss)*, and *Nimz v. Freie und Hansestadt Hamburg* (discussed in the text to notes 152–6 below).[146]

Linking pay both to 'performance' and to seniority reduces women's relative wages. In addition, making pay dependent upon overtime working disadvantages women workers as women are less able to undertake overtime work than are men. And any pay practice which disadvantages part-time workers relative to full-timers (paying part-time workers a lower rate, for example, or refusing them fringe benefits, or denying them overtime payments until they have worked more than full-time hours) will pull women's relative wage levels down.

To what extent can these pay practices be regarded as 'discriminatory'? Taking performance-related payments first, women are both less likely to be in jobs in which they are eligible for such payments and, even when they do potentially qualify for performance-related reward, appear to receive

---

[145] Bergmann, n. 113 above, argues that one of the reasons for women's shorter job tenure is their lower pay—turnover is inversely proportional to pay.
[146] N. 143 above, *Rinner-Kühn* is at [1989] IRLR 493.

lower rewards.[147] The Institute of Manpower Studies' research was mentioned above—Bevan and Thompson found that managers valued men
and women employees for different qualities and that the qualities which
were seen as worthy of performance-related reward were those which were
valued in men rather than in women. Where managers value men for
one set of (stereotypically male) characteristics and women for another
(stereotypically female) set of characteristics, they are more likely to look
for the 'male' characteristics in male employees and the 'female' characteristics in women staff. They are, as a result, more likely to find the
'male' characteristics in men and the 'female' characteristics in women.
When the male characteristics are then used as the basis upon which to
make awards, it is hardly surprising that, as in the IMS study, men get
higher awards.

Any pay disparity arising out of such a process of evaluation should be
seen as the result of discrimination—men and women employees are not
competing on a level playing field when they are judged on different attributes, particularly when 'male' attributes are those which are rewarded.
Not only is this clear as a matter of principle but such practices, to the
extent that they result in lower pay for one or other sex, also fall foul of
Article 119 of the Treaty of Rome. In the *Danfoss* case the European
Court of Justice, considering the legality of 'merit pay', ruled that where
such payments resulted in different average rewards for men and women
in the same grades of employment they breached the principle of equal
pay. 'It is inconceivable' stated the ECJ, 'that the work carried out by
female workers would generally be of a lower quality' than that done by
men in the same grade—where a merit pay system 'results in systematic
unfairness [in the form of lower average wages] to female workers it can
only be because the employer has applied it in an abusive manner.'[148]

Pay disparities resulting from differential average rewards under performance-related schemes must, therefore, be regarded as the product of
discrimination (except perhaps if the payments are transparently linked
to an objective measure of job performance, such as is the case in piece
work[149]). What of the differentials which arise because of women's lower
rates of access, within employing organizations, to performance-related
pay? The discrimination at issue here, if discrimination it is, is more

---

[147] In common with women lower down the hierarchy who are often excluded, in practice, from bonus payments as well as overtime premia. Women are also less likely to receive
incentive pay than are men. Casey *et al.*, n. 9 above, 25 report that 31% of manual women
and 40% of manual men received such payments, 17% and 13% of non-manual men and
women respectively in 1989. While the use of such payments had increased among non-
manual workers and decreased among manual workers since 1983 (using NES statistics),
women were consistently less likely to receive them than men.

[148] [1989] IRLR 532, 536.

[149] See *Specialarbejderforbundet i Danmark* v. *Dansk Industri, acting for Royal Copenhagen
A/S* case 400/93 [1995] IRLR 648.

likely to be indirect than direct.[150] Unless women's jobs are excluded from access to the payment schemes because they are women's jobs, or sex segregation as between jobs is complete and only male jobs (and *all* male jobs) qualify for performance-related pay (in which case women employees could claim, as did the plaintiff in *James* v. *Eastleigh Borough Council*, that *but for* their sex they would have been treated differently) the complaint will relate to equal but differently *impacting* treatment, rather than different treatment of men and women. In other words, it will generally be the case that women are excluded as a matter of *fact* from the performance-related pay scheme, because they are engaged in job A rather than job B. But, so long as women are considerably less likely to qualify for the scheme than are men (i.e., women account for a smaller proportion of the workers in job B than in job A), the non-application of the performance-related pay scheme to job A will amount to indirect discrimination in breach of Article 119 unless the application of the scheme to job B (and its non-application to job A) is justifiable—unless its selective application 'correspond[s] to a real need on the part of the undertaking, [is] appropriate with a view to achieving the objectives pursued and [is] necessary to that end'.[151]

The 'objective justification' test, laid down by the ECJ in *Bilka-Kaufhaus* and strengthened through cases such as *Rinner-Kühn* and *Danfoss*, is imperfect from an anti-discrimination perspective, allowing as it does for the elevation of an employer's narrow economic interest over the principle of equality. But the test does, at least, place the onus firmly upon the employer to establish the accuracy of any assumption upon which s/he relies and does not permit justification by reference to generalizations about predominantly male and/or female groups of workers. So, for example, the UK government's argument, in the 1994 *Ex p EOC* case, that part-time employment would be reduced by the grant of statutory protection to part-time workers was rejected by the House of Lords on the ground that it was not established by the evidence relied upon.[152] And in *Rinner-Kühn*, the ECJ went further in characterizing claims that part-time workers were 'not integrated into and connected with the undertaking in a way comparable to that of other workers' as mere 'generalised statements concerning

---

[150] See, however, the rather generous approach taken by the HL in *Ratcliffe* v. *North Yorkshire County Council* [1995] IRLR 439 (see Chs. 1 and 4 for discussion).

[151] *Bilka-Kaufhaus*, n. 143 above, 125–6. *James* v. *Eastleigh* is at [1990] IRLR 288. It might be interesting at this point to consider the findings made by D. Marsden and R. Richardson, 'Performing for Pay? The Effects of "Merit Pay" in a Public Service' (1994) 32(2) *British Journal of Industrial Relations* 243—the researchers found that 'merit pay' had the effect of de-motivating employees as a result, *inter alia*, of its perceived unfairness. They point out, 243, that '[i]f the scheme did not improve employee motivation, it is hard to see how it could have enhanced employee performance'.

[152] *R.* v. *Secretary of State for Employment, ex p EOC* [1994] IRLR 176.

categories of workers' which could not even potentially amount to objectively justifiable reasons for their lower payment.[153] But having said this, an employer who could establish, as the employer was considered to have done by the House of Lords in *Rainey* v. *Greater Glasgow Health Board*, that its economic or administrative interests were best served by a policy which had the effect of disadvantaging women, might successfully resist any claim for equal pay.[154]

What is true in the case of performance-related pay is true also as regards other bonus payments, seniority, and 'flexibility' payments—when the payments are disproportionately available to employees in predominantly male jobs the payment practice may be directly or indirectly discriminatory. Direct discrimination will occur only if the payments are designed or operated in order to treat men and women differently or if they are as a matter of fact *only* available to male employees, and available to *all* male employees. But indirect discrimination will be made out in any case where men are considerably more likely to qualify for the payments than are women, unless the disparately impacting nature of the payment system can be justified. Where, for example, 'flexibility' or 'seniority' payments disproportionately favour men either because they are available in male-dominated, but not in female-dominated jobs, or where they are applicable to men and women employees equally but, because men can be more flexible in terms of working hours, mobility, etc., or because they generally have more years of service, they do better on average from the payments, the ECJ ruled in *Danfoss* and in *Nimz* respectively that any inequality in pay arising from the reward of flexibility or seniority would not be justified so as to comply with Article 119, save where it could be shown that the flexibility or seniority which was being rewarded was important to the particular workers' ability to perform their jobs effectively.

The reward of overtime working is less likely to breach Article 119. Although the ability to perform overtime work may well, as Janet Siltanen showed in research into Post Office workers, make the difference between receiving a wage sufficient to support an adult independently and one which could be regarded only as a 'component wage', the additional reward of overtime work is likely, unless it bears an absurdly disproportionate relationship with the rate of pay for normal time working, to be 'objectively justifiable' within the *Bilka-Kaufhaus/Rinner-Kühn/Danfoss/Nimz* test regardless of its impact on the male/female wage ratio.[155] Some challenge might be possible where male jobs were structured so as to encourage

---

[153] [1989] IRLR 493, 496.

[154] Though see the discussions of *Ratcliffe*, n. 150 above, in Chs. 1 and 4.

[155] J. Siltanen, *Locating Gender: Occupational Segregation, Wages and Domestic Responsibilities* (London: UCL Press Ltd, 1994).

overtime work and female jobs so as to use part-time workers instead, but even this is likely to be justifiable if the different approaches have been taken in response to the level of employee willingness in particular jobs to work overtime. And, given the imperfections of the objective justifiability test itself, an employer might be able to justify the use of part-timers in such a case precisely on the basis of their lower cost to the business.

Certainly, the approach of the ECJ to the issue of overtime payment does not bode well in this respect. In *Stadt Lengerich* v. *Angelika Helmig* that court rejected a claim that part-time workers were discriminated against by having to work full-time hours before being eligible for over-time payments.[156] On the one hand, this decison can be supported on the ground that, if part-timers qualified at an earlier point, they would end up earning more, per hour, than a full-time worker if both worked, for example, thirty hours in one week when the part-timer normally worked twenty and the full-timer thirty-five hours. This appears to be contrary to the principle of equality. But if the full-timer in the example works forty hours in a week when the part-timer works only twenty, the full-timer's average hourly rate for that week will be higher than that of the part-time worker. One might say, of course, that the justification for this is that the full-time worker worked over and above his or her normal hours. But the same could be said for the part-timer who worked twenty-five, instead of twenty, hours a week.

Workplace and Occupational Segregation

What of that part of the gender–pay gap which results from women's occupational, industrial, and/or workplace segregation? I argued previously that women's segregation results from (a) direct discrimination by employers who refuse to recruit women, or to recruit them for 'male' jobs; (b) the expectation of discrimination on the part of women, whether by virtue of their own experience (a woman who leaves one fire-fighting job as a result of sexual harassment is unlikely to persist in that occupation) or otherwise; (c) *indirect* discrimination, inasmuch as 'male' jobs and workplaces are organized around patterns of work (in particular, the expectation of full-time labour) with which women as mothers are unable to comply.[157]

The result of this segregation is that women compete with other women for jobs whose wages are held down by the availability of part-time workers (who are in turn, as a result of their very restricted flexibility relating to hours, in a particularly weak bargaining position regarding wages). This, together with the general unavailability of social security benefits to women (more particularly, to women who live with men); the fact that

---

[156] Case 399/92 [1995] IRLR 216.

[157] Siltanen, n. 155 above, claims that occupational segregation is importantly caused by the pay and hours of jobs, rather than with views as to what work is 'suitable'.

many women are restricted in terms of travel-to-work distances and ability to conform to traditional (male) patterns of working time, and women's lower levels of coverage by collective bargaining arrangements results in downward pressure on women's wages in comparison with those available to men. The impact of these factors on women's pay may, in this instance, make itself felt indirectly through the women's concentration into particular jobs, particular workplaces, which in turn offer relatively poor rates of pay. But these rates of pay are no less the result of sex-based factors than if the employer explicitly determined workers' pay on the basis of the minimum for which they were prepared to work: these women's wages, no less than those of the 'dinner-ladies' who formed the subject of the House of Lords' decision in *Ratcliffe* v. *North Yorkshire County Council* (see immediately below), are held down by employers' exploitation of 'the general perception in the UK . . . that a woman should stay at home to look after her children and if she wants to work it must fit in with that domestic duty'. The approach of their Lordships to this matter is discussed below.

(B) TACKLING THE EFFECTS OF DISCRIMINATION ON PAY

In Chapters 3 to 5 we considered the flaws in the existing legislation—both the Equal Pay Act and the Sex Discrimination and Race Relations Acts. Applying the information in those chapters to the sources of the gender–pay gap identified here, we can see that much of the discrimination-tainted gap remains unaddressed by existing legislation, whether by lacunae in the actual coverage of the legislation (as in the case of inter-establishment differentials) or by shortcomings in its practical application (where, for example, difficulties associated with the individual model and the complexities of the law prevent women from challenging effectively that part of the gap which results from the reward of seniority, etc.).

In summary, the Equal Pay Act is powerless against disparities which arise between workplaces and greatly flawed even in relation to differences which arise in the same workplace between men and women doing different jobs (the law is hugely complex, procedures cumbersome and productive of massive delay; no increase in pay is available in the absence of an *equal* job, as distinct from one which is merely overpaid relative to its value; the individual focus largely overlooks the fact that discriminatory pay differentials are endemic within pay structures—both as regards the relative value assigned to 'male' and 'female' work and the rewards associated with seniority, overtime, full-time working, and the like). Anti-discrimination legislation could operate so as to break down the barriers between 'male' and 'female' jobs, 'male' and 'female' workplaces, and to facilitate women's advancement within organizations. But neither the Sex Discrimination Act nor its sister legislation, the Race Relations Act, has had much impact on segregation. Some advances have been made by women who have, in small numbers, struggled through various gaps in the glass ceiling. But for the most part women remain subordinate to men in those occupations and workplaces where some degree of mixing by sex occurs. Again, the reasons behind these apparent failures include the individualistic focus of the Sex Discrimination and Race Relations Acts, the enormous difficulties of proof faced by applicants, and the patchy approach taken by the courts to discrimination based on women's unequal burden of parenting responsibilities.

The question which arises concerns how the problem of women's unequal pay may best be addressed. It is one thing, for example, to accept that at least part of the gender–pay difference which is associated with occupational and workplace segregation is the result of discrimination—if women were given the same access to jobs (both formally and in practical terms) employers would not have such a marked advantage over them relative to men. And it is another thing to require that part of the gender–wage gap to be tackled by direct action in the form of equal pay legislation, as distinct from measures aimed at the discrimination which produces segregation in the first place. The link between broad 'market' discrimination may be considered too tenuous to give rise to an obligation on a woman's employer to pay her what she would be able to command in the absence of discrimination in other employers' recruitment practices.

Article 119 of the Treaty of Rome, and its implementation in section 1(1)(c) of the Equal Pay Act, provides a partial answer—the 'equal pay for work of equal value' claim presumes that pay differences between men and women engaged in equally valuable work are discriminatory (or, at least, that they should be eliminated) unless the employer can prove that they are not caused by the difference of sex but are, rather, genuinely the result of other factors. (This is explicit in the 'material factor defence' laid down in section 1(3) of the Equal Pay Act and implicit in Article 119 as interpreted in Council Directive 75/117 (Equal Pay) and the many decisions of the ECJ thereon.[158])

Factors justifying a pay difference between jobs of equal value might include a geographical difference between the man and the woman (if, for example, she works in Shropshire and he in London where his job attracts 'London weighting'), or the fact that his salary had been 'red circled' after demotion on grounds of ill-health or incompetence from a more 'valuable' job. But, to the extent that reliance upon the factor in determining wages disadvantages women in general, and an equal pay applicant in particular, an employer will be able to defend an equal pay claim only

---

[158] *Bilka-Kaufhaus, Rinner-Kühn, Danfoss, Nimz,* nn. 143 and 146 above and discussed following n. 146 above.

if that reliance is 'justifiable' in line with the test set out above. An employer who sought, for example, to argue that, although widget-moulders and widget-finishers performed work of equal 'value', nevertheless the wage generally commanded by (predominantly male) widget-moulders was simply higher than that generally paid to (predominantly female) widget-finishers, would not defeat a widget-finisher's claim for equal pay—the employer would merely have explained the difference but would not have justified it. This issue was clouded somewhat by the Employment Appeal Tribunal's approach in *Reed Packaging Ltd* v. *Boozer*, and in *Enderby* v. *Frenchay Health Authority & Secretary of State for Health* (see the discussion in Chapter 2—in the first case the EAT accepted as a justification the fact that the jobs were covered by separate bargaining structures; in the second that they were different jobs). But the ECJ rejected these approaches in the *Enderby* case and ruled that a significant difference in pay between predominantly male and predominantly female jobs of equal value was itself sufficient to establish a *prima facie* case of discrimination.[159] In such a case the burden shifted to the employer to show 'that the difference is based on objectively justified factors unrelated to any discrimination on grounds of sex' and that an explanation in terms of separate collective bargaining processes, even if these were carried out by the same parties in respect of both jobs and 'taken separately, have in themselves no discriminatory effect' did not amount to sufficient justification.[160] Equally, an employer who appeals more explicitly to 'market forces', as the employer did in the *Ratcliffe* case, will still be obliged to demonstrate that this 'material factor' is not the difference of sex within section 1(3). In *Ratcliffe*, the fact that, according to the tribunal, the wages in the applicant's female job were held down by the danger of undercutting by employers prepared to exploit women's position as disadvantaged workers meant, according to the House of Lords, that the council 'paid women less than their male comparators because they were women'. This amounted to 'direct discrimination and ex hypothesi cannot be shown to be justified on grounds "irrespective of the sex of the person" concerned' as required by section 1(3).[161]

It is clear from the above that pay differences which result from occupational segregation can (to the extent that men doing 'male' jobs and women doing 'female' jobs are employed 'in the same employment' by the same employer, and that 'male' and 'female' jobs can be found which are of equal value one to the other) be challenged under the existing 'equal pay' law. The inadequacies of this law have been discussed in Chapters 3 and 4. But, at least at the level of principle, sex-wage differences which result from occupational segregation should, under Article 119, be

---

[159] [1993] IRLR 591.   [160] *Ibid.* 595.
[161] See A. McColgan, 'Equal Pay, Market Forces and C.C.T.' (1995) 24 *Industrial Law Journal* 368.

considered contrary to the principle of equal pay. What of the sex–wage gap which results from *workplace* segregation? And what of the gap which exists between white and ethnic minority workers?

The latter problem is not addressed at all by Article 119. Nor, as it is currently interpreted, does that provision go so far as to require the elimination of discrimination in pay *between*, as distinct from *within*, workplaces. Indeed, as it is applied in the United Kingdom it imposes no obligation upon employers not to discriminate against women in terms of their pay—it simply requires that women are not paid less than comparable men actually are paid, save where the lower payment is justifiable on grounds other than those of sex.[162] But whatever the shortcomings of Article 119, it is argued here that an adequate approach to the gender–wage gap (and, indeed, to the race–wage gap) requires the elimination of sex discrimination (whether direct or indirect) in remuneration.

_If we were to embrace a principle requiring that all discriminatory pay differences be eliminated, it is clear that the disadvantage suffered by ethnic minority women whose experience and expectation of race discrimination in the labour market drives them into low-paid, racially segregated employment, must be addressed. The slightly more problematic question which arises is whether, to the extent that women's wages are held down by virtue of their childbearing and caring responsibilities, we should nevertheless regard reliance upon these factors as *justifiable* (and hence not discriminatory). Polachek accepts that 'if division of labour in the family is equated with discrimination, all of the [human capital] gap is by definition a symptom of discrimination', and Becker that 'discrimination and other causes of sexual differences in basic comparative advantage can be said to explain the *entire* differences in earnings between men and women, even though differences in human capital may appear to explain most of it'.[163] But these protests are out of kilter with human capitalists' general approach—these theorists appear to believe that, at root, workers are free (or, if constrained at all, are constrained only by influences *outside* the workplace) to make decisions about the jobs they do, the training they undertake, etc.

Polachek accepts that 'labour market activities of women are less likely to contain skill training and learning components as a result *both* of women's decisions *and decisions of employers*, who may be expected to invest in workers' skills to some extent' (my emphasis).[164] But the predominant tone evokes well-meaning employers helpless in the face of women's commitment to low-paid, low-skilled jobs which they choose in preference to well-paid, highly-skilled, fulfilling occupations.

---

[162] Or were—in *Murphy* v. *Bord Telecom Eireann*, case 157/86 [1988] ECR 673 the ECJ allowed a comparison to be drawn with a predecessor in employment.

[163] Polachek and Mincer, n. 92 above, S. 76; Becker, n. 35 above, S. 42.

[164] Polachek and Mincer, n. 92 above, S. 86.

Women who take time out of the labour market (and/or who return to it part-time) are heavily penalized in salary terms. The explanations of the orthodox economists—that women who *choose* the joys of mother-hood over the demands of 'work' diminish their human capital, allow their skills to rust; that those who return are less committed and that they will reap part of the 'wages' for their labour in the form of convenient hours, etc—fail to take into account the wider picture.

Society has an interest in the reproduction of itself. While global 'over-population' may be causing experts to lose sleep, the United Kingdom's population is falling. This has the effect that the average age and the pro-portion of elderly persons (in particular, pensioners) is increasing, which in turn places in jeopardy their expectations of being state-funded dur-ing retirement. While the most sensible solution to this problem may lie in the abandonment of (inherently racist) immigration policies, it must be said that this is an unlikely prospect. It is, therefore, in the collective interest that our present population is encouraged to reproduce (or, at any rate, not unduly inhibited from so doing).

At present, the *benefit* of child-production falls to us all, at least in the event of our reaching old-age. But the bulk of the *cost* associated with child-rearing falls upon the individual. Only when the individual is dis-advantaged to the extent of being significantly dependent upon the state is the burden really shared. And the position of the family dependent upon social security is hardly an enviable one. The burden of child-production does not merely fall upon the individual family unit. More precisely, it falls predominantly upon the mother. While fathers (at least those who are present) may provide an equal or greater share of finan-cial *outlay*, the job-costs associated with childbearing and rearing mean that women often bear the greater long-term financial *costs*.

The estimated cost to the average British woman of childbearing (57.4 per cent of life-time salary after 25 for a mother of two) was discussed in Chapter 2. Part of the cost results from women being squeezed into jobs for which they are over-qualified because higher skilled and better paid jobs do not give them the option to work part-time.[165] Part results from their being penalized, even when they return to their old or to com-parable jobs, in terms of future promotion prospects etc. Both of these factors represent a cost to overall welfare as well as to the individual women penalized—because many employers are wedded to the idea that 'normal' workers are men who do not have babies, do not need mater-nity leave or one or more career breaks, however short; they fail fully to utilize women's potential productivity. Jobs which would, all else being equal, go to women go to men instead and, where those men are less able, employers suffer. It goes without saying that the women who are

---

[165] Rubery *et al.*, n. 101 above.

denied promotion and whose wages are held down for reasons connected with their sex bear a disporportionate burden of discrimination's costs.

One could argue that men's wages subsidise those of women, *family* incomes doing away with much of the *individual* gender–wage gap. The 'family wage' argument has been around for many years and gained prominence recently as a government justification for the abolition of the Wages Councils in 1993. But many, and increasingly more, families are supported wholly or mainly by a female lone parent (this is particularly true for black women), and the notion that men are the main breadwinners condemns these families to grinding poverty and, not infrequently, dependence on the state.[166] Whereas 'non-manual men earn full wages for a two adult, two child household' and 'manual men earn full wages for a one adult household', '[t]ypically, women earn component wages' insufficient fully to support even themselves.[167]

Even where mother and father are together it cannot be argued that the combination of male and female earnings suffices, in the family context, to equalize overall economic well-being. Studies of lone parents have found that many women's economic well-being actually *improves* as a result of divorce, even in those cases where they are dependent upon social security. Graham, in the mid-1980s, found that over half of the women she studied (all but one of whom enjoyed incomes below supplementary benefit level) perceived themselves as better off after divorce, and in Northern Ireland Evanson reported that, of a sample of women 70 per cent of whom lived below the poverty line, 48 per cent said their living standards had improved after divorce.[168] Single parenthood, according to Evanson: 'represented a movement from poverty as a result of *the inequitable distribution of resources between husband and wife* [my emphasis] to poverty as a result of the lowness of benefits'.[169]

Many women in two-adult households do not have the same access to resources as the men with whom they live. This appears to be the case even where women have paid work—men's money is often ring-fenced for personal use, whereas the calls upon women's earnings are high.[170]

---

[166] See H. Graham, 'Being Poor: Perceptions and Coping Strategies of Lone Mothers' in J. Brannen and G. Wilson (eds.), *Give and Take in Families: Studies in Resource Distribution* (London: Allen and Unwin, 1987), 64–8. 28 of her sample of 38 lone mothers (in common with half of all lone mothers in the UK) relied upon state benefits; all but one lived below the supplementary benefit level; 24 of the 38 said they could not afford healthy food for their children.

[167] Siltanen, n. 155 above, 115.

[168] Graham, n. 166 above, 64; E. Evanson, *Just Me and the Kids: A Study of Single Parent Families in Northern Ireland* (Belfast: Northern Ireland EOC, 1980) cited by Graham, *ibid*.

[169] Evanson, n. 168 above, 22–3, cited by Graham, n. 168 above.

[170] See, e.g. J. Brannen and P. Moss, 'Dual Earner Households' and G. Wilson, 'Money: Patterns of Responsibility and Irresponsibility in Marriage' both in Brannen and Wilson, n. 166 above.

Researchers have also noted an unwillingness in some married women earners to 'rock the boat' by calling attention to the importance of their contributions to the household economy.[171] But the notion that men are (and indeed should be) primarily or entirely responsible for bringing home the bacon and, as a result, that they are entitled to primary control of (as distinct from day-to-day responsibility for) household resources, can persist only for as long as women are denied the opportunity to earn wages which are comparable to those of men. It is one thing for a woman to demand equal access to resources of which she supplies (in pounds and pence, as distinct from hours' paid and unpaid work) the smaller part— in such cases it seems that the man is likely to have first call on the total sum.[172] It is another to demand such access where the hard financial contributions are comparable.

Women's lower earning power contributes to a situation where men control the home. Even before they have children, women generally earn less than their partners, with the effect, in many cases, that men have a louder voice in the home. And the production of children only exacerbates the situation—even if all other things were equal, women's lower earning power frequently renders them the more obvious candidates for primary childcare duties which, in addition to alienating many men from their children, itself reduces women's future earning potential. Not only does economic dependency disable women from leaving violent men but, when relationships do break down, women are often unable adequately to support themselves and their children. Women earn less than men do in any event and their lack of experience (or full-time experience) in the labour market reduces their earning potential still further.

The economic arguments also favour action on this front. These arguments in favour of labour standards generally have been summarized by Frank Wilkinson and Simon Deakin as follows:

- 'By paying poverty wages, inefficient firms, which are technologically and managerially backward, can remain in business. This prevents more efficient firms from expanding their share of the market';
- 'Because the more efficient firms are held back in current markets they are less able to invest sufficiently in the development of new products and services [but] long term competitive survival depends on improving the quality of services and products, rather than competing on price alone';
- 'A strategy of competing on quality requires cooperation between management and labour. Low pay and poor conditions are not the way to achieve this. Low paying employers are the least likely to train workers and low paying industries likely to suffer from shortages of skilled workers';

---

[171] Wilson, n. 170 above.   [172] Brannen and Moss, Wilson, n. 170 above.

- 'Substantive standards . . . aim to forestall destructive competition by setting an "inderogable" level below which conditions may not fall . . . [they] effectively require firms to adopt strategies based on enhancing the quality of labour inputs';
- 'Labour standards have the function of avoiding the use of social security and/or the tax system to subsidise wages. Such subsidisation often succeeds only in transferring income to low-paying employers, thereby exacerbating the problem which the transfers were intended to deal with';
- An unequal distribution of income has a detrimental effect on both the level and structure of consumer demand. As incomes rise so does the demand for products embodying and produced by the latest technology . . . the more equal the distribution of income the higher the rate of technological progress'.

These arguments were, as was noted above, put forward in support of labour standards generally but, aimed as they are at reducing the overall levels of inequality in the labour market, they are equally appropriate to gender–wage inequalities in particular.

V. LEGISLATING EQUALITY

It is imperative that action is taken to improve women's wages. But what form should this action take? Assuming that the answer lies in a legislative approach, should that legislation best be directed at the pay gap itself? Or might direct action on *low* pay or on sex segregation in occupations and/or establishments prove more effective?

It is clear from Chapters 3 to 5 that the existing UK legislation, even as influenced by European law, has been ineffective in addressing the real causes of women's lower pay. We saw in Chapter 2 that part of the gender–pay gap arises from the horizontal and vertical segregation of women in the workforce: women are generally found in female-dominated workplaces and/or occupations and, even where they do work in the same occupations and/or workplaces as men, they tend to be found at the bottom of the hierarchy. This segregation by sex is due, at least in part, to discrimination. Some employers are unwilling to employ women, or to employ them in particular jobs. This not only has the effect of reducing the openings actually available to women, but it discourages women from training and/or applying for male-dominated jobs. The relative cost of job searching is greater for women than for men, at least in those areas in which they are likely to encounter discrimination in recruitment (whether that discrimination is 'statistical', or the result of employers', workers', or customers' 'tastes') and so women are inhibited from even trying to break out of female-dominated workplaces and/or occupations.

It might be argued, then (and economists such as Mark Killingsworth adopt this line), that if men and women workers were integrated the problem of women's underpayment would disappear and that action on this front would be more effective, in the long run, than the bureaucracy likely to result from any major programme of pay regulation.[173] There is no dispute that the existing legislation is inadequate, that twenty years of the Sex Discrimination Act have done little to break open male occupations to women, and that further action is needed on this front. But, as to any suggestion that such measures should replace, rather than complement, a drive specifically directed at women's pay, a number of points should be made.

If sex segregation in employment resulted, primarily, in the exclusion of women from the bulk of the 'good' jobs ('good' being defined in terms of the skills and/or qualifications required, the responsibilities entailed, etc., rather than the salaries paid), the answer to the gender–pay gap might indeed lie in ensuring that women got their fair share of those 'good' jobs and, therefore, of the better levels of pay associated with them, rather than in increasing the wages in 'women's jobs'. There is little doubt that access to 'good' jobs needs to be widened—women at present account for only 30 per cent of managers and 45 per cent of professionals. Such a widening will require rethinking the demands made of *all* workers in fields such as surgery and high-finance (which, at present, are simply incompatible with *any* family responsibilities save for the purely financial); as well as tackling the employee and employer attitudes which keep women out of predominantly male jobs such as printing, engineering, and the higher echelons of the police service (in September 1995 the *Observer*, remarking upon a drop in the proportion of high-ranking to low-ranking policewomen, reported that recent rule changes had blocked women from returning part-time after childbirth to the ranks of superintendent and inspector[174]).

Some part of the pay gap between men and women may well result from women's lower representation within the most responsible, skilled, or demanding jobs (though this in turn, of course, may be the result of discrimination). But a significant part of the problem, it is submitted, lies in the differential payment, as between men and women, of jobs that are *equally* skilled, *equally* demanding[175]—at the risk of making unwarranted assumptions about the relative merit of 'male' and 'female' jobs, it is difficult to see, on the face of it, why (predominantly female) probation officers and social workers earned, in 1996, less than two-thirds of civil engineers'

[173] See generally M. Killingsworth, *The Economics of Comparable Worth* (Kalamazoo, Mich.: W. E. Upjohn Institute for Economic Research, 1990), 282 ff..

[174] *Observer*, 3 Sept. 1995.

[175] Or, at the very least, of the existence of pay differentials which are greater than the differences in skill/demands, etc., warrant.

272 Just Wages for Women

hourly wages, why (female) speech/occupational and psychotherapists earned less than three-quarters of the hourly wages paid to (male) environmental health officers.[176] And while greater integration of the workforce may be a major factor in the *long-term* solution, it does not address this particular issue and, as a result, fails to help many women *now*.[177] In any event, the United Kingdom is bound, at the level of the individual employer as well as of the state, by Article 119 of the Treaty of Rome which requires the elimination of discriminatory pay differences *between*, as well as *within*, jobs. At least as far as *occupational* segregation is concerned, Article 119 requires action on the pay-related impact of the segregation, rather than on the segregation itself.

Leaving principle aside, for a moment, 'pay equity' or 'comparable worth' is sometimes opposed on the ground that it serves to perpetuate sex-stereotyping of jobs by removing the incentive for women to break into male jobs. But even if employers were effectively prevented from discriminating in terms of access to jobs, the practicalities of achieving a sex-integrated workforce are daunting. In the United States, for example, a 1990 estimate suggested that over 50 per cent of either men or women would have had to move into occupations usually performed by the opposite sex in order to achieve a sex-integrated workforce.[178] And if segregation was addressed at the level of *jobs*, rather than occupations, 70 per cent of men or women would have had to move in order to balance the workforce by sex.[179] Some estimates have put the level of occupational segregation (measured in terms of the proportion of men or women who would have to move) as low as 32–3 per cent in the United Kingdom.[180] But this figure takes into account only the very broadest

---

[176] NES 1996, tables 8 and 9—the figure refers to full-time employees and includes male as well as female probation officers and social workers (no statistics are given for women civil engineers). If female probation officers and social workers are considered in isolation, they earn 68.6% (as opposed to 69.9%) of male civil engineers' hourly rates: NES 1995, tables 86 and 87—no figures are given for women environmental health officers or for male therapists.

[177] Only pay can be considered under the directly effective Art. 119 EC but, in the public sector (widely defined after the decision of the ECJ in *Foster & Ors.* v. *British Gas*, case 188/89 [1990] 2 CMLR 833), the Equal Treatment Dir. is also directly effective and the decision of the ECJ in *Frankovich & Bonifaci* v. *Italy*, cases 6 & 9/90 [1991] ECR I-5357 [1992] IRLR 84 is a substantial incentive on Member States to conform with EU law.

[178] B. Reskin, 'Segregating Workers: Occupational Differences by Race, Ethnicity and Sex', paper presented at the Annual Meetings of the Industrial Relations Research Association in Boston, Jan. 1994 and cited by J. Jacobs, *Gender Inequality at Work* (Newbury Park, Cal.: Sage, 1995), 9.

[179] Jacobs, n. 178 above. D. Tomaskovic-Devey, 'Sex Composition and Gendered Earnings Inequality' in Jacobs, n. 178 above, (25) estimates that this figure is as high as 77% in North Carolina. He states (26) that 'sex segregation is dramatically underestimated when measured at the occupational rather than the job level'. See also, in the UK, Hakim, n. 30 above, 151–2.

[180] Z. Tzannatos, 'Employment Segregation: Can We Measure it and What Does it Mean?' (1990) 28(1) *British Journal of Industrial Relations* 105, 108—this was stable between 1901 and 1978.

occupational groupings, at which level the degree of occupational segregation in the United Kingdom is actually higher than it is in the United
States.[181] Dividing occupations into 350, Jill Rubery estimated in 1989
that the level of sex segregation in the United Kingdom was 65 per cent
(for all employees, 57 per cent for full-time employees only[182]). Again,
if segregation is addressed at the level of jobs, rather than occupations,
this figure is likely to be considerably higher.[183] Whatever the precise
figures, complete integration of the UK workforce would require a truly
massive transfer of men and/or women workers between jobs. The possibility of this (or anything close to it) happening in the relatively short
term must be zero, even with the most effective anti-discrimination programme imaginable.

Even if women were to move in great numbers into previously male-
dominated workplaces and/or occupations, there is little reason to suppose that this would have the desired effect in terms of improving their
wages. Research carried out in Australia showed that women actually
earned more in predominantly female jobs than in more integrated or
male-dominated jobs. While the *overall* average levels of pay in female-
dominated jobs were lower than those in male-dominated jobs, the wages
of *women* were higher in the former.[184]

Glancing at the UK statistics, too, while the four most predominantly
female occupations (clerical and secretarial, personal and protective, selling, and 'others'[185]) occupied the four lowest positions in terms of the
average wages of *all* their employees; average *female* wages in these categories occupied fourth, sixth, fifth, and ninth (last) place respectively in
the *female* occupational hierarchy.[186] The first three places in this hierarchy,

---

[181] See A. Dale and J. Glover, *An Analysis of Women's Working Patterns in the U.K.,
France and the U.S.A.* (London: Department of Employment, 1990), Research Paper No
75, 15. Dale and Glover detail the distribution of men and women in the UK and the US
respectively among 7 occupational categories (professional, technical and administrative,
administrative and managerial, clerical and related, sales, service, agriculture and production and related, transport and labourers). If the disparity between the proportion of men
and women who work in each occupational group is totalled for the UK and the US, the
UK figure is considerable higher (88.3 as against 74.4).

[182] J. Rubery (ed.), *Women and Recession* (London: Routledge and Kegan Paul, 1988), 32.

[183] See Ch. 2, especially the discussion of Millward and Woodland—even where men
and women are engaged in the same occupations, they tend to do them in different workplaces (i.e. have different jobs).

[184] F. Vella, 'Gender Roles, Occupational Choice and Gender Wage Differential' (1993)
69 *Economic Record* 382: 'females are located in sectors in which they experience less discrimination. Accordingly, at the current wage rates, any attempt to change the occupational
distribution of females, in the direction of the male distribution, may produce a larger wage
differential'. See also B. Chapman and C. Mulvey, 'An Analysis of the Origins of Sex
Differences in Australian Wages' (1986) 18 *Journal of Industrial Relations* 504.

[185] Women comprised 76%, 66%, 63%, and 52% of the employees in these categories
respectively, and 62% of all women worked in these occupations.

[186] These figures relate to full-time women—for part-time women the positions are 4th,
5th, 8th, and 9th respectively.

as in the overall pay hierarchy, went to the managerial, professional, and associate professional and technical jobs (not necessarily in that order) and, in 1995, women accounted for between 30 per cent (managerial) and 53 per cent (associate professional and technical) of the employees in these categories. But as far as very predominantly male occupations such as craft and related work, and plant and machine operatives are concerned, women who work in these categories earn less than all other women except for those in the 'other' category. The position of these occupations in the overall wage hierarchy (fourth and fifth respectively) would appear to have more to do with the relative absence of women from the ranks of the workers employed in them (women constitute 12 per cent and 23 per cent of craft and related workers and plant and machine operatives respectively) than with any other factor.

A closer examination of the New Earnings Survey supports this. Taking the 1995 figures, full-time women's average hourly rate would decline dramatically if such women were to redistribute themselves into the manual/non-manual pattern occupied by men while retaining the existing levels of pay in manual and non-manual jobs—the figure of £7.14 per hour would fall to £6.27 and women would earn a mere 69.9 per cent of men's hourly rate instead of the then 79.6 per cent. If women were, instead, to occupy the same broad occupational categories as men currently did in 1995 (again, men's and women's wages within each category remaining static), women's relative hourly wage would fall to 77.1 per cent. If, by contrast, women remained where they were in 1995 but had their salaries within each broad occupational group equalized with those of men, women's hourly rate would rise to £8.78 and their relative pay to 97.8 per cent.[187]

Even where occupational position is examined at the narrower level (using seventy-two categories rather than the nine broad occupational groups), the repositioning of women along male workers' lines has little impact on the gender–pay gap. If, for example, women are distributed across the seventy-two categories in the same pattern as men, their weekly wage would have increased in 1995 by less than £3 to £272.31 (from £269.8) to reach a figure of 72.7 per cent as opposed to 72 per cent.[188] And if women within the existing broad occupational groups were simply redistributed to match male patterns, those working in management, personal and protective services, sales, craft, and 'other' would have gained between 2.8 per cent (managers) and 32.9 per cent (personal and protective occupations) of their hourly salaries, but women professionals,

[187] Calculations based on the NES, 1995 (Department of Employment, London: HMSO, 1995), tables 86 and 87.
[188] It is necessary to fill in some gaps by assuming the same relationship between narrower and broader occupational pay as is the case for men where no figures are available for women in the narrower occupational group.

associate professionals and technicians, clerical and secretarial workers, and plant and machine operatives would have lost out by between 0.2 per cent (plant and machine operatives) and 8.7 per cent (clerical and secretarial workers) and the overall effect on women's hourly wages would be a slight reduction (two pence).[189]

The same point is illustrated by studies in the United States and in Canada which have shown that the rates of pay within any given occupations decline in proportion to the number of women in those jobs, *all other wage-related factors held constant*—one US study found, for example, that fifteen factors explained 90 per cent of the variation in wages between different jobs but that, *independently of these factors*, wages were inversely proportional to the number of women in a given job.[190] These results have been held out as displaying a *causal* connection between 'percent female' and wages which, as Francine Blau points out, is not necessarily the case.[191] But whether an increasing proportion of women in a given job drags down the wages paid to *individual* workers (as, for example, occurred when previously male clerical work was 'feminized' from the late nineteenth century[192]) or whether it simply reduces *overall* average wages (because relatively higher paid male workers are replaced by relatively poorly paid female workers) the studies do suggest that getting women in to male occupations is not necessarily a solution to the gender–pay gap.

More generally, too, figures published by the EEC in 1985 illustrated an apparent lack of relationship between the degree of sex segregation

---

[189] The figure for personal and protective services is high because 'security and protective services occupations', which accounted in 1995 for 52% of men in the broad occupational category but only 7.5% of women, paid half as much again as the rest of the broad category for men, almost twice as much for women: the exact figures are 49% and 85%—see tables 86 and 87—sales would have gained by 11.9%, craft workers by 2.9%, and 'other occupations' by 8.2%; associate professional and technicals by 1.4%, and professionals by 6.7%. See also D. Lewis and B. Shorten, 'The Wage Effect of the Occupational Segregation of Women in Britain' (1991) 97 *The Economic Journal* 885; B. Reilly, 'Occupational Segregation and Selectivity Biases in Occupational Wage Equations: An Empirical Analysis Using Irish Data' (1991) 23 *Applied Economics* 1.

[190] R. Steinberg *et al.*, *The New York Pay Equity Study: A Research Report* (New York: State University of New York at Albany, 1986). For the relationship between female occupational proportion and pay see also E. Sorensen, *Comparable Worth; Is It a Worthy Policy?* (Princeton, NJ: Princeton University Press, 1994) and in M. Killingsworth (ed.), *Comparable Worth: Analyses and Evidence* (New York: New York State School of Industrial and Labour Relations, Cornell University, 1989), 78–9 'studies indicate that 10 to 30 per cent of the male–female earnings gap is due to the sex composition of an occupation. My own research indicates that employment in a job held predominantly by women reduces individual earnings significantly. Furthermore, this particular variable explains 23% of the male–female earnings disparity. Thus the impact of this variable on earnings is not only significant but substantial.' For the Canadian figures see D. Lewis, 'Just Give Us the Money' (Vancouver: Women's Research Centre, 1988), 120.

[191] N. 33 above.

[192] See generally G. Anderson (ed.), *The White Blouse Revolution: Female Office Workers Since 1980* (Manchester: Manchester University Press, 1988); G. Love, *Women in the Administrative Revolution* (Cambridge: Polity Press, 1987), 144–51.

and the relative earnings of women by country. Denmark, Ireland, and the Netherlands all exhibited higher degrees of segregation by sex than was the case in the United Kingdom, and all these countries together with Belgium, France, and West Germany showed higher levels of segregation than the United States.[193] Yet, as is evident from tables 9.2 and 9.3, women in the United Kingdom do worse in terms of wages than those in any other EC countries. And women in the United States earn even less than those in the United Kingdom.

A further point to add here is that an influx of women into jobs previously held predominantly by men would, according to the normal rules of supply and demand, reduce the wages payable for those jobs (this would apply equally to an influx of *any* workers). A reduction in wages would result in a flow of men out of them, in increasing feminization and in the further reductions in wage levels (because women are, as we saw in Chapter 2, generally less well placed to demand relatively high wages than are men). If discrimination in recruitment was adequately controlled, women should have equal freedom of movement with men, and any increase in the proportion of women within a job would not lead to the reduction of wages—women would be as free as men to take their labour elsewhere and employers would be unable to attract any staff at the lower levels of pay. Again, however, this state of affairs simply does not exist at the moment: until it does, the relative underpayment of female dominated jobs must itself be addressed.

Finally, there is evidence that the movement of women into previously male occupations is accompanied by a subdivision of those occupations into 'male' and 'female' areas—the latter being characterized by lower wages.[194] As women have moved into medicine, for example, they have not only remained concentrated in the lower ranks (in 1983 women were only 12 per cent of hospital consultants; by 1993 this figure had improved by only 5 per cent[195]) but, where they have advanced to registrar and consultant level, have done so disproportionately in the areas of paediatrics

[193] The dissimilarity indices for Denmark, Ireland, the Netherlands, Norway, Sweden, the U.K., Austria, Belgium, Finland, and the U.S. were, respectively, 28.5, 31, 32, 31.5, 35, 28, 27.5, 27, 25.5, 23.5—EEC, *The Economic Role of Women in the E.E.C. Region* (UN publication, Geneva, 1985) cited by D. Barbezat, *Equality for Women in Employment: An Interdepartmental Project* (Geneva, ILO, 1993), table 31. In 1990, too, the EC countries ranked by degree of segregation (most segregated first) were Denmark, the UK, Luxembourg, France, Ireland, West Germany, the Netherlands, Belgium, Spain, Portugal, and Greece (Rubery and Fagan, *Occupational Segregation of Women and Men in the E.C.*, Network of Experts on the Situation of Women in the Labour Market, Synthesis Report cited by Barbezat, *op. cit*, table 34.). The rank in terms of women's relative pay (highest first) was Denmark, Greece, France, Italy, Portugal, the Netherlands and West Germany, Belgium, Spain, Ireland, Luxembourg, and the UK—see table 9.3.

[194] For discussion of this see B. Reskin and P. Roos, 'Job Queues, Gender Queues' (Philadelphia, Penn: Temple University Press, 1990).

[195] 58 *Equal Opportunities Review*, 6–7. Women in 1993 were 38% of senior house officers and 47% of house officers, 53% of medical school entrants in 1992–3.

and psychiatry (54 per cent and 25 per cent respectively at registrar level, over 25 per cent of consultants) while remaining almost entirely absent from the prestigious and lucrative area of surgery (where they accounted for only 8 per cent of registrars and 4 per cent of consultants in 1993). Also within the NHS, women are not only under-represented in top management posts but, where they are present, they are concentrated in provider rather than purchaser units, and in the less prestigious areas of care in the community and of the elderly and those with learning disabilities.[196] The areas in which women managers are mainly to be found pay less, and this contributes to the pay gap between men and women managers in the NHS (in 1993, 9 per cent of men but no women earned more than £70,000 a year, 30 per cent and 16 per cent of men and women respectively earned more than £60,000 and 58 per cent of women but only 24 per cent of men earned less than £25,000).

And what is true within the NHS also holds for management more generally. Gregg and Machin's study of 29,000 managers showed that women managers were relatively crowded into only four of the ten management categories (*relatively* being stressed, as women accounted for no more than 23.7 per cent of any category and as little as 9.3 per cent of one of those (legal and financial) in which they were classified as being concentrated), as well as being crowded into predominantly female workplaces. It was to their workplace segregation that Gregg and Machin put down a good part of the pay gap which existed between men and women managers (6–9 per cent at the lower rungs of management, over 50 per cent at the top) and to segregation in job function (personnel rather than property, non-technical support rather than production) that they attributed much of the gap which existed at the level of individual companies. In the ten years to 1990 women had almost doubled their share of management jobs but had done little, if anything, to break into the very top jobs, or into areas such as property, production and general management (where they accounted for 1.3 per cent, 3 per cent, 3.3 per cent respectively of managers in 1990).[197] On the same note, while women have increased their share of appointments to statutory and advisory boards and to other public appointments from 18.5 per cent in 1983 to 23 per cent in 1989, women received a mere 5 per cent of those appointments made by the Ministry of Agriculture, Fisheries and Food (up from 3.2 per cent) in comparison with 43 per cent of those made by the Cabinet Office—the latter figure was inflated by appointments to the exclusively

---

[196] *Creative Career Paths in the N.H.S. Report No 1: Top Managers* (London: Department of Health, 1995) IHSM Consultants report for NHS Women's Unit. Women were concentrated in community and mental health also further down the line—see *Creative Career Paths—(NHS No 3): Managers in 15 NHS Organisations* (London: Department of Health, 1995).

[197] Machin and Gregg, n. 92 above, 4 and 8.

female Women's National Commission.[198] And while, in 1992, women accounted for 50 per cent of the membership of the Hotel, Catering, and Management Association and of the Institute of Health Service Management (up from 48 per cent and 39 per cent respectively in 1986) and for 60 per cent of the Institute of Personnel Management (up from 42 per cent); in the same year they comprised less than 2 per cent of the membership of the Chartered Institute of Building, 6.5 per cent of the Institute of Directors, and 12 per cent of the Institute of Chartered Accountants of England and Wales.

All this is not to say that the barriers to women's horizontal and vertical segregation should not be challenged, and challenged at the level illustrated by Gregg and Machin's research (i.e. that of specialisms within occupational categories) as well as at the broader occupational level. But such a programme, while it may do much to eradicate the discriminatory pay differentials between men and women workers, is a very long-term solution. In particular, it will do little if anything to assist those women who are already educated or trained to perform particular jobs. Nor will it address the apparent undervaluation of those skills associated with and attributes demanded by stereotypically 'female' jobs such as nursing and secretarial work—unless this issue is tackled, the potential will remain that, to the extent that men and women exercise occupational choices differently, 'women's' work will carry lower rates of pay.

(A) EQUAL PAY LEGISLATION

If we are to tackle the gender–pay gap by means of legislation aimed at pay, as opposed to occupational segregation alone, what form might that legislation most usefully take? Inasmuch as the individualistic focus of the current equal pay legislation is seen as its major flaw, one solution might simply be to allow group actions. But it is possible that a more radical approach should be adopted. Group actions permit individual claimants to share the risk and, if successful, the benefits of equal pay claims. But they still require employees to initiate legal action without imposing any obligations upon employers to examine their pay structures for evidence of discrimination, much less to do anything to eliminate any such discrimination. It has been argued in earlier chapters that pay structures still bear the marks of discrimination; that women are still paid on the basis of their sex; that old attitudes about the 'family wage' for men and 'pin money' for women die hard. Part of the pay difference between men and women does result from men's working longer hours. Another part of it may be explained by men's having greater levels of education, skill, or

[198] Women's National Commission, *Women Into Public Appointments* (London: Women's National Commission, 1987 and 1990), cited by Hammond and Holton, n. 91 above.

experience relevant to the jobs they do. But there is powerful evidence to support the argument that men are paid more because they are men, that the gender–pay gap is attributable to differential *returns* to human capital, rather than to any substantial differences in the amount of human capital possessed by men and women; that what is considered 'education', 'skill', and 'relevant experience' depends upon whether its possessor is male or female. It may be that, in order effectively to tackle this, it is necessary to start from the presumption that pay structures are discriminatory, and to require that they be scrutinized on that basis. This would get away from the present situation whereby employers can simply do nothing and concern themselves with whether their pay structures discriminate only in the (extremely unlikely) event of an equal pay claim.

To the extent that the existing legislation has improved women's relative wages, a good deal of its success has been due to its initial (although limited) collective approach. Zabalza and Tzannatos drew attention to this in 1985: '[a]n explicit channel through which the legislation sought to implement equal pay was the removal of differentiated female rates in the wage structure of collective agreements and wage orders, and this was promptly and thoroughly achieved'.[199] It was to this mechanism, restricted as it was by the judiciary and later abolished entirely by the 1986 Sex Discrimination Act (see Chapter 3), that the pair ascribed the significantly greater improvements made in women's wages in the United Kingdom than in the United States, in which exclusively individualistic legislation was in place. Certainly the advances made immediately after the implementation of the Equal Pay Act in 1975 dwarfed any improvements in the immediate aftermath of the equal pay for work of equal value claim in 1984.[200] And, as we saw in Chapter 4, much of the improvement which has taken place since 1984 can be ascribed to factors such as women's move from manual to non-manual work, and to the increasing proportion of women in higher-paying jobs such as the professions and management, rather than to any improvement in the relative wages paid in 'female' jobs.

It seems, then, that the best legislative approach must take the form of a collective machanism. But should that mechanism consist simply of requiring employers to eradicate discrimination from their own pay structures? Or might it better be tackled by encouraging trade union organization in those sectors and occupations which are currently relatively under-organized? (According to one recent major survey, unionized women earned almost 25 per cent more than non-unionized women.[201] Other research has suggested that one seventh of the 9 per cent decline in the gap in the United Kingdom between 1973 and 1988 was due to the 9.5

---

[199] Zabalza and Tzannatos, n. 1 above, 1.   [200] See Chs. 3 and 4.
[201] Sloane, n. 15 above, 161.

per cent greater decline in male than in female unionism.[202]) The difficulty with these approaches is that they are ineffective in dealing with the
pay differentials which arise *between* workplaces. In addition, as far as the
trade union organization approach is concerned, if women's workplaces
are more difficult to organize than men's (see Chapter 2), even greater
sex–pay disparities might result from further imbalances in the impact of
the union-wage effect. In any event, relatively recent research suggests
that, while a number of unions are at the forefront of the equal pay struggle in the United Kingdom, a great deal of improvement remains necessary in the collective bargaining arena.[203]

   In order to determine how a collective approach might best be
structured, it is useful to look at how other legal systems have tackled
the 'equal pay' issue. The methods adopted are as various as the states
expressing commitment (verbal or otherwise) to equal pay: some rely predominantly on collective bargaining to promote equality (this is typical
of the Scandinavian countries); some operate both collective-bargaining
and individual complaints-based approaches (France, Spain, the Netherlands); others approach the problem wholly or mainly through individual
challenges (the United States); and some merely express their agreements with the principle and have done very little indeed to give effect
to it (Japan stands as a particularly notable example of this).[204]

   I propose to look at three very different collective approaches which
have, or were intended to have, a significant impact on the gender–pay
gap. The first is to be found in Ontario, Canada, whose 1987 Pay Equity
Act is seen by many as the most advanced legislative approach yet to
women's underpayment. The second approach consists not of any legislation directed specifically at the gender–pay gap but, rather, of a centralized system of pay determination coupled with a common minimum
wage for men and women. This is the pattern which prevailed, until
recently, in Australia—a country in which, despite extremely high levels
of labour force sex-segregation and the absence of any effective 'equal pay'
legislation, women were among the most highly paid (relative to men) of
any in the world.[205] Finally, I shall consider the role of minimum wage
regulation in reducing the gender–pay gap. While this is not, strictly speak-
ing, a collective approach, it does differ from the individualistic approach

---

[202] W. Even and D. Macpherson, 'The Decline of Private Sector Unionism and the
Gender Wage Gap' 28(2) *The Journal of Human Resources* 279.

[203] T. Colling and L. Dickens, *Equality Bargaining: Why Not?* (London; HMSO, 1989),
EOC Research Series. In Canada, see A. Forrest, 'Women and Industrial Relations Theory:
No Room in the Discourse' (1993) 48(3) *Industrial Relations* 409. See also Collinson *et al.*,
n. 100 above, 110 on defects in the approaches taken by some unions.

[204] See C. Pettiti, 'Equal Pay in France' in F. Eyraud (ed.), *Equal Pay Protection in
Industrialised Market Economies: In Search of Greater Effectiveness* (Geneva: ILO, 1993), 79;
A. Okuyama, 'Equal Pay in Japan' in Eyraud, *ibid.* 95.

[205] There was some equal pay legislation but it gave rise to no cases—see Ch. 9.

currently in force in the United Kingdom in that it is not dependent upon an individual complaint-based mechanism. There are many examples throughout the European Union of such legislation and their impact upon women's wages will be considered before I go on to examine in some length the history of minimum wage regulation in the United Kingdom itself, together with the effects of this regulation upon British women's wages.

As far as the centralized collective and directed legislative approaches are concerned, there are several reasons for choosing Australia and Ontario for analysis. In the first place, while both approaches can properly be categorized as 'collective' and while both, at least in part (in the case of Ontario) involve trade unions, it is hard to imagine two more different ways of dealing with 'equal pay'. Ontario's legislation is technical and precise, it is specifically addressed towards the issue of sex discrimination in pay, and, for the most part, it deals with differences which arise between workers employed by the same employer. It can properly be characterized as a bureaucratic approach to equal pay—the legislation established a Pay Equity Commission which is recognized as expert in the field and which is, through its 'judicial' arm (the Pay Equity Hearings Tribunal), empowered to reach binding decisions on the scope of the legislation. Ontario is chosen as the best example of the 'pro-active' approach because, while neighbouring Manitoba (and Minnesota, together with various municipalities in the United States) introduced such legislation prior to Ontario, and while six of the remaining eight Canadian provinces had embraced the concept by 1993, Ontario is the only place in which it has been applied across the private as well as the public sector.[206] This, as we shall see in Chapter 7, brings with it some unique problems of enforcement and funding which would need to be considered if a 'pro-active' route to equal pay were to be adopted in the United Kingdom.

Australia, by contrast, dealt with the problem of unequal pay, at least until very recently, by general measures of wage-fixation rather than by legislation specifically addressed to the issue. The traditional Australian approach to wage setting could not, by any stretch of the imagination, have been described as 'technical' or 'precise'—instead it consisted of conciliation between the industrial parties with, if necessary, binding arbitration. While the Australian system recognized a right to 'equal pay' in 1969, and while it applied this to work of 'equal value' in 1972, this was only ever done in a crude and incomplete way. In particular, the Australian system did not accept the notion of 'comparable' worth, with its implication of widespread comparisons between significantly different jobs,

---

[206] *Calgary Herald*, 25 Apr. 1994. See also M. Gunderson, *Comparable Worth and Gender Discrimination: An International Perspective* (Geneva: ILO, 1994)—Newfoundland and British Columbia put the onus on unions to negotiate—61—but all except Ontario limited legislation to the public sector.

until the 1990s. Further, this recognition coincided with a movement away from the traditional, industry, and occupation-wide approach to wage fixation, and with a reduction in women's relative wages. I consider the development and demise of the peculiarly Australian approach to wage-setting in general, and to 'equal pay' in particular, in Chapter 8.

Australia's traditional system might be described as an example of a 'collective bargaining' approach to equal pay. The state and federal wage-fixing tribunals had the power to prescribe terms and conditions of employment, but did so, to a significant extent, along collectively agreed lines. But the greater the degree of prescription involved, the more closely the Australian system resembled one of state-imposed minimum wage regulation. Australia's Federal government is constitutionally prevented from interfering directly with terms and conditions of employment, it is true, but a high degree of regulation by the industrial courts, albeit after attempts to conciliate between the social partners, has little to distinguish it (save in the detail and particularity of the regulation imposed) from a system of minimum wage regulation.

The most significant difference between the two systems does not lie even in trade union and employer involvement (as these parties may be incorporated into a minimum wage fixing body, as in the case of the United Kingdom's Wages Councils) but, rather, in the relative aspirations of the systems to control actual, rather than merely minimum, rates of pay. It is for this reason that the Australian system, although heavily influenced by the judicial arm of the state, is usefully considered as an example of a collective bargaining, rather than a typical wage-regulation approach. It will be considered in this context and together with some wider evidence relating collective bargaining to the gender–wage gap.

Britain itself provides the main focus for the examination of a minimum wage approach to the gender–pay gap, simply because the degree of speculation associated with attempting to transpose approaches from elsewhere to the UK context is avoided. Some general lessons can be gleaned from the picture throughout Europe and the study of the British experience in minimum wage regulation (both through the Wages Councils and the various Fair Wages Resolutions which operated between 1891 and 1983) tells us a great deal about the potentials and the pitfalls of a number of possible minimum wage mechanisms, while also providing clues about the possible operation of a national minimum wage. The minimum wage approach is considered in Chapter 9, and in Chapter 10 I attempt to draw some conclusions about how Britain's gender–pay gap, including the particular disadvantages suffered by specific groups of women workers, might best be approached.

[7]
Ontario: The Pay Equity Act

I. INTRODUCTION

The Government of Ontario, Canada's most populous province, passed the Pay Equity Act in 1987. The term 'pay equity' meant simply that 'excluding non gender-related factors which influence pay, work performed by women which is equivalent in value to that performed by men in the same establishment is to be paid the same'.[1] Prior to the Pay Equity Act, women workers in Ontario (unless they came under federal jurisdiction) were entitled to be paid the same as men only if their jobs were substantially the same *and*, in addition, were equal in terms *each* of skill, effort, responsibility, and working conditions.[2] Ontario's Pay Equity Act was intended to redress this. In addition, it went beyond the complaints-based model adopted by the United Kingdom (and, in Canada, under federal equal pay legislation) and embraced a pro-active approach which required employers actively to implement 'pay equity' rather than, as in the United Kingdom, being free to do nothing in the absence of complaint.

The Pay Equity Act was shaped by struggle between Ontario's Liberals (who were sympathetic to the business lobby and sought limited reform) and the NDP (who demanded much more radical change). The NDP made the passage of 'equal pay for work of equal value' law a price of their support for the Liberal minority government, but the details of the legislation were the subject of much dispute. By the time the Pay Equity Act was in draft form the Liberals had won an election outright and, according to one commentator, 'business opposition to pay equity was unleashed'.[3]

Despite this, the passage of the Pay Equity Act was hailed as a great victory for women's rights. By contrast with the United Kingdom's approach, Ontario's legislation started from the premise that women were underpaid and that their underpayment was the result of discrimination. It declared that its purpose was 'to redress systemic discrimination in

---

[1] Government of Ontario, *Green Paper on Pay Equity* (Ontario: Government of Ontario, 1985), 3.

[2] *Ibid.* 14.

[3] J. Fudge, 'Fragmentation and Feminization: The Challenge of Equity for Labour Relations Policy' in J. Brodie (ed.), *Women and Canadian Public Policy* (Toronto: Harcourt Brace, 1996).

284   Just Wages for Women

compensation for work performed by employees in female job classes'.[4] And it, uniquely, combined the proactive approach (which had previously been adopted in neighbouring Manitoba and in various US municipalities) with coverage of both public and private sector employers.

The Act generated a great deal of excitement among equal pay advocates. For all the horse-trading that had been necessary in securing the legislation, it was widely seen as a model for the future of anti-discrimination legislation. In 1989 Ontario's Minister of Labour, addressing an Intergovernmental Conference on Pay Equity, claimed that: '[a] few years from now . . . any reasonable commentary analyzing the progress of social, cultural and economic development will point to the Ontario experience . . . and say . . . that pay equity was a milestone toward the achievement of true equality for women, not only in the province of Ontario, but also across Canada'.[5] In the same year, the *New York Times* characterized Ontario as 'having gone the furthest in the world' in promoting equal pay.[6]

The general scheme laid down by the Pay Equity Act was as follows:[7]

• employers were obliged to examine their pay structures for evidence of discrimination—predominantly male and predominantly female jobs had to be assessed to determine their relative values, and predominantly female jobs 'matched' where possible, to predominantly male jobs having comparable value;
• employers (with exceptions) had to draw up 'pay equity plans' which detailed how jobs had been compared, which male and female jobs had been determined to be of comparable value and what was to be done about any pay discrepancies between them;
• 'pay equity adjustments' had to begin to be paid in line with deadlines which depended on the size and nature (public/private sector) of the employer, and had to continue to be paid until all matched male and female job classes had reached parity.

These were the very bare bones of 'pay equity'. But the three points serve to illustrate some of the most important features of Ontario's approach. First, and perhaps most important, comparisons were possible only between those employed by the same employer (more narrowly still, in fact, between those employed within the same 'establishment': defined as all those employed within the 'county, territorial district or regional municipality' by the same employer). Secondly, comparisons were to be made

---

[4] PEA, s. 4(1).
[5] Reported in the Pay Equity Commission's *Annual Report 1989–90* (Toronto: Pay Equity Commission, 1990), 14.
[6] 27 July 1989, cited by P. McDermott, 'Pay Equity: Closing the Gender Gap' in D. Drache, *Getting on Track: Social Democratic Strategies for Ontario* (Kingston: McGill-Queen's University Press, 1992), 142.
[7] The past tense is appropriate because the legislation required particular results to be achieved in accordance with a timetable.

between *jobs* (or, even more widely, job classes or job groups, of which more after note 17 below), rather than between particular employees. Thirdly, the jobs which are compared are those which are mainly done by women, and those mainly done by men. Fourthly, entitlement to 'pay equity' adjustments was triggered by a finding that a female job class was of comparable (i.e. equal or almost equal) value to that of a higher-paid male job.

The procedure laid down by the Pay Equity Act will be considered in rather more detail under 'The Pay Equity Process' below. First it is important to note that, where trade unions were recognized by employers, they had to be involved in the 'pay equity' process. The involvement of trade unions proved generally beneficial, but did have the effect of restricting the scope of comparison available to female job classes. Where a female job class was within a 'bargaining unit', a male match had to be sought, in the first place, from within that same unit.

Unions in Ontario organize in workplaces within groups of workers. Once a union has gained sufficient support within such a group it applies to Ontario's Labour Relations Board for certification. If the Board takes the view that the group constitutes a unit of 'community interest' it will certify the unit as a pay bargaining unit and the employer will be obliged to negotiate with it ('community interest' is determined by reference to the skills and nature of work performed by the workers, their conditions of employment, interdependence, functional coherence, geographic circumstances, and administration). Agreements reached between employer and union are then binding on the parties to the agreement and on the workers in the unit to which the agreement relates. The union may go on to target other units of 'community interest' for organization, but the achievement of recognition for other units will not generally result in the amalgamation of the units into larger bargaining units. Thus, just as a number of units may each have a bargaining unit (covering different categories of employees) within a workplace, so a single union may have a number of different bargaining units within the same workplace.

Where one or more bargaining units existed within an organization, the employer had to 'do' pay equity separately for each unit, and to do it in co-operation with the relevant union in each case. The union would be involved in the determination of which job classes (defined as 'positions ... that have similar duties and responsibilities and require similar qualifications, are filled by similar recruiting procedures and have the same compensation schedule, salary grade or range of salary grades'[8]) were 'male' and which were 'female' (see 'Identifying Gendered Job Classes', below); how information about the various jobs would be gathered, how the jobs could be compared and how any wage disparities would be remedied.

---

[8] PEA, s. 1(1).

Significantly, where union and employer failed to reach agreement by the deadline for the posting of the 'pay equity plan', the enforcement body (the Pay Equity Commission) had to be called in. When this happened a 'review officer' was dispatched to facilitate agreement between the parties, failing which he or she issued an order determining the rights and obligations of the parties. Either party could challenge the order, in which case the issue would be litigated from scratch in the Pay Equity Hearings Tribunal whose decision was final, save for the possibility of judicial review. Review officers would also be sent out at the request of one or other party during the pay equity process.

It is evident from this that trade unions could exert a beneficial effect on the 'pay equity' process. Their effective veto was a valuable counterbalance to employers' natural temptation to minimize the costs of pay equity. And women in organized job classes were much more likely to find male comparators and benefit from the process than were their unorganized colleagues.[9]

On the other hand, the narrowness of most pay bargaining units exerted a downward pressure on many pay equity adjustments. Female-dominated jobs within such units had to be compared, in the first instance, to male job classes within the same units. But the Labour Relations Board's narrow approach to 'community interest', coupled with its reluctance to allow the amalgamation of existing pay bargaining units, frequently resulted in small bargaining units consisting, for the most part, of similarly situated workers. In particular, those units which contained female-dominated jobs would also generally contain male job classes whose wages were held down by virtue of their association with the female job classes. Judy Fudge, a prominent anti-discrimination advocate, pointed out that '[t]he separation of office employees from production employees . . . is a well-entrenched policy' and that the Board also 'has a policy of separating part-time and student workers from full-time workers' at the request of employer or union. In addition, '[h]omeworkers have been excluded from a unit of production workers employed in a factory in the garment industry'.[10] Any requirement that comparisons were sought within such units, therefore, served to reinforce rather than eliminate pay discrimination.

Where female job classes were not organized, employers were entitled to 'do' the pay equity process alone. The Pay Equity Commission (the educational and enforcement body created by the Pay Equity Act) counselled that employers set up a pay equity committee consisting of workers

---

[9] See text to nn. 11–13 below.

[10] J. Fudge, 'The Gendered Dimension of Labour Law: Why Women Need Inclusive Unionism and Broader-based Bargaining' in L. Briskin and P. McDermott (eds.), *Women Challenging Unions: Feminism, Democracy and Militancy* (Toronto: University of Toronto Press, 1993), 235.

as well as management in order to ensure that job classes were properly compared.[11] But employers were under no obligation so to do, and a 1992 survey of the implementation of pay equity by private sector employers of 100–499 employees found that only 5 per cent followed this advice.[12] According to one critic, the job comparison process was generally carried out by firms which were the same ones 'that have been undervaluing women's work for years'.[13]

II. THE PAY EQUITY PROCESS

(A) IDENTIFYING THE EMPLOYER

The first step was to identify the employer for the purposes of pay equity. This was pertinent to a number of issues: if the employer employed fewer than ten employees within Ontario, the Act did not apply; a private sector employer with fewer than 100 employees was not required to post a 'pay equity plan' (of which more under 'Pay Equity Plans' below); and the deadline within which the 'pay equity' process had to be started depended upon the size of the employer, as did the amount of adjustment which had to be paid to those employees determined to be underpaid— private sector employers were not obliged to spend more than 1 per cent of their previous year's payroll in Ontario on pay equity adjustments in any one year.[14]

The size of the employer (where that employer was in the private sector) also determined the pace at which the pay equity process had to be determined. Whereas all public sector employers were required to post pay equity plans and to have begun to make adjustments by 1 January 1990, only those private sector employers with at least 500 staff were obliged to have posted plans by this date (they had to begin pay adjustments by 1 January 1991). Those employers with between 100 and 499 employees had to post plans by 1 January 1991, and begin adjustments by 1 January 1992 and those with between fifty and ninety-nine employees, and with between ten and forty-nine employees, if they chose to post plans, had to do so by 1 January 1992 and 1993 respectively and to begin to make adjustments by the first anniversary of these deadlines. Small private sector employers which chose not to post plans had to achieve 'pay

[11] See, e.g. PEC, *Step by Step to Pay Equity: A Guide for Small Business, Volume 1, The Workbook* (Ontario: PEC, 1992), 13 ff.

[12] 64% consulted female employees whose jobs were being evaluated. These statistics come from Canadian Facts *Outcomes of Pay Equity for Organisations Employing 100 to 499 Employees in Ontario* (Toronto: Canadian Facts, 1992), 29–30.

[13] MacDermott, n. 10 above, 138.

[14] S. 13(4)–(7), PEA, although public sector employers must have completed adjustments by 1 Jan. 1995.

equity' (i.e. to have adjusted fully all those female job class salaries which required adjustment under the 1987 Act) by 1 January 1993 (for those having between fifty and ninety-nine employees) or 1994 (for those with between ten and forty-nine). Public sector employers had to achieve pay equity by 1 January 1995, but private sector employers which posted pay equity plans had no deadline (subject to the 1 per cent minimum adjustment rule).

Despite the importance of the concept, the Pay Equity Act failed to define 'employer'. Where collective bargaining existed within a workplace the identity of the employer would have been settled, for this purpose, by the Ontario Labour Relations Act. This, however, was not necessarily conclusive as regards the implementation of pay equity. Further guidance resulted from litigation. The most important decision to date on the identity of the employer was that in *Ontario Nurses Association* v. *Regional Municipality of Haldimand Norfolk (No 3)* where nurses sought to have the Regional Municipality, rather than the hospital, identified as their employer.[15] The Hearings Tribunal, deciding in ONA's favour, stated a number of factors should be taken into account in identifying the employer. These included: who had overall financial responsibility; who had overall responsibility for compensation practices; what was the nature of the business, service, or enterprise; and what definition was most consistent with achieving the purposes of the Act. The decision granted nurses access to highly paid police officers as male job class comparators. Nevertheless, given the number of relevant factors and the non-conclusive nature of each, the definition of 'employer' for the purposes of the Act may not be a clear-cut issue.

(B) IDENTIFYING THE ESTABLISHMENT

The definition of 'establishment' has been mentioned in the introduction above. Here it is important to note the flexibility afforded by the Act to employers. Where no union was present, the employer could decide to amalgamate one or more geographic divisions for the purposes of pay equity.[16] Where unions were present, this had to be negotiated with them.[17]

(C) IDENTIFYING GENDERED JOB CLASSES

Central to the approach adopted by the Act was that the wages of male and female 'job classes', rather than of individual employees, were compared.[18] Again, the Act allowed a certain amount of flexibility in the characterization of job classes as male or female. Gender-predominance was

---

[15] (1990) 1 PER (Pay Equity Reports) 17.   [16] PEA, s. 15(2)(a).
[17] PEA, s. 14(3)(a).   [18] PEA, s. 1(1).

determined mainly in accordance with a 60 per cent threshold for female job classes and a 70 per cent threshold for male job classes, but the historical domination of a job class by members of one or other sex, together with any sex stereotype of a job as male or female, could also be taken into account. The Pay Equity Commission (PEC) suggested that, where a job class had very few incumbents or where the percentage of women in it was 'somewhat less or somewhat more' than the percentage cut-off, these other factors should be taken into consideration in so far as they were relevant to the job class.[19] Where the job class was unorganized this was an issue for the employer, although employees could challenge the employer's implementation of pay equity, of which more under 'Challenging the "Pay Equity" Process' later.[20] Where a bargaining agent was present, the question of gender predominance had to be negotiated between employer and union.[21]

Employers could choose (or, where employees were organized, agree) to use a 'group of jobs' instead of a 'job class' approach to pay equity comparisons.[22] A 'group of jobs' is defined by the Act as 'a series of job classes that bear a relationship to each other because of the nature of the work required to perform the work of each job class in the series and that are organized in successive levels'.[23] Thus, to take the example provided by the PEC's guidelines, the job classes of 'clerk', 'senior clerk', 'clerk typist', 'intermediate clerk typist', and 'senior clerk typist' might, given that promotion would typically lead from one to the next, be treated as a 'group of jobs'.[24] A 'group of jobs' approach could only be used where the group consisted of 60 per cent or more female employees overall. The method of comparison for the 'group of jobs' approach is discussed below.

(D) COMPARING JOB CLASSES

General

Once male and female job classes were identified, their relative values had to be assessed with a view to eliminating any disparity between wages paid to male and female job classes of comparable value, unless the disparity was shown to result from one of a number of permissible factors mentioned under 'Determining "Pay Equity" Adjustments' below. Where

---

[19] PEC, *Pay Equity Implementation Series #7 Determining Gender Dominance* (Ontario: PEC, 1988).
[20] PEA, s. 15(2)(b).   [21] PEA, s. 14(3)(b).
[22] PEA, s. 6(6) & 6(8).   [23] PEA, s. 1(1).
[24] PEC, *Pay Equity Implementation Series #6 Using the 'Group of Jobs' Approach* (Ontario: PEC, 1988).

the 'group of jobs' approach was used, a single job class in the series could be used as the basis for comparison with male job classes. The job class chosen had to be that with the greatest number of female employees in the series, and any adjustment determined to be required in respect of that job class had to be made also, in dollar terms, to each of the other job classes in the group. The comparison between male and female job classes had to be carried out by means of a 'gender-neutral' job comparison system created or chosen and applied to those job classes.[25] Where job classes were organized, the comparison was to be carried out within each bargaining unit and in co-operation with the relevant bargaining agent. Unorganized job classes should be compared with each other, and the employer could choose to carry out this procedure with or without assistance from employees. The PEC suggested that employers set up a pay equity committee consisting of workers as well as management, in order to ensure that job classes were properly compared.[26] But, as was noted above, this advice was largely rejected.

The Act required, in any case, that jobs be compared on the basis of the skill, effort, and responsibility they entailed, and of the conditions in which they were performed. The Act did not specify any particular type of job comparison system or give further guidance on evaluating jobs. This was, again, a matter of managerial prerogative or, where unions are present, for negotiation. But the PEC produced a mountain of leaflets and workbooks giving advice on the manner in which such job comparisons should be carried out. It stressed the importance of adequate information-gathering in the creation or adaptation and the application of a job comparison system. In *How to do Pay Equity Comparisons*, the PEC stressed that a standardized method should be applied to all jobs examined, that information-gatherers should be sensitive to gender-related issues, that the language used to describe jobs should be gender-neutral, and that the jobs, rather than those who perform them, be examined. Attention should be paid, they advised, to generally overlooked aspects of women's work.

Once information was gathered, the comparison system could be applied. In addition to the requirements laid down by the Act (that is, that the system be 'gender neutral' and that jobs be compared on the basis of skill, effort, responsibility, and working conditions) the PEC suggested that, in order to be appropriate for the purposes of the Pay Equity Act, the job comparison system had to: fit the nature of the organization and match its services and/or products; meet the organization's goals; capture the full range of work performed at the workplace, with particular regard to gender issues; and be useful for the maintenance of pay equity in the future.[27]

---

[25] PEA, s. 12.   [26] See, e.g. PEC, n. 11 above, 13 ff.   [27] *Ibid.* 27–8.

Job Comparison Systems

The PEC listed three basic types of comparison system as potentially suitable for pay equity purposes. In order of increasing complexity, they consisted of ranking, classification (grade description), and the point factor method.[28]

Ranking and classification operate on a 'whole job' basis, and consist, essentially, of placing job classes in order of their value to the organization. In order to comply with the provisions of the Act, ranking had to be done for each of the required factors: skill, effort, responsibility, and working conditions. Ranking of skill, for example, consisted of comparing the skill factor of each job class against that of every other job class in turn in order to determine their relative places within the hierarchy. The same process would then have to be undertaken for each of effort, responsibility, and working conditions. To take an example of an establishment with only four job classes: A, B, C, and D: A is found to be more skilled than B, C, and D; B is found to be more skilled than C and D; C is found to be more skilled than D. A is awarded three points under skill, B is awarded two, C is awarded one, and D receives none. The same process is then completed for effort (which the PEC suggested should be broken down into physical and mental effort to reduce gender-bias), responsibility, and working conditions and the results totalled to find the relative job values.

The Commission suggested that ranking was suitable only for small organizations given the number of comparisons required. In the example above, twenty-four comparisons would be required to cover all the required factors (thirty if mental and physical effort were separately compared): where twelve job classes were to be compared this figure would rise to 264 (330).

The classification (grade description) method requires the identification of 'job families' (such as clerical, professional, managerial) within the organization and the placing of the job classes within each family within predetermined grades relating to skill, effort, responsibility, and working conditions. The grades should apply across the job families (so that, for example, the job family of 'manual work' might contain grades one and two, each of which are defined to include factors of skill, effort, responsibility, and working conditions, while 'clerical work' might have possible gradings of one to three and professional jobs two to five). Job classes within each job family could then be compared (on the basis of their grade) to job classes within and outside the job family in order to identify comparators.

The third method suggested by the Commission was the point factor method of comparison. This method sub-divides the skill, effort, responsibility, and working condition factors into sub-headings. These sub-headings

[28] PEC, *How to do Pay Equity Job Comparisons* (Ontario: PEC), 22 ff.

should, in order to ensure that the scheme is gender-neutral, reflect accurately the nature of the jobs done within the organization. Skill, for example, might be sub-divided into knowledge, problem-solving/judgement, and interpersonal skills/contacts. Effort should include mental as well as physical effort, and responsibility might cover responsibility for human resources as well as financial, information, and material resources. Each of these sub-factors should then be given a number of different possible scores—there might be three possible scores for human resources responsibility for example, or six depending on the nature of the organization. The PEC's guidelines suggested that the sub-factors chosen and the relative importance assigned to them should reflect the organization's 'goals, products and services'. They also drew attention to the importance of taking into account factors of predominantly female jobs which are frequently overlooked. Some such factors mentioned in their guidelines were:

- the skills required to operate and maintain several different types of office and manufacturing equipment, to dispense medication to patients and to train and orient new staff;
- the mental effort required for long periods of concentration at keyboards or manufacturing equipment;
- the physical effort involved in frequent lifting of sick people or retail goods or of sitting in the same position at a keyboard for a long period of time;
- the responsibility of caring for children or patients and of maintaining confidentiality of personnel or financial information; and
- working conditions involving the stress of office noise or crowded conditions, exposure to disease and long periods of isolation.[29]

Once the job comparison system was chosen it had to be applied to all the female jobs and, the PEC suggested, 'to all male job classes which appear to be potential comparators'.[30] (It is arguable that any predetermination of potential comparators undermines the very purpose of using a job comparison system in order to determine value.) Each job class was to be analysed, by means of the careful collection and examination of information from employees and managers, in terms of each sub-factor chosen, and points awarded under each category in line with the demands of the job. The Commission drew attention to the need for consistency in the assigning of points to each sub-factor in each job-class, suggesting steps to be followed by the evaluating body. These suggestions were by way of guidance only, however. Failure to follow them would not of itself render the application of a job comparison system invalid for the

[29] PEC, n. 11 above, 27–35.
[30] PEC, *Pay Equity Implementation Series #2 Pay Equity Plans* (Ontario: PEC, 1988), 5.

purposes of the Act, nor, in the absence of complaint, would the Commission ever know about such failure.

Comparable Job Classes

Once the job classes were evaluated, comparators had to be sought from within the male job classes for all the female job classes. Where the female job class was organized, a comparator had to be sought within the bargaining unit. The Act did not define what is meant by 'comparable' value. What is clear is that 'comparable' did not mean 'identical'. The PEC recommended three ways of determining 'comparability':[31]

- by means of 'job clusters', where all job classes are listed according to points awarded by the job comparison scheme and those which 'cluster' together are deemed to be of comparable value;
- by means of 'female job class comparison bands' whereby any male job class falling within a predetermined number of points on either side of a female job class is deemed to be of equal value to the female job class;
- by means of the 'job point bands' method whereby jobs are treated as of comparable value where they fall within the same predetermined value bands. This was the most commonly used method of determining comparability.

To explain the third method in a little more detail, an employer might decide to use or develop a job comparison system which rates job classes on a possible scale of 100 to 499 with value bands of twenty-five points. Thus jobs which fall between 100 and 124, 125 and 149, 150 and 174 . . . and so on to the final band of 475 to 500, would be deemed 'comparable' for the purposes of the Act.

If no male job was found which was of comparable value to any particular female job class, the female job class was deemed to be comparable to any male job class rated as being of lower value but paid at a higher rate.[32] The same principle applied to organized female job classes, which were to be deemed comparable to a lower-valued higher-paid male job class within the bargaining unit, if no higher-paid male job class of comparable value was identified therein. Only if no such higher-paid lower-value male job class exists would a comparator be sought in other bargaining units and, finally, throughout the establishment as a whole.[33]

(E) DETERMINING 'PAY EQUITY' ADJUSTMENTS

Once comparable job classes had been assigned, where possible, to each female job class, the employer had to identify any pay disparities between

---

[31] PEC, *Step by Step to Pay Equity: A Guide for Small Business, Volume 2 The Job Evaluation System* (Ontario: PEC, 1992), 86.
[32] PEA, s. 6(2).   [33] PEA, s. 6(5).

the male and female job classes ('pay' being defined to include benefits, bonuses, commissions, etc. the value of which were to be calculated on an hourly rate). Only those disparities resulting from one of the following factors could be retained:[34]

- a formal, non-discriminatory seniority system;
- a temporary non-discriminatory training assignment leading to promotion;
- a formal, non-discriminatory and notorious merit system;
- red-circling 'where, based on a gender-neutral re-evaluation process, the value of a position has been down-graded'; or
- a skill shortage causing a temporary inflation in compensation as a result of the employer's difficulty in recruiting.

Where a female job class was rated as of comparable value to more than one male job class, the female rate had only to be adjusted to the lowest comparable male rate. Where a comparable male job class was paid the same as the female job class, no pay equity adjustment was required for the female job class. The same was true where no male job class was of comparable value to the female job class, and no lower-valued male job class was paid at a higher rate than it. The effect of these provisions on the level of adjustments payable under the Act is criticized below.

Employers were obliged to identify the female job classes requiring pay equity adjustments, determine the amount of these adjustments, and draw up a timetable for the process. The deadlines for the various stages according to employer size and sector were set out above. The Act also laid down a number of rules in accordance with which pay equity adjustments were to be calculated. All female job class rates which required adjustment were to receive some adjustment in each year until they achieved parity with their male job class comparator, and increases had to be weighted in favour of the lowest paid female job class in each bargaining unit or (for unorganized job classes), in the establishment.[35] Where a female job class contained more than one job, each job was to receive the same adjustment in dollar terms and no reduction in the wages of any employee was permitted.[36] Nor could the wage gap between a female job class and its male job class comparator be allowed to increase during the implementation of pay equity.

(F) PAY EQUITY PLANS

As was mentioned under 'The Pay Equity Process' above, all but private sector employers having fewer than 100 employees were obliged to draw up a pay equity plan. Where bargaining units existed, separate plans had to be drawn up for each and for unorganized job classes. Each plan had to:

[34] PEA, s. 8(1).   [35] PEA, s. 13(3).   [36] PEA, s. 9(3) & (1).

- identify the establishment and the workers within it to which it applied;
- list all male and female job classes in the unit to which it applied together, where necessary, with any male job classes in other units of the establishment which were to be used as comparators for female job classes within the unit;
- describe the job comparison system used and the relative values assigned by it to the job groups it covered;
- explain any wage disparities between comparable job classes permitted by the legislation (on the grounds of red-circling, merit pay, etc.);
- identify female job classes to receive adjustments and describe how these adjustments were to be made.

When a plan had been agreed between employer and bargaining agent, or posted in accordance with a review officer order or Tribunal finding, it became binding on employer and bargaining agent and on the employees within the bargaining unit to which it related.[37] But all parties remained free to complain to the PEC of any violation of the Act, and employees and bargaining agents could also complain that a pay equity plan was not being implemented according to its terms, or that a change in circumstances had rendered the plan inappropriate for the female job class to which the employees belonged.[38]

(G) MAINTAINING 'PAY EQUITY'

The Pay Equity Act required not only that 'pay equity' be achieved, but also that it be maintained. Where new male or female job classes came into existence they had to be evaluated in accordance with the original pay equity plan, or a new method of job evaluation applied across the board. Wage differences which were acceptable on one of the grounds allowed by section 8(1) (temporary employee training, or a temporary skills shortage) cease to be so when the training or skills shortage ends, in which case the job rates must be adjusted accordingly. Equally, the Act forbids any increase in the wage gap between comparable male and female job classes until pay equity has been achieved. Any across-the-board percentage increase in wages would result in a lower absolute wage rise for a female job class than for the male job class comparator to which its rate was being raised, with a consequent increase in the wage gap between them. Employers were required to compensate for any such increase in the wage gap as well as allocating the predetermined pay equity adjustments. Only the latter were subject to the 1 per cent required maximum discussed above.

[37] PEA, s. 13(9).   [38] PEA, s. 22(1) & (2).

Once pay equity was achieved in an establishment, i.e. once wage parity was achieved between male and female job classes rated as being of comparable value, section 8(2) stated that 'the Act does not apply so as to prevent differences in compensation between a female job class and a male job class if the employer is able to show that the difference is the result of differences in bargaining strength'. This particular provision has been the subject of much criticism, suggesting as it did that the pay equity process was in the nature of a 'one shot' solution to the problem of women's underpayment and that one of the very factors (differences in collective bargaining strength) which gave rise to the pay differentials regarded as unacceptable for the purposes of the process would, once that process was complete, somehow be regarded as cleansed of its potentially discriminatory impact. Given that the pay equity process is not generally regarded as complete (proportional adjustments still being calculated and made) it is too early as yet to determine the impact of the provision.

(H) CHALLENGING THE 'PAY EQUITY' PROCESS

It has been stated above that the PEC was to be contacted in the event of failure by employer and union to agree a pay equity plan, where such agreement was required by the Act. Either party was, in addition, entitled to seek the assistance of the Commission prior to the posting date on issues such as the definition of 'employer', the gender predominance of job groups, the gender-neutrality of the job comparison system, etc. Where a request or complaint was received, a review officer was appointed to investigate and to assist the parties in reaching a settlement. If no such settlement was forthcoming, the review officer could decide to issue an order which would determine the issue subject to the ability of either party to seek a tribunal ruling. If either party disputed the order of a review officer, the Hearings Tribunal considered the matter afresh, making its own decision on the facts. The decision of the Hearings Tribunal was final, there being no appeal except by way of judicial review of an allegation that the Tribunal exceeded its powers. Plans agreed between employers and bargaining agents became binding on the parties thereto, and upon the employees covered by them.

Unorganized workers had no right to negotiate their employers' implementation of 'pay equity', but did have a right to make representations to the employer within ninety days of any pay equity plan being posted.[39] If the employer chose to amend the plan in response to these representations the plan had to be reposted and employees had a further thirty days in which to challenge it to the Commission.[40] If no complaints were

---

[39] PEA, s. 15(4).   [40] PEA, s. 15(7).

forthcoming the plan was deemed to be approved by the Commission and became binding on employer and employees.[41] The employees of an employer who chose, in compliance with the Act, not to post a pay equity plan could complain to the Commission if they felt that the employer was in breach of the Act.

Where an employer failed to implement a plan according to its terms, or where a plan was rendered inappropriate in relation to a job class by a change of circumstances, an employee or group of employees in that job class or (where the job class was organized) the bargaining agent which represented it, could complain to the Commission.[42] Further, an employer, employee, or bargaining agent might complain to the PEC at any time that the Act, its regulations, or a Commission order was being contravened.[43] Such complaints are still possible and might include allegations that compensation is being reduced in order to effect 'pay equity', that an employer had intimidated employees who have exercised their rights under the Act, or that the employer has failed to establish or maintain pay equity. Where the Commission receives a complaint a review officer investigates and attempts conciliation. Failing this, the officer may either issue an order or refuse to do so on the ground that the complaint is trivial, vexatious, or made in bad faith or was outside the jurisdiction of the Tribunal.[44] In either case the complainant may request a Tribunal hearing. As above, the decision of the Tribunal is final. Fines of up to $2,000 are available against an individual who contravenes an order of the Tribunal, and of up to $25,000 against any other body. The same fines may be awarded against anyone who interferes with a review officer's duties or discriminates against anyone exercising their rights under the Act.

III. THE IMPACT OF THE PAY EQUITY ACT

(A) INITIAL IMPACT

The rolling implementation of the Act made its impact on wages rather difficult to assess, and matters were complicated further by the amendments made to the Act in 1993 (of which more later). To these difficulties were added the Pay Equity Act's failure to require any systematic monitoring of the pay equity process. Judy Fudge has pointed out that '[t]here is ... simply no way of telling which women workers ... are receiving pay equity adjustments or how much they have received'.[45] While annual surveys were conducted of employers as the obligation to post pay equity plans crystallized, these surveys were one-off affairs, and no ongoing monitoring took place over the pay equity implementation programme. Nor are

[41] PEA, s. 15(8).   [42] PEA, s. 22(2).   [43] PEA, s. 22(a).
[44] PEA, ss. 22(3)(a) & (b).   [45] Fudge, n. 3 above.

statistics available on any changes which have taken place in the male: female earnings ratio in Ontario since the Act came into force.

What the surveys have shown, however, is that employers in all categories lagged behind the deadlines imposed by the Act.[46] Fewer than half of those employers required to post pay equity plans by January 1990 had completed the process, by between September and December 1990 (up to a year after the deadline). Of public sector employers (who were supposed to have begun pay adjustments on 1 January 1990), only 46 per cent had posted nine to twelve months later: this fell to a mere 9 per cent of those public sector organizations employing 1,000 plus employees.[47] And in late 1992 a survey of private sector employers of fifty to ninety-nine employees (who had to have posted by the beginning of that year or completed adjustments by January 1993) found that only about 10 per cent had posted on time, a further 14 per cent still intended to post, and 45 per cent had yet to decide whether to post or not. Only 30 per cent of the employers surveyed declared that their pay equity processes were complete (i.e. either plans had been posted or adjustments made)—the survey took place between nine and twelve months after plans should have been posted or, if employers had chosen not to do so, no more than three months prior to the deadline for completion of pay equity adjustments.[48] In 1994 one commentator characterized compliance with the Act as 'very poor'.[49]

The second major issue which has been highlighted by the various surveys conducted is the alarmingly low cost of 'pay equity'. The Green Paper on which the Act was based stated that women in Ontario earned about 78 per cent of men's hourly earnings (much the same as in the United Kingdom). It estimated that just under one quarter of this was attributable to 'wage discrimination': 'paying women less than men for equal work or substantially the same work'; a further half to occupational segregation (both into equally skilled, etc. jobs and into those requiring less skill); and the rest to differences in experience, education, and unionization. The Green Paper recognized that each of these factors, as well as that of hours worked, might be affected in turn by discrimination:

---

[46] SPR Associates carried out the 1990 study (*An Evaluation of Pay Equity in Ontario: The First Year* (Toronto: SPR Associates Inc, 1991)), Canadian Facts the 1991 study, n. 12 above. The 1990 study dealt with employers whose posting deadline was 1 Jan. 1990, the 1991 study with those who were to have posted by 1 Jan. 1991. Some indication is however to be found in the studies carried out for the Pay Equity Commission in late 1990 and 1991. The studies found widespread failure on the part of employers to post by the relevant deadlines, but in both years the vast majority of employers posted or were close to posting at least some of their pay equity plans within a short period of the deadlines. Factors such as the unexpected length of time taken to complete job comparison studies and the delay caused by challenges to the gender-neutrality of chosen systems affected employers' readiness to post by the relevant deadlines. Of much more importance are the findings relating to the cost at which employers were claiming to have achieved pay equity.

[47] SPR Associates Inc., n. 45 above.   [48] Canadian Facts, n. 12 above.

[49] M. Gunderson, *Comparable Worth and Gender Discrimination: An International Perspective* (Geneva: ILO, 1994), 80.

'differences in hours worked may reflect an inequitable division of labour within households [and d]ifferences due to . . . education and training may reflect screening prior to entry into the labour force'.[50] But it went on to state that a 'pay equity' policy could address only that part of the wage gap which was due to the undervaluation of women's work, a gap it estimated at about 10 per cent of men's average wage (i.e. about half of the 22 per cent difference[51]).

If the Pay Equity Act were to halve the gap between men's and women's average earnings, a very rough estimate suggests that the total additional cost to the wage bill should have been in the order of 5 per cent. But the largest private sector employers reported an average total adjustment cost of a mere 0.6 per cent of previous annual payroll, employers of between 100 and 499, 1.1 per cent, and employers of between fifty and ninety-nine estimated, in late 1992, an average total adjustment cost of only 0.5 per cent of payroll.[52] Far from the 1 per cent annual maximum acting as a break on the pay equity process, it turned out to be largely irrelevant. And even in the public sector (where many more employees are organized) the figures were scarcely more impressive: in 1990 the total pay equity adjustments required amounted to a mere 2.2 per cent of the previous year's payroll.

(B) LACK OF COMPARATORS

The costs of pay equity were held down primarily because many female job classes lacked a higher-paid male comparator class. That this was not entirely fortuitous (at least for employers) is suggested by the differences displayed by organized and unorganized workplaces. Comparatorless jobs were markedly more common in non-unionized workplaces. In 36 per cent of non-unionized workplaces, some employees in female job classes were excluded from adjustments by the lack of a comparator for their job class. In unionized workplaces this figure fell to 16 per cent. And in 82 per cent of non-unionized workplaces, but only 63 per cent of unionized workplaces, less than 50 per cent of female job classes received adjustments.[53]

Further, unions' involvement in the pay equity process was associated with fewer female job classes being denied adjustments on the ground that their rate was equal to or higher than that of a comparable male job class. Taking, first, those private sector employers with between 100 and

---

[50] N. 1 above.   [51] *Ibid.* 12–13.
[52] Gunderson, n. 49 above; Canadian Facts, n. 11 above.
[53] Canadian Facts, n. 12 above, 33 and 36. L. Ames, 'Fixing Women's Wages: The Effectiveness of Comparable Worth Policies' (1995) 48(4) *Industrial and Labor Relations Review* 709, 723, criticizes the Pay Equity Act for creating 'new, capricious instances of inequity' by its failure to cover all women workers.

499 employees, more than 50 per cent of female job classes were denied adjustment on the basis that they were earning as much as a comparable male job class in 67 per cent of non-union plans but in only 40 per cent of unionized plans. The figure for plans reported by employers of between fifty and ninety-nine employees, only 20 per cent of which were unionized at all, was 57 per cent.

These figures might appear to suggest that, where employees are unionized, the gender–wage gap between men and women workers is higher. But this runs contrary to all evidence, and it is probable that the answer lies, rather, in the power of trade unions to counterbalance the interests of employers in the pay equity process and minimize manipulation.

Many women denied comparators worked in overwhelmingly female workplaces where few or no male job classes existed (in such predominantly female sectors as social services and the service sector, for example, 66 per cent and 75 per cent respectively of women in female job classes lacked comparators[54]). But many others worked in mixed workplaces where male job classes existed, but where the job comparison system as applied did not assign a comparable value to any such job class having a higher wage rate.[55] Taken together, these facts point to three problems inherent within the Act's concept of 'pay equity'. All of these problems stem in essence from the job-to-job comparison upon which the Act relies.

First was the legislation's initial failure to require the proportional adjustment of wage rates where, for example, a female job was found to be 80 per cent as valuable as a male job which was paid 150 per cent of the female job rate. The absence of such a requirement impacted most on women in predominantly female workplaces where few male job classes existed for comparison. But it also impacted on women in mixed workplaces whose jobs were not evaluated as comparable to any male job class. Besides the practical problem this gave rise to—that many women were left without comparators—the reliance of pay adjustments upon an initial determination of 'equality' was, even if such a determination could be made in an objective and scientifically verifiable fashion, objectionable in principle. Once it is accepted that predominantly female jobs are undervalued for reasons associated with the sex of their incumbents, to restrict jobs selected for wage adjustments to those which happen to be capable of being 'matched' to a male job is utterly arbitrary: there is no reason to favour a job whose value is assessed at 100 per cent of any given male job but whose current wage is 80 per cent over one whose assessed value and wage are, respectively, 80 per cent and 67 per cent, or 120 per cent and 100 per cent.

[54] This figure relates to private sector organizations having between 100 and 499 employees. The 1990 study found that 30% of female job classes in private sector organizations having 500 or more employees lacked comparators.

[55] Or a lower value but higher job rate.

Secondly, given that 'pay equity' had to be achieved only within establishments, the Act did not deal with the underpayment of women in women-only workplaces, or in workplaces where so few men work that there are no male job classes. We saw, in Chapter 2, that women in the United Kingdom are segregated by sex not only in terms of occupation but also in the workplaces in which they are to be found. The same is true in Ontario.

These problems were recognized by the Pay Equity Act itself, section 33(2)(e) of which imposed an obligation on the Commission to investigate those sectors of the economy where the workforce was predominantly female, and to report and make recommendations to the Minister about how discrimination in these sectors could be addressed. Of the recommendations made by the Commission, the Government adopted the suggestion that proportional value comparisons be made available and that female job classes in workplaces with no or very few male job classes should be allowed to seek comparators outside the establishment. The latter method ('proxy' comparisons) was recommended only for the public sector. Both recommendations formed the basis of amendments to the Act, discussed under 'The Amendments' below. The amendments did not seek to address the problem of inter-establishment pay differentials: indeed the Green Paper, upon which the Act was based, had assured employers that 'gender based comparison [would be] required only within a particular establishment'.[56]

Before going on to deal with the third problem inherent in the job-to-job comparison method, it is useful to note that the Act's failure to define 'employer' and to prohibit contracting-out allowed employers to deny female job classes comparators by adopting a narrow view of the employer in cases of doubt (effectively closing the issue for workers unrepresented by unions and requiring expensive litigation if the representatives of organized workers are to challenge the decision), and by hiving off female job classes to outside contractors.[57]

The third problem associated with the job-to-job comparison approach is its dependence on job-evaluation to assess the relative value of jobs. Job evaluation is not an exact or an objectively verifiable scientific procedure, the assessment of 'value' within numerous available sub-categories of skill, effort, responsibility, and working conditions and the choice of value bands within which jobs are deemed comparable being a question of judgement and degree. In the United Kingdom, for example, a study of reports compiled for industrial tribunals by independent experts found 'remarkably little consistency' in the approach taken to the assessment of

---

[56] N. 1 above, 4.
[57] To a certain extent the effects of this could be mitigated by the Pay Equity Hearing Tribunal's broad approach to the interpretation of 'employer—see *ONA* v. *Haldimand-Norfolk (No 3)*, n. 15 above.

value.[58] The twenty-four reports studied (40 per cent of those commissioned by 1991) showed extensive differences in the choice of factors analysed, the method of scoring, the weighting of various factors, and the interpretation of equal value. The decision whether or not a complainant's job was of equal value to that of her comparator seemed, to a great extent, to depend on the method applied. Ontario's legislation gave employers unfettered discretion, where workers were unorganized, to choose or create and apply any job comparison system so long as it took into account the factors of skill, effort, responsibility, and working conditions and so long as it was 'gender-neutral'.

The question of gender neutrality is a ferociously difficult one to judge. In the few cases in which the gender neutrality of job-comparison processes was challenged before the Hearings Tribunal, the processes were found wanting. In *Ontario Nurses' Association* v. *Regional Municipality of Haldimand-Norfolk (No 6)* the Tribunal found that the respondent employer's job comparison process failed adequately to capture the demands of nurses' jobs by failing to recognize the different skills and job contents inherent in typically female work.[59] And in *ONA* v. *Women's College Hospital* the Hearings Tribunal again decided that the hospital's job-evaluation process was not gender-neutral.[60] Not only were the job information sheets which were distributed to staff incapable of capturing all the demands made upon nurses (the emotional demands of nursing, the teaching and communication skills and manual dexterity required, etc.), but the evaluation criteria applied did not assign value to many aspects of nurses' work (communication skills, problem-solving, ethical decision-making, etc.), and were weighted so as to favour those (male) jobs at the top of the hierarchy.

Where the Pay Equity Hearings Tribunal was required to address the issue of gender neutrality, it adopted a rigorous approach. But its refusal to establish generally applicable rules, or even to disapprove of the job evaluations systems examined (as opposed to their application in the particular workplaces), deprived other workers of a valuable negotiating tool, and required them to engage in their own litigation if they wished to challenge the gender neutrality of their employers' systems.[61] This was a wildly expensive tactic, and one which ONA was able to pursue only because it had at its disposal a large strike fund which, due to the inability of most of its members to strike, it was able to divert to the cause. In addition, and unlike most other large unions, the vast majority of ONA's members were (and are) women, so it was spared any demands to bal-

---

[58] A. Plumer, *Equal Value Judgments: Objective Assessment or Lottery?* (Coventry: University of Warwick, 1992), Industrial Research Unit, School of Business Studies.

[59] (1991) 2 PER 105.   [60] *ONA* v. *Women's College Hospital (No 4)* (1992) 3 PER 61.

[61] *ONA* v. *Haldimand-Norfolk (No 6)*, n. 59 above, *ONA* v. *Women's College Hospital (No 4)*, n. 60 above.

ance the costs of 'pay equity' against the potentially conflicting demands of male members.

Job evaluation, regardless of how detailed the analysis it employs, depends ultimately on subjective judgements of value. Even if such an exercise was to be undertaken by an employer wholeheartedly committed to the elimination of discrimination, there would still remain the task of examining minutely the demands made by each job, of assessing which of these demands are most important to the organization without unduly favouring either male- or female-dominated jobs, and of allocating values to each job in terms of the chosen factors. To require all of this while demanding also that the assessor remain uninfluenced by stereotypical notions such as the idea that 'caring' is a facet of the female character, rather than a rewardable skill, or that manual jobs typically done by men require more physical effort than those done by women, is a tall order indeed.

(C) EMPLOYER MANIPULATION

In the context of legislated pay equity, these problems are magnified by the fact that pay equity costs money. Employers' realization that the allocation of high valuations to predominantly female jobs will result, more often than not, in high pay equity adjustments for those jobs, must have acted as a downward pressure in the evaluation process. Value judgements, being subjective, can be made to reflect any particular aim. The Pay Equity Commission stated that it was the value of the jobs *to the, employer* that was to be assessed in the pursuit of pay equity, and that the job comparison system chosen should 'fit the nature' and 'meet the goals' of the organization in which it was to be applied while capturing 'the whole range of work performed' by men and women within the organization.[62] This approach did little to challenge existing hierarchies which tend to place women at the bottom and men at the top of the wage ladder, particularly when the job ranking or grade classification methods were used. The job ranking method could hardly fail to perpetuate existing hierarchies, given that evaluators' instinctive responses to the skill rating of 'executive' and 'secretary' would be shaped by the very hierarchy they were supposed to be examining. The same is true of grade classification. Further, neither method is capable of capturing subtle gradations of skill, effort, responsibility, and working conditions. Nor are they capable, without substantial moderation, of weighing the relative values to the organization of skill, effort, responsibility, and working conditions or sub-factors thereof.

[62] PEC, n. 11 above, 28.

The points factor method is typically seen as more appropriate for the elimination of pay discrimination, given its capacity to analyse job demands under a relatively large number of sub-headings, to assign weights to reflect the relative importance of each, and to value different jobs accordingly. While it depends, ultimately, on the comparison of jobs in terms of their value to the employer, and is therefore favourable to existing hierarchies, its analytical approach does have the potential for uncovering and rewarding previously unrecognized aspects of jobs. The PEC appeared to favour the points factor system, presumably for this reason, and most of its material which dealt with job comparison did so on the basis of the points factor system. Nevertheless, this system provided room for the manipulation of results to minimize pay equity costs. If an employer wished to assign a particular male job class comparator to any given female job class (or to deny the female job class a comparator), he or she could do so by assigning appropriate values to the various job classes. If this resulted in a nurse's job being rated as equivalent to that of a porter, the possible gender bias in the system would be apparent. But if the manipulation was done more subtly, it would be much more difficult to recognize. The historical under-valuation of women's jobs, and the hierarchies thereby established, have become entrenched into most people's views of the order of things. A job evaluation scheme which rates a nurse's job as equivalent to that of a senior security officer may not offend against these views, but may have been specifically designed in order to reflect the current wage position.

(D) JOB EVALUATION

Given the common faith in job evaluation as a means by which gender–pay discrimination can be eliminated, it is useful to examine it in some detail in order to show how it can be manipulated to frustrate its declared aims. The best way to do this is to provide an example of a points factor system in operation. The system values jobs on the basis of skill, effort, responsibility, and working conditions, as required by the Act. It subdivides each of these factors into four sub-headings which, as the Commission suggested, are designed to reflect the 'goals, products and services' of the organization. The sub-factors have also, it is assumed, been chosen in order to reflect the demands made by both male and female job within the organization. The imaginary job evaluation scheme is in place in a publishing organization which, being unorganized, has developed a single job comparison system to cover everyone from the managing director to the most junior typist. The system has four sub-factors of each skill, effort, responsibility, and working conditions. Each of the sub-factors has the possible scores listed below, so that a minimum score on each would give a total points rating of 100, a maximum score on each the maximum 500.

Table 7.1 — sample job-evaluation scheme

skill	effort	responsibility	working conditions
education: 10–40	attention demanded: 10–40	cost of errors: 5–40	interruptions: 5–20
creativity: 5–50	people stress: 5–30	supervision: 5–30	physical env.: 5–10
manual quickness: 5–20	pressure of work: 10–40	financial: 5–20	multiple demands: 5–30
problem solving: 5–40	manual effort: 5–20	detail: 5–40	time pressure: 10–30
max.: 150	max.: 130	max.: 130	max.: 90

It will be assumed (and this is no small assumption) that the sixteen chosen sub-factors are potentially gender neutral in that, if properly applied, they will accurately reflect the work of both male and female job categories within the organization. It will further be assumed that the weighting assigned to each sub-factor (the low 'manual quickness' maximum, for example, in contrast with the high maxima for 'cost of errors', 'problem-solving', and 'creativity') is reasonable within the criteria suggested by the PEC, i.e. they accurately reflect the importance of each sub-factor to the nature and aims of the organization. Assume that the initial application of the system to the job class of 'secretaries' produces the following results:

Table 7.2 — possible point rating for each sub-factor

skill	effort	responsibility	working conditions
education: 30	attention demanded: 30	cost of errors: 20	interruptions: 20
creativity: 10	people stress: 20	supervision: 5	physical env.: 10
manual quickness: 20	pressure of work: 20	financial: 5	multiple demands: 20
problem solving: 20	manual effort: 10	detail: 20	time pressure: 20
total: 80	total: 80	total: 50	total: 70

The job class 'secretary' therefore receives a total points score of 280. The comparison system utilizes twenty-five point bands (100–124, 125–149 . . . 475–499), so the secretary class falls within that 275–299 band of comparability. Assume also that the job rate for the secretary is $11 an hour (about £10,000 pa), and that the closest scoring male job classes have been scored as below:

Table 7.3 — male and female job scores

job class	points	value band	wage
male A	248	225–249	$10.8
male B	278	275–299	$15.5
female I	280	275–299	$11

If the secretaries' score is left at 280, the employer will be obliged to make pay equity adjustments amounting to $3 an hour (over £2,500 pa). In order to avoid such adjustments, the employer need only nudge the secretaries' total point score downwards by ten points, which could be done by reducing scores for creativity and manual effort from ten to five, for example, or for attention demanded from thirty to twenty. The temptation so to do may prove overwhelming, given the lack of any comparator in the 250–274 band, and the fact that no male job class in the band below that (225–249) earns more than the secretary class.

This is a fairly straightforward example of how a female job class might find itself without a male job class comparator. The failure of the legislation to provide for the systematic monitoring of pay equity plans renders such manipulation very difficult to discover.

(E) LOW PAID MALE JOB CLASSES

Just as a female job class could be denied an adjustment on the basis that no comparator existed, so too it could be denied adjustment because a male job class of comparable value is paid the same or a lower rate. While this appears on its face to be reasonable, the presence of low-paid male job classes suggesting that low wages are the result of factors other than sex discrimination, the reality may be somewhat different. The rate of a particular male job class could be held down by a number of factors including the presence of a relatively large proportion of women (up to 29 per cent before the job class ceases to be classified as male), or, perhaps, of ethnic minority men. In the following example, the rate paid to male job class D is considerably lower than those paid to E, F, and G, there being a $3 gap (and a five-point difference) between D and E in comparison with only a $1 (and five-point) gap between E and F, and F and G respectively. Female job class II will be denied an adjustment here because of the presence of D, while the rate of D itself may be the result of factors not unconnected with discrimination.

Table 7.4 — avoiding female wage rises

job class	points	value band	wage
male D	250	250–274	$8
male E	255	250–274	$11
male F	260	250–274	$12
male G	265	250–274	$13
female II	260	250–274	$8

The presence of D within the 250–274 value band may be a matter of the employer's good luck. It may, on the other hand, be the result of manipulation. Had D originally been scored at 245 rather than 250 points, it would have been easy for the employer, given the inherent subjectivity of value judgements, to nudge a five-point score for pressure of work up to ten and thereby avoid having to increase the wages paid to female job class II.

Given the inherent subjectivity of any evaluation process, it is impossible to determine whether the scoring of 'pressure of work', for example, at twenty rather than ten, is the result of unbiased evaluation or whether it is motivated by a desire to place the job within a particular value band. Only the application of a balancing force in favour of adjustments can limit the effect of such temptation.

(F) LEVEL OF ADJUSTMENTS

Even where female job classes received pay equity adjustments as a result of the Act, the level of these adjustments was not, typically, high. There are a number of reasons for this. First, the Act itself provided for a poor measure of 'pay equity'. Where more than one comparable male job class existed the Act allowed the male job class with the lowest wage to be chosen as the comparator job class for the purposes of pay equity.[63] This is illustrated by Table 7.5.

Table 7.5 — minimizing female wage rises

job class	points	value band	wage
male H	300	300–324	$17
male J	310	300–324	$18
male K	320	300–324	$20
female III	320	300–324	$16

[63] PEA, s. 6(3).

All three male job classes are within the same value band as that of the female job class (300–324 points). The male job class paid at $20 dollars an hour is rated at exactly the same value as the female job class, but the female job class is entitled only to the *lowest* paid comparable male job class rate and will be entitled therefore to an adjustment of only $1, rather than $4 an hour (with the effect that the incumbents of female job class III will continue to be paid more than £2,500 less *per annum* than employees in male job class K, with whose job their own has been rated as exactly equal.

The Act also allowed, where there was no male job class rated as equivalent to that of a particular female job class, that the female job class rate be adjusted to that of the *highest paid lower valued* male job class, if that job class rate was higher than that of the female job class. This served to provide a comparator of sorts for some female job classes which would otherwise have been denied adjustments, but to depress adjustments particularly for organized female job classes. Where a job class formed part of a bargaining unit, the comparator job class had first to be sought within that bargaining unit. Only in the absence of a higher paid and lower or equally rated male job class within that unit could comparators be sought within other bargaining units or the establishment as a whole. Thus, in the following example, the presence of male job class L within bargaining unit A will deny female job class V the $4 adjustment otherwise available (if male job class M were available as a comparator) given that it (L) is higher paid than female job class V despite the lower value assigned to it by the job comparison system.

Table 7.6 — bargaining units and female wage rises

job class	points	value band	wage
bargaining unit A			
male L	260	250–274	$9.5
female IV	255	250–274	$8
female V	285	275–299	$9
bargaining unit B			
male M	280	275–299	$13

The restriction of comparisons to the bargaining unit, where possible, was defended on the basis that inter-bargaining unit differences could be explained in terms of union strength rather than sex discrimination. This is not an argument that washes particularly well, particularly given that the sex-segregated nature of many jobs and the 'community interest' approach to the delineation of bargaining units frequently resulted in bargaining units which are predominantly male or female. The wages of male job classes within such units would frequently have been depressed by their structural position within a predominantly female bargaining unit, with the effect that the adoption of the male job class as a comparator for the female job classes within the unit served simply to reinforce rather than eliminate discrimination. Given the Green Paper's explicit recognition that the wage gap was due, in part, to occupational segregation between workplaces and to the different levels of organization between men and women, this failure to require wider comparisons is noteworthy. Its explanation lies partly in the strength of Ontario's business lobby which, against labour-feminist alliance demands for across-the-board comparisons, had argued that cross-bargaining unit comparisons would result in wage spirals, violated employees' freedom of choice, and would 'undermine our entire democratic history of freedom of association'.[64]

Further, pay equity adjustments could be minimized in certain cases by the 'job group' approach. It was stated above that employers could choose (or, where employees are organized, negotiate) the comparison of jobs on a 'job group' rather than 'job class' approach, enabling the comparison of a single 'representative' female job class on behalf of the group. This approach could save time by reducing the number of comparisons an employer was obliged to carry out. It could also save the employer money where the 'representative' job class was better paid, comparative to its assigned value, than the other job classes within its group. The 'representative' job class chosen might even be gender-neutral or male dominated, so long as there were at least 60 per cent women in the group of jobs as a whole. An example of how the 'group of jobs' approach might keep pay equity adjustments low was provided by the Commission itself:

Table 7.7 — job groups and female wage rises

job class	salary	adjustment	'pay equity' salary	subsequent differential
I	$14,000	$2,000	$16,000	0
II	$16,000	no comparator	$16,000	$3,000
III	$18,000	$1,000	$19,000	$3,500
IV	$20,000	$2,500	$22,500	$3,500
V	$22,000	$100	$22,100	−$400

source: Pay Equity Commission[65]

[64] Canadian Manufacturers' Association Submission, 11.
[65] *Pay Equity Implementation Series #6*, n. 24 above, 6.3.

The guideline explains how a 'job class' approach would here disturb the existing differentials between job rates within the group of jobs, and suggests that a group of jobs approach might be useful. If job class II is the job class with the largest number of females, however, this approach will deny all the other job classes adjustments as no comparator is available for job class II. If job class V is the 'representative' job class, job class II will at least get some increase but I, III, and IV will be condemned to increases of only $100 *per annum* rather than increases of between $1,000 and $2,500. It is unlikely, to say the least, that an employer would choose to adopt the 'group of jobs' approach if job class IV were the representative job class here, but the same employer would be overwhelmingly likely to choose this method where job class II or V is the largest. In the absence of union strength the Pay Equity Act does nothing to prevent this.

Finally, the flexibility of the definition of 'establishment' within which pay equity must be achieved provided a certain amount of scope for employer manipulation. The Act allowed employers to amalgamate two or more geographical divisions into a pay equity 'establishment' either by unilateral decision or, where unions were present, by negotiation. Where employers had a free hand, they were likely to amalgamate divisions only where this permitted lower pay equity adjustments to be made, i.e. where it provided low paid male job classes as comparators for female job classes which would otherwise have had access to highly paid male job classes against which pay equity adjustments could be claimed.

(G) THE IMPACT OF TRADE UNIONS ON 'PAY EQUITY'

Table 7.6 illustrates the downward impact that organization could have on pay equity adjustments. But, in the main, organization was beneficial to women seeking pay equity adjustments. The possibilities of employer manipulation of the pay equity process have been outlined under 'The Impact of the Pay Equity Act' above, as have the sometimes impoverished concepts of 'equity' employed by the Act. Where workers were represented, the trade union was involved at every stage of the process, i.e. in determining:

- the scope of the 'employer' and the establishment within which pay equity was to be achieved;[66]
- the male, female, and gender-neutral job classes;
- the aspects of each job upon which remuneration should be based;
- the relative importance of these aspects;
- the value given to each job on the basis of them;

[66] *ONA* v. *Haldimand-Norfolk*, n. 15 above. Union pressure can also force a wide approach to the definition of the 'employer', particularly within the public sector where ONA, in particular, has achieved significant legislative victories allowing otherwise comparator-less nurses to compare themselves to highly paid police officers.

- the choice of appropriate comparators for each female job class; and
- the adjustments required by 'pay equity'.

The Act required that employer and union 'shall negotiate in good faith and endeavour to agree' the job comparison system, the pay equity plan for the relevant bargaining unit, the 'establishment' and characterization of job classes as male and female.[67] This could provide a counter-balance to the natural inclination of employers to minimize the costs of pay equity. Not only were unions in a position to reduce the conscious flouting of the legislation (by means of the deliberate assigning of particular values to particular job classes), but they were also able to negotiate in order to achieve more for their members than the sometimes minimal provisions of the Act. They could negotiate the definition of 'establishment', for example, in order to provide comparators for female job classes which would otherwise lack them, and influence the characterization of job classes as male or female. In table 7.4 above, it is possible that job class D might have only just reached the 70 per cent threshold for male job classes, and might perhaps have been a job traditionally done by a fairly high proportion of women. In such a case the presence of a trade union might have resulted in its characterization as gender-neutral with the result that female job class II could have used male job class E as a comparator and therefore been entitled to a $3 hourly increase. Trade unions could also discourage the use of the 'group of jobs' approach where it would have disadvantaged workers.

In addition to all of this, trade unions were able, even before the amendment of the Pay Equity Act (see under 'Proportional and Proxy Comparisons' below) to negotiate proportional adjustments for those female job classes which lacked comparators and to agree higher pay equity adjustments than would otherwise be required by the Act. The employer was originally under no obligation to agree to such demands, but unions could exert pressure on employers by threatening otherwise to challenge, for example, the gender neutrality of the job comparison system. Given the costs of defending a claim, should it have gone to the Hearings Tribunal, and the impossibility of ensuring that a system would be accepted as gender-neutral, such tactics were capable of exerting a strong upward pressure on pay equity adjustments. In any case, the union could refuse to agree to the employer's proposed pay equity plan in which case the Commission had to be notified by the employer and would investigate.[68]

By contrast, unorganized workers had no control over the pay equity process, and could challenge their employers only after the pay equity plan was posted or, where the employer chose not to post such a plan (and was entitled to do so by the Act), after the relevant deadline had expired. They were certainly in no position to provide a balance to the natural

[67] PEA, s. 14(2) & (3).   [68] PEA, s. 14(6).

temptation for employers to avoid finding highly paid male comparators for female job classes. Only if the choice and application of a job comparison system was overtly designed to maintain existing wage differentials would it be readily susceptible to challenge by unorganized workers. Further, where the employer had fewer than 100 employees, no pay equity plan had to be posted and employees were thrown back on an essentially intuitive complaints-based mechanism with no greater knowledge of their employer's pay system than is available to the average UK employee.

It is hardly surprising, then, that the pay equity process operated more to the benefit of organized, rather than unorganized, workers.

IV. THE AMENDMENTS

It is apparent from the foregoing discussion that many women were denied the benefit of the Pay Equity Act: not only did the Act exempt those employers covered by (weaker) federal equal pay legislation and those employers having fewer than ten employees in Ontario (these restricted the coverage of the Act to 1.7 million of Ontario's 2.2 million women workers) but, as we have seen above, many women who worked in establishments covered by the Act did not have any suitable male job class against which their job could be compared. The Pay Equity Commission estimated, in 1991, that the lack of comparators denied the benefits of 'pay equity' to a further 500,000 women workers.[69] And Judy Fudge, a prominent critic of the Act's shortcomings, estimated that '[a]lmost 50% of the women in workplaces covered by the Act are unable to claim pay equity adjustments under it'.[70]

These shortcomings, together with others, were drawn to the attention of the government and in 1993 the NDP, which had by that time taken power, passed amending legislation to address the problem of predominantly female workplaces. The amendments, which promised to bring a further 420,000 of Ontario's women workers within the scope of the Act, allowed proportional and proxy job comparisons. No change was made, however, to the small employer exclusion.

(A) PROPORTIONAL AND PROXY COMPARISONS

Proportional comparisons were to be available in both the public and the private sectors. They were designed, in essence, to allow female job classes which were rated as (say) 90 per cent as valuable as their nearest male comparator but were only paid 70 per cent of the wage, to improve their

---

[69] PEC, *Report to the Ministry of Labour by the Pay Equity Commission on Sectors of the Economy Which Are Predominantly Female* (Toronto: Pay Equity Commission, 1991).

[70] S. Findlay, 'Making Sense of Pay Equity: Issues for a Feminist Political Practice' in J. Fudge and P. MacDermott (eds.), *Just Wages* (Toronto, University of Toronto Press, 1991), 81.

wages. This was to be done by means of a 'wage line' which displayed the value-to-wage relationship for 'representative' male job classes in the organization (or, where the female job class was organized, the bargaining unit). An example of a wage line is shown in figure 7.1.

Figure 7.1 — male wage line

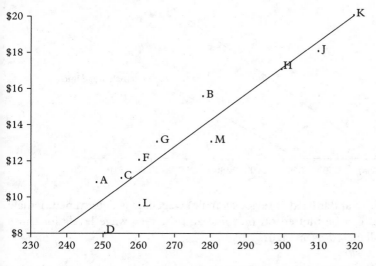

In order to determine proportional adjustments, male and female wage lines would be drawn separately and the female wage line brought up to match the male line. This process is illustrated in figures 7.2 and 7.3.

Figure 7.2 — female wage line

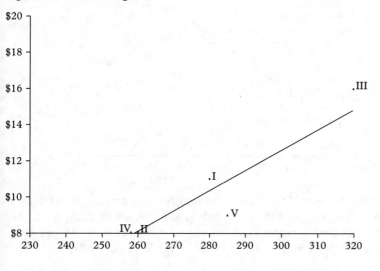

Figure 7.3 — standardizing wage lines

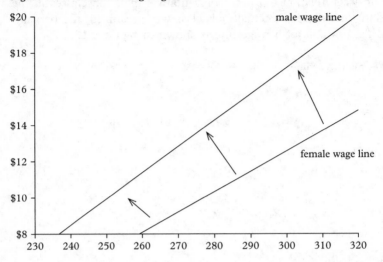

Once the standardized (previously male) wage line is determined, female job classes can be plotted on that line and the new wage levels for those classes calculated as in figure 7.4.

Figure 7.4 — female wages after 'pay equity' adjustments

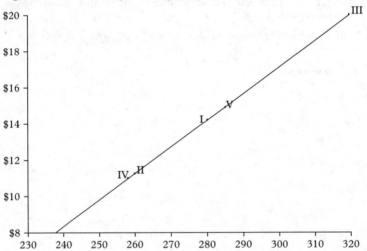

Reading from figure 7.4, the new wages for female job classes I to V would be $13.8, $11.2, $20, $11, and $15, increases of $2.8, $3.2, $4, $3, and $6 per hour (25 per cent, 40 per cent, 25 per cent, 38 per cent, and 67 per cent) for classes I, II, III, IV, and V respectively.

Figures 7.1 to 7.4 assume that there are no bargaining units within the establishment (or, alternatively, that all the male and female job classes whose wages are plotted are in a single bargaining unit). Where different bargaining units existed this process was to be performed separately for each. In addition, female job classes which had already received adjustment under the original job-to-job approach did not have to receive any further adjustment under the proportional approach even where such an adjustment would have been greater and even where the original adjustment was held down, for example, by the presence of a low-paid male job class whose impact would be reduced where a wage line was drawn.

It was estimated that the implementation of the proportional method would extend the benefits of pay equity to 340,000 women previously denied adjustments. Some women, however, would still be left with no comparisons where the organizations within which they worked contained too few male job classes to allow a male wage line to be constructed from representative male job classes. The proxy method was intended to provide pay equity adjustments for some (around 80,000) of these women. Unlike proportional value, it was made available only to female job classes in the public sector. Given that it required the comparison of salaries between different employers this was hardly surprising: the Green Paper had started from the 'fundamental premise' that 'job comparisons will be confined to an employer's establishment . . . thus obviating the concern that an industry-wide or province-wide wage-setting system is under discussion'.[71]

The election of a Conservative Government in Ontario in summer 1995 resulted in the abandonment, within a period of months, of the proxy method.[72] This is further discussed in the next section below. But even for the short time during which the proxy approach formed part of the Pay Equity Act, it was very much a method of last resort. Where employers were unable to provide pay equity adjustments, by means of job-to-job or proportional value comparison, for some or all of their female job classes, they had to report this failing to the Pay Equity Commission which would send a review officer to verify that no comparison was possible. (Permission had to be sought before proxy comparisons could be made as government funding was available for them.) If the review officer found that no comparison was possible within the organization the employer would be allowed to seek a proxy employer (which had to be in the same or a contiguous geographical area and provide at least some similar services). Regulations made under the amended Pay Equity Act set out nine different types of 'seeking' organizations together with potentially appropriate 'proxy' organizations with which they could seek comparison.

---

[71] *Green Paper*, n. 1 above, iv.
[72] Pay Equity (Amendment) Act 1995, introduced in Nov. 1995.

The 'seeking' organization was required to provide job descriptions in respect of its main female job classes (whether these had previously been matched to male job classes or not) to a suitable 'proxy' organization. The 'proxy' organization attempted to match these job descriptions with some of its own female job classes (which had been matched with male job classes), and sent information about those job classes to the 'seeking' organization. The 'seeking' organization then had to evaluate the 'proxy' organization's female job classes in line with its own 'job comparison system' and to create a 'wage line' depicting the relationship between the value of the proxy jobs, and the rate (after 'pay equity' adjustments) paid for them by the 'proxy' organization. It then had to compare its own (already evaluated) female job classes with the wage line developed from the 'proxy' organization's female job classes in order to determine the appropriate pay equity adjustments for all of its female job classes. As ever, if the 'seeking' organization contained one or more bargaining units, the process had to be conducted separately for each of these units and for any unorganized female job classes.

(B)   IMPLEMENTATION OF THE AMENDED ACT

Employers whose organizations included female job classes which had been without male job class comparators were obliged to post their new pay equity plans by January 1994 (the amendments were passed in July 1993) and to begin to pay adjustments to the affected female job classes by that date (proxy adjustments had to be made only from 1 July 1994). In the case of private sector employers of between ten and forty-nine employees the adjustments were to be calculated from that date: all other employers had to make them retroactive to 1 January 1993. The public sector was to be obliged to achieve equity across the board by January 1998.[73] Other employers remain subject to the 1 per cent maximum requirement until equity is achieved.

The price of the Pay Equity Act's extension was the restriction of the scope under which the Government of Ontario would be considered the 'employer' for the purposes of pay equity. Prior to the 1993 amendments 'employer' was undefined under the legislation and the Pay Equity Hearings Tribunal had tended towards a wide approach which had, on occasion, resulted in nurses being able to compare themselves with highly paid police officers to the dismay of their 'employing' hospitals.[74]

It is too early, as yet, to assess the final impact of the amended Act on

---

[73] The deadline did not apply as regards proxy adjustments in the public sector but these were abolished, in any case, by the Pay Equity (Amendment) Act 1995.

[74] *Haldimand-Norfolk (No 3)*, n. 15 above.

the male–female wage ratio in Ontario. I am inclined, however, to suggest that it will not be very great. There are a number of reasons for this suspicion. In the first place, even if all the 340,000 women estimated to be in line to benefit from the Pay Equity Act actually do so (the original figure of 420,000 must be reduced by the 80,000 who depended on the proxy method), they will amount to well under half the number of women who have already reaped all the rewards of pay equity which are open to them (the 1993 estimate was that the lack of comparators excluded 420,000 of a total of 1.7 million otherwise eligible women—a further 500,000 women were excluded either because they were covered by federal legislation or because their employers came within the small employers' exception, and a further 420,000 women were employed in mixed or male-dominated jobs—this left around 860,000 women eligible to benefit[75]). The gains of all women employed other than by federally regulated employers or those with fewer than fifty staff have averaged between 2.2 per cent of annual payroll in the public sector and 0.5 per cent in the smaller (fifty to ninety-nine employees) in the private sector. There is little reason to suppose that the figures for private sector employers of between ten and forty-nine, when they become available, will be markedly better than those for other private sector employers (0.6 per cent, 1.1 per cent, and 0.5 per cent in descending order of size).

If we estimate the pre-amendment cost of pay equity at around 1 per cent of annual payroll throughout the economy (860,000 women workers) and inflate this by 40 per cent to cover those 340,000 employees who are expected to receive adjustments as a result of the amendments, we are still only left with a 3 per cent fall in the 22 per cent (hourly) gender–pay gap which existed in 1985 in Ontario.[76] On the Ontario government's own calculations, pay equity could be expected to get rid of around ten of those twenty-two points (the remainder being attributed to differences in experience, education, and unionization). It would appear, at this stage, that it has done nothing of the sort.

And there are other reasons to be sceptical about the possibility of radical future change. It was mentioned, above, that the 1993 amendments

[75] Figures taken from the US General Accounting Office, *Briefing Report to Congressional Requesters: Pay Equity, Experiences of Canada and the Province of Ontario* (1993).

[76] This is calculated as follows: according to the Green Paper, n. 1 above, women constituted 44% of Ontario's workforce in 1985. When differences in hours worked was taken into account, women earned 62% of men's *annual* wage—which in turn translates into 32.75% of the total wage bill. If pay equity increased the total wage bill by 1.4%, and it benefited *only* women, women would stand to receive (32.75% + 1.4%)/100% + 1.4% = 33.7% of the wage bill (in fact, since women will not be the only beneficiaries of the 1.4% increase, this is an overestimate). Assuming that women still account for 44% of Ontario's workforce, this means that they will earn only 65% of men's annual wage and, again assuming that the difference in hours worked remains static, about 81% (which is 78% pre-'pay equity' and 3% gain) of mens' hourly wages.

included a commitment on the part of Ontario's government to fund
pay equity adjustments in the broader public sector. Judy Fudge claimed,
in 1996, that '[t]he significance of the proxy method in allieviating the
wage gap . . . will depend upon the size of the pay equity fund that the
government is prepared to provide'.[77] The new Conservative administration declared, in August 1995, that pay equity was one of the items on
its 'hitlist' when Parliament reconvened on 26 September, and early that
month the government announced that pay equity funding would be
capped.[78] In November of that year it went further and introduced an
Act to abolish the proxy method of pay equity adjustments.

In addition, massive problems have arisen as a result of the Pay Equity
Act's failure to require smaller private sector employers to post their pay
equity plans. The absence of any deadline in this regard resulted in a very
widespread failure, on the part of such small employers, to take any action
to comply with the Act. This had the effect that many of the employers
of between fifty and ninety-nine staff were (leaving aside the issue of proportional value) supposed to have completed pay equity adjustments by
January 1993, and many of the smaller employers to have done so by 1994.
These deadlines were rarely met, great numbers of small employers are
in breach of the Pay Equity Act, and this unhappy situation has coincided with a severe recession. The Pay Equity Commission threatened,
in early 1995, to 'get tough' with recalcitrant employers.[79] But, at least
where small organizations are concerned, it may be a choice between
forcing these employers to pay the appropriate adjustments (even if they
know what these were) and go out of business as a result, or contenting
itself with encouraging gradual compliance.

Finally, in July 1995 the new government announced that public funding for those who wished to claim under the Pay Equity Act was to be
withdrawn: '[t]he government is committed to pay equity', the Labour
Minister claimed, '[w]e are simply opting for less costly and more efficient
ways to . . . assure working women the benefits of pay equity achievement'.[80] The new government also announced the repeal of the Employment Equity Act 1993 which had been passed by the NDP a mere eighteen
months before and had come into force in September 1994—that piece
of legislation was designed to bring the same 'pro-active' approach to

---

[77] Fudge, n. 3 above. For further discussion of the limitations placed by economic pressures on the 'pay equity' process see also R. Warskett, 'Can a Disappearing Pie Be Shared
Equally? Unions, Women and Wage "Fairness" ' in Briskin and McDermott, n. 10 above,
249.

[78] *Financial Post*, 19 Aug. 1995; *Canada NewsWire*, 11 Sept. 1995.

[79] *Kitchener News*, 30 Jan. 1995.

[80] *Ibid.* Legal aid in Ontario is administered in the form of free clinics. Pay Equity
Advocacy Legal Services (PEALS) was the clinic which took pay equity cases. According
to *Canada NewsWire*, 25 July 1995, its funding of $600,000 pa was to cease at the end of
1995 and the $950,000 promised for the major review of the Act was slashed to $100,000.

discrimination in access to jobs, promotion, etc. as the Pay Equity Act had brought to discrimination in pay.[81]

Ontario's new Prime Minister, Mike Harris, announced that the 1993 Act was 'not the vehicle to fight discrimination in the workplace' and declared that it was the Conservative Government's goal 'to take down barriers to equality of employment' (in particular, it would appear, those barriers confronting white, able-bodied men). The 1993 Act, he stated, was 'symbolic' of the NDP's 'indifference' to the pressures under which Ontario's business community was labouring.[82] We saw, above in this section, that the government has already curtailed public sector spending on pay equity. It may only be a question of time before it turns its attention to the unreasonable demands made on the pockets of that business community by the Pay Equity Act. Certainly, advocates of pay equity reacted with alarm to the legislative review announced by Ontario's government in March 1996.[83]

V. CONCLUSIONS

Ontario's Pay Equity Act could be described as the ultimate in existing 'comparable worth' legislation. Leaving aside for a moment issues such as the lack of any comprehensive monitoring mechanism and the impoverished notion of equality which accepted as sufficient the raising of women's salaries to the lowest male salary in a job of equivalent value, here was legislation which both embraced the concept of equal pay for work of equal value (later, of pay according to the *proportionate* value of jobs) and required the comparison of male and female jobs in order to determine their relative worth. In this latter characteristic, at least, Ontario's legislation provides a potential model for reform of the United Kingdom's law.

Ontario's legislation is flawed, not least by its restriction of job comparisons to those done by men and women working for the same employer. While the Pay Equity Tribunal's generous approach to the meaning of 'employer' allowed many poorly paid women in the broader public sector to compare their salaries with those of well paid men in very different types of workplaces (the tribunal, for example, declared that employees working in a Toronto public library were employees of the city of Toronto rather than of the library board, that those working in a children's aid society were employed by the province rather than the society, and that police officers were employed by the Municipality rather than the Board of Commissioners of the Police[84]); the test adopted did not invariably prove favourable to broad comparisons and was, in any case, of little benefit to employees in the private sector. The Pay Equity Act did not enable

[81] *Financial Post*, 20 July 1995.   [82] *Ibid.*   [83] *Canada NewsWire*, 9 Apr. 1996.
[84] *Haldimand-Norfolk (No 3)*, n. 15 above.

women to challenge pay disparities which arose by virtue of sex segregation at the workplace and industry, rather than the occupational, level.

This problem might not be insurmountable if 'pay equity' were to be embraced in the United Kingdom along the (modified) lines of the Ontario legislation. But perhaps the most valuable lesson to be learned from the Pay Equity Act concerns the ease with which grand schemes can be neutered by apparently minor details. Factors such as the exclusion of employers with fewer than ten employees and the initial demand for parity of worth before any adjustment was required, rather than mere lack of proportionality between 'value' and wages in predominantly male and female jobs, combined to exclude almost one third of Ontario's women workers from the scope of the Pay Equity Act. And given the reliance of Ontario's approach upon undefined concepts of 'male' and 'female' jobs, and upon the essentially untestable mechanism of 'gender-neutral' job evaluation, it is impossible to know what proportion of the almost 40 per cent of women denied pay rises on the ground that they did not work in predominantly female jobs, or (at least until the implementation of the amendments) that no comparable male job class existed, were cheated out of the benefits of the Act. (In the case of the latter women, manipulation of the job evaluation scheme would still enable employers to minimize any potential pay rises, if not to deny them completely.) One critic of the Pay Equity Act went so far as to claim that 'devices were set up in the legislation whereby pay equity would not cost employers any more in terms of labour expenditures than they would otherwise have to bear in the absence of pay equity'.[85]

Perhaps more than anything else, the Pay Equity Act should serve as a warning about the difficulties of establishing any radical attempt to overhaul the gender–wage relationship upon the foundation of job evaluation. (Both the Pay Equity Act and the Pay Equity Commission insisted on using the term 'job comparison' rather than 'job evaluation', but the information-gathering and relative evaluation process are indistinguishable —neither indicates absolute values; both merely suggest the relationship of jobs one to another.) Job evaluation is so complex, the demands made by jobs so many and so various that unless the result, rather than the process, of comparison is dictated (or, in any event, subject to rigorous scrutiny), it is very difficult to see how bias can be avoided.

Treiman and Hartmann, early 'comparable worth' advocates, claimed that '[w]hat a job is "worth" to an employer depends largely on how the employer chooses to structure it'.[86] Burton et al., who considered the

[85] C. Cuneo, 'The State of Pay Equity: Mediating Gender and Class Through Political Parties in Ontario' in Fudge and MacDermott, n. 70 above, 56.

[86] D. Treiman and H. Hartmann (eds.), *Women, Work and Wages: Equal Pay for Jobs of Equal Value* (Washington, DC: National Academy Press, 1981), 52, cited in C. Burton, R. Hag, and G. Thompson, *Women's Worth: Pay Equity and Job Evaluation in Australia* (Canberra: Australian Government-Publishing Service, 1987), 103.

possibilities of improving Australian women's pay using the job evaluation tool, said of their experience with the implementation of the Hay scheme by one large employer, that women's jobs were re-designed in order to exclude the use of discretion where this was perceived as necessary in order to avoid an unwelcome finding of parity with male jobs.[87]

Finally, the dependence of the pay equity process upon the job evaluation technique has, in the view of many of the Act's critics, technicalized what is an essentially political process. The 1990 survey (of public sector employers and those in the private sector having at least 500 employees) found that 34 per cent of the former and 44 per cent of the latter had used outside consultants to develop a job comparison system.[88] A further 17 per cent of public and 21 per cent of private sector organizations bought a new plan, while 16 per cent of public and 22 per cent of private sector employees simply applied their existing job evaluation system without modification. A mere 53 per cent of public and 52 per cent of private sector employers consulted female employees about the implementation of pay equity. In 1992 the study of private sector organizations having between 100 and 499 employees found that 37 per cent had purchased a new system, 24 per cent developed a new one either with or without the assistance of outside consultants, and 12 per cent used the unmodified existing job evaluation system.[89]

This technicalization of the discrimination issue has been much criticized, even by those commentators who express the view that the consciousness-raising associated with the Pay Equity Act may have long-term beneficial effects upon women's wages. Pat and Hugh Armstrong assert that:

[m]en are paid mainly on the basis of their power to demand wages, not primarily on the basis of some objective definition of the work they do. They are paid as the result of struggles or the potential for struggle and on the basis of their access to the means of production and of their control over techniques. What men do is more highly priced because worth is primarily negotiated, whether or not this is done through collective bargaining. Women, on the other hand, have, to a large extent, been excluded from these negotiations, regardless of whether they are part of a formal bargaining process.[90]

Ontario's Pay Equity Act fails to address this problem. Its technicalization of the discrimination issue, and the ensuing entrenchment of pay differentials legitimated by job evaluation systems whose gender-neutrality has usually not been tested, has done nothing to empower women, and relatively little to improve their wages.

[87] Burton *et al.*, n. 86 above.   [88] SPR Associates, n. 46 above, 23, display 8.
[89] Canadian Facts, n. 12 above, 29 exhibit IV–18.
[90] P. Armstrong and H. Armstrong, 'Lessons from Pay Equity' (1990) 32 *Studies in Political Economy* 29.

[8]
Collective Bargaining and Equal Pay

I. INTRODUCTION

In the previous chapter I considered one legislative approach to the gender–pay gap. In this and the following chapter, I will consider two types of pay regulation which are not directed specifically at the gender–pay gap but which may, on the evidence from the United Kingdom and elsewhere, have a significant impact upon it.

The gender–pay gap and, more generally, the degree of wage dispersion in any particular country are affected by the degree of collective bargaining coverage within that country. One of the reasons the United Kingdom has among the worst gender–pay ratios in the EU (see Chapter 4 for discussion of this) is the fact that the gap between the best and the worst-paid workers in the United Kingdom is much wider than that in most of the other Member States. Thus, even if women in the United Kingdom were no more likely than those elsewhere to be found in lower paid jobs than those done by men, the size of the wage disparity between the poorly- and the well-paid would make the gender–wage gap wider than elsewhere.

Tables 8.1 and 8.2 show the gender–wage gap in the various EC (as it then was) Member States in 1991 and attempt to rank those states in order. Table 8.3 shows the levels of wage dispersion in most of those Member States.

Of those Member States included in table 8.1, the United Kingdom has the largest proportion of workers earning less than 66 per cent and less than 80 per cent of the median wage.

Women tend to be concentrated at the bottom of the earnings ladder —the longer the ladder, therefore, the greater the degree of their relative disadvantage. The degree of wage dispersion is, in part, affected by the existence or otherwise of minimum wage regulation (a matter discussed in Chapter 9). But it is also significantly affected by the extent to which workers are covered by collective bargaining. Table 8.4 shows the degree of collective bargaining coverage in each of the Member States included in table 8.3.

Table 8.1 — women's relative wages by EU Member State (1991)

	women's wages	
	manual (hourly)	non-manual (monthly)
Belgium	75.6	65.2
Denmark	84.5	n/a
France	80.3	67.2
Greece	79.2	68.6
Ireland	69.5	n/a
Italy	79.3!	n/a
Luxembourg	68.0*	55.2*
Netherlands	76.2*	64.8*
Portugal	70.8	70.7
Spain	72.2	60.9
United Kingdom	67.2	58.3
West Germany	73.8	67.1

source: Eurostat, *Earnings, Industry and Services*, 1992[1]
* figures for 1990
! estimate from 1989 figures

Table 8.2 — EU Member States ranked according to women's relative wages

	women's wages (1991)		
	1: manual	2: non-manual	3: average of 1 and 2[2]
Belgium	6	5	8
Denmark	1	n/a	1
France	2	3	3
Greece	4	2	2
Ireland	10	n/a	10
Italy	3	n/a	4
Luxembourg	11	9	11
Netherlands	5	6	6
Portugal	9	1	5
Spain	8	7	9
United Kingdom	12	8	12
West Germany	7	4	6

source: Eurostat, *Earnings, Industry and Services*, 1992[3]
* figures for 1990

[1] Reported in C. Hoskyns, *Integrating Gender* (London: Verso, 1996), App. 6.4.
[2] The average is meaningless save for the purposes of this table—various states use monthly or hourly figures and there are different proportions of manual and non-manual women by Member State.
[3] N. 1 above.

Table 8.3 — wage dispersion by EU Member State

% of workers earning less than

	50% overall median	66% overall median	80% overall median
Belgium	0	5	19
Denmark	0	0	1
France	0	14	28
Greece	10	16	26
Ireland	10	18	30
Italy	9	15	25
Netherlands	5	11	24
Portugal	5	12	31
Spain	9[a]	19	32
United Kingdom	7	20	35
West Germany	6	13	25

source: Bazen and Benhayoun[4]
[a] 42% median

Table 8.4 — collective bargaining coverage by EU Member State

	% covered by collective bargaining
Belgium	90
Denmark	83
France	92
Greece	—
Ireland	57
Italy	100
Luxembourg	70
Netherlands	71
Portugal	79
Spain	68
United Kingdom	47
West Germany	100

source: Bazen and Benhayoun,[5] OECD *Economic Outlook*, 1994[6]

Those countries with very high levels of collective bargaining coverage (Belgium, Denmark, France, Italy and West Germany) tend to show

---

[4] S. Bazen and G. Benhayoun, 'Low Pay and Wage Regulation in the European Community' (1992) 30 *British Journal of Industrial Relations* 623, 629.
[5] *Ibid.*   [6] The figure for Luxembourg is taken from the OECD material.

relatively low degrees of wage dispersion (if each country is rated 0–10 in order of wage dispersion under each category: percentage of workers paid under 50 per cent, 66 per cent, and 80 per cent of the minimum wage, their overall ranking, starting with the state with the least dispersion, is Denmark, Belgium, the Netherlands, France, West Germany, Portugal, Italy, Greece, Ireland, Spain, the United Kingdom[7]). The Netherlands and Portugal also show low levels of wage dispersion: the Netherlands has a relatively high level of collective bargaining coverage, and it, together with Portugal, has a national minimum wage (set, respectively, at 77 per cent, and 74 per cent of the median wage) which tends to offset relatively low levels of collective bargaining coverage (see further Chapter 9).

The relationship between wage dispersion and the gender–wage gap was mentioned above. Table 8.5 shows the chances, relative to men, of women being low-paid in some of the Member States of the EU (where 100 is in each case the risk of a worker of either sex being underpaid).

Table 8.5 — women's relative chances of being low-paid by EU Member State

	50% overall median	66% overall median	80% overall median
Belgium	0	200	167
France	0	145	137
Greece	154	163	172
Ireland	172	163	150
Italy	166	160	150
Netherlands	274	263	230
Portugal	<150	<150	158
Spain	221	n.a.	155
United Kingdom	189	191	166
West Germany	287	248	217

source: Bazen and Benhayoun[8]

Women are always and everywhere in the EU more disadvantaged than men, and women are *relatively* more likely to be in each of the low-paid groups in the Netherlands and in West Germany. Again ranking the Member States under each of the categories, the overall hierarchy (in terms of

[7] The same order exactly (save that Portugal and Italy draw) is obtained if scores are just averaged across the three categories—Italy should lag in that case anyway since it scores higher on % under 50%.

[8] Bazen and Benhayoun, n. 4 above, table 1, 625 taken from Centre d'Etudes des Revenues et Coûts, *Les Bas Salaires en Europe* (Paris: CERC, 1991), Report No 101; V. Koutsogeorgopolou, 'Minimum Wages in Greece', unpublished Ph.D thesis, 1992, University of Kent.

the increasing relative likelihood of women being in the low-paid groups)
is France, Italy and Portugal, Ireland, Belgium, Greece, the United Kingdom, West Germany, and the Netherlands (figures for Spain and Denmark being unavailable). But this hierarchy is meaningless until taken into
account, with the overall proportions of workers in each Member State
falling within each category of low pay (in the Netherlands, for example,
women are most likely to be low paid relative to men, but the proportion of workers, and therefore the proportion of women workers, who are
low-paid is very small in comparison with other Member States). When
tables 8.4 and 8.5 are considered together, the results shown in table 8.6
emerge.

**Table 8.6 — proportion of low-paid women by
EU Member State**

	50% overall median	66% overall median	80% overall median
Belgium	0	7	12
France	0	16	33
Greece	12	20	33
Ireland	13	22	36
Italy	11	18	30
Netherlands	7	16	33
Portugal	<6	<14	37
Spain	12	n.a.	39
United Kingdom	9	26	45
West Germany	9	19	34

source: Bazen and Benhayoun[9]

What is perhaps most immediately noticeable is the very high proportion of women in the United Kingdom who earn less than 80 per cent
of the median wage—this figure is well beyond the nearest rival (Spain)
and considerably above the average 33 per cent.[10] The United Kingdom
is also noticeably behind in terms of the proportion of women being paid
less than 66 per cent of the overall median wage (the overall average is
18 per cent[11]) but women in Spain, Greece, Ireland, and Italy do worse
in terms of the proportion being paid less than 50 per cent of the median
wage. If Member States are ranked overall, women in Belgium do best,
followed by those in France, Italy, the Netherlands, Portugal, Greece, West
Germany, the United Kingdom, and Ireland. Again, as before, Belgian,
French, Italian, and Dutch women benefit from high levels of collective
bargaining coverage and those in Portugal from a minimum wage. In the

---

[9] N. 8 above.   [10] 36% if Belgium is omitted.   [11] 19% excluding Belgium.

United Kingdom and Ireland, on the other hand, neither of these apply. Only West Germany bucks the trend by combining high levels of collective bargaining with a large female wage disadvantage.

It can be seen that those countries with relatively few low-paid women are generally those with the smallest gender–wage gaps (Greece and Belgium being the exception, the first having large numbers of low-paid women and a small gender–wage gap and the reverse being true in Belgium). In addition, those countries with low levels of wage dispersion generally have low gender–wage gaps (again, with exceptions for Greece and Belgium as well as Italy, which combines relatively high levels of dispersion with a narrow gender–wage gap).

In considering in rather more detail the possible impact of a collective bargaining approach to the gender–pay gap, this chapter will focus upon the Australian model. Australia is chosen because it combines a particularly high degree of collective bargaining coverage with a very low gender–pay gap and a common law background which perhaps has more in common with the UK system than does, for example, any of the Nordic countries. The Australian approach does not itself typify a collective bargaining one, given its reliance (discussed in section II below), on a system of administrative tribunals. Nevertheless, the application of the 'awards' made by those tribunals through the collective bargaining system makes the approach suitable for study as one form of collective model.

II. AUSTRALIA'S WAGE-SETTING SYSTEM

(A) INTRODUCTION

In order to understand how Australia qualifies as a possible model for 'pay equity' reform it is necessary to appreciate how, until recently, its wage-setting structure operated.[12] What follows is an explanation of the traditional system which governed wages in Australia between 1907 and the early 1990s. Initially, and until 1972, this system institutionalized direct and explicit sex-based wage discrimination: it set wages for male and female jobs expressly by reference to the sex of their occupants. In 1969 this practice was halted in so far as men and women engaged in the *same jobs* were concerned, and in 1972 the same principle was applied to those doing work of *equal value*. The impact of this change was enormous—in 1966, Australian women had earned 71.4 per cent of men's weekly and 71.8 per cent of their hourly 'award rates' (see the section below). In 1972, after 'equal pay for work of equal value' had been implemented, these figures increased to 77.4 per cent and 78.2 per cent respectively.

---

[12] More accurately, 'qualified'—the system here described has, as we shall see under 'The Threat to Australian Women's Pay' below, been replaced by a decentralized model.

By 1975, weekly and hourly award rates had reached 91 per cent and 91.9 per cent.[13]

Australia is a useful subject for study because its approach to equal pay, in common with wage determination in general, is at the far end of the spectrum from that of the United Kingdom. Not only did Australia operate an extremely centralized and market-resistant method of pay determination but, until very recently, it took no significant legislative steps to deal with pay discrimination. In addition, recent changes have resulted in a move away from centralized towards enterprise bargaining and some evidence is already emerging of the effect of this shift on women's relative position.

(B) TRADITIONAL APPROACH

Wages in Australia have traditionally been fixed centrally, being determined by state and federal tribunals which set minimum terms and conditions (including wages) for particular occupations and industries and which, until recently, also restricted maximum pay levels to a significant extent.[14]

The system was established in 1904 by the Commonwealth Conciliation and Arbitration Act which created the Court of Conciliation and Arbitration (CCA).[15] (This was replaced in 1956 by the Australian Conciliation and Arbitration Commission which was in turn replaced, in 1988, by the Industrial Relations Commission—ACAC and IRC respectively.) The CCA's (then the ACAC's and IRC's) job was to provide mandatory conciliation for parties to industrial disputes which spread across state lines, and to arbitrate where necessary. Tribunals were set up at the state level to deal with intra-state disputes.[16] In either case, conciliation and/or arbitration would result in the imposition of 'awards' by the tribunal.

The 'awards' system in Australia largely took the place, until very recently, of any direct legislative intervention in the employment relationship. Although Australian states can and do legislate for minimum standards in employment, the constitution prevents the federal government from intervening in employment matters except in relation to its employees (and those in the State Capital Territories) and in order to comply with international obligations.[17] Awards typically included terms relating to termination of employment, hours of work, holidays, sick-leave, safety

[13] M. Killingsworth, *The Economics of Comparable Worth* (Kalamazoo, Mich: W. E. Upjohn Institute for Employment Research, 1990), 240–1. The wages including overaward payments were 76.5% hourly in 1973, 82.3% in 1975, and 84% in 1978.

[14] See S. Deery and D. Plowman, *Australian Industrial Relations* (2nd edn., Sydney: McGraw-Hill, 1985), 274–82.

[15] For a discussion of the events preceding the establishment of the awards system see *ibid*.

[16] See D. Plowman and J. Niland, 'Australia' in R. Blanpain (ed.), *Bulletin of Comparative Labour Relations* (special issue: *Flexibility and Wages, a Comparative Treatment*), (Deventer: Kluwer, 1990), 119.

[17] *Australian Boot Employees Federation* v. *Whybrow & Co.* (1910) 11 CLR 311.

provisions, and long-service leave, etc. In addition, they established rates of pay. But awards might remain in force for years at a time during which period wages might be expected to change substantially while, at least until 1970, employees could not take industrial action during the life-span of any award by which they were covered (and even after this, while contempt of court actions became largely redundant, unions could still face serious administrative sanctions for taking industrial action[18]). Not surprisingly, therefore, federal and state tribunals upgraded the wage rates in awards automatically—from 1921 the federal tribunal decided an annual *National Wage Case* and then applied the increase granted in this case across all federal awards.[19] A very important principle applied by state and federal tribunals was 'comparative wage justice'—pre-existing relativities between various categories of workers were retained over time unless special circumstances (such as a change in the 'value' of a job—of which more later) intervened.[20] Thus, not only did the federal tribunal apply the wage increases from its *National Wage Case* across the board each year, but state tribunals almost invariably followed suit in respect of wage rates in their awards.[21] Small wonder, then, that the annual *National Wage Case* became a focus of concern with many employer and employee representatives together with governments and various interest groups intervening in order to try to influence the outcome.[22]

[18] Although the maximum duration of an award under the Conciliation and Arbitration Act 1904 was 5 years, awards did not lapse after this time but remained in force until replaced or dissolved by the ACAC—see Deery and Plowman, n. 14 above, 139. See generally Deery and Plowman, 274–82. The penal sanctions were much used in the 1960s in a period which culminated in the imprisonment of O'Shea, Secretary of the Tramways Union, for contempt of court in 1969. His fine was paid by a lottery winner and legislation passed in 1970 to change the method of enforcement in favour of a conciliation and arbitration approach which preceded any penalty. In 1976 deregistration became an option once more; in 1979 the power to impose this penalty was taken on directly by the government (it had belonged to the Industrial Relations Board); and in 1983 the emphasis changed to co-operation between government and unions in the Accord (see after n. 98 below). Even after 1970: '[a]n award . . . is in the nature of a *legislative act*. It is something which, authorised to be made by statute, is, when made, covered by and made of binding force by the statute' ((1923–4) 34 CLR 528–9, cited by Deery and Plowman, 139)—'parties must strictly adhere to the terms of the award' (139–40). Administrative sanctions could include deregistration of the trade union—this happened, in 1985–6, to the Building Labourers' Federation—see L. Bennett, *Making Labour Law in Australia: Industrial Relations, Politics and Law* (Melbourne: The Law Book Company, 1994), 52.
[19] Deery and Plowman, n. 14 above, 288 ff for a history of the National Wage Cases.
[20] *Ibid.* 139—the uniformity of holiday and general conditions throughout industries was an explicit aim of the ACAC in making awards.
[21] Prior to the 'total wage' concept, of which more in the text to n. 35 below, the decisions on the metal workers' margins cases were used to establish patterns throughout industry—see generally R. O'Dea, *Principles of Wage Determination in Commonwealth Arbitration* (Sydney: West Publishing Corporation Pty. Ltd, 1969).
[22] D. Plowman, 'Developments in Australian Wage Determination, 1953–83: The Institutional Dimension' in J. Niland (ed.), *Wage Fixation in Australia* (Sydney: Allen & Unwin, 1986) records that, in 1952, in the Metal Trades Case, 20 unions, 8 employer associations, 11 state 'state instrumentalities', 6 large private employers, and 3 state governments intervened.

Federal awards covered about 40 per cent of Australian employees in 1990 and state awards a further 40 per cent.[23] The result was, in the words of one critic in 1990, that 'wage determination is probably more centralised in Australia than in any other country in the developed capitalist world'.[24]

In the early years the CCA set wages on the basis of minimum (basic) rates payable to all workers, however unskilled, and skill margins which were to be paid on top of these minima. The division of wages into minimum or basic and additional components persisted until 1967 when the ACAC embraced the notion of the 'total wage'.

Institutionalized Discrimination

The basic rate was first established for men in 1907 in *Ex p. McKay* (the *Harvester* case), in which the CCA interpreted a statute relating to the payment of 'fair and reasonable wages' to require a basic wage for male workers which allowed them to support a wife and three children.[25]

No mention was made of women workers in the *Harvester* case, but five years later, when they were considered, the court rejected the argument that their minimum rate should be the same as that of men.[26] Justice Higgins, then President of the CCA, accepted that women's work could be as valuable as that done by men, and agreed that their skill margins should be the same as those received by men. But he took the view that women's smaller needs meant that these margins should be established on a lower base except where women were actually doing the same work as men, in which case lower wages would encourage employers to use them in preference to men. For male jobs, the bottom line was that sufficient to support a man, his wife, and family in a 'civilized community', work value margins to be additional thereto. No ruling was made on the appropriate minimum payable to women.

In 1916 the minimum rate for women was fixed at 54 per cent of that payable to men, at which level it remained until 1949, although major fluctuations occurred during the Second World War when responsibility for women's rates (in men's jobs) passed from the CCA to the Women's Employment Board. Women's lower award rates were justified on the basis that, whereas men needed to support wives and families, women were secondary earners who, at most, were responsible only for themselves.[27] One particularly clear articulation of this view, as well as of the

[23] Killingsworth, n. 13 above, 219. Cf. R. Mitchell and R. Naughton, 'Australian Compulsory Arbitration: Will it Survive into the Twenty-First Century?' (1993) 31(2) *Osgoode Hall Law Journal* 265, 267—they estimate coverage of 33% and 50% respectively in 1993.
[24] Killingsworth, n. 13 above, 218.   [25] (1907) 2 CAR 1.
[26] *Rural Workers' Union and United Labourer' Union* v. *Mildura Branch of the Australian Dried Fruits Association* (1912) 6 CAR 61.
[27] See D. Sells, 'Wage Regulation in Australia and New Zealand' (1924) 10 *International Labour Review* 779; J. Stackpool-Moore, 'From Equal Pay to Equal Value in Australia: Myth

reasoning behind the 'equal pay for equal work' practice, came in the 1919 *Clothing Trades Case*: Higgins J not only declared that the wage for a predominantly female job 'should be that suitable for a single woman supporting herself only' (that for a male job had to be sufficient to support the worker, his wife, and three children) but went on to state, in support of requiring equal pay for equal work, that 'the lower rates habitual for women are the cause of the gradual disappearance of men from the industry . . . it is . . . serious to drive men out of employment by prescribing unequal wages . . . it is better for society—if the candidates are equally qualified—that most of the jobs should go to the men'.[28] In another case, the chair of Western Australia's state tribunals declared, in ruling that women bar staff should be paid the same as men, that 'if the effect of making no distinction between the wage is that barmaids are more or less abolished in hotels, I think the result would be a good one'.[29] It followed from this approach that, where lower rates of pay for women would not, for one or other reason, prejudice men's job opportunities, equal pay was not applied.

Even during the Second World War, a time during which the US National War Labor Board embraced the principle of 'equal pay for equal work', the Australian Women's Employment Board continued to fix women's rates lower than men's[30] (presumably at this time women were not seen as threatening men's jobs). The Board provided, for example, that women engaged in munitions work were to be paid no more than 90 per cent of the male rate, and that only after a probationary period on 60 per cent of the male rate.[31] By this stage, wage discrimination was being defended on the basis of worth rather than that of need.[32] Women,

---

or Reality?' (1990) 11 *Comparative Labor Law Journal* 273; M. Thornton, 'Equal Pay in Australia' in F. Eyraud *et al.*, *Equal Pay Protection in Industrialised Market Economies* (Geneva: ILO, 1993), 23.

[28] (1919) 13 CAR 692, 692 & 701–2.

[29] West Australian Arbitral Tribunal, WAAR 112, cited in E. Sykes and H. Glasbeek, *Labour Law in Australia* (Sydney: Butterworths, 1972), 617.

[30] See Z. Clark Dickinson, 'Men's and Women's Wages in the US' (1943) XLVII *International Labour Review* 693. Some states had acted prior to this. In 1931, e.g., Michigan Statute Act 328 s. 556, Public Acts of 1931 (Mich.) provided that '[a]ny employer of labour in this State, employing both males and females in the manufacture or production of any article, who shall discriminate in any way in the payment of wages as between the sexes or who shall pay any female engaged in the manufacture or production of any article of like value, workmanship or production a less wage, by time or by piece work, than is being paid to males similarly employed in such manufacture, production or in any employment formerly performed by males, shall be guilty of a misdemeanour; provided, however, that no female shall be given any task disproportionate to her strength or her potential capacity for motherhood' (cited at 701).

[31] (1943) 47 *International Labour Review* 92.

[32] See A. Curthoys, 'Equal Pay, A Family Wage, or Both?' in B. Caine, E. Grosz, and M. de Lepervanche (eds.), *Crossing Boundaries: Feminisms and Critiques of Knowledge* (Sydney: Allen & Unwin, 1988), 132—the trend towards fixation of wages on the basis of worth rather than need had been evident since 1931 and particularly after the Second World War.

it was declared, were not as productive as men. Even though they were 'at least as efficient' in some things, limitations on heavy work and 'regular periods of lessened efficiency and productivity peculiar to women' rendered them less valuable employees than men. But despite the general shift from needs-based to worth-based arguments, the former continued to be used to justify women's lower pay: the bottom line wage for female occupations, in contrast to that for male jobs, was fixed by reference to 'the needs of a single woman who has to pay for her board and lodging, has to maintain herself, out of her earnings, but has no dependants to support'.[33]

Australia was peculiar amongst nations in so openly devaluing women's work. In 1944 the CCA again resumed jurisdiction on the matter of women's wages and rejected calls for equalization[34] (many unions saw 'equal pay' as communist-inspired and campaigned against it after the war ended). But in 1949, women's minimum rate was raised to 75 per cent, and twenty years thereafter the principle of 'equal pay for equal work' was embraced by the ACAC to become fully effective from 1972. This step followed the replacement, in 1967, of the 'minimum and margin' approach to wage setting with the 'total wage' approach. This was intended to place more emphasis on the needs of the economy and of employers, less on those of workers themselves.[35] Logically, this change in emphasis should have opened the way to the equal pay principle, and it was perhaps in recognition of this that the tribunal awarded a standard dollar increase to men and women employees in that year. But it was not until 1969 that the principle of equal pay was formally accepted.

The Advent of Equal Pay

By the time the ACAC accepted 'equal pay', all of the states had taken some form of action on their own account, giving into union pressure which had mounted in the wake of the International Labour Organization's (ILO's) 1951 Convention No 100 on Equal Remuneration.[36] The first of these was New South Wales which provided, in 1958, that men

[33] *In the Matter of the National Security (Industrial Peace) Regulations and of the Arms Explosives and Munitions Workers Federation of Australia* v. *Director-General of Munitions* (1943), 50 CAR 191, 211, cited by J. Purdy, 'Women, Work and Equality: The Commonwealth Legislation (1989) 19 *Western Australian Law Review* 352, 352. Having said this, Curthoys n. 32 above, at 133–7 describes the upward pressure exerted on salaries in 'female jobs' by competition from openings to women in 'male' jobs—this resulted in an increase in salaries in 'female' jobs that were rated as essential to the war effort.

[34] *Basic Wage Inquiry*, (1944) 68 CAR 698; Curthoys, n. 32 above, 133–7.

[35] See Commonwealth of Australia, *Equal Pay: Some Aspects of Australian and Overseas Practice* (3rd edn., Melbourne: Department of Labour and National Service, 1968).

[36] See Curthoys, n. 32 above, 137 ff—the House of Representatives approved the principle in 1951 but declared that it was for the courts to implement. The ACAC did not fully accept the challenge until 1974 (when the minimum wage was equalized) and the Convention was ratified in the same year.

and women should receive equal pay when they performed 'the same work or work of a like nature . . . and [did] the same range and volume of work . . . under the same conditions'.[37] But, however restricted the scope of this principle was, it was narrowed still further by the proviso that it should 'not apply to and in respect of those provisions of any awards and industrial agreements which are applicable to persons engaged in work essentially or usually performed by females but upon which male employees may also be employed'.[38] Women were, in other words, entitled to be paid the same as men when they were worked in 'male' jobs (there being very few mixed sex jobs).

In the words of one critic, the exclusion from the right to equal pay of women in 'female' jobs 'rendered the rest of the Act virtually irrelevant to the majority of women in the occupationally segregated workforce'.[39] Others condemned it as a 'blatantly sexist piece of legislation'.[40] The Act really only impacted on the wages of women teachers and lecturers.[41] And even in those sectors where the Act did apply, it did so only at the cost of new promotion criteria which favoured men over women (as in teaching) or only to those women who transferred into male occupational paths with the loss of their existing seniority (public sector clerical workers[42]).

The initial adoption of the equality principle at the federal level was as narrow as the legislation of New South Wales. In 1969, in its first equal pay case, the ACAC ruled that pay awards should lay down the same rates for adult men and women who were covered by the same award or determination, where the award covered men and women doing work which was the same or of a like nature *and* of equal value[43] (men, of course, were entitled to the same wages for the same work regardless of whether equal value was established). In assessing whether the work was the same or of a like nature and of equal value the issue whether the women did the same range and volume of work as the men could be taken into account, as could whether the working conditions were the

---

[37] Female Rates (Amendment) Act (NSW 1958), s. 88D(2).

[38] *Ibid.*, s. 88D(9)(b).   [39] Stackpool-Moore, n. 27 above, 277.

[40] E. Ryan and A. Conlon, *Gentle Invaders: Australian Women at Work 1788–1974* (Melbourne: Thomas Nelson (Australia) Ltd, 1975), 147.

[41] *Ibid.*

[42] *Ibid.* 277–8. The legislation in NSW was followed by similar enactments in Queensland 6 years later, Tasmania in 1966 (though this applied only to government employees), Western Australia in 1968. All states had some provision by 1969 at least within state public services though, in the case of Victoria, it applied only to teachers.

[43] C. Short, 'Equal Pay—What Happened?' (1986) 28(3) *Journal of Industrial Relations* 315, 318, remarks that 'the effect of the 1969 decision was to restore the principles set up by Higgins in 1912 and to allow equal pay for work where women did the same work as men and were likely to replace them'. In fact, and despite the move from basic to total wage, Short, 318, reports that the equalization was meant to apply only to the basic part of the wage and, 320, that unions were only advised, not required, to follow it. Bob Hawke, later Prime Minister of Australia, was counsel for ACTU in this case and argued for equal pay on the basis of justice rather than to protect men's wages.

same for the men and the women, together with any other relevant matters. In particular, where the award covered more than one establishment, consideration should not be restricted to the establishment in respect of which the claim was made, but should extend to the 'general situation' prevailing under the award or determination. 'Equal value' should not be taken here to mean 'of equal value to the employer' but, instead, 'of equal value, at least from the point of view of wage or salary assessment'. Finally, equal pay should not be awarded where, as in the New South Wales provision, the work in question 'is essentially or usually performed by females but is work for which male employees may also be employed'.[44] These women should already have been in receipt of equal pay according to the (male) protectionist policy established by the CCA as early as 1919 (see the text to note 28 above).[45] But, as a publication issued by the Women's Bureau of Australia's Department of Education, Employment, and Training pointed out in 1987, in practice, three different regimes co-existed between 1912 and 1967 (when the 'total wage' approach was adopted by the ACAC). Sometimes women who worked in 'men's' jobs were awarded the same basic wage and the same skills margins as men received, sometimes they received between 54 per cent and 75 per cent of men's basic wage but 100 per cent of the skill margins, and sometimes they received between 54 per cent and 75 per cent both of the basic wage and the skill margins.[46]

The restrictions in this articulation of 'equal pay for equal work' were such as to render it irrelevant to most women—in 1969, 82 per cent of women worked in 'female jobs' and were therefore excluded from the scope of the principle.[47] And one response on the part of employers to the 1969 case was further to segregate men and women workers. According to its critics:

[g]reat care was taken at all levels of clerical work to keep women from pencil work alone; they were expected to be able to use the typewriter. Most . . . spent up to a year doing a secretarial course to learn short hand and typing only to receive less money than the boys and men who took no such training.[48]

But despite tactics such as these, women's average 'award rates' increased from 72.1 per cent of men's weekly rates, 72.7 per cent of their hourly rates in 1969, to 77.4 and 78.2 per cent respectively in 1972 (the year that the equal pay principle was meant to have been fully phased into pay awards). And in 1972 the Commission ruled that awards should also pay equal rates to men and women for work of equal *value* (even when

[44] *Equal Pay Case* (1969) 127 CAR 1147, 1158.
[45] See comments regarding the federal case in the text to n. 46 below.
[46] K. MacDermott, *Pay Equity: A Survey of 7 O.E.C.D. Countries* (Canberra: Australian Government Publishing Service, 1987), Women's Bureau, Information Paper No 5, 6. See also Short, n. 43 above, 316–18.
[47] Thornton, n. 27 above, 25.   [48] Ryan and Conlon, n. 40 above, 147.

it was not the same or of a like nature).[49] Value was to be assessed in terms of the relativities already established in awards rather than by any new assessment of the job's worth to the employer, and the principle was to be fully incorporated by 1975. Finally, in 1974 the minimum wage (which had been imposed by the federal tribunal in 1966) was extended, at the male rate, to women workers.[50] Before this time men, but not women, whose award rates were lower than the minimum had their wages raised to the minimum with the effect that *actual* wages differed as between men and women.

(c) AUSTRALIAN WOMEN'S PAY

We have already seen that Australian women closed the gap between their award rates and those of men by about five percentage points between 1969 and 1972. In the wake of the 1972 decision the female job rates within awards increased by between 25 and 30 per cent, relative to those of male jobs and, by 1977, had reached 93 per cent.[51] But rates set out in awards were not necessarily the rates that employees were actually paid—actual rates might include overtime payments, performance-related pay, and 'over-awards' (additional payments bargained for at the enterprise level), and actual pay statistics would also take into account the 10 per cent or so of employees (mainly managerial staff) who were not covered by awards. In terms of actual pay, women's relative position lagged behind their position in terms of award rates by about 4 per cent in 1973 and, from 1975 onwards, consistently by about 10 per cent.[52] But even in terms of their actual wages, Australian women saw their position improve, relative to that of men, from 68 per cent (hourly) in 1970 to 81 per cent in 1976, and by 1985 full-time women workers earned 80 per cent and

---

[49] *National Wage and Equal Pay Cases 1972*, (1972) 147 CAR 172, 179 'female rates [shall] be determined by work value comparisons without regard to the sex of the employees concerned'.

[50] According to Short (n. 43 above, 319), the tribunal had refused to do this in 1972 'because the male minimum rate takes account of family considerations' ((1972) 149 CAR 179)—in 1966 the tribunal had replaced the basic with the minimum rate so they could increase this without improving wages at the top of the ladder. Ryan and Conlon (n. 40 above, 169–70) report that the ACTU had rather reluctantly applied for the extension of the minimum in 1974 after the federal government, under pressure from the ILO, had legislated so as to allow (but not require) the minimum wage to be extended to women.

[51] R. Gregory and V. Ho, *Equal Pay and Comparable Worth* (Canberra: Australian National University, 1985), Centre for Economic Policy Research, Discussion Paper no 123, 7. From 0.72 in 1969 and 0.77 in 1972—see M. Gunderson, 'Male–Female Wage Differentials and Policy Responses (1989) 27 *Journal of Economic Literature* 46, 67.

[52] Short, n. 43 above, 321—in 1973 the award and actual hourly rates (including overtime) were 80.3% & 76.5%; in 1974, 86.2% & 77.7%; in 1975, 91.9% & 82.3%; 1976, 93.4% & 84.3%; 1977, 94.1% & 84.9%; 1978, 93.9% & 84%; 1979, 93% & 82.2%; 1980, 92.7% & 85.2%; 1981, 93.7% & 84.4%; 1982, 93% & 82.9%; 1983, 93.2% & 83.5%; 1984, 94% & 85.8%.

full- and part-time women together two-thirds of Australian men's *weekly* rate.[53] Full-time women's weekly earnings peaked at 84.5 per cent of men's in 1991 before declining slightly thereafter. By contrast, British full-time women workers earned 56 per cent of men's weekly rate in 1970, 64 per cent in 1976, and 71 per cent in 1991.

Australia does not only compare favourably with Britain. UN statistics put Australian women top of the wage ladder (relative, of course, to men in the same countries) with women in Tanzania and Vietnam, ahead not only of the United States and the United Kingdom, but also in front of countries, such as Sweden, which tend to be viewed as particularly successful in having minimized pay discrimination.[54] Comparisons are difficult, because countries calculate relative earnings on different bases (hourly/ weekly/monthly or even annually) and the league tables do not always compare like with like. But it is clear that women in Australia do better, relative to men, than do women almost anywhere else in the world.

(D)   EXPLAINING AUSTRALIA'S GENDER–PAY GAP

Shortcomings of the 'Equality' Approach

The strides which Australian women have made towards equal pay are remarkable for two reasons. First of all, until 1993 Australia lacked any legislation directed at the 'equal pay' issue save in the narrowest terms— while the Industrial Relations Act 1988 required the IRC to take account of the principle of non-discrimination in making awards, awards were exempted almost completely from the scope of the (federal) Sex Discrimination Act 1984 and so could not be challenged by the individuals covered by them[55] (the position varied between states). Claims could be made in relation to over-award payments, and by those who were not covered by awards. But by 1987 not one 'equal pay' claim had ever been made under either state or federal anti-discrimination legislation[56] (as distinct from

---

[53] ILO, (1985)(2) *Women at Work* 10–11.

[54] The world average is 75%—*USA Today*, 24 Aug. 1995 (source: UN Development Programme, *UN Human Development Report* (Oxford: OUP, 1995)). In 1992, ILO figures put women in Iceland at the top of the league with 91% (down from 94% in 1984)—*Courier Journal*, 21 Sept. 1992.

[55] See M. Thornton, *The Liberal Promise: Anti-discrimination Legislation in Australia* (Melbourne: OUP Australia, 1990), 134; T. MacDermott ('Equality of Opportunity in a Decentralised Industrial Relations System' in R. McCallum, G. McCarry, and P. Ronfeldt, *Employment Security* (Sydney: The Federation Press, 1994), 94) claims that 'discrimination issues have been traditionally regarded as secondary to industrial issues, largely through the maintenance of statutory exemptions of awards and agreements from the application of anti-discrimination legislation'.

[56] MacDermott n. 46 above, 38. Nor, despite the power of the Human Rights and Equal Opportunities Commission to intervene in National Wage Cases, had this ever occurred (25). The Industrial Relations Act 1988 required the IRC to take the Sex and Race Discrimination Acts into account—see generally C. Ronalds, *Affirmative Action and Sex Discrimination* (2nd

the award system). Further, while 'equal pay' was imposed by the federal tribunal in 1972 and 1975, more women were covered by state than by federal awards (in 1974 the figures were 62 per cent and 30.2 per cent respectively, whereas 40.6 per cent of men were covered by state and 43.7 per cent by federal awards[57]). As late as 1983, the New South Wales tribunal was still awarding women different rates and Western Australia did not equalize its minimum rates until 1981.[58]

Secondly, and despite the fact that Australia's workforce is just as segregated by sex as Britain's (in 1988 the OECD's *Economic Outlook* rated Australia as having the most sex-segregated workforce of all[59]), the wage gains that have been made by Australian women have not resulted from any real attempt to assess the relative 'value' of male and female jobs.

Not until 1993 did Australia embrace the concept of 'equal pay for work of equal *value*' as we understand it in the United Kingdom. The 1972 case allowed, and indeed encouraged, the comparison of male and female jobs and even envisaged the possibility that these comparisons could be made *between*, as distinct from merely *within*, awards.[60] As a result, it promised to go some way towards alleviating the wage effects of occupational segregation. But a 1987 survey for the Women's Bureau of Australia's Department of Employment, Education, and Training reported that '[t]he suggestion that comparisons of work value might be made between female and male classifications was never followed'.[61]

The ACAC was as firm in 1972 as it had been in 1969 that 'the value of the work refers to worth in terms of award wage or salary fixation, not value to the employer'. On the one hand, this meant that jobs should be valued in terms of factors such as skill, effort, responsibility, and working conditions (the standard 'pay equity'/'equal value'/'comparable worth' approach), rather than marginal productivity to the employer. But no real effort was ever made to analyse the relative 'value' of jobs, save in terms

edn., Leichhardt, New South Wales: Pluto Press Australia Ltd, 1991), 180—commenting upon the exclusion from the jurisdiction of the Sex Discrimination Act of any 'court or tribunal having power to fix minimum wages or other terms and conditions of employment': 'its exclusion is an overt recognition that the industrial jurisdiction should be able to operate without regard to the principles embodied in the Sex Discrimination Act'. This exclusion did not, however, cover over-awards.

[57] Short, n. 43 above, 325.   [58] *Ibid.*

[59] See also F. Vella, 'Gender Roles, Occupational Choice and Gender Wage Differential' (1993) 69 *Economic Record* 382. For example, while 60% of working females are in either clerical or sales related occupations the corresponding figure for males is 22%. Similarly, while 35% of males are in trade related occupations, only 5% of females are located in this sector. F. Rafferty, 'Equal Pay: The Evolutionary Process 1984–1994' (1994) 36(4) *Journal of Industrial Relations* 451 at 453 states that the 1969 equal pay decision 'exacerbated the already severe gender segregation of the Australian workforce'.

[60] See Thornton, n. 27 above, 27.

[61] MacDermott n. 56 above, 27. Indeed, according to Short, n. 43 above, 323, only one case ever openly proceeded upon an attempt scientifically to assess the value of one job relative to others—*The Journalists' Case* (1967) 120 CAR 169—this was not an equal pay case.

of their traditional places within a hierarchy which had been constructed with an explicit purpose of paying men more than women.

Trade unions could certainly challenge the relative pay of women (and men) in particular jobs—according to one earlier commentator: 'the hunting down of [wage] anomalies [between job classifications] . . . remains a popular sport'.[62] But unions were not unanimous in their support for the concept of equal pay—Margaret Thornton, a leading Australian discrimination theorist, stated in 1990 that '[t]he Australian union movement has traditionally been a bastion of white, Anglo-Celtic, male heterosexist values which has been insensitive, until relatively recently, to the working conditions of women, immigrants, Aborigines, gays and those with physical or intellectual impairments'.[63] Some unions 'even went on strike to prevent equal award wages being introduced in their industry or occupation' and by 1981 only fifty-three wage cases had been brought specifically on the issue of equal pay (thirty-five were successful).[64] In only two of these cases did the federal tribunal carry out any inspection of the jobs, and in only one did any reassessment of the relative value of jobs take place—this despite the ACAC's recognition, in the 1972 *Equal Pay/ National Wage Case* that '[t]he gap between the level of male and female rates in awards generally is greater than the gap, if any, in the comparative value of work performed by the two sexes *because* rates for female classifications in the same award have generally been fixed without a comparative evaluation of the work performed by males and females' (my emphasis).[65]

One commentator observed that the 'equal value' cases which were brought before the tribunal turned in essence upon whether 'female' jobs could be slotted into previously 'male' classifications in order to be granted equal rates of pay: '[b]efore 1972 male and female work was compared

---

[62] J. Hutson, *Six Wage Concepts* (Sydney: AEU, 1972), 14 cited by Plowman and Niland, n. 16 above. 131–2.

[63] N. 16 above, 135.

[64] M. Power *et al.*, 'Women, Work and Labour Market Programs', prepared for the Committee of Enquiry into Labour Market Programs, Department of Economics (NSW: University of Sydney, 1985), 59 cited by Killingsworth, n. 13 above, 234. See also Deery and Plowman, n. 14 above, 311: '[i]n some instances, because of union and management opposition to females doing some work, they are denied access to the better paid classifications within awards' and K. MacDermott, 'Women's Productivity: Productivity Bargaining and Service Workers' (1993) 35(4) *Journal of Industrial Relations* 538 at 549: 'the trade union movement has been built around trades, not services, and trades have been built around male workers'. See also Thornton, n. 17 above, and Short, n. 43 above, 324.

[65] According to Short, n. 43 above, they were more akin to attempting to fit female jobs within male classifications—the 53 figure includes only those cases listed as 'female rates' or 'equal pay' so the number of cases where these issues were touched upon may have been greater: (1972) 147 CAR 172 at 179. T. MacDermott, n. 55 above, 95 characterises the ACAC's 'failure to establish effective mechanisms . . . to provide a systematic gender neutral method of comparing female occupations with male occupations' as the 'major shortcoming' of the 'equal pay' process in Australia.

to see if it was exactly the same or very nearly; after 1972 work was compared to see if it was similar'.[66] According to another:

the improvements that occurred were based on conventional 'rule of thumb' views about the value of different sorts of work rather than on any systematic or analytical method of comparing male occupations with female occupations . . . women's jobs were slotted into existing classifications without any real attempt to assess their value. Typing, for example, was simply placed at the bottom of the clerical range since it was assumed to be inferior to other, male-defined clerical tasks.[67]

The failure of the ACAC thoroughly to compare male and female jobs for the purpose of establishing 'equal pay for work of equal value' could not, as Christine Short pointed out in 1986, really be considered surprising. Prior to the 1972 decision the only case in which the ACAC had systematically attempted to compare the value of truly different jobs was the *Metal Trades Work Value Inquiry* of 1966–7, and then it had come across substantial resistance both from employers and trade unions.[68] Interestingly, it was this very inquiry which led to the ACAC's discovery that women were doing 'work that was in every way the equal of that done by males' and was, in some cases, even more valuable.[69]

For all the shortcomings of the ACAC's approach to 'equal pay for work of equal value', even it was sufficient substantially to improve women's relative rates of pay. But the issue of 'comparable worth' rumbled on and demands for such an approach grew as Australia slipped into recession and women's relative wage gains ceased in the early 1980s. A number of interest groups intervened in the 1983 *National Wage Case* in an attempt to persuade the ACAC to require that predominantly female jobs be reevaluated in order to give full effect to the 1972 decision, but this was to no avail. Three years later the Australian Council of Trade Unions brought a test case (the *Nurses Test Case*) in which it requested that the ACAC reaffirm the 1972 decision and declare that it was still available for implementation; that it allow the processing of 'equal pay' claims through the normal (National Wage) mechanisms; and that it endorse the 'comparable worth' concept as integral to that 1972 decision.

The ACAC agreed that the 1972 decision was still to be regarded as correct, but rejected the ACTU's other arguments. It declared that comparisons should not be allowed between different types of jobs for the purposes of establishing an equal value claim and rejected the notion of 'comparable worth', with its associated requirements for job evaluation methodologies and the threat to established relativities:

---

[66] Short, n. 43 above, 325.
[67] Thornton, n. 27 above, 27 and 33. Short, n. 43 above, 325 points out that typing is distinguished from clerical work on the basis that 'typists require a special skill (typing) in addition to the ability to carry out clerical work'.
[68] Short, n. 43 above, 322–5.   [69] Ryan and Conlon, n. 40 above, 155–7.

[c]omparable worth is capable of being applied to any classification regarded as having been improperly valued, without limitation on the kind of classification to which it is applied, with no requirement that the work performed is related or similar. It is capable of being applied to work which is essentially or usually performed by males as well as to work which is essentially or usually performed by females. Such an approach would strike at the heart of long accepted methods of wage fixation in this country and would be particularly destructive of the present Wage Fixing Principles [of which more in the text to notes 74–6 below].[70]

In particular, the ACAC was exercised by the understanding that 'comparable worth' would have to be determined in terms of the value of work to the employer—a practice which would be out of line entirely with the approach taken in Australia. This concern was perhaps misguided inasmuch as, although 'comparable worth' in the United States is so determined, 'equal value', under the Equal Pay Act 1970 as amended, has to be determined 'in terms of the demands made on' the workers—there was no reason why the latter approach could not have been adopted in Australia.[71]

The ACAC did accept that equal pay claims could be made. But they had to be made in line with the 1972 decision (whatever that meant— the later decision seemed to deny the potential of the former for allowing cross-award comparisons between men's and women's jobs), rather than with the notion of 'comparable worth'. There was a suggestion also, and this was embraced in later decisions, that equal pay claims could be made only where the 1972 decision had not been implemented at all[72] (rather than where it had, allegedly, been inadequately implemented within an award). And, in any case where it was alleged that the 1972 'equal pay' principle had not been applied, the claim would have to be decided under the 'anomalies' procedure rather than in the ordinary way.

This last qualification was an extremely effective way of restricting the ambit of 'equal pay'. It had been recognized for many years that the content of various jobs would change over time as would, in consequence, their appropriate wage relative to that in other jobs. 'Work value' cases were designed to challenge the position of particular jobs within the hierarchy, although at times any increases awarded in respect of such changes ended up being reflected throughout the generality of awards.[73] Concern

---

[70] *Re Private Hospitals Nurses & Doctors Australian Capital Territories Award*, ACAC Print 92250 (1986), 9.

[71] Equal Pay Act, s. 1(2)(c).

[72] 1986 case at 113 '[w]e . . . confirm that claims for the application of the 1972 Principle in awards in which it has not been applied may still be made and determined in accordance with that decision'. This was taken to mean that claims could only be made where the 1972 principles had not been implemented at all (rather than inadequately implemented) by the ACAC in the *Australian Capital Territories Nurses* Case in April 1986 (discussed by Short, n. 43 above, 330–1).

[73] See Deery and Plowman, n. 14 above, 303—between 1978 and 1980 'work value rounds' had actually taken place: 'a supposedly restrictive and selective principle was transformed into a mechanism for a generalised wage increase'.

about this tendency to 'flow on' led to the establishment, in the 1976 and 1977 National Wage Cases, of an 'anomalies and inequities' procedure under which, in very tightly defined circumstances, changes could be made to jobs' positions in the wage hierarchy. This procedure had been embraced again in the 1983 National Wage Case in which a wage freeze previously applied had been removed—the 1983 National Wage Principles were designed to restrict wage inflation by regulating, *inter alia*, the circumstances under which jobs could receive increases in remuneration over and above the indexed rate of inflation.[74]

According to the 1983 case, wages could be adjusted under the 'anomalies' principle only in the most exceptional circumstances: the 'overriding concept [is that] . . . any claim under this Principle will not be a vehicle for general improvement in pay and conditions and that the circumstances warranting the improvement are of a special and isolated nature . . . doctrines of comparative wage justice and maintenance of relativities should not be relied upon'.[75] It need scarcely be pointed out that only rarely would equal pay cases come within this definition, designed as it was to enable the adjustment of wages in cases such as where, for example, a supervisor whose wages were determined in accordance with a federal award was being paid less than a supervisee whose wages were determined at the state level. In ordinary equal pay claims, by contrast, the complaint is more usually that wage relativities are out of line with the value of work. Equally, there would be every possibility in such cases that any wage improvement granted would 'flow on', at least to the other 'female' jobs in the award.[76]

According to one commentator, the insistence upon the use of the anomalies procedure in this respect 'reflected the ongoing tensions between the economic cost of implementing equal pay and community acceptance of the concept identified by the commission in its 1972 decision'.[77] Not only were the terms under which equal pay adjustments could be made defined in an extremely restrictive manner, but most of the potential for publicizing equal pay cases was lost at a stroke. Where it was alleged that a particular wage rate was out of line with that available in comparable jobs, a closed hearing (an anomalies conference) would first establish whether an arguable case had been made out and then, if it had, appoint an inspector to determine whether such an anomaly or inequity existed. Only if the parties failed to resolve matters between themselves after a report favourable to the applicant would the matter go to a full (open)

---

[74] See generally R. McCallum and M. Pittard, *Australian Labour Law: Cases and Materials* (3rd edn., Sydney: Butterworths, 1995), Ch. 12 and text after n. 98 below for the discussion of the Accord.

[75] Deery and Plowman, n. 14 above, 312 reproduce the 1983 principles.

[76] It was also supposed to be a one-off—Rafferty, n. 59 above, 455 points out the difficulties with applying this in the equal pay arena.

[77] *Ibid.* 454.

hearing of the ACAC: '[t]he secretiveness of the process attaching to the principle made it difficult to identify and follow precedent cases as it had the effect of removing all but the most disputaceous of anomalies cases from the public arena'.[78]

The secretiveness of the anomalies procedure means that few equal pay claims made after 1986 are in the public domain. However, the *Australian Capital Territories Nurses Case*, decided in April 1986, illustrates how narrow the approach of the ACAC to these cases was: in granting the nurses their claim for increased wages Madden J stressed the existence of 'compelling circumstances of a special and isolated nature' and the lack of potential for flow-on.[79] And in another nurses' case determined by the Victorian state tribunal two months later, the increase granted under the anomalies procedure was not applied to junior nurses—according to one commentator, these nurses were widely used by non-nursing hospital staff as comparators for wage purposes.[80]

In 1988 the structural efficiency principle (discussed below in the text beginning at note 89) was adopted by the ACAC and in 1991 the anomalies procedure done away with. The principle assisted some women in their struggle for improved pay, requiring as it did that minimum rates within awards were organized on the basis of examinations of the 'work value' of the various jobs therein and that awards were restructured, often by broad-banding jobs and doing away with many of the rigid narrow job classifications which had developed.[81] In addition, complex multiple pay structures within workplaces, industries, or broad occupational groups were replaced with single common pay structures.

On the one hand these changes made pay structures within awards much more transparent than had previously been the case. But some revised awards merely reproduced old pay inequalities within the new structures —the Australian Public Service Agreement, for example, amalgamated all professional occupations within a single salary structure in which 82 per cent of women counsellors, but only between 34 and 44 per cent of (predominantly male) scientists and engineers were in the bottom two of the five grades.[82] At least in such cases the old inequalities were made more apparent than might previously have been the case. But whether, in any particular instance, such inequalities were capable of challenge was, of course, another matter. One critic pointed out that, while the:

process of minimum rates adjustments has allowed for some inter-occupational comparisons of traditional women's jobs with men's jobs . . . the process . . . uses

---

[78] Rafferty, n. 59 above, 454–5.   [79] Short, n. 43 above, 330.   [80] *Ibid.* 331.
[81] See Rafferty, n. 59 above, 456—dental therapists made as much as 84% from the combination of this and the anomalies procedure which had given them 27%. Rafferty, 458, points out however that, while this was potentially helpful, work value comparisons were not necessarily rigorous.
[82] See Rafferty's discussion (*ibid.*) of the *Family Court Counsellors' Case.*

the metal/building industry tradesperson rate as the basis for comparison of relative skill, responsibilities and working conditions. The use of a male benchmark assumes that the value assigned to the benchmark is a consequence of value-neutral market forces rather than entrenched social values.[83]

Certainly in jurisdictions in which job evaluation provides the basis of 'equal pay' legislation, it is well recognized that the use of male benchmarks for the assessment of relative value itself results in many of the skills, etc. involved in typically female jobs being overlooked and hence in those jobs being undervalued.[84] But in any event, the 'potential of the structural efficiency principles for processing claims for equal pay—[was] truncated by the advent of enterprise bargaining' in 1991.[85] 'Enterprise bargaining' is discussed in the text to notes 90–103 below.

Collective Bargaining and the Gender–Pay Gap

It should be clear from the foregoing that the major strides towards equal pay which have taken place in Australia have been achieved in the absence of any enforceable right to 'equal pay', much less any requirement that male and female jobs be compared in terms of skill, effort, responsibility, etc. and paid equally on the basis of these features. This is not to say that discrimination did not hold down the level of women's wages in Australia —despite early claims that the 1972 case had eliminated pay discrimination, the more general consensus was that a fair amount remained.[86] The estimated extent of this amount varies between 4 per cent and 13 per cent where 100 per cent was men's average wage.[87] But whatever the true figure, the impact of discrimination upon Australian women's pay was very substantially reduced by the centralized adoption and implementation of the notion, however impoverished, of equal pay—first for the same work and then, albeit under a very narrow definition, for work of equal value. And the improvements which took place over the 1980s are particularly impressive in view of the fact that, during that decade, large pay rises for

[83] MacDermott n. 55 above, 95–6.   [84] See Ch. 7.

[85] Rafferty, n. 59 above, 461.

[86] Contrast R. Gregory and R. Duncan, 'The Relevance of Segmented Labor Market Theories: The Australian Experience of Equal Pay for Women' (1981) 3 *Journal of Post Keynesian Economics* 403 with Thornton, n. 55 above, 134; Short, n. 43 above, 320–1; and K. Mumford, *Women Working: Economics and Reality* (Sydney: Allen & Unwin, 1989), Ch. 4, generally and, in particular, her discussions of B. Chapman 'Sex Differences in Earnings: Changes over the 1980s in the Australian Public Service', B. Chapman, J. Issac, and R. Niland (eds.) *Australian Labour Economics: Readings* (3rd edn., Sydney: MacMillan, 1984) and B. Chapman and C. Mulvey, 'An Analysis of the Origins of Sex Differences in Australian Wages' (1976) 18 *Journal of Industrial Relations* 504. See also Vella, n. 59 above, and S. Rummery, 'The Contribution of Intermittent Labour Force Participation to the Gender Wage Differential' (1992) 68 *Economic Record* 351 for a survey of recent work on the issue.

[87] R. Drago, 'The Extent of Wage Discrimination in Australia' (1989) 15(4) *Australian Bulletin of Labour* 313; Chapman and Mulvey, n. 86 above. See also MacDermott n. 64 above, 545 on differential returns to schooling and further education between Australian women and men.

those highly paid (managerial) employees not covered by awards substantially increased the overall level of earnings inequality in Australia. In the absence of a strong countervailing force this would have had the effect of reducing women's relative wages.[88]

It appears that the strength of centralized pay determination, coupled with equal minimum wages for men and women, has been more effective than any attempt to compare male and female jobs and to determine their pay accordingly. The strides which have taken place in Australia appear threatened by the move away from centralized pay determination, but the Australian experience points to the potential associated with this mechanism of regulation. If such centralized pay determination were to be coupled with an attempt to rationalize the pay differentials between male and female jobs (in terms of the work 'value', however determined, rather than in terms of *traditional* 'value' hierarchies) the potential would be enormous indeed.

(E) THE THREAT TO AUSTRALIAN WOMEN'S PAY

Legislative Change

Just as the promise of centralized wage determination can be seen in the increase in Australian women's relative wages between 1969 and 1991, so the dangers of deregulation are illustrated by what has happened in Australia more recently. In 1991 the IRC introduced the principle of enterprise bargaining in its *National Wage Case*. The door to this had been opened in the 1987 *National Wage Case* in which the ACAC introduced a two-tier wage system which, while allocating a flat-rate increase across the board, made the remainder of the increase (up to 4 per cent) dependent on collective bargaining which was to take place around a 'restructuring and efficiency' principle—in order to qualify for this part of the increase, employers and trade unions had to show that any increase was matched by the elimination of formal and informal restrictive practices. This approach was taken further in the 1988 *National Wage Case* in which the whole of the permissible wage increase was made dependent upon the principle, mentioned earlier, of 'structural efficiency'. The principle was intended to encourage skill formation and flexible work organization with a view to creating macro-economic growth and required unions to agree to a complete overhaul of existing awards (in terms of job classifications, wage relativities, etc.) in order to gain access to any wage increases for employees.[89]

---

[88] P. Gregg and S. Machin, *Is the U.K. Rise in Inequality Different?* (National Institute of Economic and Social Research, 1993), Discussion Paper No 45, 28–9.

[89] *National Wage Case 1988* [1988] AILR 327. See generally Mitchell and Naughton, n. 23 above. Also the Industrial Relations Act 1988 allowed certification of agreements reached outside the compulsory arbitration arena—see Mitchell and Naughton, op. cit.

We saw, in the text to notes 81–2 above, that the structural efficiency principle did, at least in theory, have the potential to improve women's position. But the National Wage Cases of 1987 and 1988 established the movement towards decentralization of the wage-setting process. According to the Minister for Industrial Relations in 1988: '[n]egotiations at the industry and award levels need to be complemented by discussions at the enterprise level: it is, ultimately, at the enterprise level that restructuring agreements will be implemented and the benefits derived'.[90] The 1988 decision was followed by the 1991 *National Wage Case* which was in turn followed in 1992 and again in 1993 by legislation designed to encourage enterprise-level agreements. Whereas, under the 1988 Industrial Relations Act, agreements reached at workplace level could only be certified (rendering them binding on the parties thereto[91]) if they complied with a number of requirements including a stipulation that they be in the public interest, in 1992 the power to refuse certification on public interest grounds was removed from the IRC which was placed under an obligation to certify any agreement which was not disadvantageous to the employees covered by it.[92] It was not until 1993 that the legislation stipulated that employees must be made aware of the content of agreements intended to be binding upon them.[93] Since that time, the election of a right-wing Liberal government, the scrapping of the Accord between the Government and the ACTU (see below after note 98), and further attacks on the powers of the IRC have shifted the focus of wage-setting even more to the level of the workplace.

The 1991 decision and the 1992 amendments to the Industrial Relations Act 1988 (IRA) had the effect of increasing radically the relative importance of workplace, as opposed to federal or state level bargaining. This process was continued by further amendments to the IRA made by the Industrial Relations Reform Act 1993, described by the then President

---

[90] P. Morris, 'Award Restructuring: the Task Ahead', Statement by the Minister for Industrial Relations (Canberra: Australian Government Publishing Service, 1989), 6.

[91] And potentially preventing subsequent access to the ACAC (e.g., on an equal pay claim) by employees covered by them—for discussion of this issue see Rafferty, n. 59 above, 463. The 1992 amendments allowed certified enterprise agreements even in cases where the employees bound by them did not know of their terms.

[92] Because of perceived hostility to enterprise bargaining—see Rafferty, n. 59 above, 461. See Mitchell and Naughton, n. 23 above, and M. Short and J. Buchanan, 'Wages Policy and Wage Determination in 1994' (1995) 37(1) *Journal of Industrial Relations* 119. The public interest remained relevant only if the agreement covered more than a single business and in the negative sense that, even if an enterprise agreement laid down terms less favourable than those in the relevant award, there would be 'no disadvantage' to the employees unless the departure from the award was not in the public interest. See also L. Bennett, 'Women and Enterprise Bargaining; The Legislative and Institutional Framework' (1994) 36(2) *Journal of Industrial Relations* 191.

[93] See D. O'Connor (President of the IRC), 'Equality in the Workplace: The Implications of the Industrial Relations Reform Act 1993' (1995) 37(1) *Journal of Industrial Relations* 63 and T. MacDermott, n. 55 above, 100.

of the IRC as the 'most fundamental change' to the industrial relations system made since 1904.[94] These amendments extended enterprise bargaining beyond those workplaces where a trade union was recognized—employers could reach (binding) enterprise 'flexibility agreements' with employees who were unrepresented by a trade union (or even where they were represented, but the employer refused to reach agreement with the union[95]). And in 1994, the IRC ruled that the traditional award system would apply only to those employees in respect of whom no enterprise agreement had been reached. From that point on, the IRC ruled in the *Safety Net Adjustments and Review Case*, the award system would act to protect those 'who may be unable to reach enterprise agreements, while maintaining an incentive to bargain for such agreements'.[96] The incentive was to be provided by the fact that the IRC awards would be extremely modest and would lag some months or even years behind those agreed at the enterprise level.[97] Most recently, the President of ACTU remarked that, whereas enterprise agreements were running at between 2–4 per cent (for small unions) and 6 per cent (for the large and powerful) in 1996, the 'safety net' provided for wage increases of only between 1 and 2 per cent.[98]

The shift to workplace bargaining was motivated by a perceived need to modernize a rigid and inefficient industrial relations framework in the face of increasing pressure from the global market. The changes took place in the context of the continuing Accord which had been struck in 1983 between the then opposition Labour Party and the ACTU. Under the Accord the Labour Party (which was elected into government in the same year) and the ACTU would agree a package of wage outcomes and other conditions which would be presented to the ACAC in the form of the annual National Wage Case. The ACTU agreed to moderate its demands and, on behalf of its member unions, to refrain from making any additional wage demands ('over-award' claims) in return for government promises relating to price control, tax reform, national health insurance, and improvements to minimum wages.

Until 1987 the Accord followed the traditional centralized approach to wage determination (indeed, in so far as it did away with 'over-award' payments, increased this centralization) but, from 1987 onwards, the parties to it pushed increasingly towards decentralization.[99] By April 1991 the

---

[94] O'Connor, n. 93 above, 63.

[95] See generally Short and Buchanan, n. 92 above. The 1993 Act, which permitted 'enterprise flexibility agreements' to be reached with employees (by a simple majority) in the absence of or without the consent of the union, established a 'public interest' test for their certification.

[96] O' Connor, n. 93 above, 65.   [97] Short and Buchanan, n. 92 above, 131.

[98] *RWE Business News*, 7 Aug. 1996.

[99] This was the result (Mitchell and Naughton, n. 23 above) of the government's retreat from indexation which had been a powerful reason for unions to agree to the Accord.

push towards decentralization had reached the point where the parties to the Accord put to the IRC the principle of 'enterprise bargaining'[100] (suggesting a small flat-rate increase of $12 coupled with 4.5 per cent increase in respect of enterprise-level productivity increases). Such was the concern of the IRC about the possible implications of this suggestion (specifically, the Commission drew attention to the difficulties of measuring productivity increases, the inability of the economy to sustain a 4.5 per cent level of wage increase and the threat to women's relative wages) that it refused to endorse the ACTU–government agreement and instead required a 2.5 per cent increase in line with the 'structural efficiency' approach.[101] By October of the same year, however, the Commission capitulated and, in the *National Wage Case 1991*, embraced enterprise bargaining.

Even in 1991, concern was expressed about the impact that the shift from state or national to enterprise-level wage determination would have on women's relative pay. We have already seen the substantial difference between women's relative pay at the (centralized, regulated) level of the award and at the (decentralized, largely unregulated) level of *actual* wages (taking into account, *inter alia*, the effects of over-award payments and performance-related pay[102]). On the one hand, the move to enterprise bargaining did not, at least initially, remove the role of awards as minimum floors of rights—unions and employers had, in any case, been free before 1991 to negotiate at establishment level in order to improve terms and conditions above those specified in awards. But these 'over-awards', as they were known, were generally unavailable in the public sector, were tightly controlled after the 1983 Accord, and, in any event, had a tendency to 'flow on' in subsequent National Wage Cases (i.e. to increase the wage demands made by workers not covered by them which in turn resulted in higher tribunal awards and the loss of relative advantage to the original beneficiaries). In any event, while 'over-awards' had been made in 52 per cent of workplaces having at least twenty employees in 1989–90, they only accounted for between 1.5 per cent (women) and 2.3 per cent

---

[100] For more detailed discussion about the move towards enterprise bargaining see Plowman and Niland, n. 16 above.

[101] See J. Buchanan and R. Callus, 'Efficiency and Equity at Work: The Need for Labour Market Regulation in Australia' (1993) 35(4) *Journal of Industrial Relations* 515, 517 for discussion of the reaction of Paul Keating, then Minister for Labour, to the Apr. decision.

[102] In 1987, e.g. (Australian Bureau of Statistics, *Labour Statistics Australia* 1987 (Canberra: Commonwealth of Australia, 1990), table 6.5) men's salaries consisted 87.3% of award or agreed base—women's 95.7%. Much of the difference was overtime, but men earned an additional 2.4% but women only 1.5% from over-awards. Given the relatively small part played by over-awards, perhaps what is most significant is the difference—men got almost half as much again. (By 1993 these figures were, respectively, 87%, 95.8%, 1.8%, and 1.2%). See also M. Short, A. Preston, and D. Peetz, 'The Spread and Impact of Workplace Bargaining: Evidence from the Workplace Bargaining Research Project' (Canberra: Australian Government Publishing Service, 1993), 24 and K. MacDermott, n. 46 above, 549.

(men) of non-managerial adults' pay.[103] 'Enterprise bargaining', by contrast, was largely to take the place of state or federal wage determination.

Small wonder, then, that the move to workplace level bargaining was criticized by many 'equal pay' activists at the time on the ground that it would serve to increase the wage inequality which already existed between women and men.[104] It was in part these arguments which helped to persuade the IRC in April 1991 to reject enterprise bargaining which, it claimed: 'places at a relative disadvantage those sections of the labour force where women predominate'.[105] But, as we saw above, by October of the same year the government had intervened and the IRC had changed its approach. Instead of remaining the normal method of wage determination for 90 per cent of Australia's workers' tribunal awards were, from that point on, to provide only a floor for wages and other conditions (and later to do this only for employees lacking access to enterprise bargaining).

Peter Morris, Minister of Labour in 1989, had declared that the structural efficiency principle embraced by the ACAC would encourage a more equitable distribution of rewards: '[l]ow paid workers, particularly women, will benefit from more equitable pay levels with reduced labour market segmentation and access to career paths based on training and skills'.[106] To a certain extent this was true—'structural efficiency' did present a challenge to award structures which had, on occasion, disadvantaged women by enforcing sex segregation within very narrow occupational classifications.[107] But the pressure towards enterprise determination of pay presented serious threats to women's relative wages and, in 1991, the then Minister for Labour (Peter Cook) claimed, to a National Women's Consultative Council forum, that only the retention of the awards system as a floor for wages 'protects the interests of all workers, particularly those who are vulnerable because they have little or no bargaining power'.[108] But he did not attempt to argue that workplace bargaining would be

---

[103] 1989–90 AWIR reported by Buchanan and Callus, n. 101 above, 524. 32% of workplaces used profit related pay, 8% profit-sharing, and 13% share options. Australian Bureau of Statistics, *Labour Statistics Australia* 1990 (Canberra: Commonwealth of Australia, 1990), table 98. Men and women earned, respectively, a further 1.3% and 0.4% in performance related pay and a further 10.5% and 2.5% in overtime payments—in all, agreed or award basic rates accounted for 95.6% of womens' salaries in 1990, 86% of men's.

[104] These concerns were noted in 1992 by the report of the House of Representatives' Standing Committee on Legal and Constitutional Affairs, *Half Way to Equality* (Canberra: Australian Government Publishing Service, 1992), paras. 4.6.1.–9. See also Women's Electoral Lobby, *Impact of Enterprise Bargaining on Women: Statement of Concerns* (Sydney: Women's Electoral Lobby, 1992).

[105] (1991) 36 Ind. Rep. 120 at 173. See also Rafferty, n. 59 above, 463 and National Women's Consultative Council, *Women and Enterprise Bargaining: Who Benefits?* (Canberra: Australian Government Publishing Service, 1992), 1—the Australian Federation of Business and Professional Women intervened to argue against Enterprise Bargaining—according to the NWCC report, the AIRC expressed misgivings about the disadvantage to women.

[106] N. 90 above, 8.   [107] See comment regarding typing at text to n. 67 above.

[108] National Women's Consultative Council, n. 105 above, 5.

positively good for women. Certainly, the experience of decentralization of wage-setting in New Zealand was that the gender–wage gap widened— a fact recognized, according to the Federal Sex Discrimination Commissioner in 1993, by the federal government.[109]

Enterprise Bargaining and Women's Wages

In the short time which has elapsed since the introduction of enterprise bargaining, the critics appear to have been proven right—between 1991 and 1993 women's wages fell slightly, relative to those of men. If 'ordinary time' earnings alone are considered, full-time adult women's weekly wages fell from 84.1 per cent of men's in 1991 to 83.7 per cent in 1993. If total hours worked are taken into account the decline was from 80.6 per cent to 79.5 per cent—this despite the ratio of hours worked by full-time women to those worked by full-time men remaining stable at 0.90.[110] The figures appear more alarming in view of the fact that male wage growth was twice that of women's in the year to August 1993; that, to June 1994, the gender–wage gap was continuing to increase;[111] and that, in the year to February 1995, men's wages rose by an average of 5 per cent, women's by only 3.7 per cent.

Perhaps even more significant, as far as predicting future trends is concerned, are the recent findings from the Workplace Bargaining Research Project.[112] The project, which was undertaken by Australia's Department of Industrial Relations, set out to determine the impact of the 1991 *National Wage Case* decision and the subsequent legislative changes. In 1993 it reported that 24 per cent of men, but only 15 per cent of women, were covered by agreements negotiated at the level of their workplaces in December 1992.[113] The far greater portion (eight of the nine percentage points) resulted not from women's exclusion from agreements reached within their workplaces, but from their over-concentration in workplaces where no such agreements existed: 'females' lower access to wage increases was explained not so much by their exclusion from such agreements where they were negotiated, but rather because they were less likely to work at a workplace where such an agreement was negotiated at all'.[114]

---

[109] S. Walpole (Sex Discrimination Commissioner, Human Rights and Equal Opportunity Commission), *The Sex Discrimination Act 1984: Future Directions and Strategies* (Canberra: Australian Government Publishing Service, 1993), 26.

[110] Australian Bureau of Statistics, *Labour Statistics Australia 1987 & 1993* (Canberra: Commonwealth of Australia, 1987 & 1993), tables 6.3 and 7.2—if all workers (part- and full-time, young and adult) are considered, women's earnings fell from 66.7% in 1991 to 66.0% in 1993 while overall average hours retained the female: male ratio of 0.72.

[111] R. Green, 'Wages Policy and Wage Determination in 1993' (1994) 36(1) *Journal of Industrial Relations* 108.

[112] See also NSW Department of Industrial Relations Education Training and Further Education, Women and Work Unit 1993 publication, *Women and Equality Bargaining*, discussed by MacDermott n. 55 above, 92.

[113] Short, Preston and Preetz, n. 102 above; Short, n. 43 above, 24–5.

[114] Short, n. 43 above, 25.

Having said this, those workplace agreements which did exclude some groups (in addition to management) usually excluded such female occupations as 'clerks and sales and personal service workers'.[115] Such groups were less likely to be regarded as central to the increased productivity on which wage increases tended to rely, with the effect that their representatives were not always included in workplace collective bargaining.

The authors of the survey considered whether the gap in coverage might result from extra difficulties in measuring increased 'productivity' in those workplaces where women are concentrated (the whole purpose of the move towards enterprise bargaining was to restrict wage increases, so far as possible, to those linked with productivity gains). On the contrary, however, they report that, whereas 'productivity grew in 72% of workplaces in which females constituted three quarters or more of the employees . . . it increased in only 65% of workplaces in which females constituted less than half the workforce'.[116] Nor was there any difference in the distribution of men and women between workplaces which did and did not measure productivity. They concluded that 'the employees in workplaces with high female employment were, on average, less likely to have the bargaining strength or support to obtain wage increases as workplace change occurred and productivity increased'.

Part-timers suffered particularly badly in the move towards enterprise level bargaining. Whereas a 9 per cent gap existed between the workplace level coverage of women and men, the gap stretched to 14 per cent in the case of full- and part-time workers. Not only were workplaces with a high proportion of part-timers less likely to be covered by negotiated agreements (this explained five of the fourteen percentage points), but part-timers were also likely to be excluded from such agreements as did cover the workplaces in which they were located[117] (this accounted for a further six). The Workplace Industrial Relations Bill 1996, which aims to increase the extent to which enterprise agreements are reached between employers and unrepresented employees, will probably increase the number of women and part-time workers covered by enterprise agreements but, given the poor bargaining position of unrepresented employees and the ever-decreasing influence of the awards system, the position of these workers is set to decline still further.

(F) ANTI-DISCRIMINATION LEGISLATION

In 1993, in recognition of the concern about the impact of enterprise bargaining upon women's relative wages, Australia's federal government implemented amendments to the Sex Discrimination Act which, *inter alia*,

---

[115] Short, n. 43 above, 30. More evidence of this is available from Fruin and Hall cited by Bennett, n. 92 above, 196.
[116] Short, n. 43 above, 27.   [117] *Ibid.* 28.

enabled complaints to be made about discrimination in new awards and enterprise agreements.[118] The effect of these amendments was to allow individuals, for the first time, to complain to the Industrial Relations Commission (via the Sex Discrimination Commissioner at the Human Rights and Equal Opportunities Commission) about perceived discrimination, whether direct or indirect, in the terms of awards or agreements. If the Commissioner is satisfied that discrimination exists she must refer the matter to the IRC which must, in turn, review the award. The Commissioner may be a party before the IRC which, if it takes the view that any term is discriminatory, must remove the discrimination.

According to the Commissioner, prohibited discrimination includes 'discrimination on the grounds of sex, marital status, or pregnancy, in employment and superannuation, for commission agents, and for contract workers. Discrimination can be either direct or indirect.'[119] However, where awards or agreements were already in existence prior to the implementation of the amendments, they cannot be challenged. Thus, the existence of 'a separate pay table . . . for the payment of women at a rate approved by the employer' in the railway industry; the restriction of women's employment 'in jobs exclusively performed by men' to cases where the union agrees in the meat industry; and the payment of 'different travel allowances for men and women' by airlines remain legal.

The Industrial Relations Reform Act 1993 also empowered the IRC to award 'equal pay for work of equal value' to those employees who do not have an adequate alternative means under either federal or state law to secure equal pay.[120] Such orders can be made only on the application of an employee, a trade union, or the federal Sex Discrimination Commissioner. In addition, the Commission has the residual power to arbitrate disputes and, as a result of this, could make an order for equal pay regardless of any other existing legislative coverage in the event of an equal pay dispute. In neither case, however, is any guidance afforded on how the relative value of jobs might be assessed. It is likely, therefore, that the IRC will exercise its powers in these respects predominantly in relation to men and women doing similar jobs.

It is perhaps too early as yet to draw any firm conclusions about Australia's change of direction, and the effect that this will have on women's relative wages.[121] But what is evident from the Australian experience is that, despite the many imperfections of the traditional approach to equal pay, women did better under a system which, as late as 1981 in Western

---

[118] Sex Discrimination and Other Acts Amendment Act 1992 (implementation 13 Jan. 1993)—see MacDermott, n. 55 above, 102 for discussion thereof.

[119] Short, n. 43 above, 34.

[120] See MacDermott, n. 55 above, and McCallum and Pittard, n. 74 above, 669.

[121] In Mar. 1995 a senior adviser to the Sex Discrimination Commissioner characterized progress on the equal pay issue as 'glacial'—Reuters World Service, 8 Mar. 1995.

Australia and until 1983 in New South Wales, retained differential minimum wages and basic rates respectively and which never in practice embraced a comparative approach to job value, than they have done in the United Kingdom under legislation which is, at the level of theory, much more rigorous in its approach to discrimination and much more committed to the concept of 'comparable worth'. The move to enterprise bargaining in Australia, in particular the restriction of the notion of 'equal pay' to equal pay *within*, as distinct from *between*, workplaces,[122] is a massive blow to the pursuit of the 'comparative wage justice' so formerly beloved of the Australian system and so intrinsically favourable to women's relative pay.[123]

III. CONCLUSION

Australian commentators are extremely bleak as regards the future of women's relative wages in Australia. The President of the IRC claimed, in 1995, that enterprise bargaining did not disadvantage women and that the new system actually improved matters by:

- allowing women to challenge discriminatory over-awards which had, in her view, previously been the major source of the wage differential;
- requiring the IRC to refuse to certify discriminatory agreements;
- requiring the tri-annual review of awards to identify and remedy deficiencies including discrimination;
- allowing individuals to complain to the Sex Discrimination Commissioner about discriminatory award provisions; and
- allowing the IRC to award equal pay for work of equal value to those employees not otherwise able to secure it.[124]

But it is perhaps instructive to note, not only that the gender–wage gap widened up to June 1994 but that, twenty-one months after the amendments allowing individual complaints to the Sex Discrimination Commissioner, '[t]o date, no activity has occurred in this area'.[125] By far the more common view is that enterprise bargaining will significantly damage the prospects of Australia's women.

One commentator rather chillingly remarks that '[t]he implications [of enterprise bargaining] are that different rates of pay may apply to persons performing identical work under the same award and in the same industry but with different employers. The resultant confusion could render even the narrow 1969 equal pay for equal work principle unworkable.'[126]

---

[122] Or at any rate employers—it depends on the ambit of the agreement itself.

[123] Change at the state level has, in some cases, been considerably more radical—see R. Reitano, 'Legislative Change in 1994' (1995) 37(1) *Journal of Industrial Relations* 84 and Bennett, n. 92 above.

[124] O'Connor, n. 93 above, 64.   [125] *Ibid.* 68.   [126] Green, n. 111 above, 466.

Another points out that, in those countries (such as Japan and the United States) in which bargaining traditionally takes place at the workplace level, this has 'encouraged particularistic bargaining . . . divided workers . . . encouraged a focus on . . . short-term, sectional gains rather than a broader concern with fairness and social justice . . . exacerbated the divide between powerful [male] unions . . . and weak [female] unions'.[127] She goes on to claim that:

where agreements have been secret (as in overaward payments) discrimination has flourished and been substantially unchecked. . . . The move to enterprise bargaining is generally accompanied by a push towards secrecy . . . the move to decentralised wage fixation is likely to swamp any compensating effects associated with the introduction of anti-discrimination provisions.[128]

Even such limited assistance as was provided by the anti-discrimination legislation is likely to be lost: the Liberal Government's Workplace Relations Bill 1996 proposes to remove the IRC's power to remove pay discrimination, as well as to restrict the Commission's power to oversee the content of workplace agreements.

Women's pay is set to worsen in Australia over the coming years. But the changes wrought by the ever-increasing drive towards individual pay determination do not detract from the Australian message concerning the potential of centralized pay determination for women's wages. However flawed was the detail of Australia's approach to pay regulation, the impact of its centralization on women's wages was profound and its utility proven as much by the decline in women's position since its dismantling as by the gains women enjoyed under it. The role of collective bargaining and of centralized systems of pay determination in improving women's wages will be considered further in Chapter 10.

[127] Bennett, n. 92 above, 194.   [128] *Ibid.*, 205–6.

[9]
Minimum Wage Regulation

I. INTRODUCTION

Centralized collective bargaining and specific equal pay legislation have already been considered. Now it is useful to turn to the possible role of minimum wage regulation in reducing the gender–pay gap. There is little doubt that the implementation of some form of minimum wage regulation can have a significant impact on that gap: when Portugal introduced a national minimum wage in the early 1970s, women's monthly wages soared from 50 per cent to 72 per cent of men's in a space of two years.[1] But it is equally clear that minimum wage regulation is not, of itself, a complete answer: the existence of a minimum wage in the United States has not prevented women there enjoying among the lowest levels of pay, relative to men, in the developed world.

In order to consider the potential impact on the gender–pay gap of a minimum wage regulation approach, this chapter will look at the position in a number of European countries which operate some form of minimum wage regulation, and will then examine the various minimum wage fixing mechanisms which have operated in the United Kingdom.

I have pointed out the degree of overlap which exists between minimum wage regulation and collective bargaining—the Australian system, dealt with in Chapter 8, could be viewed as an example of either approach as, to a certain extent, could those of Finland, Germany, and Austria in each of which countries, while there is no established minimum wage as such, collectively agreed standards are extended to the majority of workers. Extension is common also in Portugal, Belgium, and France where it operates alongside established minimum wages. Despite these overlaps, it is useful to consider minimum wage regulation as an option—whether alternative or additional—to the collective bargaining approach. Generally the extension of collectively bargained standards will take the form only of a minimum floor for wages as distinct from, as was the case under the traditional Australian model, establishing the comprehensive regulation of wages for distinct groups of workers. Minimum wage regulation also performs

---

[1] K. MacDermott, *Pay Equity: A Survey of 7 O.E.C.D. Countries*, (Canberra: Australian Government Publishing Service, 1987) 64 and 67.

different functions from the collective bargaining approach: first it is capable of reaching further (subject to satisfactory enforcement); secondly, it may be a separate measure where unions are too weak or the implementation of, for example, sectoral or national bargaining policy is politically or otherwise impossible.

Minimum wage regulation has a long history. The establishment of wages boards in the Australian state of Victoria in 1896 is generally taken as its first manifestation—the practice rapidly spread throughout Australia, and in 1899 New Zealand passed its first minimum wage.[2] Britain was next in line with the Trade Boards Act 1909[3] and the International Labour Organization (ILO), established in 1919, was interested in minimum wage regulation from its earliest days. The ILO Constitution declared the need to improve conditions of work by, among other things, 'the provision of an adequate living wage'.[4] The first inquiry into systems of minimum wage fixation was begun in the same year, and in 1928 Convention No 26 (Minimum Wage-Fixing Machinery) was adopted. Further Conventions followed in 1951 (Convention No 99, on Minimum Wage Fixing Machinery (Agriculture)) and in 1970 (Convention No 131, on Minimum Wage Fixing).[5]

Convention No 26 requires that ratifying states undertake:

to create or maintain machinery whereby minimum rates of wages can be fixed for workers employed in certain of the trades or parts of trades (and in particular in home working trades) in which no arrangements exist for the effective regulation of wages by collective agreement or otherwise and wages are exceptionally low [Article 1.1]

and to 'take the necessary measures by way of a system of supervision and sanctions, to ensure that the employers and workers concerned are informed of the minimum rates of wages in force and that wages are not paid at less than these rates in cases where they are applicable'. Convention No 99 requires the creation or maintenance of machinery 'for workers employed in agricultural undertakings and related occupations' and imposes the same obligations as Convention No 26 in respect of

---

[2] The minimum wage was not of general application—see G. Starr, *Minimum Wage Fixing: An International Review of Practices and Problems* (Geneva: ILO, 1981), Ch. 1.

[3] Again, this was of limited application, see the text to n. 20 below.

[4] ILO, *Convention and Rules* (Geneva: ILO, 1921), 17.

[5] In addition to these provisions directed expressly at the minimum wage issue, a number of other Conventions, together with several Recommendations and ILO Conference resolutions refer to minimum wages: Conventions 94, 95, and 117 (on Labour Clauses (Public Contracts), Protection of Wages, and Social Policy (Basic Aims and Standards) respectively); Recommendations 84, 85, and 90 (on Labour Clauses, Protection of Wages, and Equal Remuneration respectively)—see generally ILO, *Minimum Wages* (Geneva: ILO, 1992), ILO, 79th Session Report III (Part 4B) General Survey of the Reports on Conventions 26, 99, 131.

UNIVERSITY OF WINCHESTER
LIBRARY

enforcement of the minimum rates, and Convention No 131 requires the establishment of 'a system of minimum wages which covers all groups of wage earners whose terms of employment are such that coverage would be appropriate'.

Convention No 26 is one of the most widely embraced of all the ILO's Conventions. By 1994, 101 countries had ratified it, fifty-one countries had ratified Convention No 99, and thirty-eight countries Convention No 131.[6] The United Kingdom, which had been one of the first countries to ratify Convention No 26, denounced it in 1985 in order to facilitate the abolition of the Wages Council machinery (discussed in the text to notes 36–48 below). Although ratification, in particular of Convention No 26, is common, a number of the twelve Member States of the European Community (now the fifteen Member States of the European Union) had not ratified any of the Conventions in 1994 and only three (France, the Netherlands, and Spain) had ratified all three. Five of the fifteen (Austria, Belgium, Ireland, Italy, and Germany) had ratified Conventions Nos 26 and 99 and one (Portugal), Nos 26 and 131. Luxembourg had ratified only Convention No 26; the United Kingdom only Convention No 99; neither Denmark nor Greece, Finland nor Sweden had ratified any.

The failure of most EU Member States to ratify one or more of the ILO minimum wage Conventions should not be taken as indicative of any general lack of regard for minimum wage regulation. Of the fifteen current Member States, eight (Belgium, France, Greece, Ireland, Luxembourg, the Netherlands, Portugal, and Spain), embrace some form of minimum wage (whether by the application of collective bargaining, as in Belgium and Greece; administrative dictat, as in Spain and France; or a very limited Wages Council system as in Ireland) and ten (Austria, Belgium, Denmark, Finland, France, Germany, Italy, Sweden, the Netherlands, and Portugal) enjoy very high levels of collective bargaining which cover between 71 per cent (the Netherlands) and 100 per cent (Italy) of the workforce (in Luxembourg, about seven in ten workers are covered by extended collective agreements).[7] In those countries with very high degrees of collective bargaining coverage (whether the result of high levels of union membership or the extension of collective agreements[8]), collective agreements apply a *de facto* minimum wage for most, if not all, workers, even

[6] ILO, *International Labour Conference 1994 Report III (5)*, List of Ratifications by Convention and Country (as at 31 Dec. 1993) (Geneva: ILO, 1994)—the total of 101 ratifying countries includes the UK which had, by that stage, deratified.

[7] Statistics taken from OECD, *Economic Outlook* 1994 (Paris: OECD, 1994), and S. Bazen and G. Benhayoun, 'Low Pay and Wage Regulation in the European Community' (1992) 30 *British Journal of Industrial Relations* 623. On OECD figures coverage in Sweden and Portugal is in the region of 80%, Denmark 85%, France, Germany, and Belgium 90%, Finland and Austria 95%). Figures for Luxembourg are taken from A. Trine, *Employers' Liabilities Under Social Legislation* (Brussels: Chispeels), looseleaf.

[8] In Germany, Austria, Belgium, Greece, and Italy. See ILO, n. 5 above, para. 248.

in the absence of any specific additional minimum wage-fixing mechanism. Collective bargaining coverage, and its impact on the general level of wage dispersion and on the gender–pay gap in particular, is discussed in Chapter 8.

Countries such as Denmark, Finland, France, and Germany, whether or not they ratify Conventions Nos 26, 99, and 131, are generally in keeping with the spirit of the ILO provisions. Convention No 26, for example, requires only that minimum wage-fixing machinery is established in those trades in which 'no arrangements exist for the effective regulation of wages by collective agreement or otherwise and wages are exceptionally low'. In Germany, it has been precisely because workers are comprehensively covered by collective bargaining that the 1952 legislation permitting the establishment of minimum rates has never been utilized.[9] And while Conventions Nos 99 and 131 impose more general obligations, they both, in common with Convention No 99, permit the machinery used to be that of collective bargaining and Convention No 117 of 1962 (the Social Policy (Basic Aims and Standards) Convention) stipulates that minimum wage-fixing by freely negotiated collective agreements 'shall be encouraged'.[10] There would not therefore appear to be, and is not, in the view of the ILO's Committee of Experts, any incompatability between the provision of minimum rates by way of collective bargaining and the requirements of Conventions Nos 26, 99, and 131.

The United Kingdom and Ireland stand as the only countries in the European Union in which very significant proportions of the workforce are without minimum wage protection. While both countries enjoy a degree of collective bargaining coverage and, in addition, some statutory regulation (Ireland has Wages Councils along the old British lines and the United Kingdom still has Agricultural Wage Boards), the combined coverage of collective bargaining and statutory regulation is in each case low.[11] The United Kingdom abolished the few remaining Wages Councils in 1993 and, with them, the last vestiges of minimum wage regulation save in the agricultural sphere. But even when the Wages Councils were at their greatest strength, they never covered more than about 17 per cent of the working population (this figure includes those whose wages were regulated by the Agricultural and Scottish Agricultural Wages Boards) and this figure declined to around 11 per cent in the years before abolition.[12]

---

[9] Starr, n. 2 above.   [10] Art. 10(1).

[11] In both countries, collective bargaining affected the wages of less than 60% of workers and minimum wage levels a further 6 and 12% respectively. See Bazen and Benhayoun, n. 7 above, 629. Since the abolition of the Wages Councils, only a handful of UK workers are covered by statutory wage regulation.

[12] Department of Employment, *Wages Councils: 1988 Consultation Document* (London: Department of Employment, 1988).

358   Just Wages for Women

The methods of wage regulation in each of the EU's Member States can be seen in table 9.1.

Table 9.1 — minimum wage and collective bargaining coverage by EU Member State

	minimum wage	% median wage	% covered by collective bargaining
Austria	✗		98
Belgium	✓	66	47
Denmark	✗		83
Finland	✗		95
France	✓	61	80
Greece	✓	70[a]	—
Ireland	✗		57
Italy	✗		100
Netherlands	✓	77	70
Norway	✗		75
Portugal	✓	74	58
Spain	✓	60	61
Sweden	✗		83
United Kingdom	✗		55
West Germany	✗		100

sources: Bazen and Benhayoun;[13] OECD 1994
[a] 70% average wage

Reading table 9.1 together with tables 8.1 to 8.6, the Member States with the lowest levels of wage dispersion, of low-paid women, and of gender–pay gap all regulated wages either *de facto*, with high collective bargaining coverage (as was the case in Denmark and West Germany in terms of overall wage dispersion, in France and Italy in terms of low-waged women) or *de jure* by means of a national minimum wage (as was the case in Belgium, the Netherlands, France, and Portugal in terms of both general wage dispersion and low-waged women). The relative (to men), as opposed to absolute, likelihood of women being low paid was also lowest in those countries (France, Italy, and Portugal) which had either a minimum wage or high levels of collective bargaining coverage, or, as was the case in France, both. Equally, when the gender–wage gap in the various Member States is considered, those in which women did relatively well in 1991 either enjoyed high levels of collective bargaining (Denmark, France, Italy, and West Germany) or a national minimum wage (Greece, Portugal, the Netherlands, and Belgium). The other four Member States,

[13] N. 7 above.

in which the gender–wage gaps were considerably larger, either had no national minimum wage or one set at a low level (Spain, at 60 per cent of the median wage[14]) and had low levels of collective bargaining coverage.

Greece and Spain alone combine minimum wages with high levels of wage dispersion (and, perhaps even more significantly, very high numbers of workers earning less than 50 per cent of the overall median wage). Given the level of the minimum wage at 60 per cent and 70 per cent of the median wage in Spain and Greece respectively, these figures suggest high degrees of non-compliance, a suspicion borne out by Bazen and Benhayoun who report that these countries, together with Portugal, had large informal sectors and believed that non-compliance was high. As Bazen and Benhayoun remark: 'the presence of minimum wage legislation *per se* does not ensure that vulnerable workers are protected'.[15]

II. MINIMUM WAGE REGULATION IN THE UNITED KINGDOM

(A) INTRODUCTION

We have considered the current state of play, as far as minimum wages are concerned, in the various Member States of the EU. While few firm conclusions can be drawn from such a broad survey—questions remaining unanswered about the relationship between minimum wage regulation and extensive collective bargaining arrangements in minimizing the gender–wage gap, it is possible to assert that the existence of one or other of these mechanisms appears to have a beneficial impact. In Chapter 8 we looked at one model of the collective bargaining approach (albeit in a form which comes very close to state regulation, but at a level of detail which is characteristic of collective bargaining, as distinct from minimum wage regulation). Here we turn to consider the extent to which the United Kingdom itself has operated minimum wage regulation, and the impact which such regulation has had on the degree of wage dispersion in general and, in particular, on the gender–wage gap.

(B) HISTORY OF MINIMUM WAGE REGULATION IN THE UNITED KINGDOM

Wages Councils

The United Kingdom is currently the only Member State to boast neither minimum wage regulation nor high levels of collective bargaining.

---

[14] The figure for France is not much higher at 61%, but the country has 80% collective bargaining coverage.

[15] Bazen and Benhayoun, n. 7 above, 629.

But the United Kingdom was the first country in Europe, third only in the world to Australia and New Zealand, to embrace minimum wage regulation in modern times (earlier legislative provisions in the United Kingdom having been repealed at the turn of the nineteenth century).

Britain's first modern legislative attempt at minimum wage regulation took place in 1909, when Winston Churchill, then President of the Board of Trade, successfully shepherded his Trade Boards Act through Parliament. The Act was directed at 'sweating', defined by a Select Committee reporting in 1890 as work with wages 'barely sufficient to sustain existence, . . . hours of labour . . . such as to make the lives of the workers periods of almost ceaseless toil . . . insanitary conditions . . . injurious to the health of the persons employed and . . . dangerous to the public'.[16] Concern over sweating had increased over the final years of the nineteenth century, particularly after the report of that Committee whose recommendations, however, confined themselves to government contracts and resulted in the Fair Wages Resolution 1891 (discussed after note 46 below).

Pressure built over the succeeding decades; Beatrice and Sidney Webb proposed minimum wages to counteract the impact of sweated labour on its workers (who earned insufficient to remain healthy) and, thereby, on the economy as a whole; public outrage was excited by a Sweated Industries Exhibition staged in London in 1906; the National Anti-Sweating League was established; and the Select Committee on Homework reported in 1908. The Committee's conclusions, that sweating was widespread and extended beyond the homeworking sector to factories, resulted in the passage of the Trade Boards Act the following year.[17] Introducing the legislation, Winston Churchill MP declared:

[i]t is a national evil that any class of Her Majesty's subjects should receive less than a living wage in return for their utmost exertions . . . where you have what we call sweated trades, you have no organisation, no parity of bargaining, the good employer is undercut by the bad and the bad by the worst; the worker, whose whole livelihood depends upon the industry, is undersold by the worker who only takes up the trade as a second string . . . where these conditions prevail you have not a condition of progress, but a condition of progressive degeneration.[18]

The Trade Boards Act, which enjoyed wide support from employers concerned at undercutting by those paying poverty wages, permitted the Board of Trade to establish Trade Boards in industries whose wages were

---

[16] Select Committee on the Sweating System, *5th Report* (Parliamentary Papers, 1890), xvii. For further discussion of the events leading up to the introduction of the Trade Boards Act see J. Morris, *Women Workers and the Sweated Trades* (Aldershot: Gower Publishers, 1986).

[17] The Act was a compromise—the Committee had recommended wages boards in line with the Australian arbitration committees (see Ch. 8) but, according to S. Blackburn, 'The Problem of Riches: From Trade Boards to a National Minimum Wage' (1988) 19(2) *Industrial Relations Journal* 124, 127, 'suspicion of state intervention' made for a more moderate approach.

[18] 155 HC Debs. (24 Apr. 1906), col. 1888.

'exceptionally low as compared with [those] in other employments'.[19] Four industries were provided for in the Act itself and Parliament was to determine which additional industries should be covered. Each board (and there could be many regional boards in each industry or trade) would consist of three permanent members who would sit on every board in that particular trade, together with representatives both of employers and employees.[20] Wages were to be fixed at the rates which the Boards saw fit, subject to a three-month period during which objections could be made, and the Board of Trade was entitled to make the rates mandatory after a further six months.[21]

Trade Board (later Wages Council) orders functioned by incorporating terms into the contracts of those workers covered by them. Employers were obliged to display notices of the working conditions required by the relevant Board and to keep adequate records of wages and hours as well as observing the terms imposed. The power of enforcement lay in the Wages Inspectorate which had powers of inspection and prosecution to that end. Workers paid less than the appropriate rates could, either on their own account or through a Wage Inspector, sue on their contracts. Alternatively, back pay was recoverable by summary criminal proceedings taken by the Wages Inspectorate.

The initial emphasis of the Trade Boards Act was simply upon the extremely low-wage industries, despite the emphasis which had been given by Churchill in the House of Commons to the lack of trade union organization in many poorly-paying trades.[22] Only 200,000 workers benefited from the 1909 Act and the demand for a minimum wage grew from 1911.[23] In 1913, trade boards were set up in a further five industries, and the war years which followed saw the implementation of minimum wages initially in munitions and agriculture and, in 1918, almost universally. But the Liberal Government resisted calls from the Labour Party for a permanent national minimum wage and, in 1918, chose instead to reform the Trade Boards Act to enable new trade boards to be established more easily (by the Minister of Labour without the previous requirement for an Act of Parliament) and to widen the scope of regulation beyond the sweated industries to those in which 'no adequate machinery exist[ed] for the effective regulation of wages throughout the trade'.[24] The hope

---

[19] See generally V. Hart, *Bound by Our Constitution: Women, Worker, and the Minimum Wage* (Princeton, NJ: Princeton University Press, 1994), Ch. 3.

[20] The permanent members were, according to Churchill himself, intended 'to grip, guide and coordinate the operations of local Wages boards' (in a letter to Asquith, 12 Jan. 1909 reproduced in R. Churchill, *Winston S. Churchill: Volume II, Companion, Part 2, 1907–1911* (London: Heinmann, 1969), 870 cited in Hart, n. 19 above, 56.

[21] N. 19 above, 58–9.

[22] F. Bayliss, *British Wages Councils* (Oxford: Blackwell, 1962), 9.

[23] Blackburn, n. 17 above, 128.

[24] Cited by P. Beaumont, 'The Extent of Compliance with Minimum Wage Regulations: The West of Scotland' (1978) 9(2) *Industrial Relations* 4.

was that trade boards would succeed in making themselves redundant by promoting collective bargaining, and eventually the formation of Joint Industrial Councils in the industries in which they were established. But the Trade Boards Act 1919 did not extend the scope of trade boards beyond manufacturing into the service industries.

The number of trade boards shot up to sixty-three by 1921 (between them covering in the region of three million workers). Agricultural wages boards were added by the first Labour Government in 1924,[25] and the 1930s saw a modest expansion in the number of boards as employers softened their resistance to state intervention in the wake of the depression. Nevertheless, the number of boards and of workers covered by them declined, respectively, to forty-seven boards and around one million workers by 1936 as a result of determined employer resistance during the 1920s depression and the impact of the hostile Cave Committee report in 1922.[26] But trade boards, rendered generally redundant during the war because of the widespread use of compulsory arbitration (see after note 55 below), received a boost towards the end of that period when Ernest Bevin (then Minister for Labour) placed the emphasis on statutory wage regulation in order to protect wages during the slump anticipated (but not actually experienced) in the wake of the Second World War. According to Fred Bayliss, while the immediate aims of the Wages Councils Act 1945 were to extend wage regulation to the retail trades and to make minor adjustments to the existing legislation, its main purpose lay in 'the provision of a legislative framework for collective bargaining which would guarantee to all workers certain industrial rights of citizenship.[27]

The Catering Wages Act 1943 had established wages boards in the catering industry and the 1945 Act renamed trade boards as Wages Councils in an attempt to 'remove the stigma of being associated with the sweated trades';[28] increased the number of workers covered by them by including within them for the first time workers in the service industries; and extended their power to fix minimum remuneration beyond basic rates to include holidays and holiday pay. Wages Councils were established in a number of other (predominantly female) industries over the subsequent few years and in 1959 incorporated miscellaneous wage-fixing measures (with the exception of the Agricultural Wages Board[29]) within

[25] Their remit was severely curtailed to combatting subsistence wages.

[26] See B. Bercusson, *Fair Wages Resolutions* (London: Mansell, 1978), 127; C. Craig, J. Rubery, R. Tarling, and F. Wilkinson, *Labour Market Structure, Industrial Organisation and Low Pay* (Cambridge: CUP, 1982), 15—although the election of a Labour government avoided the most radical of that committee's recommendations (a return to the 1909 Act's emphasis on low pay rather than inadequate organization, limitation of the boards' power to fix anything other than a subsistence minimum), the report did halt any further expansion of the system during the 1920s.

[27] *British Wages Councils* (Oxford: Blackwell, 1945), 54.

[28] Cited by Beaumont, n. 24 above, 5.

[29] The 1945 Act repealed the 1943 Act and converted wages boards thereunder established to Wages Councils.

the Wages Councils System,[30] and returned to the Minister of Labour the power to create wages councils.[31] The Minister was empowered also to order the abolition of Wages Councils or variations in the scope of their operations.[32] By 1962 Wages Councils covered three and a half million workers, and Agricultural Wages Boards a further 500,000.

But Wages Councils were not universally popular. Trade unions had always been ambivalent about them. And, whereas the Government's initial reluctance to intervene in the wage-setting process had largely been put aside over the course of the centuries, and many employers looked upon the Councils favourably as a weapon against undercutting by the very worst of their competitors, the 1960s witnessed a growth in trade union opposition to the Councils.[33] Prior to this unions had complained that Wages Council rates were too low and that the Councils hindered the development of organization in those industries in which they operated. Although this latter view has not gone unchallenged,[34] it was later supported both by the Donovan Commission and the National Board for Prices and Incomes (NBPI).[35] But no real attempts had been made to abolish any Councils (none had, in fact, been abolished prior to the 1960s) until 1962, in which year the TUC listed those Councils which, in its view, should be abolished.[36]

Government incomes policies also became commonplace during the 1960s and the wage increases recommended by Wages Councils, though

[30] The Road Haulage Wages Act 1938 had already been incorporated as a Wages Council by the Wages Council Act 1948 but the 1938 Act continued as regarded the arbitration issue.

[31] Councils could be established by the Minister on his own initiative, or after reference to a commission of inquiry where he felt that no adequate negotiating machinery existed for the wages of any group or (in the case of a reference) where he felt such machinery might not survive. A reference could also be made on the application of a joint industrial council, other body representing employers and workers, or any organization which claimed habitually to take part in settling the wages and conditions of employment of the workers.

[32] Following the procedure outlined in n. 31 above.

[33] Bayliss, n. 22 above, 8 (on the failure of the Trade Boards Act 1909 itself to establish a minimum): '[t]he legitimacy of state interference was acknowledged but suspicion of such interference was so strong that the state itself could not be given the power to settle the actual amount of the wage . . . the state's power was minimised, and the practical effect of the legislation was to leave the determination of wages to representatives of the individuals and independent parties sitting as a Trade Board, with the state only using its power to enforce what the Trade Board decided'.

[34] See Craig et al., n. 26 above, 15–21.

[35] The Royal Commission on Trade Unions and Employers' Associations (1965–8, Report (London: HMSO, 1968), Cmnd. 3623, 66); National Board for Prices and Incomes, Report No 110, Pay and Conditions in the Clothing Manufacturing Industries (London: HMSO, 1969), Cmnd. 4002, both cited by J. Greenwood, 'On the Abolition of the Wages Councils' (1972) 3(4) Industrial Relations 30, 31. See Greenwood also for criticism of the argument that Wage Councils increases served to improve the pay of workers in the industries generally, rather than benefiting most those on the minimum rates.

[36] See S. Keevash, 'Wages Councils: An Examination of Trade Union and Conservative Government Misconceptions about the Effect of Statutory Wage Fixing' (1985) 14 Industrial Law Journal 217, 221. The union movement continued to agitate against Wages Councils, a TUC conference in 1969 showing a majority of union speakers in favour of abolition.

themselves affected by these policies (see the text to notes 102–8 below), were widely seen as inconsistent with them. At the same time, the 1960s saw increasing calls for the establishment of a national minimum wage. These conflicting pressures did little for the image of the Wages Council system, and many councils were abolished or merged with others over the 1960s and 1970s (abolition having been made easier in the latter decade by the Industrial Relations Act 1971[37]) with the result that thirty Councils covered three (rather than three and a half) million workers by 1981.

Simultaneously with the abolition of many Wages Councils during the 1970s, the jurisdiction of the remaining Councils was extended to cover all terms and conditions of employment, and their orders were made binding without the need for referral to the Minister of Labour. The Wages Council Act 1979 consolidated existing legislation, but the election of a Conservative Government in the same year spelt the beginning of the end for the Wages Council system. The Wages Inspectorate was reduced in size and a subsequent reprimand from the ILO's Committee of Experts was followed by the government's announcement of its intention to deratify ILO Convention No 26 on Minimum Wage-Fixing Machinery (the government had already deratified Convention No 94 (Labour Clauses (Public Contracts) Convention of 1949)[38] in order to permit the abolition of the Fair Wages Resolution, discussed in the text after note 46 below). The Institute of Personnel Management criticized this withdrawal: '[n]o country which has ratified Convention No 26 has denounced it. The Government's denunciation of the Convention will, as the CBI commented last year, embarrass the UK internationally, particularly in the context of penalizing competition from less developed countries on the ground that they are sweatshop labour.'[39]

---

[37] See generally E. Armstrong, 'Wages Councils, Retail Distribution and the Concept of the Cut-off' (1970) 1 *Industrial Relations Journal* 9, 10—the 1971 Act replaced abolition criteria requiring the existence of adequate voluntary collective bargaining machinery which was capable of sustaining adequate levels of terms and conditions with the statement that the Commission of Industrial Relations (which was to replace the previous *ad hoc* commissions of inquiry into the abolition of particular councils) could recommend abolition 'if of the opinion that it is expedient to do so'. It also allowed abolition on the application of the trade union alone, rather than (as previously) jointly by trade union and employer, and required the CIR to investigate the bulk of the Councils to consider whether they should be abolished or reformed.

[38] The TUC made a complaint to the ILO in 1983 as a result—in Mar. 1984 the Committee of Experts report expressed hope that 'the Government will be able to take appropriate measures to ensure full observance of the minimum wages set by Wages Councils—*Report of the Committee of Experts on the Application of Conventions and Recommendations* (Geneva: ILO, 1984), 69, cited by Keevash, n. 36 above, 224. Keevash reports John Selwyn Gummer's statement (*The Times*, 15 Feb. 1984). See also J. Clark and Lord Wedderburn, 'Modern Labour Law: Problems, Functions and Policies' in Wedderburn, R. Lewis, and J. Clark, *Labour Law and Industrial Relations: Building on Kahn-Freund* (Oxford: Clarendon Press, 1983), 241 n. 382.

[39] Low Pay Network, *Save Wages Councils: A Briefing Paper on the Abolition of Wages Councils* (London: Low Pay Network: 1992), 6.

The Government was undeterred. In 1985 an Employment Department Consultation Paper on Wages Councils put forward the possibility of abolition; employers' organizations as well as unions came out against this suggestion;[40] and the Government eventually enacted the Wages Act 1986 which, instead, removed from the scope of minimum wage regulation those workers aged under 21 and prohibited Councils from fixing any terms other than a single standard and overtime rate for workers covered by them. The Act also contained provisions making it easier for the Secretary of State to abolish and modify the scope of Wages Councils.

The final death blow for the Wages Councils was heralded by the Employment Department's 1988 Consultation Document on Wages Councils. The document began with the assertion that 'excessive pay rises hit jobs' (this at a time when the Wages Council rates of between £1.96 and £2.49 per hour were set at a mere 37 and 47 per cent respectively of the average hourly rate for all full-time employees, 34 and 43 per cent of the average hourly rate for full-time men[41]), and went on to state that 'requests for the abolition of particular councils, the exclusion of individual firms, or the release of particular sectors of a trade from regulation . . . experience of the working of the legislation since 1986 and the needs of the 1990s all point to a strong case for further change'.[42] Minimum wage fixation was characterized as inflationary and inflexible, leading to knock-on effects throughout industry, and the clustering of up to a third of those workers covered on or around the minimum rates set was interpreted as:

evidence that council minima continue to be above the levels required to fill jobs . . . most workers in Wages Council trades are part-time, many of them contributing a second income to the home. . . . It has become increasingly clear that Wages Councils' decisions continue to prevent employers from developing pay structures wholly in accordance with the best interests of their businesses.[43]

In 1990 Michael Howard, then Secretary of State for Employment, announced that the Wages Council system 'should have no permanent place in the labour market'[44] and, according to a report in the *Independent*, a Cabinet sub-committee agreed in June 1991 that abolition would follow re-election in 1992.[45] The Conservatives were re-elected and in 1993 the Trade Union Reform and Employment Rights Act abolished the councils entirely. Agricultural Wages Boards remain, the Government having failed to take the opportunity open to it in 1993 to denounce Convention No 99.[46]

---

[40] Blackburn, n. 17 above, 125.   [41] NES 1988, table 1.   [42] N. 12 above, 3.
[43] *Ibid.* 4–5.
[44] Written answer 6 Mar. 1990 cited by the Low Pay Network, n. 39 above, 7.
[45] 31 Dec. 1991, reported *ibid.* 7.
[46] The UK government was expected to denounce this Convention in 1993, but has not done so despite threats from the then Secretary of State for Employment, Michael Portillo MP, in 1995 to withdraw entirely from the ILO (*Financial Times*, 6 June 1995).

Fair Wages Resolutions

Those Wages Councils abolished in 1993 represented the last attempts by the United Kingdom to regulate minimum wages outside the agricultural arena. But even at their height, the Councils and the Agricultural Wages Boards together never covered more than about 17 per cent of the workforce, and those in only a limited range of industries.[47] But from 1891 to 1983, Fair Wages Resolutions passed by the House of Commons aimed to ensure that government contractors provided their employees with terms and conditions that were no less favourable than those generally established by collective bargaining in the trade[48] (many local authorities also imposed fair wages clauses on private sector companies with which they contracted).

The forces which led to the passage of the 1891 resolution were mentioned in the text to notes 16–46 above: it was very general and unspecific[49] and was succeeded in turn by the 1909[50] and 1946 Resolutions, both of which were considerably more detailed, and the later of which also required government contractors to permit workers the freedom to join trade unions. The 1946 Resolution was, in addition to being administered by the executive in the allocation and content of government contracts, incorporated into a number of statutes including the Road Traffic Act 1960,[51] the Road Haulage Wages Act 1938, the Television Act 1954, and

---

[47] The estimate includes Agricultural Wages Board (0.5 million) and Wages Councils (3.5 million). Coverage peaked between 1953 (Consultation Paper, n. 12 above) and 1962 (Craig et al., n. 26 above).

[48] See generally Bercusson, n. 26 above.

[49] 'That in the opinion of this House, it is the duty of the Government in all Government contracts to make provision against the evils recently disclosed before the Sweating Committee, to insert such conditions as may prevent the abuses arising from sub-letting, and to make every effort to secure the payment of such wages as are generally accepted as current in each trade for competent workmen.' According to Bercusson, ibid. 46, the resolution was: 'so vague and so general that . . . the problem was not one of interpreting the Resolution in those situations in which it applied, but of finding situations where it could be said to apply at all'. In addition, very low levels of trade union membership (48) and poor administration by government departments rendered the first resolution little more than useless.

[50] 'The contractor shall, under a penalty of a fine or otherwise, pay rates of wages and observe hours of labour not less favourable than those currently recognised by employers and trade societies (or in the absence of such recognised wages and hours, those which in practice prevail amongst good employers) in the trade in the district where the work is carried out. Where there are no such wages and hours recognised or prevailing in the district, those recognised or prevailing in the nearest district in which the general industrial circumstances are similar shall be adopted. Further, the conditions of employment generally accepted in the district in the trade concerned shall be taken into account in considering how far the terms of the Fair Wages Clauses are being observed. The contractor shall be prohibited from transferring or assigning, directly or indirectly, to any person or persons whatever any portions of his contract without the written permission of the department. Sub-letting other than that which may be customary in the trade concerned shall be prohibited. The contractor shall be responsible for the observance of the Fair Wages Clause by the sub-contractor.'

[51] Previously the Road Traffic Act 1930 as amended.

the Civil Aviation Act 1946 in which it was given statutory force although, as in the case of the Resolution itself, the obligations were not directly enforceable by the employees concerned.[52]

The 1891 and 1908 Resolutions will not be considered in any detail. Certainly the first of these was not regarded as extending to female workers —certainly not, at any rate, so as to apply 'male rates' to them—and the exclusive enforcement of the first two resolutions by the government departments concerned means that information on their implementation is limited.[53] The 1946 Resolution required contractors:

1 (a) to pay rates of wages and observe hours and conditions of labour no less favourable than those established for the trade or industry in the district where the work is carried out by machinery of negotiation or arbitration to which the parties are organisations of employers and trade unions representative respectively of substantial proportions of the employers and workers engaged in the trade or industry in the district.

   (b) In the absence of any rates of wages, hours or conditions of labour so established [to] pay rates of wages and observe hours and conditions of labour which are no less favourable than the general level of wages, hours and conditions observed by other employers whose general circumstances in the trade or industry in which the contractor is engaged are similar.[54]

Contractors were, in addition, responsible for ensuring compliance by any sub-contractors. The Fair Wages Resolution gave no individual rights of enforcement to workers but operated so as to make compliance with its terms a condition of the contract between government department and employer. Alleged infringements were referred through the government department concerned to the Ministry of Labour, which could attempt conciliation before referring the matter for arbitration first to the Industrial Court, from 1971 to the Industrial Arbitration Board, and after February 1976, to the CAC. A decision by either body that the Resolution had been infringed did not itself give rise to any rights but permitted the contracting department to take the appropriate contractual measures. The 1946 Resolution remained in place until 1983 when the Conservative administration repealed it.[55] Its efficacy, both in general terms and, in particular, in relation to women's relative wages, is considered below.

Other Wage-Fixing Mechanisms

Fair Wages Resolutions were only ever designed to benefit the employees of those who contracted with government bodies. By contrast, Orders

---

[52] *Simpson* v. *Kodak Ltd* [1948] 2 KB 184.

[53] See Bercusson, n. 26 above, 35–100, 142–207.

[54] The Resolution also imposed an obligation to permit trade union membership and to display the Resolution in the workplace.

[55] Repeal took place on 21 Sept. 1983 following a Commons vote to rescind on 16 Dec. 1982.

368   Just Wages for Women

1305 of 1940 and 1376 of 1951, section 8 of the Terms and Conditions of Employment Act 1959, and, finally, Schedule 11 of the EPA 1975 were intended to provide some measure of protection to all employees.

The Conditions of Employment and National Arbitration Order 1940 (Order 1305), like the Fair Wages Resolution 1946, resulted from a pre-Second World War agreement between the TUC and National Confederation of Employers' Organizations (the forerunner to the CBI). By contrast with the Resolution, Order 1305 and its successors (Order 1376 of 1951 (the Industrial Disputes Order) and section 8 of the Terms and Conditions of Employment Act 1959) simply operated so as to extend collectively agreed terms and contained no provision akin to the Resolution's clause 1(b) (which provided for the extension of generally observed terms in the absence of any collectively agreed). Order 1305 also prohibited the taking of industrial action.[56]

Order 1305 required that employers observed terms and conditions which were 'not less favourable' than those 'settled by machinery of negotiation or arbitration to which the parties are organizations of employers and trade unions representative respectively of substantial proportions of the employers and workers engaged in that trade or industry in the district' and 'in force' within the trade or industry in the district.[57] It went on to provide that terms and conditions would not be regarded as less favourable if they complied with the terms of any major collective agreement, statutory provision, or any one of a number of bodies.[58]

Order 1305 was repealed in 1951 after the Attorney General's prosecution, under its provisions, of unofficial gas strikers in that year[59] but its principle of wage protection was replaced at once by Order 1376. This provision permitted those trade unions or employers' organizations which 'habitually t[ook] part in the settlement of terms and conditions in [a] trade or industry or section of trade or industry' to complain to the Ministry of Labour that an employer's terms and conditions were less favourable than those 'settled by machinery of negotiation or arbitration to which the parties are organizations of employers and trade unions representative respectively of substantial proportions of the employers and workers engaged in th[e] trade or industry or section of trade or industry in [the] district' in which the employer operated.[60] These complaints were referred to the Industrial Disputes Tribunal (IDT) which, if the claim were upheld, would order that the disputed terms be incorporated into the contracts of those employees in respect of which the complaint was made.

Order 1376 was repealed in 1958 but, such was the opposition from trade unions, employers and the Labour Party, that section 8 of the Terms and

[56] See P. Davies and M. Freedland, *Labour Law: Text and Materials* (2nd edn., London: Weidenfeld and Nicholson, 1984), 89 ff.
[57] Part III, para. 5(1).   [58] Para. 5(2).   [59] Davies and Freedland, n. 56 above.
[60] Para. 2.

Conditions of Employment Act established a similar procedure.[61] Section 8 was very similar to the Orders which preceded it, save that the Industrial Court (IC) replaced the IDT and the date to which any incorporated terms could be backdated (for the purpose of assessing damages awardable to the employees) was fixed as the date at which the employer was notified of the claim, rather than the date at which any failure to observe the relevant terms was found to have begun.

Section 8 allowed action to be taken against an employer who failed to observe 'terms or conditions of employment . . . established in any trade or industry, or section of a trade or industry, either generally or in any district, which have been settled by an agreement or award'.[62] The agreement or award had to be made between 'organisations of employers and organisations of workers, or associations of such organisations' (or representatives of the same) which represented '(generally or in the district in question, as the case may be) a substantial proportion of the employers and of the workers in the trade, industry or section, being workers of the description . . . to which the agreement or award relates'. In addition, only those trade unions or employers' organizations party to or represented by a party to the agreement or award could bring a complaint under section 8.

The Ministry first attempted to conciliate between the parties before, if necessary, referring the issue to the IC to determine what, if any, agreement applied; if such an agreement did exist, whether the terms were being observed by the employer, and, if they were not being so observed, whether the employer's terms and conditions were 'less favourable' than those laid down in the agreement. If the complaint was upheld the Industrial Court could order that the relevant terms be incorporated into the contracts of employment of those workers in respect of whom the claim was made,[63] and the terms would remain until any new collective agreement was reached. The terms so incorporated could then be enforced either by the employees themselves (by means of a contractual claim) or by another claim by the trade union or employer organization. In practice only the former method was ever used.

Section 8 was never regarded as particularly successful, not least because of its failure to provide a general fair wages clause (along the lines of the Fair Wages Resolution) in addition to the provision providing for the extension of collective agreements.[64] Schedule 11 of the EPA 1975, which replaced it, included such a clause and permitted complaints against employers whose terms and conditions were less favourable than:

---

[61] G. Latta, 'The Legal Extension of Collective Bargaining: A Study of Section 8 of the Terms and Conditions of Employment Act 1959' (1974) *Industrial Law Journal* 215.

[62] S. 8(1)(a).   [63] Again, no earlier than the date of notification.

[64] B. Bercusson, 'The New Fair Wages Policy: Schedule 11 to the Employment Protection Act' (1976) 5 *Industrial Law Journal* 129, 130.

(a) the 'recognised' terms and conditions (agreed or awarded between
substantially representative employers' organization(s) and independent trade unions representative, either 'generally or in the district
in question', of a 'substantial proportion of the employers and of
the workers in the trade, industry or section, being workers of the
description to which the agreement or award relates') 'of workers
in comparable employment in the trade or industry, or section of
a trade or industry' in which the employer operated, 'either generally or in the district in which he is so engaged',[65] or,

(b) *where no such agreement existed* (or existed in respect of the particular term challenged), the 'general level' of terms and conditions
(those applying to comparable workers of comparable employers
in the same industry, trade, or section and district).[66]

Complaints were to be made in the first instance to the Advisory
Conciliation and Arbitration Service (ACAS) which, if no settlement was
possible, referred the matter to the IAB (after 1 February 1976, the CAC).
Section 8 and Order 1376 had permitted complaints to be made only
by trade unions or employers' organizations representing a 'substantial
proportion of workers or employers' in the relevant industry, restricting
the scope of those collective agreements capable of extension to multi-
employer agreements. Schedule 11 reiterated this requirement in respect of
claims under clause 2(a) of Part I, which had to be brought by employers'
associations or trade unions which were party to the relevant agreement,
but permitted any employers' association having members in the industry and district in which the claim arose to make a 'general level' claim
under clause 2(b). In addition, any trade union could bring a general level
claim in respect of a member 'concerned' with the claim, so long as the
employer did not recognize any other union. The CAC interpreted 'concerned' to mean employed by the employer whose payment practices were
being challenged under clause 2(b).[67]

Schedule 11 also went beyond previous legislation in its approach to
Wages Council industries. Whereas section 8 had not in practice permitted claims in relation to workers covered by Wages Council Orders
until 1974 (because of the 1971 Act's restriction of claims to registered
trade unions—see the text to note 151 below—its extension of section
8's protection to Wages Council workers was of no real effect), Schedule

---

[65] Cl. 2(a), Prt. I. See P. Wood, 'The Central Arbitration Committee's Approach to
Schedule 11 to the Employment Protection Act 1975 and the Fair Wages Resolution 1946'
(1978) 7 *Industrial Law Journal* 65, 72. Workers did not have to be 'of the description
to which the agreement related' as under s. 8 which had blocked claims in relation to non-
federated employers.

[66] See M. Jones, 'C.A.C. and Schedule 11: The Experience of Two Years' (1980) 9
Industrial Law Journal 28, for a general discussion of the CAC's approach to Sched. 11.

[67] The position was possibly even narrower—see Wood, n. 65 above, 81 on the Grunwick
Processing Laboratories Ltd and APECCS Award (No 329).

11 permitted claims in respect of those workers covered by Wages Councils and the Agricultural Wages Board. In addition, Part II of the Schedule permitted trade unions which were party to collective agreements covering a 'significant number of establishments within the field of operation' of a Wages Council, statutory joint industrial council, the Agricultural or Scottish Agricultural Wages Board, to apply for the extension of the 'lowest current rate' of remuneration laid down in the collective agreement to trade union members working in establishments in which the employer's circumstances were similar to those covered by the agreement.[68] This provision, unlike Part I, allowed claims by trade unions which were not representative of a substantial proportion of employees in the trade or industry, etc., and which could not establish a 'general level' of terms and conditions prevailing in the trade or industry, etc. Despite this, Part II found little favour with trade unions (perhaps because of its application only in respect of remuneration, and only of its lowest current rate) and in the first two years of Schedule 11's operation only a single claim under Part II was determined by the CAC, by contrast with almost 700 under Part I.

Schedule 11 came into operation on 1 January 1977. On 7 December 1979 the new Conservative government indicated its intention to repeal the Schedule, arguing that it had not been directed towards eliminating the pockets of lowest pay, that it had been used to circumvent government pay policy, and that unequal access to legal assistance had resulted in its differential utilization by various groups of workers.[69] These claims will be examined below. Whatever their truth, however, Schedule 11 was repealed in 1980, thirteen years before the final vestiges of UK minimum wage regulation fell to the ground with the abolition of the last wages councils.

(C) IMPACT OF MINIMUM WAGE REGULATION IN THE UNITED KINGDOM

We have now considered the history of minimum wage regulation (more precisely, fair standards regulation) in the United Kingdom. The next point to address is the extent to which these provisions impacted on the wages of low paid sectors of the workforce in general, and of women in particular. It is clear from the picture elsewhere in Europe that minimum wage regulation can have a profound impact on the gender–pay gap (by placing a bottom line under the wages of the poorest paid workers in the formal economy, and thereby under the wages of many women). It is

---

[68] *Ibid.* 66—no offset (see text to n. 138 below) but worked only in relation to remuneration and allowed raise only to minimum level payable under collective agreement.

[69] Jones, n. 66 above, 44 challenged this: 'the Schedule appears to be achieving one of its principal objectives, that of helping the low paid'.

useful to consider whether the particular models adopted in the United Kingdom (wages councils, contract compliance, and administrative extension of collective bargaining and general wage levels) had such an effect in the UK.

Wages Councils

From the outset the main beneficiaries of the Trade Boards Act were women. This was not surprising: much of the pressure which finally resulted in the 1909 Act was concerned specifically with the issues of female wages and female work, and many of the supporters of legislation had campaigned exclusively for the regulation of the wages of (predominantly female) home workers. The Trade Boards Act was gender-neutral and did not restrict the scope of the Wages Boards to home workers. Nor were the industries first covered by boards by any means exclusively female (tailoring: 46 per cent female; paper boxes: 90 per cent; lace: 62 per cent; chain-making: 30–40 per cent). But the predominance of women among the very lowest paid workers in any trade ensured that they generally accounted for about two-thirds of the workers who directly benefited from the Trade Boards Act.[70] Studies carried out between 1912 and 1915 found significant increases in the wages of those, particularly women, covered by the early Trade Boards.[71] And the coverage of female-dominated industries increased over time to the extent that, by 1975, the bulk of the three million workers covered were to be found in the predominantly female retail, hairdressing, and catering industries (by 1980, 90 per cent of the two and a half million covered were in retail, catering, and clothing manufacturing industries[72]). In 1993, when Wages Councils were finally abolished, 75 per cent of those stripped of protection were women. Of these, about two-thirds worked part-time.

Women were not the primary beneficiaries of the Wages Councils only in the sense that they comprised the bulk of workers covered. Research carried out in the 1960s showed that, contrary to the assumption of the Donovan Commission and the NBPI, very significant numbers of workers were paid at or near the minimum rates established either by national agreements or by Works Councils.[73] Further, clustering around these minima was considerably more pronounced among women

[70] Jones, n. 66 above, 57.

[71] R. Tawney, *The Establishment of Minimum Rates in the Chain-Making Industry* (Bell, 1913); R. Buckley, *The Establishment of Legal Minimum Rates in the Box Making Industry* (Bell, 1915); R. Tawney, *The Establishment of Minimum Rates in the Tailoring Trade* (Bell, 1915); all cited in F. Field and S. Winyard, *Low Wages Councils* (Nottingham: The Spokesman, 1975), 2–3.

[72] Low Pay Unit, *Minimum Wages for Women: An Examination of Women's Earnings in Industries Covered by Wages Councils* (London: Low Pay Unit and Equal Opportunities Commission, 1980), 16.

[73] J. Greenwood, 'On the Abolition of Wages Councils' (1972) 3(4) *Industrial Relations* 30.

than men.[74] This suggests that, without the protection of Wages Councils orders, women (but not necessarily men) would have seen their wages fall below the established minima.

More recently, research carried out for the Pay Equity Project in the early 1990s found that the gender–wage gap was lower in Wages Council industries than elsewhere and warned that 'the abolition of Wages Councils will lead to an increase in dispersion of wages in those industries [and in turn] to a decrease in the female/male earnings ratio in those industries'.[75] The improved gender–pay ratio in Wages Councils industries was not, the research found, simply the result of the generally low wage levels in the industries: rather it held at all deciles (though the difference was particularly significant towards the bottom).

Wages Councils and their predecessors, the Trade Boards, did have an impact on the wage disparity between men and women. But their effect was limited by three major factors. In the first place, the levels of wages set by the boards and councils themselves discriminated between men and women as late as the start of 1976.[76] In the late 1930s, for example, Wages Boards set women's hourly rates at between 48 per cent and 72 per cent of men's (the average rate was 57 per cent)[77] and in 1946 the Agricultural Wages Boards set women's hourly rates at 75 per cent of those of men and the Laundry Wages Council at 65 per cent except where women were directly substituted for men (in which case they were paid male rates).[78] In this practice, boards and councils mirrored the approach of collective agreements and, later, of Joint Industrial Councils (JICs): not only did agreements and JICs typically provide for more categories of male than of female work[79] (thereby permitting greater scope for improvement over time in male than in female wages), but they also set female rates at lower levels than those for men.

The second shortcoming of the trades boards and wages councils as a vehicle for improving women's pay was the relative poverty of the rates

---

[74] *Ibid.* 33 ff.

[75] *Narrowing the Gender Gap: How Wages Councils Work For Women* (London: PEP, 1993), 1.

[76] Ministry of Labour and National Service Statistics Department. The Agricultural Wages Board, e.g. laid down minima for women at 80% of the male rate (up from 75% in 1968) until 1976.

[77] D. Sells, *Wages Boards* (Washington, DC: The Brookings Institution, 1939), 177.

[78] *Ibid.* Women toolmakers, e.g. earned between 44% and 66% of men's rates, women in heavy chemicals 66%, and women needle fishhook and fishing tackle makers between 69% and 100% of men's rates.

[79] The toolmakers' agreement, e.g. distinguished 2 categories of male toolmakers over 25 and a further category aged 21–5, 2 categories of male chargehands over 21 and 'other' men over 21. Women, by contrast, were categorized as only one group aged at least 18. The wool textile collective agreement for West Yorkshire contained 20 categories of men, 2 of women and the JIC for needle fishhook and fishing tackle makers provided three categories of male workers, each with grading according to skill and experience, in comparison with 2 categories of women: those aged at least 20 with at least 12 months' experience and others.

they set, together with the large numbers of very low paid workers left unprotected by them.[80] In the words of one early critic: '[t]he Trades Boards Act allowed the status quo to be continued. It imposed requirements that narrowed inequalities at the bottom of the economic hierarchy but did nothing to abolish that hierarchy or to deliniate an alternative'.[81]

Thirdly, the enforcement of Wages Council orders was always far from perfect. As early as 1923, the operation of the wages boards was criticized on the ground that there were inadequate numbers of wages inspectors.[82] By 1974, 142 inspectors were responsible for supervising the wages of 3.5 million workers, and the Commission on Industrial Relations estimated that those firms in the clothing industry which were covered by wage council orders could expect an inspection only once every eleven years.[83] The number of inspectors reached 158 in 1979, but was reduced in the wake of the Wages Act 1986, the government arguing that reduced numbers would be 'adequate in view of the simplified Wages Council system introduced by [that Act]'.[84] By 1988 the Inspectorate had been run down to the extent that seventy-one inspectors were responsible for overseeing compliance in respect of 2.5 million workers in 376,000 establishments. It is difficult to imagine how this group of people was expected to fulfill the task of checking even the 30,000 establishments targeted in that year.

In areas both of relatively full employment and of high unemployment, high and rising levels of underpayment were recorded during the 1970s.[85] One study carried out between 1969 and 1976 in the West of Scotland found that the proportion of inspected establishments in which underpayment was detected rose from 14.6 per cent to 31.5 per cent in that period, the proportion of workers affected from 3.7 per cent to 15.7 per cent.[86]

Levels of underpayment did not appear to be related to levels of unemployment (in some years the underpayment levels recorded in the West of Scotland were higher, and in other years lower, than Great Britain as a whole, while the unemployment rates for the region remained above the British average) but did show a distinct rise over the period studied both in the region under examination and in Great Britain as a whole[87]

---

[80] Blackburn, n. 17 above, 133. In 1988 'public sector workers, contract cleaners, laundrettes (but not laundries), photography processing, and the growing "new sweated trades" . . . video and rental shops; electrical assembly and plastic works' were all outside the protection of the Wages Councils.

[81] Sells, n. 77 above, 60.

[82] D. Sells, *The British Trade Boards System* (London: King & Son, 1923).

[83] Latta, n. 61 above, on Report No 77 of the Commission on Industrial Relations.

[84] 118 HC Debs. (30 June 1987), col. 61, cited by C. Barclay, *Low Pay and Wages Councils* (London: House of Commons Library Research Division, 1987), Background Paper No 6, 11.

[85] Beaumont, n. 24 above, dealt with the statistics for Scotland and the UK generally.

[86] *Ibid.* 6.   [87] *Ibid.* 9–12.

(establishment underpayments increasing from 16.8 per cent to 35.4 per cent, individual underpayment from 4.8 per cent to 16.1 per cent between 1969 and 1976).

Nor were all workers equally vulnerable to underpayment. A major study conducted in Birmingham between 1962 and 1964 found that, while the city enjoyed among the lowest levels of unemployment in Great Britain, the level of arrears owed by Wage Council industries in that city was well above average.[88] One possible explanation offered was the high rate of employment in that city of:

part-time workers, which in reality, generally means married women. Numbers of such workers are likely to be more concerned about setting their own hours of work in a shop not too far from home or school, than they are about the precise level of wages . . . many of the women may be quite unaware of the legislation which provides a floor to their earnings.[89]

Armstrong, who conducted the Birmingham study, reported that, although the proportion of men underpaid was 'surprising[ly]' higher than that of women, the average sums of money owed to women were greater: '[g]enerally, women timeworkers would seem to be most open to "exploitation", inadvertent or otherwise'.[90]

In 1974 the Commission on Industrial Relations reported, in the context of retail distribution, that women workers were considerably more likely than men to be underpaid (9.5 per cent of full-time adult women, as against 2.4 per cent of adult men). Part-time workers were particularly vulnerable—a staggering 36 per cent of part-time women workers were paid less than the minimum rates. And in 1980, the Low Pay Unit estimated that 25 per cent of establishments underpaid some workers and that, 'given the greater proximity of women's earnings to statutory minimum rates . . . we may assume that women are more vulnerable to underpayment'.[91] The LPU's report noted that homeworkers were particularly vulnerable to underpayment—that these workers were so poorly protected by the Wages Councils is ironic in view of the fact that it was their plight, above all, that had resulted in the enactment of the original Trade Boards Act 1909.

Many underpayments escaped notice by the under-staffed Wages Inspectorate. The possibility of enforcement was not enhanced by the absence of any requirement for those employers covered by Wages Councils to register with the Wages Inspectorate.[92] Even when employers were inspected, as many as 61.5 per cent kept inadequate time records and 13.9 per cent inadequate wage records.[93] This made underpayment more difficult to

[88] E. Armstrong, 'Minimum Wages in Fully Employed City' (1966) 4 *British Journal of Industrial Relations* 22, 23.
[89] *Ibid*. 24.   [90] *Ibid*. 38.   [91] *Ibid*. 27   [92] Beaumont, n. 24 above, 13.
[93] *Ibid*. 1969 and 1971 were the worst years respectively. The lowest rate of default was 47.2% and 9.4% respectively in 1974.

detect and increased the time required for inspections[94] (thereby reducing the number of inspections undertaken).

The degree of worker knowledge of their entitlements under the Wages Council Orders was seriously impaired by the incidence (19.8 per cent–35.7 per cent[95]) of employers' failure to post details, particularly in view of the fact that Wages Councils refused to circulate the rates set to the general public in order to avoid the problem of 'misrepresentation'.[96] One commentator, having studied the operation of Wages Councils in the West of Scotland, rather bleakly concluded that:

[t]he very reason for establishing wages councils is that there is little capacity for joint, voluntary regulation due to the limited development of trade union organisation and collective bargaining arrangements in these industries. But this limited capacity for self-regulation seems to be seriously compounded by the lack of individual worker knowledge of both the details of wage regulation orders and the existence and functions of the wages inspectorate.[97]

The Commission on Industrial Relations concluded that: 'lack of awareness . . . is the most important single explanation for the lack of compliance with the provisions of wage regulation orders.[98]

None of these findings boded particularly well for women, given their disproportionate concentration in industries in which workers were dependent upon wages councils for wage regulation. Even when underpayments were detected, prosecutions were rare—between 1969 and 1976, not one prosecution was carried out in the West of Scotland, despite estimated underpayments which ran to over one milllion pounds.[99] Wages inspectors never prosecuted first offenders and, with only very limited resources, the emphasis was very much on persuasion rather than penalty.[100]

The absence of prosecutions reduced the deterrent possibilities of the Wages Councils. When underpayment was detected it was generally put right without the need for prosecution,[101] but, as we saw above, many cases of underpayment went undetected and unremedied, and there was little incentive for employers to comply with Wages Council orders.

---

[94] Beaumont, n. 24 above.

[95] This fig. related to 1976—there was a fairly steady rise after 1971.

[96] Craig et al., n. 26 above, 42.

[97] Beaumont, n. 24 above, 13—the Commission on Industrial Relations report on the clothing trade found that 66% of employees had never heard of the wages inspectors and only 10% had any reasonable grasp of their functions.

[98] N. 24 above, 71.   [99] Ibid., table 6.

[100] See also Barclay, n. 84 above, 11 on the levels of prosecution and recovery in the mid-1980s.

[101] Beaumont, n. 24 above. An estimated 85–90% of those underpaid received, or themselves refused, their arrears after a verbal instruction to the employer by the visiting wages inspector, and all but 1% of the remainder did so after a written reminder to the employer and without the need for court action. This picture appeared to be deteriorating by the mid-1980s when (Barclay, n. 84 above), citing 116 HC Debs. (14 May 1987), cols, 311–16, reported that only about 67% of arrears discovered by the Wages Inspectorate were paid with about 16% waived and the remainder not pursued.

Perhaps worse than any of these shortcomings was the finding, reported by Steele, that Wages Councils actually hampered wage growth in the industries in which they operated during periods of government incomes policies.[102] Whereas, until the 1940s, wage rates increased at a higher level in Wages Council than in non-Wages Council sectors,[103] and Wages Councils were fairly effective at protecting workers against the effects of slumps,[104] Wages Council rates began to lag behind thereafter, and, during the operation of incomes policies from the mid-1960s, really began to suffer.[105] From then until the mid-1970s, governments, as they had during previous attempts at wage restraint, used varying degrees of coercion to block or delay Wages Council recommendations.[106] The 1964–7 policy, which was imposed by a Labour Government, was presented as an instrument of social justice as well as of inflation control and, to this end, permitted improvements to the position of low paid workers even in the times of most severe restraint.[107] It might have been expected that the position of workers in Wages Council industries would have improved, relative to that of other workers, as a result of these policies. But the approach taken to the definition of 'low paid' by the NBPI (which had responsibility for enforcing the policy) was ungenerous and certainly did not extend to cover generally those dependent upon wages councils. The NBPI itself recognized in 1971 that 'what little improvement took place in the relative position of the low-paid in the earlier years of the prices and incomes policy was later lost'.[108] The Conservative government's subsequent incomes policy permitted the Secretary of State for Employment to delay the implementation of Wages Council awards in order to reduce wage inflation.

Between 1967 and 1975 the average hourly rate in Wages Council industries fell from 85 per cent to 70 per cent of the average rates in non-council industries. Frank Field reported (of 1973 statistics) that:

[w]ithout exception we find the gap widening between the earnings of the lowest decile of male and female workers in . . . Wages Councils and the average for the period since 1970. The period of voluntary incomes policy, which the

[102] R. Steele, 'The Relative Performance of the Wages Council and Non-Wages Council Sectors and the Impact of Incomes Policy' (1979) 17(2) British Journal of Industrial Relations 224.

[103] R. Bowlby, 'Union Policy Toward Minimum Wage Regulation in Postwar Britain' (1957) Industrial and Labour Relations Review, 72, cited by Steele, n. 102 above, 225.

[104] Field and Winyard, n. 71 above, 3.

[105] B. McCormick and H. Turner, 'The Legal Minimum Wage: An Experiment' (Manchester School, 1957), 289, cited by Steele, n. 102 above, 225.

[106] See Field and Winyard, n. 71 above, 5 ff. Wage restraints had also been imposed in 1948, 1952, and 1961.

[107] See R. Banks, 'Wages Councils and Incomes Policy' (1967) 5 British Journal of Industrial Relations 338.

[108] National Board for Prices and Incomes, Report No 169, General Problems of Low Pay (London: HMSO, 1971), Cmnd. 4648.

Conservative government practised when first in office, appears to have done nothing to close the gap between the living standards of the poorest in work and those on average earnings. In fact the very opposite occurred.[109]

One explanation for this deterioration is provided by Steele:

once Incomes Policies, though rigidly applied to start with in all sectors, began to be more loosely applied and ignored by employers and employees in the 'private' sector, then the Wages Council machinery operated as an effective policing and restricting device for increases in the Council sector . . . the Council sector's settlements [remained] within guidelines while widespread evasion allowed non-Council rates to forge ahead.[110]

Steele suggested, as had Bayliss, that the independent members of Wages Councils (upon whose votes the final recommendations depended in the case of non-agreement between employers and trade unions) 'have what one might regard as a "conservative" bias in their occupational composition' (predominantly university staff, lawyers and ex-Civil Servants). This, together with the requirement that Council orders be ratified by the Secretary of State for Employment before becoming enforceable, 'precluded the possibility of Councils breaching policies' even after the policies had been abandoned elsewhere[111] (as was the case between 1967 and 1970). At times, Wages Council orders were returned for reconsideration or subject to mandatory delay prior to implementation.

Given all the problems outlined above, it could not sensibly be asserted that Wages Councils proved a particularly effective policy for the maintenance or improvement of women's wages, relative to those of men. Even after men's and women's rates were equalized, the disproportionate 'bite' of the government's incomes policies upon statutorily-regulated wages resulted in a widening of the wage gap between Wages Council and non-Wages Council industries which persisted until 1979.[112] And although relative wages in the Wages Council industries reached pre-incomes policy levels in this year, the average earnings of non-manual workers in Wages Council industries, in particular, declined over the succeeding years until the abolition of the last remaining Councils in 1993.[113]

---

[109] With Winyard, n. 71 above, 7.   [110] Steele, n. 102 above, 224.

[111] Ibid. 229. Wages Councils made wages regulation proposals to the Minister of Labour after having issued notice of the proposals, so far as practicable, to all those affected by them; allowed the opportunity for written representations to be made, and considered any such representations (1959 Act, s. 11(3)). The Minister, having received the wages regulation proposal, was obliged to issue a wages regulation order giving effect to the proposals from a date specified in the order (s. 11(4)). Before issuing the order the Minister could refer the regulation proposal back to the Wages Council with suggestions for its amendment, but the council could decline to make any amendments suggested and the Minister was required by the 1959 Act to give effect to the wages regulation proposals (s. 11(4)).

[112] Craig et al., n. 26 above, 124 support Steele, on this point.

[113] NES table 1, for the relevant years. Non-manual men and women in Wages Council industries each earned 73% of those in non-Wages Council industries in 1979, respectively

But for all of the criticism which can justifiably be levelled at the Wages Councils we saw, in the text to notes 70–5 above, that they did provide a degree of protection to many of those at the bottom of the earnings distribution ladder and, in particular, to women. Certainly, the prospects for many women workers have become decidedly more grim in the years since their abolition. The Low Pay Network reported that, within three months of abolition, 22.3 per cent of employers in industries previously covered by the Wages Councils were paying less than the previous minimum updated for inflation. Five months thereafter the proportion had risen to 36.5 per cent,[114] while, in the retail sector, the proportion stood at almost 60 per cent. And separate research carried out by the Scottish Low Pay Unit found that 12.3 per cent of employers in those industries previously covered were offering jobs at less than the previous minima (in absolute levels), and a further 34.9 per cent less than the minima updated for inflation.[115] More than half the retail jobs advertised in Scottish job centres paid less than the National Insurance threshold (then £58 per week) with the result that their incumbents would qualify neither for unemployment benefit nor for a pension (women account for 74 per cent of more than three million employees whose earnings are lower than the NI threshold). And almost four out of every five jobs in previously covered industries paid wages below the level of income support for a family with two children.[116]

The Employment Department regarded the possibility of reduced wages as ammunition for the argument in favour of abolition: '[c]ouncil rates continue to be above the levels required to fill jobs'. But it is important to stress that the bulk of those employed in these industries are women. Most (80 per cent) of the jobs paying wages below income support level were occupied by women,[117] and, more generally, the greater concentration of women at and around the minima heralds a worsening of the gender–wage gap as a result of abolition.[118] Labour's Scottish Employment spokesman, John McFall MP, claimed in July 1995 that the gender–pay gap in Scotland was widening as a result of abolition.[119]

Fair Wages Resolutions

The information with which to determine with any degree of precision the impact of the Fair Wages Resolution upon women's wages is not available.

61 and 69% in 1993. Manual workers did not experience so great a relative decline (no doubt the result of the overall decline in manual workers' wages), slipping from 79% and 88% respectively for men and women in 1979 to 86% and 74% in 1993. All figures relate to full-time workers.

[114] *Priced into Poverty*, reported in the *Independent*, 30 Aug. 1995.
[115] *Scotsman*, 31 Aug. 1995.   [116] *Glasgow Herald*, 31 Aug. 1995.
[117] *Glasgow Herald*, 10 July 1995.   [118] *Glasgow Herald*, 10 July 1995.   [119] *Ibid.*

Certainly the earliest version of the Resolution could be expected to have had little positive effect, in light of the generally held views that 'the Fair Wages Resolution says nothing as to the standard rate of wages for women', that 'we do not think that it was the intention of the resolution to enforce the payment to women of the rate "current" for men employed on the same class of work'.[120] Not only this, but until 1970 the provisions of the Resolutions were applicable only to those workers actually employed on governmental contracts, in early years they applied only during those hours in which workers were so employed,[121] and there was a great deal of government departmental resistance to the first Resolutions. According to Bercusson the Treasury: 'had not in fact bothered to communicate the [1891] Resolution to the other departments—an administrative action normally undertaken in the event of new policies being introduced' (emphasis omitted) and government departments frequently failed to include the terms of the resolution within their contracts and required complaints from workers before making any attempts to enforce the Resolution. Such complaints were generally unforthcoming as a result of worker ignorance of the terms of the Resolution and lack of organization.[122] Further, many departments undermined the entire purpose of the Resolution by taking the view that: '[i]f the Government is to have its work executed at the ordinary market price it cannot require the contractor to pay more than the market rate of wages'.[123] This intransigence persisted during the operation of the 1909 Fair Wages Resolution whose impact was, as a result, very limited.[124]

Matters improved after 1946 and, even given the paucity of information specifically relating to the Resolution and women's wages, the positive relationship between wage regulation in general and women's relative wages in particular makes it useful to consider the impact of the 1946 Resolution (and, below, of Order 1305 and its successors) on the pay and conditions of employment of those workers who fell within its scope.

What is perhaps most remarkable is the very small number of complaints which the Resolution gave rise to in the almost four-decade period of its operation. The 1946 Resolution provided for determination by an independent tribunal, rather than by the government department concerned, because the administration of the previous Resolutions had been far from satisfactory, with a fairly widespread lack of concern on the part of these departments for the implementation of those Resolutions.[125] It was hoped that the provision of a complaints system external to the government departments concerned would 'dispel some of th[e] suspicion

---

[120] Bercusson, n. 26 above, 36–7.　　[121] Ibid. 145 ff.

[122] Ibid. 56 & 62 ff. Inclusion was particularly patchy in goods supply contracts.

[123] Report of the Fair Wages Committee 1908, Cmnd. 4422, para. 22 cited by Bercusson, n. 26 above, 31.

[124] Bercusson, n. 26 above, 133 ff.　　[125] See generally ibid.

[that] the contracting departments were applying the fair wage standard correctly'.[126] But history records very little use of the Resolution despite the improved enforcement procedure.

Records of complaints settled prior to referral either to the IAB or the CAC are incomplete, but between 1957 and 1972 only fifteen such complaints were made and either withdrawn or settled prior to referral. In the three subsequent years a huge rise occurred, and fifty-six complaints were received and disposed of by the Ministry of Labour. As for those complaints which were actually referred to arbitration, figures varied between one in 1966–9 and twenty-four in 1970–4. Leaving these two extreme cases aside, the average number of complaints received each year between 1946 and 1974 was only 1.5, with no discernible rise over the period to 1970 but a sharp increase thereafter.[127] In all, the period 1946–75 saw only fifty-eight Fair Wages Resolution arbitrations, of which forty-eight concerned clause 1 (wages) either exclusively or together with some other issue.[128]

The success rate of claims made under the Fair Wages Resolution of 1946 was very poor indeed. Although twenty of the fifty-eight claims were successful, nine of these involved attempts to circumvent government incomes policies in the period 1972–4[129] (during which time nine of the twenty-four complaints consisted of such attempts and a further ten were made in response to a government policy of contracting-out of cleaning in the public sector[130]). In all, there were only eleven findings of breaches of the Fair Wages Resolution in cases of genuine dispute in the first thirty years of its existence.

One reason for the very limited use and success rate of claims under the Fair Wages Resolution lay, according to both Clegg and Bercusson, in the growth in workplace bargaining which took place after the Second World War.[131] The expansion of local bargaining resulted in increasing disparities between nationally agreed and generally observed terms and conditions, with the effect that the national terms would constitute little improvement for all but the most poorly paid workers. This development, and its impact on the operation of the 1946 Resolution, was particularly paradoxical in view of the decades of struggle put up by the TUC for

---

[126] N. 26 above, 135.

[127] P. Beaumont, 'Experience Under the Fair Wages Resolution of 1946' (1977) 8(3) *Industrial Relations* 34, 36. See also Bercusson, n. 26 above.

[128] According to Bercusson, n. 26 above, table 2. In addition to the 58 Resolution cases determined by the IC and IAB, a further 23 complaints each concerned the Road Traffic Act 1930 and the Road Haulage Wages Act 1938, and 14 the Civil Aviation Act 1946 (the combined number of complaints under these statutes varied between none and five annually).

[129] A finding that wages breached the Resolution would permit their increase without breach of the policy.

[130] See Beaumont, n. 127 above, 36.

[131] H. Clegg, *The System of Industrial Relations in Great Britain* (Oxford: Blackwell, 1970), 349 cited by Beaumont, n. 127 above.

the recognition in the Fair Wages Resolution of nationally negotiated terms. Previous Resolutions had referred, not to these national terms (which was the effect of the 1946 Resolution's reference to terms agreed by 'organizations of employers and trade unions', as opposed to 'employers and trade unions'), but simply to those 'generally accepted as current for a competent workman in his trade' (1891) or 'commonly recognized by employers and trade societies' (1909). Both of these were taken in practice to refer simply to the terms generally applied by employers in the district in which the employer operated, and departments proved resistant to embracing collectively agreed terms, whether national or local.

The 1946 Resolution referred (albeit in a circular fashion) to nationally agreed terms, but did so at a time in which such nationally agreed terms were increasingly being superseded by local and workplace bargaining in a period of almost full employment and relative union strength. Merely to impose nationally agreed terms on employers would generally, as a result of this wage drift, come nowhere close to having them apply the terms and conditions generally observed in the trade or industry concerned. There is, as Bercusson put it in 1978:

no need to emphasize the irony entailed in the T.U.C.'s insistence on national agreements as the post-war fair wages standard . . . once again the legal instrument of protection was at variance with what it sought to achieve . . . [t]he nemesis of incompatibility with the industrial relations system was to dog the Fair Wages Resolutions to the end.[132]

The IAB attempted to circumvent this problem in *Crittal-Hope Ltd* v. *The Pay Board*, in which it applied section 2(b) of the Resolution (the 'general level') even though a national agreement existed under section 2(b).[133] Because the national agreement laid down only minimum rates these rates could not, according to the IAB, be regarded as the 'fair' rates to be applied under section 2(a). This approach was disapproved of by the High Court in *Racal Communications Ltd* v. *The Pay Board*[134] but the IAB stuck to its guns in subsequent decisions so as, according to one commentator, 'to maintain the long-term relevance of the resolution in an institutional context in which shop-floor negotiations were an all-important fact of industrial life'.[135]

The decision in *Crittal-Hope* went some way towards addressing the problem caused by wage drift. But it did not address all the problems associated with the 1946 Resolution. The emphasis in clause 1(a) upon the district meant that national agreements were not *per se* enforceable

---

[132] Bercusson, n. 26 above, pp. xxii–xxiii.   [133] 1974 Award No 3290.
[134] [1974] 3 All ER 263.
[135] Beaumont, n. 127 above, 38. Award 3300 of the IAB and in the CAC, *Kelvin Hughes and AUEW (Eng Section)* Award No 78. See also see Wood, n. 65 above, 68.

against all those employers operating in the industries covered: clause
1(a) did not render such agreements operative unless they were the product of bargaining between employers' organizations and unions representative of employers and workers *in the district* in which the employer
operated, and the standards had been established *in that district*. As
Bercusson pointed out:

the introduction of the national element by limiting agreements to those negotiated by organisations, as opposed to single employers and trade unions, was
severely curtailed by demanding a strict district emphasis. National agreements
were only applicable where they established district rates and satisfied the criterion
of representativeness in the district. Obviously, however, where the trade unions
did represent substantial proportions of workers in a trade or industry in a district
and had national agreements which determined rates for the district, they would
have had little need for a fair wages policy. It was the recognition and enforcement of nationally agreed standards, held to be 'fair' standards, on government
contractors that were sought, regardless of district rates or representatives.[136]

In 1964 the TUC condemned the Resolution as 'absolutely inadequate'
because of its 'weak wording' and 'flimsy text'.[137] Certainly, as we saw in
the text to notes 129–30 above, the success rate of claims under the
Resolution was very low (eleven out of a total of forty-nine excluding
complicitous claims). Among the problematic issues encountered by complainants were the precise scope of the 'industry' against whose nationally agreed or generally observed terms the employer's should be compared
(this was of particular concern in those contracting-out cases where contractor's terms were compared with those of other contractors in the field,
rather than those observed in the public sector); the definition of the 'district' within which clause 1(a) comparisons should be made; and the
extent to which terms other than those in dispute could be set off against
the disputed term in determining whether the employer's terms were 'less
favourable' than those nationally agreed or generally observed. In addition,
where claims under clause 1(b) (the 'general level') were concerned, enormous difficulties arose as a result of the IAB's failure to specify how this
level was to be calculated.[138]
The result of these shortcomings was that the Fair Wages Resolution
1946 had relatively limited impact on the wages even of those employees
engaged on government contracts. Where the Resolution might have proven
most useful—in cases where the government contracted out work to the
private sector (as occurred in the early 1970s with cleaning work)—its

---

[136] Bercusson, n. 64 above, 136. At 138 Bercusson claims that the district emphasis was
applied even to cl. 1(b) 'the general level' though not required by the legislation.
[137] 1964 *Annual Report* cited by Beaumont, n. 127 above, 38.
[138] Bercusson, n. 64 above, 144–5.

impact was severely undermined by the IAB's decision that the appropriate comparators for workers in the private sector firms were not firms within the office and factory cleaning industry, much less those government employees whose jobs had been contracted out but, rather, the contract cleaning industry.[139]

If complaints alone are considered the Fair Wages Resolutions appear to have affected the pay and conditions of a very small number of workers. But their impact is likely to have been considerably wider than this. To the extent that the Resolutions regulated the terms and conditions of workers in firms which entered into contracts with government departments, women, who were likely to enjoy less favourable terms than those of their male colleagues, would have gained some benefit. Equally, where a trade or industry was generally mixed or male-dominated but the workplace in respect of which a particular government contract was awarded was female-dominated, women should have benefited from the application of nationally agreed terms or, failing this, the 'general level' of terms observed by employers in the relevant trade or industry (assuming in the first case that the national agreement was observed in the district in which the workplace was situated and, in the second, that the female-dominated workplace would be regarded as sharing the same 'general circumstances' as those in which men predominated[140]). But where entire trades or industries were female-dominated, the Resolution would have done little to advantage women as (a) national bargaining (or, indeed, bargaining at any level) was less likely to be in place,[141] and (b) the level of terms generally observed within the relevant trade or industry was likely to be lower than those prevailing in male-dominated industries or trades.

It would appear that the bulk of questions raised under the Resolution concerned male workers. If a random sample is taken from the CAC's 1977 decisions, for example, ten of the fifteen questions raised[142] concerned workers who were identifiably either exclusively or mainly employed in predominantly male jobs (heavy engineering manual workers, for example;

[139] See Beaumont, n. 127 above, 39–40. Despite this, the IAB found against the employers in 5 of the 9 contract cleaning cases.

[140] See, e.g. the decision of the CAC regarding contract cleaning—if the situation then was similar to that prevailing today, contract cleaning was probably more predominantly female, as well as lower paid, than cleaning in general (see Ch. 2).

[141] This would equally apply when the trade or industry in a particular district was female-dominated, in which case the district would be less likely to have engaged in the bargaining from which any national agreement was produced, and such nationally agreed terms would be unlikely to be established within that district.

[142] Awards 84, 115, 137, 155, 168, 218, 167, 292, 313, 326, 331, 334, 348, 359, & 370. The sample was selected by taking every 8th award, arranged in alphabetical order, as listed in the CAC's *Annual Report 1977* (London: CAC, 1977). Award 334 was selected in the same manner for the sample of Sched. 11 complaints (see n. 165 below) but was added to the Fair Wages Resolution sample because it had been incorrectly categorized in the CAC report.

senior foremen engaged in the manufacture of mining equipment; draughts-men working in the shipbuilding industry; maintenance workers; engi-neers; and technical staff[143]). Of the other five questions raised, three included a substantial or unspecified number of clerical and administrat-ive staff[144] and two were made in respect of workers who may well have included a significant number of women.[145]

Other Wage-Fixing Mechanisms

Little can be said about the impact either of Order 1305 or of its imme-diate successor Order 1376, information on their implementation being sparse. But section 8 of the 1959 Act spawned more complaints than did the Fair Wages Resolution (171 between 1959 and 1972), of which 157 proceeded to judgment with a success rate of just over 50 per cent.[146] The success rate declined from almost 70 per cent in the years to 1964 to 40 per cent in 1965–72, this decline being attributed by Latta to a change in attitude by the IAB.

The difficulties experienced in relation to section 8 claims were fairly similar to those presented by the Fair Wages Resolution: of the seventy-one cases rejected by the arbitration tribunal, in twenty-one the union failed to establish that the workers were employed in the industry to which the collective agreement applied, in seventeen the employer established that the terms on which the workers were employed were 'no less fav-ourable' than those generally observed and in ten the union failed to prove that the employer was not observing the agreed terms.[147]

The operation of section 8 was, like that of the Fair Wages Resolution 1946, criticized on the grounds of its 'conservatism': its drive towards nationally agreed rates at a time when enterprise bargaining was becom-ing more common. The result of this was that section 8 caught not only those employers who were unaware of or unwilling to apply standards set out in the nationally agreed terms—because it was concerned with the observance of particular terms, employers could be found in breach of section 8 even when their (locally agreed) package of terms was more favourable overall than that nationally negotiated—but employers who sought uniform terms and conditions across large plants or multi-plant companies (constituent elements of which were located in different indus-tries) could be required to comply with different national agreements in respect of groups of workers within the plant or in respect of the various

---

[143] Awards 326, 292, 331, 370, 115, 137, & 168.   [144] Awards 84, 267, & 348.
[145] Award 359: design development, inspection, sales, and accounting staff engaged in the production of sound recording equipment, and Award 326: camera equipment produc-tion workers and administrative and clerical staff.
[146] G. Latta, 'The Legal Extension of Collective Bargaining: A Study of Section 8 of the Terms and Conditions of Employment Act 1959' (1974) 3 *Industrial Law Journal* 215, table 1, 218.
[147] *Ibid.* 221.

plants.[148] It was also criticized for its impact on the incomes policies adopted by the government in the 1960s. The IAB did not consider itself bound by the pay policies of the late 1960s in implementing section 8 and the Conservative policy of 1972–4 specifically exempted awards made under section 8 from its scope (although, see the text to note 151 below, the provision was effectively inoperative by this time[149]).

These criticisms are not of primary concern in a consideration of the impact of section 8 on wage differentials. Despite the relatively large number of complaints (in comparison with those under Order 1305 or 1376 or the Fair Wages Resolution), section 8 only directly benefited a small number of workers: of the 157 cases in which judgment was reached, 45 per cent concerned fewer than ten workers (17 per cent a single worker) and only six complaints were brought in respect of 500 or more workers.[150]

Nor did section 8 impact evenly in terms of industries. The overwhelming majority of section 8 complaints were brought on behalf of workers in the engineering and building industries, and no claims could be made in respect of workers in parts of the public sector in which wages were regulated by statute or, until 1971, in industries in which Wages Councils operated. The restriction regarding Wages Councils was removed by the Industrial Relations Act 1971 (which reconstituted the IC as the IAB), but this Act permitted only registered trade unions to bring claims under section 8. Since trade unions were very reluctant to register, section 8 became practically inoperative after 1971 (according to Latta, there was only a trickle of claims in 1972, and these from subsequently deregistered unions, and none in 1973[151]). No claims were received in 1974. Latta concluded in 1974 that 'the economic effect of section 8 was very small . . . around 8,000 [workers] were involved in a successful decision . . . where pay was directly involved the amounts of money were usually small. . . . Section 8 . . . did not even serve as an efficient means of bringing "undercutting" employers into line.'[152]

Section 8 revived somewhat after 1974 but was replaced in 1975 by Schedule 11 to the Employment Protection Act whose approach, permitting comparison with 'general levels' as well as with collectively agreed terms and conditions, was considerably wider. But Schedule 11 was not as wide in its scope as the Fair Wages Resolution—sections (a) and (b) of Part I of the Schedule applied in a strictly hierarchical order: in other

---

[148] The Donovan Commission focused on the first of these problems in criticizing the operation of s. 8 (para. 275). The Labour Government's 1970 Industrial Relations Bill amended s. 8 to require that CAC consider the whole package of terms) but Latta (n. 146 above, 229) suggested that the impact of s. 8 on uniformity of terms and conditions within plants was most problematic. The CAC's recognition of this issue resulted in its adoption of a more rigorous approach by the IAB to small groups of workers in the latter half of the 1960s.

[149] See Latta, n. 146 above.   [150] *Ibid*. 218.   [151] *Ibid*. 217.
[152] *Ibid*. 229–30.

words, where collectively agreed terms did exist, no recourse could be had to the 'general level' where the latter was more favourable. The government had sought to avoid the application of the IAB's approach in *Crittal-Hope* by providing that, where the collective agreement established minimum, as distinct from actual, rates, the minimum rates were to be applied for the purposes of Part I (a),[153] and the CAC's limited attempt to get around this restriction was quashed by the High Court in *R. v. CAC, ex p. Deltaflow*.[154]

This aspect of Schedule 11 was strongly criticized, in particular by Brian Bercusson, who pointed out that it left workers with national level agreements worse off than those who had none.[155] The latter could claim the 'general level' going in their district of the particular trade or industry in which they operated, whereas the former were restricted to the nationally agreed rates even if, in practice, these had been overtaken almost universally by local agreements.[156] The 'most serious criticism' of Schedule 11, he wrote in 1976, was that, 'far from escaping from the innate conservatism of section 8 . . . it still restricts its continuing and overriding concern for collective bargaining to multi-employer agreements, which in practice usually mean national agreements, without regard to their contents'.[157]

Large numbers of workers were excluded from the protection of Schedule 11 by clause 3, which provided that no claim could be made under Part I in relation to workers 'whose remuneration or terms and conditions is or are fixed (otherwise than by the employer, with or without the approval of any other person) in pursuance of any enactment' other than the Acts establishing Wages Councils and Agricultural Wages Councils or Schedule 11 itself. In *R. v. CAC, ex p. NWRHA*, the High Court ruled that this provision excluded from the scope of Schedule 11 ambulance workers whose terms and conditions, in common with those of NHS workers generally, were regulated by Whitley Council agreements. The exclusion operated because, under the National Health Service (Remuneration and Conditions of Service) Regulations 1974, the Secretary of State must approve the negotiated terms before they come into effect. Thus many public-sector employees whose terms were similarly regulated were denied the protection of Schedule 11.

[153] Para. 2(a) in addition, changed from the district emphasis in 1(a) to 'generally or in the district'—see Wood, n. 65 above, 69 and 364 HL Debs. (25 Sept. 1975), col. 529.

[154] [1977] IRLR 486, quashing the CAC's decision in *TGWU* v. *Deltaflow Ltd* (Award 236), in which the CAC ruled that the minimum rate established by a national collective agreement reached 2 years prior to the claim had been intended to be supplemented by plant level agreements and that, since this had not happened in the intervening period, it did not represent the true minimum rate, with the effect that Pt. I(b) applied.

[155] It also seriously impacted on efficacy against wage freezes of which 9/13 successful claims between 1970–4 inclusive under the Fair Wages Resolution had been examples (Bercusson, n. 64 above, 140–1).

[156] *Ibid.*   [157] Wood, n. 65 above, 73.

For all of these criticisms, Schedule 11 was massively more used than either the Fair Wages Resolution or section 8 of the 1959 Act. It was noted, above, that in the first twenty-two months of its existence almost 2,000 complaints were made to ACAS and, of these, two-thirds were referred to the CAC[158] (awards made by CAC in the first two years of Schedule 11's operation directly benefited over 50,000 workers and the vast bulk of these claims—82 per cent—concerned wages[159]).

But these benefits were not evenly distributed. Just as had been the case under section 8, complaints from the engineering industry accounted for a large proportion (45 per cent) of the whole.[160] Many of the claims (at least 35 per cent in 1977) consisted of attempts to get around the government's incomes policy rather than to improve the position of particularly low-paid workers (the CAC, like the IAB, refused to be bound by such policies).[161] According to one commentator: '[t]he exemption of C.A.C. awards from any scrutiny was an invitation to parties to use the provisions in order to "get around pay restrictions", allowing Schedule 11 to operate as a "safety-valve" for incomes policies'.[162]

The success rate under Schedule 11 was somewhat higher, at 58 per cent (68 per cent if partial successes are included), than that enjoyed under section 8.[163] But this success rate was distorted by the incomes policy-related claims which had a much higher success rate than other claims.[164]

What of the effect of these wage-fixing mechanisms on the gender–wage gap? Given the small number of workers involved, their concentration in predominantly male industries such as engineering, and the exclusion, for

---

[158] See Jones, n. 66 above, 28 for discussion.

[159] *Ibid.* 39—this despite the fact that 57% of awards related to 50 or fewer employees, 74% to 100 or fewer, and only 6% to at least 500. In common with the experience under the Fair Wages Resolution and s. 8 of the 1959 Act, complaints frequently gave rise to problems with the scope of the appropriate industry, the 'district' under cl. 2(b) and the question whether, if different, an employers' terms and conditions were nevertheless not 'less favourable' than those applied elsewhere. In addition, problems were experienced in this context, as in relation to the 1946 Fair Wages Resolution, in determining the 'general level' under cl. 1(b) where no claim was possible under cl. 1 (Sched. 11 had attempted to meet the problem of trade-offs between various terms and conditions by providing, (cl. 9) that 'regard shall be had to the whole of the terms and conditions observed by the employer as respects the workers to whom the claim relates' but the CAC interpreted this provision narrowly, considering 'the main terms such as basic pay, hours, holidays and overtime rates in isolation, unless there is evidence of a negotiated reduction in relation to one item in return for a compensatory increase in another'. See also Wood, n. 65 above, 78–9 on Awards 235, 202, & 165.

[160] Jones, n. 66 above, 33–4.

[161] J. Harris, 'Schedule 11 of the Employment Protection Act: An Analysis of the 1977 Awards' (1979) 10(1) *Industrial Relations* 51, 52—the CAC, like the IAB, refused to be bound by such policies. See also Wood, n. 65 above, 82 on the CAC in Award 89 '[t]he Committee . . . does not sit to decide what is, or is not, in accordance with current pay policy'. Nevertheless, recognition of cases involving complicity led the CAC to depart from IAB precedent by refusing necessarily to determine complaints solely on the evidence of the parties before it—see Wood, 68.

[162] Jones, n. 66 above, 42.   [163] *Ibid.* 36–7.

[164] Harris, n. 161 above, 54 and Jones, n. 66 above.

the most part, of the predominantly-female Wages Council and Whitley Council industries from the scope of their protection, it is difficult to imagine that either section 8 or Schedule 11 had much impact on the wages of women workers. Again, taking a random sample from the complaints heard by the CAC in 1977,[165] seventeen of the nineteen concerned male jobs such as road haulage drivers, fitters and operators; baggage handlers; printers; Port Authority police; production foundry workers; engineering foremen and manual workers; bricklayers; car production workers; metal manufacturing workers; civil engineers and manual mining workers; maintenance and technical workers.[166] Only two of the complaints raised related to any substantial degree to clerical and administrative workers or to light manufacturing workers.[167] If this sample is representative of the whole, Schedule 11 cannot have had any significant effect on the general level of women's wages (save to the extent that it disadvantaged them in relative terms by operating to the advantage of male groups of workers).

(D) CONCLUSIONS—MINIMUM WAGE REGULATION AND EQUAL PAY

What can we conclude from the British experience of minimum wage regulation? It is clear that such regulation can have a significant impact both upon the levels of wage dispersion in general and, in particular, on women's wages. Even in the UK context, there is substantial evidence that such wage regulation as did exist in the form of the Wages Councils did have an impact on the gender–pay gap in the industries in which they operated and, indirectly, on the gender–pay gap more generally. But it is equally clear that the method of minimum wage regulation chosen is very important to its success in reducing wage dispersion and the gender–pay gap. The same is true in respect of contract compliance and the wider regulation of terms and conditions of employment.

The approach adopted in the United Kingdom, both in terms of the various fair wages clauses and the statutory minimum wage, was far too narrow to impact significantly on economy-wide levels of wage dispersion and gender–pay gap. Between them, the Wages Councils and Agricultural Wages Boards never regulated the wages of more than a very small minority of workers and the impact of the various fair wages clauses (Orders

[165] Awards 269, 89, 200, 256, 243, 158, 250, 142, 351, 135, 77, 375, 122, 154, 180, 226, 85, 354, & 94. Again, the sample was drawn by taking every 8th award listed in alphabetical order in the CAC's *Annual Report 1977* (London: CAC, 1977), with the omission of Award 334 which was incorrectly categorized in the report as relating to Sched. 11 but which, in fact, concerned the Fair Wages Resolution.
[166] Respectively, Awards 180, 200, 89, 154, 142, 122 & 351 & 354, 85, 375, 77, 226 & 256, 269, & 334.
[167] Awards 135 & 158 respectively. The latter failed on the ground that the appropriate 'general level' to be applied was not, as the union argued, that prevailing in (the predominantly male) engineering sector.

1305 and 1376, section 8 and Schedule 11, as well as the Fair Wages Resolutions; those imposed by various local authorities as well as those discussed here) is impossible to determine, given the lack of monitoring of compliance with such clauses. Given the comments made above, however, it is unlikely that they had any significant effect on low-paid workers in general, or on the wages of women in particular.

The minima provided by the Wages Councils were widely flouted, generally poor, and applied only to particular industrial sectors (there being many low-paid workers scattered across other industrial sectors who were denied even the bare protection afforded by the Councils[168]). Fair Wages Resolutions and the various other wage-fixing mechanisms in place over much of the twentieth century only ever applied in practice, whatever the theory, to a handful of workers; benefited men for the most part; and, to a significant extent, assisted already relatively well-paid workers in their attempts to circumvent incomes policies rather than providing protection for the poorest. While the Wages Council Orders at least enjoyed some measure of pro-active enforcement by wages inspectors, the Fair Wages Resolutions and other mechanisms by which collectively bargained terms could be extended were dependent upon individual complaint or action taken by a small number of eligible trade unions or employers' organizations. To the extent that they were used, their benefit appears to have been enjoyed primarily by men. Even if the detail of the Resolutions and other provisions had been more satisfactory, there was no centralized mechanism by which the minimum standards set by collective bargaining could be generally enforced. This had the effect, similar to that noted in connection with Wages Council Orders, that those employees most in need of the protection afforded by the fair wages clauses were least likely to be in a position to benefit from it.

For all of the shortcomings of the peculiarly British approach to minimum wage regulation outlined in this chapter, however, there is little doubt that the implementation of minimum wage regulation, whether by means of the extension of collective agreements, as is the case in Germany and, de facto, in many of the Nordic countries, or a national or sectorally determined minimum wage, could have a significant effect on the salaries of the lowest-paid workers (mainly women) and, in turn, on the gender–pay gap. Our experience in the United Kingdom of the Trade Boards, Wages Councils, Fair Wages Resolutions, and various other extension arrangements should point out a number of pitfalls to be avoided in the implementation of any new minimum wage policy. The role which such regulation might play, its limitations and potential, are further considered in Chapter 10.

---

[168] See J. Marquand, 'Which are the Lower Paid Workers?' (1967) 5 British Journal of Industrial Relations 359.

[10]
Conclusion

I. INTRODUCTION

It is clear from Chapters 2 to 6 that the current position of women in the UK labour market—both in terms of their job status and prospects and their pay—cannot be considered satisfactory. Despite substantial progress over the last few decades women remain clustered at the bottom of the job hierarchy, vertically and horizontally segregated from men, and a significant gender–pay gap remains. Women of colour and those who work part-time are particularly disadvantaged, but no women fare as well as men who are equivalently qualified, trained, and employed. These remaining inequalities are, at least in part, the result of discrimination (both direct and indirect—the latter particularly where part-time work is concerned) and the situation is not set to improve given increasing deregulation, particularly in the public sector, and the ever more powerful impetus towards 'flexibility'.

Much has been made of the 'feminization' of the labour market and the increased opportunities open to women as the service sector, within which they are traditionally concentrated, expands. But 'feminization' can often be taken to indicate the downgrading of jobs in terms of status and pay, the much-vaunted new 'flexibility' operates, almost invariably, predominantly in the interests of employers rather than employees ('zero hours' contracts and shift working frequently spell instability and anxiety for workers unable to predict the size of their next pay cheque or to plan their time) and many of the new jobs created are of poor quality with low status, prospects, and pay. Again, this is particularly true in respect of part-time jobs which have, over the past three or four decades, accounted for the vast bulk of new female jobs created, a trend which looks set to continue. Men may, as the EOC reported recently, have accounted for the majority of those complaining to the Commission in 1995 about sex discrimination in recruitment, but typically the jobs for which men are not considered are those considered too boring, routine, badly-paid, and dead-end for anyone but women. By contrast, women tend to be discriminated against in recruitment to jobs with promotion prospects and relatively high rates of pay (see Chapter 5).[1]

[1] M. Curran, *Stereotypes and Selection: Gender and Family in the Recruitment Process* (London: HMSO, 1985), EOC Research Series—see Ch. 5 for discussion.

The question which must be addressed relates to how this persisting inequality may best be tackled. In Chapter 6 the role of improved anti-discrimination legislation was considered: such legislation is, no doubt, required and may be modelled along the lines of the existing Fair Employment Act 1989 (applicable only in Northern Ireland) or Ontario's recently scrapped Employment Equity Act—both pieces of legislation require positive action and monitoring of employees in terms, respectively, of their religion and their sex/colour, etc.). A system of contract compliance may also usefully be considered. Certainly, voluntary action by employers cannot be relied upon. Much has been made of the government-sponsored Opportunities 2000 initiative. But a study of a number of workplaces participating in the scheme found that 'equal opportunity had not been tackled in the United Kingdom in a way in which the necessary cultural and structural changes could be sustained'.[2] Hammond and Halton's study, which compared equal opportunities approaches in the United Kingdom with those in other European countries, the United States, Canada, and Australia, reported that:

- 'line managers tended to regard equality of opportunity to be in direct competition with the attainment of strategic goals';
- '[c]hampions for equal opportunities tended to have responsibility but little power';
- '[a]ttempts to change behavior were limited almost entirely to training for women, with little effort to amend the content or style of training more generally. U.S. companies typically used payment systems and promotion criteria to support behavior change, while Scandinavians opted for family-friendly policies. Neither were typically used in the U.K.'; and
- 'the development of women was perceived to be at the expense of men and, by inference, not in the best interests of the company. This last point seems to be linked to the scale of the investment which in the U.K. tended to be minute. Equal opportunity was rarely a senior appointment, but more typically part-time, low-priority work with little or no budget—the first place to make a cut.'[3]

But even if satisfactory equal opportunities legislation were to be adopted it is the case, as I concluded in Chapter 6, that such legislation can improve matters only in the very long term (many women already having chosen and trained in predominantly female occupations in which wages are held down by virtue of their predominantly female composition). Much of the disadvantage in terms of pay which is currently suffered by part-

[2] V. Hammond, and V. Holton, *A Balanced Workforce: Achieving Cultural Change for Women, A Comparative Study* (Berkhamsted: Ashridge Management Research Group, 1991).
[3] *Ibid.*

time workers could be remedied by integrating them more fully into the workforce to remedy the current situation whereby part-time workers are stuck in dead-end jobs for which they are over-qualified because employers will not permit 'proper' jobs to be done on a part-time basis. But again, this will do little to help the many women who, as a result of past discrimination, have long since suffered downward occupational mobility and are presently working in jobs which, while they may be beneath the educational or other qualifications of their incumbents, are nevertheless underpaid even taking into account their demands.

A further difficulty with the equal opportunities approach relates to the changing nature of the labour market. Although there is much to be said for the view that the apparent trend towards 'flexibilization' of the workforce serves merely to place white men in a similarly vulnerable position to that in which women and people of colour have traditionally laboured, it has been pointed out that traditional 'equal opportunities' approaches rely, to a significant extent, upon the internal labour markets generally regarded as typical of 'pre-flexible' employment.[4] If, for example, much employment is temporary, sub-contracted, or classified in terms of 'self-employment', severe difficulties arise in terms both of substantive law, information-gathering by prospective claimants, and the problem of proving discrimination by an employer (even if defined so as to capture the 'employer' of the nominally self-employed).

It is imperative, as a result, that an adequate approach to 'equal pay' be developed. The current UK legislative approach fails even in theory to address those pay disparities which arise between workplaces and, as we saw in Chapters 3 and 4, is so flawed as to be of extremely limited practical value even as against those discriminatory pay disparities which actually fall within its scope. But how might an alternative approach best be shaped? Chapters 7, 8, and 9 respectively considered a specific legislative approach aimed at gender–pay discrimination; a system under which high levels of centralized collective bargaining (this was the effect of the Australian tribunal system) resulted in a very low gender–pay gap; and a variety of approaches concerned with the regulation of minimum wages and employment standards. These chapters dealt with the various advantages and drawbacks of each particular model examined, and some of the factors raised will be mentioned again in the next section below. But it is useful here, in order to determine the role, if any, which such approaches might play in the United Kingdom, to take a more general look at some of the benefits and disadvantages, in terms of their impact on the gender–pay gap, of the broader legislative, collective bargaining, and minimum wage approaches to pay determination.

---

[4] This point was made by Alan Hyde at the Transformative Labour Law Conference held at the University of Kent at Canterbury, July 1996.

II. CHANGING THE GENDER–PAY GAP

(A) EQUAL PAY LEGISLATION

The primary shortcoming of any legislation directed specifically at the
gender–pay gap is that it fails to address issues of *substantive*, as opposed
to *relative*, justice. Even if legislation were to be drawn so as to require
the adjustment of wages on a proportional basis (rather than only after
an initial determination of equality—see further Chapter 7), equal pay
legislation will not, as a rule, prevent an employer from paying male and
female employees *equally* badly. Nor, in general, will it do anything to
combat wider issues of wage dispersion; increasing inequality (between
'core' and 'marginal' workers, 'skilled' and 'unskilled' workers, rather than
simply between men and women); the rising levels of exploitation resulting from the globalization of markets; and the drive towards an ever more
'flexible' workforce. This problem was particularly apparent in Ontario
during the implementation of the Pay Equity Act, Judy Fudge remarking that:

[i]t is precisely the current legislation's emphasis on equality of opportunity which
undermines its ability substantially to improve the working conditions of women
and other designated groups. Employment equity will do nothing to halt the shrink-
age in the share of employment in large firms and the increase in non-standard
employment. The chief problem with the legislation is that it ignores the fragmentation and feminization of the labour market.[5]

But the issue was not unique to the particular approach adopted by that
Act: US studies have shown that part of the decrease in the gender–pay
gap there over the last number of years has resulted from the decline in
male, rather than any rise in female, wages. One study estimated the proportion due to male decline to be in the region of 50 per cent.[6] Recent
evidence has also shown that women are 'swimming upstream' in the
United States and that their 'relative skills and the manner in which they
are treated in the work force will have to improve for the pay gap merely
to remain constant'.[7] Not only this, but a good part of the gender–pay
gap in the United States, as in the United Kingdom (see Chapter 8), is
attributable precisely to the large wage disparity which exists there: recent

---

[5] J. Fudge, 'Fragmentation and Feminization: The Challenge of Equity for Labour
Relations Policy' in J. Brodie (ed.), *Women and Canadian Public Policy* (Toronto: Harcourt
Brace, 1996).
[6] Testimony of H. Hartmann and S. Aaronson of the Institute for Women's Public Policy,
to the Capitol Hill Hearings regarding the Fair Pay Act 1994, 21 July 1994. See also F.
Blau and L. Kahn, *The Impact of Wage Structure on Trends in U.S. Gender Wage Differentials:
1975–87* (Washington, DC: National Bureau of Economic Research Inc. 1994), Working
Paper No 4748.
[7] Francine Blau and Lawrence Kahn, respectively, quoted in the *Harvard Business Review*
Sep./Oct. 1993.

estimates suggest that, whereas in the early to mid-1980s US women earned 67 per cent of men's pay, if the overall level of wage inequality in the United States had mirrored that in Australia, women's relative earnings would have been of the order of 80 per cent.[8] In Britain, as in the United States, the level of wage inequality is increasing, particularly in the wake of the Wages Councils' abolition in August 1993.[9] It is most unlikely, against this background, that equal pay legislation alone could make a great deal of impact.

The other issue which arises in respect of specific equal pay legislation is the apparent lack of fit between those countries which have implemented comprehensive equal pay legislation, and those in which the gender–pay gap is narrow. According to Gillian Whitehouse's recent survey of OECD countries, for example, many of those in which women earn relatively high wages (comparative to those of men) have only recently, if at all, implemented equal pay (or, indeed, equal opportunities) legislation. Whitehouse's survey reported that women in Denmark, Finland, Norway, Sweden, Australia, France, Germany, and the Netherlands earned more than 70 per cent of men's wages in 1980–8, women in the first four of these countries also having labour market participation rates of more than 70 per cent.[10] By contrast, women in the United Kingdom, the United States, Canada, Switzerland, and Japan earned less than 70 per cent of men's wages and had participation levels lower than 70 per cent.[11] While virtually all the countries surveyed had both equal pay and equal opportunities legislation by 1986, in 1975 only the United States and the United Kingdom had had both equal pay and equal opportunities legislation; Australia, Canada, France, Japan, and the Netherlands had equal pay (but not equal opportunities) legislation; Germany had equal opportunities (but not equal pay) legislation; and Denmark, Finland, Norway, Sweden, and Switzerland had neither.

Just as there seems to be no (or, if any, a negative) relationship between women's relative wages and the historical regulation of discrimination (particularly in the field of pay), so the same appears to be true in the present day. The European Commission's recently published *Memorandum on Equal Value* placed the United Kingdom at the bottom of the league of Member States in terms of women's relative wages—only women manual workers

[8] F. Blau and L. Kahn, 'The Gender Earnings Gap: Some International Evidence' (Washington, DC: National Bureau of Economic Research, 1992), Working Paper No 4224.

[9] For the US see L. Katz, G. Loveman, and D. Blanchflower, *A Comparison of Changes in the Structure of Wages in 4 O.E.C.D. Countries* (paper presented at the National Bureau of Economic Research Comparative Labour Markets Conference, Cambridge 1992)—now NBER *Working Paper No 4297*—(Cambridge, Mass.: NBER, 1993).

[10] G. Whitehouse, 'Legislation and Labour Market Gender Inequality: An Analysis of O.E.C.D. Countries' (1992) 6(1) *Work, Employment and Society* 65, fig. 1.

[11] Though the first three had near 70% wages and higher participation rates than some countries with higher than 70% wages.

UNIVERSITY OF WINCHESTER
LIBRARY

in Luxembourg and Ireland did worse, and then only marginally.[12] The *Memorandum* used statistics from 1990—table 8.1 shows that the position in the United Kingdom has deteriorated still further since then, only non-manual women workers in Luxembourg now trailing equivalent British women. Yet the United Kingdom's legislation relating to equal pay is in some respects the most sophisticated of any in Europe.[13] Italy, on the other hand, lacks any explicit mechanism by which equal pay claims can be made.[14] But in 1985 Italian women did relatively better than women anywhere else in the EC,[15] and in 1992 they were third as far as manual women workers were concerned, fourth overall.[16]

The failure of legislation specifically to require equal pay for work of equal value is common to Luxembourg, Spain, and Portugal as well as to Italy, despite the obligation imposed upon Member States by Article 119 of the EC Treaty to 'ensure and subsequently maintain the application of the principle that men and women should receive equal pay for equal work', Article 1 of Council Directive 75/117 (the Equal Pay Directive) stipulating that 'equal work' covers not only like work, but also 'work to which equal value is attributed' (see Chapter 1). In addition, by 1994, neither France nor Luxembourg, Greece nor Italy had seen any litigation in the equal value arena. Yet, although the gender–pay gap in Luxembourg is similar to that in the United Kingdom and in Ireland (both of which have explicit legislative commitments to equal pay for work of equal value); Greek, Spanish, Portuguese, and Italian women workers fare considerably better than their UK counterparts.[17]

It is clear that equal pay legisation is not sufficient to achieve a narrow gender–wage gap and that the existence of a high degree of regulation in the labour market, as is the case in Germany, or of flat-rate national wage increases designed to advantage lower-paid workers (as was the case in Italy during the 1970s and 1980s) can, even in the absence of any effective equal pay legislation, have a substantial impact on that gap.[18]

What does this tell us about the potential of specific equal pay legislation? First impressions might suggest that it is next to useless and that attention would be more profitably paid to the pursuit of other strategies designed to improve the wages of low-paid workers generally. If the

[12] See also J. Rubery, 'Pay, Gender and the Social Dimension to Europe' (1992) 30(4) *British Journal of Industrial Relations* 605, 610–11.

[13] British women have among the most favourable distribution (in terms of their concentration in relatively highly paid non-manual jobs) of women anywhere in the EC— Rubery, *ibid.*, thought this is not important here as the statistics for manual and non-manual workers are disaggregated.

[14] *Ibid.* 615–16.

[15] *Ibid.* Note this did not include a large number of atypical, mainly part-time, workers.

[16] Note the artificial nature of final statistics—see discussion of table 8.2.

[17] EC Commission, *Memorandum on Equal Pay for Work of Equal Value* (Brussels: EC Commission, 1994).

[18] See Rubery, n. 12 above, 614.

gender–pay gap results, to a large extent, from the wider pay disparity between low and highly paid workers, a strategy of reducing the earnings disparity will have a profound impact on women's relative underpayment, as well as on poverty pay more generally.

But such a conclusion would be over-hasty. While overall pay inequalities determine the absolute financial penalties on workers clustered at the bottom of the pay hierarchy, strategies aimed exclusively at the overall level of pay inequality do little to challenge women's position within the hierarchy. The fact that women's wages have increased, albeit very gradually, relative to those of men since 1983, while the overall levels of pay inequality have widened during that time, suggests that the existence of equal pay legislation has had some impact on the relative payment levels of men and women within the hierarchy.

The implementation of a national minimum wage or, indeed, the adoption of any other mechanism aimed at reducing the level of wage disparity across the board, would not be sufficient to address the gender–pay gap in its entirety. While women at the very bottom of the wage ladder are most urgently in need of improvements to their wages, women earn less than men right across the board. A minimum wage will do little to close the 13 per cent gap between men and women doctors, the 16 per cent gap between men and women accountants, the 23 per cent gap between male and female solicitors.[19] And even amongst the very poorly paid, when Wages Council minima were in force, women in the industries covered by them were far more likely to be paid at or around the minimum level than were men. In 1993, for example, manual women earned 83.4 per cent and non-manual women 76.4 per cent of men's hourly rate in Wage Council industries.[20] These figures were substantially better than those for the labour force as a whole (72 per cent and 67 per cent for manual and non-manual women respectively). But they are still far from indicating equality between men and women. And although a bottom limit on exploitation is better than none at all, there is no reason why women should have to put up with being paid less and exploited more than men.

Equal pay legislation may not in itself be sufficient to deal with the gender–pay gap, but it a necessary element in any solution. In any case, to remove the commitment to legislation specifically directed at the gender–pay gap would remove the potential for further change, quite apart from contravening the United Kingdom's obligations under EC and international law.[21] The shape that such legislation might take is considered after the text to note 61 below.

[19] NES 1995, tables 86 & 87.
[20] Pay Equity Project, *Equal Pay Now!*, Briefing paper for Pay Equity conference held in Leicester, 29 Jan. 1994. See generally Ch. 8.
[21] See discussion of EC legislation in Ch. 4, and ILO Equal Remuneration Convention No 100 (1951).

(B) COLLECTIVE BARGAINING

The experience in Australia suggests that collective bargaining can provide an effective way in which the gender–pay gap can be reduced. Australia cannot, given the extent to which its awards system depended upon third-party intervention into the collective-bargaining process, be regarded as typical of a 'collective bargaining' approach. But this conclusion is born out by the experience elsewhere in Europe (see Chapter 9).[22] However, the link between collective bargaining and the gender–pay gap is not entirely straightforward: in countries such as the United Kingdom, in which male and female (full-time) workers are equally likely to belong to trade unions, unionization has a greater upward impact upon men's than upon women's pay, with the effect that the overall result of unionization is to reduce women's pay.[23] A number of unions have recently been at the forefront of the struggle to improve women's wages, but much collective bargaining which takes place, particularly at the local level, leaves a great deal to be desired.[24]

Colling and Dickens' report *Equality Bargaining: Why Not?*, which was based on research carried out in the late 1980s, found 'among negotiators generally an unquestioning acceptance of the existing distribution of jobs and rewards' and, very important in our context, a view of the 'actual process of job evaluation . . . as a matter of technical expertise or management skills rather than negotiation'.[25] Negotiators were overwhelmingly male and:

where issues of particular importance to women are raised or female stewards attempt to push the interests of their members within male-dominated negotiations they risk being accused of sectionalism . . . serving men's interests and upholding existing structures and arrangements tended to be equated not with sectional concerns but with serving *members*' interests. Trade union negotiators . . . were often resistant to (and at times amused by) the idea that they might raise issues of particular importance to women . . . because they took the view that they were there to represent 'all the members', not men or women.[26]

---

[22] And negatively by the US and Japan. See also Whitehouse, n. 10 above, 75–6. The best countries (i.e. those in which both female participation rates and women's relative pay were over 70%) in 1985 had an average density of 76.4% as against a density of 30.1% in the worst countries (those having lower levels of both female participation and female pay).

[23] Although it increases the pay of those women who are unionized—according to one recent survey, by as much as 25%—P. Sloane, 'The Gender–Wage Differential' in A. Scott (ed.), *Gender Segregation and Social Change: Men and Women in Changing Labour Markets* (Oxford: OUP, 1994), 161.

[24] For a critique of unions' role in creating the gender–pay gap, in particular through their support for seniority payments, separate jobs, and the differential analysis of 'skill' in male and female jobs, see A. Forrest, 'Women and Industrial Relations Theory: No Room in the Discourse (1993) 48(3) *Industrial Relations* 409. In the UK context see T. Colling and L. Dickens, *Equality Bargaining: Why Not?* (London: HMSO, 1989), EOC Research Series.

[25] Colling and Dickens, n. 24 above, 22.   [26] *Ibid.* 33–4.

But for all of these criticisms, there is no doubt that unionization has a significant upward impact upon women's pay. The importance of trade union organization to the gender–pay gap appears to lie in the degree to which bargaining and, therefore, pay determination generally, is centralized. Whitehouse found that, where the level of centralization of wage determination was rated between one and ten for the OECD countries studied, those countries in which women fared best (both in terms of participation rates and pay) averaged a score of 8.7 as against the worst countries' (again, in terms both of participation rates and pay) average of 3.5.[27] Whitehouse reported a 'statistically insignificant . . . association between union density and the relative earnings of women'. But:

centralised wage fixation is . . . positively and strongly associated with the relative earnings of women, such that a change in institutional arrangements from the bottom to the top of the centralised wage fixation scale . . . would be associated with a change in the relative earnings of 16.8 percentage points. Even a small change of 2 units on the scale (equivalent, for example, to increasing the scale of industry wide bargaining) yields a rise in relative earnings for women of 3.36 percentage points.[28]

As Whitehouse points out, the average increase in women's relative earnings for women between 1974 and 1986 across the thirteen countries studied was a mere 3.2 per cent.

Rubery reports that women in Denmark and Italy saw their relative wages fall throughout the 1980s as those countries moved towards decentralized determination of wages.[29] Luxembourg combines decentralized wage fixation with a large gender–wage gap. By contrast, France, Portugal, the Netherlands, and West Germany all combine highly centralized collective bargaining with relatively narrow gender–wage gaps.

There is no doubt that unions have a very important role to play in the eradication of the gender–pay gap. But it is not sufficient simply to encourage collective bargaining at the enterprise level and to express the pious hope that those female workplaces which have previously proved so resistant to organization will somehow become more open to it. Some method must be found by which collective bargaining can be both encouraged and harnessed as a means by which women's pay, specifically, can be improved.

The importance of centralized pay determination to the impact of unionization on women's wages was mentioned in the text to notes 22–9 above. Not only does collective bargaining which takes place at the national or sectoral level benefit women workers, it also extends the coverage of collective bargaining generally and appears to render that coverage more stable than is the case with enterprise level bargaining. The relationship

[27] The top scoring countries were Denmark, Finland, Norway, and Sweden, those in which women earned more than 70% of men's wages but had participation levels lower than 70% were Australia, France, Germany, and the Netherlands, and those countries scoring poorly on both counts were the UK, the US, Canada, Switzerland, and Japan.
[28] Whitehouse, n. 10 above, 77–9.   [29] Rubery, n. 12 above, 281.

between the level at which bargaining takes place, the extent of coverage and of stability was highlighted by the OECD in its 1994 *Economic Outlook*. The OECD reported that the decline in collective bargaining coverage which occurred over the last few decades in the United Kingdom was associated with enterprise level bargaining and was more pronounced in Great Britain than in any of the other ten states studied (Australia, Canada, Finland, France, Germany, Japan, the Netherlands, Portugal, Spain, and the United States).[30]

The suggestion of any movement towards centralized pay determination might appear extraordinary in view of the current trend in the United Kingdom. But there is nothing particularly radical about such pay determination: according to the 1994 OECD figures some form of economy-wide bargaining took place in the early 1990s in Australia, Belgium, Finland, France, the Netherlands, Norway, Portugal, and (decreasingly) in Sweden and Spain while sectoral bargaining was common in Austria, France, Germany, the Netherlands, and Switzerland. Figure 10.1 reproduces the OECD's findings for coverage and levels of collective bargaining in a large number of industrialized economies in 1994.

(C) MINIMUM WAGE REGULATION

We saw in Chapter 9 that those European countries which regulated minimum wages (whether by legislative or administrative dictat or the extension of collectively agreed terms) tended to have smaller gender–wage gaps and, in particular, fewer very low paid women than is the case in the United Kingdom and in Ireland. But we also saw that the adoption of a national minimum wage is not a panacea: in particular, those countries such as Spain and Greece whose economies contain large informal sectors and which, as a result, have high levels of non-compliance.

The United Kingdom's own experience with minimum wages in the form of the Wages Council system was also marred by significant problems with compliance, most notably when it came to those sectors of the workforce (most notably, homeworkers, part-time, and women workers) who were among the least likely to be in a position to challenge their underpayment. The minima established by the Councils were very low indeed and, as we saw in Chapter 9, at times served to hinder rather than encourage wage inflation in the covered sectors. To the extent that the contract compliance system of the Fair Wages Resolutions and the collective agreement extension mechanism of Order 1305 and its successors

---

[30] Rubery, n. 12 above, 185. Of these countries, all but Canada, Japan, and the US had some degree of economy-wide or sectoral bargaining and the coverage in those 3 countries was extremely poor to begin with—OECD, *Economic Outlook 1994* (Paris: OECD, 1994), 170; S. Bazen and G. Benhayoun, 'Low Pay and Wage Regulation in the European Community' (1992) 30 *British Journal of Industrial Relations* 623.

Figure 10.1[31] — trade union density and collective bargaining coverage rates 1990

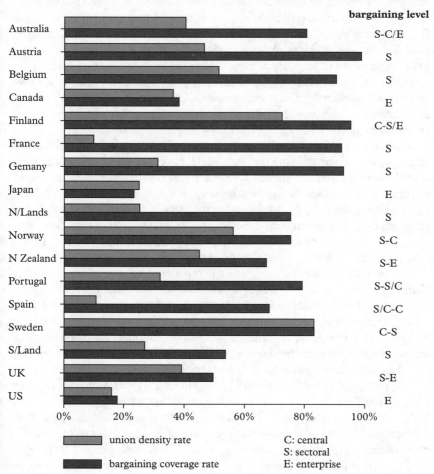

bargaining level

Australia	S-C/E
Austria	S
Belgium	S
Canada	E
Finland	C-S/E
France	S
Gemany	S
Japan	E
N/Lands	S
Norway	S-C
N Zealand	S-E
Portugal	S-S/C
Spain	S/C-C
Sweden	C-S
S/Land	S
UK	S-E
US	E

union density rate   C: central

bargaining coverage rate   S: sectoral

E: enterprise

source: OECD, *Employment Outlook 1994* (Paris: OECD, 1994). The figures for France, Germany, Japan, and Portugal are for 1985, 1992, 1989, and 1991 respectively.

can be regarded as forms of minimum wage regulation, they too suffered from poor enforcement mechanisms and the standards which they did impose were often inadequate.

Another significant problem with the UK approach, in common with that in the Netherlands, concerned the exclusion of many low-paid workers from entitlement to minimum wage protection. In the Netherlands, part-time workers are excluded from wage protection; in the United Kingdom

[31] S-C/E indicates change in the direction of centralized and enterprise bargaining from sectoral wage determination; S-E from sectoral to enterprise-level bargaining.

the Wages Council system operated only within particular sectors of the economy, working as it did on the assumption that, in those sectors where average pay was relatively high, there was no real problem with low wages. But low-paid workers are to be found throughout the economy, in highly paid industrial sectors as well as in those in which the low-paid predominate. Even the banking, insurance, and finance sector, which rates as the highest paid of all sectors, accounted in 1987 for 7 per cent of all low-paid male workers.[32] The same was true in respect of the Fair Wages Resolutions, which applied only to workers engaged in government contracts (later to all employees of firms so engaged) and, in practice, of the other wage regulation mechanisms which were enforced only in respect of a narrow range of workers. Adequate coverage of a minimum wage would require its extension to low paid workers wherever they are found. Of particular concern is the fact that, as a result of flawed enforcement mechanisms, the benefits afforded by the Wages Councils and other UK wage regulation mechanisms failed to reach many of those workers who were most in need of them (see Chapter 9). Regard must be had to this in the design of any system of minimum wage regulation.

The issues discussed above concern the detail of minimum wage regulation and enforcement, rather than the question whether such regulation is a useful mechanism in addressing the gender–pay gap. There is no doubt that such a mechanism can help to address the gap by providing a floor below which wages cannot fall and by helping the disproportionate number of women workers who comprise the poorest-paid workers.

Minimum wage regulation is necessary. But, as we have seen, it should not be regarded as sufficient—the provision of a base level for wages does little to regulate the distribution of wages (either in terms of their overall levels of dispersion or, more particularly, of their distribution as between women and men, workers of different racial groups). Nevertheless, the implementation of a minimum wage would have a significant impact on the United Kingdom's gender–pay gap. If such an approach is to be embraced, the form in which it is most likely to be widely recognized, and arguably therefore most easily enforced, consists of a single, national minimum figure. A contract compliance approach such as that used by the 1946 Fair Wages Resolution would, even if it were considerably improved, constitute only the most partial attack on the problem of low wages: while such a mechanism is to be welcomed as an additional means of enforcement, whether of minimum wage rates, anti-discrimination legislation, or any other employment standards, it cannot replace a comprehensive regulation of such standards.

---

[32] P. Brosnan and F. Wilkinson, *Cheap Labour; Britain's False Economy* (London: Low Pay Unit, 1987), cited by C. Barclay, *Low Pay and Wages Councils* (London: HMSO, 1987), House of Commons Library Research Division, Background Paper No 206, 2.

In 1991, using a national minimum wage figure of £3.40 per hour, Frank Wilkinson estimated that 20 per cent of female full-time and 50 per cent of female part-time workers (but only 7 per cent of full-time male workers) would benefit from a national minimum wage.[33] The most recently suggested figure is in the region of £4.15 an hour: if this is applied to 1995 wage statistics, 22.5 per cent of full-time manual women workers would see their wages rise by at least 65 pence per hour as would a similar proportion of all part-time women workers and almost 40 per cent of manual women working part-time.[34] A further 22 per cent of full-time manual women workers, together with around 10 per cent of full-time non-manual women workers and 20 per cent of part-time women workers (27 per cent of part-time manual women workers) would benefit to some extent from such a minimum as would over 10 per cent of male manual workers.[35]

A figure in the region of £4/£4.15 per hour is about half of the male median wage (the latter being calculated weekly and divided by the average number of hours worked by all). But the Low Pay Unit defines as 'low pay' any wage which is less than two-thirds of the male median, and the Council of Europe decency threshold is 68 per cent of the national average wage. If one of these standards were to be adopted as a minimum (and neither will be), the majority of women workers would see their wages increase. Taking the LPU figure of about £5.40 per hour and 1995 wage statistics, of the nine major occupational groups all but three (managerial and administrative, professional, and associated professional and technical) pay part-time women average hourly wages less than this figure,[36] and only these, together with the clerical and secretarial group of jobs, offer full-time women workers average hourly rates in excess of this figure. By contrast, men's hourly wages in every occupational group are above this minimum (though, in the case of 'other occupations', only barely so[37]).

There is no chance that a minimum wage will be pitched at anywhere near the £5.40 level, even though a Labour Government was elected in May 1997. Indeed, although the Labour Party in 1992 adopted a minimum wage formula based on the median male wage, it is at present committed only to the establishment of a Low Pay Commission which, it is envisaged, would set various minimum figures for different industrial

[33] F. Wilkinson, *Why Britain Needs a Minimum Wage* (London: Institute for Public Policy Research, 1992), 6.

[34] *The Times*, 2 Sept. 1995—this is reported as having been adopted by the TGWU and the GMB.

[35] NES 1995, table 95. Figs. are given for hourly earnings less than £4 and £4.60, and the estimate for £4.15 is reached by increasing the £4 per hour figure proportionate with the rate of increase in the number of workers earning below the various sums. See tables 1 and 178 of the NES 1994.

[36] At £5.40, calculated as two-thirds of the median male hourly rate.

[37] £5.42 in 1994.

sectors. Given that party's efforts, in both 1995 and 1996, to deter the TUC from naming a figure in the region of £4.15, it will be interesting to see what kinds of figures eventually emerge. Not even the Low Pay Unit itself is seriously pushing for a figure in excess of £5.00: according to *The Times* the Unit 'admits that would be disruptive and would settle for an initial half' of the median.[38]

The establishment of a national minimum wage may, as yet, appear an unlikely prospect. But even if a sectoral approach is taken, minima pitched at around half of male median earnings would be a major improvement on the current position, in particular for women. The Low Pay Unit calculates that such a rate, if established as a single minimum, would raise the wages of four million workers, 70 per cent of them women.[39] The danger with sectoral minima is that the lowest-paying sectors, in which most of the potential beneficiaries of a national minimum wage are located, would be precisely those sectors in which the minima would be pitched at a lower rate and their benefit, as a result, denied to many of the four million who would otherwise see their wages rise.

Whether a minimum wage is set at a national or sectoral level, it is vital that the minimum or minima are applied to the broadest possible extent if the gender–pay gap is to be tackled effectively. In particular, there must be no exceptions for small workplaces, domestic employment, or the employment of homeworkers. Small workplaces are disproportionately the employers of women, and women are more likely than men to work in their own and in other people's homes. These women are amongst the lowest paid of all and, certainly at present, the least likely to benefit from any legislation specifically directed to *unequal*, as opposed to *low*, pay. Not only would they be hard pressed to find any male co-workers with whom to compare their jobs and wages for the purpose of an equal pay claim, but many are denied even the status of employees. And while the Equal Pay Act requires only that the claimant is 'employed under a contract of service or of apprenticeship or a contract personally to execute any work or labour'[40] (encompassing, therefore, even homeworkers who frequently do not qualify as 'employees' for the purposes of the Employment Protection (Consolidation) Act 1978 (EP(C)A), now replaced by the Employment Rights Act 1996[41]), the inability of such workers to claim unfair dismissal must act as a disincentive for all but the most determined—the victimization protection provided in respect of equal pay claims is far from satisfactory.[42] In any case, homeworkers will

[38] *The Times*, 5 Jan. 1995.   [39] *Ibid.*   [40] EPA, s. 1(6)(a).
[41] See *O'Kelly* v. *Trust House Forte plc* [1983] IRLR 369; *Nethermere (St Neots) Ltd* v. *Taverna and Gardiner* [1984] IRLR 240.
[42] For the shortcomings of victimization protection see the decision of the CA in *Aziz* v. *Trinity Street Taxis* [1988] ICR 534—the decision is made under the Race Relations Act but the protection afforded under the Sex Discrimination Act (which applies also to victimization related to equal pay claims) is the same.

not generally be able to point to appropriate male comparators—even if they do have the information upon which to choose a comparator, they are most unlikely to be employed under the same terms and conditions as men in a factory run by the same employer. It goes without saying, therefore, that minimum wage legislation should apply to those not currently defined as 'employees' but who, nevertheless, exchange their labour for payment other than in the clearest cases of arm's length independent contracting.

One of the fears most frequently expressed regarding the implementation of a national minimum wage relates to its perceived threat to jobs: this, indeed, was the UK government's principal articulated reason for abolishing the Wages Councils and is the primary reason relied upon by business opponents of a national minimum wage. It also lies behind the Labour Party's refusal to commit itself to a single national figure, as opposed to sectoral minima. But the jury is still very much out on the question of the extent to which the minimum wage will damage employment prospects. One study in California found that increases in the minimum wage there actually increased employment,[43] and the research that suggests large negative impacts upon employment tends, as Bazen and Benhayoun have pointed out, to be based 'on the assumption that wage differentials above the minimum wage will be substantially restored'.[44] This, they pointed out: 'amounts to saying that firms have no say in the wage determination process and are not committed to containing costs'.[45] Those authors, together with Craig and others in 1982, estimate much more modest job losses than those commonly threatened. According to Craig et al.:

the aim of minimum wage protection would be to ensure that no one is paid below some minimum socially acceptable level of wages. In general people do not have a notion of customary differentials, and certainly not of a 'fair' differential, vis-à-vis low paid workers, and indeed most are probably unaware that anyone is paid at such low levels. Thus, although the inflationary possibilities of the price and relative wage effects of minimum wages cannot be denied, it is unlikely that they would be of any great significance.[46]

Jobs will probably be lost in the short term but, to take Deakin and Wilkinson's argument (see Chapter 6), the removal from the market of those firms which have to pay very poor wages in order to survive will

---

[43] D. Card, *The Effects of Minimum Wage Legislation; A Case Study of California 1987–89* (Princeton, NJ: Princeton University Press, 1990), Industrial Relations Sector Discussion Paper No 278 cited in Bazen and Benhayoun, n. 30 above.
[44] N. 30 above, 632.   [45] *Ibid.*
[46] C. Craig, J. Rubery, R. Tarling, and F. Wilkinson, *Labour Market Structure, Industrial Organisation and Low Pay* (Cambridge, CUP, 1982), 132. See also R. Dickens, P. Gregg, S. Machin, A. Manning, and J. Wadsworth, 'Wages Councils: Was There a Case for Abolition?' (1993) 31 *British Journal of Industrial Relations* 515; and C. Barclay, *Wage Flexibility and Employment Creation* (London: House of Commons Library Research Division, 1988), Background Paper No 208, for review of the material.

benefit more efficient firms which are able to compete other than by relying on poverty wages, and will also reduce the extent to which government is required to subsidize the inefficient to the detriment of investment in, for example, research and development designed in the long term to encourage high-wage jobs in expanding product markets. Certainly, the very poor wages in the British manufacturing industry (relative to France, Germany, and the United States) did nothing during the 1980s to advantage that industry against its international competitors. According to one commentator, '[w]e would expect to find more labour-intensive techniques in the UK, which often means older machinery, and that finding is partly borne out. This has not resulted in improved performance and profitability but rather in a series of chronic problems'.[47]

What is true as regards the minimum wage is true also in relation to other mechanisms of wage regulation, such as the centralized Australian model and, more specifically, equal pay programmes. Many economists (together with the Australians themselves) have associated Australia's economic difficulties (and, in particular, the problem of unemployment) with its centralized pay determination. Figures recently published in *Gender, Work and Organisation* appear to give the lie to this, at least in comparison with the United Kingdom.[48] Between 1979 and 1993, the proportion of UK women and men in employment rose and fell respectively by 18 per cent and 8 per cent. Women in full-time employment increased by 5 per cent and in part-time employment by 37 per cent. In Australia, women's employment increased by 52 per cent in the same time, men's by 14 per cent. The proportion of women in full-time employment increased by 36 per cent, and those in part-time employment by 83 per cent. These figures cast some doubt on the common notion that decentralization of pay and the dismantling of employee protection is the way to tackle the problem of unemployment.[49]

Research in the United States into the employment effects of various 'comparable worth' policies has also given an encouraging picture as regards the effect of improved women's wages on female employment rates. Just as Zabalza and Tzannatos found little or no negative impact on female employment in the wake of the Equal Pay Act 1970,[50] so Kahn found significant female growth (while male employment in the same jobs remained static) in the aftermath of the 'pay equity' process carried out in the Californian municipality of San José in the 1980s.[51] The growth, which

[47] Barclay, n. 46 above, 9.

[48] L. Hunter and S. Rimmer, 'An Economic Exploration of the U.K. and Australian Experiences' (1995) 2 *Gender, Work and Organisation* 140.

[49] For a traditional economist's view of centralized pay determination see S. Rhoads, *Incomparable Worth* (Cambridge: CUP, 1993).

[50] A. Zabalza and Z. Tzannatos, *Women and Equal Pay: The Effects of Legislation on Female Employment and Wages* (Cambridge: CUP, 1985).

[51] S. Kahn, 'Economic Implications of Public Sector Comparable Worth: The Case of San José, California (1992) 31(2) *Industrial Relations* 270.

Kahn attributed to the combined effect of 'comparable worth' (pro-active equal pay for work of equal value) and 'pro-female hiring policies' took place predominantly in those jobs which were targeted for comparable worth increases although women also increased their share of non-targeted jobs.

III. CONCLUSION

What is being put forward as an effective response to the gender–pay gap in particular and, more generally, to the problem of serious and increasing levels of inequality in the labour market, is a three-pronged approach. We have seen that the gap results in part from the sheer size of the wage disparity between the best and the worst paid workers, coupled with women's concentration in the United Kingdom, as elsewhere, at the bottom of the wage hierarchy. The first step towards tackling the gender–pay gap must consist of improving the lot of the most disadvantaged, male and female, by means of a minimum wage. A single national figure is to be favoured, not only in the interests of equality but also because of the extent to which it eases enforcement problems. But whether a national or sectoral approach is embraced, the level of the minimum or minima is crucial. The figures which tend to be put forward in the United Kingdom are very low indeed: the Wages Councils were setting minima as low as 34 per cent of the average male earnings by the late 1980s (see Chapter 9) and 31.2 per cent in 1993[52], and the figure most recently favoured by the TUC was, as we saw in the text to notes 33–5 above, around half the male wage. Perhaps the most significant problem with the sectoral approach favoured by the Labour Party is that, given the role which it is envisaged that employers will play in their selection, the figures may be set at levels akin to the Wages Council minima.

The figure(s) chosen will in the end, and whether by action or default, be a matter for political compromise. But it is worth noting that the current levels in other EU states such as Belgium, France, Greece, the Netherlands, Portugal, and Spain are between 60 and 77 per cent of the median wage (an average of 67 per cent of the median). On current UK figures this would work out at a level of well over £5.00 per hour. In addition, the ILO's Recommendation No 30 (which accompanies Convention No 26 which, it is to be hoped, would be re-ratified in the event of a change of government in the United Kingdom) requires that, in determining the minimum rates of wages, 'the wage fixing body should in any case take account of the necessity of enabling the workers concerned to maintain a suitable standard of living'.[53] In 1967 the ILO's Committee of Experts interpreted this to require that the wage be fixed at a rate:

[52] NES 1993, table 1.   [53] Para. 34.

408 Just Wages for Women

considered sufficient to satisfy the vital necessities of food, clothing, housing, education and recreation of the worker, taking into account the economic and cultural development of each country. In some cases the needs of the family are also taken into account in the same manner as those of the worker, and in other cases they are covered by family allowances and other measures of social security.[54]

The second issue which needs to be considered, in relation to the matter of a national minimum wage (whether that wage were to be set by the executive or, as currently looks more likely, by a Low Pay Commission) is that of enforcement. The Wages Inspectorate was never adequate to the task required of it: criticism was voiced of the low numbers of inspectors by Dorothy Sells as early as the 1930s and, as was pointed out in Chapter 9, those whose under-payment was most difficult to police were the very workers who were most in need of protection.[55] Consideration will have to be given to more effective enforcement mechanisms and, in particular, to the argument that a single nationally-applicable figure would prove easier in terms of worker awareness of any under-payment.[56]

Even if the minimum wage were set at a generous level (this being very unlikely in the foreseeable future) and to be adequately enforced, the minimum wage approach can only form the beginning of any equal pay strategy. We saw in Chapters 2 and 6 that the gender–wage gap exists at the level of the well-paid as well as the disadvantaged. Women doctors earn less than their male colleagues, women social workers and probation officers less than male environmental health officers. The establishment of a minimum wage, however it is structured, will do nothing to attack these wage disparities. Nor will it do anything to encourage or enable workers to put themselves in the position where a change of government is capable of dismantling the protection afforded by the minimum wage.

In order to address these issues, action is needed both on the collective bargaining and specifically on the equal pay front. The approach adopted to the latter can depend, in large part, on the structures established to deal with the former, and it is to collective bargaining that we now turn once more.

We saw above and in Chapter 8 that collective bargaining generally has an upward impact on women's relative wages. We also saw that enterprise-level action is insufficient as a measure by which the gender–pay gap might be reduced: not only does centralization play a much greater role than unionization *per se* in improving women's wages, but the major differences in unionization rates between workplaces (in particular, the difficulties

---

[54] M. Gunderson, *Comparable Worth and Gender Discrimination: An International Perspective* (Geneva: ILO, 1994), 84–5—at worst in the US it led to slower job growth, rather than absolute decline: 1992 ILO report, para. 100.

[55] See P. Beaumont, 'The Extent of Compliance with Minimum Wage Regulations: The West of Scotland' (1978) 9(2) *Industrial Relations* 4, discussed in Ch. 9.

[56] See discussion about the difficulties of Wages Council orders' complexity in Ch. 9.

associated with organizing predominantly female workplaces as well as those in which ethnic minority workers are concentrated) renders any such policy very high-risk for women. Much of the wage inequality between women and men, full-time and part-time workers, ethnic minority and white workers, arises at the inter-workplace level. In other words, although there is evidence of the inequitable distribution of wages within particular firms, there is also evidence that women and part-time workers in particular and, most probably, ethnic minority workers, are concentrated in workplaces in which low wages are a problem generally. It is vital that this inter-workplace inequality is not lost sight of in seeking to reduce the gender–wage gap.

How might centralized collective bargaining be encouraged? The Australian approach utilized tribunals which were given the final responsibility for wage fixation and whose rulings were binding upon trade unions, employers, and employees; Scandanavian countries have traditionally opted for national-level collective bargaining; Denmark, Greece, and Portugal for occupational bargaining at the national scale (thereby leaving differentials between workers in the same firms largely unaffected) while industry-level bargaining is common in Belgium, France, Spain, Germany, Italy, and the Netherlands.[57]

What approach might be taken in the UK context? National-level bargaining is increasingly uncommon here in the wake of almost two decades of government-led drive towards local wage determination, primarily at the dictat of the employer. Despite the international acceptability of national and sectoral bargaining arrangements, Deakin and Ewing point out the hostility with which UK employers regard bargaining other than at the enterprise level (and often even then) and suggest the establishment of sectoral employment commissions.[58] If wages were fixed at a sectoral level, this would be a tremendous advance for the many women concentrated in small, poorly-paying workplaces. What is perhaps significant here is, as we saw in Chapter 2, that women's pay is not held down by virtue of the (broad) sectors in which they work—in 1994, for example, banking, insurance, and finance, etc. and 'other services' employed 59 per cent of all women workers and ranked second and third (in terms of the average wages of *all* employees) of the nine industrial sectors then listed; and men accounted for a lower proportion (37 per cent as against women's 59 per cent) of the three top paying industries (energy and water supply; banking, finance, and insurance, etc., and other services). If wages

[57] J. Rubery and C. Fagan, 'Equal Pay Policy and Wage Regulation Systems in Europe' (1994) *Industrial Relations Journal* 281, 284—these 6 countries also have various degrees of enterprise-level bargaining.

[58] S. Deakin and K. Ewing, 'Inflation, Economic Performance and Employment Rights' in J. Michie and J. Grieve-Smith (eds.), *Managing Without Unemployment* (Oxford: Clarendon Press, forthcoming).

were fixed at a sectoral level, the concentration of women workers within predominantly female, currently very low paying, workplaces would cease to exert such a powerful downward influence on their pay.

The very existence of centralized wage regulation would, on the evidence of Australia and elsewhere, tend to operate so as to improve women's wages and reduce the gap between them and men. But it should not be regarded as sufficient—Jill Rubery and Colette Fagan remark that the '[n]ational systems of job grading' which frequently form a part of such determination 'are inherently conservative and there may be considerable problems in achieving any changes in job grading'.[59] If centralized bargaining or other wage determination were simply to be imposed on the existing position (even if this were to entail a standardization of wage rates for particular jobs, however narrowly defined, across workplaces within or across industrial sectors), those jobs whose wages are currently held down by virtue of their being predominantly female would be slotted further down in the hierarchy than might otherwise be justified. And once that hierarchy had been constructed it might, as Rubery and Fagan warn, prove very difficult to change.

Any movement towards centralized pay determination (whether on a national or a sectoral level) will require a rethinking of the place which particular jobs currently hold in the hierarchy of wages. The very standardization of wage rates across workplaces should itself serve to improve women's wages (concentrated, as they currently tend to be, in relatively low-paying workplaces) and, in particular, to increase the wages of ethnic minority workers. But regard must also be paid to the differences which arise between predominantly male and female jobs at the more general level (e.g. to the large pay gaps between predominantly female probation officers and social workers and predominantly male civil engineers; between (female) speech, occupational and physiotherapists and male environmental health officers[60]). The major strides towards equal pay which took place in Australia between the mid-1970s and the early 1980s were achieved even absent any requirement that male and female jobs be compared in terms of skill, effort, responsibility, etc., and paid equally on the basis of these features. If such centralized pay determination was coupled with an attempt to rationalize the pay differentials between male and female jobs (in terms of the work 'value', however determined, rather than in terms of *traditional* 'value' hierarchies), the potential would be enormous indeed.

Finally, the role of 'equal pay' legislation must be considered. Chapters 3 to 5 highlight the problems with the existing legislative models, and

---

[59] Rubery and Fagan, n. 57 above, 287–8.
[60] NES 1995, tables 86 & 87.

Chapters 2 and 6 bear witness to the failures of both the Sex Discrimination and the Equal Pay Acts. Consideration of how the former Act might be amended is beyond the scope of this book, but some discussion of possible amendments to the Equal Pay Act will be attempted. The proposals set out here mirror in large part those recently made by the Institute of Employment Rights (IER) in *Working Life: A New Perspective on Labour Law*.[61]

The first point which can be made concerns the individual/collective model. Whereas it might be possible simply to amend the Equal Pay Act in order to entitle similar workers to reap the benefits of an individual woman's equal pay claim, the impact of such a change would be relatively minor, confined in practice to women (and men) doing exactly the same work as the successful applicant. Nor would such an approach avoid the potential for victimization by employers or the inhibiting effect that fear of such victimization has on potential equal pay applicants.

Group actions permit individual claimants to share the risk and, if successful, the benefits of equal pay claims. But they still require employees to initiate legal action without imposing any obligations upon employers to examine their pay structures for evidence of discrimination, much less to do anything to eliminate any such discrimination.

It has been argued in earlier chapters that pay structures still bear the marks of discrimination; that women are still paid on the basis of their sex; that old attitudes about the 'family wage' for men and 'pin money' for women die hard. Part of the pay difference between men and women does result from men's working longer hours. Another part of it may be explained by men's having greater levels of education, skill, or experience relevant to the jobs they do. But there is powerful evidence (see Chapter 6) to support the argument that men are paid more because they are men, that the gender–pay gap is attributable to differential returns to human capital, rather than to any substantial differences in the amount of human capital possessed by men and women; that what is considered 'education', 'skill', and 'relevant experience' depends upon whether its possessor is male or female. The same is true as between white workers and those from ethnic minority groups. Such differences are catered for, at least in so far as they apply between women and men and between jobs of *equal* value (as opposed to those in respect of which payment is simply disproportionate to value) under the existing Equal Pay Act. But in practice, the Act's utility is severely constrained by the many flaws discussed in Chapters 3 and 4.

Much more effective than the individual or group action approach

[61] K. Ewing (ed.), *Working Life: A New Perspective on Labour Law* (London: Institute of Employment Rights and Lawrence & Wishart, 1996).

would be the institution of a specifically collective legislative approach to the issue of equal pay. Rather than requiring workers individually to challenge their pay and/or conditions to an industrial tribunal, the collective model would give a body (preferably, in the light of its experience in this matter, the CAC) responsibility for examining collective agreements for discriminatory effect (whether these agreements covered entire sectors, as above or, in the absence of such sectoral agreements or in the event of gaps in their coverage, individual workplaces). The body would take account of those differences which arise between white and ethnic minority workers and, where sectoral employment commissions were in place, their orders too could be referred (indeed, would for preference be referred by them before promulgation) to the body for 'equality-proofing'. To the extent that workplaces which were not covered by collective bargaining continued to exist, pay structures could also be referred. In order to achieve the maximum utility from the system, the power to refer should be widely drawn (being available to trade unions, employers, and individual workers affected by the agreement) and individual complaints should be permitted to be made under the cloak of anonymity.

The IER proposals further suggest the retention of an individual right of complaint to the (suggested replacement of the) industrial tribunal which would be obliged to refer all equal value claims to the CAC but which could, after the CAC's determination of the issue, award compensation to the individual. The CAC would be obliged to consider the *proportional* undervaluation of jobs, as well as the relationship between *equally* valuable male and female jobs (or jobs with male and female incumbents, or incumbents of different racial groups, or, in contrast with the existing legislation, jobs done by black women and those done by other workers) and would have regard to the wider employment market as well as to the individual workplace in determining the appropriate wage for any particular job. The result of a CAC award would be to amend the collective agreement or pay structure.

If equal pay legislation were to be amended along these lines, coupled with an appropriately pitched minimum wage and a drive towards more centralized pay determination (with a specific view to the remedying of traditional undervaluation of female jobs), the gender–pay gap in the United Kingdom and the under-payment of workers of colour could really begin to dissolve away. Some sex inequality would remain, and will continue to do so for as long as men and women share unequal burdens of domestic and childcare responsibility. But the improvement of women's wages would itself do much to address this wider inequality: if women were not so underpaid, relative to men, the 'choice' of which parent takes primary responsibility for childcare would perhaps be more neutral as between men and women and the change in pattern of both men's and women's employment would do much to undermine the wider discrimination which persists against women in the workforce. It would also do much to enable fathers to spend more time with their children and to alleviate the intolerable burden of poverty which is frequently the lot of those women and children who live in one-parent families.

Bibliography

ALDRICH, M., and BUCHELE, R., *The Economics of Comparable Worth* (Cambridge, Mass.: Ballinger Publishing Co., 1986)

AMES, L., 'Fixing Women's Wages: The Effectiveness of Comparable Worth Policies' (1995) 48(4) *Industrial and Labor Relations Review* 709

AMSDEN, A. (ed.), *The Economics of Women and Work* (Harmondsworth: Penguin, 1980)

ANDERSON, G. (ed.), *The White Blouse Revolution: Female Office Workers Since 1980* (Manchester: Manchester University Press, 1988)

ARMSTRONG, E., 'Minimum Wages in Fully Employed City' (1966) 4 *British Journal of Industrial Relations* 22

—— 'Wages Councils, Retail Distribution and the Concept of the Cut-off' (1970) 1 *Industrial Relations Journal* 9

ARMSTRONG, P., 'If Its Only Women's Work It Doesn't Matter So Much' in WEST, J. (ed.), *Work, Women and the Labour Market* (London: Routledge and Kegan Paul, 1982)

ARROW, K., 'The Theory of Discrimination' in ASHENFELTER, O., and REES, A. (eds.), *Discrimination in Labour Markets* (Princeton, NJ: Princeton University Press, 1973)

—— 'Economic Dimensions of Occupational Segregation: Comment I' (1976) 1(3) *Signs* 233.

ARTHURS, A., 'Equal Value in British Banking: The Midland Bank Case' in KAHN, P., and MEEHAN, E. (eds.), *Equal Value/Comparable Worth in the U.K. and the U.S.A.* (Basingstoke: Macmillan, 1992)

ASHIAGBOR, D., 'The Intersection Between Gender, "Race" and Class in the Labour Market', paper presented at the Transformative Labour and Employment Law: Democratic Perspectives in a Changing World conference at Rutherford College, University of Kent, 6–8 July 1996

BANKS, R., 'Wages Councils and Incomes Policy' (1967) 5 *British Journal of Industrial Relations* 338

BARBEZAT, D., *Equality for Women in Employment: An Interdepartmental Project* (Geneva: ILO, 1993)

BARCLAY, C., *Low Pay and Wages Councils* (London: HMSO, 1987), House of Commons Library Research Division, Background Paper No 206

—— *Wage Flexibility and Employment Creation* (London: HMSO, 1988) House of Commons Library Research Division, Background Paper No 208

BAYLISS, F., *British Wages Councils* (Oxford: Blackwell, 1962)

BAZEN, S., 'On the Employment Effect of Introducing a National Minimum Wage in the U.K.' (1990) 28(2) *British Journal of Industrial Relations* 215

—— and BENHAYOUN, G. 'Low Pay and Wage Regulation in the European Community' (1992) 30(4) *British Journal of Industrial Relations* 623

BEAUMONT, P., 'Experience Under the Fair Wages Resolution of 1946' (1977) 8(3) *Industrial Relations* 34

—— 'The Extent of Compliance with Minimum Wage Regulations: The West of Scotland' (1978) 9(2) *Industrial Relations* 4

BECKER, G., *The Economics of Discrimination* (Chicago, Ill.: University of Chicago Press, 1957).

—— 'Investment in Human Capital: A Theoretical Analysis' (1962) 70(5) (II) *Journal of Political Economy* 9

—— 'Human Capital, Effort, and the Sexual Division of Labour' (1985) 3(I) (2) *Journal of Labor Economics* S.33

BELLER, A., 'Trends in Occupational Segregation by Sex and Race, 1960–1981' in RESKIN, B. (ed.), *Sex Segregation in the Workplace: Trends, Explanations, Remedies* (Washington, DC: National Academy Press, 1984)

BENNETT, L., *Making Labour Law in Australia: Industrial Relations, Politics and Law* (Melbourne: The Law Book Company, 1994)

—— 'Workplace and Enterprise Bargaining; the Legislative and Institutional Framework' (1994) 36(2) *Journal of Industrial Relations* 191

BERCUSSON, B., 'The New Fair Wages Policy: Schedule 11 to the Employment Protection Act' (1976) 5 *Industrial Law Journal* 129   ·

—— *Fair Wages Resolutions* (London: Mansell, 1978)

BERGMANN, B., 'The Economic Case for Comparable Worth' in HARTMANN, H. (ed.), *Comparable Worth: New Directions for Research* (Washington, DC: National Academy Press, 1985)

—— *The Economic Emergence of Women* (New York: Basic Books, 1986)

—— 'Does the Market for Women's Labor Need Fixing?' (1989) 3(1) *Journal of Economic Perspectives* 43

BEVAN, S., and THOMPSON, M., *Merit Pay Performance Appraisal and Attitudes to Women's Work* (Brighton: University of Sussex, 1992), Institute of Manpower Studies Report No 234

BHAVNANI, R., *Black Women in the Labour Market: A Research Review* (Manchester: EOC, 1994)

BIELBY, W., and BARON, J., 'A Woman's Place Is with Other Women: Sex Segregation Within Organizations' in RESKIN, B. (ed.), *Sex Segregation in the Workplace: Trends, Explanations, Remedies* (Washington, DC: National Academy Press, 1984)

BLACK, D., 'Discrimination in an Equilibrium Search Model' (1995) 13(2) *Journal of Labor Economics* 309.

BLACKBURN, M., and BLOOM, D., *Changes in the Structure of Family Income Inequality in the U.S. and other Industrial Nations during the 1980s*

(Cambridge, Mass.: National Bureau of Economic Research, 1994), NBIR Working Paper No 4754

BLACKBURN, S., 'The Problem of Riches: From Trade Boards to a National Minimum Wage' (1988) 19(2) *Industrial Relations Journal* 124

BLANCHFLOWER, D., 'Union Relative Wage Effects: A Cross-section Analysis using Establishment Data' (1984) 22(3) *British Journal of Industrial Relations* 311.

—— and CORRY, B., *Part-time Employment in G.B.: An Analysis Using Establishment Data* (London: HMSO, 1987), Department of Employment Research Paper No 57

—— and ELIAS, P., *The Occupations, Earnings and Work Histories of Young Adults—Who Gets the Good Jobs?* (London: HMSO, 1989), Department of Employment Research Paper No 68

BLANPAIN, R. (ed.), *Flexibility and Wages a Comparative Treatment* (Deventer: Kluwer Law and Taxation, 1990), *Bulletin of Comparative Labour Relations* No 19 (special edition)

BLAU, F., *Equal Pay in the Office* (Lexington, Mass.: D. C. Heath, 1977)

—— 'Occupational Segregation and Labour Market Discrimination' in RESKIN, B. (ed.), *Sex Segregation in the Workplace: Trends, Explanations, Remedies* (Washington, DC: National Academy Press, 1984)

—— 'Gender and Economic Outcomes: The Role of Wage Structure' (1993) 7(1) *Labour* 73

—— and BELLER, A., 'Trends in Earnings Differentials' (1988) 41(4) *Industrial and Labor Relations Review* S. 13

—— and FERBER, M., *The Economics of Women, Men and Work* (Eaglewood Cliffs, NJ: Prentice Hall, 1986)

—— and JUSENIUS, C., 'Economists' Approaches to Sex Segregation in the Labor Market: An Appraisal' in BLAXALL, M., and REAGAN, B. (eds.), *Women in the Workplace: The Implications of Occupational Segregation* (Chicago, Ill.: University of Chicago Press, 1976)

—— and KAHN, L., *The Impact of Wage Structure on Trends in U.S. Gender Wage Differentials: 1975–87* (Cambridge, Mass: National Bureau of Economic Research, 1994), NBIR. Working Paper No 4748

—— and KAHN, L., *The Gender Earnings Gap: Some International Evidence* (Cambridge Mass.: National Bureau of Economic Research, 1992), NBIR Working Paper No 4224; also in R. FREEMAN, and L. KATZ (eds.), *Differences and Changes in Wage Structures* (Chicago Ill: University of Chicago Press, 1995)

BLAXALL, M., and REAGAN, B., *Women in the Workplace: The Implications of Occupational Segregation* (Chicago, Ill.: University of Chicago Press, 1976)

BOOTHBY, D., *The Determinants of Earnings and Occupation for Young Women* (New York: Garland Publishing Inc., 1984)

BOSCH, G., DAWKINGS, P., and MICHON, F. (eds.), *Times are Changing: Working Time in 14 Industrialised Countries* (Geneva: ILO, 1993)

BRAH, A., ' "Race" and "Culture" in the Gendering of Labour Markets: South Asian Young Muslim Women and the Labour Market' (1993) 19(3) *New Community* 38

—— and SHAW, S., *Working Choices: South Asian Women and the Labour Market* (London: Department of Employment, 1992), Research Paper No 91)

BRANNEN, J., and MOSS, G., 'Dual Earner Households' in BRANNEN, J., and WILSON, G. (eds.), *Give and Take in Families: Studies in Resource Distribution* (London: Allen and Unwin, 1987)

—— and MOSS, P., *Managing Mothers: Dual Earner Households after Maternity Leave* (London: Unwin Hyman, 1991)

—— Mészáros, G., MOSS, P., and POLAND, G., *Employment and Family Life: A Review of Research (1980–1994)* (London: Employment Department, 1994)

—— and WILSON, G., *Give and Take in Families: Studies in Resource Distribution* (London: Allen and Unwin, 1987)

BREUGEL, I., 'Sex and Race in the Labour Market' (1983) 32 *Feminist Review* 49

—— 'Labour Market Prospects For Women from Ethnic Minorities' in LINDLEY, R. (ed.), *Labour Market Structures and Prospects for Women* (Manchester: EOC, 1994)

BRISKIN, L., and McDERMOTT, P., *Women Challenging Unions: Feminism, Democracy and Militancy* (Toronto: University of Toronto Press, 1993)

BROWN, C., *Black and White in Britain* (London: Policy Studies Institute, 1984)

BROWN, D., and McCOLGAN, A., 'U.K. Employment Law and the I.L.O.; The Spirit of Co-operation?' (1992) *Industrial Law Journal* 265

BROWN, J., '*Why Don't They Go to Work? Mothers on Benefit* (London: HMSO, 1989) Social Security Advisory Committee Research Paper No 2

BUCHANAN, J., and CALLUS, R., 'Efficiency and Equity at Work: The Need for Labour Market Regulation in Australia' (1993) 35(4) *Journal of Industrial Relations* 515

BURCHELL, B., and RUBERY, J., 'Divided Women: Labour Market Segmentation and Gender Segregation' in SCOTT, A. M. (ed.), *Gender Segregation and Social Change: Men and Women in Changing Labour Markets* (Oxford: OUP, 1994)

BURTON, C., *Gender Bias in Job Evaluation* (Canberra: Australia Government Publishing Service, 1988), Affirmative Action Agency Monograph No 3

—— *Redefining Merit* (Canberra: Australia Government Publishing Service, 1988), Affirmative Action Agency Monograph No 2

—— HAG, R., and THOMPSON, G., *Women's Worth: Pay Equity and Job Evaluation in Australia* (Canberra; Australian Government Publishing Service, 1987)

CCH, INDUSTRIAL LAW EDITORS in consultation with PUNCH, P., *Law of Employment in Australia* (New South Wales: CCH Australia Ltd, 1989)

CENTRAL STATISTICAL OFFICE, *Social Focus on Women* (London: HMSO, 1995)

CENTRAL YOUTH EMPLOYMENT EXECUTIVE, *Choosing Your Career: Choice of Careers No. 1* (London: National Youth Employment Council, Office of Information and Department of Employment, 1971)

CAMPBELL, A., *The Industrial Relations Act* (London: Longman, 1971)

CASEY, B., LAKEY, J., and WHITE, M., *Payment Systems: A Look at Current Practice* (Sheffield: Department of Employment, 1992), Research Paper No 5

CHAMBERS, G., and HORTON, C., *Promoting Sex Equality: The Role of Industrial Tribunals* (London: Policy Studies Institute, 1990)

CHAPMAN, B., and MULVEY, C., 'An Analysis of the Origins of Sex Differences in Australian Wages' (1986) 18 *Journal of Industrial Relations* 504

CHIPLIN, B., and SLOANE, P., *Sex Discrimination in the Labour Market* (London: Macmillan, 1976)

—— and —— *Tackling Discrimination in the Workplace* (Cambridge: Cambridge University Press, 1982)

CLARK, A., *Diaries* (London: Weidenfeld & Nicholson, 1993)

CLARK DICKINSON, Z., 'Men's and Women's Wages in the U.S.' (1943) 47 *International Labour Review* 693

CLARK, J., and WEDDERBURN, K. W., 'Modern Labour Law: Problems, Functions and Policies' in WEDDERBURN, K. W., LEWIS, R., and CLARK, J. (eds.), *Labour Law and Industrial Relations: Building on Kahn-Freund* (Oxford: Clarendon Press, 1983)

COCKBURN, C., *Brothers* (London: Pluto Press, 1983)

COLLING, T., and DICKENS, L., *Equality Bargaining: Why Not?* (London: HMSO, 1989), EOC Research Series

COLLINS, H., 'Equal Pay for Work of Equal Value' (1987) 16 *Industrial Law Journal* 196

COLLINSON, D., *Barriers to Fair Selection: A Multi-Sector Study of Recruitment Practices* (London: HMSO, 1988), Equal Opportunities Commission Research Series

—— KNIGHTS, D., and COLLINSON, M., *Managing to Discriminate* (London: Routledge, 1990)

COMMISSION FOR RACIAL QUALITY (CRE), *The Race Relations Code of Practice in Employment: Are Employers Complying?* (London: CRE, 1989)

COMMISSION ON INDUSTRIAL RELATIONS, *Report No 89: Retail Distribution* (London: HMSO, 1974).

COOK, A., LORWIN, V., and KAPLAN DANIELS, A., *The Most Difficult Revolution: Women and Trade Unions* (Ithaca, NY: Cornell University Press, 1992)

CORCORAN, M., 'The Structure of Female Wages' (1978) 68(2) *American Economic Review* 165

—— 'Work Experience, Labour Force Withdrawals and Women's Wages: Empirical Results Using the 1976 Panel of Income Dynamics' in LLOYD, C., ANDREWS, E., and GILROY, C. (eds.), *Women in the Labor Market* (New York, Columbia University Press 1979)

—— DUNCAN, G., and PONZA, M., 'Work Experience, Job Segregation and Wages' in RESKIN, B. *(ed.)*, *Sex Segregation in the Workplace: Trends, Explanations, Remedies* (Washington, DC: National Academy Press, 1984)

COURT, G., *Women in the Labour Market* (Brighton: Institute of Employment Studies, 1995), Report No 294

COUSSINS, J., *The Equality Report* (London: NCCL, 1976), Rights for Women Unit

COX, G., *Working Women: A Study of Pay and Hours* (Manchester: Greater Manchester Low Pay Unit, 1989)

COYLE, A., 'Sex and Deskilling in the Organisation of the Clothing Industry' in WEST, J. (ed.), *Work, Women and the Labour Market* (London: Routledge & Kegan Paul, 1982)

CRAIG, C. 'Towards National Job Evaluation? Trends and Attitudes in Britain and the Netherlands' (1977) 8(1) *Industrial Relations* 23

—— GANSEY, E., and RUBERY, J., *Payment Structures in Small Firms: Women's Employment in Segmented Labour Markets* (London: HMSO, 1985), Department of Employment Research Paper No 48

—— RUBERY, J., TARLING, R., and WILKINSON, F., *Labour Market Structure, Industrial Organisation and Low Pay* (Cambridge: Cambridge University Press, 1982)

CREIGHTON, W., 'Enforcing the Sex Discrimination Act' (1976) 5 *Industrial Law Journal* 42

—— *Working Women and the Law* (London: Mansell, 1979)

—— FORD, W., and MITCHELL, R., *Labour Law Materials and Commentary* (Sydney: The Law Book Company, 1983)

CROMPTON, R., 'Occupational Trends and Women's Employment Patterns' in LINDLEY, R. (ed.), *Labour Market Structures and Prospects for Women* (Manchester, EOC, 1994)

—— and JONES, G., *Deskilling and Gender in Clerical Work* (London: Macmillan, 1984)

—— and SANDERSON, K., 'The Gendered Restructuring of Employment in the Finance Sector' in SCOTT, A. M. (ed.), *Gender Segregation and Social Change: Men and Women in Changing Labour Markets* (Oxford: OUP, 1994)

CURRAN, M., *Stereotypes and Selection: Gender and Family in the Recruitment Process* (London: HMSO, 1985), EOC Research Series

CURTHOYS, A., 'Equal Pay, A Family Wage, or Both?' in CAINE, B., GROSZ, E., and de LEPERVANCHE (eds.), *Crossing Boundaries: Feminisms and Critiques of Knowledge* (Sydney: Allen & Unwin, 1988)

DALE, A., and GLOVER, J., *An Analysis of Women's Working Patterns in the U.K., France and the U.S.A.* (London: HMSO, 1990), Department of Employment Research Paper No 75

DANIEL, W., and MILLWARD, N., *Workplace Industrial Relations in Britain: The E.D./P.S.I./E.R.S.C. Survey* (London: Heinemann Educational, 1983)

DAVID, M., and STARZEC, C., 'Women and Part-time Work: France and Great Britain Compared' in FOLBRE, N., BERGMANN, B., AGARWAL, B., and FLORO, M. (eds.), *Issues in Contemporary Economics: Volume 4, Women's Work in the World Economy* (New York, New York University Press, 1992)

DAVIES, P., 'The Central Arbitration Committee and Equal Pay' [1980] *Current Legal Problems* 170

—— and FREEDLAND, M., *Labour Law: Text and Materials* (2nd edn., London: Weidenfeld & Nicholson, 1986)

DE BURCA, G., 'Giving Effect to European Community Directives' (1992) 55 *Modern Law Review* 219

DEAKIN, S., and EWING, K., 'Inflation, Performance and Employment Rights', in MICHIE, J. and GRIEVE-SMITH, J. (eds.), *Managing Without Employment* (Oxford: Clarendon Press, 1997), forthcoming

—— and MORRIS, G., *Labour Law* (London: Butterworths, 1995)

DEERY, S., and PLOWMAN, D., *Australian Industrial Relations* (2nd edn., Sydney: McGraw-Hill, 1985)

DEPARTMENT OF EMPLOYMENT, *Equality for Women* (London: HMSO, 1974), Cmnd. 5724

—— *Race Discrimination* (London: HMSO, 1975), Cmnd. 6234

—— *Wages Councils: 1988 Consultation Document* (London: Department of Employment, 1988)

—— *Resolving Employment Rights Disputes: Options for Reform* (London: HMSO, 1994), Cm 2707

DEPARTMENT OF LABOUR AND NATIONAL SERVICE, *Equal Pay: Some Aspects of Australian and Overseas Practice* (3rd edn., Melbourne: Department of Labour and National Service, 1968)

DEX, S., *Women's Occupational Mobility: A Lifetime Perspective* (Basingstoke: Macmillan, 1987)

—— *Women's Attitudes Towards Work* (Basingstoke: Macmillan, 1988)

DICKENS, L., JONES, M., WEEKES, B., and HART, M., *Dismissed: A Study of Unfair Dismissal and the Industrial Tribunal System* (Oxford; Blackwell, 1985)

DICKENS, R., GREGG, P., MACHIN, S., MANNING, A., and WADSWORTH, J., 'Wages Councils: Was There a Case for Abolition? (1993) 31 *British Journal of Industrial Relations* 515

DISNEY, R., GOSLING, A., and MACHIN, S., 'British Unionism in Decline: Determinants of the 1980s Fall in Union Recognition' (1995) 48(3) *Industrial and Labor Relations Review* 403

DOERINGER, P., and PIORE, M., *Internal Labour Markets and Manpower Analysis* (Lexington, Mass.: DC. Heath, 1971)

DOLTON, P., MAKEPEACE, G. and INCHLEY, G., *The Early Careers of 1980 Graduates* (London: HMSO, 1990), Department of Employment Research Paper No 78

DRACHE, D., *Getting on Track: Social Democratic Strategies for Ontario* (Kingston: McGill-Queen's University Press, 1992)

DRAGO, R., 'The Extent of Wage Discrimination in Australia' (1989) 15(4) *Australian Bulletin of Labour* 313

DRAKE, C., and BERCUSSON, B., *The Employment Acts 1974–1980 with Commentary* (London: Sweet & Maxwell, 1981)

EQUAL OPPORTUNITIES COMMISSION, *Review of the Training Opportunities Scheme* (Manchester: EOC, 1978)

—— *Equality Between the Sexes in Industry: How Far Have We Come?* (Manchester: EOC, 1978)

—— *Equal Pay . . . Making it Work* (Manchester: EOC, 1989)

EATON, S., *Women Workers, Unions and Industrial Sectors in North America* (Geneva: ILO, 1992)

EDGEWORTH, F., 'Equal Pay to Men and Women for Equal Work' (1992) 32 *Economic Journal* 431

—— 'Women's Wages in Relation to Economic Welfare' (1923) 33 *Economic Journal* 487

EDWARD, R., REICH, M., and GORMAN, D., *Labor Market Segmentation* (Washington, DC: Heath, 1975)

EHRENBERG, R., 'Empirical Consequences of Comparable Worth' in KILLINGSWORTH, M. (ed.), *Comparable Worth: Analyses and Evidence* (New York: New York School of Industrial and Labor Relations, Cornell University, 1989)

ELIAS, P., 'Part-time Work and Part-time Workers: Keeping Women In or Out?' in McRAE, S. (ed.), *Keeping Women In: Strategies to Facilitate the Continuing Employment of Women in Higher Level Occupations* (London: Policy Studies Institute, 1990)

ELLIS, E., 'A Welcome Victory for Equality' (1988) 51 *Modern Law Review* 781

EMPLOYMENT GAZETTE, 'Ethnic Origins and the Labour Market', February 1991, 59.

—— 'Lone Parents and the Labour Market: Evidence from the Labour Force Survey', November 1992, 559.

—— 'Ethnic Origins and the Labour Market', February 1993, 25.

—— 'Part-time Employment and Attitudes to Part-time Work', May 1993, 213.

—— 'Estimating Britain's Ethnic Minority Populations Using the L.F.S.', September 1993, 429.

—— 'Trends in Pay Flexibility', September 1993, 405.

—— 'Ethnic Groups and the Labour Market', May 1994, 147.

—— 'Trade Union Membership and Density 1992–93', June 1994, 189.

—— 'The Flexible Workforce and Patterns of Working Time in the U.K.', July 1994, 239.

—— 'Working Parents: Trends in the 1980s', October 1994, 343.

—— 'Women and Training: Data from the Labour Force Survey', November 1994, 391.

—— 'Mothers in the Labour Market', November 1994, 403.

—— 'Trade Union Recognition: Data From the 1993 L.F.S.', December 1994, 441.

—— 'Patterns of Pay: Results from the 1994 N.E.S.', December 1994, 453.

—— 'Part-time Working in Great Britain—an Historical Analysis', December 1994, 473.

—— 'Highly Qualified Women', March 1995, 115.

—— 'Trade Union Membership and Recognition: Data from the 1994 L.F.S.', May 1995, 191.

—— 'An Analysis of Working Time 1979–1994', May 1995, 211.

—— 'Membership of Trade Unions Based on Information from the Certification Officer', May 1995, 205.

—— 'Ethnic Groups and the Labour Market: Analyses from the Spring 1994 L.F.S.', June 1995, 251.

ENGLAND, P., 'The Failure of Human Capital Theory to Explain Occupational Sex Segregation' (1982) 17(3) *Journal of Human Resources* 358

—— 'Wage Appreciation and Depreciation: a Test of Neoclassical Economic Explanations of Occupational Sex Segregation' (1984) 62(3) *Social Forces* 726

—— FARCAS, G., KILBOURNE, R., and DOU, T., 'Explaining Occupational Sex Segregation and Wages: Findings From a Fixed Effects Model' (1988) 53(4) *American Sociological Review* 544

EQUAL OPPORTUNITIES REVIEW, 'Changes to Sex Equality Law Proposed by the EOC', 19, 18.

—— 'The Employment Act and Equal Opportunities: An EOR Guide', 29, 27.

—— 'Contract Compliance Assessed', 31, 26.

—— 'EC Recommendation and Sexual Harassment Code', 41, 38.

—— 'The Rising Cost of Injury to Feelings', 41, 30.

—— 'Compensation Awards: Employers Pay More for Race and Sex Bias', 49, 11.

—— 'Government Responds to EOC Proposals for Reforming the SDA', 52, 29.

—— 'Job Advertising and the SDA', 52, 12.

—— 'Paternity Leave', 55, 14.

—— 'Employment Forecasts for Women to the Year 2000', 56, 20.

—— 'Taking the Cap off Discrimination Awards', 57, 11.

—— 'Equal Value Update', 58, 11.

—— 'The Gender Impact of Compulsory Competitive Tendering', 61, 19.

—— 'EOC Issues Draft Pay Code', 61, 25.

—— 'EOC Issues Part-Timers Guidance', 63, 37.

—— 'Maternity Arrangements '95: Part 1', 63, 8.

—— 'Maternity Arrangements '95: Part 2', 64, 11.

—— 'Flexible Working: The Impact on Women's Pay and Conditions', 65, 19.

—— 'The Rising Cost of Discrimination', 67, 13.

—— 'Contract Compliance in the 1990s', 354, 11.

ERMISCH, J., and WRIGHT, R., 'Differential Returns to Human Capital in Full-time and Part-time Employment' in FOLBRE, N., BERGMANN, B., AGARWAL, B., and FLORO, M. (eds.), *Issues in Contemporary Economics: Volume 4, Women's Work in the World Economy* (New York: New York University Press, 1992)

EVEN, W., and MACPHERSON, D., 'The Decline of Private Sector Unionism and the Gender Wage Gap' 28(2) *The Journal of Human Resources* 279

EWING, K. D., *Britain and the I.L.O.* (London: Institute of Employment Rights, 1995)

—— (ed.), *Working Life: A New Perspective on Labour Law* (London: Institute of Employment Rights and Lawrence & Wishart, 1996).

EYRAUD, F. (ed.), *Equal Pay Protection in Industrialised Market Economies: In Search of Greater Effectiveness* (Geneva: ILO, 1993)

FIELD, F., and WINYARD, S., *Low Wages Councils* (Nottingham: Institute for Workers' Control, 1975)

FIELDS, D., and MORRISON, K., 'Comparable Worth: the Next Step to Pay Equity Under Title VII' (1985) 62 *Denver University Law Review* 417

FIELDS, J., and WOLFF, E., 'The Decline of Sex Segregation and the Wage Gap, 1970–80' (1991) 26(4) *Journal of Human Resources* 608

FLETCHER, J., and GILL, S., 'Union Density and Women's Relative Wage Gains' in FOLBRE, N., BERGMANN, B., AGARWAL, B., and FLORO, M. (eds.), *Issues in Contemporary Economics: Volume 4, Women's Work in the World Economy* (New York: New York University Press, 1992)

FOLBRE, N., BERGMANN, B., AGARWAL, B., and FLORO, M. (eds.), *Issues in Contemporary Economics: Volume 4, Women's Work in the World Economy* (New York: New York University Press, 1992)

FORD, I., 'Women's Wages' in ROBERTS, M., and MIZUTA, T., *The Exploited: Women and Work* (London: Routledge/Thoemmes Press, 1993)

FORREST, A., 'Women and Industrial Relations Theory: No Room in the Discourse' (1993) 48(3) *Industrial Relations* 409

FRIDMAN, G., *The Modern Law of Employment* (London: Stevens and Sons, 1963)

FUCHS, V., *Women's Quest for Economic Equality* (Cambridge, Mass.: Harvard University Press, 1988)

—— 'Women's Quest for Economic Equality' (1989) 3(1) *Journal of Economic Perspectives* 25

FUDGE, J., 'Fragmentation and Feminization: The Challenge of Equity for Labour Relations Policy' in BRODIE, J. (ed.), *Women and Canadian Public Policy* (Toronto: Harcourt Brace, 1996)

GHOBADIAN, A., and WHITE, M., *Job Evaluation and Equal Pay* (Policy Studies Institute) (London: Department of Employment, 1986), Research Paper No 58

GOLDIN, C., *Understanding the Gender Gap* (New York: Oxford University Press, 1991)

—— *The U Shaped Female Labor Force Function in Economic Development and Economic History* (Cambridge, Mass.: National Bureau of Economic Research, 1994), NBIR Working Paper 4707

GORDON, P., WRIGHT, J., and HEWITT, P., *Race Relations Rights* (London: NCCL, 1982).

GOSLING, A., MACHIN, S., and MEGHIR, C., *What Has Happened to Wages?* (London: Institute of Fiscal Studies, 1994), Commentary No 43

GRAHAM, C., and LEWIS, N., *The Role of A.C.A.S. Conciliators in Equal Pay and Sex Discrimination Cases* (Manchester: EOC, 1985)

GRAHAM, H., 'Being Poor: Perceptions and Coping Strategies of Lone Mothers' in BRANNEN, J., and WILSON, G. (eds.), *Give and Take in Families: Studies in Resource Distribution* (London: Allen and Unwin, 1987)

GREEN, F., 'Sex Discrimination in Job-Related Training' (1991) 29(2) *British Journal of Industrial Relations* 295

GREEN, R., 'Wages Policy and Wage Determination in 1993' (1994) 36(1) *Journal of Industrial Relations* 108

GREENWOOD, J., 'On the Abolition of Wages Councils' (1972) 3(4) *Industrial Relations* 30

GREGG, P., and MACHIN, S., *Is the Glass Ceiling Cracking? Gender Compensation Differentials and Access to Promotion Among U.K. Executives* (National Institute of Economic and Social Research, 1993), Discussion Paper No 50

—— and —— *Is the U.K. Rise in Inequality Different?* (London: National Institute of Economic and Social Research, 1993), Discussion Paper No 45

—— and WADSWORTH, J., *More Work in Fewer Households* (National Institute of Economic and Social Research, 1994), Mimeo Discussion Paper No 72

GREGORY, J., *Discrimination, Employment and the Law* (London: LSE, 1985: PhD thesis)

—— *Trial by Ordeal: A Study of People who Lost Equal Pay and Sex Discrimination Cases in the Industrial Tribunals During 1985 and 1986* (London: HMSO, 1989)

GREGORY, R., and DUNCAN, R., 'The Relevance of Segmented Labor Market Theories: The Australian Experience of Equal Pay for Women' (1981) 3 *Journal of Post Keynesian Economics* 403

—— and HO, V., *Equal Pay and Comparable Worth* (Canberra: Australian National University, 1985), Centre for Economic Policy Research, Discussion Paper No 123

GUNDERSON, M., 'Descrimination, Equal Pay and Equal Opportunities in the Labour Market' in RIDDELL, W. (ed.), *Work and Pay: The Canadian Labour Market* (Toronto: University of Toronto Press, 1985)

—— 'Male–Female Wage Differentials and Policy Responses' (1989) 27 *Journal of Economic Literature* 46

—— *Comparable Worth and Gender Discrimination: An International Perspective* (Geneva: ILO, 1994)

GUTEK, B., STROMBERG, A., and LARWOOD, L. (eds.), *Women and Work: An Annual Review* (III) (Newbury Park, Cal.: Sage Publications, 1988)

GWARTNEY-GIBBS, P., 'The "Rusty Skills" Hypothesis' in GUTEK, B., STROMBERG, A., and LARWOOD, L. (eds.), *Women and Work: An Annual Review* (III) (Newbury Park, Cal.: Sage Publications, 1988)

HAIG, B., 'Sex Discrimination in the Reward for Skills and Experience in the Australian Labour Market' (1982) 58 *Economic Record* 1

HAKIM, C., 'The Myth of Rising Female Employment' (1993) 7 *Work, Employment and Society* 97

—— *Key Issues in Women's Work: Female Heterogeneity and the Polarisation of Women's Employment* (Athlone, NJ: London Atlantic Highlands, 1996)

HAMMOND, V., and HOLTON, V., 'The Scenario for Women Managers in Britain in the 1990s; Competitive Frontiers: Women Managers in the Triad' (1993) 23 *International Studies of Management & Organization* 71

HANCOCK, K., and RAWSON, D., 'The Metamorphosis of Australian Industrial Relations' (1993) 31(4) *British Journal of Industrial Relations* 489

HARE, I., 'Gender Discrimination and Grooming Codes in the Labour (Super)market' (1995) 1 *International Journal of Discrimination and the Law* 179

HARKNESS, S., MACHIN, S., and WALDFOGEL, J., *Evaluating the Pin Money Hypothesis* (London: LSE Suntory-Toyota International Centre for Economics and Related Disciplines), Working Series Paper, 108

HARRIS, J., 'Schedule 11 of the Employment Protection Act: An Analysis of the 1977 Awards' (1979) 10(1) *Industrial Relations* 51

HART, V., *Bound by Our Constitution: Women, Worker, and the Minimum Wage* (Princeton, NJ: Princeton University Press, 1994)

HARTMANN, H. (ed.), *Comparable Worth: New Directions for Research* (Washington, DC: National Academy Press, 1985)

—— and AARONSON, S., 'Capitol Hill hearings testimony regarding the Fair Pay Act 1994' (Federal Document Clearing House Congressional Testimony, 21 July 1994)

HASTINGS, S., 'Equal Value in the Local Authorities Sector in Great Britain' in KAHN, P., and MEEHAN, E. (eds.), *Equal Value/Comparable Worth in the U.K. and the U.S.A.* (Basingstoke: Macmillan, 1992)

—— and COLEMAN, M., *Women Workers and Unions in Europe: An Analysis by Industrial Sector* (Geneva: ILO, 1992)

HEBDEN, J., 'Men's and Women's Pay in Britain, 1968–75' (1978) 9(2) *Industrial Relations* 56

HEPPLE, B., *Race, Jobs and the Law in Britain* (London: The Penguin Press, 1968)

HEWITT, P., *Rights for Women* (London: NCCL, 1975)

HILL, M., 'The Wage Effects of Marital Status and Children' (1979) 14(4) *Journal of Human Resources* 579

HOEL, B., 'Contemporary Clothing "Sweatshops", Asian Female Labour and Collective Organisation' in WEST, J. (ed.), *Work, Women and the Labour Market* (London; Routledge and Kegan Paul, 1982)

HOMANS, H., 'Man-made Myths: The Reality of Being a Women Scientist in the NHS' in SPENDER, A., and PODMORE, D. (eds.), *In a Man's World: Essays on Women in Male-Dominated Professions* (London: Tavistock Publications Ltd, 1987)

HONEYBALL, S., *Sex, Employment and the Law* (Oxford: Blackwell, 1991)

HORNSTEIN, Z., *Trends in Female Employment 1967–75* (London: Department of Employment, 1977)

HORRELL, S., and RUBERY, J., *Employer's Working Time Policies and Women's Employment* (London: HMSO, 1991), EOC Research Series

—— and —— 'Gender and Working Time: An Analysis of Employers' Working Time Policies' (1991) 15(4) *Cambridge Journal of Economics* 373

—— —— and BURCHELL, B., 'Unequal Jobs or Unequal Pay?' (1990) 20 *Industrial Relations Journal* 176

HORRIGAN, M., and MARKEY, J., 'Recent Gains in Women's Earnings: Better Pay of Longer Hours?' (1990) 113 *Monthly Labor Review* 11

HOSKYNS, C., *Integrating Gender: Women, Law and Politics in the European Union* (London: Verso, 1996)

HOUSE OF LORDS SELECT COMMITTEE ON SCIENCE AND TECHNOLOGY, *Report on Research Careers for Graduate Scientists* (London: HMSO, 1995)

HUMPHRIES, J., and RUBERY, J., 'The Reconstitution of the Supply Side of the Labour Market: The Relative Autonomy of Social Reproduction' (1984) 8 *Cambridge Journal of Economics* 331

HUNT, A., *Management Attitudes and Practices Towards Women at Work* (London: HMSO, 1975), Office of Population Censuses and Surveys

HUNTER, L., and McINNES, J., *Employers' Labour Use Strategies—Case Studies* (London, HMSO, 1991) Department of Employment Research Paper No 87

—— and RIMMER, S., 'An Economic Exploration of the U.K. and Australian Experiences' (1995) 2 *Gender, Work and Organisation* 140

HUWS, U., *Home Truths: Key Results from a National Survey of Homeworkers* (Leeds: National Group on Homeworking, 1994), Report No 2

INTERNATIONAL LABOUR ORGANISATION, *Equal Remuneration* (Geneva: ILO, 1986), ILO 72nd Session Report III (4b), General Survey of the Reports on Convention No 100

—— *Minimum Wages* (Geneva: ILO, 1992), ILO 79th Session Report III (Part 4B) General Survey of the Reports on Conventions Nos 26, 99 & 131

—— *International Labour Conference 1994 Report III* (5) (Geneva: ILO, 1994)

INCOMES DATA SERVICES, *The New Race Law and Employment* (London: IDS, 1976)

—— *Equal Pay, Sex Discrimination, Maternity Rights* (London: IDS, 1979)

—— *Maternity and Paternity Leave* (London: IDS, 1985), Study No 351

INDUSTRIAL RELATIONS SERVICES, *Pay and Gender in Britain: A Report for the EOC* (London: IRS, 1991)

—— *Pay and Gender in Britain (2): A Report for the EOC* (London: IRS, 1992)

JACOBS, J. (ed.), *Gender Inequality at Work* (Newbury Park, Cal.: Sage Publications, 1995)

JEFFERSON, M., 'The Effects of Equal Value Claims on Businesses' (1990) 21(1) *Industrial Relations Journal* 7

JENKINS, R., *Racism and Recruitment* (Cambridge: Cambridge University Press, 1986)

—— and SOLOMOS, J., *Racism and Equal Opportunity Policies in the 1980s* (Cambridge: Cambridge University Press, 1987)

JEWSON, N., MASON, D., WATERS, S., and HARVEY, J., *Ethnic Minorities and Employment Practice* (London: Department of Employment, 1990)

JONES, M., 'C.A.C. and Schedule 11: the Experience of Two Years' (1980) 9 *Industrial Law Journal* 28

JOSHI, H., and DAVIES, H., *Childcare and Mothers' Lifetime Earnings* (London: Centre for Econonic Policy Research, 1992), Discussion Paper Series No 600

KAHN, P., and MEEHAN, E., *Equal Value/Comparable Worth in the U.K. and the U.S.A.* (Basingstoke: Macmillan, 1992)

KAHN-FREUND, O., *Labour Law: Old Traditions and New Developments* (Toronto: Clark, Irwin & Co., 1968)

KATZ, L., LOVEMAN, G., and BLANCHFLOWER, D., *A Comparison of Changes in the Structure of Wages in 4 O.E.C.D. Countries* (Cambridge, Mass.: National Bureau for Economic Research, 1993), NBER Working Paper No 4297

KEENAN, D., and CRABTREE, C., *Essentials of Industrial Law* (London: Pitman, 1970)

KEEVASH, S., 'Wages Councils: An Examination of Trade Union and Conservative Government Misconceptions about the Effect of Statutory Wage Fixing' (1985) 14 *Industrial Law Journal* 217

KIDD, M., 'Sex Discrimination and Occupational Segregation in the Australian Labour Market' (1992) 69 *Economic Record* 44

KILLINGSWORTH, M., 'The Economics of Comparable Worth: Analytical, Empirical, and Policy Questions' in HARTMANN, H. (ed.), *Comparable Worth: New Direction for Research* (Washington, DC: National Academy Press, 1985)

—— (ed.), *Comparable Worth: Analyses and Evidence* (New York: New York State School of Industrial and Labor Relations, Cornell University, 1989)

—— *The Economics of Comparable Worth* (Kalamazoo, Mich.: W. E. Upjohn Institute for Employment Research, 1990)

KUMAR, V., *Industrial Tribunal Applicants under the Race Relations Act 1976* (London: CRE, 1986)

LABOUR MARKET TRENDS, 'Membership of Trade Unions in 1994: An Analysis Based on Information from the Certification Officer', February 1996, 49

—— 'What Happens to Men and Women with SET Degrees?', February 1996, 63

—— 'Family and Working Lives Survey: Preliminary Results', March 1996, 115

—— 'Women in the Labour Market: Results from the Spring 1995 LFS', March 1996, 91

—— 'Earnings Data from the LFS, and the NES', April 1996, 161

—— 'Ethnic Minority Participation in the Labour Market: Trends from the LFS 1984–95', June 1996, 259

LARWOOD, L., STROMBERG, A., and GUTEK, B. (eds.), *Women and Work: An Annual Review* (I) (Newbury Park, Cal.: Sage Publications, 1985)

—— SZWAJKOWSKI, E., and ROSE, S., 'When Discrimination Makes Sense: the Rational Bias Theory' in GUTEK, B., STROMBERG, A., and LARWOOD, L. (eds.), *Women and Work: An Annual Review* (III) (Newbury Park, Cal.: Sage Publications, 1988)

LATTA, G., 'The Legal Extension of Collective Bargaining: A Study of Section 8 of the Terms and Conditions of Employment Act 1959' (1974) 3 *Industrial Law Journal* 215

LAWRENCE, B., 'The 5th Dimension: Gender and General Practice' in SPENDER, A., and PODMORE, D. (ed.), *In a Man's World: Essays on Women in Male-Dominated Professions* (London: Tavistock Publications Ltd, 1987)

LEONARD, A., *Judging Inequality: The Effectiveness of the Tribunal System in Sex Discrimination and Equal Pay Cases* (London: Cobden Trust, 1987)

—— *Pyrrhic Victories: Winning Sex Discrimination and Equal Pay Cases in the Industrial Tribunals, 1980–1984* (London: HMSO, 1987)

LEWIS, D., *Just Give Us the Money* (Vancouver: Women's Research Centre, 1988)

LEWIS, D. and SHORTEN, B., 'The Wage Effect of the Occupational Segregation of Women in Britain' (1991) 97 *The Economic Journal* 885

LINDLEY, R. (ed.), *Women's Employment: Britain in the Single European Market* (London: HMSO, 1992), EOC Research Series

—— (ed.), *Labour Market Structures and Prospects For Women* (Manchester: EOC, 1994)

LLOYD, C., ANDREWS, E., and GILROY, C. (eds.), *Women in the Labor Market* (New York: Colombia University Press, 1979)

—— and NIEMI, B., *The Economics of Sex Differentials* (New York: Colombia University Press, 1979)

LOVE, G., *Women in the Administrative Revolution* (Cambridge: Polity Press, 1987)

LOVERING, J., 'Restructuring and the Sex-Typing of Jobs' in SCOTT, A. (ed.), *Gender Segregation and Social Change: Men and Women in Changing Labour Markets* (Oxford; OUP, 1994)

LOW PAY NETWORK, *Save Wages Councils: A Briefing Paper on the Proposal to Abolish Wages Councils* (Manchester: Low Pay Unit, 1992)

LOW PAY UNIT, *Minimum Wages for Women: An Examination of Women's Earnings in Industries Covered by Wages Councils* (Manchester: EOC, 1980)

—— *Who Needs the Wages Councils* (London: Low Pay Unit, 1983), Production No 24

LUCAS, R., 'Remuneration Practice in a Wage Council Sector: Some Empirical Observation in Hotels' (1991) 22(4) *Industrial Relations Journal* 273

MACDERMOTT, K., *Pay Equity: A Survey of 7 O.E.C.D. Countries* (Canberra: Australian Government Publishing Service, 1987), Women's Bureau Information Paper No 5

—— 'Women's Productivity: Productivity Bargaining and Service Workers' (1993) 35(4) *Journal of Industrial Relations* 538

MACDERMOTT, T., 'Equality of Opportunity in a Decentralised Industrial Relations System' in MCCALLUM, R., MCCARRY, G., and RONFELDT, P., *Employment Security* (Sydney: The Federation Press, 1994)

MACDONALD, H., 'Equal Employment Opportunities and the Invisible Family' in SAYERS, J., and TREMAINE, M. (eds.), *The Vision and the Reality: Equal Employment—Opportunities in the New Zealand Workplace* (Palmerston North: The Dunmore Press Ltd, 1994)

MACDONALD, I., *Race Relations: The New Law* (London, Butterworths, 1977)

MACHIN, S., and WALDFOGEL, J., *The Decline of the Male Breadwinner: Changing Shares of Husbands' and Wives' Earnings in Family Income* (London: LSE, 1994), Discussion Paper WSP 103.

MALONE, M., *Discrimination Law: A Practical Guide for Management* (London: Kogan Page, 1993)

MANNING, A., *The Equal Pay Act as an Experiment to Test Theories of the Labour Market* (London: LSE Centre for Economic Performance, 1993), Discussion Paper No 153

MARINI, M., 'Sex Differences in Earnings in the U.S.' (1989) 15 *Annual Review of Sociology* 343

—— and BRINTON, M., 'Sex Typing in Occupational Segregation' in RESKIN, B. (ed.), *Sex Segregation in the Workplace: Trends, Explanations, Remedies* (Washington, DC: National Academy Press, 1984)

MARQUAND, J., 'Which are the Lower Paid Workers?' (1967) 5 *British Journal of Industrial Relations* 359

MARSDEN, D., and RICHARDSON, R., 'Performing for Pay? The Effects of "Merit Pay" in a Public Service' (1994) 32(2) *British Journal of Industrial Relations* 243

MARSHALL, B., 'Job Evaluation: Who's Worth What?' in SAYERS, J., and TREMAINE, M. (eds.), *The Vision and the Reality: Equal Employment Opportunities in the New Zealand Workplace* (Palmerston North: The Dunmore Press Ltd, 1994)

MARTIN, B., 'Understanding Class Segmentation in the Labour Market: An Empirical Study of Earnings Determination in Australia' (1994) 8(3) *Work, Employment and Society* 357

MARTIN, J. and ROBERTS, C., *Women and Employment: A Lifetime Perspective* (London: HMSO, 1984)

MATHYS, N., and PINCUS, L., 'Is Pay Equity Equitable? A Perspective That Looks Beyond Pay' (1993) 44 *Labor Law Journal* 351

MCAULEY, J., 'Women Academics: A Case Study in Inequality' in SPENDER, A., and PODMORE, D. (eds.), *In a Man's World: Essays on Women in Male-Dominated Professions* (London: Tavistock Publications Ltd, 1987)

MCCALLUM, R., MCCARRY, G., and RONFELDT, P. (eds.), *Employment Security* (Sydney: The Federation Press, 1994)

—— and PITTARD, M., *Australian Labour Law: Cases and Materials* (3rd edn., Sydney: Butterworths, 1995)

MCCOLGAN, A., 'Equal Pay, Market Forces and C.C.T.' (1995) 24 *Industrial Law Journal* 368

MCCRUDDEN, C., 'Equal Pay For Work of Equal Value: The Equal Pay (Amendment) Regulations 1983' 12 *Industrial Law Journal* 197

—— and KNOX, J., *Racial Justice at Work: Enforcement of the Race Relations Act 1976 in Employment* (London: Policy Studies Institute, 1991)

MCDERMOTT, P., 'Pay Equity: Closing the Gender Gap' in DRACHE, D., *Getting on Track: Social Democratic Strategies for Ontario* (Kingston: McGill-Queen's University Press, 1992)

MCLAUGHLIN, E. and INGRAM, K., *All Stitched Up: Sex Segregation in the Northern Ireland Clothing Industry* (Belfast: Northern Ireland EOC, 1990)

MCQUEEN, H. (ed.), *Sex Equality: Law and Economics* (Edinburgh: Edinburgh University Press, 1993), Hume Papers on Public Policy, Vol. 1(1)

McRAE, S. (ed.), *Keeping Women In* (London: Policy Studies Institute, 1990)

MEULDERS, D., PLASMAN, R., and VANDER STRICHT, V., *Position of Women on the Labour Market of the E.C.* (Aldershot: Dartmouth, 1993)

MILLER, P., 'The Wage Effect of Occupational Segregation of Women in Britain' (1987) 97 *Economic Journal* 885

MILLWARD, N., *Workplace Industrial Relations in Transition* (Aldershot: Dartmouth, 1992)

—— *Targeting Potential Discrimination* (Manchester: EOC, 1994), Research Discussion Series No 11

—— *The New Industrial Relations?* (London: Institute for Public Policy Research, 1994)

—— STEVENS, M., SMART, D., and HAWES, W., *First Findings from the 1990 Workplace Industrial Relations Survey* (London: Department of Employment, 1992)

—— and WOODLAND, S., *Gender Segregation and Male/Female Wage Differences* (London: LSE, 1995), Centre for Economic Performance Discussion Paper No 220

MINCER, J., 'Wage Differentials: Comment' in LLOYD, C., ANDREWS, E., and GILROY, C. (eds.), *Women in the Labor Market* (New York, Columbia University Press, 1979)

—— and POLACHEK, S., 'Family Investments in Human Capital: Earnings of Women' (1974) 82(2) *Journal of Political Economy* S. 76.

—— and —— 'Women's Earnings Re-examined' (1978) 13 *Journal of Human Resources* 118

MITCHELL, R., and NAUGHTON, R., 'Australian Compulsory Arbitration: Will it Survive into the Twenty-First Century?' (1993) 31 *Osgoode Hall Law Journal* 265

MOENS, G., and RATNAPALA, S., *The Illusions of Comparable Worth* (St Leonards, New South Wales: Centre for Independent Studies Ltd, 1992)

MORRIS, A., and NOTT, S., *Working Women and the Law: Equality and Discrimination in Theory and Practice* (London: Routledge, 1991)

MORRIS, J., *Women Workers and the Sweated Trades* (Aldershot: Gower Publishers, 1986)

MORRIS, P., *Award Restructuring: the Task Ahead* (Canberra: Australian Government Publishing Service, 1989), Statement by the Minister for Industrial Relations.

MUMFORD, K., *Women Working: Economics and Reality* (Sydney: Allen & Unwin, 1989)

NATIONAL COUNCIL FOR CIVIL LIBERTIES, *The Sex Discrimination Act* (London: NCCL, 1975)

NATIONAL WOMEN'S CONSULTATIVE COUNCIL, *Women and Enterprise Bargaining: Who Benefits?* (Canberra: Australian Government Publishing Service, 1992)

NASH, P., and GOTTHEIL, L., 'Employment Equity: A Union Perspective', 2 *Canadian Labor Law Journal* 49

NATIONAL BOARD FOR PRICES AND INCOMES, *General Problems of Low Pay* (London: HMSO, 1971), Report No 169, Cmnd. 4648

NEATHEY, F., 'Job Assessment, Job Evaluation and Equal Value' in KAHN, P., and MEEHAN, E. (eds.), *Equal Value/Comparable Worth in the U.K. and the U.S.A.* (Basingstoke: Macmillan, 1992)

NEUMARK, D., *Sex Discrimination and Women's Labour Market Interruptions* (Cambridge, Mass.: National Bureau of Economic Research, 1993), NBER Working Paper No 4260

NEWTON, P., 'Who Becomes an Engineer? Social and Psychological Antecedents of a Non-traditional Career Choice' in SPENDER, A., and PODMORE, D. (eds.), *In a Man's World: Essays on Women in Male-Dominated Professions* (London: Tavistock Publications Ltd, 1987)

NIELSEN, R., and SZYSZCZAK, E., *The Social Dimension of the European Community* (Denmark: Handeldhøjkolens Forlag, 1993)

NILAND, J. (ed.), *Wage Fixation in Australia* (Sydney: Allen & Unwin, 1986)

O'CONNOR, D., 'Equality in the Workplace: The Implications of the Industrial Relations Reform Act 1993' (1995) 37(1) *Journal of Industrial Relations* 63

O'DEA, R., *Principles of Wage Determination in Commonwealth Arbitration* (Sydney: West Publishing Corporation Pty Ltd, 1969)

O'NEILL, J., 'Role Differentiation and the Gender Gap in Wage Rates' in LARWOOD, L., STROMBERG, A., and GUTEK, B. (eds.), *Women and Work: An Annual Review* (I) (Newbury Park, Cal.: Sage Publications, 1985)

—— and POLACHEK, S., 'Why the Gender Gap in Wages Narrowed in the 1980s' (1993) 11(1) *Journal of Labor Economics* 205

OECD, *Economic Outlook* 1994 (Paris: OECD, 1994)

OKUYAMA, A., 'Equal Pay in Japan' in EYRAUD, F. (ed.), *Equal Pay Protection in Industrialised Market Economies: In Search of Greater Effectiveness* (Geneva: ILO, 1993)

OSTERMAN, P., 'Employment Structures within Firms' (1981) *British Journal of Industrial Relations* 349

PANNICK, D., *Sex Discrimination Law* (Oxford: Clarendon Press, 1985)

PARLIAMENT OF THE COMMONWEALTH, THE HOUSE OF REPRESENTATIVES SELECT COMMITTEE ON LEGISLATIVE AND CONSTITUTIONAL AFFAIRS, *Half Way to Equal* (Canberra: Australian Government Publications, 1993)

PATERSON, P., and ARMSTRONG, M., *An Employers' Guide to Equal Pay* (London: Kogan Page, 1972)

PAY EQUITY PROJECT, *Narrowing the Gender Gap: How Wages Councils Work For Women* (London: PEP, 1993)

PETERSON, J., and BROWN, D., *The Economic Status of Women under Capitalism* (Aldershot: Edward Elgar Publishing Ltd, 1994)

PETTITI, C., 'Equal Pay in France' in EYRAUD, F. (ed.), *Equal Pay Protection in Industrialised Market Economies: In Search of Greater Effectiveness* (Geneva: ILO, 1993)

PHELPS, E., 'The Statistical Theory of Racism and Sexism' (1972) 62(4) *American Economic Review* 659

PHIZACKLEA, A., and WOLKOWITZ, C., *Homeworking Women: Gender, Racism and Class at Work* (London: Sage Publications, 1995)

PLOWMAN, D., 'Developments in Australian Wage Determination, 1953–83: The Institutional Dimension' in NILAND, J. (ed.), *Wage Fixation in Australia* (Sydney: Allen & Unwin, 1986)

—— and NILAND, J., 'Australia' in BLANPAIN, R. (ed.), *Flexibility and Wages a Comparative Treatment* (Deventer: Kluwer Law and Taxation, 1990)

PLUMER, A., *Equal Value Judgments: Objective Assessment or Lottery?* (Coventry: University of Warwick, 1992), Industrial Research Unit, School of Business Studies

POCOCK, B., 'Women in Unions: What Progress in South Australia?' (1985) 37(1) *Journal of Industrial Relations* 3

POLACHEK, S., 'Sex Differences in College Majors' (1978) 31 *Industrial Labour Relations Review* 498

—— 'Occupational Self-selection: A Human Capital Approach to Sex Differences in Occupational Structure' (1981) 63 *Review of Economic Statistics* 60

POWER, M., 'Women's Work is Never Done—by Men: A Socio-Economic Model of Sex Typing in Occupations' (1975) 17(3) *Journal of Industrial Relations* 225

PURDY, J., 'Women, Work and Equality: The Commonwealth Legislation' (1989) 19 *Western Australian Law Review* 352

RAFFERTY, F., 'Equal Pay: The Evolutionary Process 1984–1994' (1994) 36(4) *Journal of Industrial Relations* 451

RASHID, A., 'Women's Earnings and Family Incomes' (1991) *Statistics Canada Perspectives* 27

REILLY, B., 'Occupational Segregation and Selectivity Biases in Occupational Wage Equations: An Empirical Analysis Using Irish Data' (1991) 23 *Applied Economics* 1

REITANO, R., 'Legislative Change in 1994' (1995) 37(1) *Journal of Industrial Relations* 84

RESKIN, B. (ed.), *Sex Segregation in the Workplace: Trends, Explanations, Remedies* (Washington, DC: National Adacemy Press, 1984)

—— and PADAVIC, I., *Women and Men at Work* (Thousand Oaks, Cal.: Sage Publications/Pine Forge Press, 1994)

—— and ROOS, P., *Job Queues, Gender Queues* (Philadelphia, Penn.: Temple University Press, 1990)

RHOADS, S., *Incomparable Worth: Pay Equity Meets the Market* (Cambridge: Cambridge University Press, 1993)

RICHARDS, M., 'The Sex Discrimination Act—Equality For Women?' (1976) 5 *Industrial Law Journal* 35

RIDDELL, W., *Women and Pay: The Canadian Labour Market* (Toronto: University of Toronto Press, 1985)

ROBACK, J., *A Matter of Choice: A Critique of Comparable Worth by a Skeptical Feminist* (New York: Priority Press Publications, 1986)

ROBERTS, M., and MIZUTA, T., *The Exploited: Women and Work* (London: Routledge/Thoemmes Press, 1993)

ROBINSON, O., and WALLACE, J., 'Part-time Employment and Low Pay in Retail Distribution in Britain' (1974) 5(1) *Industrial Relations* 38

RONALDS, C., *Affirmative Action and Sex Discrimination* (2nd edn., Leichhardt, New South Wales: Pluto Press Australia Ltd, 1991)

ROOS, P., and RESKIN, B., 'Institutional Factors Contributing to Sex Segregation in the Workplace' in RESKIN, B. (ed.), *Sex Segregation in the Workplace: Trends, Explanations, Remedies* (Washington, DC: National Academy Press, 1984)

ROYAL COMMISSION ON TRADE UNIONS AND EMPLOYERS' ASSOCIATIONS 1965–68, *Report* (London: HMSO, 1968), Cmnd. 3623

RUBENSTEIN, M., 'Discriminatory Job Evaluation and the Law' (1985–86) 7 *Comparative Labour Law* 172

RUBERY, J., 'Structured Labour Markets, Worker Organisation and Low Pay' (1978) 2(1) *Cambridge Journal of Economics* 17. Also in AMSDEN, A. (ed.), *The Economics of Women and Work* (Harmondsworth: Penguin, 1980)

—— (ed.), *Women and Recession* (London: Routledge and Kegan Paul, 1988)

—— *Equal Pay and Institutional Systems of Wage Determination: A Comparative Study* (Brussels: EC Commission, 1991)

—— 'Pay, Gender and the Social Dimension to Europe' (1992) 30 *British Journal of Industrial Relations* 605

—— *The Economics of Equal Value* (Manchester: EOC, 1992), Research Discussion Series No 2

—— and FAGAN, C., 'Equal Pay Policy and Wage Regulation Systems in Europe' (1994) 25(4) *Industrial Relations Journal* 281

—— and —— 'Occupational Segregation . . . *Plus ça Change?*' in LINDLEY, R. (ed.), *Labour Market Structures and Prospects for Women* (Manchester: EOC, 1994)

—— HORRELL, S., and BURCHELL, B., 'Part-time Work and Gender Inequality' in SCOTT, A. (ed.), *Gender Segregation and Social Change: Men and Women in Changing Labour Markets* (Oxford: OUP, 1994)

—— and TARLING, R., 'Women's Employment in Declining Britain' in RUBERY, J. (ed.), *Women and Recession* (London: Routledge and Kegan Paul, 1988)

RUMMERY, S., 'The Contribution of Intermittent Labour Force Participation to the Gender Wage Differential' [1992] *Economic Record* 68

RUSSO, A., and KRAMARAE, C., *The Radical Women's Press of the 1850s* (New York: Routledge, 1991)

RYAN, E., and CONLON, A., *Gentle Invaders: Australian Women at Work 1788–1974* (Melbourne: Thomas Nelson (Australia) Ltd, 1975)

SANDELL, S., and SHAPIRO, D., 'An Exchange: The Theory of Human Capital and the Earnings of Women' (1978) 31(1) *Journal of Human Resources* 103

SAYERS, J., and TREMAINE, M. (eds.), *The Vision and the Reality: Equal Employment Opportunities in the New Zealand Workplace* (Palmerston North: The Dunmore Press Ltd, 1994)

SCHOFIELD, P., 'Equal Pay: Permitted Comparisons' (1988) 17 *Industrial Law Journal* 241

SCHUR, L., and KRUSE, D., 'Gender Differentials in Attitudes Towards Unions' (1992) 46(1) *Industrial and Labor Relations Review* 89

SCOTT, A. (ed.), *Gender Segregation and Social Change: Men and Women in Changing Labour Markets* (Oxford: OUP, 1994)

SELECT COMMITTEE ON THE SWEATING SYSTEM, 5th Report (Parliamentary Papers, 1890)

SELLS, D., *The British Trade Boards System* (London: King & Son, 1923)

—— 'Wage Regulation in Australia and New Zealand' (1924) X(5) *International Labour Review* 779

—— *Wages Boards* (Washington, DC: The Brookings Institution, 1939)

SHORT, C., 'Equal Pay—What Happened?' (1986) 28(3) *Journal of Industrial Relations* 315

SHORT, M., and BUCHANAN, J., 'Wages Policy and Wage Determination in 1994' (1995) 37(1) *Journal of Industrial Relations* 119

—— PRESTON, A., and PREETZ, D., *The Spread and Impact of Workplace Bargaining: Evidence from the Workplace Bargaining Research Project* (Canberra: Australian Government Publishing Service, 1993), Department of Industrial Relations Workplace Bargaining Research Project

SILTANEN, J., *Locating Gender: Occupational Segregation, Wages and Domestic Responsibilities* (London: UCL Press Ltd, 1994)

SINGLETON, G., *The Accord and the Australian Labour Movement* (Melbourne: Melbourne University Press, 1990)

SLOANE, P., 'The Gender Wage Differential' in SCOTT, A. (ed.), *Gender Segregation and Social Change: Men and Women in Changing Labour Markets* (Oxford: OUP, 1994)

SNELL, M., GLUCKLICH, P., and POVALL, M., *Equal Pay and Opportunities: A Study of the Implementation and Effects of the Equal Pay and Sex Discrimination Act in 26 Organisations* (London: Department of Employment, 1981), Research Paper No 2

SOKOLOFF, N., *Black Women and White Women in the Professions* (New York: Routledge, 1992)

SORENSEN, E., 'Comparable Worth: Is it a Worthy Policy?' in KILLINGSWORTH, M. (ed.), *Comparable Worth: Analyses and Evidence* (New York:

New York State School of Industrial and Labor Relations, Cornell University, 1989)

—— 'The Wage Effects of Occupational Sex Composition: A Review and New Findings' in KILLINGSWORTH, M. (ed.), *Comparable Worth: Analyses and Evidence* (New York: New York State School of Industrial and Labor Relations, Cornell University, 1989)

—— *Exploring the Reasons Behind the Narrowing Gender Pay Gap in Earnings* (Washington, DC: Urban Institute Press, 1991)

—— *Comparable Worth: Is It a Worthy Policy?* (Princeton, NJ: Princeton University Press, 1994)

SPENCE, M., *Market Signaling: Information Transfer in Hiring and Related Screening Processes* (Cambridge, Mass.: Harvard University Press, 1974)

SPENDER, A., and PODMORE, D., *In a Man's World: Essays on Women in Male-Dominated Professions* (London: Tavistock Publications Ltd, 1987)

—— and —— 'Women Lawyers—Marginal Members of a Male Dominated-Profession' in SPENDER, A., and PODMORE, D. (eds.), *In a Man's World: Essays on Women in Male-Dominated Professions* (London: Tavistock Publications Ltd, 1987)

STACKPOOL-MOORE, J., 'From Equal Pay to Equal Value in Australia: Myth or Reality?' (1990) 11 *Comparative Labor Law Journal* 273

STAMP, P., and ROBARTS, S., *Positive Action: Changing the Workplace* (London: NCCL, 1986)

STARR, G., *Minimum Wage Fixing: An International Review of Practices and Problems* (Geneva: ILO, 1981)

STEELE, R., 'The Relative Performance of the Wages Council and Non-Wages Council Sectors and the Impact of Incomes Policy' (1979) 17(2) *British Journal of Industrial Relations* 224

STEINBERG, R., *et al.*, *The New York Pay Equity Study: A Research Report* (New York: State University of New York at Albany, 1986)

STEINBERG, R., *et al.*, *Worth and Gender Discrimination: An International Perspective* (Geneva: ILO, 1994)

STROMBERG, A., LARWOOD, L., and GUTEK, B. (eds.), *Women and Work: An Annual Review* (II) (Newbury Park, Cal.: Sage Publications, 1987)

SYKES, E., and GLASBEEK, H., *Labour Law in Australia* (Sydney: Butterworths, 1972)

THOMAS, D., *Gender Differences in Household Resource Allocations* (Washington, DC: World Bank, 1991), LSMS Working Paper No 79

THORNTON, M., *The Liberal Promise: Anti-discrimination Legislation in Australia* (Melbourne: OUP Australia, 1990)

—— 'Equal Pay in Australia' in EYRAUD, F. (ed.), *Equal Pay Protection in Industrialised Market Economies: In Search of Greater Effectiveness* (Geneva: ILO, 1993)

TOWERS, B., *British Incomes Policy* (University of Leeds and the University of Nottingham, 1978), Occasional Papers in Industrial Relations

TOWNSHEND-SMITH, R., 'Equal Pay and the Material Factor/Difference Defence' (1987) 16 *Industrial Law Journal* 114

—— '*Tower Boot Co. Ltd* v. *Jones, Waters* v. *Commissioner of Police of the Metropolis*' (1996) 2 *International Journal of Discrimination and the Law*, forthcoming

TRADE UNION CONGRESS, *The New Divide: Part Time Workers' Pay in the 90's* (London: TUC, 1995)

TREIMAN, D., and HARTMANN, H. (eds.), *Women, Work and Wages: Equal Pay for Jobs of Equal Value* (Washington, DC: National Academy Press, 1981)

TRINE, A., *Employers' Liabilities Under Social Legislation* (Brussels: Chispeels looseleaf)

TZANNATOS, Z., *A General Equilibrium Model of Discrimination and its Effects on Incomes* (London: LSE, 1986), Centre for Labour Economics Discussion Paper 1986

—— 'Equal Pay in Greece and Britain' (1987) 18(4) *Industrial Relations Journal* 275

—— 'Employment Segregation: Can We Measure it and What Does it Mean?' (1990) 28(1) *British Journal of Industrial Relations* 105

—— and ZABALZA, A., 'The Anatomy of the Rise of British Female Relative Wages in the 1970's: Evidence from the New Earnings Survey' (1984) 22(2) *British Journal of Industrial Relations* 177

UK ACTION COMMITTEE ON ISLAMIC AFFAIRS, *Muslims and the Law in Multi-Faith Britain: Need for Reform* (London: UK Action Committee on Islamic Affairs, 1993)

VELLA, F., 'Gender Roles, Occupational Choice and Gender Wage Differential' (1993) 69 *Economic Record* 382

WALBY, S., *Patriarchy at Work* (Cambridge: Polity Press, 1986)

WALDFOGEL, J., *Women Working For Less: A Longitudinal Analysis of the Family Gap* (London: LSE, 1993), LSE Suntory and Toyota International Centre for Economics and Related Disciplines, Discussion Paper WSP 93

SEX DISCRIMINATION COMMISSIONER, HUMAN RIGHTS AND EQUAL OPPORTUNITY COMMISSION (Walpole, S.), *The Sex Discrimination Act 1984: Future Directions and Strategies* (Canberra: Australian Government Publishing Service, 1993)

WANNELL, T., 'Male–Female Earnings Gap Among Recent University Graduates, Statistics Canada' (1990) *Perspectives* 19

WATTS, M., 'Divergent Trends in Gender Segregation by Occupation in the United States: 1970–92' (1995) 17(3) *Journal of Post Keynesian Economics* 357

—— and RICH, J., 'Equal Opportunity in Australia? The Role of Part-time Employment in Occupational Sex Segregation' (1991) 17(2) *Australian Bulletin of Labour* 155

—— and —— 'Occupational Sex Segregation in Britain, 1979–89: The Role of Part-time Work' (1992) 6(3) *International Review of Applied Economics* 286

WEDDERBURN, K. W., *Cases and Materials on Labour Law* (Cambridge: Cambridge University Press, 1967)

—— LEWIS, R., and CLARK, J. (eds.), *Labour Law and Industrial Relations: Building on Kahn-Freund* (Oxford: Clarendon Press, 1983)

—— and MURPHY, W. (eds.), *Labour Law and the Community: Perspectives for the 1980's* (London: IALS, 1982)

WELSH, C., KNOX, J., and BRETT, M., *Acting Positively: Positive Action Under the Race Relations Act 1976* (London: Employment Department, 1994), Research Series No 36

WEST, J. (ed.), *Work, Women and the Labour Market* (London: Routledge & Kegan Paul, 1982)

WHITEHOUSE, G., 'Legislation and Labour Market Inequality: An Analysis of OECD Countries' (1992) 6(1) *Work, Employment and Society* 65

WILKINSON, F., *Why Britain Needs a Minimum Wage* (London: Institute for Public Policy Research, 1992)

WILSON, G., 'Money: Patterns of Responsibility and Irresponsibility in Marriage' in BRANNEN, J., and WILSON, G. (eds.), *Give and Take in Families: Studies in Resource Distribution* (London: Allen and Unwin, 1987)

WILSON, R., 'Sectoral and Occupational Change: Prospects for Women's Employment' in LINDLEY, R. (ed.), *Labour Market Structures and Prospects for Women* (Manchester: EOC, 1994)

WOMEN'S ELECTORAL LOBBY, 'Impact of Enterprise Bargaining on Women: Statement of Concerns, April 1992' in TULLY, K., *Women and Enterprise Bargaining: Who Benefits?* (Canberra: Australian Government Publishing Service, 1992), Final Report of the National Women's Consultative Council

WOOD, P., 'The Central Arbitration Committee's Approach to Schedule 11 to the Employment Protection Act 1975 and the Fair Wages Resolution 1946' (1987) 7 *Industrial Law Journal* 65

WOOD, R., CORCORAN, M., and COURANT, P., 'Pay Differences Among the Highly Paid: The Male and Female Earnings Gap in Lawyers' Salaries' (1993) 11(3) *Journal of Labor Economics* 417

WRIGHT, J., HEWITT, P., and SEDLEY, A., *Race Relations Guide* (London: NCCL, 1978), Know Your Rights Series, No 1

ZABALZA, A., and TZANNATOS, Z., *Women and Equal Pay: The Effects of Legislation on Female Employment and Wages* (Cambridge: Cambridge University Press, 1985)

ZELLNER, H., 'The Determinants of Occupational Segregation' in LLOYD, C. (ed.), *Sex Discrimination and the Division of Labour* (New York: Columbia University Press, 1975)

ZOLATH, S., and STELLMAN, J., 'Hazards of Healing: Occupational Health and Safety in Hospitals' in STROMBERG, A., LARWOOD, L., and GUTEK, B. (eds.), *Women and Work: An Annual Review* (II) (Newbury Party, Cal.: Sage Publications, 1987)

Index

UNIVERSITY OF WINCHESTER
LIBRARY